Knowledge Management
Lessons Learned

Knowledge Management Lessons Learned

What Works and What Doesn't

Edited by
Michael E. D. Koenig, Ph.D.
Dean, College of Information and Computer Science
Long Island University

and

T. Kanti Srikantaiah, Ph.D.
Director and Associate Professor, Center for Knowledge Management
Dominican University

American Society for
Information Science
and Technology

Published for the
American Society for Information Science and Technology by

 Information Today, Inc.
Medford, New Jersey

Knowledge Management Lessons Learned: What Works and What Doesn't

Library of Congress Cataloging-in-Publication Data

Knowledge management lessons learned : what works and what doesn't / edited by Michael E.D. Koenig and T. Kanti Srikantaiah.
    p. cm. -- (ASIS monograph series)
    Includes bibliographical references and index.
    ISBN 1-57387-181-8
    1. Knowledge management. I. Koenig, Michael E. D.   II. Srikantaiah, Taverekere.   III. American Society for Information Science.   IV. Series.
  HD30.2.K6633 2003
  658.4'038--dc22

                                                                2003015556

Publisher: Thomas H. Hogan, Sr.
Editor-in-Chief: John B. Bryans
Managing Editor: Deborah R. Poulson
Project Editor: Michelle Sutton-Kerchner
Graphics Department Director: M. Heide Dengler
Cover Designer: Jacqueline Walter Crawford
Indexer: Sharon Hughes

Contents

Introductory Chapters

Part I: Strategy and Implementation

Part II: Cost Analysis

Part III: Knowledge Management Applications— Content Management

Part IV: Knowledge Management Applications— Communities of Practice

Part V: Knowledge Management Applications— Competitive Intelligence

Part VI: Education and Training—Organizational Learning

Bibliography

Introduction

Four years ago, the editors wrote parts of, and compiled a book on, KM: *Knowledge Management for the Information Professional* (Srikantaiah and Koenig, 2000). At that time, such a publication was created to satisfy the need for a book on KM that was addressed to the information practitioner, as well as to be a tool on which to center an undergraduate or master's level KM course. Those reasons are still valid today.

The reason for another book on KM only a few years later is obvious. The domain of KM (see the Road Map beginning on page xv for pointers to various definitions of KM) is growing and changing rapidly. In our predecessor monograph to this book, the terms "content management" or "enterprise content management" were hardly mentioned. In fact, neither term even appeared in the rather detailed 28-page index; yet, content management is a term frequently discussed in this book. Many of the topics related to content management previously existed; however, they were not seen as related in the fashion that they are now, particularly in the development described as Stage III in Chapter 1. Not only has the KM industry grown, but it also has changed its direction and perspective.

A fascinating indication of KM's growth is that in *Knowledge Management for the Information Professional*, we included a rather comprehensive, although we made no pretense to its being exhaustive, bibliography of over 600 items. Only a few years later, it is no longer feasible to even attempt an exhaustive bibliography in a book such as this. Less than a year after the predecessor volume, an updated version of its bibliography was issued as a separate volume (Burden, 2000). To produce such a resource a year after publication of this book would probably result in a multivolume publication. Therefore, constrained by practicality, for this book we have included a bibliography of items relating specifically to the topic of KM lessons learned.

Another reason for a new book on KM so soon is that KM is different from the typical business or management topic. As Ponzi's research in Chapter 2 demonstrates, KM is not just another management fad. The typical management fad or enthusiasm appears from almost nowhere (as measured by the number of articles in business literature discussing the topic), grows rapidly, peaks in five years, falls off just as rapidly, and 10 years from its birth has returned to almost zero. When graphed, the result looks like a spike on an oscilloscope. In contrast, KM experienced that same dramatic five-year growth period, 1995 to 2000, but since then has not fallen back. It dipped a bit for a year, but then continued to grow, albeit less dramatically and at a more conventional pace, but still faster than business literature as a whole. Knowledge management is either, at the least, an unusual, very broad-shouldered fad, or a rather permanent topic of interest and concern, as shown by its long-term consistent growth.

One of the reasons, perhaps the principal reason, to construct a book of this type is to assemble in one publication the experiences, perceptions, knowledge, and wisdom of a number of KM practitioners and theoreticians. The careful reader inevitably receives a richer view than if the book were authored by only one or two writers.

The joy of editing such a book is to review the chapters and see the patterns and the tensions emerge—to observe, for example, Durham and Borbely writing about thought leaders in Chapters 20 and 21, Koenig writing about opinion leaders in Chapter 8, and Palmquist writing about knowledge champions in Chapter 32. These authors are noticing and stressing the importance of the same phenomenon—Durham from the operations perspective, Borbely from experience at Towers Perrin, Koenig from the study of research productivity, and Palmquist from the sociology of learning. The confluence of authors and perspectives provides the reader with more depth on the topic than any one author could provide. Even more importantly, this consistency on a theme gives the reader a greater confidence in both the importance of the phenomenon and the reliability of the reportage than any single author could deliver.

Of course, there will not always be uniformity. For example, a number of authors, either explicitly or implicitly, recommend building KM systems from the bottom up. Note: Short and Azzarello's focal points, Chapter 3; Durham's pain points, Chapter 20; and Droitsch's conclusion, Chapter 22. Arnold in Chapter 12—although certainly not rejecting this approach, and implying that the state of technology makes it almost inevitable—indicates the unavoidable collision with enterprise resource management (ERM) systems that will result from a bottom-up approach to building KM systems. Borbely in Chapter 21, by contrast, advocates central administrative support with local content control. However, such lack of uniformity is typically a virtue in itself. Often, as in this example, it picks up a tension within the KM field. In this case, it is more a tension inherent in the different contexts of KM than a tension between experts, and the KM implementer would do well to consider this. Similarly, compare Malhotra's genuine and well-founded emphasis in Chapter 7 on the importance of security issues as KM expands to include suppliers, contractors, and customers with Koenig's evidence in Chapter 8 that an emphasis on the protection of proprietary information is negatively correlated with research productivity, and with Barth's analysis in Chapter 28 of the tension between the emphasis on sharing and communication of KM versus the need to not only undertake competitive intelligence but also guard against it.

Our hope is that just as we were further informed about KM by putting together this book, the readers of this book will be informed as well—and informed to the point of illumination about the fascinating and multifaceted field of KM.

We suggest you use the Road Map to the book, rather than merely perusing the Table of Contents for likely looking chapters. Knowledge management is multifaceted and, although a chapter may fit logically in one section of the book, it will almost certainly report on other topics as well. The editors are not at liberty to cut the chapters into smaller pieces and rearrange them. (Even if they could, the same problem of faceting and classification would exist.) Hence, we created the Road Map, an annotated thematic index that guides the reader—something more detailed than a table of contents but less granular and more conversational than an index. For example, the Road Map indicates that Chapter 22 on KM implementation at the Department of Labor contains very informative developments on just-in-time education and training, which is something that is not obvious from scanning the Table of Contents. The reader who not only peruses the Table of Contents but also uses the Road Map will have a much richer understanding of what this book contains, and can be directed to material that might not otherwise be found.

A final and sad note is that our colleague, Jeffrey A. Flint, passed away suddenly and tragically while this book was being published. There is a brief celebratory note about his life and his contribution to the fields of KM and competitive intelligence by his co-author, Gary D. Maag, at the end of Chapter 26.

REFERENCES

Srikantaiah, T. Kanti and Koenig, Michael E. D., eds. 2000, *Knowledge Management for the Information Professional*, Medford, NJ: Information Today, Inc. for the American Society for Information Science.

Burden, Paul. 2000, *Knowledge Management—The Bibliography*, Medford, NJ: Information Today, Inc. for the American Society for Information Science and Technology.

Acknowledgments

The editors would like to acknowledge the contributions of the chapter authors. In this rapidly changing field, this book would not have been feasible without their speedy cooperation. We would like to thank them not only for their specific chapters but also for the insights, suggestions, and further education that they have provided for the editors.

We would also like to thank the editorial staff at Information Today, Inc. who, having worked with us before, were still willing to undertake it again.

T. Kanti Srikantaiah	Michael E. D. Koenig
Dominican University	Long Island University

The Road Map—A Thematic Guide to *Knowledge Management Lessons Learned*

Probably very few readers, other than the editors and the editorial staff, will read this book in its entirety. Most will come to this book with particular interests in mind, and with specific information interests or needs. The intent of this "road map" is to allow entry into the book by subject and theme, at a level of specificity greater than that of the table of contents but broader than that of the back-of-the-book index. This entry route also provides an analytical guide—a road map that allows one to use the book for researching a specific subject of interest, as well as for browsing and pursuing serendipity, and doing either with a real feel for the terrain.

Major Themes and Topics Covered Here

- What Is KM?
- KM Strategy
- Lessons Learned
- Implementing KM
- Education for KM and Learning in KM
- Communities of Practice
- Content Management
- KM Costs and Economics
- KM Measurement
- Trust
- Find the Focal Points
- KM Stars and Thought Leaders
- Taxonomy
- Standards
- Roles in KM
- Portals and Visual Design
- KM Applications in Government

- Competitive Intelligence in KM
- The Future of KM

What Is KM?

This book does not attempt to define KM, it is a follow-up to a book that attempted to introduce KM to information professionals and, in the process, define it (Srikantaiah and Koenig, 2000); however, inevitably, this second book also contains definitions of KM. Probably the most complete discussion is in Ponzi's "Knowledge Management: Birth of a Discipline" (Chapter 2), where the issue is not only discussed but quantitatively analyzed in terms of works used and cited in the field of KM and the relationships between them, and in which graphics based on co-citation links are developed using factor analysis and multidimensional scaling. The combination of Ponzi's data (including extensive lists of key journals ranked by bibliometric importance) and Burden's update to his previous bibliography (Burden, 2000) certainly gives the closest and most thorough examination currently existing of the scope and extent, and even the shape, of literature in the KM field.

The chapters by Hasanali (Chapter 4) and Hubert and O'Dell (Chapter 5), both written from the perspective of the American Productivity and Quality Center's (APQC's) extensive research on KM, contain definitions of KM. Hasanali addresses the managerial components of KM and what the critical success factors are for each. Hubert and O'Dell attack the issue from the sequence of steps with which one initiates a KM program. Chen (Chapter 17) reviews the Gartner Group's multitiered KM architecture, which is a de facto definition of KM in an operational sense. The Gartner Group's emphasis on IR (information retrieval) as the core of KM architecture nicely complements Koenig and Srikantaiah's discussion of the development stages of KM and the emergence of a third stage of KM (Chapter 1). In developing those stages of KM, Koenig and Srikantaiah inevitably discuss what KM has been and what it is now, showing how the emphasis has shifted over time. Koenig's chapter on KM and user education (Chapter 29) uses an IBM table to demonstrate that of which KM consists, and he develops it further, to delineate the realms where KM education can contribute. Malhotra in his chapter on KM in human enterprises (Chapter 7) similarly develops that discussion from a useful overview of what KM is. Droitsch (Chapter 22) reviews several definitions of KM, as does D. Bennet (Chapter 31) at the beginning of his chapter. Powell (Chapter 9) delineates the various operational components of KM.

Borbely (Chapter 21) provides a quick operational definition of KM and then provides a description by enumerating the components of KM at Towers Perrin. Barth (Chapter 28) discusses the overlapping definitions of KM and competitive intelligence (CI). Koenig offers a novel definition of KM in Chapter 8. He describes it as "the extension, broadly across the firm, of the information environment that has been shown by research to be conducive to successful R&D."

Combined, these discussions not only provide a very complete description of where KM is now but also lend an in-depth discussion of how KM has developed over time. Also provided are discussions of content management (CM). Arnold (Chapter 12), in an extensive discussion of CM, defines KM as one bullet item under CM. This opposes the opinion believed by most authors in this book but is well argued and illustrative of the fact discussed by Ponzi that there is still no broad consensus on what KM is and what is or is not included within the fold.

KM STRATEGY

Knowledge management strategy is discussed in a number of chapters. Droitsch (Chapter 22) discusses the issue of "grand plan" versus a more ad-hoc programmatic approach. He generally opts for the latter, and specifically recommends a focal-point approach to accomplish KM implementation, at least in large bureaucratic organizations. In discussing CM and the issues therein, Arnold (Chapter 12) presents exactly the same argument but approaches the problem of implementing KM from a different direction and arriving at conclusions that are totally congruent with those of Droitsch (Chapter 22). Arnold also indicates in Chapter 12 the difficulties of fitting CM into flat organizations. Content management tends to "want" structure and hierarchy—and the more, the better, to facilitate data access structure. Short and Azzarello (Chapter 3) similarly take a bottom-up approach to KM implementation, and Barth (Chapter 28) takes the approach of "apply KM to specific problems."

By contrast, A. Bennet in Chapter 19 discusses KM in the context of the U.S. Department of the Navy and stresses the importance of rapidly building to an enterprise-wide approach. Borbely, from Towers Perrin, also emphasizes the advantages of quickly developing an enterprise-wide approach in Chapter 21. The "lesson learned" is that the right strategy for KM implementation is very context specific. Koenig (Chapter 6) discusses strategy along the codification versus personalization spectrum, and argues that it is a far more complex and context-specific issue than has been argued in the past. In Chapter 29, he argues for user education and its planning as a fundamental part of KM strategy development.

In summary, KM strategy is complex and context specific and is likely to be a mixture of both bottom up and top down, sometimes simultaneously, and a mixture of codification and personalization.

(Also see the theme, "Find the Focal Points.")

Lessons Learned

The subtitle of this book is "What Works and What Doesn't" with regard to KM lessons learned. All of the chapters address this theme at least implicitly. However, where can the time-constrained reader find good, sharp lists of lessons learned? Check out the following:

- Short and Azzarello focus on nine lessons learned; review several cases; and, after each, have sections entitled: The Lesson, The Learning, and How to Apply This Lesson. (Chapter 3)
- Durham's chapter is essentially a list of lessons learned, primarily in the KM area of communities of practice. (Chapter 20)
- Arnold's Section 3 is specifically on lessons learned in CM, and his observations in Section 4 are really further lessons learned. (Chapter 12)
- Koenig's chapter covering research on research is specifically a recounting of the lessons learned relevant to KM from the last quarter century of research on research, including what the effective correlates of successful research are. Research is, after all, the quintessential knowledge work. This is a very relevant body of research, but it is surprisingly little connected to the literature of KM. (Chapter 8)
- Hubert and O'Dell provide a list of lessons learned set in the context, and ordered by the stages, of development of KM implementation. (Chapter 5)
- Hasanali looks at issues of KM implementation (such as leadership, culture, and IT) and supplies lessons learned for each issue. (Chapter 4)
- In Borbely's chapter, the weft is KM implementation at Towers Perrin, and the warp is lessons learned. (Chapter 21)
- Koenig's chapter on KM and user education is an exposé of lessons not learned in the importance of user education, and a recap of what those lessons are. (Chapter 29)

- Malhotra similarly lists some lessons not learned, and his section on enablers and constraints is, in effect, a discussion of lessons to keep in mind when designing KM systems. (Chapter 7)
- Barth provides some lessons learned from the viewpoint of CI but also applicable to KM in general. (Chapter 28)

IMPLEMENTING KM

The following are some sources specifically on implementing KM:

- Short and Azzarello: the consultant's viewpoint; identifying where to start first (Chapter 3)
- Durham: who does what; acknowledging success (Chapter 20)
- Koenig: planning user education into the development of KM (Chapter 29) (Durham's and Koenig's chapters nicely complement each other.)
- Arnold: KM and enterprise resource planning—the complexities and pitfalls of which to beware in planning and implementing CM systems (Chapter 12)
- Chen: Dataware's, Delphi Group's, and Accenture's formulae for KM implementation (Chapter 17)
- Borbely: very frank review of the implementation of KM at Towers Perrin (Chapter 21)
- Hasanali: drawing from APQC's extensive experience and lessons learned from the study of numerous KM implementations (Chapter 4) and the following:
- Hubert and O'Dell: drawing from the same experience as Hasanali provide guidelines for KM implementation (Chapter 5)
- Droitsch: KM implementation and programmatic approach in the U.S. Department of Labor (Chapter 22)
- A. Bennet: KM implementation, the more wholistic approach, in the U.S. Department of the Navy (Chapter 19)
- Stuedemann: implementing KM at Caterpillar University, the incorporation of commercial "others" into communities of practice (Chapter 23)
- Srikantaiah: tacit knowledge, KM-system development at the World Bank (Chapter 24)
- Palmquist: communities of practice and "yellow pages" (Chapter 32)

(Also see the themes: "KM Stars and Thought Leaders," "Lessons Learned," and "Communities of Practice.")

EDUCATION FOR KM AND LEARNING IN KM

Srikantaiah reviews training and education for and about KM offered by both academic institutions and nonacademic institutions, such as professional associations and nonprofits like the APQC and the Conference Board (Chapter 30). Koenig uses KPMG Consulting data to demonstrate the extent of KM failures attributable to inadequacies in user education and training, and focuses on tactics to correct those inadequacies (Chapter 29). Hasanali in Chapter 4 similarly indicates that "The role of training is not given the attention that it deserves ...," and emphasizes teaching, grading, and coaching. In Chapter 5, Hubert and O'Dell, drawing from APQC experience, not surprisingly also point out the importance of training, and they further indicate that if it emanates from a central resource pool, it also serves the function of demonstrating institutional commitment to KM.

A. Bennet, in discussing KM in the U.S. Department of the Navy, focuses on information literacy and learning objectives for KM, providing a useful list of the latter and references to much of the seminal material produced by the U.S. Department of the Navy (Chapter 19). Palmquist (Chapter 32) and D. Bennet (Chapter 31) both emphasize the relationship between KM and active learning: first, KM as a way of accomplishing active (or action) learning; and second, the importance of designing KM systems with an understanding of active learning. Palmquist also discusses the technique of building "learning histories." In Chapter 22, although the term "just-in-time" (JIT) is not used, Droitsch addresses the JIT learning theme, specifically the Advanced Distributive Learning (ADL) Initiative, and the development of standards to make it implementable.

COMMUNITIES OF PRACTICE

Communities of practice are addressed in some considerable detail by Durham in Chapter 20. She focuses on their composition, the roles of participants, and the identification of the right people for the right roles. In particular, she stresses the role of the moderator, and the importance of that role in making communities of practice work effectively. Palmquist also dedicates a considerable portion of Chapter 32 to communities of practice. D. Bennet (Chapter 31) gives specific examples. The largest part of Borbely's Chapter 21 is about lessons learned in implementing communities of practice. Chapter 25 by Davenport is about designing communities of practice to enable people to cooperate across different companies whose relationship may be comparatively short term. Hasanali, in Chapter

4 when discussing structure and roles/responsibilities, includes communities of practice. In Chapter 23, Stuedemann's discussion of communities of practice at Caterpillar University is particularly interesting because it is one of few cases reported in the literature of communities of practice in the for-profit environment that extend beyond the parent organization. Srikantaiah (Chapter 24) examines extended communities of practice at the World Bank, perhaps the best-known example but in the nonprofit environment.

(Also see the theme, "Roles in KM.")

CONTENT MANAGEMENT

Srikantaiah, in Chapter 11, provides a brief overview of the issues in CM, and two further chapters address it in depth. Specifically, Chen's Chapter 17 focuses on data mining and, in the process, covers CM rather broadly, providing a good introduction to definitions and techniques. This is important as the field of data mining has incorporated and renamed a variety of existing techniques, and many people may not recognize the tried–and–true under their new names. In reading the literature of data mining, some may feel like Molière's character, Monsieur Jourdain, who was pleased to discover that he had been speaking prose all his life and never knew it. Equally pointedly, Arnold, in Chapter 12, discusses CM in considerable depth, focusing on tactical issues and their implications, both short and long term. He identifies a number of troubling issues, particularly integration and scale-up problems. In addition, some of the technical aspects of handling data and information in CM are addressed by Cervone and Fichter in Chapter 13, and by Krichel's focus on the semantic Web in Chapter 14.

KM COSTS AND ECONOMICS

In Chapter 9, Powell discusses the challenge of preparing a return on investment/net present value justification for KM and, in the process, explains the technique for nonfinancial managers and professionals. Koenig informs in Chapter 10 that using "time saved" as a justification for KM is one that, for reasons that are not intuitively obvious, is fraught with peril and must be used sparingly. Arnold provides some useful "rules of thumb" on software costs and license costs in Chapter 12.

KM Measurement

The measurement of KM is always a key topic and always difficult. The emphasis on storytelling to sell KM is not happenstance. However, a number of chapter authors do have useful contributions to make. Borbely discusses the importance of establishing KM measurement function and provides some techniques in Chapter 21. In Chapter 19, A. Bennet touches on some of the metrics used by the U.S. Department of the Navy's KM initiatives. Hasanali's Chapter 4 identifies measurement as one of the five principal "critical factors" for KM, and discusses some of the problems involved in accomplishing good measurement. Hubert and O'Dell correspondingly identify "creating measures" as one of the five key components of KM implementation (Chapter 5).

(Also see the theme, "KM Costs and Economics.")

Trust

A long-term, by KM standards, topic in KM implementation is that of trust: How does one implement KM without trust, or develop the trust necessary for an effective implementation of KM? In Chapter 7, Malhotra presents developing trust and commitment as a key issue in implementing KM. D. Bennet discusses trust and team building as part of the KM planning process (Chapter 31). Intriguingly, Davenport, in her discussion of a design exercise for a KM system to enable groups from different organizations to collaborate, speculates on the possible development of a "Trust Mark-Up" language (Chapter 25). Barth emphasizes trust from two aspects: the conventional view of employees needing trust in the organization, and that of decision makers who need to trust the KM/CI system to use it in an effective and timely fashion (Chapter 28).

Find the Focal Points

The importance of finding the critical points or functions for the design and implementation of a KM project or system is a key theme. In Chapter 3, Short and Azzarello, as consultants who focus on KM, emphasize these focal points as the key to delivering a solution to the customer. Durham (Chapter 20) similarly emphasizes locating the "pain points," and Hasanali refers in the same vein to "pain areas" (Chapter 4). Droitsch, in Chapter 22, discusses overall strategy— grand plan versus a more ad-hoc programmatic approach—and opts, in general, for the latter, specifically recommending a focal-point approach to accomplish that, as does Arnold (Chapter 12).

KM STARS AND THOUGHT LEADERS

The importance of identifying KM stars and thought leaders in KM implementation is discussed and emphasized by Durham (Chapter 20), and by Koenig (Chapter 8), who refers to "gatekeepers" in this chapter on findings pertinent to KM that have been revealed by the corpus of research on research. Palmquist uses the term "knowledge champion" to express the same notion in Chapter 32. The same concept emerges in Borbely (Chapter 21) who, like Durham, uses the phrase "thought leaders."

TAXONOMY

Taxonomies are the topic of Bedford's Chapter 15, and both types and applications are discussed. Taxonomies are also discussed in some depth by Palmquist (Chapter 32), who provides an appropriate "sea story" of KM development at Siemens Industrial Services. Koenig and Srikantaiah emphasize the importance of taxonomies to KM in Chapter 1. They make it the focal point of the transition of KM from Stage II to Stage III. Chen, in Chapter 17, similarly emphasizes its importance.

Powell develops a taxonomy, laying out knowledge assets and knowledge content classes in a matrix designed to rationalize and standardize thinking about the K components in a KM system (Chapter 16). For those in the information field, for some time, something of a wonder has been the KM field's failure to build upon the fairly extensive previous work done in trying to develop knowledge audits of an organization's knowledge assets. Part of the reason for this is what might be called the one-dimensional aspect of the previous work and its failure to cast knowledge auditing in the business context, a failure that Powell attempts to remedy.

(Also see the themes: "The Future of KM" and "Content Management." There is clearly a congruence of view: that KM is moving in the direction of a greater appreciation of CM's importance; and of the centrality of taxonomy and knowledge structuring to that development.)

STANDARDS

The issue of KM standards are not only addressed by the chapters specifically about relevant standards—Cervone and Fichter on XML (Chapter 13) and Krichel on the semantic Web and Resource Description Framework (Chapter 14)—but they also appear organically elsewhere. Droitsch emphasizes the importance of developments like the ADL Initiative and the Sharable Content Object Reference Model (SCORM), which developed from ADL. Arnold, in discussing CM in Chapter 12, similarly stresses the importance of standards.

ROLES IN KM

One of the themes that emerges in this book is who does what in KM, and how to match skills and competencies to roles. Durham's Chapter 20 is based on this topic specifically. Chapters 21 and 32, by Borbely and Palmquist, respectively, also cover the topic in some depth.

(Also see the themes: "Education for KM and Learning in KM" and "Communities of Practice." A number of the chapters there also are applicable to this generally under-appreciated topic.)

PORTALS AND VISUAL DESIGN

In Chapter 17, Chen discusses several aspects of portals and visual design, and gives examples from HelpfulMed. Palmquist also addresses the topic in Chapter 32 but more from the perspective of user participation.

KM APPLICATIONS IN GOVERNMENT

Chapter 19, by A. Bennet on the U.S. Department of the Navy, and Chapter 22, by Droitsch on the U.S. Department of Labor, specifically discuss the implementation of KM in government agencies. Quite interesting is the difference in approach that is recommended, primarily top down (A. Bennet), or primarily programmatic or bottom up (Droitsch).

(Also see the theme, "KM Strategy.")

CI in KM

In Chapter 26, Maag and Flint provide a comprehensive introduction to Competitive Intelligence (CI), and Shelfer, in Chapter 27, discusses CI as a subset of KM, indicating the overlap and also discussing benchmarking as a clear overlap area between CI and KM. Barth (Chapter 28) stresses the tension between KM and the protective preventative aspects of CI, and addresses issues in trying to simultaneously satisfy both.

The Future of KM

Malhotra (Chapter 7) and Arnold (Chapter 12) both make useful predictions about the future of KM. Arnold is particularly cogent on the problems of scaling up CM in KM. At the end of Chapter 5, Hubert and O'Dell have a section, Continuing the Journey, that roughs out future trends and likely developments. Koenig and Srikantaiah's Chapter 1, describing three stages of KM, discusses the stages that have led to where KM is now and that, in turn, leads to speculation as to where KM will go. Stage III leads directly to Hubert and O'Dell's first bullet item. Chen speculates on a number of primarily technology-based developments, both hardware and software, which are likely to have an impact on KM, and what that impact will be (Chapter 17). Davenport (Chapter 25) discusses what are, as of yet, only experimental design projects intended to move KM from the reactive to the proactive stages, a theme that Malhotra (Chapter 7) also emphasizes. A perusal of Davenport indicates where KM may be going and how difficult it will be to get there, and, by doing so, indicates what are some of the practical limitations to KM in the near future.

References

Srikantaiah, T. Kanti and Koenig, Michael E. D., eds. 2000, *Knowledge Management for the Information Professional*, Medford, NJ: Information Today, Inc. for the American Society for Information Science.

Introductory Chapters

CHAPTER 1

Three Stages of Knowledge Management

Michael E. D. Koenig, Long Island University

T. Kanti Srikantaiah, Dominican University

A third stage of knowledge management has emerged. If one peruses the content of the 2000 and 2001 KMWorld conferences, one can see it clearly. At KMWorld 2000, a track on content management appeared for the first time. At KMWorld 2001 in October/November, content management was the dominant track, constituting the largest cluster of topics. *Taxonomy/content* has emerged as the third state.

THE THREE STAGES OF KM

Stage I is the "by the Internet out of intellectual capital" stage and consists of

- Information technology
- Intellectual capital
- The Internet (including intranets, extranets, and so on)

The key phrase is *best practices,* later replaced by the more politic *lessons learned.*

Stage II is the human and cultural dimensions, the human relations stage, and consists of

- Communities of practice
- Organizational culture
- The learning organization (Senge, 1990)
- Tacit knowledge (Nonaka et al., 1995) incorporated into KM

The key phrase is *communities of practice.*

Stage III is the content and retrievability stage and consists of structuring content and assigning descriptors (index terms). The key phrases are *content management* and *taxonomies*.

First, let us review the developments to date and the first two stages. Note that new stages do not replace earlier stages, they merely emphasize aspects of KM that, although there, were inadequately recognized previously.

Stage I

The initial stage of KM was driven primarily by IT. Stage I has been described in an equestrian metaphor as "by the Internet out of intellectual capital." Organizations, particularly the large international consulting organizations, realized that their stock in trade was information and knowledge; that often the left hand, as it were, had no idea what the right hand knew; and if they could share that knowledge, they could avoid reinventing the wheel, underbid their competitors, and increase profits. When the Internet emerged, organizations realized that the intranet flavor of the Internet was a god-given tool to accomplish that knowledge coordination and sharing. The first stage of KM was about how to deploy that new technology to accomplish those goals.

In Stage IB, if you will, those large international consulting organizations also realized quickly that many of their customers shared exactly the same problems, and that the expertise they were building for themselves could also be a product, that is, an expertise they could purvey to those customers. A new product needs a name and a theme or rationale. The name for their new product was KM, and the theme/rationale justifying it was *intellectual capital*. This theme coincidentally had emerged as a hot topic in the business literature only a couple of years earlier and provided a wonderful rationale for the importance of KM. The first stage might be described as the "If only Texas Instruments knew what Texas Instruments knew" stage, to revisit a much quoted aphorism. The hallmark phrase of Stage I first was *best practices*, to be replaced by the more politic *lessons learned*.

Stage II

The second stage of KM, described simply, added recognition of the human and cultural dimensions. Stage II might be described as the "If you build it they will come is a fallacy" stage; that is, the recognition "If you build it they will come" is a recipe that can easily lead to quick and embarrassing failure if human factors are not sufficiently taken into account. As this recognition unfolded, two major themes from the business literature were brought into the KM fold. The first was the work by Senge (1990) on the learning organization. The second was the work by Nonaka et al. (1995) on tacit knowledge and how to discover and cultivate it. Both were not only about the human factors of KM implementation and use, they were also about knowledge creation as well as knowledge sharing and communication. The hallmark phrase of Stage II is *communities of practice.*

The Conference Board has been organizing meetings on the subject of KM since 1995. Information technology people overwhelmingly populated the early meetings. A good marker of the shift from the first to the second stage of KM is that for the 1998 Conference Board conference on KM there was, for the first time, a noticeable contingent of attendees from human resources (HR) departments; and by 1999 HR was the largest single group.

Stage III

The third stage is the awareness of the importance of content and, in particular, an awareness of the importance of the retrievability and therefore of the importance of the arrangement, description, and structure of that content. A good alternate description for the second stage of KM is the "It's no good if they don't use it" stage. Thus, in that vein, perhaps the best description for the new third stage is the "It's no good if they can't find it" stage, or perhaps "It's no good if they try to use it but can't find it." Another bellwether is that the TFPL report on the October 2001 CKO (Chief Knowledge Officer) Summit stated that, for the first time, taxonomies emerged as a topic, and it emerged full blown as a major topic. Figure 1.1 shows the graphic with which TFPL summarized the results of that summit. Note that the largest, boldest word is **taxonomy**. The hallmark phrases emerging for the third stage are *content management* (or enterprise content management) and *taxonomies.*

What Does That Tell Us?

Recognizing the stages of development of a concept is foremost, of course, a good way to recognize where one is and where the field is. It also leads one to ask the following questions: Am I up on things? Have I missed anything?

Another advantage is the recognition that a new stage is also a change of direction, and when changing direction one should ask two questions: What are the rocks and shoals out ahead? What are the new opportunities?

Various ramifications of this change of direction will undoubtedly unfold, but one important corollary already stands out. There seems to be a very clear missed opportunity, at least so far. The KM community seems to be trying to reinvent the

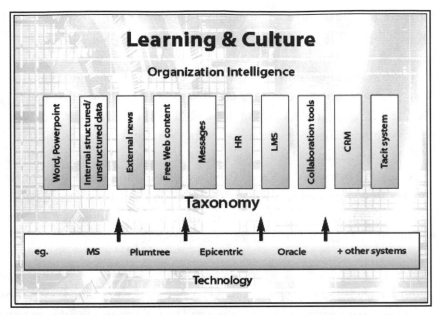

Figure 1.1   TFPL's summary of the context of knowledge management. (From KMWorld. March 2002, 11(3):20.)

domain of taxonomy, even though there are plenty of taxonomic specialists out there. The KM community seems to be almost completely unaware of their existence and looking entirely in the wrong direction. Taxonomies are perceived by the KM community as emanating from natural scientists, not from librarians and information scientists. To be sure, meaning No. 2 in Webster's Dictionary for the term *taxonomy* is "classification, especially the orderly classification of plants and animals." Meaning No. 1, however, is "the study of the general principles of classification," that is, librarianship and information science. If business professionals and KM staff could visualize what they have in mind when they talk about taxonomies—and only a few could adequately do that—what would constitute that picture is something very similar to MESH (medical subject headings), the carefully structured compendium compiled by the National Library of Medicine. But there is precious little awareness that taxonomies and classificatory structures such as MESH are the natural domain of librarians and information scientists.

An interesting token of that gap in comprehension was a presentation at KMWorld 2001 by members of the staff of the American Productivity and Quality Center (www.apqc.org), an important "opinion leader" organization in the world of KM and organizer of an important KM conference. The presentation was entitled

"Managing content and knowledge"; its theme was the *critical success factors* for successful implementation of KM. It was clearly a Stage III presentation. The most heavily stressed point was the prescriptive offered for successful KM implementation: "Taxonomy before technology."

Even more interesting was what emerged indirectly. A number of examples and case studies were briefly described. One of those was the implementation by the Washington State Library of a system to deliver state agency and related information to small business in particular and to the public at large. Some dollar figures were given, and indeed the Washington State Library project was striking for its impact per dollar, a fact commented on by the audience. The phenomenon should not be surprising, however; after all, the project had a running head start because it was spearheaded by librarians, taxonomic specialists. Unfortunately, while there was no opportunity to ask the question in public, because the content filled session ran into overtime, one question was obvious: Had the team examined whether the central involvement of such staff was also a generic critical success factor for KM implementation? If so, what had the team found? The answers to the question of whether involvement of information professionals was a critical success factor, delivered privately after the talk, were "Yes, the question had been asked," and "Yes, very much so."

To be sure, content management and librarianship are not a simple one-to-one relationship, but the area of core overlap is substantial and critical.

An important corollary is that one area where the KM community should take advantage of the expertise of information professionals (librarians and information scientists), as opposed to IT, is in software selection, particularly software that offers some sort of automatic classification, categorization, or indexing, an area of great interest in Stage III KM. By way of illustration, 25 software packages were submitted for the *KM Promise Award* at the KMWorld 2001 Conference. They provide a snapshot of where the vendors think the field is going, and where they think there is a need that they can address. The largest cluster of nine products attempted, in some algorithmic fashion, to structure and index a body of documents. The next largest cluster consisted of eight "communities of practice"/"yellow pages" products. These attempted, at some level, to identify and classify who in the organization or the extended organization possessed which particular subject knowledge or expertise, and then facilitate an appropriate linkage. In either case, but particularly the former, program or product selection should centrally involve information professionals who are familiar with taxonomies, thesauri, indexes, and the world of textual information retrieval in general.

The bottom line in this new third stage of KM is that information professionals need to make their skills known to the KM community, and the KM community needs to seek out information professionals and bring them more into the KM fold. If that does not happen, there will be much needless reinvention of the taxonomic wheel.

ENDNOTE

For a discussion of the developments through Stages I and II, see Koenig, M. E. D., and Srikantaiah, T. K. (2000). The evolution of knowledge management. In: *Knowledge Management for the Information Professional*, Srikantaiah, T. K. and Koenig, M. E. D., eds. Medford, NJ: Information Today, Inc. for the American Society for Information Science, Chapt. 3, pp. 23–36.

REFERENCES

Nonaka, I. and Takeuchi, H. (1995). *The Knowledge-Creating Company: How Japanese Companies Create the Dynamics of Innovation*, New York: Oxford University Press.

Senge, P. M. (1990). *The Fifth Discipline: The Art and Practice of the Learning Organization.* New York, Doubleday/Currency.

TFPL. (2001). *Knowledge Strategies—Corporate Strategies.* TFPL's 4th International CKO Summit, London, TFPL, 2001; see also www.tfpl.com.

CHAPTER 2

Knowledge Management: Birth of a Discipline

Leonard J. Ponzi, IBM

INTRODUCTION

The birth of a discipline can be said to occur when researchers become interested in the new idea or problem. Its survival, however, is reflected first by changing patterns of informal communication, then by changing formal communication. Cronin (1982) refers to this as "formalizing the informal."

The growth in formal communications, better referred to as published works, has been observed by Price (1963) and Crane (1972). Price (1963) presented statistical evidence showing, with impressive consistency and regularity, that when a segment of science is measured in terms of its citations the resulting graph depicts a logistic curve. Crane (1972) added that the number of new publications in a specialty would have four distinct stages of growth:

1. An initial formation stage, in which the absolute number of publications is small and the growth rate shows signs of increasing;
2. Emergence of a growth period. During this time the absolute number of publications grows exponentially (doubling the number of publications at regular intervals) and the growth rate is constant and large;
3. A subsequent stage whereby the annual growth of publications returns to being incremental and the growth rate shows signs of decline;
4. The growth rate and absolute number of publication declines to zero.

Countless potential disciplines emerge in the literature on every new publication, and those that survive for any length of time do so against immense odds. Knowledge management is one emerging discipline that remains strong and does not appear to be fading.

Knowledge management was born in the mid-1990s and has been deemed a broad-based concept. A survey of the literature suggests that KM appears to be borrowing theories and practices from such disciplines as organizational science, management science, and management information systems. It also suggests that this amalgamation of literature is aimed at addressing today's need to leverage some mix of business processes, people, and technology to create a competitive advantage.

While much has been published about the concept, only recently has a critical mass of work been published to enable the concept to be viewed from a bibliometric perspective. This perspective is needed because it provides an empirical structure that can be used to describe the emergence of and the contributors to KM. To this end, the objective of this fundamental research is to describe the KM concept using a "structural" interpretation of the 1991–2001 academic and industry literature as represented by three databases.

METHODOLOGY AND LIMITATIONS

The structural approach used in this research identifies published KM works and then reviews citation patterns in the literature. More specifically, this chapter reveals patterns relating to (1) publishing activity by year, (2) disciplinary breadth, (3) journals supporting KM, (4) most influential authors, (5) most cited works, and (6) the metabolic rate of the academic literature.

Source records were retrieved in the Spring of 2002 from three DIALOG files. Two files are considered academic in nature (Science Citation Index, File 34 and Social Science Citation Index, File 7), and the third file is representative of industry literature (ABI Inform, File 15). The selection of these files was based on their broad and comprehensive coverage of the academic and industry literature.

The retrieved records are articles that include the key search phrase *knowledge management* in the title, abstract, or descriptor field of the record. (See the Appendix for DIALOG search strings and commands.) This capture configuration is a more exacting search strategy than simply retrieving any records where KM appears. The assumption made is that retrieved records that include "knowledge management" in these fields represent writings focused on KM.

The capture included 2,240 source records that, in turn, were used to develop the measure mentioned above by specific bibliometric techniques (Table 2.1). Of course, this research is not without limitations. The limitations lie within the use of the three data sources, which restrict this study in five ways. First, monographs are not included in the collection. As a result, the cited reference may be a book, but the citations are not from books. Second, works indexed in two academic databases are listed by the first author only, leaving second-named authors of multi-authored works unseen and unacknowledged in the intellectual structures. The industry database does not have a "cited" field. Third, none of the databases index papers from research conferences. These technical deficiencies of the sources presently are consistent across all bibliometric research.

Table 2.1   Summary of measure and bibliometric techniques.

Measures		Methods
Publishing activity by year	⇒	Annual Counts
Disciplinary breadth	⇒	The number of disciplines contributing to a field
Journals supporting KM	⇒	Ranked journal names in both academic and industry databases
Influential authors	⇒	Ranked cited authors
Most cited works	⇒	Ranked cited references
Metabolism rate of the literature	⇒	Ranked cited year

The fourth limitation of the study is the lag time when works are indexed and when they are uploaded. As a result, the research activity captured quantitatively by the method in early 2002 might not fully reflect information published in 2001.

Lastly, while these data sources have proved to be important in the development of the bibliometric techniques used in this study, the absence of a proven cross-indexing mechanism is another limitation. This research required that monographs and journal names from ABI Inform be coded into ISI (formerly known as the Institute for Scientific Information) Subject Category Codes. To control for this variable, coding was performed by two independent coders. Each coder was given a list of ISI Subject Category Codes and scope notes, both provided by ISI.

RESULTS

Next we report on the results of each of the bibliometric measures. Each sub-section includes a brief review of the measures and the findings from this study. An interpretation and a brief discussion of the results are given in the next section.

Publication Activity

Publication activity is time-series data of occurrences. In this case, it is the KM search phrase charted by year to form a life-cycle curve similar to that of a "product life-cycle curve." The y-axis is measured this way in article counts; the shape of this type of curve offers insight into the amount of discourse surrounding a concept.

Figure 2.1 diagrams 2,240 source articles, with more than 98 percent concentrated in the six-year period from 1996 to 2001. In fact, KM remained relatively flat until 1995. Then, in 1996, KM expanded rapidly from 26 articles to its peak of 584 articles in 1999. In 2000, the publication occurrence of KM decreased by almost 20% then rebounded to about the same level in 2001.

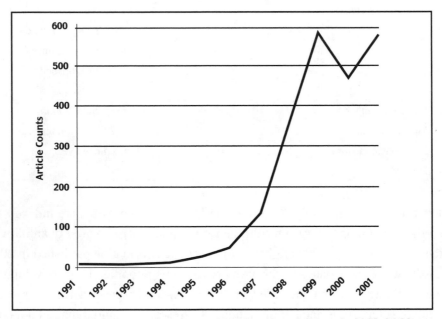

Figure 2.1   Knowledge management publication activity life cycle, 1991–2001.

Disciplinary Activity and Breadth

Disciplinary activity and breadth are interdisciplinary measures that indicate how many and which disciplines are contributing theories or methods to the development of other disciplines (Ponzi, 2002).

The method used to address these measures allows for the inclusion of all three databases by ranking the journal-name field of KM source articles. This list was then coded into ISI Subject Category Codes by two independent coders.

Assuming a threshold count of three or greater, Table 2.2 shows the proportion of disciplinary affiliation of journals over time. The threshold is justified because three co-occurrences dramatically reduce the number of random counts in journals and indicate the concentration of publication activity. This is a partial view of the activity surrounding KM.

Table 2.2   Disciplinary breadth, 1996–2001.

Discipline	1996	1997	1998	1999	2000	2001
Computer science	35.7%	43.1%	42.0%	38.8%	28.7%	36.2%
Business	21.4%	16.9%	32.4%	25.6%	18.0%	20.7%
Management	42.9%	7.7%	5.3%	12.8%	13.2%	17.2%
Information and library science		15.4%	10.6%	7.9%	16.9%	14.2%
Engineering		10.8%	4.3%	8.6%	13.6%	7.7%
Psychology		6.2%	5.3%	1.7%	1.8%	1.5%
Multidisciplinary sciences				2.0%	4.0%	
Energy and Fuels				0.7%	3.7%	0.7%
Social sciences						1.7%
Operations research and management science				1.0%		
Planning and development				1.0%		
Total	14	65	207	407	272	401
Breadth	3	6	6	10	8	8

Journals Supporting KM

The growth in the literature can be described by the type of contributing journal. This is of interest because it further narrows disciplinary activity by indicating whether activity is of academic or industry origin.

Contributions to the literature can occur in one of three ways. In the first, one or several events are popularized in the field, for example, an announcement of a new product that is later reviewed by trade journals. This type of event generally would be reflected in the industry literature. The second event that could have an impact comes from theoretical developments or seminal research. These developments often are debated through formal communications and would mainly appear in academic journals. The third possibility is a combination of the two. The most common occurrence is an academic journal reporting research conducted on industry followed by trade journals popularizing the work. At granular level, the life cycle of KM can be divided into academic (DIALOG Files 7, 34) and industry (DIALOG File 15) sources (Figure 2.2).

In the 1995–2001 publishing period, 639 source articles were found in the academic literature and 1,562 source articles in the industry literature. Figure 2.2 reveals that while the academic literature showed steady growth, the industry literature

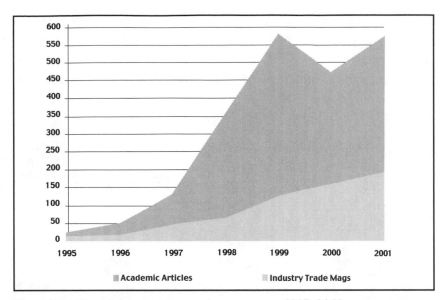

Figure 2.2   Knowledge management by source type, 1995–2001.

experienced exponential growth between 1997 and 1999 and is the focal point for the 2000 contraction seen in Figure 2.1.

The amount of KM content published by any one particular journal can be measured easily by ranking the source articles by journal name. In this research, industry and academic journals are ranked separately and then compared.

Applying a threshold of greater than 0.5 percent, Table 2.3 shows the top 44 industry journals that have published KM information during its growth period. The top five industry journals, which represent 20.8 percent of the total KM publication count, are *InformationWeek* (5.6 percent), *ComputerWorld* (4.5 percent), *CIO* (4.2 percent), *InfoWorld* (3.3 percent), and *Information World Review* (3.1 percent).

Table 2.4 shows the top 25 academic journals that publish KM research. The top 5, which represent 44.6 percent of the total KM count, are *International Journal of Technology Management* (15 percent), *Expert Systems with Applications* (9 percent), *Decision Support Systems* (8.9 percent), *NFD Information-Wissenschaft Und Praxis* (6.4 percent), and *Journal of Universal Computer Science* (5.6 percent).

Most Cited Authors and Works

The most cited authors measure ranks cited authors from academic source articles. Herein, a threshold of one or more citations per year, or a total of seven, was selected. This set represented 262 authors and 4,151 citation counts. Authors that

Table 2.3   Industry journals supporting knowledge management, 1995–2001.

Rank	Journal	Counts (%)	Rank	Journal	Counts (%)
1	InformationWeek	5.57	23	British Journal of Administration Management	0.77
2	ComputerWorld	4.48	24	European Management Journal	0.77
3	C/O	4.23	25	Journal of KM	0.77
4	InfoWorld	3.33	26	Software Magazine	0.77
5	Information World Review	3.14	27	Document World	0.70
6	Computer Reseller News	3.07	28	Executive Excellence	0.70
7	Computing Canada	2.05	29	Fortune	0.70
8	InternetWeek	1.98	30	KMWorld	0.70
9	Information Today	1.92	31	Management Review	0.70
10	Chief Executive	1.66	32	Industry Week	0.64
11	Inform	1.54	33	Competitive Intelligence Magazine	0.58
12	Network World	1.47	34	Management Today	0.58
13	Business Information Review	1.28	35	Oil & Gas Investor	0.58
14	Journal of Intellectual Capital	1.28	36	Oil & Gas Journal	0.58
15	Journal of Business Strategy	1.15	37	Sloan Management Review	0.58
16	People Management	1.15	38	American Society for Information Science Bulletin	0.51
17	Training	1.15	39	Asia Pacific Journal of Management	0.51
18	Competitive Intelligence Review	1.09	40	HR Magazine	0.51
19	Information Management Journal	0.90	41	Journal of General Management	0.51
20	International Journal of Technology Management	0..90	42	Management Services	0.51
21	R & D Management	0.83	43	Midrange Systems	0.51
22	Automotive Manufacturing & Production	0.77	44	National Underwriter	0.51

Table 2.4   Academic journals supporting knowledge management, 1995–2001.

Rank	Journal	Counts (%)
1	International Journal of Technology Management	15/02
2	Expert Systems with Applications	9.01
3	Decision Support Systems	8.58
4	NFD Information-Wissenschaft Und Praxis	6.44
5	Journal of Universal Computer Science	5.58
6	International Journal of Human-Computer Studies	5.15
7	Wirtschaftsinformatik	5.15
8	Journal of Management Information Systems	4.72
9	Long Range Planning	4.72
10	ASLIB Proceedings	4.29
11	California Management Review	4.29
12	Knowledge-Based Systems	4.29
13	Research-Technology Management	4.29
14	International Journal of Information Management	3.86
15	Journal of The American Medical Informatics Association	3.86
16	Kybernetes	3.86
17	Training & Development	3.86
18	European Journal of Information Systems	3.43
19	IEEE Intelligent Systems & Their Applications	3.43
20	Information Systems Management	3.43
21	Journal of Scientific & Industrial Research	3.43
22	Journal of Strategic Information Systems	3.43
23	IBM Systems Journal	3.00
24	Journal of Information Science	3.00
25	Journal of Management Studies	3.00

represented 0.5 percent or greater of the total were selected and presented in Table 2.5. The top five authors, representing 14.6 percent of the total count, are Nonaka, Davenport, Senge, Leonard, and Polanyi.

In the 1995–2001 period, 639 academic articles were published. All have added to the intellectual development of KM; however, not all have been influential. To address this, the most cited references in the academic literature were examined.

Table 2.5 Most cited authors, 1995–2001.

Rank	Author	Counts (%)	Rank	Author	Counts (%)
1	Nonaka I	4.818	24	Hamel G	0.747
2	Davenport T	3.927	25	Simon H	0.747
3	Senge P	2.048	26	Porter M	0.723
4	Leonard-Barton D	1.951	27	March J	0.699
5	Polanyi M	1.855	28	Mintzberg H	0.699
6	Drucker P	1.831	29	O'Dell C	0.699
7	Argyris C	1.566	30	Liebowitz J	0.675
8	Brown J	1.518	31	Barney J	0.650
9	Grant R	1.156	32	von Krogh G	0.650
10	Stewart T	1.108	33	Blackler F	0.602
11	Teece D	1.108	34	Edvinsson L	0.602
12	Wiig K	1.108	35	Stein E	0.602
13	Quinn J	1.084	36	Wenger E	0.602
14	Kogut B	1.060	37	Orlikowski W	0.578
15	Spender J	1.060	38	Hedlund G	0.554
16	Nelson R	1.036	39	Lave J	0.554
17	Huber G	0.964	40	Vonhippel E	0.554
18	Hansen M	0.867	41	Tsoukas H	0.530
19	Weick K	0.867	42	Daft R	0.506
20	Prahalad C	0.819	43	Malhotra Y	0.506
21	Ruggles R	0.795	44	Nahapiet J	0.506
22	Cohen W	0.771	45	Winter S	0.506
23	Sveiby K	0.771			

References from the academic KM source articles were ranked, and a threshold of one citation per year, or seven, created a list of 121 works. Appendix B lists the top 50 references. The entire list is available on request. Interestingly, of the total cited reference count (1,868), about half (935) were articles and the rest (933) were monographs. The top five cited works represent 19.2 percent of the total citation count.

Metabolic Rate of the Literature (Ranked by Cited Year)

An important characteristic of papers in a fast-growth field is the predominance of references to recently published works, or the metabolic rate of the literature. One measure of that is Price's Index. Price's Index (1970) corresponds to the percentage of items that refer to materials published within the last five years. The method used in this measure ranks KM source articles by cited year.

DISCUSSION

This section discusses the overall KM life cycle then centers on unpacking the 1995–2001 period in order to illuminate the emergence of and contributors to KM.

Figure 2.1 illustrates the publication activity life cycle of KM and is evidence of the emergence of the discipline. The shape of the KM life cycle suggests it might be a fad. This research, however, shows that KM does not fit the fad profile. According to Rogers (1995), a fad is described as an innovation adopted very quickly then sharply discontinued. The jury is still out on whether KM is a fad, but Ponzi and Koenig (2002) provide a general rule to determine fads.

Ponzi and Koenig (2002) charted the life cycles of three well-known fads (i.e., quality circles, total quality management, and business process re-engineering) and introduced empirical evidence that asserts a typical management movement generally reveals itself as a fad in about five years after having gained some type of momentum. The research by Ponzi and Koenig revealed that when comparing the three life cycles, each fad peaked between four and six years after some momentum began, and then declined just as dramatically. More specifically, in 1979, quality circles appeared to have momentum, only to peak in five years. The same holds true for total quality management (starting in late 1989 and peaking in 1993) and business process re-engineering (starting in 1991 and peaking in 1995). To this end, assuming that KM emerged in 1995 (defined here as the first year with a count greater than 1% of the total), the five-year rule of thumb suggests that KM is at least living longer than typical fads and perhaps is in the process of establishing itself as a new aspect of management.

In sectioning the KM life-cycle curve, three distinct stages can be described. More specifically, the life cycle can be divided into its introduction (pre-1995), growth period (1995–1999), contraction (2000), and rebound (2001). This research used bibliometric measures to explore further the last three areas.

The growth period of KM started in 1995 and continued through 1999. Nonaka and Takeuchi's 1995 seminal work, *The Knowledge-Creating Company,* marked this period. Establishing the birth year of KM, this work was the first expanded KM model. Nonaka and Takeuchi described a "spiral model of knowledge creation" and argued that knowledge is created out of a dialogue between people's tacit and explicit knowledge. This work not only conceptually framed KM but also became the most influential work of the period (Table 2.6).

In 1996, the contributing disciplines, or disciplinary activity, were concentrated into three core areas of study: computer science, business, and management. The number of contributing disciplines, or disciplinary breadth, expanded from the three in 1996 to 10 disciplines in 1999 (see Table 2.2). According to Koenig (2000), this expansion was in response to new developments in technology and to organizations seeking an advantage in an increasingly competitive market.

Table 2.6   Top five most cited references, 1995–2001.

Rank	Work	Counts (%)
1	Nonaka, I., and Takeuchi, H. (1995). *The Knowledge-Creating Company; How Japanese Companies Create the Dynamics of Innovation.* New York: Oxford University Press.	7.12
2	Davenport, T., and Prusak, L. (1998). *Working Knowledge; How Organizations Manage What They Know.* Boston, MA: Harvard Business School Press.	3.85
3	Senge, P. (1990). *The Fifth Discipline: The Art and Practice of the Learning Organization.* New York: Doubleday.	3.16
4	Nonaka, I. (1994). A dynamic theory of organizational knowledge creation. *Organization.* 51:24–38.	2.94
5	Argyris, C., and Schon, D. (1978). *Organizational Learning: A Theory of Action Approach.* Reading, MA: Addison Wesley.	2.09

In 2000, KM experienced a contraction in disciplinary activity and breadth. To improve our understanding of the event(s) that caused the 2000 pullback, it is important to narrow the KM discourse activity. Comparison of Tables 2.3 and 2.4 reveals that the percentage of publishing activity is much more concentrated among academic journals than industry journals. That is, the top five academic journals represent 45 percent of the KM counts as compared with 21 percent of the industry journals. In Tables 2.3 and 2.4, the top five journals are oriented more toward computer science and business.

Table 2.2 reveals that the 2000 computer science and business literature decreased, whereas the remaining six disciplines increased. According to Abrahamson (1991; 1996), downswings in popularity might be the direct result of shortfalls in realized benefits experienced by organizations. One such study indicating that KM was coming up short was conducted by Bain & Company. Their well-known survey on management tools and techniques reported that KM "not only had relatively low utilization but also very low satisfaction scores relative to the average" (Rigby, 2001).

The rebound in 2001 included eight disciplines contributing to the development of KM. Four disciplines (computer science, business, management, and information and library science) are each contributing more than 10 percent of the total count and together represent 88 percent of the publishing activity in the industry and academic literature. The rebound of KM observed in Figure 2.1 appears to lie within the computer science discipline and, more specifically, the industry literature.

Reflected in the 2001 computer-trade literature, the approach to KM became accepted by the industry, not strictly as a technology solution but as technology used as a supporting element in an organizational learning construct. The organizational learning proposition originally was posed in the academic literature. Table 2.6 demonstrates that four of the top five citations during the 1995–2001 period (Nonaka, 1994; 1995; Senge, 1990; Argyris and Schon, 1978) originate from the organizational science literature, supporting the idea that KM has emerged from the organizational sciences and predominately is a social science construct.

The growth of the academic literature surrounding the KM concept appears to be strong throughout the 1995–2001 period (Figure 2.3). According to Price (1970), whereas references from fast-growing hard sciences (e.g., physics and biochemistry) would consist of approximately 60 percent or more of research published within the last five years, social sciences would weigh in at 42 percent. Application of Price's social science figure to the KM 2001 academic literature

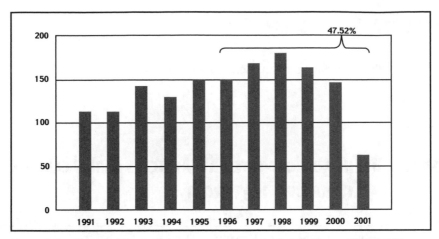

Figure 2.3   Knowledge management source articles by cited year, 1991–2001.

suggests that the academic community is metabolizing recently published works at the fairly rapid rate of 47.5 percent.

Conclusion and Future Research

The structural view of a discipline can reveal its birth and is a starting point for further research. This view allows researchers and practitioners to observe empirically the linkage and cross-fertilization of the literature. This research has revealed several interesting conclusions that lend a hand in describing the emergence of KM and that researchers may find useful in their own research.

Most notable is that KM is a multidiscipline management theory that has roots in the discipline of organizational science. Throughout the expansion years, KM drew from a number of literature domains, each contributing theories and practices to its development. The most influential author identified in this research is Nonaka. As stated previously, Nonaka and Takeuchi's 1995 seminal work, *The Knowledge-Creating Company*, not only was the most influential work but also marked the birth year of KM.

While continuing to grow and define itself, the intellectual development of KM remains unclear. This research suggests the underlying KM value proposition argues that the theories and processes from a variety of disciplines as a whole are extensively greater than the sum of their parts. This author recommends additional research to further explore how each discipline and each author—beyond the most cited—has contributed to the development of KM.

Appendix A: Dialog Search Commands

B 7,15,34
? S (Knowledge()Management)/de,ti,ab and py=Year
S1
? rd
S2 2240

Appendix B: The 50 Most-Cited KM Articles from Academic Literature, 1995–2001

Rank	Citation	Counts (%)
1	Nonaka, I., and Takeuchi, H. (1995). *The Knowledge-Creating Company; How Japanese Companies Create the Dynamics of Innovation*. New York: Oxford University Press.	7.12
2	Davenport, T., and Prusak, L. (1998). *Working Knowledge; How Organizations Manage What They Know*. Boston, MA: Harvard Business School Press.	3.85
3	Senge, P. (1990). *The Fifth Discipline: The Art and Practice of the Learning Organization*. New York: Doubleday.	3.16
4	Nonaka, I. (1994). A dynamic theory of organizational knowledge creation. *Organization Science*. 51:24–38.	2.94
5	Argyris, C., and Schon, D. (1978). *Organizational Learning: A Theory of Action Approach*. Reading, MA: Addison Wesley.	2.09
6	Polanyi, M. (1966). *The Tacit Dimension*. New York: Doubleday.	1.98
7	Polanyi, M. (1962). *Personal Knowledge Toward a Post-Critical Philosophy*. Chicago, IL: University of Chicago Press.	1.87
8	Nelson, R., and Winter, S. (1982). *Evolutionary Theory of Economic Change*. Cambridge, MA: Harvard University Press.	1.77
9	Nonaka, I. (1991). The knowledge-creating company. *Harvard Business Review*. 96–104. Nov.-Dec.	1.71
10	Huber, G. (1991). Organization learning: The contributing processes and the literatures. *Organization Science*. 2(1):88–115.	1.66

Rank	Citation	Counts (%)
11	Leonard-Barton, D. (1995). *Wellsprings of Knowledge.* Boston, MA: Harvard Business School Press.	1.66
12	Grant, R. (1991). The resource-based theory of competitive advantage: Implication for strategy formulation. *California Management Review.* Spring:114–135.	1.61
13	Stewart, T. (1997). *Intellectual Capital; How the Knowledge Economy Is Creating New Challenges for Corporations and New Opportunities for the People Who Work for Them.* New York: Doubleday.	1.55
14	Cohen, W. (1990). Absorptive capacity: A new perspective on learning and innovation. *Administrative Science Quarterly.* 35:128–152.	1.45
15	Drucker, P. (1993). *The Post-Capitalist Society.* New York: Harper Business/HarperCollins.	1.39
16	Hansen, M., Nohria, N., and Tierney, T. (1999). What's Your Strategy for Managing Knowledge? *Harvard Business Review.* 77(2) (March–April):106–116.	1.39
17	Kogut, B., and Zander, U. (1992). Knowledge of the firm, combinative capabilities, and the replication of technology. *Organization Science.* 3(3):383–397.	1.39
18	Quinn, J. (1992). *Intelligent Enterprise: A Knowledge and Service Based Paradigm for Industry.* New York: The Free Press.	1.39
19	Rubin, M., and Huber, M. (1986). *The Knowledge Industry in the United States, 1960–1980.* Princeton, NJ: Princeton University Press.	1.34
20	Barney, J. (1991). Firm Resources and Sustained Competitive Advantage. *Journal of Management.* 17(1):99–121.	1.28
21	Nonaka, I. (1998). The concept of "ba": Building a foundation for knowledge creation. *California Management Review.* 40(3):40–55.	1.23%

Rank	Citation	Counts (%)
22	Brown, J. (1991). Organizational learning and communities of practice: Toward a unified view of working, learning, and innovation. *Organization Science*. 2(1):40–57.	1.12
23	Brown, J. (1998). Organizing knowledge. *California Management Review*. 40(3):90–112.	1.12
24	Leonard, D. (1998). The role of tacit knowledge in group innovation. *California Management Review*. 40(3):112–143.	1.12
25	Wenger, E. (1998). *Communities of Practice: Learning, Meaning, and Identity*. Boston, MA: Cambridge University Press.	1.12
26	Blacker, F. (1995). Knowledge, knowledge work and organization: An overview and interpretation. *Organization Studies*. 16(6):1021–1048.	1.07
27	Spender, J. (1996). Competitive advantage from tacit knowledge? Unpacking the concept and its strategic implications. In: *Organizational Learning and Competitive Advantage*. Mosingeon, B. and Edmondson, A., eds. London: Sage; pp. 56–73.	1.07
28	Sveiby, K. (1997). *The New Organizational Wealth: Managing and Measuring Knowledge-Based Assets*. San Francisco, CA: Berrett Koehler.	1.07
29	Lave, J., and Wenger, E. (1991). *Situated Learning: Legitimate Peripheral Participation*. Boston, MA: Cambridge University Press.	1.02
30	Davenport, T., De Long, D., and Beers, M. (1998). Successful knowledge management projects. *Sloan Management Review*. Winter:43–57.	0.96
31	Edvinsson, L., and Malone, M. (1997). *Intellectual Capital: Realizing Your Company's True Value by Finding Its Hidden Brainpower*. New York: Harper Business/HarperCollins.	0.96
32	Nahapiet, J. (1998). Social capital, intellectual capital, and the organizational advantage. *Academy of Management*. 23(2):242–267.	0.96

Rank	Citation	Counts (%)
33	Tsoukas, H. (1996). The firm as a distributed knowledge system: A constructionist approach. *Strategic Management Journal.* 17:11–25.	0.96
34	O'Dell, C. (1998). If only we knew what we know: Identification and transfer of internal best practices. *California Management Review.* 40(3):154–175.	0.91
35	Walsh, J. (1991). Organizational memory. *Academy of Management Review.* 16(1):57–91.	0.91
36	Grant, R. (1996). Towards a knowledge-based theory of the firm. *Strategic Management Journal.* 17(Winter special issue):109–122.	0.86
37	Hedlund, G. (1994). A model of knowledge management and N-form corporation. *Strategic Management Journal.* 15:73–90.	0.86
38	Stein, E., and Zwass, V. (1995). Actualizing organizational memory with information systems. *Information System Research.* 6(2):85–118.	0.80
39	Teece, D. (1998). Capturing value from knowledge assets: The new economy, markets for know-how, and intangible assets. *California Management Review.* 40(3):55–75.	0.80
40	Wernerfelt, B. (1984). A resource-based view of the firm. *Strategic Management Journal.* 5(2):171–181.	0.80
41	Polanyi, M. (1967). *The Tacit Dimension.* New York: Doubleday.	0.75
42	Szulanski, G. (1996). Exploring internal stickiness: Impedi–ments to the transfer of best practice within the firm. *Strategic Management Journal.* 17:27.	0.75
43	Hamel, G., and Prahalad, C. (1994). *Competing for the Future.* Boston, MA: Harvard Business Schools Press.	0.70
44	Starbuck, W. (1992). Learning by knowledge-intensive firms. *Journal of Management Studies.* 29:713–740.	0.70

Rank	Citation	Counts (%)
45	Stein, E. (1995). Organizational memory: Review of concepts and recommendations for management. *International Journal of Information Management.* 15(1):17–33.	0.64
46	Von Hippel, E. (1994). Sticky information and the locus of problem solving: Implications for innovations. *Management Science.* 40(4):429–439.	0.64
47	Winter, S. (1987). Knowledge and competence as strategic assets. In: *The Competitive Challenge.* Teece, D., ed. Boston, MA: Harvard Business School Press, pp. 159–184.	0.64
48	Davenport, T. (1996). Improving knowledge work processes. *Sloan Management Review.* 37(4):53–65.	0.59
49	Davenport, T. (1997). *Information Ecology: Master the Information and Knowledge Environment.* New York: Oxford University Press.	0.59
50	Fahey, L. (1998). The eleven deadliest sins of knowledge management. *California Management* Review. 40(3):265–277.	0.59

References

Abrahamson, E. (1996). Managerial fashion. *Academy of Management Review.* 21(1):254–285.

Abrahamson, E. (1991). Managerial fad and fashion: The diffusion and rejection of innovations. *Academy of Management Review.* 16(3):586–612.

Crane, D. (1972). *Invisible Colleges; Diffusion of Knowledge in Scientific Communities.* Chicago, IL: University of Chicago Press.

Cronin, B. (1982). Invisible colleges and information transfer: A review and commentary with particular reference to the social sciences. *Journal of Documentation.* 38(3):212–236.

Koenig, M. (2000). Information services and productivity: A backgrounder. In: *Knowledge Management for the Information Professional.* Srikantaiah, T. K., and Koenig, M. E. D., eds. Medford, NJ: Information Today; pp. 77–98.

Price, D. (1970). Citation measures of hard science, soft science, technology, and nonscience. In: *Communications Among Scientists and Engineers.* Carnot, C. E. and Donald, D. K., eds. Lexington, MA: Heath Lexington Books; pp. 3–22.

Price, D. (1963). *Little Science, Big Science.* New York: Columbia University Press.

Ponzi, L. (2002). The intellectual structure and interdisciplinary breadth of knowledge management: A bibliometric study of its early stage of development. *Scientometrics.* 55(2):259–272.

Ponzi, L., and Koenig, M. (2002). Knowledge management: A management fad? *Information Research.* 8(1). Available online: http://informationr.net/ir/8-1/paper145.html.

Rigby, D. (2001). Management tools and techniques: A survey. *California Management Review.* 43(2):139–160.

Rogers, E. (1995). *Diffusion of Innovation.* New York: Free Press.

Part I

Strategy and Implementation

Strategy and Implementation
INTRODUCTORY NOTES

If there is one clear lesson learned in perusing the many chapters in this volume that address KM strategy and implementation, it is that the appropriate strategy for KM implementation is very context specific. While there are many lessons learned, there is no one template for all KM implementations. A major issue is clearly whether to take a bottom-up, one-project-at-a-time approach to implementing KM, an organizationwide top-down approach, or perhaps even more likely, some simultaneous combination of the two. This, in turn, leads to the issue of how that seemingly contradictory simultaneous combination can best be managed.

These and similar themes are described in the Road Map following the Table of Contents. The reader interested in either KM strategy or in KM implementation is encouraged to use the Road Map because these are two of the themes on which it elaborates. The reader is also encouraged to look at the theme, "Find the Focal Points."

Additional chapters that call attention to those themes but are outside of this section include:

Chapter 12	Content Management: Role and Reality Stephen E. Arnold, Information and Online Systems Consultant
Chapter 17	Knowledge Management and Text Mining: Overview and Case Study Hsinchun Chen, University of Arizona
Chapter 19	Alive with the Fire of Shared Understanding: Implementing Knowledge Management in the Department of the Navy Alex Bennet, Mountain Quest Institute
Chapter 20	Three Critical Roles for Knowledge Management Workspaces: Moderators, Thought Leaders, and Managers Mary Durham, Genzyme Corporation

CHAPTER 3

Knowledge Management in Action: Nine Lessons Learned

Tom Short, IBM

Richard C. Azzarello, Reality Consulting, Inc.

EXECUTIVE SUMMARY

IBM Global Services management consultants Tom Short and Richard Azzarello performed a number of KM engagements for clients in a variety of industries. Two client examples are used to illustrate nine lessons learned from their collective work in the field.

The nine lessons learned from these two projects relate to change management, solution development, and solution implementation:

1. A focal point for KM improvement ensures an appropriate KM solution is developed.
2. A KM solution blueprint provides a long-lasting reference point for action.
3. Successfully addressing a KM issue in one area often addresses it in many other areas of a firm.
4. The best KM solutions address a business issue that is already perceived to be important.
5. A passionate, committed line business leader is key to successful KM initiatives.
6. Dedicated, competent, respected business unit members make excellent KM team members.
7. Involve IT and human resources (HR) from the start to expedite KM implementation.
8. Walk a mile in the client's shoes.

9. Improve knowledge worker productivity by reducing time spent on information management tasks.

Taken together, these lessons suggest that the most useful knowledge in an enterprise is the tacit skill and expertise residing in the minds of knowledge workers. As such, knowledge itself cannot be "managed" in the traditional sense of the word the way other resources may be managed. Therefore, the tools and methods of KM are best used to address process- or resource-based issues. Successful KM results in maximizing the value employee knowledge contributes to the business operations of the firm.

A demanding discipline, KM requires a solid foundation in the practice of change management, process analysis, and business operations improvement.

INTRODUCTION

We, like many consulting practitioners, came to KM from other consulting pursuits. The common thread for us linking KM to other kinds of consulting work we performed (e.g., business process re-engineering; activity-based costing) is that KM focuses on improving business operations; and it does so by identifying ways in which the firm might better use the resources under its control.

In this regard, the promise of KM is not unlike the promise of any other operations improvement effort: Change the way business is performed internally to improve productivity, reduce waste, and generally increase effectiveness. The difference is that KM focuses on resources—such as employee skill and knowledge, the complete spectrum of information-based resources, communications infrastructures, and so forth—along with the work processes, culture, and employee behavior of the firm.

Taking all this into consideration, it is not surprising that many of the lessons of effective KM practice are ones that most people in the field already have learned. For example,

- Focus on change management.
- Include client staff on every project team.
- Understand the current state before undertaking the design of the improved, future state.
- Overcommunicate planned changes.
- Identify meaningful metrics, and link them to business value.
- Gain executive sponsorship early on.

- Develop line-level ownership of the proposed solution.
- Use client-supplied data as the basis for developing recommendations.
- Remember that a solution that works for one client may not work for another.

Although the lessons above are not KM-specific and are well known, we found ourselves rediscovering the importance of these lessons in the practice of KM. We present them here as a reminder to anyone involved in KM or other business improvement projects—these lessons are applicable to almost any project one may undertake.

The nine lessons presented here are based on our work with two client companies who looked to KM as a way of addressing real business issues. We have changed the names of both companies in order to maintain confidentiality.

Each lesson is presented in the same way. We first describe what the lesson is and why it is important. We then describe how we came to learn the lesson, in the context of one of the two client cases ("PetCo," Lessons 1–3, and "SupplyCo," Lessons 4–9). We conclude with our advice to KM practitioners as to how they might use the lesson in the practice of KM either within their own organizations or in their work with clients.

LESSON 1. A FOCAL POINT FOR KM IMPROVEMENT ENSURES DEVELOPMENT OF AN APPROPRIATE KM SOLUTION

The Lesson

As a field of study, the number of KM-related topics is daunting. A look at the list of "related topics" on one KM Web site reveals over 80 topics, ranging from communities of practice to XML, from complex systems to data mining.

One frustrated client mentioned a project list containing over 60 projects, all part of the KM program of his company. How can a line manager running a profit center, or for that matter a chief information officer or even a chief knowledge officer, possibly make sense out of this mass of possibilities. As a challenge, it is similar to attempting to put together a jigsaw puzzle without the picture on the top of the box it came in. There are so many pieces that all belong, but what goes where? How does one fit with another?

Our approach to addressing this complexity is to begin by creating a knowledge strategy by identifying a focal point for improvement and then developing a KM improvement blueprint. The completed strategy development work is followed by pilot implementation of the blueprint, and then extrapolation of the successful portions of that implementation out to other areas of the business.

This lesson provides a technique for identifying an initial focal point for your KM initiative. In Lesson 2, we describe how to construct a KM improvement blueprint.

PetCo Case Study: An Overview

PetCo is a manufacturer of consumer products with an international network of independent distributors. In order to optimize the success and effectiveness of its distribution network, PetCo established an internal consulting group (ICG) that offered a variety of services to the distributors, including process re-engineering, inventory management, and market strategy. In the five years since it was created, the ICG developed a repeatable methodology for each of these services, along with how-to guides and templates for its consultants.

The consultants from ICG come from other parts of the business and spend three years working as internal consultants before moving back out into the company, usually with a promotion and greatly improved career prospects. A key challenge for ICG was how to get their new consultants up to speed quickly, so they could be contributors on any of various engagement types from the start. Because the model ICG developed uses two-person teams on all the engagements, the obvious solution was to pair an experienced consultant with a newer one as a form of on-the-job training. This worked well for the most part; however, there were engagements that would have benefited greatly from the experience of several of the ICG members, not just the two who happened to be on the project.

Tim, the ICG manager, decided that KM might have something to offer. He contracted IBM Global Services to help him develop a solution.

We worked closely with Tim and his leadership team to develop an objective for KM within the ICG. This objective can be summarized as follows: "To access the full range of the group's experience and expertise on every consulting engagement." The next step was to develop a knowledge strategy, including a statement of intent for KM (similar to a mission statement), a KM solution blueprint, and a set of implementation plans for the various KM solution blueprint components.

The Learning

This lesson is drawn from the PetCo client engagement. Tim, the manager, was committed to pursuing KM in some way but was not yet clear as to how KM could best be used to improve ICG performance. He was following his gut instinct, which told him that KM was something good. Following good consulting practice, we elected to inventory the current set of work practices and processes of the ICG and learn as much as we could about ICG history and current way of operating, including an inventory of work processes.

We then identified which work process appeared to be the best candidate for "KM-enabling" and which step within that process was the source of greatest business risk or variance when the work process was executed. In following this approach we were really conducting a "drill down" into ICG, assessing what KM-related issues existed and developing hypotheses for ways of addressing them. On this engagement, we ultimately developed an approach to identify a clear focal point for creating a knowledge strategy, which we would reuse on all subsequent KM strategy engagements.

The lesson we learned was that by having a clear focal point within the work processes of the business, we could develop an integrated KM solution blueprint. A subsequent lesson in this chapter addresses an important corollary: Solving a KM-related issue in one place solves it everywhere. Hence the value of identifying a focal point, that is, finding a place to focus KM efforts, is the key to beginning that process. Further benefits will result when the approach and solution are applied more broadly.

How to Apply Lesson 1

The focal point for developing a KM strategy is, by definition, a task or work step within a business process that shows the most promise of benefiting from a KM initiative. Therefore, the process model for a given functional area is a good place to begin a KM strategy effort.

Here are some key criteria to consider when determining on which process to focus:

- The process represents a significant amount of activity (high transaction rate) undertaken by a significant number of people (high labor input).
- The process represents a source of significant financial risk to the business.

- The process relies on a high degree of individual judgment to produce a "good" outcome (and hence a high level of variance in process performance is likely).
- Management or employees perceive room for, or there is a real business need for, improvement.

The ideal focal point is within a work process that conforms to all the criteria listed. A good candidate process will always meet the last criterion, regarding perceived or actual business need. Engagement consulting using repeatable methods as practiced by large consulting firms and commodity trading as practiced by large financial organizations are two examples of work activities based on processes that conform to these criteria: They involve a high number of transactions over a given period of time, a large number of people perform the same process, the process represents a source of financial risk to the business, and successful outcomes are almost entirely dependent on individual judgment.

Once the candidate process has been identified, the next step is to determine which point within that process is most critical to a successful outcome and the greatest source of variance and, therefore, business risk. If this is not obvious, an easily applied tool called knowledge process mapping (KPM) may be used to help divine the answer.

Knowledge process mapping is a means of extending a process flow diagram by adding a second dimension: knowledge resources. The knowledge resources we use include tacit knowledge (or expertise), content, social capital, and infrastructure (including processes, information technology, and physical infrastructure). Figure 3.1 shows how these are oriented to the focal process to form a knowledge process map. The map is set up by providing the name and overall objective of the work process, along with all process steps and their individual objectives across the top.

Populating the map can be done either linearly from beginning to end, or by starting with a probable focal point. The probable focal point approach is faster and is identified by answering the following question: "When we fail to achieve the desired outcome for this process it is usually due to poor performance in which step?"

Regardless of how the focus of a KM strategy development effort is established, we recommend having a clearly defined focal point and associated improvement objective before undertaking the development of a knowledge strategy or other KM initiatives.

Process Name Overall Objective	Step 1 Objective	Step 2 Objective	Step 3 Objective	Step 4 Objective
Tacit Knowledge				
Content				
Social Capital				
Infrastructure				

Figure 3.1   Setup for a knowledge process map.

Lesson 2. A KM Solution Blueprint Provides a Long-lasting Reference Point for Action

The Lesson

Identifying the focal point for a KM initiative does precisely what the term says: It provides focus for the development of a KM strategy. The KM strategy, however, is a set of initiatives and projects aimed at addressing whatever issue is at the focal point. A KM solution blueprint is a diagram depicting a systemic solution to whatever issue was flagged as the focal point within a work process. The KM solution blueprint provides the aforementioned "top of a jigsaw puzzle box" for a complex KM solution. It reminds the solution implementers of what the larger solution is composed of and how the various components are connected to one another, bringing needed context to each of the components.

The Learning

After we completed the KPM work and identified the focal point for KM improvement for ICG, we needed to identify specific tasks and projects that could be undertaken to address the focal point issues. We ran a series of workshops and focus groups in which ICG staff identified the universe of KM-related projects or interventions that might provide some improvement. This list was distilled to those projects that the ICG viewed to be highly relevant and relatively easily implemented within 12 months.

This was still only a list of projects, including mentoring, after-action reviews, staff location updates, and more. The real work involved configuring these various initiatives into a coherent solution. We began by grouping the initiatives based on similarity and then took a conceptual "step back" to have a look at the groupings in the context of the whole, keeping in mind the overall objective (which was to be able to access the full resources of the group on every consulting assignment).

After several iterations, the KM solution blueprint in Figure 3.2 emerged. It depicts 11 discrete solution components, each of which needed to be created and implemented. The components are like jigsaw puzzle pieces. The KM solution blueprint is like the top of the jigsaw puzzle box; that is, it is a picture of what all the pieces look like when fully assembled. Without this top-level picture, the risk is that a KM initiative will focus on implementing one puzzle piece or another without ever creating the top-level picture. The result will be that the pieces will not fit together and function as a whole system.

Therefore, the KM solution blueprint is critical. In fact, one year after the blueprint was created, the ICG KM implementation leader showed us a laminated copy of the blueprint. He said, "I carry this with me everywhere I go. There is enough here to keep us busy for three years."

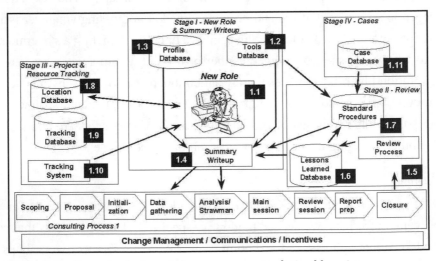

Figure 3.2   Example of a knowledge management solution blueprint.

How to Apply Lesson 2

Solution blueprints are as unique as the KM issues they are designed to address. The objective of the blueprint is to provide a view of a whole-system solution, situated in the context of the work process it is designed to improve. The blueprint should show new KM-related work processes, roles, information flows, information sources, computer applications, manual steps, automated steps, reports, and so on, all in the context of the focal point and work process defined in Lesson 1. For each solution component shown on the blueprint, a project plan should be developed, providing at least a high-level description of how that component could be implemented.

Components to include in the blueprint can be identified using brainstorming and voting, focus groups, or individual interviews. The key is to identify those actions, tools, or other changes that could positively impact the issues identified at the KM focal point. The list of potential components created from brainstorming is reduced to a list of KM blueprint solution components based on ease of implementation within a fixed time period (e.g., within 12 months), estimated cost, and anticipated level of acceptance.

Affinity clustering is a powerful way to identify logical groupings of the solution components. Orientation of these logical groupings to the focal point and focal work process is how the solution blueprint is created. The resulting blueprint shows not only the entire system that the solution components comprise but also individual projects required to implement the blueprint.

If the blueprint is sufficiently complex, it may be desirable to group the individual blueprint components into separate stages and arrive at the best sequence for implementation, considering cost, dependence on implementation of other components, and anything else that might have an effect on the sequence.

LESSON 3. SUCCESSFULLY ADDRESSING A KM ISSUE IN ONE AREA OF A FIRM OFTEN ADDRESSES IT IN MANY OTHER AREAS

The Lesson

In our view, KM solutions rely heavily on the softer, human behavior and cultural aspects of business rather than on computer systems and technology. Therefore, once a KM-related issue has been identified related to a specific focal point, it is likely that a solution to effectively address this issue will have broader applicability—even though it was initially developed to address an issue closely associated with a specific work step in a particular process.

This is great news for KM implementers. It means that a solution can be developed and proved for a specific issue and that access to the solution can be extended to other work processes and staff to deliver equally effective results. The trick is to convince the management team, who will likely be skeptical of the truth of this lesson.

The Learning

"When you've seen one, you've seen them all."

The consulting group for PetCo offered its clients a half dozen distinct service types, each with its own consulting method. After we explained our KPM approach, Tim, the manager, expected us to map each of the methods as a separate process because each was composed of different steps.

During the mapping exercise for the first process selected, however, it became apparent that we would not need to map out the other processes. We identified the focal point around which we could develop our KM solution blueprint, and Tim agreed that the root cause of the problem was common to the other methods and that solving it for one method would carry over to the others without any adjustment whatsoever.

The reason for this carryover is that KM issues often can be traced to two sources. One is the willingness of the performers of a given process to share and reuse knowledge and information related to that process. In broadest terms, this "willingness" is culturally based and is mediated by other factors of the culture of a firm, such as the measurement system and leadership. The other source of KM issues is the information infrastructure used to support work processes. This may include databases, applications, and workflow tools, along with virtual collaboration and communication tools.

We accept that both culture and information systems' infrastructure are common across many if not all of the processes of an enterprise. Thus, it is not surprising that when a given root cause of a KM issue can be traced to either or both of these systems (rather than unique issues related to a particular work process), a KM solution developed to address an issue in one area is also likely to translate to many other areas.

How to Apply Lesson 3

Knowledge management issues are often common across various processes and functional areas within a firm. Directing attention to a single area and developing a KM solution for it provides an excellent basis for piloting KM solutions that, once proven effective, can be deployed elsewhere. Keep this in mind as potential focal points and solution approaches are evaluated—KM solutions usually apply more broadly across the business than the area for which they were developed.

Lesson 4. The Best KM Solutions Address a Business Issue Already Perceived to be Important

The Lesson

As the popularity and currency of KM has increased, the number of tools and methods aimed at supporting KM has soared. Some of these offerings are repositioned versions of things that have been around for years; others are novel and innovative. Most if not all *appear* to have merit, at least from the perspective of KM. A challenge many enterprises face is to figure out which tools or methods to pursue.

We identified a way to address this challenge, a way to provide clients with a set of tasks and projects that enable concrete, meaningful action. Our approach is based on discovering the answer to a very simple question: "What is the business ready to do next?" A good place to start is to identify the parts of the business that are broken.

Imagine you are in your backyard digging a hole to plant a tree. You do not know what a shovel is, so you are using what you have at hand, a discarded soup can. Your neighbor spies you doing this, walks over, and lays a shovel on the ground next to you. Would you require any explanation or instruction as to the use of the shovel? No. Would you require any convincing to pick up the shovel and continue your hole-digging using it instead of the soup can? No.

So it is, too, with effective KM solutions. In fact, in a perfect world all business improvement efforts would be "shovels" laid down before legions of "soup can users." Failed KM efforts, we have learned, ignore this approach.

The essence of a successful KM solution, then, is one that addresses a perceived issue among those who are affected by the solution, and it does so in a way that is consistent with prevailing cultural and behavioral norms. When a solution is aligned in this fashion, the likelihood of acceptance is maximized.

SupplyCo Case Study: An Overview

SupplyCo is a large multinational enterprise whose operations include supplying basic ingredients to processed food manufacturers. In order to hedge against currency fluctuations and ensure a continuous supply of raw agricultural products, SupplyCo established a commodity trading division that includes traders located worldwide.

Commodity trading is both information and knowledge intensive. Traders must track global commodity prices and the wide array of variables that impact those prices, including weather, natural disasters that might impact crop yields (e.g., drought, the effects of El Niño), transportation pricing, economic growth, and currency prices. The trader must gather and assimilate this information in near real time, merge it with his or her own personal experience and judgment, and make decisions to buy or sell positions in a given commodity.

SupplyCo was interested in piloting KM in one of its divisions and approached IBM Global Services for assistance. We conducted a Discovery Workshop aimed at identifying the business units that would be the most receptive to, and derive the most value from, a KM intervention. We concluded that the commodity trading business would be the best place to start. Further work within the trading operations highlighted several potential KM-related issues. The one we decided to pursue was e-mail overload, with each trader receiving 150 to 300 messages per day, requiring about four hours to read through.

When we asked the traders what they would do if we could give them an extra hour or two in their trading day, they replied without hesitation, "We would turn it into money." We found our group of people "digging holes with soup cans." Our job was to work with them to create a "shovel."

The solution we developed included automatic e-mail categorization, new job role definitions, and new incentives and performance metrics. In developing the solution, we worked closely with traders and executive management as well as with the HR and IT functions.

The solution was designed, built, and implemented in less than six months and was well received by both the users and HR and IT functions that supported the users. After the solution was fully implemented for this pilot group, it was further deployed to other trading groups in SupplyCo. Having similar needs and challenges, these groups also quickly "put down their soup cans" and "picked up their shovels."

The Learning

Our client was determined to identify a KM pilot and prove the value of KM to his firm, SupplyCo (see the SupplyCo case study). The problem was that he had no idea where to start. We designed and conducted a workshop with him and a group of managers representing various parts of the business in order to identify some potential starting points. Our goal was to identify those parts of the business that were both knowledge intensive and represented a high degree of financial risk.

The term *knowledge intensive* refers to the degree to which achieving a given objective relies on effective use of key knowledge resources. These resources could be anything from content resources, such as structured and unstructured information, to soft resources, such as social capital or tacit knowledge and expertise. A knowledge-intensive task or process is one that relies on one or more knowledge resources.

So how did we find the "soup can" for SupplyCo? After the Discovery Workshop, we spent two days interviewing managers and traders to gain a deeper understanding of how the group was structured, which jobs they performed, how they were measured, and what they thought their challenges were.

We then developed a short list identifying six potential focal processes. After prioritizing these six processes, we concluded that the best process for focusing our KM efforts would be information overload among the commodity traders.

Although the workload of the traders was high throughout the workday, they made time to meet with us for interviews and focus groups. This helped us to gain an understanding of the shape of their information overload issue and then to provide input and feedback toward a potential solution design. We interpreted this as a positive indication of their level of commitment to supporting our KM work. The traders had a vested interest in helping us determine what the "shovel" would look like so they could be relieved of using their "soup cans."

Our proposed solution included redefining trader job roles and filtering e-mail. The result was greater clarity regarding information requirements for each newly defined role and less e-mail clutter in everyone's inbox. We involved the traders at each step of the solution development and, as a result, they not only supported our project but readily embraced the implemented solution. The result was a 40 percent reduction in their e-mail and a corresponding increase in the amount of time available to perform their jobs.

How to Apply Lesson 4

Sometimes the focal point as described in Lesson 1 above provides a pointer to the soup-can users. In other cases, however, the issue may not manifest itself as a suboptimal process outcome. Instead, the issue may have more to do with personal productivity of knowledge workers who are performing the task in the best manner possible given the available tools, and generating acceptable outcomes as they go. In that case, the challenge may not be one of the knowledge workers ignoring available tools that would increase productivity but, rather, their lack of familiarity with available tools or alternatives. In other words, knowledge workers continue to use soup cans because they have never seen or heard of shovels. The challenge for the KM implementer is that they themselves may be similarly unaware of better alternatives to the current practices.

We will address how to spot productivity issues in a subsequent lesson. For KM implementers, the important aspect of this lesson is to maintain an awareness of the range of acceptance with which a proposed solution may be met. On one end of that spectrum lies complete rejection, in which case the proposed solution is not addressing any perceived need or, perhaps, is in conflict with the prevailing cultural and behavioral norms. Conversely, the proposed solution may be readily embraced, in which case it likely addresses a widely perceived critical need of the business in a manner consistent with the norms and values of the stakeholders and end users.

All proposed solutions lie somewhere on this continuum. Successful KM implementers give highest priority to those solutions that will be readily embraced, even if they lack the glamour of available alternatives.

Lesson 5. A Passionate, Committed Line Business Leader Is Key to Successful KM Initiatives

The Lesson

A line business manager who truly sees the connection between KM and the value it will bring the business is essential. Skepticism makes it easy for a manager to allow a project to languish as soon as any issues emerge. A Discovery Workshop is one approach to identifying a line manager who is committed to KM principles. In such a workshop, we bring together managers from various lines of business or functional areas. After a brief overview of what KM is, we give them the opportunity to examine their respective business functions and identify KM-related issues and challenges.

During this type of exercise we "discover" which participants understand KM and wish to pursue it and which ones either fail to see the value in it or simply have no significant KM-related issues that need to be addressed.

The Learning

A number of pilot project selection criteria were developed and agreed on during the Discovery Workshop we conducted for SupplyCo. The group:

- Has high value at the core
- Is globally dispersed (unless this poses an unrealistic challenge)
- Is a workable size
- Represents or controls a major cost driver for the business
- Represents or controls a major revenue driver for the business
- Is strategically significant to the business
- Is willing and able to undertake a KM project
- Has agreement and support from the executive sponsor
- Has strong, passionate sponsorship within it

Of these, the only one that we viewed as a firm requirement was the last one, "strong, passionate sponsorship." The manager of the commodity trading area, Sue, enthusiastically engaged in the workshop process and signaled to us her willingness to sponsor a KM pilot initiative in the trading area. It was clear to her that if the traders could recover some of the time they spend reading, analyzing, and responding to e-mails, they could convert it into real value in the form of increased margin for SupplyCo.

The trading function also scored well against the other selection criteria, and we ultimately contracted with Sue and SupplyCo to undertake the company's first KM pilot. Throughout the pilot we had excellent access to the traders and to internal reports and other documents from the department, largely because of Sue's commitment.

After the KM solution blueprint was finished, the rollout also went well. In fact, the pilot solution found a standing place on the weekly global team call agenda. All this was accomplished without the need for a lot of convincing or active client management on our part—Sue picked up the blueprint and ran with it from the start.

We contrasted this with our experience on other consulting projects where a line manager was handed the assignment of being the pilot case for a new solution without being given a chance to voice agreement or dissent. In such cases the engagement generally went poorly, and the solution implementation lost momentum almost as soon as we left the client site.

How to Apply Lesson 5

The committed line business leader is essential to the success of a KM project. Beware of situations where the line business leader for the project has been selected by the chief information officer or the program office that has the seed money for the project. The line business manager must be personally committed to the project, the degree of change it will require, and the value it will create. Workshops and pre-engagement interviews of various line managers are two ways of determining which business managers are interested in pursuing KM.

Lesson 6. Dedicated, Competent, and Respected Business Unit Members Make Excellent KM Team Members

The Lesson

All projects that involve change, particularly KM projects, require someone to help make and sustain the changes required on a day-to-day basis. Like the committed and passionate line business leader, this person must also understand the changes required and have the requisite focus to address challenges along the way. The person must also have the appropriate level of authority to make day-to-day decisions regarding the project. Ultimately, this person's effectiveness depends on his or her competence and the respect he or she commands.

This individual needs to sustain the change after the project team and consultants have gone and thus must be deeply involved from the start. We recommend committing the implementation leader full time to the solution rollout. If this is not possible, a minimum of 50 percent may be workable.

The Learning

On starting the formal KM solution design for SupplyCo, we asked Sue, the commodity trading manager, to commit one of her traders as a member of our project team. We estimated a time commitment of up to 50 percent and specified that this person should be someone who is at least knowledgeable of, if not proficient at performing, the various trading tasks within the function.

Sue assigned Mike, one of her best traders, to our project team and committed him to nearly full-time involvement on the project. She wanted to ensure that when we left there would be someone at SupplyCo who was familiar with our work methods and the solution we developed and who could carry the work forward in the trading function and other areas.

As our project progressed, it became clear that Mike was genuinely interested in learning about KM and applying KM principles to the work of the traders. More than that, because Mike was a seasoned and respected trader, he was able to gather support for the solution design and implementation from his peers. He was a trusted equal and thus was not seen as someone from outside the group or from management imposing a solution on the traders.

When our project was finished, Mike went on to become the project leader for implementation and ongoing support for KM within the commodity trading group. He also served as a key KM resource for the company well after this particular project concluded, participating in several other KM enabling projects within SupplyCo.

Mike harvested new approaches and refinements to existing approaches developed from these subsequent implementations and fed them back into the solution of the pilot group as appropriate. Mike became a KM specialist for SupplyCo.

How to Apply Lesson 6

In addition to the KM subject matter expertise that internal or external consultants bring to a project team, a team member who is a respected member of the business area where KM is being pursued can help ensure the success of a KM initiative. Insist on including such a person on every KM project. Also, because KM is not a one-time event for many enterprises, having at least one person participate on successive KM initiatives along with members of the target function ensures continuity of knowledge and experience across those initiatives, resulting in harvesting and reuse of valuable experience. This continuity can contribute to successful KM implementation across a large, complex enterprise.

Lesson 7. Involve Information Technology and Human Resources from the Start to Expedite KM Implementation

The Lesson

The IT and HR departments in large firms will likely be called on to support most KM solution implementations. From an IT perspective, KM solutions may require introducing a new software application, modifying an intranet portal, or adding a content database. From an HR perspective, significant changes to annual performance evaluations or incentive programs may be called for.

In either case, the sooner the IT and HR functions are incorporated into the solution design and deployment phases of a KM project, the better. Waiting to involve these functions until the design is completed and deployment is under way can result in delays and even intentional attempts to undermine the success of the project.

The Learning

At SupplyCo, we involved both HR and IT in the solution design phase of our project. We asked for their involvement in analyzing the issues related to e-mail overload, and in providing ideas for potential solutions. As a result, the changes we proposed were backed with the conceptual and financial support of both functions.

The SupplyCo solution involved changes to job roles, job descriptions, and associated incentive plans. The HR staff was included on the project team from the start. As a result they readily supported and implemented the proposed HR-related changes for the commodity trader job function. Had they not been brought in until the changes were actually required, a great deal of "selling" would have been needed and the changes may never have taken place.

The involvement of IT was equally important. The IT organization included a number of developers of Lotus Notes. Some of these developers were involved in the early solution design stages of the project, and they immediately began to recognize opportunities for capturing and extracting information needed by each of the redefined job roles. The IT staff also used their knowledge of the existing and planned corporate IT infrastructure to help tailor the KM-related IT components so they would fit together seamlessly, and within the budgetary commitments already in place. They designed the IT portion of the solution and drove the rollout.

How to Apply Lesson 7

Involve the IT and HR departments in a KM intervention from the start. Doing so ensures that needed changes and adjustments to information and HR-related systems and policies are done smoothly and in concert with existing plans and budgets within these functions. Ensure that representatives from both functions are included on the project governance team, consulted regarding proposed solution components, and provided with regular project updates.

LESSON 8. WALK A MILE IN THEIR SHOES

The Lesson

Knowledge management project teams employ a variety of traditional data- and information-gathering techniques. These include document reviews, interviews, surveys, workshops, facilitated discussions, and the like. Reliance on these techniques may result in a limited understanding of the true situation of a given business function, especially regarding the way work is actually performed versus the way it was designed to be performed.

This gap must be addressed, and the nuances and true nature of the work being performed must be discovered. Knowledge management project team members, especially those from outside the targeted functional area, should consider the various jobs and roles associated with a given work process and "walk a mile in their shoes." Make direct observations of the work being done. If possible, do the job for a period of time. Direct experience of a given work process provides insight and opens lines of inquiry regarding what a person is doing and why they are doing it that otherwise might have been missed.

The Learning

In order to develop a useful solution for the SupplyCo traders, we needed to gain a solid understanding of their work. We sought answers to questions such as these: How does one trader sort through e-mail versus how another trader does so? Which factors cause one trade to be successful and another unprofitable?

We asked Sue, the trading manager, if we could spend a day sitting with a trader at a trading desk and ask questions about what the trader was doing. Sue agreed, and the experience was eye opening. We gained an understanding of the trader's need to carefully sift through e-mail, looking for potentially valuable nuggets of information that could greatly affect the degree of financial risk associated with a given trade. This observation triggered more questions regarding the ways each trader sorted through and prioritized daily e-mail. In retrospect, had we missed this experience we would have missed important subtleties surrounding the way the traders created value for SupplyCo, and our proposed solution would have been less robust.

How to Apply Lesson 8

Modify the approach used to gather data, and gain an understanding of the way processes are performed.

Use direct observation and experience of the work process under review to supplement data and information gathered through more traditional techniques. In doing so, remember to remain open-minded. The objective is to experience the work process from the same perspective as those who perform it every day. Which information is used to make which decisions? What is the nature of personal judgment that is brought to bear? Knowledge work is often marked by idiosyncratic subtlety and nuance. Open-mindedness and sensitivity to this fact will increase the likelihood of crafting a solution that addresses that which needs to change while respecting the norms and practices of the area under review.

Lesson 9. Improve Knowledge Worker Productivity by Reducing Time Spent on Administrative or Non-Value-Adding Tasks

The Lesson

Not all KM initiatives are undertaken to address poor process outcomes (e.g., PetCo). In some cases, the issue is the reduced productivity of knowledge workers, who may spend more time hunting for or sifting through needed information than applying their judgment and experience to a given situation to make a decision. In this case, the actual outcome of the work process may be in line with the expected outcome. The KM opportunity is to improve the productivity of these knowledge workers by reducing the time spent on wading through ever-increasing amounts of information.

These opportunities are addressed by "reallocating the dollar." That is, reduce the percentage of time knowledge workers spend searching through vast amounts of content for information needed to make a decision or otherwise perform a task. One way to achieve this is to put in place content filters, which can free up time for knowledge workers to apply their knowledge to prescribed work tasks, share their knowledge with colleagues, and build their own personal knowledge in formal and informal ways.

The Learning

As mentioned in the case study, when asked what they would do if we could free up time for them, the traders immediately responded that they would "turn it into money," benefiting both SupplyCo and themselves. This flagged the importance the traders attached to their own productivity. That productivity, however, was compromised by the traders' self-imposed requirement to read all the e-mail they received on the chance it *might* contain an important piece of information for a future trade.

Our analysis of the e-mail overload issue at SupplyCo led us to believe two things. First, reducing the e-mail workload was possible. Second, doing so would give the traders more time to collaborate with their colleagues, analyze trades, or otherwise apply their expertise more productively to trading without any further encouragement. Either way, it seemed to us that "reallocating the dollar" made sense, given the number of traders and amount of time they spent sifting through their e-mails.

The solution we developed and implemented included a number of elements described in previous lessons here. In terms of productivity improvement, the solution focused on filtering out e-mails according to a custom profile developed for each of the newly defined trading roles. The filtered out e-mails were stored in a database and available to the traders if needed. The result was an approximate 40 percent reduction in the number of e-mails in each trader's inbox and a corresponding 40 percent reduction in the time required to read e-mail for each trader. On average, the traders gained the two hours per day we originally estimated during the Discovery Workshop.

One of the unexpected benefits of freeing up time for the traders was that they were able to spend more time talking with their customers and, in the process, developing relationships that enabled them to sell these customers commodity products at a slight premium over the market price. This was proof positive that if we gave the traders more time, they could, in fact, turn it into money.

How to Apply Lesson 9

Conducting simple work analysis using data collected from face-to-face interviews can spot productivity issues. Use work analysis to create a breakdown of the tasks a knowledge worker performs and the amount of time spent on each task, expressed as a percentage. Then evaluate and categorize the tasks. If the work analysis shows that a group of knowledge workers is spending a significant portion of their time sifting through or otherwise manipulating information or content, then it is likely that an opportunity to improve productivity exists.

Use this analysis to support a KM solution that simplifies information search, retrieval, or analysis. Evaluate content management tools, such as text mining, federated search, data visualization, and decision support. We call this "reallocating the dollar," referring to the way in which a dollar's worth of time is spent between sifting and hunting through information, and applying judgment and experience to that information. Reallocating the dollar results in improving productivity of knowledge workers.

CONCLUSION

Truly useful knowledge is based on experience and expertise. Because each person's life experience is unique, it follows that knowledge may be thought of as *sticky* (i.e., not easily transferred from one person to another) and unique. Knowledge also is not easily managed through controls or efforts that treat it as separate from the "knower." The best we can do is identify process inefficiencies or breakdowns that reduce knowledge worker efficiency or effectiveness, and then devise coherent solutions that are culturally and behaviorally consistent with prevailing norms to address them. In other words, KM is a misnomer.

In the future, KM as a discipline will likely be folded into more traditional business disciplines, such as "operations improvement" or "productivity improvement." Although KM is a legitimate area of inquiry today, the business world will be better served when the various adherents of KM recognize KM for what it is: a continuation of the inquiry into how the internal operations of an enterprise can be improved by proactively managing the resources and infrastructure under its control.

The previous lessons learned are not presented as an exhaustive accounting of all we have learned in the practice of KM. Indeed, much of that knowledge is tacit and not readily reducible into any meaningful text. Rather, these lessons are presented here as a selection of highlights from our own work with clients. In some cases, we learned these lessons "the hard way," having suffered the consequences of not knowing about them. In other cases, we learned the lessons by examining retrospectively an unanticipated success. We present them here in the hope that other practitioners can benefit from our experiences and continue to build on the collective knowledge and wisdom surrounding the practice of effective KM.

CHAPTER 4

Critical Success Factors of Knowledge Management

Farida Hasanali, American Productivity & Quality Center

"You said that if I gave you $500,000 and two full-time people, you would get people to share information with one another!" Has your boss ever confronted you at a progress review meeting regarding your attempt to implement knowledge management? "So, what went wrong?" You mull over the events of the past year.

You are John Webber, sales manager for an organization that supplies paint to builders, retail stores, wholesalers, and even small interior decorators. Sales were dropping, and as you discussed the problems with your sales staff, you heard the following complaints: "The other salesperson was able to get a solution to the customer's problem a week before I was able to." "I don't even know where to go to get information, much less translate it into a complete solution for the customer." Or, your absolute favorite: "After I had lost the sale, I came back to the office and found that Joe knew the answer to my problem. How was I to know that?"

All these complaints from the sales staff made you think of a simple solution: If I can get my salespeople talking to one another and sharing information, they can win sales. Of course, to do that I would need a technology that would enable them to save what they know so that others can access that knowledge when they need it. Next, you started researching technologies. What would enable my sales staff to input and access information on products, customers, and tips? You found several software packages that managed sales information. The one that seemed to best suit your situation is called KnowledgeSales, with the tag line: "Sell effectively by managing your sales knowledge."

It is perfect—exactly what you are looking for. The software enables your sales staff to enter customer names, activities, challenges they have had with their customers, and how they resolved customer issues. It has a chat area for salespeople to talk with each other, a bulletin board to post new problems, a private area to upload their personal pictures, and even a lead-generation process by which the system tells the salesperson whether the customer is a good lead.

Because you know that you cannot implement this software completely on your own or within your existing budget, you decide to go to your boss and ask for help. You hear yourself say, "I need $500,000 and two people. In six months I can have the salespeople talking to one another and using the information from the database. The increased sales will more than cover the cost of this initiative."

As you embarked on your project, you realized you needed some input from your salespersons. You asked two of your top local performers for help. It was difficult to get to those located outside the country. The top two salespeople shared with you that they usually carried a lot of information with them to every sale. In that way, they always had the information at hand and were able to answer customer questions. They also said they spoke to each other often and discussed potential sales before they proposed a solution. "Right on the mark," you thought. If I can start by obtaining all the documents (that these two salespeople carry around), putting them into an electronic format, and providing a chat area where salespeople can talk with one another, I will have enabled the rest of my sales staff to sell more.

So what went wrong? Why is it that six months later, your sales team is still struggling?

This story is a classic example of an organization taking the correct steps to provide its employees with the tools they need for managing and sharing knowledge but forgetting to account for certain critical elements that enable knowledge sharing.

CRITICAL SUCCESS FACTORS

One of the critical success factors of KM is to have a common understanding of the term knowledge management, or knowledge sharing, and how it applies to your situation and needs. Some organizations choose not to use the term at all, because it is not a recognized or an accepted word within their culture. By recognizing this fact, an organization is actually adhering to one of the other critical success factors of KM: Listen to your employees and customers. For the purpose of this chapter, I will use the term knowledge management.

The definition of KM has evolved quite a bit over the last six years. It started simply as valuable information in action, with value being determined by the organization and the recipient. Although this definition still holds true today, over time KM has developed into a more rigorous discipline subject to the same scrutiny as are most other business processes within an organization and even expected to show a return on investment (ROI).

The American Productivity and Quality Center (APQC) currently defines KM as an emerging set of strategies and approaches to create, safeguard, and put to use a wide range of knowledge assets (e.g., people and information). Thus, these assets flow to the right people at the right time so that they can be applied to create more value for the enterprise.

If we break down this definition of KM, we can see that some critical success factors are built into it. KM is a set of strategies and approaches, implying that there is a definite structure or a way to do things. The APQC Road Map to Knowledge Management Results: Stages of Implementation™ is one such approach and is described in Chapter 5 (see Figure 4.1). Another critical piece of this definition is that this approach enables information to flow to the right person at the right time. Otherwise, an organization would be managing its knowledge just for the sake of managing it and not to create value. Here it is important to point out that the information needs to do more than flow through wires; it needs to flow from people to people. Systems and computers do not make decisions, people do. That brings us to the most critical aspect of this definition, creating more value for the enterprise. The most elaborate of knowledge-sharing procedures means absolutely nothing if the knowledge shared within an organization

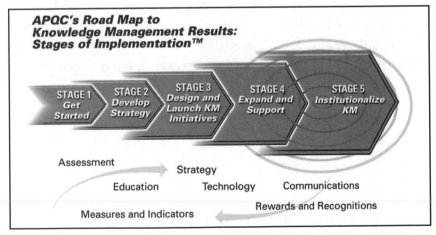

Figure 4.1   The American Productivity and Quality Center road map to knowledge management results: Stages of Implementation™.

does not enable its recipient(s) to create value, be it through increased revenue, time savings, or cost savings.

The success of a KM initiative depends on many factors, some of which are within our control and some that are not. The cascading effect of a tumbling economy resulting in a loss of business is not within the immediate control of any one party within an organization. In contrast, not having an IT infrastructure that enables employees to capture and share information can be changed in an organization to promote knowledge sharing.

Typically, critical success factors can be categorized into five main categories:
- Leadership
- Culture
- Structure, roles, and responsibilities
- IT infrastructure
- Measurement

LEADERSHIP

Leadership plays a key role in ensuring success in almost any initiative within an organization. The impact of leadership on KM is even more pronounced because KM is a relatively new discipline and, therefore, not as established as other disciplines, such as quality or shared services. An individual leading a KM initiative should primarily believe in and support the message. Nothing makes a greater impact on an organization than when its leaders model the behavior they are trying to promote among employees. For example, at Buckman Laboratories, a chemical company, the chief executive officer (CEO) who champions the cause for KM within the organization personally reviews submissions to its knowledge bank. When the CEO notices that a particular employee has not been active within the system, the CEO sends the employee a message that reads:

> Dear Associate,
> You haven't been sharing knowledge. How can we help you?
> All the best,
> Bob

Several other best-practices organizations have demonstrated this commitment to KM. At the World Bank, CEO James Wolfensohn boldly stated, "We are not a lending bank, we are a knowledge bank." His support led to the creation of an infrastructure that promoted and supported the growth of communities of practice not only throughout the bank but worldwide. Today, the World Bank has sustained its KM initiative through its communities of practice. Its knowledge managers constantly search for new approaches to knowledge sharing. Steve Denning, former director of KM at the World Bank, introduced the concept of storytelling in the organization. Denning's premise is that a story is worth more than a thousand numbers. His belief is that humans are natural storytellers; that is how we hand down our knowledge from generation to generation. Stories are remembered because people can relate to them.

We return to our story of John Webber and ask, "What went wrong with the leadership commitment at his organization?" John realized later that although his boss had given him the money and the resources, he did not mention the project at all in the monthly department meeting, he did not provide any input into the design, and he did not come to the launch meeting. John himself had gotten so involved in trying to deploy the software that he did not have time to notice these things or to communicate his progress or vision to the rest of his sales staff. Consequently, when the software was launched, it seemed to the sales staff that it was just a new piece of software that required more time to maintain, decreasing the time they had to contact customers. If John's boss had mentioned the initiative at the department meeting and asked the salespeople to support John, and had attended the launch meeting to reinforce that he understood the importance of using this system and that he would be the first one on it come Monday morning, the sales staff would have been more motivated to model his behavior.

CULTURE

Although leadership plays a critical role in the success of the KM initiative, the "culture" factor can be just as or even more important to the success of KM within your organization.

Culture is the combination of shared history, expectations, unwritten rules, and social mores that affects the behaviors of everyone, from managers to clerks. It is the set of underlying beliefs that, while never exactly articulated, are always there to color the perception of actions and communications.

If your organization naturally has a tendency to share knowledge, your job as the person who is charged with enabling people to share becomes a little easier. It is important, however, not to give up in the face of "culture." At the APQC, we share three basic principles in dealing with culture:

- Your culture will not change first. Get over it!
- Culture change is a result of knowledge sharing, not an antecedent.
- Design KM around your culture.

If your organization harbors a nonsharing culture, do not give in to it. As long as your organization has not created negative consequences for sharing, we believe that people really want to share their knowledge. They want others to know that they are knowledgeable. And if you have created negative consequences for sharing, then address those first. Break down some of the existing barriers to knowledge sharing, and give people the tools and environment they need to share knowledge. By designing KM initiatives around your culture, you in fact will be initiating a cultural change.

Cultural issues usually arise as a result of the following:

Lack of common perspectives. Sharing must be inspired by a common vision. All employees affected by the new process or technology must buy into this vision and believe it will work. This includes the leadership team, who must articulate and act on the same principles of sharing being preached to the employees.

Lack of time. This is probably the most commonly used excuse for a lack of knowledge sharing. In reality, with the advent of merging companies and loss of jobs, people are being expected to work more than they used to. Here the goal is not to encourage the employees to work more but to work more effectively. The processes, technologies, and roles designed during your KM initiative must attempt to save employees time, not burden them with more work. This can only be accomplished if the employees' work patterns are accounted for during the initial design and planning phase of the initiative.

Nonaligned reward systems. Reward systems and their effectiveness are highly debated in all fields, not just KM. A fine balance exists between intrinsic and explicit rewards, which organizations must maintain to encourage employee behavior. Whether you will need more of one or the other of course will depend on the group of employees you are targeting. Through its various studies on the topic of KM, the APQC has found that knowledge-sharing behaviors are sustained over longer periods of time in organizations where people share because they want to, because they like to see their expertise being used, and because they like being respected and trusted by their peers. Intrinsic rewards can translate into explicit rewards. The recognition received can mean that the employee will be considered for a promotion or another growth opportunity. The most effective use of explicit rewards has been to encourage sharing behaviors at the onset of a KM initiative, that is, when a new technology is introduced or when employees are being encouraged to attend a face-to-face meeting or to provide personal information. The use of small explicit rewards, such as t-shirts and coffee mugs, is an effective and inexpensive way to attract participation. Again, if the attendees do not find value in either the meetings or the information on the system, providing incentives will not sustain their participation.

No formal communication. What makes the world go round? Communication, communication, communication. Although some of us realize its importance in our personal lives, we fail to carry over communication into our professional lives. Just as it is critical that you know where your loved ones are, or your child is, at all times, so it is important for employees and customers to know about the changes occurring in your organization. While designing and implementing KM initiatives, overcommunicate. According to marketing professionals, a person needs to hear the same message at least three times before the brain registers it. While implementing KM within your organization, market yourself. Make sure everyone knows what you are attempting to do; build anticipation for the launch. Best-practices organizations in the APQC consortium studies have shared that they print posters advertising the initiative, arousing people's curiosity in the upcoming change. Thus, when it does come about, employees or customers already have some awareness and familiarity with it and feel as if they have been part of the process.

STRUCTURE AND ROLES/RESPONSIBILITIES

Many organizations overlook creating a structure for a KM initiative. Take our example of John Webber. As a manager of a sales team, John chose to tackle the issue of lack of information and sharing by himself. He went straight to his boss who, in turn, did not see the big picture. John's sales team was not the only one in the organization, and a customer contact system already existed. How would that system interact with this one? More than half the sales force is abroad. Would those salespeople get access to the system? These were all organizationwide issues that John or his boss did not consider.

Although there are many variances in how organizations structure the governance of their KM initiatives, the APQC has found one that seems to have proven itself in many best-practices partner organizations. In this model, there is a steering committee and a central KM core group, and there may be some individuals spread out within the organization who are responsible for KM. It is a combination of a centralized and decentralized approach (Figure 4.2).

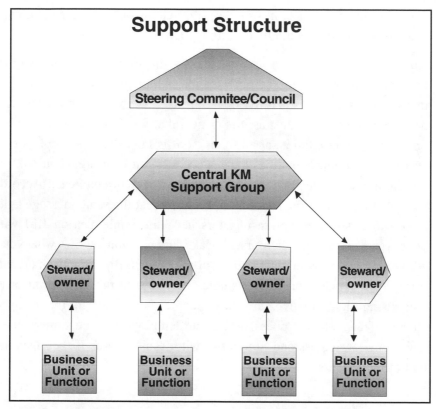

Figure 4.2   Flowchart for the American Productivity and Quality Center's approach to knowledge management model.

The steering committee usually consists of executives at the top level. They buy into the concept and are willing to provide guidance, direction, and support. If the KM initiative is being conducted at a division level, the steering committee can be a group of top-level divisional managers.

Typically, the central KM group is made up of three to four people who support the cause of KM. Projects or initiatives may start with the central KM group but usually are handed over to the business owners once they are implemented. In this way, the business owners see the value of sharing themselves, and a greater chance of sustaining the behavior change exists than if a central group is seen as owning an initiative. The central group usually consists of people with project management, facilitation, and excellent communication skills.

The stewards or owners are people in the business units who are responsible for knowledge sharing and acquisition. As mentioned previously, until the business itself sees the value of knowledge sharing, the initiative will not sustain itself. The core KM group and the stewards are the agents of change for the organization. They model and teach employees the principles of knowledge sharing.

Even with a structure and roles in place, organizations must watch out for a few pitfalls. If your team does not have a common vocabulary, there will be misunderstandings. Most organizations are also plagued by *departmental or divisional silos*, groups of individuals who are concerned only about themselves and never see the organization and its overall success as theirs as well. Having a silo mentality inhibits team building. Identify individuals with silo mentalities, and get them on board early so that they feel they are a part of the process.

Last, the structure is put into place to give ownership and accountability. However, if there is no overall ownership of knowledge and learning within the organization and the leadership does not "walk the talk," then sustaining sharing behavior will be difficult.

INFORMATION TECHNOLOGY

Good technology really does matter. As most of the APQC studies have shown, KM is not about IT, but KM most certainly is enabled by IT. Without a solid IT infrastructure, an organization cannot enable its employees to share information on a large scale. The trap that most organizations fall into is not lack of IT but rather too much focus on IT only. A KM initiative is not a software application. Having a platform to share information and to communicate is part of a KM initiative—sometimes a very important part, but just a part nonetheless.

So where do organizations fall short in providing an IT infrastructure for sharing. The most common ones seen so far by the APQC follow:

Use of the wrong approach. Most of these mistakes arise from the basic premise that the people who are charged with implementing KM within their organizations do not take the time to understand their users' needs. Matching the KM system with the KM objectives is essential. If the overwhelming need of the users is to have an area that allows them to communicate with one another, then look for technology that provides real-time chat, bulletin boards, discussion threads, collaboration space, and so on. Providing these users with a structured database where they must key in information to templates will not meet their needs and, therefore, will not be used.

Lack of great content. Content is finally starting to get the attention it deserves. It follows the exact same principles: If your users need information on matching paint colors and you provide them information on painting techniques, they are not going to find value in coming back to the system. Great content also includes having processes in place to acquire, manage, validate, and deliver the right information, at the right time, to the right people. That is the basis of KM.

Lack of common platforms. A standard, companywide architecture ensures the sustainability and scalability of KM efforts. Having a hodgepodge of technologies that may or may not communicate with one another can hamper the ability of an organization to provide its employees with a solid infrastructure for sharing. This is where a steering committee can play a strong leadership role. By understanding the infrastructure of the organization at a high level, the steering committee can guide the KM team in making the right decision while picking the appropriate technology. Sometimes organizations realize that they need a complete overhaul of their IT infrastructure before they can expect their employees to share knowledge. Five years ago, a best-practices partner company involved in an APQC study invested millions of dollars to get the whole company on one standard platform so that all of its employees could share information and knowledge with one another. Today, many organizations have eliminated or are in the process of phasing out customized legacy systems and replacing them with market-standard operating systems, such as MS DOS™, UNIX, and Linux. This enables organizations to build on the existing architecture by using off-the-shelf software written to support these platforms, thus avoiding costly customized packages. This is not to imply that there is anything wrong with customization. Sometimes off-the-shelf software may cost more than a customized piece because it has significantly more functionality than the organization needs. However, in general, maintaining custom software over a long period of time, especially if the needs of the company are constantly changing, is more difficult and more expensive.

Complicated technology. If it takes more than three clicks to find knowledge on your system, your users will be frustrated. Of course, you must temper that with the amount of information you are attempting to deliver, along with the complexity of information being demanded by the user. For example, if you are catering to a research department, its users' needs for refined information may be much higher than the needs of others. Therefore, the researchers may not mind clicking 10 times to get exactly what they are looking for, because they are drilling down into a particular topic to understand its every facet. In such cases, you are still meeting your user's needs without adhering to a three-click rule, which is standard in information delivery. Another common mistake made in information delivery is the emphasis on explicit knowledge. Although technology is primarily used to deliver explicit knowledge, placing too much emphasis on it causes the user to lose the context within which the information was shared and leads to misunderstandings about how to interpret and use the knowledge.

Inadequate technology and inadequate knowledge to use it. An organization can be unsuccessful in its attempts at knowledge sharing if it fails to provide adequate technology to its users or, more importantly, fails to train them on how to use the system. You can have a great system, but it is worth nothing if your users do not know how to use it. At best-practices partner companies, the central KM group spends most of its time (after deployment) teaching, guiding, and coaching users on how to use the system to interact, communicate, and share information and knowledge with one another.

John Webber, for instance, forgot to take into account that half of his sales staff members were positioned internationally. The same features that he felt were "cool," such as posting photographs on the Web site, were the very ones that caused the system to hang up on his international sales representatives as a result of bandwidth failure.

MEASUREMENT

Highly misunderstood and feared by most is the measurement factor. Most people fear measurement because they see it as being synonymous with ROI, and they are not sure how to link KM efforts to ROI. Although the ultimate goal of measuring the effectiveness of a KM initiative is to determine some type of ROI, many intervening variables also affect the outcomes.

The first step is to know the objectives and desired outcomes and what you are going to measure right up front while you are planning and designing your KM initiative. Measures are of two types: activities and outcomes. Measuring the number of hits on a site, or the number of registered users, is considered an activity measure. Although it does not tell you if your employees saved time or money, it is essential to gauge the interest in and the progress of a KM initiative. Outcome measures are focused on finding a change in the numbers reflecting outcomes, such as sales or margins, hours spent preparing proposals, or cycle time to respond to a customer request. As most of us agree, these are more difficult to track. However, the organization may already be collecting some of these measures.

Many variables may affect an outcome. Thus, it is important to show the correlation of KM activities with business outcomes but not claim a pure cause-and-effect relationship. Increased sales may be a result not only of the sales representatives having more information but also of the market turning, a competitor closing down, or prices dropping 10 percent since the same time last year. Owing to the inability to exactly pinpoint a cause-and-effect relationship between knowledge sharing and results, tracking the correlations over time is important.

This is not to say that KM activities have not shown results that can be directly linked to knowledge-sharing activities. Chevron Corporation used communities of practice to transfer best practices internally within its organization, resulting in a $2 billion reduction in operating costs. In contrast, Schlumberger used a combination of communities of practice among its technicians and a robust intranet platform to save $10 million in the first year of activity.

Collecting, exchanging, and publishing anecdotal success stories can be a powerful adjunct to hard measures. Success stories do more than relate financial success. They put the act of sharing in common terms and make it easier for employees to identify with them and encourage employees to share information. This is best described by an example of a success story that made it to the Xerox shareholder portfolio.

A technician in Brazil was having much difficultly with one of his customer's Documentum machine. At the time, the Documentum cost $40,000. If the technician could not fix it, Xerox would have to replace it. This was a very cost-intensive solution, but it would have to be done to keep the customer happy. The technician shared this problem on the Xerox Eureka network, a system that stores tips provided by Xerox technicians worldwide. Technicians share how they find solutions to problems at customer sites not necessarily found in any manual. What the technician in Brazil found was that someone else had the same issue and had resolved it. The solution: A 50-cent capacitor in the copier kept heating up and shorting out the machine. Once replaced, the machine worked just fine.

Actual savings in dollars: about $40,000. The effect of sharing this story in the whole company: invaluable. It encouraged technicians worldwide to share and access Eureka before going to a customer site.

This anecdote also helps illustrate another point. Measures do not reflect the value proposition. Although the amount saved was obvious, the measure of success for Xerox and for the technicians could not be put into numbers.

In this chapter we have covered leadership, culture, structure, IT, and measurement as the critical success factors for a successful KM initiative. However, it is important for us to mention other enablers that have the potential to derail an initiative or affect the outcomes of a KM initiative. They are assessment, training, and strategy:

> **Assessment.** It is important to know what you already have before embarking on a KM initiative. For example, determine if communities already exist in your organization. If they do, then the strategy would be to support them rather than to try to create a new approach for knowledge sharing. For organizations wishing to embark on KM, it is important to know the major pain areas in the organization. Where can you get the most for your money? When you focus on those first, it leads to an early win. This, in turn, builds credibility and support from other players in the organization as well as the sponsor who committed resources to you.

> **Training.** The role of training is not given the attention it deserves in most organizations. The best system in the world will be a graveyard of information if employees are not trained to use it. Training must cover more than just technology. The people who will be affected by this change must know the vision, goals, expected behavior, desired behavior, the measures (if any), and

rewards (if any). If KM is going to change the way people work, then employees must get some guidance on the new process, too. For example, if new roles have been created—such as editors, validators, and knowledge managers—employees must know who is supporting those roles. One of the lessons learned shared by best-practices organizations is that employees must feel like someone owns the KM initiative and that there is always someone that they can go to when they need help.

Strategy. A whole chapter could be written on strategy. Typically, leaders are charged with this great feat of looking into the future and determining what to do now, based on what might happen later. Although leadership plays an important role in the strategy of a KM initiative, this really should be a team effort. The steering committee is charged with devising a strategy because it has a broader view of the organization as a whole. However, it is the business owners who typically validate the strategy because they are the ones to operationalize it. One of the key components of strategy is that of creating a business case. No matter how obvious it may be to the organization that the change is needed, a written document should outline the initiative, especially the expected outcomes.

Conclusion

So, let us conclude John Webber's story. How could he have been successful in his attempt to get the sales representatives to share knowledge. We will touch on a few of the key points. First, he needed more commitment from his boss, or even his boss's boss. The lack of visibility of management made this a low priority in the eyes of the sales representatives.

Second, John needed to consider more than just technology as a solution. He did not take the time to talk to the salespeople who were not selling (they are the ones to focus on). His focus only on the best salespeople meant he was designing only for that audience. Had he talked to more salespeople, they would have shared with him the bandwidth issues they face working abroad. John also missed something very important that his top sales performers shared with him. They talked to one another before a sales meeting. John did not create an environment for sharing. Until the salespeople knew each other, they would not be comfortable sharing information in a public forum on a Web site.

Third, John did not decide up front what his measures of success would be. His promise to his boss that "the increased sales will more than pay for this" could not be fulfilled, because he could not make a cause-and-effect case that any increase in sales would be due to the system he implemented. The market could have improved, a competitor could have closed down, or prices could have dropped. There were too many variables for John to prove to his boss that the KM initiative had worked.

One last thought on critical success factors that transcend KM and apply to almost everything in our lives. Listen! Listen to your users, your customers, your managers—whatever audience for whom you are designing. They will tell you how you can meet their needs and have a successful KM initiative.

CHAPTER 5

Successfully Implementing Knowledge Management: Lessons Learned and Best Practices

Cindy Hubert and Carla O'Dell, American Productivity & Quality Center

Knowledge management has reached the tipping point. Eighty percent of major corporations have explicit KM initiatives, and more than 300 organizations have joined the American Productivity & Quality Center (APQC) to benchmark best practices in KM since 1995. Furthermore, global firms have hundreds of communities of practice (see Figure 5.1). As a result, KM approaches are maturing. Organizations are using portal and collaborative technologies to deliver "magnet" and dynamic content to the desktop. Knowledge workers are able to access and connect to information and knowledge "just in time, just for me." Communities are not only stewarding core organizational knowledge but also creating new knowledge to meet ever-changing customer needs. Combine all of these components with a staff committed to publishing, validating, and adapting knowledge, and a dynamic new culture becomes institutionalized.

In addition to this good news is the existence of a road map to implement KM processes, tools, and principles. The APQC developed a methodology based on research and experience from working with hundreds of organizations pursuing KM as part of their business strategy. Using best practices and lessons learned, the APQC developed the Road Map to Knowledge Management Results: Stages of Implementation™ to guide organizations through the five stages of KM implementation, with relevant advice concerning processes, structure, and enablers.

THE "NOT SO GOOD" NEWS

When embarking on KM implementation many organizations continue to repeat the mistakes of others. The age of the early adopters is over, and organizations

World Bank = 120
Daimler Chrysler = 140
Siemens = 345
Chevron = 100

Communities of practice are groups of people who come together to share and to learn from one another, face-to-face and virtually. They are held together by a common interest in a body of knowledge and are driven by a desire and need to share problems, experiences, insights, templates, tools, and best practices. Community members deepen their knowledge by interacting on an ongoing basis.

Figure 5.1   Communities of practice in global firms.

should learn from the KM pioneers and instead make "new mistakes." Capitalizing on best practices and lessons learned will propel an organization to a faster implementation as well as more effective results.

Organizations often find that organizing and managing their explicit knowledge—for example, content—is a beginning step that leads to reuse and contributes to efficiency. As these same organizations evolve their KM efforts, they begin to see how to more effectively share and transfer their tacit knowledge. While more difficult to articulate and capture, sharing experience and expertise provides a higher competitive advantage and decreases time to competency.

The obvious lesson is that KM is not just about sharing documents. Knowledge cannot exist without information as well as experience. Knowledge is information in action. It includes what people *know* about any process or approach. With good information, people can make better decisions and take intelligent action.

Knowledge management is a systematic process to

- Identify important knowledge
- Create a space and system for people to share what they know and create new knowledge
- Capture, collect, and manage best practices and useful information in a form that other people can use in the future
- Transfer information, knowledge, and best practices to others who can use it

Early KM adopters paved the way for successful implementation. In 1999 and 2000, 52 organizations participated and contributed to the APQC Road Map to Knowledge Management Results: Stages of Implementation. The following lessons learned are based on early adopters and best-practices organizations and highlight the critical success factors, approaches, and options to implement a KM initiative.

Stage 1: Get Started

The most common lesson learned for organizations when implementing a KM initiative is that form should follow function. Some organizations have eagerly organized KM teams to "do" KM. Unfortunately, as has been proved time and time again, these team members assigned to new roles and responsibilities are falling into the same pitfalls as did the early adopters. In order to quickly prove the value of KM to the organization, misguided KM teams begin by focusing on activities that are "nice to do" instead of activities that lead to outcomes and business results. And, these activities must be embedded in everyday workflow.

If KM advocates fail to learn from more experienced KM practitioners, they may fall into the same traps, such as addressing the wrong problem, failing to link and leverage into existing processes that can be improved, working on changing the culture without giving a reason for doing so, and creating an IT solution before determining the demand and process. Instead, KM advocates should find an executive sponsor, capitalize on existing technologies to connect people and allow collaboration, and create a compelling picture of how KM can solve current and real business problems. A common tool used for developing this picture is storytelling.

Storytelling can be a springboard for organizational change. Stories can entertain, convey information, preserve cultures, build relationships and communities, and most important, change organizations. Storytelling has become a valuable tool for engaging the support of people in organizations. At the World Bank, the term knowledge management risked being confused with some kind of computer system or a "brain in the sky" that was unrealistic in terms of and irrelevant to the goals of the organization. Storytelling proved to be the most memorable way to enable managers and staff members to understand the concept and, by analogy, reinvent the concept for their own work environments.

The World Bank KM champion began with stories about a staff person in an underdeveloped country who needed the best information on treating malaria in a particular situation. They connected virtually with others who had experience and quickly received useful answers. Listeners could identify with the story, which prompted them to imagine what else they might be able to do if only they could connect with others.

Sometimes, painful reminders of the cost of not knowing are more powerful than stories of gains. At Xerox, not knowing that a technician had fixed a $40,000 machine with a 90-cent part could have cost the company plenty. Fortunately, because of the Eureka knowledge-sharing system, a technician in Brazil did know of the Canadian technician's feat, and other machines were fixed rather than returned at a significant loss to Xerox.

Stage 2: Develop Strategy

Stage 2 is the turning point from individual interest or local efforts in KM to an organizational experiment. It is characterized both by the decision to explore potential benefits and an evolution from individual passion to organizational action. Best practices include forming a cross-functional KM advisory group; developing a KM strategy that is aligned with organizational goals and objectives; and identifying opportunities to test and understand how KM practices, principles, and approaches can be applied in selected business focus areas.

A common lesson learned is the failure to develop the appropriate governance model and structure to drive change and orchestrate various KM efforts at the enterprise level. The lack of a senior steering committee, a core-coordinating group, or an advisory group—and the lack of dedicated resources at the business unit level—will compound the inability to leverage investments in infrastructure, process, and people. The advisory group usually functions as the key decision-making body and as a sounding board for problems that may arise in any of the KM efforts. The advisory group must have a strong grounding in KM principles. Strategy development, communication, training, and a plan for rewards and recognition are proper topics for the advisory group to discuss and implement. The advisory group is also the main vehicle for corporatewide communication and support of KM.

Stage 3: Design and Launch KM Initiatives

The goals of Stage 3 are simple: Conduct successful pilots, provide evidence of the business value of KM, and capture lessons learned. Creating replicable processes and methodologies in Stage 3 is key to successfully expanding any of the lessons discovered in this stage. The most critical mistakes made in Stage 3 are not engaging people who are involved with the business process in the knowledge-sharing design process. Additionally, it is important in developing and tracking measures that show how knowledge sharing contributes to business results.

Forming Design Teams

Because learning and sharing knowledge are social activities, culture and people are the keys to enable practices and ideas to flow seamlessly across time and space. Processes are embedded in culture, people, and context; processes also are complex and rich. Descriptions yield less. Dialogue and demonstrations can help enrich learning opportunities. To ensure practices and knowledge do not just transfer, but transfer effectively and make a difference, organizations must connect people who can and are willing to share their tacit knowledge.

Design teams are made up of people who represent the business unit or functional area where knowledge sharing and transfer will provide value. Typically, this group includes both management and line representation. The purpose of the design team is to refine the scope of the KM initiatives, identify the potential users and "high-voltage knowledge" to achieve early success, and analyze the costs and infrastructure required. A design team will create the tactical rollout plan with staged activities and milestones. This plan includes communication and training plans, rewards, recognition, key indicators of success, and other issues affecting cultural acceptance of a KM approach.

The key lesson learned about culture is that people cannot be expected to change the way they work without a reason to do so. Demanding that the culture change to support KM is the wrong thing to do. The key is to tap into people's motivation to share by giving them a valid business reason for doing so. You will find that people's behavior, and hence company culture, will change when that reason exists and tools to do so are readily available. Involving people in the change process from the beginning, as the design-team process does, will lead to a more successful deployment of the KM approaches and processes.

Creating Measures

By not tracking and measuring your KM activities and results, practitioners will have a hard time understanding what is working (or what is not) and what the payoffs are. Measures can provide an assessment of where you are, a picture of where you want to be, and vital information about the routes you need to take to get there.

What an organization measures depends on the overall purpose and expectations of KM. If a practitioner wants to know if KM efforts are achieving their objectives, then it is important to identify the business results that match the original value proposition and measure those. If a practitioner wants to know how well KM tools and applications are being used and accepted, it is critical to measure the activity level and ask users how useful the new processes are in improving their daily jobs.

There are two general types of measures that can be used to evaluate KM activities:

1. **Results.** The measurable impact of the initiative on the outcomes of the projects or processes targeted for improvement

2. **Activities.** Usage and participation rates in KM activities

Measuring KM is not simple. Determining the pervasiveness and impact of KM is analogous to measuring the contribution of marketing, employee development, or any other management or organizational competency. Nonetheless, it is a necessity if KM is to sustain and have significant impact in an organization.

STAGE 4: EXPAND AND SUPPORT

By the time an organization reaches Stage 4, KM has proved valuable enough to be officially expanded to become part of the funded activities of the organization. Demand for KM support by other parts of the organization tends to be high, providing additional evidence of its value.

As experienced KM practitioners know, high visibility and the authority to expand are a mixed blessing. The added costs and visibility of resources devoted to KM will require more formal business evaluation and return on investment (ROI) justification. Competition to "own" the KM program also may exist. The good news is that unless unforeseen factors derail the efforts, KM is on its way to being considered a strategic and necessary competency.

Rapid expansion inevitably will entail some confusion and missteps; these can be alleviated somewhat by an active, central, and cross-functional advisory group. This group must create an expansion strategy and identify required resources. Sustaining the core KM team and forming a network of business unit KM managers and champions will continue to provide support to knowledge-sharing efforts, will align multiple initiatives, and will combat isolation among business units.

Best-practices organizations have passed on the passion for knowledge sharing by creating marketing and public relations campaigns. At Siemens, some of the KM promotional activities included sending a letter of endorsement from the senior leadership to all local employees, publishing a KM article in the local company paper, and placing KM articles on the intranet with a link to the knowledge-sharing network of the organization.

A lesson learned is that constant communication prohibits a regression of the KM activities and provides continuity to the KM efforts of the enterprise. Communicating the KM strategy and its rationale to the organization requires the same kind of vigorous marketing as does any other large-scale initiative.

STAGE 5: INSTITUTIONALIZE KM

An organization does not reach Stage 5 unless KM is part of the business model. One striking difference between early-stage adopters and advanced firms is that experienced KM practitioners see financial support as one their biggest issues. Once KM becomes part of the mainstream and part of the normal budgeting process, it is subject to the same expectations and pressures of any other function.

Early-stage adopters should expect that the realities of organizational life would catch up with KM; they can expect financial pressure to increase as they move through the stages. In contrast, organizations with advanced initiatives do not report that functional silos are barriers, and early-stage adopters see them as one of the biggest barriers they face. Early-stage adopters ranked both lack of incentives and lack of definition as their primary obstacles to implementing KM in their organizations.

In order to proceed successfully with Stage 5, KM leaders must work to realign the structure and budget of the organization to include KM initiatives. The following are suggested topics to address:

- Budget realignment
- Who pays for KM efforts
- Central KM budgets versus business units
- Infrastructure versus projects and local applications
- Where do KM resources reside
- Costs to build and maintain skill sets needed for maintenance

One of the challenges of making KM part of the business model is that divisions within the business will actualize the model in their own autonomous ways. Some ways to successfully manage this certainty are to enact a standards board, to have readily accessible and written policies, and to use communities of practice as a vehicle for local innovation.

It is clear that KM must "go native" for acceptance; however, it also is clear that some common standards and policies can help. Business need should drive policy formulation, not the details of how a unit deploys policy. Even the policy should be determined by practitioners, and the common institutional policy should allow variation where needed. The exception is for knowledge repositories that must be shared across the enterprise.

Aligning rewards and adding knowledge-sharing objectives to the performance evaluations are best practices used to institutionalize knowledge sharing across the enterprise.

CONCLUSION: KEY LESSONS

Even with a road map based on lessons learned and best practices, KM implementations can fail. Why? We still have naïve beliefs about human and organizational behavior; forgetting change management principles and expecting people to share their knowledge on demand are major roadblocks. It has been said that a major business change initiative will not work unless the culture also changes. Of course, organizational culture will not change unless the business is transformed first. Can this argument be won? Compare this story with that of the chicken and the egg, and the answer will be clear.

Without an understanding of how change management requires work force collaboration at each stage, an organization may mistakenly insert an imperative to "change the culture" as an initial step in the KM implementation process. It may seem like a simple and plausible endeavor: Knowledge-sharing advocates spread the word; and the work force readily embraces the process of finding, sharing, and using knowledge. And from this acceptance, organizations assume that the work force will eagerly employ portals and best practices repositories. Why wouldn't the work force adopt a process to eliminate redundant work, as well as improve productivity and work processes?

Despite the efforts of an organization to train newly acquired or hired employees in change management concepts, establish methodologies and frameworks to guide employees through major software implementation, or communicate the value of KM, people will inevitably be resistant to changing the way they work. And no single gesture of support that begins a change-management initiative will create organizationwide acceptance.

In addition to capable tools and senior management support, knowledge sharing and its requisite culture necessitate a systematic inclusion of four factors at every turn: people, process, content, and technology. This may not seem like novel or contentious information, but the inclusion and engagement of people—experts, stewards, team members, management, trainees, system users, content authors, editors, and so on—are often disregarded in various stages with detrimental effects. No matter what the change initiative, KM is the platform to overcome resistance. Well-founded objectives need to be well communicated.

In the APQC best-practices report entitled "Creating a knowledge-sharing culture," based on a 1999 benchmark consortium study, the study team found that everyone affected by a change initiative needs to see the connection between sharing knowledge and the business purpose. With strong management and peer pressure to collaborate and share, knowledge sharing can become a core cultural value within an organization. Consequently, barriers to change break down. But knowledge sharing must be integrated with employees' responsibilities through knowledge-sharing events and routine work processes. Organizations facilitate this environment by aligning knowledge sharing with rewards and recognition and by creating human networks with facilitators to own knowledge and ensure participation.

A Focus for Organizationwide Engagement

When an organization makes the strategic decision to share and transfer its knowledge, it also commits to changing the way people work. After all, we all share our knowledge. But do we do so in a systematic way with shared processes and tools? Consider the following elements of change, and identify which one has the biggest impact on knowledge sharing and initiating change:

- Collaboration
- Communication
- Creativity
- Empowerment
- Enthusiasm
- Involvement

- Open-mindedness
- Positive attitude
- Sharing
- Synergy
- Trust

Now, ask yourself the following questions for each of the elements in the previous list:

1. Why is this element important?
2. What happens without it?
3. How can we ensure that we have it?

A legitimate case can be made for each element; all have a significant impact on the outcome of a KM initiative. But what is the lynchpin? Best-practices organizations have found that the most critical success factor for managing change is to involve (i.e., to engage thoroughly, or to employ and absorb) people in the process. Employees will support what they help to create.

The following steps to involve people in the planning, design, and deployment of changing work are cited in the APQC Stages of Implementation™:

- Focus on processes and business critical areas that people are passionate about.
- Create a governance structure to bring together a cross-functional thought leadership group that provides guidance, makes strategic decisions, and removes obstacles.
- Empower people closest to the process to decide, design, and deploy any new activities and tools needed to embed knowledge sharing and transfer into the everyday workflow.
- Provide support, such as training, IT, and HR, from a central resource pool. Dedicated resources show commitment to making changes.
- Organize face-to-face events (e.g., training, workshops, and miniconferences) where people with common issues and opportunities can meet to build relationships.

If resistance is recognized as inevitable, an organization can prepare for the following dynamics of change.

- **Confusion.** Explain that some confusion is expected, and educate the participant.
- **Isolation.** Break down silos, and arrange participants in human networks.
- **Anxiety.** Give participants the facts, and explain what will happen.

- **Resources.** Define priorities for the organization.
- **Readiness.** Assess who is ready.
- **Saturation.** Implement the change initiative in manageable chunks.
- **Reversion.** Monitor progress to sustain the initiative.

With these recommendations in hand, an organization can plan how to aggressively engage all participants at each stage of a change-management initiative. The key is to use KM as the platform for change. Only with the support of those who will facilitate the change can an organization hope to make lasting improvements.

Continuing the Journey

It can be said that KM is a journey, not a destination. So what are the signposts of the future? What can we expect? Based on the APQC study of KM and KM thought leaders, some predictions and assumptions can be made:

- Content management systems are becoming vital to organizing and managing the explicit knowledge of organizations.
- E-learning will continue to converge with KM. A best-practices organization will strive to connect people to the best practices, knowledge, and expertise they need when they need it. An organization must be there at the teachable moments!
- E-business will result in more ways to deliver more knowledge to customers and will extend to virtual collaboration with customers and business partners, creating new organizations and distributed work processes.
- Ways of building knowledge capture, sharing, and reuse into everyday work processes will be pursued continuously.
- Portals customized to deliver just-in-time information matching the preferences and roles of individual employees will become commonplace.
- Increasing bandwidth will make connections with international employees more practical, especially for sharing large, seismic data sets. Increasing bandwidth also will lead to the proliferation of Web-based training, particularly streaming video. This may make video conferencing a more effective communication mechanism.
- For accounting reasons, measuring intellectual capital in a formal and consistent manner will become important.

CHAPTER 6

Knowledge Management Strategy: Codification Versus Personalization (A False Dichotomy)

Michael E. D. Koenig, Long Island University

One of the points that long has been made about KM is that most KM initiatives can usefully be categorized as either focusing on the codification or the personalization of information and knowledge. For example, for several years—that is, from very early on in the growth of KM—IBM (http://www.ibm.com/us) employed the graphic in Figure 6.1 to help explain the domain of KM. The vertical dimension of the graphic makes precisely that distinction (collecting [stuff]) versus personalization (connecting [people]).

	EXPLOIT	EXPLORE
COLLECT (stuff)	HARVEST Examples: best practices	HUNTING Example: data mining
CONNECT (people)	HARNESS Example: response teams	HYPOTHESIZE Examples: brainstorming, scenario analysis

Figure 6.1   Knowledge management strategies (From: Tom Short, Senior Consultant, Knowledge Management, IBM Global Services).

AN 80–20 BALANCE?

In a recent and much referenced article, however, Hansen et al. (1999) have seized on the codification–personalization distinction to argue that not only are most specific KM undertakings oriented to either codification or personalization, but that overall organizational strategies for KM are similarly either heavily codification or heavily personalization. Hansen et al. (1999) argue that KM systems are almost inevitably an 80–20 balance, with some firms emphasizing the codification and others the personalization. For example, Andersen Consulting (now Accenture) and Dell emphasize codification; McKinsey and Hewlett-Packard emphasize personalization. Hansen et al. (1999) point out that the KM strategy must be carefully thought out and aligned with the business operations and goals of the firm. Codification can be the KM strategy when the company products are standardized and mature and when people rely primarily on explicit knowledge. Personalization can be the KM strategy when the company products are customized and innovative and when people rely primarily on tacit knowledge.

The arguments of Hansen et al. (1999) are straightforward and relatively unexceptionable up to this point. However, the authors go on to make an additional argument: Not only are KM strategies almost always fish or fowl (either 80 percent codification and 20 percent personalization, or the reverse) but, further, straddles (about a 50–50 mix) are a sign of a lack of strategic focus and are to be avoided. Their advice is very specific: "DO NOT STRADDLE" (Hansen et al., 1999, p. 112, their capitalization).

A 50–50 BALANCE?

Whereas the advice to match one's strategy with the context is admirable, the "Do not straddle" advice is overly simplistic. Indeed, it is dangerously misleading. An analysis of the pharmaceutical industry, for example, reveals a situation where a 50–50 straddle is precisely what is called for. Koenig[1] studied the relationship between the research productivity of pharmaceutical companies and the information–knowledge characteristics of their research environments and found a fascinating phenomenon. In the pharmaceutical industry, a heavy emphasis on codification is of course required; codified access to research notebooks, compounds synthesized, screening results, clinical trials, and so on, is *de rigueur*. However, the research revealed that the most salient difference between the less successful and the more successful pharmaceutical companies is that the former have an information–knowledge environment that indeed has an 80–20 emphasis on codification, and the latter, though placing no less emphasis on codification, place an equal emphasis on personalization. These companies have deliberately adopted the 50–50 straddle that Hansen, Nohria, and Tierney precisely advise us to avoid. It should be pointed out that this research is not anecdotal; it is quantifiable and rigorous.

Conclusion

Companies should think carefully about their KM strategy and align it with their business operations and goals. However, the 80–20 and 20–80 emphases are not either–or choices; they are the practical limits of the range in which the appropriate KM strategy mix lies. The correct balance for overall KM implementation may lie anywhere within that 20–80 to 80–20 range. Furthermore, the correct balance is likely to differ within different functions or units of the organization. Do *not* fall for the advice: "Do not straddle."

Endnote

The measure of research performance was the number of new pharmaceutical agents per billions of dollars of research budget, limited to chemically novel new agents, and refined by the evaluation by the Food and Drug Administration of the importance of each new agent and by the patent position of the company on the agent. See Koenig, M. E. D. (1992). The information environment and the productivity of research. In: *Recent Advances in Chemical Information*, Collier H., ed. London, Royal Society of Chemistry; pp. 133–143. Reprinted in *Information Culture and Business Performance* (1995). Grimshaw, A., ed. (Information Strategy Report 2, prepared for the British Library by Hertis Information and Research), Hatfield, Hertfordshire: University of Hertfordshire Press.

Reference

Hansen, M. T., Nohria, N., and Tierney, T. (1999). What's your strategy for managing knowledge? *Harvard Business Review*. 77(2):106–116.

CHAPTER 7

Why Knowledge Management Systems Fail: Enablers and Constraints of Knowledge Management in Human Enterprises

Yogesh Malhotra, Syracuse University

INTRODUCTION

The advent of the era characterized by high uncertainty was announced by a *Business Week* (2001) cover story that determined September 11, 2001, as the day of the watershed event. On this day, the unprecedented combination of *conventional* means of terrorism inflicted wrath on thousands of lives in the World Trade Center twin towers despite policymakers' preoccupations with *unconventional* means of terror. The basic premises guiding the knowledge processes of the intelligence machinery and policy makers' decision models surmised the following:

- *Unconventional* means pose greater risk compared with those posed by *conventional* means.
- *Conventional* means cannot reconfigure in unpredictable ways to pose greater risk than *unconventional* means.
- The impact of human and technology inputs can be determined with a safe margin of predictability.
- *High-tech* inputs always have greater impact than *low-tech* inputs.
- *Human* inputs play a lesser role compared with *technology* inputs and *financial capital* inputs in the input–outcome equation.
- Inputs rather than the execution strategy primarily determine the outcomes.

In retrospect it was found that all these assumptions were questionable. A review of the assumptions guiding policy-making decisions offers some interesting revelations listed here:

- Prespecified and predetermined notions of *unconventional* and *conventional* means and *low-tech* and *high-tech* inputs may not necessarily always be applicable.
- Technology inputs and financial capital inputs may be less relevant factors in the input–outcome equation given unconventional *strategy of execution,* which defines how creatively and innovatively inputs are deployed to produce unprecedented outcomes.
- Human inputs may not necessarily play a lesser role than technology inputs or financial capital inputs in the input–outcome equation. Given highly committed and motivated humans and their leaders, technology inputs and financial capital inputs may assume a lesser role in the input–outcome equation.

Extending the same analysis to understand the recent debacle of "new economy" enterprises also offers some interesting insights. Given the euphoria about the Internet technologies and the pitch of the venture capitalists and tech stock analysts and underwriters, Internet technology–based businesses were summarily branded as *unconventional* in contrast to the *conventional* enterprises of the brick-and-mortar economy. It was assumed that *conventional* enterprises must get on the Internet bandwagon if they were to survive in the future. It was assumed that given enough investment of venture capital, technology, and hype, any company could create and sustain successful business performance outcomes within a very short time. In summary, the following premises guided the euphoria about the Internet-based companies, which was compounded by the overexuberance of media network reporters and the analysts:

- *Unconventional* means pose greater risk compared with those posed by *conventional* means.
- *Conventional* means cannot be reconfigured in unpredictable ways to pose greater risk than *unconventional* means.
- The impact of human inputs and technology inputs can be determined with a safe margin of predictability.
- *High-tech* inputs always have greater impact than *low-tech* inputs.
- Human inputs play a lesser role compared with technology inputs and financial capital inputs in the input–outcome equation.
- Inputs rather than the execution strategy primarily determine the outcomes.

Given the recent spate of Internet-based company failures, reversal of faith in these companies has been pervasive. This has happened even though widespread weaknesses are being observed in many sectors of the economy, including many industries and companies that represent the tried-and-tested "old economy." It is time to reflect on the lessons learned from the biggest failures of KM in recent world history and the debacle of the new economy enterprises. This is important to dispel the prevailing myth about the intrinsic infallibility of old economy enterprises in contrast with the new economy enterprises despite dependence of both on the same fundamentals.

Based on the earlier analysis, the following propositions are suggested as a more robust basis for defining, implementing, and executing effective KM systems.

- The impact of human and technology inputs cannot be determined with a safe margin of predictability because the business performance outcomes are separated from these inputs by intervening variables. Such variables include effective acceptance and use of technologies by humans; motivation and commitment for adoption of these technologies and for achieving the specified performance outcomes; and contextual interpretation of information, resulting in diverse subjective decisions and actions. Prespecified outcomes may also become marginalized with the changing business environment when the inputs are utilized for *doing the thing right* even though it may not be the *right thing* anymore.

- *Low-tech* and *high-tech* inputs are constrained or enabled by knowledge workers who utilize these inputs as well as by the strategy of execution that may together produce different outcomes despite a similar mix of the inputs. The contrast between *low-tech* and *high-tech* is based on context-specific perspectives and as business contexts change, these contrasts may change or become immaterial with the emergence of newer and unprecedented inputs.

- The contrast between *unconventional* and *conventional* means of producing business performance outcomes is based on context-specific perspectives. As business contexts change such contrasts may become marginalized with the emergence of newer and unprecedented means as well as unprecedented outcomes. Such contrasts may also become marginalized if *conventional* means are configured in unprecedented ways to achieve unprecedented outcomes. In this discussion, it is observed that unprecedented business performance outcomes are realized as a result of new business value propositions and customer value propositions.

This article explains how both old and new economy enterprises having any mix of brick-and-click strategies are vulnerable to these failures. Such failures result from the gaps between the input resources and the business performance outcomes, and the gaps between the value these enterprises create and the value changing market conditions demand. Such market transitions include changing consumer preferences, competitive offerings, and changing business models and industry structures.

Knowledge management systems (KMSs) are often defined in terms of inputs such as data, IT, best practices, and so on, which by themselves may inadequately explain business performance outcomes. Often, moderating and intervening variables may play a significant role in skewing the simplistic relationships based on correlation of the inputs with business performance outcomes. Also, usefulness of such inputs and how they are strategically deployed are important issues often left unquestioned as "expected" performance outcomes are achieved. However, the value of such performance outcomes becomes eroded by the dynamic shifts in the business and competitive environments. The remaining discussion will explain the following: why KMSs fail; how *enablers* of KMSs designed for the "knowledge factory" engineering paradigm become *constraints* in adapting and evolving such systems for business environments characterized by high uncertainty and radical discontinuous change; and how risk of such failures may be minimized.

KM FOR ROUTINE AND STRUCTURED INFORMATION PROCESSING (MODEL 1 KMS)

Given the centrality of computerized information processing in most mainstream conceptualizations of KM, most KMSs primarily depend on routines that are programmed in the logic of computational machinery and on data residing in data warehouses.[1] Based on the prespecification and predetermination of the programmed logic connecting "information inputs" and consequent "information outcomes," such systems are based on consensus, convergence, and compliance to ensure adherence to organizational routines. The mechanistic model of information processing and control based on compliance is not only limited to the computational machinery, but extends to the specification of goals and tasks and the best practices and institutionalized procedures to achieve those prespecified outcomes.

Motivated by emphasis on optimization and efficiencies of scale, the logic of KM described above has evolved from "scientific" Taylorism and the assembly line techniques applied by Henry Ford in the production of the Model T.

Not surprisingly, the original versions of such KMSs were reified in the interpretations of some information systems researchers who seemed to believe that technology inputs, rather than knowledge workers, would play a predominant role in the performance outcome equation discussed earlier. One example of such systems was offered in an earlier edition of a popular information systems textbook published by professors at the Harvard Business School (Applegate et al., 1988):

> Information systems will maintain the corporate history, experience and expertise that long-term employees now hold. The information systems themselves—not the people—can become the stable structure of the organization. People will be free to come and go, but the value of their experience will be incorporated in the systems that help them and their successors run the business.

Trained in similar reasoning, many business technology executives have been trying to push for adoption of computer technologies for *storing* their employees' *knowledge* in computerized databases and programmed logic of the computing machinery, and gotten mixed results. Best practices, benchmarks, and rules tend to define the assumptions that are embedded not only in information databases, but also in the strategy, reward systems, and resource allocation systems of the organization.

A recent interpretation of the same reasoning, illustrated in Figure 7.1, is based on predefinition, prespecification, and predetermination. It is offered in a definition popularized by the Gartner Group (cf.: *Oracle Magazine*, 1998):

> Knowledge Management promotes an integrated approach to identifying, capturing, retrieving, sharing, and evaluating enterprises information assets. These information assets may include databases, documents, policies, procedures, as well as the un-captured tacit expertise and experience stored in individual's heads.

Such inputs-oriented mechanistic and static representations of knowledge do not provide any hint of how these inputs would affect business performance. Nor do they suggest how to deal with "associated emotions and specific contexts" (Nonaka and Takeuchi, 1995) that characterize tacit knowledge.

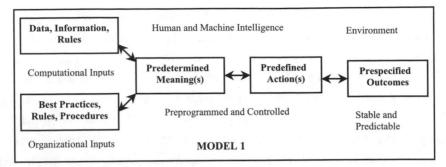

Figure 7.1   Model 1: Knowledge management for routine and structured information processing.

The recent thrust of some organizational KM initiatives on archiving "best practices" and "what we know" to guide future decisions and actions is also based on a relatively predictable view of the business environment. Not surprisingly, this model of KM guided by prespecification and predetermination of business logic with primary emphasis on optimizing the use of existing knowledge (embedded in best practices, computational logic, data warehouses, and so on) has primarily focused on *knowledge reuse* over *creation of new knowledge*. This model is based on managerial focus on seeking consensus and compliance to minimize variance so that prespecified business performance outcomes are achieved. In this model of KM, conformance to prespecified and predetermined business logic is expected to ensure that prespecified and predetermined business performance outcomes are achieved.

Not surprisingly, many KM practitioners and researchers who identify with Model 1 discussed here consider *information* and *knowledge* as synonymous constructs. In this perspective, both these constructs can be expressed in the computational rule-based logic as well as in the form of data inputs and data outputs that trigger predefined and predetermined actions in preprogrammed modes. There is limited, if any, scope for diverse interpretations of the same information by different agents, nor is there any need for multiplicity of *meanings* based on the same information. Homogeneity of information processing and control logic is desirable as it ensures that the model works as prespecified. Inclusion of feedback and feedforward loops may often provide the mechanism for reactive fine-tuning of inputs for optimal conversion of the inputs into outcomes.[2]

Not surprisingly, the goal of KMSs based on Model 1 is often characterized as "getting the right information to the right person at the right time." This model is based on the assumption that all relevant knowledge, including *tacit knowledge,* can be stored in computerized databases, software programs, and institutionalized rules and practices. The distinguishing features of this model are derived from the following assumptions:

1. The same knowledge can be reused by any human mind or computer to reprocess the same logic to produce the same outcomes.
2. The same outcomes will be needed and delivered again and again through optimal use of input resources.
3. The primary objective of the system is to achieve the most efficient means for transforming prespecified inputs into predetermined outcomes.
4. There is no need for subjective interpretation of information—criticism and conflict must be minimized to achieve conformance and compliance.

Model 1 KMSs are based on *doing the thing right* where the prespecified inputs, processing logic, and outcomes are assumed to represent *the right thing*. The overriding belief is that designers of the systems and the knowledge managers have accurate and complete knowledge about the viability of the input–output transformation process as well as the viability of the predefined performance outcomes.

The next section explains the contrasting Model 2 of KMSs, which is more suited for nonroutine and unstructured sense making when deterministic controls encounter uncertain environments characterized by a "wide range of potential surprise" that defy predictive logic (Landau and Stout, 1979). Interestingly, many limitations of Model 1 may be considered to be strengths in Model 2 as the premises of predetermination, predefinition, and prespecification of meanings, actions, and outcomes become less relevant.

KM for Nonroutine and Unstructured Sense Making (Model 2 KMS)

In Model 2, the construct of knowledge may be better represented as *intelligence in action*. This is because it is a composite construct resulting from interaction of data, information, rules, procedures, best practices, and traits, such as attention, motivation, commitment, creativity, and innovation. This contrasting representation of knowledge as *intelligence in action* rather than static computerized representations of Model 1 is notable for several reasons. The *active*, *affective*, and *dynamic* representation of knowledge makes better sense from a pragmatic perspective and is better aligned with theoretical representations of this construct beyond the domain of IT management. It is *active* because knowledge is best understood in action—it is not the theory but the practice of theory that makes the difference. It is *affective* because it takes into consideration not only the cognitive and rational dimensions but also the emotional dimensions of human decision making. It is *dynamic* because it is based on ongoing reinterpretation of data, information, and assumptions while proactively sensing how the decision-making process should adjust to future possibilities. From a pragmatic perspective, the dynamic representation of knowledge provides a more realistic construct where human and social interactions are present while situating this construct closer to performance outcomes. This is illustrated in Figure 7.2.[3]

Model 2 provides a better representation of reality because it takes into consideration two key characteristics:

1. What is done with data, information, and best practices depends on subjective interpretation ("construction") of individuals and groups that transform these inputs into actions and performance.
2. Performance outcomes need to be continuously reassessed to ensure that they indeed represent best business performance for the enterprise with respect to changing market conditions, consumer preferences, competitive offerings, and changing business models and industry structures.

This view of KM is consistent with some other perspectives that have attempted to address the limitations of Model 1, which is based on "overdefinition of rules and overspecification of tasks" (Landau and Stout, 1979). For

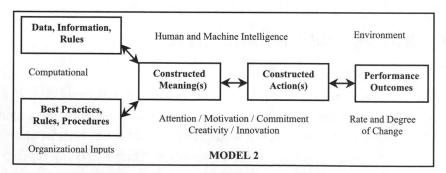

Figure 7.2   Model 2: Knowledge management for nonroutine and unstructured sense making.

instance, Churchman (1971) has emphasized that "To conceive of knowledge as a collection of information seems to rob the concept of all of its life... Knowledge resides in the user and not in the collection." Similarly, Nonaka and Takeuchi (1995) had proposed the conceptualization of knowledge as *justified belief* in their argument that "knowledge, unlike information, is about *beliefs* and *commitment*." On a complementary note, Davenport and Prusak (1998) have defined knowledge as deriving from minds at work:

> Knowledge is a fluid mix of framed experience, values, contextual infor-
> mation, and expert insight that provides a framework for evaluating and
> incorporating new experiences and information. It originates in the minds of
> knowers. In organizations, it often becomes embedded not only in docu-
> ments or repositories but also in organizational routines, processes, prac-
> tices, and norms.

As represented in Model 2, knowledge is a *dynamic* construct, in contrast to the *static* representations of Model 1, because diverse (individual and shared) mean-ings are possible based on diverse interpretations of the same information inputs across different contexts and at different times. Processing of knowledge through the machinery of ITs may still be represented by simplified, highly routine, and structured forms that permit predefinition, preprogramming, and predetermina-tion of data inputs for achieving prespecified performance outcomes. In contrast, human sense-making processes represent a complete contrast, and human deci-sion making is influenced by attention, motivation, commitment, creativity, and innovation of individuals and groups.[4]

CONTINUUM OF KM SYSTEMS BETWEEN MODELS 1 AND 2

Model 1 works well in predictable and stable environments, with the primary focus on knowledge harvesting, reuse, and replication. Under moderate control levels, this model could be used for knowledge workers' goal-and-task specifica-tions to achieve prespecified performance outcomes. This model may be suscep-tible to failure when the creativity and innovation of knowledge workers overwhelm the controls inherent in the prespecified logic of the input–output transformation process. It is also vulnerable to failure where the attention and actions of knowledge workers are significantly influenced by their intrinsic moti-vation (rather than organizational or institutional rewards and punishments) and commitment to personal goals (rather than organizational or institutional goals). The ideal scenario is to achieve perfect congruence between extrinsic motivation and intrinsic motivation, and between organizational goals and individual goals. However, this is a formidable challenge for designers of most organizational KMSs.[5]

While Models 1 and 2 represent the extreme archetypes of KMSs, most organizations need some combination of both, depending on their emphasis on knowledge harvesting and knowledge creation (cf.: Yuva, 2002). Also, organizations and inter-enterprise value networks contain some business processes that primarily depend on knowledge harvesting and others that primarily depend on knowledge creation. This point can be appreciated by considering the two worlds of business that often coexist in many organizations—the world of bulk-processing industrial economy and the "world-of-re-everything" of the knowledge economy (Arthur, 1996):

> The two worlds are not neatly split. Hewlett-Packard, for example, designs knowledge-based devices in Palo Alto, California, and manufactures them in bulk in places like Corvallis, Oregon, or Greeley, Colorado. Most high-tech companies have both knowledge-based operations and bulk-processing operations. But because the rules of the game are different for each, companies often separate them—as Hewlett-Packard does. Conversely, manufacturing companies have operations such as logistics, branding, marketing, and distribution that belong largely to the knowledge world. And some products—like the IBM PC—start in the increasing returns world, but later in their life cycle become virtual commodities that belong to Marshall's processing world.

Model 1 is relevant to the industrial world of bulk-economy production, and Model 2 is relevant to the "world-of-re-everything." Optimization-based routinization of organizational goals and convergence is relevant for "freezing" the meaning for achieving optimization-based efficiencies. However, unfreezing of meaning embedded in information is critical for reassessing and renewing the routines embedded in business logic and business processes. Business enterprises will need to be facile in both modes, despite the apparent contradiction in terms of the business logic and related assumptions. For instance, a key challenge for most organizations with institutionalized best practices is to ensure that such practices remain open to critique (Malhotra, 2002e), adaptation, and replacement so that the enterprise is not caught in the death spiral (Nadler and Shaw, 1995) of doing *more of the same better and better*, with diminishing marginal returns (Drucker, 1994). Discontinuously changing environments impose on the organization the need for "creative synthesis," resulting from a "dialectical confrontation of opposing interpretations" (Mason and Mitroff, 1973). Although companies often separate the operations pertaining to the two worlds of business related to Models 1 and 2, both worlds need to be integrated in their business models. For example, given the diminishing margins in the PC markets owing to increased competition, computer distributor Dell may need to shift its focus to distribution of servers or to hosting services. To do so effectively, however, it would need to start *harvesting* (using Model 1) knowledge that it *created* (using Model 2) earlier through experimentation, adaptation, and innovation related to servers or hosting. It also would be time to redefine the customer value propositions and the related business value propositions.[6]

Because most business environments would include a combination of both stabilizing and destabilizing factors, real-world KMS implementations should contain combinations of characteristics of both models. The processes of *knowledge reuse* and *knowledge creation* need to be balanced by integration of routine and structured *information processing* and nonroutine and unstructured *sense making* in the same business model. Figure 7.3 depicts this representation of a business model that includes simultaneous and parallel sets of knowledge harvesting and knowledge creation processes.

Prior arguments suggest the need for skepticism about the myth of intrinsic infallibility of old economy enterprises in contrast with the new economy enterprises, despite dependence of both on the same fundamentals. Both old and new economy enterprises that have any mix of *conventional* and *unconventional* brick-and-click strategies are vulnerable to the failures resulting from the gaps between their inputs and the business performance outcomes as well as from gaps between the values they create and the value demanded by their customers. Also, despite similarity of inputs and sought market shares, the relative success of any business model will be determined more by its execution than by the inputs, especially in the case of rapidly changing environments.

As illustrated in Figure 7.4, new business models for the knowledge economy need to consider Internet and Web simply as elements of the overall business strategy without getting caught up in "irrational exuberance" or despair about these means of producing business value. Just like other inputs and intervening variables,

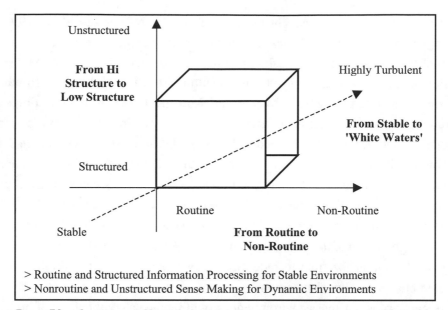

Figure 7.3   Continuum of knowledge management systems between stable and dynamic environments.

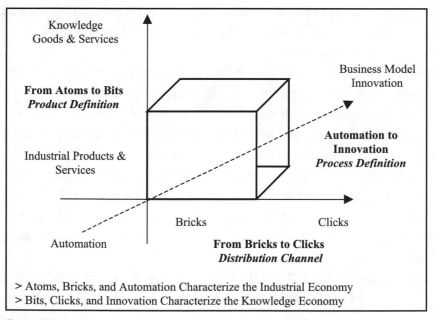

Figure 7.4   Continuum from industrial economy to knowledge economy.

inadequate understanding or application of the Internet and Web should not become the basis for outright rejection or degradation of these technologies.

ENABLERS AND CONSTRAINTS OF KM SYSTEMS

Prior discussion has highlighted that KMSs fail because of two broad reasons. First, KMSs are often defined in terms of inputs (such as data, IT, best practices, and so on) that alone may be inadequate for effective business performance. For these inputs to result in business performance, the influence of intervening and moderating variables (such as attention, motivation, commitment, creativity, and innovation) must be better understood and accounted for in business model design. Second, the efficacy of inputs and how they are strategically deployed are important issues often left unquestioned as "expected" performance outcomes are achieved; however, the value of such performance outcomes may be eroded by the dynamic shifts in the business and competitive environments. These enablers and constraints are presented in the following discussion as seven *challenges* that need to be met for successful KM. These are called challenges (Table 7.1) because they represent *both* enablers and constraints in different contexts, as represented by Models 1 and 2.

The following discussion highlights how the seven challenges relate to the recent evolution in thinking about business and technology strategy, organizational control, information-sharing culture, knowledge representation, organization structure, managerial command and control, and economic returns.

Table 7.1 Comparison of enablers and constraints of knowledge management systems: Models 1 and 2.

Enablers and Constraints	Model 1 KMS	Model 2 KMS
Business and technology strategy	Predefinition of outcomes	World of re-everything
Organizational control	Control for consistency	Self-control for creativity
Information-sharing culture	Based on contracts	Based on trust
Knowledge representation	Static and prespecified	Dynamic and "constructed"
Organization structure	Insular and top-down	Inclusive and self-organized
Managerial command and control	For achieving compliance	For achieving commitment
Economic returns	Decreasing returns	Increasing returns

Business and Technology Strategy Challenge of Next Generation KMS

In the world of re-everything, automation of functions, rationalization of work-flows, and redesign of business processes that characterize Model 1 KMSs will be inadequate (Malhotra, 2000d). Rather, most organizations will need to develop adaptive capacity for redefining their *business value propositions* that add greatest value to the business enterprise. Competitive survival and ongoing sustenance would depend on the ability to continuously redefine and adapt the goals, purposes, "way of doing things" of the organization. The digital business models will need to accommodate relatively rapid obsolescence of traditional concepts of industries, organizations, products, services, and channels of marketing, sales, and distribution (Malhotra, 2000b; Mathur and Kenyon, 1997). The critical challenge for most business enterprises will lie in the ability to redesign and reinvent their business processes and business models for realizing more interesting *customer value propositions*, while harvesting the knowledge flows embedded in the current setup.

The next generations of KMSs will need to accommodate the need for ongoing questioning of the programmed logic and a very high level of adaptability to incorporate dynamic changes in business models and information architectures. Designers of information architectures will need to ensure that they deliver efficiency and optimization for knowledge harvesting, while providing for flexibility for facilitating innovative business models and value propositions. Designers will need to provide loose coupling between technology and business architectures so that existing technology infrastructure should not straitjacket the evolution of the business model. Greater technological integration will help to achieve more efficient optimization for knowledge harvesting. However, there will be a critical need for ensuring rapid adaptation of the business performance outcomes to the dynamic shifts in the business environment while keeping them loosely coupled with prespecified technology architectures. The new paradigm of flexible, adaptive, and scalable systems will accommodate real-time changes in information and data across the business ecosystems network.

Organizational Control Challenge of Next Generation KMS

Organizational control is imperative in Model 1 KMSs to ensure viability of predetermined meanings, predefined actions, and prespecified outcomes.

Consistency is imperative for ensuring homogeneity of processing of the same information in the same manner to ensure the same outcomes and is achieved by minimizing criticism and questioning of the status quo. However, this may take its toll by suppressing innovation and creativity. Even despite organizational control that demands absolute conformance, knowledge workers' attention, motivation, and commitment may moderate or intervene in its influence. Control is often based on rules and, hence, is difficult to maintain in a world where competitive survival often depends on questioning existing assumptions. Given an environment characterized by radical and discontinuous change, the survival of the organization would hinge on ongoing assessment of assumptions underlying the business logic as well as ensuring that the definition of business performance outcomes is aligned with the changing market conditions, consumer preferences, competitive offerings, business models, and industry structures.

Design of the next generation KMS should ensure that they are not constrained by overemphasis on consistency. Whereas the traditional business logic is based on control, the dynamics of the new business environment require a business model that assumes existence of few rules, some specific information, and a lot of freedom. Within the proposed model, the designers of organizational systems can at best facilitate the "self-designing" of the organization. In this organizational design, not only would the knowledge workers define problems and generate their own solutions but would also evaluate and revise their solution-generating processes. By explicitly encouraging experimentation and rethinking of premises, this model promotes reflection-in-action, creation of new knowledge, and innovation. Organizations will need to be comfortable with the *dialectic* of harvesting their existing knowledge while being able to rethink and redefine their current models of success before they are marginalized by environmental change.

Integration of data and processes across inter-enterprise value networks will also impose certain challenges of organizational control. On the one hand, the players in the inter-enterprise supply chains and extended value chains will need to share information and collaborate with their upstream and downstream partners to ensure streamlined information flows. On the other hand, ironically, they may also perceive the upstream and downstream players as potential competitors vying for the most attractive and dominant position in the value chain networks. Sharing accurate information related to goods or services flowing across the supply chain will be necessary; however, it increases the peril inherent in the paradoxical roles of collaboration and competition adopted by various players in the same supply chain.

Information-Sharing Culture: The Challenge of Next Generation KMS

Success of the next generation KMS will depend on integration of not only data and processes across inter-enterprise supply chains and value chains, but also integration of decision making and actions across inter-enterprise boundaries. Effectiveness of integrated information flows will depend on the accuracy of information that is shared by diverse stakeholders across inter-enterprise boundaries. The challenge of information sharing will result from the potentially competitive nature of various enterprises across the value chains because access to privileged information may often determine the dominant position in the inter-enterprise value networks. Similarly, access to customer and supplier data residing in databases or networks that are hosted on the infrastructure of outsourcing providers and Web service providers may pose increased privacy and security challenges. This is particularly important in situations where sharing of proprietary strategic or competitive information about customer or supplier relationships needs to be safeguarded from third parties. This issue will be particularly relevant if vendor knowledge of the customers or specific customer relationships of the company may be used against the best interests of the company. There will be a need for trusting the vendor(s); however, given the changing business environment, the basis for trust will need to go beyond a simple contractual agreement that would have been sufficient in the deterministic and predictable logic of Model 1.

Often, individuals may not willingly share information with their departmental peers, supervisors, or other departments because they believe that what they know provides them with an inherent advantage in bargaining and negotiation. Despite the availability of most sophisticated knowledge-sharing technologies, such human concerns may often result in sharing of partial, inaccurate, or ambiguous information. In absence of enabling technologies, lack of knowledge sharing is detrimental to the viability of relationships between partners in supply-chain and value-chain networks. However, use of such "knowledge sharing" technologies per se cannot eliminate competitive concerns that may result in intentional hoarding of information or sharing of incomplete, incorrect, or ambiguous information. Reliability of integrated information flows depends upon the motivation of people to share accurate information on a timely basis across intra-enterprise and inter-enterprise information value chains. Motivation of employees, organizations, customers, and suppliers to share accurate and timely information is based on trust, despite the potential to use information in unanticipated ways. This in turn depends on the overriding inter-enterprise and intra-enterprise information-sharing cultures. As community and commerce paradigms increasingly intermingle, business enterprises will be challenged to inspire trust and motivation for sharing needed information with their stakeholders over which they may often have little control. Given the lack of these enabling factors, it will be almost impossible to ensure that accurate information is available for integration despite the presence of *enabling* technologies that can facilitate such integration.

Knowledge Representation Challenge of Next Generation KMS

Static and predefined representation of knowledge is particularly suited for *knowledge reuse* and offers an interesting contrast against the dynamic, affective, and active representation of knowledge needed for *knowledge creation*. The premise of the digitized memory of the past as a reliable predictor of future success is valid for a business environment characterized by routine and structured change. The digitized logic and databases can facilitate real-time execution of the inter-enterprise information value chains. However, their efficacy depends on real-time adaptation of underlying assumptions to continuously account for complex changes in the business environment. Often, such changes cannot be recognized or corrected automatically by computerized systems because these changes cannot be preprogrammed given an indeterminate and unpredictable future. The adaptability of a KMS is therefore dependent on its capability of sensing complex patterns of change in business environments *and* of using that information for adapting the digitized logic and databases to guide decision making, actions, and resulting performance outcomes.

Artificial intelligence (AI) and expert systems-based KMSs can deliver the "right information to the right person at the right time." However, this can occur only *if* the right information, right person to use or apply it, and right time when specific information is needed are *all* known well in advance. Detection of non-routine and unstructured change in business environments would still depend on the sense-making capabilities of knowledge workers for correcting the computational logic of the business and the data it processes. A related challenge lies in tapping the tacit knowledge of executives and employees for informing the computational logic embedded in the KMS. It may be possible to gather information about the decision-making logic from human experts if such decisions are based on routine and structured information processing. AI and expert systems-related technologies enable complex computation of specific and clearly defined areas of domain expertise by compiling inferential logic derived from multiple domain experts. The challenge of "scanning the human mind and its sense-making capabilities" lies in the problem that most individuals may know more than they think they know. This is particularly true about their information-processing and decision-making capabilities related to nonroutine and unstructured phenomena and to knowledge that spans multiple domains. The meaning-making capacity of the human mind facilitates dynamic adaptation of tacit knowledge to new and unfamiliar situations that may not fit previously recognized *templates*. The same assemblage of data may evoke different responses from different people at different times or in different contexts. Hence, storing explicit *static* representations of individuals' tacit knowledge in technology databases and computer algorithms may not be a valid surrogate for their *dynamic* sense-making capabilities.

Organization Structure Challenge of Next Generation KMS

Developing an information-sharing technological infrastructure is an exercise in *engineering design,* whereas enabling use of that infrastructure for sharing high-quality information and generating new knowledge is an exercise in *emergence*. The former process is characterized by predetermination, prespecification, and preprogramming for knowledge harvesting and exploitation. The latter process is typically characterized by creation of organizational cultural infrastructure to enable continuous information sharing, knowledge renewal, and creation of new knowledge.

Organizational routines embedded in standard operating procedures and policies can become formalized by their implementation in computer programs and databases as the dominant business logic of the firm becomes reinforced. Such formalized information systems become inflexible when they are based on *static* assumptions about the business environment. With increasingly rapid, dynamic, and nonlinear changes in the business environment, such systems are increasingly vulnerable because of out-of-date assumptions inherent in their processing logic and the data processed by them. To overcome these vulnerabilities, it is necessary to design technological systems that are sensitive to the dynamic and divergent interpretations of information necessary for navigating unforeseen changes in the business environment. Subjecting the extant business logic to critique from diverse customer, supplier, and partner perspectives can help in defining innovative customer value propositions and business value propositions by early detection of complex changes in the business environment. Online and offline communities (cf.: Malhotra, 2002a; Wenger et al., 2002) of customers, suppliers, and partners could provide the means for enabling critical analysis of the assumptions underlying given business models.

The expanded role of the customers, suppliers, and partners includes their involvement in the creation of "content," in generating product and service reviews, and in helping out each other on shared concerns. It is important to note that such roles often *assumed* voluntarily by *external* communities of customers, suppliers, and partners in the new world have been traditionally *delegated* to *internal* customer service representatives and technical support personnel. Hence, in the emerging business models, virtual communities could rightfully be treated as external extensions of the service and support infrastructure of the company. Executives must understand the distinction between the lack of structure and lack of controls that characterize self-selected communities and the command and control systems embedded in their formal organizational structures. Such communities may defy enforcement of compliance as they represent "self-organizing" ecosystems built on self-control and autonomy. As knowledge work gets transformed and dissipated across the inter-enterprise value networks, enterprise managers will need to become more comfortable with the model of the enterprise as "anything, anywhere, anyhow" *dynamic structures* of people, processes, and technology networks.

Managerial Command and Control Challenge of Next Generation KMS

Organizational controls tend to seek compliance with predefined goals that need to be achieved using predetermined best practices and standard operating procedures. Such organizational controls tend to *ensure* conformity by enforcing task definition, measurement, and control, yet they may *inhibit* creativity and initiative. Enforcement of such controls is essentially a negative activity because it defines "what cannot be done" (Stout, 1980) and reinforces a process of single-loop learning with its primary emphasis on error avoidance (Argyris, 1994). Given the premium on innovation of customer value propositions, business value propositions, and business models, organizations in dynamically changing environments need to encourage experimentation. Design of new information architectures thus needs to take into consideration ambiguity, inconsistency, multiple perspectives, and impermanency of existing information. Such architectures need to be designed along the principles of flexible and adaptive information systems. These systems should facilitate exploitation of previous experiences while ensuring that memory of the past does not hinder ongoing experimentation and adaptation for the discontinuous future.

A key challenge for managers in the forthcoming turbulent environment will be cultivating *commitment* of knowledge workers to the organizational vision. As it becomes increasingly difficult to specify long-term goals and objectives, such commitment would facilitate real-time strategizing in accord with the organizational vision and its real-time implementation on the front lines. Knowledge workers would need to take autonomous roles of self-leadership and self-regulation, because they would be best positioned to sense the dynamic changes in their immediate business environment. Compliance will lose its effectiveness as the managerial tool of control as managers removed from the front lines would have less and less knowledge about the changing dynamics for efficient decision making. Managers would need to facilitate the confidence of knowledge workers in acting on incomplete information, trusting their own judgments, and taking decisive actions for capturing increasingly shorter windows of opportunity. In the new world of business, the control over employees will be ultimately self-imposed.

Argyris (1990) has referred to the transition from traditional external control mechanisms to the paradigm of self-control as "the current revolution in management theory." Complementary views have been expressed by other scholars (cf.: Bartlett and Ghoshal, 1995; Ghoshal and Bartlett, 1996; Malhotra, 2002b; Malhotra, 2002d) to de-emphasize conformance to the status quo so that such prevailing practices may be continuously assessed from multiple divergent perspectives. The explicit bias of *command and control* systems for seeking compliance makes these systems inadequate for motivating divergence-oriented interpretations that are necessary for surviving in ill-structured and complex environments. Systems designed to ensure compliance might ensure obedience to given rules. However, they do not facilitate the detection and correction of gaps between the institutionalized inputs, logic, and outcomes, and those necessary for the survival and competence of the organization.

Economic Returns Challenge of Next Generation KMS

Some economists (cf.: Arthur, 1996) have argued that the production and distribution of knowledge-based goods and services should create and sustain increasing returns in contrast to diminishing returns characteristic of industrial goods and services. The traditional factors of production are constrained by a threshold of scale and scope as every unit increase in land, labor, or capital results in diminishing returns on every incremental unit beyond that threshold. In contrast, information and knowledge products seem to be governed by a different law of economic returns: Investment in every additional unit of information or knowledge created and utilized could result in progressively higher returns. However, it is important to observe that the actual realization of such returns requires fundamental rethinking of not only the nature of the product or service but also of its distribution channels, as well as the processes underlying its creation, distribution, and utilization. Increasing digitization and virtualization of business processes without rethinking of the fundamental premises of the traditional models of products and service definitions has been responsible for the demise of many over-hyped venture capital-funded enterprises.

Whereas plug-and-play technologies could enable rapid adaptability of integrated technology infrastructures, success of the business performance outcomes will still depend on sustained business relationships with collaborators and potential competitors. Designers of the next generation KMS would need to understand how enterprise information architectures for intra- and inter-enterprise integration of business processes could enable relationship-building capabilities. This will facilitate sharing of accurate, complete, and timely information by stakeholders across inter-enterprise boundaries to achieve true integration of information flows. Understanding how information sharing occurs in emergent and self-designed communities of practice, such as those supporting open-source technologies, could perhaps facilitate this process.

A related issue is that of the incentives and rewards often used for justifying the economic rationale for knowledge sharing by employees and outsiders, such as customers and suppliers. Knowledge managers responsible for the success of KMSs and knowledge sharing will need to reconcile contractual measures such as punitive covenants with the need for trust and loyalty of customers, employees, partners, and suppliers. This is particularly true about information-sharing environments that *emerge* from self-selection of organizations and entities that cooperate with each other based on shared concerns despite the absence of formal controls, rewards, or incentives. These issues will gain greater importance with the emergence of Internet-based exchanges and global knowledge economies for knowledge, expertise, skills, and intellectual capital in which the free market of knowledge is just a few mouse clicks away (Malhotra, 2002c). Design of incentives for knowledge sharing must consider that institutional controls as well as monetary rewards and incentives are not necessary and do not guarantee the desired knowledge-sharing behavior. The consulting firm Pricewaterhouse Coopers presents an interesting example of institutionalized formal knowledge harvesting and reuse existing side-by-side with informal ad hoc knowledge exchange and knowledge creation (Stewart, 2002). In this company, the formal and institutionalized KnowledgeCurve intranet has proved effective as a means for sharing routine and structured information relevant to worldwide employees, while the informal and ad hoc e-mail list, Kraken, has shown tremendous potential for hooking up "self-selected creatives" across various divisions and departments.

SUMMARY AND RECOMMENDATIONS FOR KM EXECUTIVES

Corporate executives are demanding better justification for investments in KMS infrastructures and expected business performance outcomes. Executives realize that the next generation KMSs must be based on ongoing innovation of business value propositions and extended inter-enterprise value networks. Many executives want to know how investments in new KMS architectures and "solutions" would contribute to the adaptability of their businesses to the unprecedented and rapid pace of change. Accordingly, in establishing the agenda for digitization of their enterprises, KM executives must recognize that their companies can create viable KMSs only by attending to the fundamentals of agility and flexibility. The unprecedented level and scope of integration of information flows within and across enterprise boundaries have motivated design of KM architectures based on highly integrated technologies.

Business environments characterized by rapid and radical change put a premium on continuous business model innovation to deliver novel, sustainable, and competitively viable customer value propositions. Hence, the design of KMSs should ensure that adaptation and innovation of business performance outcomes occur in alignment with changing dynamics of the business environment. This would prevent the failure of KMSs caused by the gaps between the value these enterprises create and the value demanded by changing market conditions, consumer preferences, competitive offerings, changing business models, and industry structures. In addition, the design of KMSs must give due consideration to moderating and intervening behavioral and sociological variables (such as attention, motivation, commitment, creativity, and innovation discussed in Model 2) to ensure that computational inputs (including enabling technologies) and organizational inputs result in effective business performance. This would prevent the failure of KMSs caused by the gaps between the data, IT, best practices, and so on, and the business performance outcomes. As explained previously, conceiving multiple future trajectories of the IT and human inputs embedded in the KMS can diminish the risk of rapid obsolescence of such systems as they can be readily adapted to innovative business value propositions and customer value propositions. The overriding challenge for the organizations is to effectively address the dialectic of knowledge harvesting and knowledge creation. Enablers and constraints of KMSs were enumerated in the form of seven challenges related to business and technology strategy, organizational control, information-sharing culture, knowledge representation, organization structure, managerial command and control, and economic returns.

The architects of next generation KMSs cannot afford to treat as afterthoughts the strategic sustainability of business models, the related organizational cultural challenges, and the dependence of these architectures on true integrated information flows. To successfully manage these challenges, KMS designers must take a holistic approach to designing inter- and intra-organizational "systems" with due consideration not only for the technological design but also for the design of strategic sustainability of these systems. This approach is expected to provide the needed balance of integration and flexibility required for next generation KMS architectures. Where "disruptive technologies" *alone* fell short of expectations, the same technologies could provide the winning recipes for success when coupled with "disruptive customer value propositions." Organizational competence and success ultimately depend on KMS architectures that can enable agile and adaptive enterprises skilled in creating innovative business models driven by unique, interesting, and competitive customer value propositions.

ACKNOWLEDGMENTS

The content, discussions, and schematic representations in this chapter are based on the author's original works, including authored and in-print publications, working papers, keynote presentations, and speeches. The contributions of the editors of this book in clarifying and updating many ideas expressed in this chapter are gratefully acknowledged. The author also acknowledges the contributions of the global virtual community of practice of the BRINT Institute (http://www.brint.com/press) in refining the framework shared herein.

ENDNOTES

1. A detailed discussion about such definitions of KM is available elsewhere (Malhotra, 2000a; 2000b). A recent historical perspective of KM is available in Prusak (2001).

2. Information systems researchers (cf.: Churchman, 1971; Mason and Mitroff, 1973; Malhotra, 1997) have discussed limitations of this model, particularly for environments characterized by uncertainty and radical change.

3. A detailed discussion about the active, affective, and dynamic representation of knowledge is available elsewhere (Malhotra, 1999; Malhotra and Kirsch, 1996; Malhotra, in press).

4. Related discussion on how "construction of meaning" differs from "the processing of information" is available in Bruner (1990), Kelly (1963), Malhotra (1999), Morris (1938), and Strombach (1986). Detailed conceptualization and empirical validation of commitment and motivation constructs as applicable to effective technology use in knowledge work are available in Malhotra (1998) and Malhotra and Galletta (1999). The contrast between information-processing capabilities of smart technologies and sense-making capabilities of humans is explained in Malhotra (2001a).

5. A detailed discussion on the contrast between extrinsic motivation and intrinsic motivation and on the contrast between various levels of commitment is available elsewhere (Malhotra, 1998; Malhotra and Galletta, 2003).

6. How the contrast between the two worlds applies to the use of IT and KM strategy is discussed in the context of business model innovation in Malhotra (2000d) and Yuva (2002). How the world of old economy and new economy connect with their representation in terms of digitized information and knowledge has been discussed in the business literature on virtual organizations, virtual products, and virtual services; see, for instance, Davidow and Malone (1992). More recent research relating KM to virtual organizations and business model innovation is available in Malhotra (2000c) and Malhotra (2001b), respectively.

REFERENCES

Applegate, L., Cash, J., and Mills, D. Q. (1988). Information technology and tomorrow's manager. In: *Revolution in Real Time: Managing Information Technology in the 1990s*, McGowan, W. G., ed. Boston, MA: Harvard Business School Press; pp. 33–48.

Argyris, C. (1990). *Integrating the Individual and the Organization*. New Brunswick, NJ: Transaction.

Argyris, C. (1994). Good communication that blocks learning. *Harvard Business Review*. July–August:77–85.

Arthur, B. (1996). Increasing returns and the new world of business. *Harvard Business Review*. 74(4):100–109.

Bartlett, C. A. and Ghoshal, S. (1995). Changing the role of the top management: Beyond systems to people. *Harvard Business Review*. May–June:132–142.

Bruner, J. (1990). *Acts of Meaning*. Cambridge, MA: Harvard University Press.

Business Week. (2001). Understanding a new world of uncertainty and risk. October 8.

Churchman, C. W. (1971). *The Design of Inquiring Systems*. New York, NY: Basic Books.

Davenport, T. H. and Prusak, L. (1998). *Working Knowledge: How Organizations Manage What They Know*. Boston: Harvard Business School Press.

Davidow, W. H. and Malone, M. S. (1992). *The Virtual Corporation*. New York: HarperCollins.

Drucker, P. F. (1994). The theory of business. *Harvard Business Review*. September–October:95–104.

Ghoshal, S. and Bartlett, C. A. (1996). Rebuilding behavioral context: A blueprint for corporate renewal. *Sloan Management Review*. Winter:23–36.

Kelly, G. A. (1963). *A Theory of Personality: The Psychology of Personal Constructs*. New York: W. W. Norton.

Landau, M. and Stout, Jr., R. (1979). To manage is not to control: Or the folly of type II errors. *Public Administration Review*. March/April:148–156.

Malhotra, Y. (1997). Knowledge management in inquiring organizations. *Proceedings of the Americas Conference in Information Systems*; pp. 293–295. [Available online at http://www.kmbook.com]

Malhotra, Y. (1998). Role of social influence, self-determination and quality of use in information technology acceptance and utilization: A theoretical framework and empirical field study. Unpublished Ph.D. thesis, Katz Graduate School of Business, University of Pittsburgh, Pittsburgh, PA.

Malhotra, Y. (1999). Bringing the adopter back into the adoption process: A personal construction framework of information technology adoption. *Journal of High Technology Management Research*. 10(1):79–104.

Malhotra, Y. (2000a). From information management to knowledge management: Beyond the "hi-tech hidebound" systems. In: *Knowledge Management for the Information Professional*, Srikantaiah, T. K., and Koenig, M. E. D., eds. Medford, NJ: Information Today; pp. 37–61. [Available online at http://www.kmbook.com]

Malhotra, Y. (2000b). Knowledge management and new organization forms: A framework for business model innovation. *Information Resources Management Journal*. 13(1):5–14. [Available online at http://www.kmbook.com]

Malhotra, Y., ed. (2000c). *Knowledge Management and Virtual Organizations*. Hershey, PA: Idea Group Publishing.

Malhotra, Y. (2000d). Knowledge management for E-business performance: Advancing information strategy to "Internet time." *Information Strategy: The Executive's Journal*. 16(4):5–16. [Available online at http://www.kmbook.com]

Malhotra, Y. (2001a). Expert systems for knowledge management: Crossing the chasm between information processing and sense making. *Expert Systems with Applications*. 20(1):7–16.

Malhotra, Y., ed. (2001b). *Knowledge Management and Business Model Innovation*. Hershey: PA, Idea Group Publishing.

Malhotra, Y. (2002a). Enabling knowledge exchanges for E-business communities. *Information Strategy: The Executive's Journal*. 18(3):26–31.

Malhotra, Y. (2002b). Is knowledge management really an oxymoron? Unraveling the role of organizational controls in knowledge management. In: *Knowledge Mapping and Management*, White, D., ed. Hershey, PA: Idea Group Publishing; pp. 1–13.

Malhotra, Y. (2002c). Knowledge assets in the global economy: Assessment of national intellectual capital. In: *Advanced Topics in Global Information Management*, Tan, F., ed. Hershey, PA: Idea Group Publishing; pp. 329–345.

Malhotra, Y. (2002d). Information ecology and knowledge management: Toward knowledge ecology for hyperturbulent organizational environments. In: *UNESCO Encyclopedia of Life Support Systems (EOLSS)*, Kiel, D. L., ed. Oxford, U.K.: EOLSS Publishers. (http://www.eolss.net)

Malhotra, Y. (2002e). When best becomes worst. *Momentum—The Quality Magazine of Australasia*. September:29–30.

Malhotra, Y. and Galletta, D. F. (1999). Extending the technology acceptance model to account for social influence: Theoretical bases and empirical validation. *Proceedings of the Hawaii International Conference on System Sciences*; pp. 6–19.

Malhotra, Y. and Galletta, D. F. (2003). Role of commitment and motivation in knowledge management systems implementation: Theory, conceptualization, and measurement of antecedents of success. *Proceedings of the Hawaii International Conference on Systems Science*; pp. 1–10.

Malhotra, Y. and Kirsch, L. J. (1996). Personal construct analysis of self-control in IS adoption: Empirical evidence from comparative case studies of IS users and IS champions. *Proceedings of the First INFORMS Conference on Information Systems and Technology*; pp. 105–114.

Mason, R. O. and Mitroff, I. I. (1973). A program for research on management information systems. *Management Science*. 19(5):475–487.

Mathur, S. S. and Kenyon, A. (1997). Our strategy is what we sell. *Long Range Planning*. 30 June.

Morris, C. W. (1938). *Foundations of the Theory of Signs*. Chicago, IL: University of Chicago Press.

Nadler, D. A. and Shaw, R. B. (1995). Change leadership: Core competency for the Twenty-First Century. In: *Discontinuous Change: Leading Organizational Transformation*, Nadler, D. A., Shaw, R. B., and Walton, A. E., eds. San Franscisco, CA: Jossey-Bass.

Nonaka, I. and Takeuchi, H. (1995). *The Knowledge-Creating Company*. New York: Oxford University Press.

Oracle Magazine. (1998). Knowledge management in the information age. May. http://www.oracle.com/oramag/oracle/98-May/cov1.html.

Prusak, L. (2001). Where did knowledge management come from? *IBM Systems Journal*. 4:1002–1007.

Stewart, T. (2002). The case against knowledge management. Business 2.0, February. http://www.business2.com/articles/mag/0,1640,36747%7C3,00.html.

Stout, R., Jr. (1980). *Management or Control?: The Organizational Challenge*. Bloomington, IN: Indiana University Press.

Strombach, W. (1986). Information in epistemological and ontological perspective. In: *Philosophy and Technology II: Information Technology and Computers in Theory and Practice*, Mitcham, C., and Huning, A., eds. Dordrecht, the Netherlands: Reidel.

Wenger, E., McDermott, R., and Snyder, W. M. (2002). *Cultivating Communities of Practice: A Guide to Managing Knowledge*. Boston, MA: Harvard Business School.

Yuva, J. (2002). Knowledge management—The supply chain nerve center. *Inside Supply Management*; pp. 34–43, July.

CHAPTER 8

Knowledge Management and Research on Research: What Has Been Learned?

Michael E. D. Koenig, Long Island University

The people served by KM are knowledge workers. The quintessential knowledge workers, and the ones most thoroughly studied, are researchers. Those studies, that is, research on research, have much to tell us in regard to KM.

Knowledge management has been described as emerging "by the Internet out of Intellectual Capital" (Koenig, 2000). It is the very pragmatic recognition by the major consulting firms that they could use the Internet, particularly in its intranet form, to link their organizations and that what was being linked and transported by way of the intranet was their intellectual capital. The next and almost immediate recognition was that here was an application that, in turn, could be marketed to their customers. This new product needed a name—hence, knowledge management.

Although it did not historically emerge this way, another very suggestive and illuminating definition, though an uncommon one, is that *KM is the extension, broadly across the firm, of the information environment that has been shown by research to be conducive to successful R&D*. The logical but unstated assumption undergirding the development of KM is that R&D is the quintessential information work, and as the age of information and knowledge unfolds, an increasingly larger proportion of the work force becomes knowledge workers. Then, what has been shown to be good for the goose should be good for all other geese and those ganders now in the knowledge worker fold.

BACKGROUND

Examining KM from this viewpoint reveals a number of illuminating insights. First, however, we provide a bit of background.

The body of research work on research reaches conclusions that are very consistent, and that are therefore robust to a surprising degree, in what is basically a fairly soft research area (Koenig, 1990). The conclusion common to all these studies is that richness and openness in communication flow and in access to information are very highly correlated with research success and productivity. And, of course, if that is not congruent with the thinking behind KM, what is?

The seminal work in this field by T. J. Allen (1977) compares the winners and losers in competing military R&D contracts and examines their information environments. Allen found that the more productive teams were particularly characterized by having had more diverse information contacts outside the project team than did the less productive teams. In particular, Allen elucidated and illuminated the rich informal communication networks, typically quite independent of the formal organizational structure, characteristic of the more successful companies, and management's relative unawareness of either the importance of, and in many cases even the existence of, those networks. Analysis by Brown and Duguid (2000) of the work and communication structures of Xerox field representatives has revealed similar phenomenon and richly confirmed these conclusions.

One surprising aspect, however, is the degree to which the business community and even the researchers themselves have been at the very least unaware and even obtuse in perceiving and acting on the consistency of these findings.

For example, one major study by Goldhar et al. (1976) that reviewed a large corpus of work on R&D innovation concluded that there are six characteristics of environments conducive to technological innovations. The first three are related to the information environment: (1) easy access to information by individuals; (2) free flow of information both into and out of the organizations; and (3) rewards for sharing, seeking, and using "new" externally developed information sources. Number six is also related to the information environment: encouragement of mobility and interpersonal contacts. Yet the authors of the studies never remarked on the win, place, and show finish of information and knowledge factors.

Another similarly rigorous study (Orpen, 1985) examined productivity in R&D-intensive electronics–instrumentation organizations. It analyzed various aspects of the behavior of research managers as perceived by the research staff. Orpen found that in the more productive organizations (as defined by growth rates and return on assets) the managers were perceived to be significantly more characterized by three aspects of their behavior, all information related: (1) they routed literature and references to scientific and technical staff, (2) they directed their staff to use scientific and technical information (STI) and to purchase STI services, and (3) they encouraged publication of results and supported professional meeting attendance and continuing education. Particularly striking was the finding that not only did information-related management behavior strongly tend to discriminate between "high-performance" and "low-performance" companies, but also that none of the non–information-related management behaviors measured had any discriminatory value. Again, the predominance of information and knowledge factors was not remarked on.

Specific Lessons

So what are the specific lessons to be learned?

Facilitate Rich and Open Communication, Internal and External

If KM is to be successful, then management must encourage openness and richness in the communication of information and knowledge. This may seem obvious; however, often, it is not so obvious to management. This is particularly so at the macro level, that is, in regard to communicating with the outside world. It is now rather taken for granted that a major component of the implementation of KM is to change the culture of the organization to encourage information and knowledge sharing rather than hoarding. What is not so well appreciated is that change needs to be implemented for inter-organizational and not just intra-organizational communication and knowledge sharing.

Use Common Sense Precautions but Do Not Get Hung Up on Confidentiality

In a classic study of the research winners and losers among two dozen major pharmaceutical companies, Koenig (1992) found the following:

> The single best correlation with research success was that researchers in the most successful companies perceived their own organization as placing less emphasis on confidentiality and the protection of proprietary information than did other companies in the industry.

More emphasis on confidentiality and proprietorship yields less research success. Less emphasis yields more. One of the best known and at the time less successful companies in terms of R&D (in the bottom third of the rankings) was notorious in the industry for requiring researchers and managers, before embarking on a business trip or attending a conference, to sign a note reminding themselves that they were employees of the company and would be careful not to reveal proprietary information. Wisely, the company has retired this policy.

This requirement for richness and openness does not mean that one should ignore protecting one's intellectual property. However, it is consistent with the argument that it is more important to get new ideas and new products into the pipeline, to be the faster learning organization, than it is to be overly concerned about protecting what one has. Openness and rich communication flow foster learning. Excess emphasis on confidentiality dampens it.

Foster Egalitarianism: It Fosters Better Information and Knowledge Use

Foster an egalitarian organizational culture. In that same study of pharmaceutical research productivity (Koenig, 1992), another finding was that the more productive companies were the more egalitarian, and were the ones where the managerial structure and the status and rank indicators were relatively unobtrusive. One major pharmaceutical company, Eli Lilly, has in the last decade very much overhauled its corporate culture, which previously was very hierarchical and very obviously so, precisely with this end in mind: to facilitate better research and to improve their competitive position. Their comparative research performance has improved markedly. And, yes, Lilly is the company referred to earlier in regard to confidentiality.

Support Travel and Professional Development

Another correlate of successful R&D in the pharmaceutical industry is greater travel and meeting attendance and greater professional development. In that same vein, Paul Strassmann [ex–Chief Information Officer of Xerox, Assistant Secretary of the Army, and Director of Defense Information; author of *The Information Payoff* (1985); and amasser of data par excellence on IT-related expenditures] reports that the only IT expenditure that he has been able to find that is strongly related to a company's financial success is the amount (proportion) of money that the company devotes to management and professional development (Strassmann, 1994).

Facilitate Serendipity and Current Awareness (Environmental Scanning)

Knowledge management often focuses on the systems that enable employees to search for and retrieve specific information, or to locate those who may be able to help. Nothing wrong here, but do not overlook the importance of browsing. The researchers at the more productive pharmaceutical companies, for example, not only use their corporate library or information center more frequently, they use it proportionately much more for browsing and keeping abreast, as opposed to using it to address a specific information need. Indeed, at the pharmaceutical company with the highest score for research success, Pfizer, the corporate message encouraging such browsing was stunningly clear. Immediately on entering the library–information center at research headquarters one saw two long tables, one prominently labeled "Today's Journals" and the other "Yesterday's Journals" (anything older than yesterday was already off the table and on the shelf, open display shelves, granted). The researcher was obviously expected to be in the library, to be there frequently, and to be following the most current literature. By contrast, another large company very near the bottom of the list, G. D. Searle, "enjoyed" a culture in which it was made very clear that researchers should be at their benches doing their jobs. When information was needed, they should ask their library–information staff or their laboratory technician to obtain it for them. Other studies corroborate this conclusion. Mondschein (1990) studied the productivity of researchers in major corporations in several industries, including pharmaceuticals and electronics. He found that scientists who used literature-alerting services heavily were more productive (as measured by publication output, patents, and internal evaluations) than their colleagues who either did not use such services or used them only infrequently. Further, the productive researchers were characterized by their use of a wider variety of information sources, particularly by the extent of their efforts to stay current and by their use of patent information sources. In studying the information use of chief executive officers (CEOs), Ginman (1988) observed a very different information style for CEOs of companies in the revival or growth phase as compared with those of companies in comparative stasis. The former are more extroverted in their style of information use and have an information culture characterized by greater width and depth, with greater use of external information sources and greater emphasis on staying abreast.

The corollaries of Facilitate Serendipity are:

- Establish a culture with clear signs, as in the case of Pfizer, that encourage browsing and other forms of information interaction. Make it clear that the organization does not regard browsing as a waste of time.
- Establish physical spaces—the company library, perhaps a chat room, a literal or virtual space around the coffeepot—where people can meet and exchange ideas. From the point of view of the company, there is precious little serendipity when someone browses the Internet for sports news and trivia. However, conversation in the workplace is more constrained and

likely to be about work or professional matters, and one person's "by the way" or "did you just see" is often another's serendipity.

- Be aware that most KM software packages are oriented toward one or the other function, directed search or current awareness, but not both.

Recognize and Utilize Your Gatekeepers

A classic finding, starting with T. J. Allen's (1977) work, is that not only in research organizations but in the workplace at large, when information flows are charted, clear stars emerge: they are the people who are sought out as information sources and provide a disproportionate share of the information distributed around the organization. The phrase Allen coined for those stars is *gatekeepers*, because he was struck not only by the role those stars played in communicating information within the company but also by the role they played as *gates* through which external and environmental information was brought into the company. Although not yet so well studied, recent studies indicate precisely the same phenomenon in business organizations. In fact, what Allen and his contemporaries termed "sociometric mapping" is being rediscovered and renamed as "social network analysis," and is being applied with gusto to the business environment, particularly in the context of KM. Social network analysis is frequently and incorrectly being touted as a new technique since, of course, "new and improved" moves consulting even more effectively than it moves detergent.

There are a number of obvious KM ramifications:

- Identify the knowledge stars. You do not have to perform elaborate sociometric studies to do so. Just ask around. In particular, ask the librarians or information officers of the organization who the knowledge stars are; they will know.

- Give knowledge stars extra attention and extra support. Knowledge stars have a leveraging effect. Support for them not only enhances their performance, it enhances the performance of others.

- Engage knowledge stars in the design and the evolutions of KM systems. They know how knowledge moves in the organization, and they know what information is needed.

- Create the climates, the coffee pots as it were, that facilitate access to the knowledge stars.

WHERE ARE WE NOW IN KNOWLEDGE MANAGEMENT?

Where are we now in KM? Looking back at the points made here, we can ask the following questions: How novel are they? Where are these precepts now in relation to the current KM literature? How well recognized are they?

- **Facilitate rich and open communication.** In some sense taken for granted in KM, but not fully thought through.
- **Do not get hung up on confidentiality.** Not yet discussed much in KM circles. In fact, some of the tone of the discussions about intellectual capital management and intellectual property asset management systems (IPAMS) tends to hide and discourage recognition of this phenomenon.
- **Foster egalitarianism.** Not yet discussed much in KM, but it is there in the "learning organization" literature.
- **Support professional development.** Not yet discussed much in KM.
- **Facilitate serendipity and current awareness.** Not adequately recognized, even yet.
- **Utilize your gatekeepers.** Recognized only obliquely in KM, and thus needs much more explicit attention.

In summary, there is much KM can learn from research on research, and KM is still in the early days in applying what already has been learned.

REFERENCES

Allen, T. J. (1977). *Managing the Flow of Technology: Technology Transfer and the Dissemination of Technological Information Within the R&D Organization.* Cambridge, MA: MIT Press.

Brown, J. S., and Duguid, P. (2000). Balancing act: How to capture knowledge without killing it. *Harvard Business Review.* May–June 78(3):73–80.

Ginman, M. (1988). Information culture and business performance. *IATUL Quarterly.* 2(2):93–106.

Goldhar, J. D., Bragaw, L. K., and Schwartz, J. J. (1976). Information flows, management styles, and technological innovation. *IEEE Transactions in Engineering Management.* February EM-23(1):51–61.

Koenig, M. E. D. (2000). The evolution of knowledge management. In: *Knowledge Management for the Information Professional*, Srikantaiah, T. K., and Koenig, M. E. D., eds. Medford, NJ: Information Today, Inc.; pp. 23–36.

Koenig, M. E. D. (1992). The information environment and the productivity of research. In: *Recent Advances in Chemical Information*, Collier, H., ed. London: Royal Society of Chemistry; pp. 133–143. Reprinted in *Information Culture and Business Performance* (Information Strategy, Report 2, prepared for the British Library by Hertis Information and Research), Grimshaw, A., ed. Hatfield, Hertfordshire, U.K.: University of Hertfordshire Press, 1995.

Koenig, M. E. D. (1990). Information services and downstream productivity. In: *Annual Review of Information Science and Technology: Volume 25*. Williams, M. E., ed. New York: Elsevier Science Publishers for the American Society for Information Science; pp. 55–56.

Mondschein, L. G. (1990). SDI use and productivity in the corporate research environment. *Special Libraries*. Fall 81(4):265–279.

Orpen, C. (1985). The effect of managerial distribution or scientific and technical information on company performance. *R&D Management*. October 15(4):305–308.

Strassmann, P. A. (1994). Skills and employment opportunities in the information age. Lazerow Lecture delivered at Dominican University (then Rosary College), River Forest, IL.

Strassmann, P. A. (1985). *The Information Payoff: The Transformation of Work in the Electronic Age*, New York, Free Press.

Part II

Cost Analysis

Cost Analysis
Introductory Notes

Almost everyone is interested in how to cost justify KM. Despite great interest, however, there is very little to show for it. The enthusiasm of a decade ago for quantifying intellectual capital (IC) has served admirably to make us aware of the importance of IC, but has produced little in the way of technique that has been adopted beyond a hard core of enthusiasts. One result was the flurry of activity in the KM community of the late 1990s for storytelling as a way of conveying the potential and worth of KM. If you cannot give them numbers, give them a compelling story. The advice is sound. This book assumes that advice is now taken for granted in the KM community; provides a review of how to apply return on investment calculations to KM; and warns of the dangers of one common justification for KM: time saved.

These and similar themes are described in the Road Map following the Table of Contents.

"KM Costs and Economics" and "KM Measurement" are two of the themes elaborated on in the Road Map.

Additional chapters that call attention to those themes but are outside of this section include:

Chapter 4	Critical Success Factors of Knowledge Management Farida Hasanali, American Productivity and Quality Center
Chapter 5	Successfully Implementing Knowledge Management: Lessons Learned and Best Practices Cindy Hubert and Carla O'Dell, American Productivity and Quality Center
Chapter 12	Content Management: Role and Reality Stephen E. Arnold, Information and Online Systems Consultant

CHAPTER 9

Knowledge Return on Investment

Timothy W. Powell, The Knowledge Agency

INTRODUCTION TO RETURN ON INVESTMENT

ROI (pronounced "are-oh-eye," and typically written without periods) is an acronym for return on investment. Herein we define ROI as a metric of the net payouts from a financial outlay over time. While discussing other ROI measures, we focus on discounted cash flow (DCF), also known as internal rate of return (IRR) and net present value (NPV). This technique is taught in most MBA programs, and is a standard way of projecting and measuring the results of capital projects in the modern enterprise.

The goals of this chapter are to explain these terms and, in so doing, give you some ways to think about the value of knowledge.

The word investment herein typically includes both capitalized and expense items.[1] All kinds of organizational projects—including IT and KM projects—are typically subjected to ROI analysis.

The ROI measurement usually has three uses: selecting among projects being considered, comparing alternative potential solutions, and evaluating projects already undertaken.

- **Selecting among projects.** Any enterprise (whether business, government, or not-for-profit) has capital constraints, and therefore, project proposals must "compete" with each other for their share of expenditure. ROI analysis is used to allocate capital resources among competing projects by providing a common framework for their evaluation.

  In this usage, ROI is essentially a pro forma estimate of what is deemed most likely to occur in the future. Because it is a forecast, it is subject to a good deal of uncertainty. Consequently, the supporting estimates often must be arrived at by negotiation and consensus, rather than by scientific proof.

- **Comparing potential solutions.** Once a particular kind of project is decided on (e.g., "Let's install an expertise profiling system"), then it remains to select among solutions offered by competing vendors. In those rare cases where vendors offer exactly the same feature sets ("apples-to-apples"), the benefits can be presumed to be the same and costs become the key feature of differentiation. In most complex projects, however, the solution sets offered by various vendors differ somewhat, or even substantially. ROI analysis offers a way to compensate for these differences. Just as when selecting among projects, comparing solutions suffers from the future estimation problems mentioned here. Moreover, these ROI estimates often are supplied by the respective vendors themselves and therefore may contain biases of various kinds.

- **Evaluating projects after the fact.** After a project has been running, it is typical to compare the actual results with the estimates prepared, as discussed. This can be useful in determining whether to continue to fund the investment and in evaluating similar future investment opportunities. Here, the challenge is to measure what already has happened, rather than estimating what probably will happen.

Alas, however, the effort often is no less problematic. The key measurement problem is attribution, that is, how can we tell whether a certain positive benefit resulted from our project or was the result of some other factors (e.g., general business conditions). In fact, in any complex system—of which the modern enterprise is a textbook example—one can only rarely truthfully isolate the effects of various "causative" forces. As a result, in practice, post facto measurements of the results of a project, as do forecasts, become subject to negotiation and consensus building.

Though few ROI analyses are precisely scientific, the *process* of developing such an analysis has inherent benefits. The discipline of thinking through the specific costs and benefits expected to result from a project typically results in both greater cost control and greater expansion of potential applications than would otherwise have been the case.

The Value of Knowledge Management

The value of better KM is intuitively obvious to some (especially those on the knowledge supply side) but often less obvious to others (including those who control the purse strings of the organization). Several studies on the perceived benefits of better KM point to areas of benefits that could be exploited in a KM initiative. A study conducted by Ernst and Young (*Information Week*, 1997) among 431 U.S. and European companies found the following reported benefits from having organized KM programs:

- Increased innovativeness
- Enhanced efficiency
- Better decision making
- Faster responsiveness
- Enhanced flexibility
- Improved quality
- Reduced duplication of effort
- Greater employee empowerment

A similar study conducted by KPMG (*PC Week*, 1999) among 43 companies found similar results—and included the numbers of companies reporting such benefits as

- Better decision making, 86 percent
- Reduced costs, 70 percent
- Improved productivity, 68 percent
- Faster response time to key issues, 68 percent
- Shared best practices, 60 percent
- Created new/additional business activity, 58 percent
- Increased profit, 53 percent
- Better staff attraction/retention, 42 percent
- Increased market share, 42 percent
- Increased share price, 23 percent

What is interesting is the trend in the 1999 study toward drawing direct correlations between KM initiatives and enterprise value in the form of reduced costs; new business activity; and increases in profit, market share, and share price. The movement toward more rigorous financial justification for KM projects was already under way.[2]

KM ROI

In a large organization, ROI analysis typically is used to determine whether a complex project lives or dies. At this writing (Summer, 2002), most KM projects are competing for IT budgets that are growing much more slowly than previously, or even shrinking. Projects related to data security now appear to claim the top spot on organizational IT wish lists, and more strategic projects such as KM seem to be undertaken more reluctantly than previously.

Knowledge management projects are especially vulnerable to "death by ROI" because KM is an overhead function, it is viewed as expendable, and its benefits are often subtle.

1. **Knowledge management is overhead.** Alone, KM rarely generates revenues nor is that typically its primary mission. It is an overhead, or staff, function the benefits of which are necessarily indirect. Therefore its benefits, even its financial ones, are subject to estimation and biases as described here.

2. **Knowledge management is expendable.** Knowledge management is a leading-edge practice and is not assumed to be necessary by all enterprises. This is not only because it is an overhead function. A typical enterprise does not subject other overhead functions (e.g., Human Resources) to continual ROI analyses, because HR is assumed to be a necessary and valuable function. In contrast, KM is relatively unproved and is not assumed to "work" in all enterprises. (In fact, it has not "worked" in many instances, though the reasons for this are beyond the scope of this chapter.)

3. **Knowledge management benefits are both far-reaching and hard to measure.** The benefits of KM are much more uncertain and subject to volatility than are other enterprise initiatives. We will discuss this further in looking at the details of a KM ROI model.

A confounding issue is that KM as a discipline is evolving so rapidly that even its name has become relatively meaningless at this writing. It is more accurate to think of KM as a *portfolio* of specific projects and larger initiatives.

Seen from this perspective, KM projects typically fall into one of the following categories:

- **Document management.** Systems that index, catalog, locate, and make available documents across the enterprise

- **Expertise profiling.** Systems that index, catalog, and locate human expertise across the enterprise
- **Best-practices repositories.** Databases that contain optimized procedures and solutions to common problems
- **Data warehousing and data mining ("business intelligence").** Software that analyzes large transactions databases for patterns and trends
- **Intellectual property management.** Cataloging and subsequent licensing of trademarks, copyrights, patents, and trade secrets
- **Collaboration.** Software that facilitates project-oriented work groups, typically across organizational and geographic boundaries

Each project type is quite different in several respects, including the costs and benefits profiles. The generalized model described subsequently will fit all of these types of projects. In the specific example that follows, we choose one of these categories to illustrate the application of this generalized model.

Generalized ROI Model

The general ROI model[3] can be diagrammed as shown in Figure 9.1. Neither project costs nor benefits are likely to be one-shot events; they are likely to be recurring. That is, there are costs associated with the initial investment ($Cost_0$) and both costs and benefits associated with each time period for which the investment is to be evaluated. Capital investments are typically evaluated by year, though more or less frequent units of measurement are also possible. Calculations are usually made on constant currency terms, such that no adjustments for inflation need be made.

The ROI model uses cash flow as its unit of measurement. Cash flow is literally the amount of cash that comes in or goes out—without any accounting adjustments. Cash flow is quite different from earnings as defined by generally accepted accounting principles (GAAP), which all U.S. corporations currently must use for reporting. For example, for financial reporting purposes the cost of a piece of capital equipment is charged in stages over a period of, say, three to five years as depreciation. In an ROI analysis, the entire outlay is treated as a single initial cash outflow.

Cash flow is the standard measurement for all capital budgeting decisions, where the relevant decision involves a choice between two alternatives: investing in the project, or not investing (Van Horne, 1977).

	INITIAL	PERIOD 1	PERIOD 2	PERIOD 3	PERIOD N
BENEFITS (cash in)		$Benefit_1$	$Benefit_2$	$Benefit_3$	$Benefit_N$
COSTS (cash out)	$Cost_0$	$Cost_1$	$Cost_2$	$Cost_3$	$Cost_N$
NET CASH FLOW	Net_0	Net_1	Net_2	Net_3	Net_N

Figure 9.1   Generalized return on investment model.

Note that this general model would fit comfortably into an electronic spreadsheet, and you are encouraged to create a template as shown in Excel or any other spreadsheet software. This will greatly facilitate revising and running the model. The formula for each column is

$$Benefit_N - Cost_N = Net_N$$

Costs

Costs for a KM-related project typically include hardware, software, labor, and other related outlays. Some costs are obvious (such as software licenses), because they appear on invoices from vendors. Others are hidden costs, for example, the time of people to learn, use, and maintain an application.

- **Hardware** includes servers, storage, routers and wiring, and telecommunications equipment. Costs include purchase or lease costs and maintenance costs.
- **Software** includes the software for KM applications operating systems, network management, and so on. Software is typically licensed, rather than purchased. There may be an initial fee and a periodic license fee. License fees for many applications are charged on a "per seat" basis, that is, how many people are using the application at any given time. License fees often cover technical support and applications maintenance and

upgrades; however, to the extent they do not, these costs must be factored in separately.

- **Labor** includes, for example, user time for training in the KM application, the costs of internal support staff, and the costs of data input to the system. The cost of staff salaries is a "sunk cost"; nevertheless, it should be included in a rigorous project analysis.
- **Other** can include related contracted costs, such as consulting support and internal marketing support for the application.

Costs are typically easier to estimate than are benefits because, by definition, costs usually are financial and often are contractually specified (where an outside vendor is involved).

Benefits

Benefits consist of the incremental (in the sense that they would not have occurred without the project) cash flows generated by the investment. These can be financial; nonfinancial but measurable; and qualitative, or nonmeasurable.

- **Financial metrics** can be top line or bottom line. Top-line financial benefits include revenue enhancements, which typically are incremental sales that would not have occurred without the project. Bottom-line improvements include cost reductions, which are outlays that can be reduced or eliminated by the project. The ROI measurement only takes financial metrics into consideration.
- **Nonfinancial metrics** are the subject of various kinds of business scorecards now in place in many enterprises. Examples include:
  - Percentage of revenues from new products
  - Employee turnover
  - Market share
  - Average number of times the phone rings before being answered
  - Percentage of a sample of customers saying they are satisfied with the product
  - Number of new patents filed
  - Though nonfinancial metrics are worth noting, they cannot be directly incorporated into an ROI analysis. Sometimes, however, it is possible to arrive at a financial equivalent for a nonfinancial metric.
- **Qualitative benefits** are assumed to exist, yet in practice typically are not measured because either they cannot be measured reliably (e.g., better

decision making) or because economically it is not worth the cost of doing so (e.g., percentage of all satisfied customers).

Benefits are relatively difficult to estimate, and may be highly uncertain, especially in "out years" farther away from the date of implementation.

Note that, strictly speaking, benefits should be *outcome measures*; that is, they should reflect measurable bottom-line results. Too often, KM proponents present *output measures* (e.g., page hits on an intranet site) as benefits. Outputs are interim goals or metrics and should not be confused with outcome measures.

Net

The net cash flow for each period N is simply the incremental cash inflow (Benefit$_N$) less the incremental cash outflow (Cost$_N$) for that period (Figure 9.2). The initial outlay (often called Period 0) is not offset by a benefit, so that its cost and net are equal.

Each "column" of our model, then, looks like those in Figure 9.2. Cash flows should be estimated for all future periods for some reasonable planning horizon. Five to seven years is a typical horizon for estimating project costs and benefits.

Cash flows for each period should be estimated independently; however, in many cases, they are based on the same value formulas. For example, benefits may "ramp up" over several periods before maturing to their full potential. Certain costs (e.g., vendor charges) tend to increase over time, whereas others

BENEFITS (cash inflows)	TOTAL BENEFITS	$
	Revenue enhancements	$
	Cost reductions	$
	(Nonfinancial)	
	(Qualitative)	
COSTS (cash outflows)	TOTAL COSTS	$
	Hardware	$
	Software	$
	Labor	$
	Other	$
NET CASH FLOW		$

Figure 9.2   Period benefits and costs.

(e.g., training) may actually decrease based on an experience curve that makes things more efficient.

Cash flows, both positive and negative, should be estimated as conservatively as possible. Wildly optimist assumptions will usually be detected in the reviews of the project proposal, and the chance to go back with a revised model may be limited. It is better to run the model conservatively (estimating costs on the high side and benefits on the low side). If the model "works," then it is robust and can be expected to provide a margin for error.

Estimates of future benefits and costs are most credible when expressed as ranges of values. Often it is useful to run three versions of your model: one optimistic (costs low, benefits high), one most likely (midpoints of the ranges), and one conservative (as discussed earlier).

Where an ROI calculation is being used to evaluate an existing project, it is possible to measure the actual financial impact of the project. In the real world, however, such measurement is time-consuming, expensive, and often not worth it in terms of its own value (the ROI of ROI analysis).

Time Value of Money

Once the cash flows are estimated for each period, we must account for the *time value of money*. Put simply, a dollar (or any other unit of currency) to be received in the future is worth less today than that same amount received today. The difference is the amount of income that could be earned in the interim if the sum were invested. (The uncertainty of future returns is also greater but, ideally, is already factored into the rate of return. Therefore we need not consider it separately.)

Each of our future cash flows must then be "discounted" by the discount rate, that is, the amount that the alternatives to this potential investment could be assumed to earn in that time. The discount rate for any given organization depends on a variety of factors, and is usually available from the office of the chief financial officer. If you cannot find this number, we suggest you run your model using 10 percent and make adjustments from there.

There are two related types of DCF calculations: IRR and NPV. These are different ways of expressing the same basic idea.[4] The IRR is the compounded percentage return the project is expected to yield over the planning time frame. Mathematically, it represents the discount rate at which the total cash inflows and outflows of the project are exactly equal. The project IRR is compared to a *hurdle rate*, that is, the rate defined as the cutoff for capital projects. If the project

IRR is greater than the hurdle rate, the project should be a "go." The NPV is the present-value financial equivalent of a stream of future cash flows. The NPV formula builds in the hurdle rate, such that any project with a positive NPV should be accepted.

Formulas for calculating both NPV and IRR from a series of net cash flows are available in most PC spreadsheets' formula libraries, in moderately priced financial hand-held calculators, and in financial software for hand-held personal digital assistants.

We have said that, ideally, any project proposal with an IRR above the enterprise hurdle rate or a positive NPV should be accepted. In the real world, however, such proposals are typically further evaluated along with other "NPV-positive" proposals in order to arrive at final budget allocations. In this capital-constrained world, these methods usually just get you to the discussion table; they do not guarantee you the funding you are seeking.

Populating the Model

So far, we have the structural outline of the model. Now we need to determine the value of each cell in Figure 9.2 by defining and calculating one (or more) *value formulas* for each cell. We will use as an example an ROI model for an *expertise profiling* system, one aspect of KM. (The entire model is shown in the Appendix to this chapter.)

For example, one of the labor costs associated with such a system is the training involved. Training might involve the cost to engage an outside trainer, as well as the training *opportunity cost* (the time spent by employees who could have been doing other things). The model also may need to account for employee turnover in that a new group of employees would need to be trained periodically.

The labor cost cells of our model might look something like this:

- Trainer cost = $25,000 first year; half that each succeeding year.
- Employee turnover = 15 percent per year.
- Employee costs = 10,000 employees x 60 minutes of online training each x $33/hour = average wage rate of $330,000 first year; $49,500 each succeeding year (or 15 percent of the annual total).

Of course, you will need to get actual figures or "best guesstimates" from your own organization.

Here is another example, this time from the benefits side. To stay with our example of expertise profiling, cost reductions could result from reducing the outside purchase of expertise, reducing hiring costs by reducing turnover, or reducing downtime by solving problems faster. Therefore, our cells might look like this:

- **Purchase of outside expertise.** This often involves the hiring of outside consultants. One company installed an expertise profiling system and as a result cut their substantial consulting expenditures by 50 percent in a short time. To estimate conservatively, our model might say something like this: current outside consultant budget $5 million/year, reduce this by 20 percent to $4 million/year. Our incremental cost reduction, therefore, is (eventually) $1 million/year.

- **Hiring costs.** Expertise profiling should reduce turnover. A certain number of people made redundant could be reassigned elsewhere in the organization based on their skill sets, rather than being let go and having new people hired. Reducing turnover by 10 percent (from 15 percent to 13.5 percent per year) would mean 150 fewer separations per year x fees of 1/3 annual compensation for the average search x average annual compensation of $68,640 = $3,432,000/year.

- **Reducing downtime.** Indexing expertise in a complex organization can result in problems being solved faster. Sometimes such problems have a debilitating impact on revenue-generating capability. Industries vary in the value of downtime caused by maintenance, accidents, and other problems. These costs tend to be relatively higher where expensive capital equipment is involved (e.g., drilling for oil). Because the value of this factor can vary substantially by industry, we recommend that an enterprise-specific value formula be developed here.

Finally, we should not assume that these "run rate" benefits would appear immediately in the first year of the project operations. Rather, they will scale up over time, say, during a three-to-five-year period.[5]

We have used a similar approach to develop each of the cells in the model shown in the Appendix.[6] As you can see, in this analysis the NPV was forecasted at over $14 million, and the IRR was nearly 69 percent. These numbers would be sufficient to earn such a project serious consideration in most organizations.

Note that although "reduced time in seeking information" (or similar) is often cited as a benefit of KM, we have not included it here. The reason is that empirical studies have shown that "time seeking information" is a relatively constant 20 percent to 25 percent of time for most knowledge workers, regardless of the kinds of knowledge support processes or systems at their disposal. This surprising finding is apparently due to the need to *satisfice* and move on with the task at hand, regardless of whether the best information has been located (Koenig, 2002).

Benefits and Limitations of ROI Analysis

The benefits of ROI analysis include the following:

- **Rationality.** Decisions should not be based on what vendors represent and not (necessarily) on what the competition is doing. The criterion should be "what creates value for stakeholders," such as customers, shareholders, and employees.[7]
- **Comparability.** Competing capital projects of differing types can be evaluated on an equivalent basis.

We have referred throughout to some of the limits of ROI analysis. To review, they include the following:

- **Uncertainty.** Cash flows may be difficult to estimate, especially in the far future. Moreover, they may be subject to substantial variability.
- **Nonmetric nature of some benefits.** Some benefits cannot be measured, and sometimes it is not worth the effort it would take to measure them.
- **Attribution.** Model organizations are truly complex, and it is difficult (if not foolish) to attribute certain benefits to specific management initiatives.

Nevertheless, we work in an economic environment in which ROI analysis of KM- and IT-related projects is regularly a requirement. It is imperative to know these techniques in order to discuss capital projects of any kind intelligently and persuasively.

Other Ways of Looking at Knowledge Value

In the appendix to his seminal book entitled *Intellectual Capital*, Thomas Stewart (1997) describes several "tools for measuring and managing intellectual capital." He characterizes these as follows: measures of the whole, human capital measures, structural capital measures, and customer capital measures.

- **Measures of the whole.** These are measures of the overall enterprise, including market-to-book ratios, Tobin's q (a similar measure that considers the replacement cost of assets), and calculated intangible value (a way of measuring the relative value of intangible assets at the enterprise level).

- **Human capital measures.** These include measures of innovation; employee attitudes, experience, and turnover; and the overall value of the accumulated "bank" of knowledge.
- **Structural capital measures.** These include intellectual property portfolio valuations, working capital turnover, measures of the amount of "bureaucratic drag," and measures of back-office productivity.
- **Customer capital measures.** These include customer satisfaction, the value of relationships and alliances, and the value of a customer over time.

Stewart provides a fascinating and well-informed discussion of each technique, including examples of how and where it has been applied. However, it is likely that the knowledge professional "competing for capital" will find these useful mostly by way of background, rather than in the executive summary of a KM project proposal. These metrics apply mostly at the enterprise or business unit level, rather than at the project level.

However, it is possible that some of the metrics described by Stewart will be useful as inputs to the kind of DCF capital projects analysis we have discussed herein. They may be among the value formulas that determine each cell of the model.

Much of Stewart's work derives from a comprehensive intellectual capital scorecard developed by Skandia, the Swedish insurance company (Edvinsson and Malone, 1997). This includes dozens of intangibles measures that are ultimately used to provide a single financial index for the efficiency of knowledge capital. Again, while this approach may provide useful ideas for some metrics, it is very "macro" in its outlook and scope.

CONCLUSION

All capital projects must be cost-justified in advance. No matter how great its promise, KM is no exception. In fact, the failure of some early KM initiatives to create value speaks to the need to manage such initiatives aggressively—before, during, and after implementation. KM is still evolving rapidly, with new success stories, technologies, and management approaches always on the horizon.

The use of rigorous business thinking and analytical tools, such as those presented herein, will ensure that KM remains at the forefront of enterprise competitiveness—and does not end in the dustbin of management fads whose time has passed.

Appendix: A Return on Investment Model for Expertise Profiling

KNOWLEDGE MANAGEMENT - RETURN ON INVESTMENT MODEL

KM PROJECT CATEGORY			Value	
	Expertise Profiling	Value Formula	One-time	Annual (Year 5)
COST CATEGORIES				
HARDWARE	Client-server architecture	Dedicated server	$15,000	$0
SOFTWARE	System license	Pricing of one system for 10,000 users (25% of employee base)	$75,000	$20,000
LABOR	Training	10,000 employees x 60 minutes online training; trainer @25K first year; half time in later years; 15% new employees/year	$355,000	$62,000
	Data population (create and maintain profiles)	10,000 employees x 30 minutes to complete initial profile x average cost of $33/hour; 2 updates/year @ 15 min. each; 15% new employees/year	$165,000	$177,375
	IT support	Two FTE people first year; one in later years	$130,000	$65,000
OTHER				
	Internal marketing		$500,000	$150,000
TOTAL COSTS			*$1,240,000*	*$474,375*
BENEFITS CATEGORIES				
FINANCIAL - Enhanced Revenues	Increase responsiveness to customer needs	Net margin (8%) on incremental sales (+1.5%, base $10 billion)		$12,000,000
FINANCIAL - Displaced Costs	Reduce costs of purchased expertise	Displace 20% of outside consulting budget ($5 million)		$1,000,000
	Reduce downtime by solving problems faster	Situation-specific		
	Reduce search/separation/hiring costs by reducing turnover by 10% (from 15% to 13.5%)	150 fewer separations/year x $68,640 annual salary x 1/3 year's salary search fees		$3,432,000
NON-FINANCIAL METRIC	Make decisions faster			
QUALITATIVE	Make better decisions (reduced risk)			
	Increase collaboration			
TOTAL QUANTIFIABLE BENEFITS			*$0*	*$16,432,000*

Endnotes

1. Capitalized items are those that must be depreciated for financial reporting purposes, such as a new plant. Expense items flow directly to the current income statement, such as salaries and other operating expenses.

2. These studies share two significant flaws: (1) they do not strictly control for what constitutes a KM initiative in each implementing organization; and (2) they were produced by vendors offering services in the KM "space," and therefore, may dwell more on upside potential than on potential pitfalls.

3. This model is actually the discounted cash flow ROI model, the most common form of ROI analysis used in the modern enterprise.

4. Nondiscounted cash flow kinds of capital projects analysis also are available, including the payback method and the profitability method. In order to be most effective, you will need to find out what kind of analysis is favored in the organization whose resources this project will consume.

5. For a more complete discussion of the model as applied here, see Herzberg, R., and Virzi, A. M. (2002). Turning knowledge intro a collective asset. *Baseline*. April:99.

6. These data were based on a composite model company with the following characteristics: sales, $10 billion/year; 10,000 employees; employee turnover, 15 percent per year; net margin, 8 percent; hurdle rate, 10 percent; other assumptions as listed. Cost estimates were developed with input from Cadenza, Inc., an expertise-profiling firm in New York City. They are intended to be illustrative only and are not quotations for services.

7. For an extended discussion of the relationship between knowledge and value, see Powell, T. (2001). The knowledge value chain: How to fix it when it breaks. In: *Proceedings of the 22nd National Online Meeting*, Williams, M. E., ed., Information Today, Inc., Medford, NJ.

REFERENCES

Edvinsson, L. and Malone, M. S. (1997). *Intellectual Capital: Realizing Your Company's True Value by Finding Its Hidden Brainpower*, New York: Harper Business/HarperCollins.

Information Week, 20 October, 1997.

Koenig, M. (2002). Time saved: A misleading justification for KM. *KM World*. 11(3):22.

PC Week, 31 May, 1999.

Stewart, T. A. (1997). *Intellectual Capital: The New Wealth of Organizations*, New York: Doubleday/Currency.

Van Horne, J. C. (1974). *Financial Management and Policy*, 4th ed., New York: Prentice-Hall.

CHAPTER 10

Time Saved: Not a Politic Justification for Knowledge Management

Michael E. D. Koenig, Long Island University

A WORD OF WARNING REGARDING "SAVING USER TIME" AS A JUSTIFICATION FOR KM

The 2001 KMWorld Conference in Santa Clara, held from 30 October to 1 November, 2001, was notable for the greatly increased emphasis on data structure and retrieval (see Chapter 1, "Three Stages of Knowledge Management"). There was also, of course, continuing emphasis on how to obtain support for KM initiatives and how to cost justify KM expenditures. The principal component of the emphasis on justification was that of justification by storytelling—the good anecdote or sea story that illustrates an effective example of KM in practice. This technique is getting increasing recognition and undoubtedly is effective. However, there was another component about which one must be a bit more cautious. That component was the advice given by several speakers, typically in the context of how a taxonomically well-structured system could improve system performance. That is, improved KM systems could save user search time and this savings could be a quantifiable justification for KM.

Indeed, a well-structured KM system can save user time, but an unrecognized danger exists in using this as a justification for investing in or improving a KM system. Of course it makes sense to save user time. Justification of the KM system, however, ultimately must be demonstrated by better decisions and improved performance.

The problem with time saving as a justification is that even if user time is saved by a KM system, management probably will not note any observable difference in user behavior, and your justification could backfire. Why won't management see a difference?

The answer is a surprising one. Over the years, a number of studies of the practices of white-collar professional employees have been conducted. The findings are quite uniform and very corroborative. White-collar professional employees spend a very consistent 20 to 25 percent of their time seeking information (Griffiths, 1982; King, McDonald, and Roderer, 1981; Nelke, 1999a; 1999b; Poppel, 1982; Roderer, King, and Brouard, 1983). A recent study by Lazard Freres & Co., reported on at the same KMWorld Conference, arrived at precisely the same proportion and the same conclusion (Normier, 2001). Workplace technology may have changed, but that 20 to 25 percent has not. This proportion is surprisingly independent of the apparent information intensity of the job domain. Line business managers and administrators spend as much of their time seeking information as do research scientists.

What Is Going on Here?

There seems to be a sort of homeostasis at work. Perhaps a more accurate term would be a *satisficing mechanism*. Knowledge workers, whether managers, administrators, or researchers, need substantial information input to perform satisfactorily. When the amount of time devoted to that function approaches 20 percent, however, then knowledge workers typically begin to *satisfice*. That is, they begin to conclude that they must get on with the rest of their job, because if they do not then they soon will incur diminishing returns in their information seeking. They know that it is time to proceed based on the information they have.

The consequence of this phenomenon is that if a KM system allows a user to save time, that time will most likely be diverted into other information-seeking behavior. Thus, the user will still spend the same 20 to 25 percent of their time information seeking. Of course, this is not bad: Both the information need served by the KM system and the information need into which time was diverted may well be better served, with better decisions being made and higher productivity resulting. The point, however, is that the bottom line for KM is better decision making and higher productivity.

Time saved is a misleading and not very convincing indicator, because you probably will not be able to demonstrate it. If justifications to management are made based on time saved, quite predictably and understandably management will expect to see that time saved now deployed into "something else," such as making sales calls or serving customers. On seeing that saved time simply directed to other information search time—if they notice any difference at all, and they probably will not—the behavior will look the same to management. Quite understandably, they will feel that they have been misled.

The bottom line is the following: Do not justify KM by time saved; justify it by sea stories and, when possible, by demonstrating better decisions and higher productivity.

REFERENCES

Griffiths, J.-M. (1982). The value of information and related systems. Products and services. In: *Annual Review of Information Science and Technology*, Williams, M. E., ed. Vol. 17. White Plains, NY: Knowledge Industry Publication for the American Society for Information Science; pp. 269–284.

King, D. W., McDonald, D. D., Roderer, N. K. (1981). *Scientific Journals in the United States: Their Production, Use, and Economics*. Stroudsburg, PA: Hutchinson Ross.

Nelke, M. (1991a). Knowledge management in Swedish corporations. In: *Knowledge Management for the Information Professional*, Srikantaiah, T. K., and Koenig, M. E. D., eds. Medford, NJ: Information Today for the American Society for Information Science.

Nelke, M. (1999b). The role of the corporate library in the knowledge management process. *Information Services and Use*. 19(1):49–54.

Normier, B. (2001). Report of a study conducted by Lazard Freres & Co. LLC in 2001. Presentation on "Natural language advances" at the KMWorld Conference, Santa Clara, California, 31 October, 2001.

Poppel, H. L. (1982). Who needs the office of the future? *Harvard Business Review*. November/December 60(6):146–155.

Roderer, N. K., King, D. W., Brouard, S. E. (1983). The use and value of defense technical information center products and services. Rockville, MD: King Research; June. (Submitted to the Defense Technical Information Center) OCLC: 12987688, 11599947. Available, by permission, from King Research, Inc., P. O. Box 572, Oak Ridge, TN 37831.

Part III

Knowledge Management Applications— Content Management

Knowledge Management Applications— Content Management

INTRODUCTORY NOTES

In following the development of KM over the last several years, one is tempted to say, from a purely operational perspective, the old core of KM consisted of communities of practice and the new core consists of content management. Therefore, it is not accidental that this section on content management is the largest in this book. The book was not consciously designed that way. Authors were solicited to write on key topics and, in assembling the book, the sections emerged as such.

Ironically, the newest part, or at least the newest major part, of KM is in many ways not new at all. To a large degree, it is the rediscovery of the overlapping domains of librarianship and information retrieval. Often, it is not as much a case of rediscovery as it is of reinvention of librarianship and information retrieval. One point of which to be aware is what amounts to the renaming of existing areas. For example, much of what is now referred to as text mining is what has been known for years as information retrieval, and much of what is now referred to as taxonomies are what have been known for years as classification schemes. It is interesting to speculate how much of this phenomenon is simply the desire to appear au-courant and how much of it is a KM case of the classic cobbler's children, with KM personnel not being provided with the opportunities for professional development that they need. The related irony is that this is also a marvelous illustration of silos in our midst, with the KM folk often in one silo and the classification experts in another; the corporate library—the very phenomenon that KM is designed to avoid.

These and similar themes are described in the Road Map following the Table of Contents.

"Content Management" is a theme elaborated on there.

CHAPTER 11

A Note on Content Management and Knowledge Management

T. Kanti Srikantaiah, Dominican University

BACKGROUND

Content is power—but only if it is readily accessible, organized, managed, analyzed, and delivered to meet an organization's needs. Too often, the right content is not found or found too late. Over the last few years, content management (CM) has emerged explosively with an interdisciplinary approach dealing with all aspects of CM, including creation, codification, organization, sharing, and application. Managing content requires many skills from a variety of fields—technology, management, and information science, among others.

DEFINITION

In simple terms, *CM* can be defined as the art of locating, selecting, acquiring, processing, managing, and disseminating content. It is certainly more than just the Web development found in today's organizations. McQueen (2001) defines CM as the strategic application of technology, content, and people resources to leverage business processes and create competitive advantage. Content management strategy should assist people in three areas: as content contributors (creators, acquiring content); as content consumers (consuming content); and as content managers (managing the content and with CM technologies) (McQueen 2001). Therefore, CM deals with managing content in organizations and making the right knowledge available at the right time to users. This knowledge must be current, relevant, and useful in application. Content management cuts through many areas and assimilating concepts, including KM, document management, competitive intelligence, Web development, library and information services, and e-commerce, among others.

Principles

Regardless of the perspective, content servicing involves five basic principles: understanding user needs; acquiring the essential content; selecting the appropriate content; storing and managing the content; and disseminating the content.

User needs assessment is an important activity in CM. The users' needs depend on the individuals involved and the culture of the organization. The needs may be met through internal resources or by reaching out to external sources. These needs are to be properly assessed and evaluated before designing and developing a CM system in the organization. According to Boiko (2002), several questions can be posed:

What does content mean to users?

How can content be acquired, processed, and stored?

Where are the content resources located in the organization?

Who has the responsibility to manage the content?

What are the information flows within the organization?

How does the organization relate to the outside world, and outside the organization?

How do people share content?

How should IT provide the necessary infrastructure to the users of content?

What are the costs and benefits?

How does it fulfill the organizational objectives?

Content is managed in organizations to increase productivity, improve efficiency, provide economic growth, enhance social capital, provide sustainability, and enhance customer satisfaction. Content management involves capturing relevant content; performing market analyses; and maintaining databases, documents, best practices, policies, procedures, products, and services, as well as previously uncaptured expertise in individual workers.

Explicit and Tacit Content

The information in a CM system generally is of three types: *unrecorded knowledge* that people carry in their heads; *recorded knowledge* generated internally;

and knowledge acquired from external sources. The first type is usually known as *tacit knowledge* and is the most difficult to deal with in accessing and sharing content. Tacit knowledge may result from:

- Face-to-face conversations
  - Formal
  - Informal
- Telephone conversations
  - Formal
  - Informal
- Video conferences and presentations
- Individual knowledge and expertise
- Customer knowledge
- Outside experts
- Mentoring
- Study Tours
- E-mail
- Best practices
- Storytelling
- Meetings
- Other sources

On the other hand, *explicit knowledge* deals with codified knowledge. It covers both internally generated knowledge and externally available knowledge. These may include:

- Data warehouses
- Internal records
- Commercial print publications
- Sound recordings, video recordings, graphic materials, etc.
- Internal databases (text, numerical)
- External databases (text, numerical)
- Intranet and extranet
- The Internet
- Groupware
- E-mail
- Self-study material
- Current awareness
- Best practices

- Newsletters
- Online chat environment
- Other sources

Content Management System

The effectiveness of a content management system (CMS) is similar to any other information system. It revolves around response time, accuracy (validity), throughput, relevancy, economy, reliability, efficiency, security, legal framework, quality, and so forth.

The creation of content maps may facilitate an understanding of an organization's content. This map may include people, processes, databases, products, documents, repositories, services, customers, and relationships.

The volume of content, internally generated and externally available, in organizations can be overwhelming. If one looks at the total possible content, including media and telephone conversations, the volume can be very high. It has been estimated that the WWW alone encompasses about six terabytes of text data (Brown, 2000), and that estimate is now out of date.

A general model of CM is given below. Content is the nucleus of tacit/explicit knowledge and an appropriate infrastructure is required to manage it. Two major components of that infrastructure are technology and the training of staff who service and support the CMS. Content management systems strategy (CMSS) must be developed in accordance with the philosophy and the direction of an enterprise's use of content.

Managing content could be centralized or distributed, depending on the policy of the organization. In a centralized service unit it may be difficult to keep content close to staff and their needs. In a decentralized situation, there may be a number of information purveyors involved in CM and distribution, such as database administrators; librarians; record managers; help desk operators; and HR, finance, and administration staff. In a decentralized environment, communities of practice can be established, giving staff with common interests a chance to voluntarily participate and share content/knowledge. Content can be organized around topical areas valuable to the community.

The CM industry has been projected to climb from $475 million in 1999 to $5.3 billion in 2004 with related services growing to $8 billion (Trippe, 2001). Another estimate by Gartner is that the CM software market should grow to $6 billion by the year 2003 (Emery, 2001). There are other similar projections for the CM industry, some indicating more than $10 billion by 2003.

Systems Study

Understanding the problem completely and with clarity is essential. In order to achieve this, a systems study is recommended. Assessing user requirements and determining costs and benefits is part of the systems study and is extremely helpful in designing a CMS. First, an overview of the organization's CM needs to be examined. Second, mapping of explicit knowledge and tacit knowledge needs to be conducted. Third, user communities need to be identified to clearly understand the communities of practice. Fourth, knowledge sharing activities in the organization need to be examined and evaluated. Once the systems study provides a solid analysis of these four, then a CMS can be designed and implemented. Analysis and evaluation of content should be the initial approach. Comparing vendor-driven systems versus what one might build in-house should be undertaken. The final stage should consist of marketing of services and implementing and monitoring the CMS.

The process of CM begins when an organization realizes that it needs a system to manage content (Warren, 2001). Content is no longer the product published on paper. Other formats are dominating the field, including electronic and CD formats.

Issues

There are numerous major issues connected with CM:

- Online/electronic: Often print material needs to be converted into electronic format for easier access.
- Legal framework: Copyright, proprietary rights, and similar issues need to be sorted out and legally protected.
- Organizational culture: Is the organization ready to implement a CMS? What kind of management is required?
- User profiles/needs analysis: What are users' real needs? Are needs profiles available to disseminate content?
- Cost: Design, implementation, installation, and ongoing maintenance costs need to be considered.

- Training: For the success of a CMS, the staff who provide services need to be well trained.
- Software: Appropriate software needs to be selected for effectiveness.

SOFTWARE APPLICATIONS

Content has become the important domain of technologists. In today's environment, content cannot be managed through manual processes. One needs an electronic platform to manage content, requiring the application of appropriate software. Apart from the software that is developed in-house, there are a large number of software packages on the market to handle many aspects of CM. The CM software chosen depends on the sector with which to be dealt and the type of application intended. There are more than 100 vendors currently claiming to offer CM products and expertise. *The KMWorld Buyer's Guide* of spring 2002 lists 27 packages available. They include: Bauter; BCI Knowledge Group; Canon U.S.A.; Citrix Systems, Inc.; Eclipsys Corporation; Entopia; Filenet Corporation; FORMTEK; Hummingbird, Ltd.; Hyperware; IBM Corporation; Identitech; iManage; IMR Alchemy; Insystems; IT Factory INC.; Neotix; Participate Systems, Inc.; Ptech, Inc.; Quiver, Inc.; SER Solutions, Inc.; Softfront Software; Softheon, Inc.; Symtrax; Tower Software; Universal Document Management Systems (UDMS); and Websoft Systems. The descriptions of these packages are provided in the guide. The scope and functionality of these packages depend upon what the organizations are trying to do with their content, such as structured versus unstructured data, document management, process integration, among others.

Priscilla Emery (2001) evaluates eight software applications of CM in her article in the *Bulletin of the American Society for Information Science & Technology*, and presents informal guidelines about what to look for in software vendors. She discusses the following packages: BroadVision, ePrise, FileNET, Intranet Solutions, Interwoven, Vignette, Cytura, and FatWire, and provides a critical evaluation of them. The software market landscape is ever changing and it can be difficult for any organization to make the right decision about which product to select for its KM efforts. Selection of software depends on the sector and the type of application. Software vendors claim that their product can manage content through creating, locating, acquiring, processing, storing, and disseminating to users. The supplier side, however, is very much in flux, with significant mergers and acquisitions, with new vendors emerging frequently, and with many vendors reducing their operations to be more in line with the reality of the market. Realistically, many of these vendors are not likely to survive (Emery, 2001).

FUTURE

A greater number of organizations will implement CMSs in the future. The industry will grow exponentially, totaling several billion dollars per year, including software and services.

REFERENCES

Adams, Katherine C. (2001) "The Web as a Database: New Extraction Technologies & Content Management" *Online*, 25:27–32.

Ball, John, Chambers, Bill, and Fenner, Joe (1998) "Bring on the Enterprise: Integrated Solutions Provide Multiple Electronic Document Management System (EDMS) Capabilities in a Single, Seamless Package" *Inform*, 12:30–34.

Boiko, Bob (2002) *Content Management Bible*, New York, Hungry Minds.

_____ (2001) "Understanding Content Management" *Bulletin of the American Society for Information Science & Technology*, 28:8–13.

Brown, Ian D. (2000) "What Can Technology Offer? Notes on Technical Developments for the Non-Technical" http://www.alpsp.uk/journal.htm

Emery, Priscilla (2001) "The Content Management Market. What You Really Need to Know" *Bulletin of the American Society for Information Science & Technology*, 28:22–26.

Guenther, Kim (2001) "Choosing Web Content Management Solutions" *Online*, 25:26–33.

Henschen, Doug (1998) "Systems in Context: Look Beyond the Label" *Imaging*, 7:26–35.

Kartchner, Chris (2001) "Fulfilling the Promise of Knowledge Management"
Bulletin of the American Society for Information Science & Technology, 28:18–21.

McQueen, Howard (2001) "Taste, Snack, & Meal: Content Management in Three Courses" *Econtent*, 24:26–31.

Messinger, Joel C. (1999) "Document Delivery on the Web" *Inform*, 12:16–18.

Robin, Murray (2001) "Better Content Management for External Resources: Today's Information Portals in Online Information" in *Online Information 2001*, London, Learned Information Europe, 57–65.

Pack, Thomas (2001) "Know Your Customer: Intranet Offers Innovations in Enterprise Wide Content Management" *Econtent*, 24:56–57.

Srikantaiah, T. K. and Koenig, M. E. D. (eds) (2000) *Knowledge Management for the Information Professional*, Medford, N.J., Information Today, Inc.

Stear, Edward B. (1998) "The Content Management Strategy: Don't Go to Work Without It" *Online*, 22:87–90.

Steiner, Ian (2001) "Serving Up to the Wireless Web: Content to Go" *Online*, 25:26–33.

Trippe, Bill (2001) "Content Management Technology: A Booming Market" *EContent*, 24:22–27.

Warren, Rita (2001) "Information Architects and Their Central Role in Content Management" *Bulletin of the American Society for Information Science and Technology*, 28:14–17.

Yeh, Jian-Hua, Chang, Jia-Yang and Oyang, Yen-Yen. (2000) "Content and Knowledge Management in a Digital Library and Museum" *Journal of the American Society for Information Science*, 51:371–379.

Yockelson, David (1998) "Netting Document Management" *Inform*, 12:16–18.

CHAPTER 12

Content Management: Role and Reality

Stephen E. Arnold, Information and Online Systems Consultant

CONTENT MANAGEMENT: IMPORTANT TODAY AND TOMORROW

A representative of a leading European consultancy began a speech on knowledge and content management (CM) by saying, "The problem addressed in this paper is essentially fuzzy." To spare the "expert" embarrassment, his name shall be kept confidential.[1]

Fuzzy is a term disliked by managers and IT professionals. Dozens, possibly hundreds, of software companies are trying to find ways to boost their sales. The economic slide after more than a decade of boom times has fostered a sales and revenue crisis in companies that build custom solutions, hook legacy systems to the Internet, and automate certain procedure-oriented functions, such as answering customer calls via a telephone hotline, keeping track of sales calls made by employees, and producing Web pages that are personalized by scripts, not programmers.

The greatest risks to an organization involve communications within and among their partners, customers, and constituents. The substance of communications is content. The Internet's biggest influence is on business process innovation, and reducing communication and interaction costs. Content management has been perceived as a pivotal software and system function.

Most people know what content is. A CM system must provide authoring, routing, updating, publishing, disseminating, archiving, and security functions for different types of content. A single PowerPoint presentation is a typical content object. These presentations usually contain one or more tables and graphics, and even multimedia. The CM system must have a way to handle the PowerPoint presentation and the bits and pieces within it. Content management systems typically have tools to manipulate:

- Textual information about products and people;
- Binary files (audio, video, programs, pictures);
- E-mail with text and rich media;
- Facts—structured in database tables or unstructured text;
- Numeric information—static or dynamic tables, visual representations
- Metadata—information about information.

The discipline of CM can have narrow or broad definitions. A presentation at Internet World (April 2002) featured a panel on CM. Among the definitions offered from the panel and the attendees at that symposium were the ideas presented in abbreviated form here:

- Content management is the collection of policies and technologies that guide and enable corporations to contribute, manage, and share their structured and/or unstructured information.
- Enterprise CM automates the production and exchange of dynamic, trusted content within and among organizations on a global scale.
- Enterprise CM does not just include communications (collaboration services and e-mail) or text (Web pages and Word files), it may embrace binaries (software code and its versions) and legacy file data (IBM Customer Information Control System material) as well.

The packaging of software is interesting because the approach is a shift from the rah-rah days of dot-com frenzy. *Return on Investment (ROI)* is a key concept, usually undefined, and not supported with hard data. The term has a ring to it, nevertheless. The idea is that if you buy a product or service, the customer must get measurable value in return. *Efficiency* is popular as well. *Cost effectiveness* vies with *competitive advantage* for the customer's taking the bait and getting the hook as well. Content management (What's content?), knowledge management (What's knowledge?), customer relationship management (What's a relationship?), and the other tawdry wrappings placed on software and system technology are indeed fuzzy.

These concepts are somehow important. Conferences are organized in Madrid, New York, London, and other centers of commerce and thought. Managers are promoted to titles such as "chief knowledge officer," "chief information officer," or "vice president, information and content relationships." Organizations are putting money where their hope is. In a chaotic, unpredictable, and uncertain world, software and systems must be able to bring some order to the behavior of humans engaged in enterprise. Figure 12.1 depicts, in a generalized way, the method used

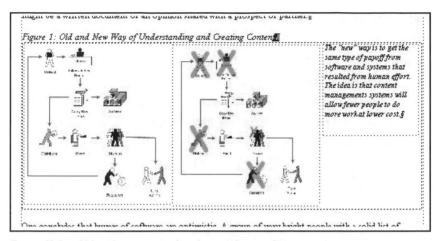

Figure 12.1   Old and new way of understanding and creating content.

by people in organizations to convert written or printed content into actionable information. The outcome might be a written document or an opinion shared with a prospect or partner.

The "new" way is to get the same type of payoff from software and systems that resulted from human effort. The idea is that CM systems will allow fewer people to do more work at lower cost.

One concludes that software buyers are optimistic. A group of bright people with a solid list of satisfied customers must have a way to get Web sites under control, provide a usable way to know what one's colleagues have written, or find out the status of a large customer's order. Most of these objectives are unmet in many organizations. Individuals working as independent consultants are not excluded. One Canadian information expert said, "My hard drives keep getting bigger and bigger. I have so much information in digital form that the search tool in Microsoft Windows runs for a half hour trying to locate a specific document. I do CM consulting, and I can't find my own content."[2]

One incontrovertible fact: The personal computer has made it possible for people to create a great deal of content. If one believes the calculations of ivory tower scholars at the University of California–Berkeley, organizations today are creating as much data every few months as all of mankind created prior to the personal computer's appearance. Scott McNealy, founder of Sun Microsystems, used to say that the number of Web pages doubled every six months. System managers use the rule of thumb that storage requirements in an organization double every 12 months. Are any of these statements true? No, but they underscore the problem that content volume poses.

Managing content is necessary. When the primary information distribution medium was speech, no one had the type of content problem facing a Webmaster in a trade association. Handwritten manuscripts and, later, printed documents were a problem because they were bulky and difficult to use. Access and storage were difficult because of the physical nature of the content object. People coped by inventing libraries, archives, and various disciplines, such as records management.

The computer and content were symbiotic. The more computers there were, the more content there was. Content was in paper printouts, long novels by word-processor-equipped writers, and the storage devices in computers, on networks, and at managed service providers. Content is increasing at a prodigious rate and will continue to skyrocket because images, video, and other rich content objects nestle comfortably in today's devices. Voice-to-text, instant messaging with photographic images, and assemblies of these text and non-text objects are second nature to mobile phone and personal digital assistant content creators.

Content, especially digital content, can come back and haunt an individual or organization. Oliver North's e-mail was not "gone." Enron's shredding eliminated the paper evidence but the digital objects remain for the forensic accountants to study. A criminal in London is captured on monitoring devices. Even though the images are of poor quality, the data must be stored, indexed, and searchable in the event the digital camera captures a crime in progress.

Defining CM

The meaning of *content management* comes from the context in which the term is used. For individuals trying to update a Web site, CM includes such functions as an interface that allows the text on pages to be changed and point-and-click functions that allow a page to be moved from the author's desktop to the server without the involvement of a systems specialist.[3] From a manager's point of view, CM implies control of content processes. One wonders how F. Scott Fitzgerald or Edgar Allan Poe would have adapted their work habits to rules-based CM online systems.

System denotes rules. Specific individuals must approve and change information before content moves to the next link in the chain of content events. Getting approvals the old-fashioned way requires an author to print out a text or graphic and walk it through the approval process. Many authors send text via e-mail and then make a follow-up telephone call to (a) make sure the content was received; (b) if received, read; and (c) if read, understood, changed, or approved. Today's cost-efficient manager wants the workflow rule to require moving the text from the author, through the approval chain, and then to the Web site. As the catch-phrase says: better, faster, and cheaper. Experienced people know that only two attributes apply to software and systems. Each company or systems manager must decide on two of these features. Better and faster will not be cheaper. Faster and cheaper may not work. And, better and cheaper may lead to many hours of debugging, despite the claims of marketing professionals.

From the financial executive's point of view, multiple Web sites and separate systems for creating Web pages are a needless duplication of expense. In large organizations, there are usually many different ways of creating content for the Web pages on intranets (intended for employees and selected contractors), the Internet (the public online space accessible to anyone with a connection), and, in some cases, an extranet (a specialized set of content and services for vendors, key customers, and some other individuals). Content management is a system that allows a single software system to provide the various services necessary to maintain a Web site. Truth be told, most financial executives have a dim concept of "authoring."

The chief executive may see the Web as a single cog in a larger machine. The "machine" is the ability to generate revenues, increase cash, and generate buzz about the company's products and services among prospects with money. The senior executive team needs to have access to orders, invoices, payroll records, and other types of financial data. With most senior executives performing sales and marketing functions, current facts are needed about proposals, contracts, inquiries from prospects and customers, the e-mail messages sent by another sales person to a major customer, and so on. If CM or any other enterprise sophistry can deliver these results, the chief executive is likely to support the initiative. Most organizations have undergone significant downsizing. Software and systems should be able to fill in the gaps like caulk fills the gaps in a wooden sailboat, correct?

The narrow definition of CM as a software or system for managing Web content is valid—to a point. Some professionals will see CM as a way to involve others in the shaping of information that will be available to different constituencies. From the top of the organization, the flow of information within and among the people in the organization embraces many different types of content.

Content management, therefore, takes its meaning from the context in which the processes for authoring, structuring, approving, publishing, and archiving digital content are used. For a one-person consulting firm, Microsoft Front Page performs these tasks reasonably well. Mid-sized organizations may want to focus on moving information to the Web but have a way to route information for approvals prior to release. Ektron, Inc. (Amherst, New Hampshire). and eMojo, Ltd. (London, England) offer mid-range products that provide basic workflow and routing functions.

Senior managers may want to consider one of the specialized enterprise software systems, such as Documentum, Inc. (Pleasanton, California) or Stellent, Inc. (Eden Prairie, Minnesota), where CM extends to a wide range of information, ranging from images created in Photoshop to reports generated by mainframe computers and stored in flat files. The chief executive may opt to use the organization's enterprise software system to handle CM chores. Within the last 12 months, SAP Aktiengesellschaft (Walldorf, Germany), J. D. Edwards & Company (Denver, Colorado), Siebel Systems, Inc. (San Mateo, California) and Oracle Corporation (Redwood City, California), among others, have extended their systems to embrace CM.

In addition, highly specialized CM tools are available to handle an organization's need to keep track of original software programs. Content management systems that maintain versions of source code are usually called configuration management software. Some configuration management features are often included in CM systems when the Web sites make use of executable code for dynamic page rendering, personalization, and other types of functions embedded in the hypertext markup language or extensible markup language for a Web site or page. There are similarly specialized software systems to manage files generated by computer-aided design systems and the databases that often accompany architectural drawings, assemblies, and other types of drawings that reference structured lists of components, facts, prices, and technical specifications.

If we ask the question, "What is CM?" after considering how the scope, functionality, and features of the system that delivers CM maps to different organizational requirements, we can make several observations:

1. Content management takes its meaning from the person or the group that has a need to handle text and other types of content object for a specific purpose. Content management can be relatively straightforward when defining the term from the point of view of a Webmaster managing a site with a handful of pages and one or two people adding information to the site manually. An off-the-shelf product can be bought, loaded, and used in a matter of days or weeks. Costs are easy to predict and control.

2. When more groups and people are involved, CM becomes a software system that must mesh with business processes used by the different people involved. Business processes when codified in software must be converted to rules and procedures. Business processes must first be identified, then converted to rules, and then tested. Most organizations, despite their managers' best efforts, do not have documented, efficient business processes. Content management requires that these processes be nailed down and converted to a formal sequence of steps. Costs are difficult to predict and control.

3. Enterprise software vendors offer tools, utilities, and functions that can be applied to CM. In large organizations, individuals or departments may have implemented a CM system from a specialist software vendor. For sound business reasons, the larger software system will play a role in the organization's CM activities. The collision of the incumbent enterprise software vendor with the one or more specialized CM systems is inevitable. Costs are likely to be high and the potential for internal turf battles even higher.

We can derive a working definition of CM from the following: *Content management* is the software, system, and business processes used by an individual or an organization to author, edit, publish, track, archive, and reuse content in electronic or printed form.

The Role of CM

Content management plays numerous roles because each user of the CM system sees a different function. The Web master sees the CM system as a way to bring order to the otherwise chaotic, complex, and inefficient processes used when Web sites are manually updated. The marketing manager sees the CM system as a way to get information in front of prospects quickly. If print versions of the information are needed, anyone can display the Web page with the information and send it to a printer for a hard copy. Marketing professionals no longer have to stand with hat in hand until the Webmaster or technical staff takes the news release, codes it, and puts it on the Web site. Financial managers see CM as a means of reducing costs and increasing the efficiency of certain information-centric operations. The senior managers of an organization will see the CM system as an important component of the firm's strategic competitiveness.

Content management is able to play the lead role, or a supporting role. The same CM system may play both roles simultaneously. When an organization wants to introduce a new product, a number of different functions are required. Each of the representatives of marketing, finance, research and development, and legal departments needs different information. Many teams work via telephone, e-mail, and face-to-face meetings. Content management systems can provide some useful functionality and services to this type of group. Content management, however, cannot handle all of the content-related tasks one might expect a modern system to perform.

Content management, then, faces a dilemma. For those using the CM system, the ebb and flow of e-mail, telephone calls, and the remarks made in face-to-face conversations are outside of most CM systems today and for the foreseeable future. If the team makes use of new collaborative technologies, such as Groove or IBM's Web Sphere collaboration functions, additional programming is required to move the content objects from these systems into the CM systems from the vendors mentioned in this chapter.

This disconnect between the CM system deployed at any level of the organization and the newest technologies used by professionals working in that organization comes as a surprise to many. Content management, like many of the other silver-bullet solutions, promises more than it delivers.

The expectations of a multimillion-dollar CM system, such as one from FileNET Corporation (Costa Mesa, California), Mediasurface, Ltd. (London, England), or Percussion Software, Inc. (Stoneham, Massachusetts) are high. The reality—like implementations of SAP R/3, Siebel Systems, or PeopleSoft enterprise applications—is different. Software marketers have taken prospects to the cliffs above the sea to watch the dawn of new efficiencies. All too often, the customer does not understand the implications of moving business processes to software. The time, the expense, the political turf battles—all teach the customer the painful lesson that reality is different from marketing hyperbole.

The solution is engineered into the fabric of software development and marketing. The vendors shift the argument. Content management exists as a separate segment in the software industry. However, companies such as BEA Systems, Inc. (San Jose, California), Microsoft Corporation (Redmond, Washington), and Sun Microsystems (Palo Alto, California) offer a suite of tools that allow an organization to build:

- A portal—this is an umbrella term for a single browser-accessible page that links an employee to applications, communications, and information needed by the organization.
- A knowledge management system—this is a class of software system that includes the functions that generate, retain, share, and exchange knowledge in an organization.
- An enterprise information system (EIS)—this is a collection of software that shares a common architectural foundation. Using industry standards, EIS allows an organization to weave the many different information, computer, and communication systems into a whole. (Think of EIS as a digital taco shell into which all other systems and data are gathered for easy and tidy handling.)
- A customer relationship management (CRM) solution—this is a class of software that can be implemented at the department level and then extended into an enterprise application or EIS solution. Anything that touches a customer is included in CRM.

What becomes evident is that a certain fuzziness exists with any of these terms unless the definition is agreed on before talking about CM, knowledge management, CRM, or any other term used to describe software that solves an organization's problem. Without a precise and agreed on definition of terms prior to looking for software or beginning a discussion of any content-centric function, the project is likely to end in failure. Hard figures are difficult to locate, but the received wisdom is that more than 50 percent of large-scale content-centric systems are failures.

Therefore, the role of CM is defined by those involved in the project. No dictionary will save a project when no one knows what it is supposed to do.

LESSONS LEARNED

Content management, like any of the newly minted phrases used to describe software that automates human-centric functions, seems to be a straightforward service. A person writes something, and software puts it on the Web site or generates a printed version of the document.

Online content is unfortunately anything but straightforward. Moving business processes that are informal and undocumented to the formal structure of rules is a difficult job, at best, and an almost impossible one in many organizations.

The lessons learned by those who have worked to define requirements for CM systems and then implement them are not well documented in trade publications. Consider these "lessons" as checkpoints, since each situation varies:

- Technology is 20 percent of the job. The real work behind CM or any information-intensive task is figuring out the business processes and codifying specific actions that take place in specific situations. Vendors of CM software derive the bulk of their revenue from services sold to the software customer. "Setting up" software is shorthand for figuring out what to have the system do in a specific situation. The cost comes from the time required to figure out the system and reconciling what really happens with what management believes is happening.

- A content management system affects business processes at a fundamental level. Despite radical downsizing in many organizations, a great deal of real work is performed by people. Whether full-time or contract workers, these individuals often innovate to do their job. What people actually do and management's ability to get them to do what management wants is a task that requires diplomacy, time, and cooperation. Moving a process from the human to the system is a radical change.

- Content management systems require time to do "right." In the era of 24/7 companies and always-on systems, the perception among many is that CM (CRM, knowledge management, or any enterprise initiative for that matter) will be quick and easy. The age of going faster does not equate to doing stupid things more quickly. Time is needed to understand, plan, research, and implement a CM system. Speed often invites failure.

- Integration with existing enterprise resource planning (ERP) applications is not flawless. Content management (like CRM and KM) systems are immature. Integrating these software systems into back-office enterprise systems that may have a longer history at an organization is difficult. Even when the exchanges are handled using extensible markup language (XML), exceptions and anomalies are common. One can undermine the economic benefits of automation by having to process exceptions manually until the scripts are completed to handle the anomalies missed in the initial build. When systems collide, the winner may be the incumbent with a long history and, hence, a greater value to the client. The newcomer may be forced out.

- Low cost means limits to scalability and functionality. At the beginning of this chapter, the relationship of cost and functionality was touched upon. The less costly a CM system, the less functionality it will provide. The most costly systems, however, require more time and money to set up and deploy in an organization. Within the next three to five years, CM systems will be less of an exercise in invention and more like installing Microsoft Word on a personal computer. At this time, the cost of CM systems is related to functionality: the greater the functionality, the higher the cost of the system.

- Support for standards is important. Support for XML, for example, is one of the standards articulated by the World Wide Web Consortium to allow information to be more easily processed and exchanged. A tornado of acronyms awaits anyone venturing into the standards arena for digital information. The battle lines are being drawn at this time between software developers who support standards-based, open-source software and proprietary solutions. The battle is not between Microsoft and IBM. The war is more complex and blurred. The key to success is to identify the standards that are meaningful to the industry or business sector in which the CM system will be deployed. The standards used must be those supported by such groups as the World Wide Web Consortium as well as any industry subgroups. Ignoring standards increases the risk associated with any software solution.

- Management support is vital. Content management, KM, CRM, or any of the content-centric systems will fail if the management of the organization does not support the effort. Projects fail if costs and complexity are not understood and bounded by a tight set of requirements and a well-conceived project plan.

One way to accelerate along the CM system learning curve is to focus on such basics as formulating a plan. Among the key checkpoints in a plan are a requirements document, a statement of work, an estimated cost, a timeline, and a "Plan B." Technologists will want to focus on the role of Web services, database architecture, and rich media. These points are important, but the project manager for the CM system must get the priorities right at the outset. The wrong priorities, coupled with skipping over the basics, means that the CM project may be headed in the wrong direction. Instead of reducing costs, the CM system becomes a black hole for resources. Although software for a workgroup may cost less than $3,000 for a basic license, the actual implementation cost may be four times that or more. A rule of thumb is that the license cost for the first year should be multiplied by 4.4 to get a quick estimate of the direct fees associated with acquiring and activating basic CM services.

THE REALITY

The reality of CM and the other labels stuck hastily on software modules is that software must be tailored to the cultural, economic, and technical environment. The institutional context—a phrase used by Max Boisot, ESADE (Barcelona)—determines the meaning of CM and, to a large degree, what CM will do, by whom, and for whom.

The management of a firm wants to consolidate software and systems to increase efficiency and reduce costs. The staff, working within a "bottoms up" department, wants the freedom to select tools that meet their needs. Content management as well as CRM, KM, or other network applications must be implemented within a *contention boundary* (see Figure 12.2). The software and system must meet the needs of different groups, each with their own different needs. Costs increase because considerable research, analysis, and customization is needed in order to deal with business process issues that may be (a) unacknowledged by management, (b) inherently unclear with no "one right way," or (c) overly complex and, therefore, unresolvable within the time and budget parameters of a project. Content management, like customer support, may seem a modest undertaking at the outset of a project. After some initial work, the project becomes larger, more costly, and more time consuming than anticipated or explained by the CM vendor/integrator.[4]

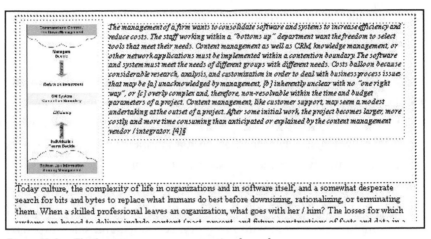

The management of a firm wants to consolidate software and systems to increase efficiency and reduce costs. The staff working within a "bottoms up" department want the freedom to select tools that meet their needs. Content management as well as CRM, knowledge management, or other network applications must be implemented within a contention boundary. The software and system must meet the needs of different groups with different needs. Costs balloon because considerable research, analysis, and customization in order to deal with business process issues that may be [a] unacknowledged by management, [b] inherently unclear with no "one right way", or [c] overly complex and, therefore, non-resolvable within the time and budget parameters of a project. Content management, like customer support, may seem a modest undertaking at the outset of a project. After some initial work, the project becomes larger, more costly and more time consuming than anticipated or explained by the content management vendor / integrator. [4]§

Today culture, the complexity of life in organizations and in software itself, and a somewhat desperate search for bits and bytes to replace what humans do best before downsizing, rationalizing, or terminating them. When a skilled professional leaves an organization, what goes with her / him? The losses for which systems are hoped to deliver include content (past, present, and future constructions of facts and data in a

Figure 12.2   The business process contention boundary.

Each of the new labels placed on software that allows more and more services to be viewed as available functions from a Web browser helps marketers and creates a tension between the customer and the purveyor of the solution. The customer wants to believe that there is a Santa Claus, a tooth fairy, and a Peter Pan. The vendor knows that "solutions" are built from what is sold to the customer. The customer wants a solution that meets specific needs at a good price and quickly. The vendor needs to install what is available and then assemble or write what is really needed. The shift in the software industry from licensing programs that work out of the box to a license with services that are 40 percent or more of the annual licensing fee puts buyers of information-centric software on notice. Content, knowledge, relationships, and other nebulous yet euphonious terms were tough to figure out when epistemology was all the rage long before there were computers.

When a skilled professional leaves an organization, what goes with her/him? These are losses of human and knowledge capital. Many CM and KM systems are intended to include:

- Content (past, present, and future constructions of facts and data in a fungible form)
- Knowledge (the ability to assemble from many different and often unacknowledged sources)

- Relationships (connections to, among, and between individuals and information)
- The interaction of these elements with others

The CM system may be a search for bits and bytes to replace the expertise that "walks out the door" when an employee leaves an organization.

The reality of CM in a pharmaceutical company boils down to knowing what the expert knew when she/he signed on with a competitor. Content management in a publishing company becomes a system that repurposes articles, artwork, and data without incurring more human editorial costs or rekeying. Content management in a distributor of steel products is knowing what orders are in the pipeline and the information associated with inventory, accounts, and sales expenses.

Content management software and the other types of what might be called "salvation systems" are often outcomes of programming jobs for a specific client. Rather than toss the code, the programmers decide to package the modules in hand and start selling a solution.

Three observations are warranted:

1. The build-it-as-we-go approach to software—particularly CM software— means that the modules will pick up functionality. Snowballs benefit from this; enterprise software does not. As CM systems become more robust, they are likely to collide with other enterprise applications.
2. The issues raised by CM systems are: technical, financial, procedural, and jurisdictional. Control of content provides a manager with considerable "influence."
3. The crossing of the boundary of contention is signaled by increased involvement of departments not directly involved in authoring content for the Web or the marketing department. The increased buzz that CM often attracts indicates that what was a software acquisition to solve a narrow problem has been perceived as a key function in an organization where various types of data and information are perceived as the keys to success.

Workflow processes are particularized in each company. Making one size fit all is a tall order in an immature, fluid niche. There are, therefore, hard limits on what CM (and by extension KM) systems can achieve. The limits are different within each organization.

The business processes associated with information, knowledge, and relationships are difficult to convert to a structured, flexible representation. Information and content, knowledge and wisdom are similar to a file compressed to reduce its size. The file cannot be reduced substantially. It is what it is.

A CM system is a concept that fits better in a top-down, hierarchical organization. Content management may be almost impossible to implement where the organization is flat, fast-moving, distributed, self-regulating, and composed of loosely coupled units or individuals.

What is the optimal path forward in this reality? As the lessons indicate, defining the project and limiting complexity are common factors in successful CM implementations. In the business climate that seems to be gripping much of the industrialized world, reduce risks through planning, careful preparation, and clearly defined expectations.

The future of computing is what might be called the executable Internet. Just as the personal computer was the development platform for such pioneer software as Lotus 1-2-3 and WordStar, the Internet is the development environment for today's innovators. Content is the muscle and sinew of applications for the executable Internet.

Coupled with this x-net is the real-time enterprise. The idea is simple. The proliferation of wireless devices and easy, low-cost connections in the U.S. and a handful of other countries allows prescient managers to make computing and communications available to every employee. One benefit is that information and access are available anytime and almost from any location. The more streamlined business processes will exploit the x-net in order to have a competitive advantage over organizations that are time constrained. With data available in these real-time systems, scripts can examine the content and provide insights into various types of business activities. With a single interface to applications and content, individuals in an organization can perform many of their job tasks more efficiently.

Content management sits dead in the center of the real-time enterprise. It is a core business issue. The future of CM consists of it being absorbed into such enterprise functions as the portal, the application server, and enterprise integration platforms. Although change in CM will be rapid and dramatic, one cannot sit on the sidelines. Content management is an important game. Organizations of all sizes and types must play it or find themselves at a disadvantage.

ENDNOTES

1. The curious may want to reference *The Proceedings of Online Information 2001*, Learned Information Europe, Ltd., Hinksey Hill, Oxford, December 2001, page 37.

2. Interview with Ulla de Stricker, April 2002, de Stricker Associates, Toronto, Ontario. See www.destricker.com for more information.

3. Those seeking a more textbook-like definition may wish to consult http://whatis.techtarget.com

4. Graphic based on a diagram on page 43 in *The New Craft of Intelligence: Personal, Public, and Political*, by Robert D. Steele, OSS, Inc.: Reston, Virginia, 2002.

CHAPTER 13

XML: Data Infrastructure for Knowledge Management

H. Frank Cervone, Northwestern University

Darlene Fichter, University of Saskatchewan

INTRODUCTION

Deriving meaning from the documents and other data within the workplace has been one of the major problems facing organizations in the last 50 years. With the arrival of corporate computing in the mid-1950s, the ability to store and retrieve data reached a new level of intensity and possibility. However, even with the advances in technology over the last 50 years, fundamental problems remain in the area of information retrieval.

Although technology allows us to retrieve data faster and in more complex ways than would have ever been thought possible, even as little as 15 years ago, the ability to derive meaning and understand relationships among data has lagged. With the arrival of low-cost computing in the form of PCs and local area networks in the early 1980s, most organizations have built up large repositories of electronic document collections.

The significance of these document collections to KM efforts is indicated in an observation from Bowman (2002): "A primary objective of knowledge management activities in organizations is to allow employees to access and utilize the rich sources of information stored in unstructured forms."

However, the very ease with which one can create unstructured documents belies the fact that this information is basically not processable in ways that would allow for meaning and context to be derived computationally. For the typical person, retrieving information from documents seems to be easy: install a full-text search engine, index the documents, create a nice user-search interface, and voila! You find things.

However, finding things and being able to uncover the relationships and meanings hidden within are two quite different concepts. With the vast amount of information available in most organizations, human-based processes cannot possibly manage the task of uncovering meaning in massive quantities of data. Even the supposedly simple task of retrieving information from document repositories is quite problematic. With the phenomenal growth of informational content within an organization, this problem has become a crisis as search engines, using existing paradigms, fail to return the best and most relevant content. The mad rush to implement KM systems has placed additional pressure to select and implement sophisticated solutions that will support a learning culture.

The genesis of XML (extensible markup language) came from the observation that the way to solve both the retrieval and meaning-making problems is to structure information from the outset because data can only be given meaning if it is placed within a contextualized structure. When data is contextualized in this manner, it becomes "semantic"; that is, the data both has meaning and can be used in operations to derive other meanings from it (Berners-Lee, et al., 2001).

XML

XML is a metalanguage used to structure data. In most cases, this structured data is represented within regular ASCII or Unicode text files through markup. Markup is derived from the publishing industry and originally was used to create the detailed, stylistic instructions within a manuscript that facilitated typesetting. Within the context of XML, markup tags are used to define data items (see Figure 13.1).

The concept of structured data is common and is represented in many familiar organizational activities, such as creating spreadsheets, financial transaction detail records, and computer system configuration information. Unfortunately, many common uses of structured data rely on proprietary binary format for storage. Binary formats, while very efficient for making the most of storage space, are not very usable outside the context of their construction. A commonly known example of a binary storage format is a Microsoft Word .doc file. Without Microsoft Word or a program that understands that particular file format, a Microsoft Word .doc file is pretty useless outside of its processing context.

Another drawback of proprietary formats, whether binary or not, is that, in most cases, these proprietary formats are not semantic. They do not indicate how

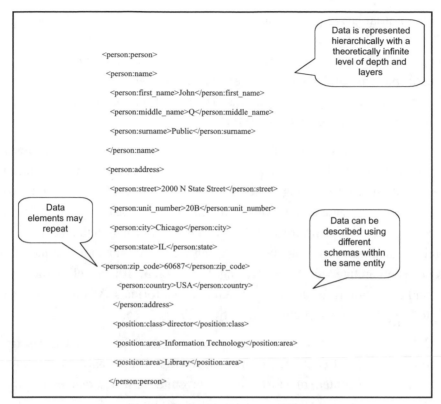

Figure 13.1   Example of an XML-encoded information entity.

the information can be used outside of the context of its creation. Referring to the Microsoft Word format as an example again: A particular problem with this format is that what is actually provided in the structured data is a "procedural markup" that defines a set of directions for how to format the document for the screen or a printer, but otherwise does not indicate what the information within the document actually is or means. This is exactly the same issue that plagues HTML on the Web. The formatting markup describes how the document should look, and not what the data within the document means.

An argument could be made that this issue is a red herring; natural language processing (NLP) can be used to extract the meaning from data—we don't need to encode data to make it meaningful. Descriptions of NLP make this sound as if it were a routine function:

Natural language processing is a complex task and involves many steps. The text is divided into sentences and each sentence is tagged according to its part of speech. … This syntactic structure is matched to pre-existing linguistic patterns and relevant content is determined. Semantic content is determined via the syntactic patterns. Then, information is extracted and a summary is produced (Adams, 2001).

However, experience shows that real world experience does not often result in this outcome. In Charles (2002), it is quite clear that reliance on NLP and other types of automated processing alone does not yield the results one would hope to gain from KM implementation. Although NLP can contribute a great deal to automatic categorization of information, assignment of information to meaningful taxonomical categories is still not possible using NLP and related techniques alone.

XML is an architecture for addressing this problem. It is a well-defined set of rules and conventions for designing structured data formats. Adams (2001) comes back to the problem of structuring data by stating:

XML is important because it facilitates increased access to and description of the content contained within documents. The technology separates the intellectual content of a text from its surrounding structure, meaning that information can be converted into a uniform structure.

XML, as a common language framework for describing how data is structured, makes it possible for a processing program to explicitly know in advance about the structure of a file (or document) before using it. The file to be processed can easily point to a reference data structure that tells the processing program how to interpret the data.

But how is that reference data structure created and what does it mean? This introduces the concepts of schemas and document-type definitions (DTDs).

SCHEMAS AND DTDS

Although the mechanics of schemas and DTDs are different, the end result of either is similar. Both are used to create the meaning of the markup within a specific XML-encoded document or data file. A DTD, or schema can be included within an XML file itself as a means for locally describing the data. But more often, the DTD or schema is defined as a separate entity and is referenced from within an XML-encoded file. By doing so, the DTD or schema can be used in multiple contexts both internally, within the organization, or externally among several organizations. It is this external cooperation that allows independent groups to exchange meaningful data.

Document-type definitions are a mature document declaration standard and were inherited from standard generalized markup language (SGML) by XML. As a result, there are thousands of DTDs available for use. Document-type definitions work well for defining traditional text documents, but otherwise DTDs are limited in many ways. One cannot, for example, declare a specific data type, such as integer or real, in a DTD. To overcome the limitations of the DTD format, schemas have been developed to provide a way of defining complex data types for data elements. Standard data types, such as currency, floating point, date, and so on can be specified or custom types can be created. In addition, standard data declaration functions, such as setting restrictions on the length of an element, are possible. This is advantageous in that it allows programs to validate not only the syntax of the document but the values of the data elements as well. Schemas also have the added advantage of being constructed in an XML syntax format, eliminating the need for programs to understand the DTD-specific syntax.

Both DTDs and schemas then are a set of syntax rules for defining the markup tags to be used within a specific type of XML-encoded data file. The DTD or schema defines

- What data elements exist
- The order in which the data elements should appear
- The hierarchical relationship of data elements within the data structure
- Which data elements have attributes in addition to, or in place of, content

Attributes are associated with specific markup tags as an additional way of encoding information within the XML-data stream. Typically, attributes are used for metadata and elements for data. However, the distinction is not always clear-cut or unambiguous. As seen in Figure 13.2, it is often possible to represent items of information in either format. The choice of form depends primarily on the use of the data; however, elements allow for more flexibility in processing, especially when the processing context diverges from the original context of creation.

XML and Namespaces

Namespaces support modularity of XML markup vocabularies. In most cases where XML-formatted data is used, rather than develop a local schema, a standard

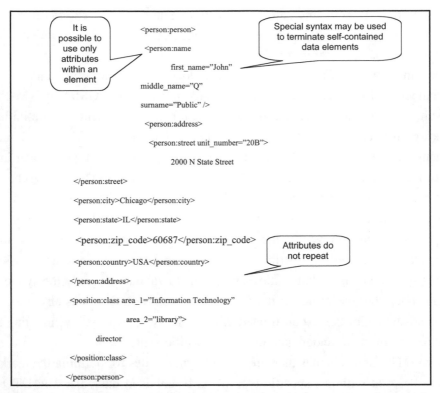

Figure 13.2   Example of an XML-encoded information entity using attributes and two namespaces.

markup format will be used. This ensures that all parties that process the program use the same predefined collections of elements rather than redefining these elements in every context in which they will be used. This is, in fact, one of the greatest powers of XML—the ability to use data across applications with opaque data descriptions. Officially, a namespace is defined as "a collection of names, identified by a uniform resource identifier (URI) reference, which are used in XML documents as element types and attribute names." [1]

Not only do XML namespaces help foster the modularized use of elements, namespaces are also used to define multiple data sources. Through the use of namespaces, conflicts of naming data elements can be avoided. When more than one data source is used, it is inevitable that elements will have the same name yet describe two very different things. For example, the element *title* in one schema may mean the title of a book in one namespace, but may refer to the land deed title holder in another namespace. Namespaces provide the means for being able to utilize elements from differing schemas by qualifying the data element name with a source definition that provides a way to reference the specific data element and prevent naming conflicts.

Namespaces are a powerful tool in promoting a semantic web where cross document and domain search-and-retrieval can be facilitated through shared namespaces and vocabularies.

XML and Unicode

Being forward thinking, the XML specification is designed to support Unicode, a character-encoding standard that enables the accurate representation of almost every character set currently used. This enables text or data using multiple character sets (such as the Latin, Cyrillic, and Hebrew character sets concurrently) to be represented accurately within a single data stream. The combination of XML and Unicode unlocks a whole new arena of international exchange of data and documents, regardless of the original language. Prior to Unicode and its adoption with XML, exchange of multilingual text files was problematic. Some languages, such as Arabic, had three dozen encoding systems, none of which were compatible with another.

Within an XML data stream or document, a specific declaration indicates the language-encoding scheme. For example, the following declaration indicates that the XML document is encoded in universal transformation format (UTF)-8:

<?xml version="1.0" encoding="UTF-8"?>

Unicode is preferably represented in UTF-16, which is an encoding scheme that represents all characters within all existing character sets as two-byte, fixed-length characters. The problem is that much of the existing software in use prefers single-byte character representation. As a result, UTF-8 is frequently used in monolingual XML documents. UTF-8 is a scheme that transforms all Unicode characters into a variable length encoding of bytes. This may seem to confuse issues, but it has the advantage that the Unicode characters corresponding to the familiar ASCII set have: The same byte values as ASCII and Unicode characters transformed into UTF-8 can be used with much existing software without extensive software rewrites.[2]

The Dublin Core—A Metadata Markup Language

The issue of encoding metadata is important because it is metadata that ascribes specific meaning to data elements. Although metadata can be created as a by-product of data analysis procedures, in most situations, metadata is created as an intentional and deliberate act. Often, this type of metadata is descriptive metadata—metadata that describes the purpose and function of the data elements. Although the importance of administrative metadata (metadata typically created as the result of automated functions of computing processes, such as a file creation date) should not be overlooked within the KM context (Fichter, 1999), descriptive metadata is a critical component in a KM environment. An example of one such descriptive metadata scheme is the Dublin Core.

The Dublin Core is a resource description scheme that can be represented in an XML markup language. Specifically, the Dublin Core is designed to enable the creation of metadata description of information resources. Although it is commonly known and used within the library community, its applicability to general KM projects has not been as well known, even though it is a convenient and relatively easy-to-use scheme for creating descriptive, as opposed to administrative, metadata.

The Dublin Core (DC) is represented through an abstract model by a qualified DC record. This qualified record is made up of one or more properties and their associated values. Each property is an attribute of the resource or data item being described, and there are 15 standard elements that correspond to properties.[3] These 15 elements include

1. Title—a name given to the resource. In most cases, this is the name by which a resource is formally known.

2. Creator—an entity primarily responsible for making the content of the resource. This might be a person, an organization, or a service.

3. Subject—the topic of the content of the resource. Usually, the subject is expressed as either keywords, key phrases, or some classification codes scheme that indicates the topic of the resource. Recommended best practice is to select a value from a controlled vocabulary or formal classification scheme.

4. Description—an account of the content of the resource. This may include, but is not limited to, an abstract, table of contents, free-text

account of the content, or reference to another resource that describes the content.

5. Publisher—an entity responsible for making the resource available.

6. Contributor—an entity responsible for making contributions to the content of the resource.

7. Date—a date associated with an event in the life cycle of the resource. In most cases, the date is associated with the creation or availability of the resource.

8. Type—the nature or genre of the content of the resource. Recommended best practice is to select a value from a controlled vocabulary, such as the list types identified in the DC.

9. Format—the physical or digital manifestation of the resource. Typically, format may include the dimensions or media type of the resource, but it may also be used to determine the software, hardware, or other equipment needed to display or operate the resource. Recommended best practice is to select a value from a controlled vocabulary, such as the list of Internet media types found at: http://dublincore.org/documents/1999/07/02/dces/#mime, defining computer media formats.

10. Identifier—an unambiguous reference to the resource within a given context. Usually, this is done through some type of formal identification system, such as a URI, including the uniform resource locator (URL), the digital object identifier (DOI), or international standard book number (ISBN).

11. Source—a reference to a resource from which the present resource is derived, whether in whole or in part. This reference is typically by means of a string or number conforming to a formal identification system.

12. Language—the language of the intellectual content of the resource. The values of the language element are defined by RFC 1766, found at: http://dublincore.org/documents/1999/07/02/dces/#rfc1766, which includes a two-letter language code (taken from the ISO 639 standard, found at: http://dublincore.org/documents/1999/07/02/dces/#iso639), followed optionally by a two-letter country code (taken from the ISO 3166 standard, found at: http://dublincore.org/documents/1999/07/02/dces/#iso3166).

13. Relation—a reference to a related resource, typically through a string or number that conforms to a formal identification system.

14. Coverage—the extent or scope of the content of the resource. This may indicate spatial location (such as a place name or geographic coordinates), temporal period (a period label, date, or date range), or jurisdiction (such as a named administrative entity).

15. Rights—information about rights held in and over the resource. Typically, a rights element will contain a rights management statement for the resource, or reference a service providing such information. Rights information encompasses intellectual property rights (IPRs), copyrights, and various other property rights.

DATA MARKUP LANGUAGES FOR ENABLING KM

Markup languages for metadata were some of the first practical implementations of XML. So it is not surprising that developments in that area are relatively advanced. Work has proceeded in other areas, but, in many cases, the current state is not as far along as is the case with metadata.

A case in point is in the area of data markup languages. Not surprisingly, the development of standards in this area has been driven greatly by the need of the marketplace. As a result, some data markup languages have been extensively developed while most are still in their nascent stages.

Rich site summary (RSS) is one of the most commonly used data markup languages today. It provides a means for distributing quick, easy, and consistent announcements that can be pushed out as content. RSS-formatted data is primarily used to incorporate news and other information feeds from external sources on Web sites, but the uses of this format can go beyond that.

Much of the allure of RSS is its simplicity. It has a very simple syntax that consists of two major placeholders for data: channel and items. The channel element (see Figure 13.3) contains

- Information about the title or name of the channel
- A short descriptive passage about the channel
- A link to the Web site from where the channel is distributed
- An indicator of what language is used in the channel
- Numerous optional elements, such as copyright notices, e-mail address of the Webmaster, publication date, and so forth

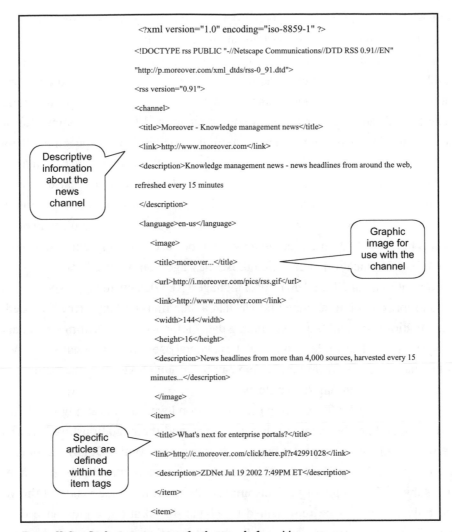

Figure 13.3   Rich site summary feed example from Moreover.com

The gist of the channel is the data delivered in its item elements. The RSS format allows a maximum of 15 item elements. Each item element contains the following subelements:

- Title—the title of the news item
- Link—a URL that serves as a link to the actual content
- Description—a short paragraph that summarizes the contents of the item

With just these simple elements, it is possible to create a news syndication service.

Other XML-data formats are being developed that can be used within the KM rubric. The outline processor markup language (OPML) is designed to structure outline-like information. Designed to be used with data that is easily browsed and editable, it is broadly applicable across a number of data formats and uses, specifications, legal briefs, product plans, presentations, screenplays, and directories.

The formal language for business communication (FLBC) is designed to provide a means for encoding business communication. Based on speech act theory, this XML-encoding scheme has been designed with an eye toward enhancing computer-assisted or -mediated communication. By providing a clear delineation between message type and content, it provides mechanisms for conversation management and dialog management. Using principals from sociolinguistics, it attempts to formally define specific message types used in communication and the range of communication over which those messages can be used.

The relational-functional markup language (RFML), in many respects, is an abstract representation language rather than a data markup language. It is used to define relationships and functions among data elements stored within formal database systems, such as tables within relational databases and relational views. With this language, context from one system can be applied to another that allows data to seamlessly map among disparate systems.

XML topic maps (XTMs) bring the abstraction level to an even higher plain, as XTMs convey knowledge about data resources and their relationships through a superimposed layer, a map as it were of the resources. Within XTMs, a topic is a named resource as represented within a computing system that stands in for a real-world subject. Examples of subjects are usually tangible objects, but, at the very least, objects that can be represented by nouns. In addition, topics have occurrences. These occurrences are the relevant information resources (in some way, shape, or form) of the subject. Most useful for KM purposes, however, is that topics can participate in relationships, also known as associations, in which they play roles as members.

At an even higher level of abstraction, we find the resource description framework (RDF), which in turn brings us back to metadata.

THE RESOURCE DESCRIPTION FRAMEWORK

The RDF is the product of a number of different communities coming together to provide a flexible architecture for supporting metadata, primarily on the Web but equally applicable in other contexts within a wide range of applications. In effect, this provides the infrastructure for enabling semantic interoperability by providing a model for describing resources. Because RDF emphasizes facilities to enable automated processing of Web resources, the range of potential RDF applications is quite wide. Potential applications of RDF that have been described include

- Resource discovery—to provide better search engine capabilities
- Cataloging and classification—to describe content and content relationships
- Intelligent software agents—to facilitate knowledge sharing and exchange
- Content rating—to provide guidelines for audience applicability
- Intellectual property rights
- Privacy preferences—for both an individual user as well as the privacy policies of the data creator or warehouser

But what is RDF? There are many similarities between XTM and RDF, but RDF is primarily a model for defining metadata so independent parties can exchange both the definitions and data implemented according to the definition. Resource description framework is represented through two constructs: properties and property values. In an RDF definition, properties correspond to attribute-value pairs where the property is an attribute of a resource. In addition, RDF properties can represent relationships between resources. Although this is similar to what XTM does, in this respect, an RDF model more closely resembles an entity-relationship diagram.[4] Whereas XTM is focused on relations, the RDF data model representation is used to evaluate equivalence in meaning. Resource description framework expressions are equivalent in meaning only if their data model representations are the same.

The basic data model in RDF consists of three object types: resources, properties, and statements. Resources encompass all things that are described by an RDF expression. Resources, however, are always named by a URI plus optional anchor IDs. [5] A property is a specific aspect, characteristic, attribute, or relation used to describe a resource. Each property has a specific meaning, and defines its permitted values, the types of resources it can describe, and its relationship with other properties. Statements bring together a named property and the value of that property. The parts of the statement are called, in order, the subject, predicate, and object—just like in natural language grammar. The object of a statement, which corresponds to the property value, can be another resource, a literal value, or XML markup (which is not evaluated by the RDF processor).

Because of this extensible design, RDF makes it possible to exchange and process metadata and metadata vocabularies among various systems. Since RDF does not define properties per se, but provides the mechanism for doing so, the strength of RDF is its ability to serve as a metadata container for communities of interest. Work in this area is already underway with the work the World Wide Web Consortium (W3C) has done in standardizing simple mechanisms for defining RDF schemas.

Furthermore, RDF provides the ability to use multiple schemas concurrently to join silos of information. For example, personal information related to the external contacts of a project may be encoded in Friend of a Friend (FOAF), a schema for contact information, while the business processes and concepts used in the project may be encoded in a schema such as RosettaNet.

Resource description framework facilitates cross-domain searching by describing the taxonomy and underlying vocabulary structure. As more standardized metadata schemas emerge and are widely adopted, these types of exchange will become even easier. A simple example would be the ability to recognize metadata schemas and construct crosswalks between taxonomies so that the search for a movie title could be concurrently mapped to the Internet movie database, one or more library catalogs, and bookstores.

Providing an Infrastructure for Promoting Information Discovery

The Open Archive Initiative (OAI) has its roots in the scholarly information community, but the principles used in the project are broadly applicable, especially in the KM realm. The OAI was created to develop and promote interoperability standards to facilitate the dissemination of content through an application-independent interoperability framework based on metadata harvesting.

Although the original focus of OAI was to consolidate and make available the content of archival material (and its associated finding aids), the fundamental technical components have been developed to facilitate the distribution of content in general. These components are not tied to a particular type of content. Therefore, the scope of the initiative has continued to broaden and it is being used to promote discoverability of many types of cultural resources.

The current OAI technical infrastructure, which is specified in the Open Archives Initiative Protocol for Metadata Harvesting (OAI-PMH), defines a mechanism for data providers to expose their metadata, but there is nothing in the OAI mission that restricts the work of the OAI to metadata alone. In fact, the OAI-PMH also defines a mechanism for harvesting XML-formatted metadata from repositories. The protocol does not mandate that a particular schema be used for encoding information; but, as a means of simplifying the exchange and distribution of metadata about the repositories, OAI-PMH requires that data providers use the Dublin Core for data description. Other metadata formats may also be exchanged, but the Dublin Core is used as the common basis for associating metadata and related content.

Within the OAI-PMH architecture, there are two primary services. Data providers create repositories and expose their metadata whereas service providers harvest the metadata to provide services based upon the data. Harvesters are specific instances of client applications that issue OAI-PMH requests on behalf of a service provider as a means of collecting metadata from repositories. A single service provider can have multiple harvesters, which allows for the consolidation of disparate information resources into a single repository.

XML and KM Challenges

Although this chapter has only scratched the surface of XML functionality, it is evident that XML can play an integral role in the technologies used to provide KM solutions: workflow, taxonomies, Web content management, enterprise portals, search engines, collaborative applications, e-learning, documentation management, analytical applications, data warehousing, and messaging. Applications built on XML will allow organizations to create, manage, personalize, and reuse content in a platform-neutral manner that allows for the seamless flow of data and information. Because of this, many content management solutions are built using XML-based technologies to provide a content repository format that allows for granular markup of information and documents for information retrieval and repurposing.

While XML is a powerful component of the IT infrastructure within an organization for supporting KM business processes, its true power lies in the ability to bring together disparate systems both within and outside the organization allowing for the effective exchange of business content. Because of the inherent separation of context, content, and format, XML provides a means for information to be easily repackaged and used in a variety of tools. As a result, XML is a key driver in allowing information to flow across departmental and organizational boundaries and in helping breaking down "information silos" that impede KM activities.

However, XML has its limitations as well. The inherent flexibility to develop any set of tags that one wishes is both a strength and weakness. On the plus side, industry- and discipline-specific groups have embarked on consultation processes to develop specific languages to facilitate their work processes. A few examples of industry-specific languages are: financial information exchange markup language (FINXML), chemical markup language (CML), court filing, and DocBook.

On the minus side, more than one language may emerge to cover a particular content type. For example, within the area of news and news syndication there are more than a half dozen standards—some of them complementary while others are overlapping in their functionality. In Darwinian fashion, some these will survive and thrive, while others will not be widely used. The multiplicity of languages developed to suit both industry- and discipline-specific needs increases the complexity of exchanging content across different DTDs and schemas. There is no doubt that crosswalks will need to be built to provide searching and retrieval across information domains.

At the heart of XML-encoded content lies the authoring process. While database information is easily converted to XML as it is retrieved from the database, converting documents is labor intensive. Ideally, documents will be created in an XML format from the start. A key challenge in XML document authoring is to ensure that documents follow the encoding standards in ways that will not slow the authoring process. In order to achieve widespread use, the XML encoding process must be as transparent to the user as formatting is in a word processing program. While many document management tools store and encode information as XML, most off-the-shelf desktop authoring tools are still not XML compliant to this degree, yet.

Conclusion

Extensible markup language serves as the infrastructure for KM processes by providing the information packet that can support a richer and more granular information base. Because of the inherent flexibility within XML, this architecture for creating markup languages has quickly become the basis of many new document formats. This is not surprising in light of the comment by Harold and Means (2002), the authors of *XML in a Nutshell*, 2nd edition, stating that "XML is simply the most robust, reliable, and flexible document syntax ever invented." As an open standard, XML has the ability to easily migrate, adapt, and embrace new technologies within its overall architecture.

Organizations are better able to create specialized content repositories and eliminate content silos by using XML to support content exchange. This is one of the key drivers in the adoption of XML. With organizations' growing interest in providing Web services, both within and outside the organization, XML provides the enabling mechanism for doing this. The use of these technologies to enhance the KM function is critical.

As we look to the future, perhaps one of the more compelling reasons to consider XML as an infrastructure choice for KM applications resides in the promise of the "semantic Web" as developed by Tim Berners-Lee and his colleagues at the W3C. In the semantic Web, information is meaningful not only within its own localized context, but in additional contexts as well. The semantic Web attempts to tackle the problems of the current Web in which meaning cannot be derived easily through computerized processing alone. Semantic-enabled search agents will be able to collect machine-readable data from diverse sources, process it, and infer new facts (Frauenfelder, 2001).

Therefore, the ability to use machine-understandable data is an important consideration in KM. Data sharing through computerized means can reach its full potential only if data can be shared and processed by automated tools as well as by people. Because of the lack of both metadata encoding of meaning in Web content and the rules that apply to the content, the computer's ability to make decisions, inferences, and carry out complex queries is inherently limited. Through enabling technology, the vision of the semantic Web—of having data defined and linked in a way that can be used by machines not just for display purposes but for automation, integration, and reuse of data across various applications—can be implemented.

ENDNOTES

1. Namespaces in XML, World Wide Web Consortium, January 14,1999. http://www.w3.org/TR/REC-xml-names

2. The Unicode® Standard: A Technical Introduction http://www.unicode.org/unicode/standard/principles.html

3. Properties can also be one of the other elements recommended by the Dublin Core Metadata Initiative (DCMI) or an *element refinement* listed in the DC Qualifiers recommendation found at: http://dublincore.org/documents/2002/04/ 14/dc-xml-guidelines/#DC

4. RDF schemas, which are RDF data models, are entity-relation (ER) diagrams.
5. Anything can have a URI. Since they are extensible, URIs can be used to identify anything imaginable, providing that a URI addressing scheme for such object exists.

References

Adams, K. C. (2001) The web as a database: New extraction technologies and content management. *Online* 24 (2) 27–32.

Berners-Lee, T.; Hendler, J.; Lassila, O. (2001) The semantic web. *Scientific American* 284 (5) 35–43.

Bowman, B. J. (2002) Building knowledge management systems. *Information Systems Management* 19 (3) 32–40.

Charles, S. K. (2002) Knowledge management lessons from the document trenches. *Online* 25 (1) 22–28.

Fichter, D. (1999) Administrative and factual metadata for Intranets–Issues and options. *Online* 23 (6) 88–91.

Frauenfelder, M. (2001) A smarter web. *Technology Review* 104 (9) 52–59.

Harold, E. R., and Means, W. S. (2002). *XML in a Nutshell,* 2nd ed. Sebastopol, CA: O'Reilly.

Web Resources

CML (chemical markup language): http://www.xml-cml.org

Court Filing (LegalXML electronic court filing): http://www.oasis-open.org/committees/legalxml-courtfiling

DocBook: http://www.oasis-open.org/committees/docbook

Dublin Core: http://dublincore.org

FinXML: http://www.finxml.org

FLBC (formal language for business communication): http://www.samoore.com/research/flbc/flbc.php

FOAF (friend of a friend): http://xmlns.com/foaf/0.1

OAI (Open Archives Initiative): http://www.openarchives.org

OPML (outline processor markup language): http://www.opml.org

RDF (resource definition framework): http://www.w3.org/RDF

RFML (relational functional markup language): http://www.relfun.org/rfml

RosettaNet: http://xml.coverpages.org/rosettaNet.html

RSS (rich site summary): http://blogspace.com/rss

Unicode: http://www.unicode.org

XTM (XML topic map): http://www.topicmaps.org/xtm/1.0

Chapter 14

The Semantic Web and an Introduction to Resource Description Framework

Thomas Krichel, Long Island University

The semantic Web is an effort promoted by the World Wide Web Consortium (W3C) to make more machine-processable information available on the Web. The Resource Description Framework (RDF) is the key infrastructure needed to build the semantic Web. This is a proposed standard for metadata encoding.

This chapter was mainly composed from documentation released by the W3C. Its prime purpose is to provide an introduction to RDF for the nontechnical audience, augmented by a somewhat personal discussion of the value of RDF. It is arguable that although RDF is technically highly competent, one cannot be certain as to whether or not it will take off because RDF implementations have too many problems related to their social and economic viability.

The relevance of this discussion to KM is very simple. As KM enters and progresses in its third stage (see Chapter 1), the integration of data and information, and the structuring of data and information to make them more accessible, will be of increasing importance. Data structuring and description standards will play a very important role. It is important that KM professionals understand the possibilities and limitations of structuring and description standards, particularly at this juncture, RDF.

Introduction

This is an introduction to RDF as proposed by the W3C. At the time of writing, the W3C has an RDF core working group (RDF Core WG) concerned with RDF. In its charter at http://www.w3.org/2001/sw/RDFCoreWGCharter, we read:

> Implementer feedback concerning the RDF model and syntax recommendation points to the need for a number of fixes, clarifications,

and improvements to the specification of RDF's abstract model and XML syntax. ... The role of the RDF Core WG is to prepare the way for such work by stabilizing the core RDF specifications. The RDF Core WG is neither chartered to develop a new RDF syntax, nor to reformulate the RDF model. However, the group is expected to re-articulate the RDF model and syntax specification in such a way as to better facilitate future work on alternative XML encoding for RDF.

What these words precisely mean is subject to interpretation, but I think it is safe to assume that an introduction to the topic—as this chapter aims to provide—is not going to be fundamentally altered by what the working group will decide. Indeed, the purpose of this chapter is twofold. As an introduction, this chapter should provide the reader with an idea of whether or not to make use of RDF when working as an information professional. But even if it is decided not to use it, I hope that the chapter stimulates interest in the underlying principles that motivate RDF, or that the concepts discussed here will be of some use to you.

I was introduced to RDF by the co-chair of RDF Core WG, Dan Brickley, in a London pub on September 2, 1998. A written chapter cannot reach the same quality of immediacy. However, I will stay faithful to Dan's ways by adopting an informal style to the discussion of these issues, which tend to be rather dry and abstract, anyway. Some familiarity with XML or a similar markup language is assumed. As for the structure, I will discuss in five sections. In the first section, I shall explain the motivation behind RDF. In the second section, I will be studying the RDF model. In the third section, I turn to RDF schema. In the fourth section, I will discuss the significance of RDF, mainly from the point of view of Web annotations. A final section will act as a summary.

MOTIVATION

The W3C has been promoting the idea of a semantic Web since the late 1990s. According to the Web edition of Webster's at http://www.webster.com, semantic can be defined as "of or relating to meaning in language." The semantic Web, thus, relates to the idea that there should be meaning in the Web. This may be puzzling since the Web is used every day to access information. This Web that is used today can be thought of as the first stage of the Web. In its most complete form, the Web offers a universal communication medium. It allows users to transport any digital entity of information. Any device that is used to produce and receive such digital information may be connected to the Web. Thus, the Web has a universal character for human communication. It is not meant for machine communication. Therefore, the Web only transports raw data, and the interpretation of that data is made by humans. The Web itself does not carry any meaning.

The idea of the semantic Web is referred to by Berners-Lee (1998) as "a plan for achieving a set of connected applications for data on the Web in such a way as to form a consistent logical web of data (semantic web)." The goal, as outlined there, is to move away from the present Web—where pages are essentially constructed for use by human consumption—to a Web where more information can be understood and treated by machines. In that case, machines may make assertions out of primary data found on the Web. Suppose, for example, that we fit each car in New York City with a device that lets a reverse geographical position system reads its movements. Suppose, in addition, that another machine can predict the weather or some other phenomenon that impacts traffic. Assume that a third device has the public transport timetables. Then, data from a collaborative knowledge picture of these machines can be used to advise on the best means of transportation for reaching a certain destination within the next few hours. Several limitations prohibit the current Web from providing such advice:

- The data is not being made available.
- The data is not being entered in machine-readable form.
- The data is not being laid out in machine-processable form.
- There is no browser where a problem can be easily and precisely entered.

It is clear that when data is not there, nothing can be done. But even if the data is there, it cannot be used until it is machine processable. The computer systems doing the calculations required for the traffic advisory are likely to be controlled by different bodies, such as the city authority or the national weather service. Therefore, there must be a way for software agents to process the information from the machine where it resides, to proceed with further processing of that information to a form in which a software agent of the final user can be used to query the dataset. At this level, another standard comes into play: the XML markup language. Assuming you are familiar with XML, you will wonder why we need a thing called RDF to encode the information.

Could the information not be encoded in XML? The answer is "yes, but … " To understand this, let us move away from the real-life, large-scale example of the traffic advice system to a another real-life example, albeit on a more intimate scale. Suppose, for example, that we want to express the fact that Thomas Krichel has a former lover named Sophie C. Rigny. There are several ways to do this in XML. What about

```
<person><name>Thomas Krichel</name><hasformerlover>
        Sophie C. Rigny<hasformerlover></person>
```

or

```
<person><name>Thomas Krichel</name><hasformerlover><person>
<name>Sophie C. Rigny</name></person><hasformerlover></person>
```

or

```
<person>Thomas Krichel<relationship type="former lover">
<person>Sophie C. Rigny</person></relationship></person>
```

The problem should be apparent. If I meet you on the street and say, "Show me your list of former lovers and I'll show you mine," and you agree, then we are fine. We can agree on an XML schema—something that formalizes any of the above syntaxes. I'll send you my data; you send me yours. A human observer would be able to get some idea if he/she understands English and if the tags are as self-explanatory as in the example above. However, a machine would not be able to make anything out of this because it would not be able to figure out which representation we have agreed upon.

Yet if the machine could understand it, it could process the data in a sensible way. For example, since the relation "former lover" is symmetric, a machine would conclude that Sophie C. Rigny has a former lover called Thomas Krichel. If, in addition, the machine knows that Thomas Krichel is a human being of male sex, it would conclude that it is highly likely that Sophie Rigny is a human, too, and that her sex is probably female. The RDF, itself, does not provide a framework for deductive reasoning; but, it provides a framework by which such information can be channeled to a machine.

To understand the message above, a machine would need to know what "Thomas Krichel" is, what a "former lover" is, and what "Sophie Rigny" is. The RDF provides tools to make that happen. Note that RDF does not provide a vocabulary of relationship terms, such as "hasformerlover," "livesataddress," and so forth. Instead, it provides for a framework where such vocabulary can be built and exchanged by communities. Thus, it is not a metadata format, but provides a framework that communities can use to express metadata. In other words, it provides a system of logic in data organizing, which, when applied to examples such as the one that I gave previously, would always result in the use of ways of expressing the information that would ease its processing by machines. This, in turn, would make data understandable by different machines. An extension of RDF, RDF schema, can be used to build metadata formats. It will be introduced in the RDF schema section.

RDF Model

Resource Description Framework is an abstract model. As such, it is syntax independent. The model has three types of things in which it is interested.

First, there are resources. A resource can be considered as something retrievable from the Web, such as a Web page, an e-mail, or a picture. However, anything else that has a uniform resource identifier (URI), see Berners-Lee, Fielding, and Masinter (1998), can be a resource. A URI is rather general. Many existing identifiers can be restated as a URI. For example, the RePEc digital library (see http://repec.org) has an identifier for me as a person: I am RePEc:per:1965–06–05:thomas_krichel. This identifier could be registered as part of a RePEc URI scheme or as part of an oai:RePEc URI scheme. I abstract from these administrative details. I will assume that this RePEc identifier is a URI reference to me. For reasons of space, I shall abbreviate it as "1965–06–05:thomas_krichel." This code is a URI reference to me. I become a resource through the reference. Since URI references can be defined for anything, anything can be a resource.

Second, there are properties. Properties are specific aspects of a resource. Each property has its own meaning. It might only admit a certain range of values, or be attached only to certain resources, but such constraints are not part of the RDF model. These constraints are part of the RDF schema.

Third, there are the two kinds of values that the property takes. First, the value may be a literal, i.e., a string that means itself. Or, second, it may be a new—possibly anonymous—resource. Let us examine the first case, where the value is a string (see Figure 14.1). I use an entity-relationship diagram with the resource in an oval box, the property name in a diamond box, and the value in a rectangular box.

In this case, we see one RDF statement. An RDF statement is a combination of a resource in the oval, a property in the diamond, and a value in the rectangular box. Now let us illustrate the case where value is an anonymous resource that has further properties (see Figure 14.2).

Here, the value of the statement is an anonymous resource. This anonymous resource is described in two other statements.

That is almost the whole basic RDF model, with the exception of two additional things. There is a container structure that covers repetitions. There are three types of containers: The first one, a "bag," is an unordered list of values. The second, a "sequence," is used when order is significant. The third, an "alternative," is used to represent alternatives for a single value (see Figure 14.3).

With several former lovers, problems cannot be far away. Assume that we know the values are a sequence. What does that actually mean? The previous example does have an order, but which one it is remains a mystery. Assume that it would be an alternative. What would that mean? The reader should begin to realize that we go down a slippery slope here.

Another tricky issue, the status of the container, is not really obvious in the previous example. A human tends to assume that the four values are meant to be distinct former lovers of our hero. However, a machine could also adopt the view that the four women collectively form a group that is the former lover of "1965–06–05:thomas_krichel". Unfortunately, the default interpretation in RDF is the latter one, rather than the former. To express what I really want to say in RDF, I must use something like what is shown in Figure 14.4.

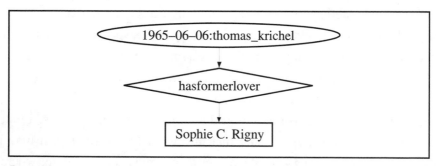

Figure 14.1

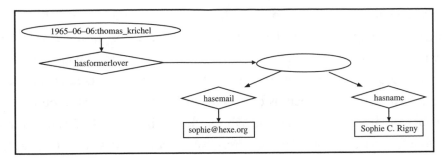

Figure 14.2

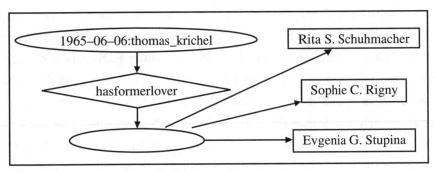

Figure 14.3

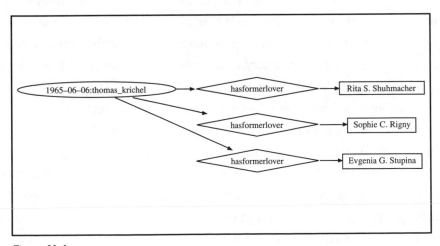

Figure 14.4

How easy it is to get this wrong! And, this is only the container architecture, a first level of complication. At the next level up (see Figure 14.5), there is what is known as "higher-order" statements. These are statements about statements. Resource Description Framework aficionados refer to such statements as "reifications." The reified statement is considered to be an anonymous resource.

In fact, as far as RDF is concerned, this statement in Figure 14.5 is transformed into four basic statements. The resource that is the reified statement is decomposed, using RDF-reserved vocabulary with an "rdf" namespace prefix. If we label the reified statement as "hexenode," any internal resource identifier would do, we get Figures 14.6 and 14.7.

This somewhat convoluted transformation is used so that the initial statement can be reconstructed from the RDF logic. The fact that a statement is added saying that it is fictitious does not imply a change in the nature of the original statement. The idea is that statements added to the existing RDF data should not be able to change the nature of the original statement. Note that a special vocabulary has to be defined; one that expresses the concept of "subject," "predicate," and "object" in such a way that all RDF applications that can read a certain application will understand it. Fortunately, there is only one standard syntax for expressing RDF, and that is XML. Therefore, referring to these special vocabularies is easy: We can use XML namespaces for that. Readers who are not familiar with XML namespaces may consult Bray (1999) for a good introduction.

To summarize, RDF is a syntax-independent way to describe things that are identified. Its mathematical structure is a graph. A graph, in mathematical terminology, is something that is composed of nodes, some of which are connected by lines. Formally, a graph is a binary relation on a set of nodes. If this relation is symmetric, the graph is said to be undirected. This is not the case in RDF, which strictly distinguished between subjects (resources) and objects (property values). Therefore, RDF is a directed graph. There are three kinds of nodes in any RDF graph: urirefs, literals, and blank nodes. A uriref is a URI referring to something that is to be described. A literal is basically just a string of characters. Blank nodes are assumed to be unique to the graph. They have no label and are unique to the specific graph. The lines that connect the nodes within the graph correspond to the properties of resources. These lines are always directed: They go from the resource to the property value.

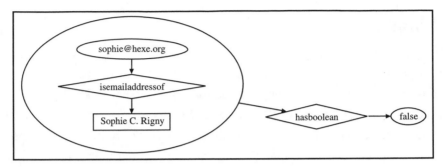

Figure 14.5

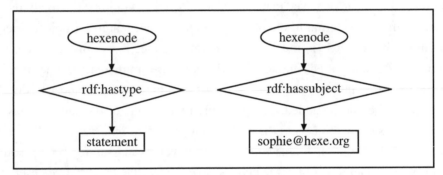

Figure 14.6

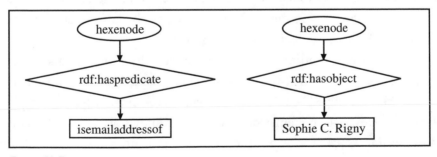

Figure 14.7

RDF Schema

Resource Description Framework does not provide a way to specify resource and property types. Once you have some instance of a resource, you can associate a property with it. However, you cannot express what kind of property and resource it is. That is the job of RDF schema. Much of the inspiration behind RDF schema comes from object-oriented programming. I will briefly explain the concept for those who are unfamiliar. (Those who are familiar with it may skip to the next paragraph.) In conventional programming, one defines variables and functions that operate on variables. In object-oriented programming, the variables and the functions that belong together are tied together in an object class. Thus, a class as "humans" groups all human beings in the world, and each person would be an object in that class. Its properties consist of "size," "name," "place of birth," and the things that it can do, like "make love" and "teach," would be the methods, i.e., functions that are internal to the object. One important feature of object-oriented programming is that it is much easier to reuse code. If I define a new object, "composer," and say it is a human, then the composer immediately inherits all the methods of the human, and specific methods that only composers do, like "orchestrate," could be added. The principle that objects of the subclass have all the properties of the objects in the higher class is called *inheritance*.

Resource Description Framework schema develops classes for both resources and properties. Defining objects in classes is very attractive for resource description because it allows the more special classes of resources to be derived from more general ones. Since everything that RDF describes is a resource rdfs:Resource is the most basic resource class. Every resource is an rdfs:Resource. The property rdf:type is used to say that a resource is of a certain type. The idea of a type of resource is expressed in the concept of a class. A class is a resource whose type is rdfs:Class. Every resource belongs to the class rdfs:Resource and all the classes used in RDF schema are subclasses of resources. Here is a, hopefully, self-explanatory graphical example for classes and subclasses (see Figure 14.8).

This is the kind of information that is conveyed by RDF schema. It says that there is a class "swine" and two subclasses "boar" and "sow." It implies that every resource that is of type "boar" or "sow" is also a resource of type "swine."

Resource Description Framework schema also allows one to specify properties. In fact, as far as RDF schema is concerned, properties are a special type of resource. The most important property is rdf:type which says that a resource is a

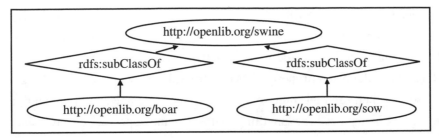

Figure 14.8

member of a certain class. rdf:subClassOf is another important property that applies to RDF resources that are of rdf:type class. This property has already been referred to in the last graph. A simple hierarchy of properties and subproperties can be specified; see Figure 14.9 for an example.

In this case, if there is a resource with the property "husband" that takes the value "Justin," then the same resource also has a spouse that takes the value "Justin," by virtue of "husband" being a subproperty of "spouse."

Properties have two important properties themselves. One is the *domain* of a property. The domain of a property refers to the zero or more classes of resources to which the property may be applied. For example, the property "sex" may be applied to man and beast and nouns in many languages. If a property has no explicit domain, it may be applied to any resource. A second important property of a resource is the range of values that it can take. The range constrains the values that the property can take. If the property has no range, it can take any value. If the property has one or more range properties, each of the values of these range

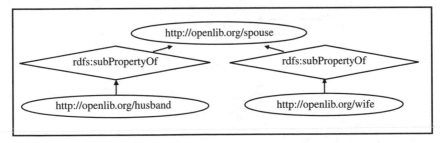

Figure 14.9

properties must be of type rdfs:Class. In that case the classes indicate the types of objects that the value of the property can take. A graphic illustration of domain and range may clarify this (see Figure 14.10).

Here I have defined a property "hassex" the value of which is something on the type "sex." I then say that three resources, "male," "female," and "neuter" are of type "sex." Finally, I say that anything that is a swine, a person, or a Russian noun can have a sex. Note that the description of the class structure and property structures is done entirely in RDF. This shows how general RDF is as a descriptive structure.

Those who are familiar with object-oriented programming should notice that there is an important difference in the way RDF schema treats inheritance. Typically, within object-oriented programming, when we define a class and the attributes that its members may have, the attributes are local to the object. In contrast, properties in RDF schema have global scope. This follows the general philosophy that within the Web anybody can make a new statement about any resource. Thus, nothing prohibits anyone from defining a new resource, say "shmoo" and say that it is also of type "http://openlib.org/sex." The universal nature of the Web is the basis for the philosophy behind this, admittedly rather liberal, way to proceed.

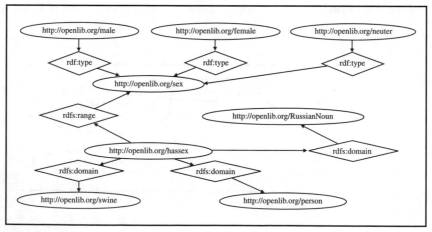

Figure 14.10

Social Obstacles to RDF

The creation of RDF seemed to be primarily motivated for the purpose of describing Web resources. The idea was that more metadata would make the Web a place where it is easier to find things. If this was the implicit promise of RDF, then clearly RDF has not lived up to it.

As far as the Web is concerned, most of the search engines on the market right now do not use any metadata. In particular, Google, at http://www.google.com, which seems to be the most widely used engine, does not use metadata. There are two problems with metadata for the Web. First, there is the problem of the vocabulary to use. Second, there is the problem of encoding that vocabulary.

In this chapter, we are concerned with the latter problem, rather than the former. However, the two problems are related. If there is no meaningful and useful vocabulary, you cannot encode anything. However, even if there is a useful and meaningful vocabulary (say Dublin Core) and if there is a way to encode it (say RDF), that still does not make for a meaningful collection until there are incentives for a majority of providers to produce good metadata. Good metadata has to be meaningful and factually correct. Finally, the user must be willing and able to use that metadata. It is in the latter stage, the good metadata stage, that Web resource description falls down, and RDF, as a tool meant to realize it, loses a good deal of its appeal. Let us briefly examine these points.

Even assuming that RDF has been a miraculous success and the Web is now annotated with good metadata—whatever that requires—it is only successful if the user uses it. If anything can summarize the studies that review how people use the Web, it is the finding that people spend a short amount of time on any one page and that the queries they issue are extremely primitive. Making use of all this metadata, even if it were assembled, would require a much more complicated search page, one that the average user would be unlikely to spend time learning how to use. Sure, users tend to get more sophisticated the longer they use a certain information system; but, since the information needs answered by the Web are so broad, there is not much hope in users learning to express their queries with structure sufficient enough that a machine can make sense of it. For example, look at the problem of shopping. I want to know where I can get convenient access to an item that I can buy. I need to tell the machine where I am, what I want to buy, and what transport options I have, and—hang-on—where my friends are who could get the item for me and give it to me the next time I see them. Entering all that data into a computer is a daunting task that is likely to cost me more effort than going to a nearby store to check if the item is there by chance. Even if I could enter all the data, the privacy issue of letting a third party know all these details about me should be a cause for concern.

A further constraint on the usefulness of RDF is that we would need to have machines that can extract a lot of information out of very limited data. Progress on that front depends on developments in artificial intelligence. My guess is that it will take a few more years to achieve results in that area, by which time RDF may have been forgotten. The progress of artificial intelligence to date has been very slow.

For a moment, assume that a semantic Web browser could be constructed. Now, turn to the problem of good metadata. Metadata is good if (1) it is factually correct and (2) it is meaningful. First, the metadata has to be factually correct. A whole industry is now laboring to get sites to the top of search engines' hit lists. If a certain term is known or suspected to be asked for a lot, such as "sex," every Web page owner will have an incentive to use this term in his/her metadata, even if this is not relevant. They can even be honest and write in the summary "Esta página no habla de sex." (which is Spanish for "This page does not have sex."), and they will still be indexed under the term "sex." This is the main reason why metadata does not work. Users are often frustrated when the page that they wish to access does not contain the term that was searched because that term was in the metadata only. This is a severe problem that limits the usefulness of any metadata that is provided by nontrusted parties. The Web, whose ultimate strength is that anyone can create pages, will have to be limited in the trust that it can place on metadata.

Recall that metadata does not only need to be factually correct but also meaningful. Creating meaningful metadata is difficult, even for Dublin Core or RDF aficionados. For example, in many cases, it is difficult to choose between the container architectures "bag," "sequence," and "alternative." Look at the case of authors writing an academic paper. In some disciplines, it is customary to sequence all authors by order of importance. In others, authors are sequenced by alphabetical order. In orders, such as high-energy physics, there are large collaboratories where scores of authors can appear on the same paper. Does the order matter there? Maybe for the first few, but as we go down the list, there is a chance we reach folks who have not even read the paper. Thus, the distinction between "bag" and "sequence" can be a difficult one. The same is true for the distinction between "alternative" and "bag" and "sequence" and "alternative."

The question of using a container is difficult, too. If we use the container, then the paper has been written by its authors acting as a committee. That may not be a realistic view as far as academic papers are concerned. But now assume that we do not use the container structure. In that case, all persons have the author property, and they all appear in different RDF triples. Now, we have to fiddle all this back together to get the "sequence"/"bag" of authors that we need for our bibliographic service and, since there is no semantics in the position of RDF statements in the file, any information that may have been intimated in the ordering may get lost. It is a recipe for a fine mess.

Another illustration of the problem of meaningful metadata is the meaning of metadata terms. For example, what does the Dublin Core community mean by "date"? If I have a Web page of the "Mona Lisa" and the "Venus de Milo," what date do I associate with it? The date when the "Mona Lisa" was painted? When the Venus de Milo was sculpted? When the pictures were taken? When the pictures where scanned? When the Web page was created or modified? Clearly, for a restricted set of resources, it is possible to agree on meaningful qualifications for "date" but, at the scale of Web resources in general, consensus on these matters would be difficult to achieve, would produce a cumbersome set of rules, and would be costly to implement.

That leads to the issue of costs. Given what we have noted here, adding good metadata, encoded in RDF to Web pages or to any other identified object (also known as "resource" in RDF terminology) is not an easy job. The labor force of such intelligent people is a rare and useful resource and, therefore, an expensive one. This is the biggest hurdle to overcome for RDF. It makes RDF a nonstarter. Its demands are beyond the reasoning skills of the average information professional, and its implementation requires computing skills that are beyond the scope of the average computing service staff. With these demands, it is likely that RDF will stay, for the foreseeable future, confined to lab experiments.[2]

To summarize this section, there is one expression that elegantly captures the problems of RDF and Dublin Core. Berners-Lee (1999) talks about "Web architecture from 50,000 feet." This is where the current efforts have serious shortcomings. They try to build a top-level application for the exchange of structured metadata between communities before there are communities that have organized internal exchanges of metadata to any significant extent. Such organized exchanges require the construction of communities. That is a social and economic process that will depend on community leaders appearing, and on the plans that they make. Given the cost of implementing RDF infrastructures, it is more likely that it will be done for high-quality resources of a specific domain. The data that will be assembled within specific domains may not need RDF for its representation and exchange. However, RDF will be a useful reference model for all communities who wish to exchange structured data.

Conclusion

Berthold Brecht wrote a famous poem about the tailor of Ulm in which a man threw himself from the cathedral spire, the highest church spire in the world, in 1592, and when he landed dead on the square, the bishop said to his flock "man will never fly."[3] Thus, I want to resist the temptation of saying that RDF will never work. It is unlikely that the whole of the Web will be covered with an RDF layer. Instead, there will be communities that use RDF and, if these communities want to open their metadata for processing by other communities (they may not wish to do that), they will surely take a close look at RDF. Therefore, it is in local domains where RDF will be used first.

About this Chapter

This chapter is available online at http://openlib.org/home/krichel/papers/ anhalter.letter.pdf and http://openlib.org/home/krichel/papers/anhalter.a4.pdf. I am grateful to Michael E. D. Koenig and Kathryn P. Read for comments on an earlier version. Please e-mail feedback on this chapter to krichel@openlib.org

Endnotes

1. To be precise, there are a couple ways of writing down RDF in XML; however, this is not the place to go into the details of the RDF XML syntax.
2. See Arms (2000) for an interesting discussion of this point.
3. The poem is a bad distortion of historical facts. The real tailor of Ulm was Albrecht L. Berblinger, 1770–1822. He made his attempt at flying on May 31, 1811, landed in the Danube, and was rescued by a fisherman. Recent research suggests that Berblinger's device could actually fly.

REFERENCES

Arms, William Y. (2000). Automated Digital Libraries: How Effectively Can Computers Be Used for the Skilled Tasks of Professional Librarianship? D-lib Magazine 6, available at http://www. dlib.org/dlib/july00/arms/07arms.html

Berners-Lee, Tim (1998). Semantic Web Road Map, available at http://www.w3.org/ DesignIssues/Semantic

Berners-Lee, Tim (1999). Web Architecture from 50,000 Feet, available at http://www.w3.org/ DesignIssues/Architecture

Berners-Lee, Tim; Roy T. Fielding; and Larry Masinter (1998). Uniform Resource Identifiers (URI): Generic Syntax. RFC 2396, available at ftp://ftp.isi. edu/in-notes/rfc2396.txt

Bray, Tim (1999). XML Namespaces by Example, available at http://www.xml.com/pub/a/ 1999/01/namespaces.html

CHAPTER 15

Designing an Information Architecture to Support Knowledge Management

Denise A. D. Bedford, The World Bank Group

INTRODUCTION

This chapter is written for the KM architect—anyone who has been charged with the task of creating or maintaining a KM system. In my experience, a KM architect comes to the task with a background in information management, educational sciences, computer science, communication sciences, or engineering. There is a high probability that basic taxonomies were not covered in the typical KM architect's education. Taxonomies are perhaps the most essential architectural component of any KM system. They are used in every KM process, and must be supported by KM technologies. This chapter provides a high-level overview of the types of taxonomies that may be used in KM systems, with references to current uses.

Full-function KM systems, by definition, have complex architectures. There is no single software product that supports all KM processes. As we have learned over the past 10 years, effective, sustainable KM systems result from the considered integration and extension of knowledge and information management functionality, and the leveraging and repurposing of existing knowledge sources. New technologies will find their role in the overall KM architecture, but there is no silver-bullet solution waiting on the shelf to be discovered. A full-function KM system is built on a full-function, integrated KM architecture. A sustainable KM system must be well suited to KM business processes. Taxonomies—all types of taxonomies—are essential structures that support KM business processes. Taxonomies are essential tools for transforming KM business processes into KM system architectures.

Most of us have a simplistic understanding of taxonomies. For example, KM literature contains advice to KM architects on how to construct hierarchical taxonomies to categorize knowledge. There are few discussions, though, on how other types of taxonomies may be used to support KM processes. A hierarchy is only one type of taxonomy; other types include: flat, faceted, and network. Each type of taxonomy plays a supporting role in KM processes and, therefore, must be considered when building a KM system. This chapter reviews the processes that comprise KM, the four types of taxonomies, and the role that each type of taxonomy plays in KM architecture.

KM Processes

As a starting point for this chapter, let us consider a definition of KM from Peter Loshin and a discussion of KM processes.

> Knowledge management is the art or science of collecting organizational data, and by recognizing and understanding relationships and patterns, turning it into usable, accessible information and valuable knowledge."[1]

By data, we mean all types of content—published information, data and data models, news stories, speeches, presentations, discussion threads, best practices, lessons learned, and so forth. From KM literature, we have synthesized the processes that comprise KM (see Figure 15.1), including:

- Knowledge creation and acquisition
- Knowledge organization and metadata creation
- Knowledge repository management
- Knowledge use and rights management
- Knowledge integration and discovery
- Knowledge distribution and promotion

Knowledge creation and acquisition includes the selection, capture, representation, transformation, review, editing, versioning, translation, and formatting of knowledge content. These processes pertain to the creation and acquisition of both explicit and implicit knowledge, knowledge fragments, and knowledge composites. Taxonomies provide the structure to represent knowledge. The more complex the knowledge is, the more complex the supporting taxonomy is. Taxonomy structures support the exposure of "deeper" knowledge or knowledge fragments. Taxonomies also help us to integrate and relate different types of content. Knowledge exists in all kinds of content—from published articles, to data sets, to

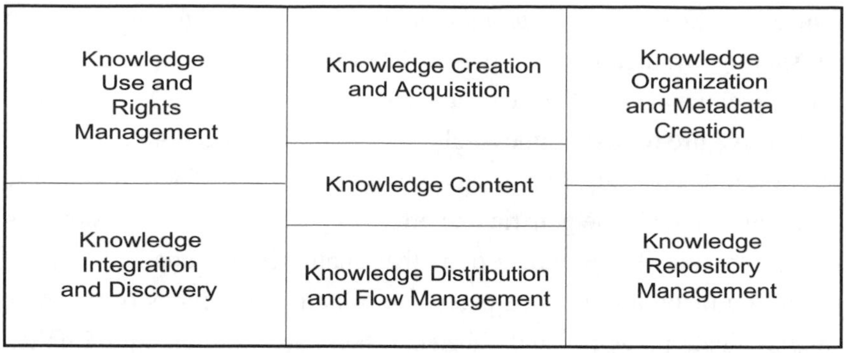

Knowledge Use and Rights Management	Knowledge Creation and Acquisition	Knowledge Organization and Metadata Creation
	Knowledge Content	
Knowledge Integration and Discovery	Knowledge Distribution and Flow Management	Knowledge Repository Management

Figure 15.1   Knowledge management processes.

tacit knowledge designed into expert systems, to video clips or digital audio recordings.

Knowledge organization and metadata creation includes describing, topic analysis, classification, indexing, and abstracting of any and all kinds of knowledge. This typically takes the form of metadata—data about data. Use of metadata for knowledge organization is a core component of the KM architecture. Metadata is to KM what middleware is to complex computer networks. It is the core component to which we apply and from which we extend other KM processes.

Knowledge repository management includes the registration and storage of knowledge sources, including traditional sources of information, best practices, stories, discussion databases, directories of expertise, communications, data and data models, and so forth. Knowledge repository management may include both content and metadata repositories.

Knowledge use and rights management includes the definition and application of security classification, use parameters, disclosure, and copyright status to knowledge content. The reference sources that control these status attributes make use of several types of taxonomies. This process also includes digital rights and workflow management—essential processes for supporting and bounding access to knowledge in disparate source systems.

Knowledge integration and discovery includes design of parametric search systems, browse and navigation structures, thesaurus design, vocabulary crosswalks, and cross-source topic maps and ontology development.

Knowledge distribution and promotion includes knowledge aggregation, repurposing, sharing, syndication, and personalization.

Knowledge management systems are designed to support KM processes. They make extensive use of taxonomies—all types of taxonomies—to accomplish this. Let us, for a moment, shift to a discussion of taxonomies. The most precise definition of a *taxonomy* is the generic one offered by Jean Graef: "a system for naming and organizing things into groups that share similar characteristics."[2] The definition of a taxonomy may be extended to include the types of taxonomies—flat, hierarchical, network, and faceted. There are explicit and implicit taxonomies. Taxonomies may be used as explicit or as implicit information governance structures.

Taxonomy Type 1: Flat Taxonomies

The purpose of a flat taxonomy is to group content into a controlled set of categories. Figure 15.2 is an example of a flat taxonomy. There is no inherent relationship among the categories in a flat taxonomy—they are co-equal members of a single structure. Users can move from one category to another without having to think about the relationship between them. The concept of a flat taxonomy may be counterintuitive to some. Consider, though, how many flat taxonomies you see implemented on Web sites, as alphabetical listings of people in a directory of expertise, in a pull-down menu of country names or geographical regions, or simple listings of product groupings.

Consider the following examples of *explicit flat* taxonomies that are commonly used on the Web or in office productivity software:

- Amazon.com's pull down list of product categories[3]
- Amazon.com's horizontal list of stores
- Nordstrom.com's alphabetical list of brand names[4]
- Microsoft PowerPoint's global functional menu[5]
- Microsoft Word's "Tools" pull-down menu[6]

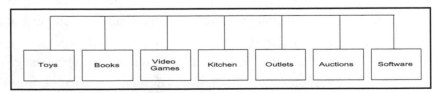

Figure 15.2   Flat taxonomy structure.

- Water Resources Directory of Expertise list of keywords[7]
- Bartleby.com's extensive pick lists of reference, verse, fiction and nonfiction listings[8]
- CyberDewey's alphabetical index to sections[9]

Consider the following examples of *implicit flat taxonomies* that are commonly used to manage knowledge, information, data, and other kinds of content:

- Report in electronic format; HTML markup
- Alphabetical list of water resource experts
- Content inventories
- Rights management values
- Information disclosure status values
- Security class values

Flat taxonomies are easy to create. Lessons learned in implementing flat taxonomies to support KM include:

- Flat taxonomies used for explicit information structures generally should consist of 30 or less categories.
- More than 30 categories may be presented in a flat taxonomy if the categories are intuitive to users (i.e., lists of countries, states, languages, etc.).
- Flat taxonomies do not require complex interface design and extensive usability testing.

Taxonomy Type 2: Hierarchical Taxonomies

Hierarchical taxonomies group content into two or more levels. Hierarchical taxonomies resemble tree structures when they are fully elaborated. Figure 15.3 is an example of a hierarchical taxonomy. The relationships among categories in hierarchical taxonomies have particular meaning. The relationship between a top-level category and a subcategory may designate group membership or the refinement of the top category by a particular characteristic or feature. To move up the hierarchy means expanding or broadening the category. To move down the hierarchy means refining or qualifying the category. Hierarchical categories typically have only one broader or parent category.

Consider the following *explicit applications* of hierarchical taxonomies that are commonly found on the Web:

- Yahoo!'s Web Site Directory; organized as a subject hierarchy[10]
- The Internet Public Library's two-tier collection structure[11]

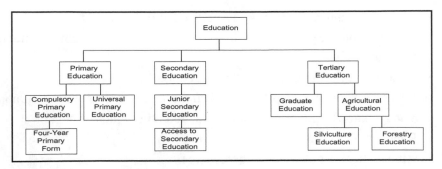

Figure 15.3   Hierarchical taxonomy structure.

- The Librarian's Index to the Internet's mixed hierarchy of topics and resource types[12]
- eBay's auction categories[13]
- CyberDewey's progressive disclosure of Dewey Decimal classes[14]
- Albertsons's Shop By Aisle grocery categories or Shop A to Z grocery product categories[15]

Consider the following *implicit applications* of hierarchical taxonomies that are commonly found in information management systems:

- Electronic news story published in XML NITF[16] format
- Classification schemes for topic areas
- Authority control lists for abbreviations and full names (alias)
- Records management hierarchical file-room structures
- Cross-source topic reference structures

Hierarchical taxonomies are easy to create but more challenging to implement in a usable way. There is more than one way to implement a hierarchy. *Explicit hierarchies* may be implemented in:

- Progressive disclosure of layers across sites or pages—eBay[17] model
- Cascading or expanding menus—Organization for Economic Cooperation and Development (OECD)[18] Web site progressive display of Themes
- Pop-up menus linked to stationary menus—OECD Web site display of Directorates
- Category and subcategory labels in a multicolumn display—Nordstrom's [19] second-level pages

The following design issues pertain to *implementing explicit hierarchical* taxonomies for KM:

- Each level in the hierarchy should have content; empty categories present empty value to users.
- There should be at least two categories for each branch in the taxonomy; do not branch for a single category.
- There should be sufficient content in each category to warrant use.
- Optimal hierarchical taxonomies balance breadth and depth; users must work harder to use a taxonomy three categories broad and nine deep than to use one that is seven wide and two deep.
- Hierarchical taxonomies should be balanced across each level of the taxonomy to provide users with a predictable experience.
- Explicit hierarchies should, in most cases, be no more than four levels.
- Use of hierarchical taxonomies should be offset with search functions.
- Hierarchies should never be designed into flat structures; a hierarchy should offer pull-down menus designed to support flat lists.
- To accommodate growth in your taxonomy, you will need to review it periodically.
- Before you add a new category, consider how the new category fits into the hierarchy and the impact it will have on others.

Taxonomy Type 3: Faceted Taxonomies

Faceted taxonomies resemble flat taxonomies when implemented. Faceted taxonomies, though, have a quite different structure and purpose. All categories in a faceted taxonomy have a defined relationship with a single object. Each category may describe a property or a value, and different views or aspects of a single topic. Like the flat taxonomy, there are no inherent relationships among categories in a faceted taxonomy.

Faceted taxonomies resemble a star structure. Figure 15.4 illustrates a faceted taxonomy. All facets pertain to the center object. The center object may be an electronic book, with each facet describing some aspect of the book, e.g., the author, the title, date of publication, and so forth. The center object may be a country, with the facets describing the country's population, geography, economic system, political system, history, and such. Each category in a faceted taxonomy may have relationships to categories in other taxonomies. A faceted taxonomy describing a book

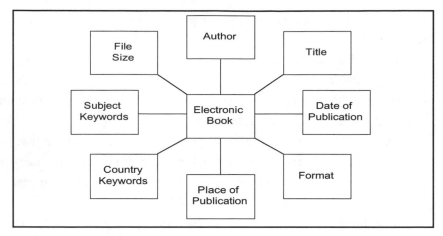

Figure 15.4   Faceted taxonomy structure.

may also have a link to a faceted taxonomy that describes a country. The book's country keyword facet would be linked to the country taxonomy.

Consider the following examples of *implicit faceted taxonomies* that are commonly used in information systems:

- Fairchild Semiconductor's product catalog[20]
- Northrup Grumann Logican Message Dissemination System's user interest profiles[21]
- Knowledge "push" or syndication profiles[22]
- Selective dissemination of information or "push" profiles.[23] The primary application of faceted taxonomies today and historically is as implicit metadata records. Traditionally, libraries have been the prime users of metadata. However, today anyone who has to describe products, services, or any other kind of content needs to use metadata. Metadata for KM systems must support all KM processes.

Consider the following professionally defined metadata schemes:

- Dublin Core Metadata Element[24]
- *Government Information Locator Service* (GILS)[25]
- *Victoria Electronic Records Strategy* (VERS)[26]
- Committee on Scientific and Technical Information (COSATI)
- Machine Readable Cataloging (MARC)[27]

- Universal Description, Discovery and Integration of Business (UDDI)[28]
- Test Encoding Initiative (TEI)[29]
- International Standard Archival Description [ISAD(G)][30]
- Consider the following commercially defined metadata schemes for describing products:
- eBay's auction item descriptions[31]
- Amazon.com's product descriptions[32]
- Albertsons's product descriptions[33]
- Nordstrom's product descriptions[34]

Parametric search, sometimes called *fielded* or attribute search, is another implementation of a faceted taxonomy. Parametric search takes advantage of metadata facets to allow users to search for a value in a specific *context*. For example, faceted taxonomies make it possible for users to search for "The Congo" as a country rather than simply searching for the appearance of the words "The Congo" in full text indexes.

Another example of a faceted taxonomy in information systems is an enterprise security scheme.[35] For each system application we describe a set of security parameters, and the set of parameters takes the form of a faceted taxonomy.

The following design issues pertain to implementing faceted taxonomies for KM:

- The most important design issue for faceted taxonomy is that it be suited to its purpose; that it contain the facets that are needed; and that the behavior of the facets is clear.
- The characteristics of each facet should be defined fully and distinctly. While all facets pertain to a common object, each has a distinct behavior.
- Facets are manipulated individually so it is important to define each facet exclusively, without overlap with other facets.
- Most faceted taxonomies are implicit structures. When they are made explicit, they are generally presented as record or table formats.

Taxonomy Type 4: Network Taxonomies

A network taxonomy is one that organizes content into both hierarchical and associative categories. A network taxonomy may look like a computer network topology. Figure 15.5 illustrates a network taxonomy. Relationships among categories may have many different meanings. In this type of taxonomy, a category

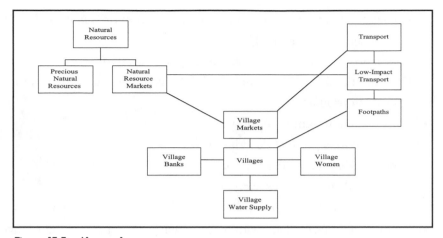

Figure 15.5   Network taxonomy structure.

may have more than one higher-level category; any category in the taxonomy may be linked to any other category. Network taxonomy applications for KM include

- Explicit topic maps or ontologies
- Implicit crosswalks for thesauri and controlled vocabularies from different knowledge domains
- Thesauri
- Semantic networks

At one end of the scale, we find simple *explicit network* taxonomies, such as topical taxonomies with "See also" references, or fully exposed thesauri. At the other end of the scale, we find more complex explicit network taxonomies, such as visual concept maps or visual semantic networks. Consider the following example of *network taxonomies* that are accessible on the Web:

- The World Bank Group Thesaurus[36]
- Unified Medical Language System (UMLS) Semantic Network[37]
- Inxight's Star Tree concept maps[38]

Thesauri, concept maps, and semantic networks can also be designed to support KM systems as *implicit taxonomies*. These tools can be designed transparently into the KM system as

- Thesaurus-facilitated search systems
- Recommender engines[39] (If you liked this, you might also like …)

- Vocabulary crosswalks from one source system to another
- Topic map crosswalks from one knowledge domain to another
- Network taxonomies are complex structures that are challenging to implement effectively. Consider the following design issues when implementing a *network taxonomy*:
- Different kinds of relationships may be implemented in different ways. A single approach to display all types of relationships may not be effective.
- You may create a single-network taxonomy to manage information, but you may have to break it into one or more types of taxonomies to implement it for users.
- Maintain a consistent level of granularity of categories. Avoid mixing pre-coordinated subject headings or broad classes with concepts.
- Network taxonomies may be implemented as three-dimensional visual presentations; however, there may be significant usability issues. This type of implementation should be usability tested with a representative group of users—particularly where the users are subject novices.
- Consider how the user will navigate a three-dimensional presentation.

OVERVIEW OF USE OF TAXONOMIES IN KM PROCESSES

Understanding the various types and uses of taxonomies is important to building a fully functional KM system. As noted, KM processes make extensive use of taxonomies. Each KM process makes use of no less than three and, in some cases, uses all four types of taxonomies. Figure 15.6 provides selected examples of the use of taxonomies in KM processes.

Knowledge creation and acquisition makes use of flat taxonomies to structure electronic content, to create alphabetical directories of experts or product listings. Hierarchical taxonomies, such as XML data-type definitions or schema are used to structure electronic content into more meaningful components. Network taxonomies can be used to capture and represent tacit knowledge as concepts and associated business rules.

Knowledge organization makes use of flat taxonomies to present controlled vocabularies or to create linear extractions of text as content abstracts. Controlled vocabularies are hierarchical reference sources used to describe ideas that are substantively treated in the content. Hierarchical taxonomies, such as classification or categorization schemes and authority control sources (e.g., use "x" instead of "y"),

KM Process	Flat	Hierarchical	Network	Faceted
Knowledge creation and acquisition	• Knowledge structure using HTML content • Alphabetical directories of experts	• Knowledge structure using XML	• Tacit knowledge structuring	• Data and data models
Knowledge organization	• Knowledge description using controlled vocabularies	• Knowledge classification and categorization • Authority control sources	• Knowledge concept relationing • Topic maps and ontologies	• Knowledge product, service, and content metadata descriptions
Knowledge repository management	• Content inventories	• File-room hierarchies • Directory structures	• Site maps	• Metadata repository management
Knowledge use and rights management	• Rights management status • Security class • Disclosure status	• Digital rights management architectures	• Workflow role definitions	• Enterprise directory schema
Knowledge integration and discovery	• Parametric search options	• Topic maps • Cross-source topic maps and ontologies	• Thesauri • Vocabulary crosswalks • Cross-source federated searching	• Integrated metadata warehouse • Search system architectures
Knowledge distribution and promotion	• Knowledge search results	• Knowledge aggregation • Knowledge repurposing	• Recommender engines—"push" systems	• User-defined "pull" or syndication profiles

Figure 15.6   Overview of use of taxonomies by knowledge management process.

help to virtually group like content. Network taxonomies, such as thesauri, help to organize knowledge at the distinct concept level, as well as to associate related knowledge. Topic maps and ontologies help to define subject domains, as well as to pull knowledge content together from disparate sources. Faceted taxonomies provide structure for product and service descriptions, as well as metadata for other types of content.

Knowledge repository management makes use of flat taxonomies to maintain knowledge content inventories. Hierarchical taxonomies are commonly used to define knowledge file-room structures or content storage directories. Network taxonomies are used to generate site maps[40] for KM systems. Site maps translate complex content management structures into simple usable directories. Faceted taxonomies are used to integrate all of the metadata created in the knowledge organization process.

Knowledge use and rights management makes use of flat taxonomies to define security classes and disclosure status of knowledge content. The digital rights management community is in the process of defining the factors and conditions associated with intellectual property protections. They use both hierarchical and network taxonomies to model the relationships among knowledge content objects, users of the knowledge, and the knowledge creator's rights. Workflow definition and management are particularly important to accessing, using, and repurposing content as new knowledge. Workflow management standards groups use network taxonomies to model the relationships among workflow actors, activities, conditions, and resources.

Knowledge integration and discovery makes use of flat taxonomies to support parametric search. While parametric search is based on a faceted metadata taxonomy, it is presented to the user as a simple flat taxonomy. The most efficient way to integrate topics across disparate source systems is to use a higher level or super hierarchical taxonomy to map topics. Similarly, thesauri use network taxonomy structures to define relationships among concepts and to integrate concepts from multiple thesauri. Network taxonomies also help us to define the maps for cross-source federated searching. Search system architectures make use of faceted metadata to construct relational database data classes and inverted indexes for searching.

Knowledge distribution and flow management uses flat taxonomies to support simple, one-dimensional browsing structures and to display search results lists. Hierarchical taxonomies are essential for aggregating knowledge fragments from multiple sources, as well as for disaggregating knowledge fragments for repurposing. Recommender engines—systems that discover similarities and make associations—make use of network taxonomies. While recommender engines may programmatically recommend content, syndication or "pull" systems rely on faceted taxonomies to maintain user interest profiles.

Conclusion

Knowledge management systems are complex, drawing on a complex functional architecture to support complex processes. Taxonomies are important building blocks in a full-function KM architecture. Knowledge management architectures that are built around well-defined taxonomies will prove to be effective, maintainable, sustainable, and extensible as technologies advance.

Endnotes

1. Peter Loshin. "Knowledge Management," *Computer World*, October 22, 2001. http://www. computerworld.com/databasetopics/data/story/0,10801,64911, 00.html

2. Jean Graef. *Introduction to Business Taxonomies*, Montague Institute, Montague, MA, 2001.

3. Amazon, Inc. Amazon.com, September, 2002. http://www.Amazon.com

4. Nordstrom, Inc. September, 2002. http://www.nordstrom.com

5. Microsoft Corporation. Microsoft PowerPoint, 2002.

6. Microsoft Corporation. Microsoft Word, 2002.

7. University of California at Riverside, Center for Water Resources. *Water Resources Directory of Expertise*, September, 2002. http://www.nceas.ucsb. edu/exp

8. Bartleby.com. September, 2002. http://www.bartleby.com

9. CyberDewey. September, 2002. http://www.anthus.com/CyberDewey/Dewey_ index.html

10. Yahoo! Inc. Yahoo!.com, September, 2002. http://www.yahoo.com

11. University of Michigan School of Information. The Internet Public Library, Web site, September, 2002. http://www.ipl.org

12. University of California. *The Librarian's Index to the Internet*, September, 2002. http://www. lii.org

13. eBay, Inc. eBay.com, September, 2002. http://www.ebay.com

14. Online Computer Library Center. CyberDewey, September, 2002. http://www.anthus.com/ CyberDewey/CyberDewey.html

15. Albertsons, Inc. Albertsons.com, September, 2002. http://www.albertsons.com/store

16. International Press Telecommunications Council. News Industry Text Format, Version 3.1, September, 2002. http://www.nitf.org

17. eBay, Inc. eBay.com, September, 2002. http://www.ebay.com

18. Organization for Economic Cooperation and Development Web site. September, 2002. http://www.oecd.org/EN/home/0,,EN-home-0-nodirectorate-no-no-no-0,FF.html

19. Nordstrom, Inc. September, 2002. http://www.nordstrom.com

20. Fairchild Semiconductors, Inc. September, 2002. http://parametric. fairchildsemi.com

21. Northrup Grumann Information Technology. September, 2002. http://www.northropgrummanit. com/mailroom/lmds.html

22. Benoit Marchal. "XML Content Syndication," *Web Developer's Journal*, November 15, 2000. http://www.webdevelopersjournal.com/articles/xml_syndication.html. Sections extracted from *Applied XML Solutions*, Indianapolis, Indiana: Sams Publishing, 2000.

23. Cheryl Gustitus. "The Push Is On—What Push Technology Means for the Special Librarian," http://www.sla.org/pubs/serial/io/1998/jan98/push.html

24. Dublin Core Metadata Initiative. *DCMI Registry*, September, 2002. http://dublincore.org/dcregistry/index.html

25. United States Government Printing Office. *Government Information Locator Service*, September, 2002. http://www.gils.net

26. Public Record Office, Victoria. *Victoria Electronic Records Strategy*, North Melbourne, Australia, 1999. http://www.prov.vic.gov.au/vers/welcome.htm

27. Library of Congress. Network Development and MARC Standards Office. *MARC Format for Bibliographic Information.* http://www.loc.gov/marc/marcdocz.html

28. Organization for the Advancement of Structured Information Standards. UDDI *Universal Description, Discovery and Integration of Business for the Web*. September, 2002. http://www.uddi.org

29. Text Encoding Initiative Consortium. *Text Encoding Initiative*, 2001. http://www.tei-c.org

30. International Council on Archives. *General International Standard Archival Description*, 2nd Edition. Ottawa, Canada, 2000. http://www.ica.org/biblio/com/cds/isad_g_2e.pdf

31. eBay, Inc. eBay.com, September, 2002. http://www.ebay.com

32. Amazon, Inc. Amazon.com, September, 2002. http://www.Amazon.com

33. Albertsons, Inc. Albertsons.com, September, 2002. http://www.albertsons. com/store

34. Nordstrom, Inc. September, 2002. http://www.nordstrom.com

35. Oliver Rist. "No Easy Trick," InternetWeek.com, July 24, 2000. http:// www.internetweek.com/indepth/indepth072400.htm

36. Denise A. D. Bedford, ed. *The World Bank Group Thesaurus*, The World Bank Group, Washington, DC, September, 2002. http://www2.multites.com/wb

37. National Library of Medicine. *Unified Medical Language System Semantic Network*, National Institutes of Health, Bethesda, Maryland, 2002. http://www.nlm.nih.gov/research/umls/META3.HTML

38. Inxight Software, Inc. Inxight Start Tree Studio, Version 1.5. http://eic.vestforsk.no/sitelense/eic.html

39. Frank Linton, "OWL: A Recommender System for Organization-Wide Learning," *Educational Technology and Society*, 3(1), 2000. http://ifets.ieee.org/ periodical/vol_1_2000/linton.html

40. United Nations Web site. September, 2002. http://www.un.org/site_index

CHAPTER 16

The Knowledge Matrix: A Proposed Taxonomy for Enterprise Knowledge

Timothy W. Powell, The Knowledge Agency

THE IMPORTANCE OF TAXONOMY

During the Middle Ages, all substances of the earth were said to be made from combinations of four elements—earth, air, fire, and water. The modern field of chemistry could not have developed as fast and as far as it has without the more complex (and meaningful) classification that we have today—the periodic table of the elements. This table was created by the Russian chemist, Mendeleyev, in 1869, and identifies key similarities and differences among the various elements.

Likewise, in the field of biology, the ancient Greek philosopher/scientist, Aristotle, classified organisms by whether or not they had red blood. It was not until the 1750s that the Swedish naturalist, Linnaeus, developed the taxonomy we use today, which starts with kingdom (like animal) and ends in genus and species (like Homo sapiens).

In both chemistry and biology, taxonomies that today we think of as "wrong," survived for centuries—mostly because they were *not* wrong. Animals *can* be classified by whether or not they have red blood—it is just not as *useful* a distinction as whether or not, say, they are warm-blooded.

Taxonomy is defined as "the branch of science, or of a particular subject, that deals with classification."[1] A taxonomy, once codified, gives us a *common terminology* for describing aspects of the world. It forms a basis for *discussion*, which in turn forms a basis for *solving problems*. We label things in order to understand them; we understand them—intellectual satisfaction aside—in order to predict, control, or improve them.

In the business world, it is a common dictum that "if you cannot document it, you cannot manage it." This is especially true of *intangible assets* (of which knowledge is one), since without documentation it is almost as if they did not exist at all.

Documentation of knowledge, then, is crucial to managing knowledge. However, most discussions of "knowledge management" fail to define exactly what it is that is to be "managed." Without such definition—the foundation of any systematic effort to manage these assets—the structure is weak, and soon collapses. We are left, for example, with systems that index *"documents,"* as if all documents contain strategically valuable knowledge (when relatively few actually do).

Knowledge "lives" in many places throughout the enterprise. It is notoriously resistant to traditional management tools of order, such as organization charts, vertical hierarchies, and geographic boundaries. As a result, as in the old fable of the three blind men and the elephant, each knowledge professional sees only a piece of the puzzle. The whole picture is not clear, and too often there is little coordination among the parts.

If one accepts the often-cited premise that well over 50 percent of the average corporation's productive assets are intangible, it becomes obvious that it is extremely important to manage those assets—and a robust taxonomy is needed as a first step.

CURRENT KNOWLEDGE TAXONOMIES

The Skandia/Canadian Imperial Bank of Commerce Model

To date, the main taxonomy proposed for intellectual capital has been the model developed at the Swedish insurance company Skandia, and as modified at the Canadian Imperial Bank of Commerce (CIBC). The Skandia model classifies all organization knowledge into two major categories with several subcategories:[2]

- *Human capital.* "All individual capabilities, the knowledge, skill, and experience of the company's employees and managers." (Edvinsson and Malone, 1997)

- *Structural capital.* "The organizational capability, including the physical systems used to transmit and store intellectual material." (Edvinsson and Malone, 1997) Structural capital itself comprises three parts:

- *Organizational capital.* "Investment in systems, tools, and operating philosophy that speeds the flow of knowledge through the organization, as well as out to the supply and distribution channels." (Edvinsson and Malone, 1997)
- *Innovation capital.* "Renewal capability and the results of innovation," including:
  - Intellectual properties, such as trademarks
  - Other intangible assets, such as the theory by which the business is run
- *Process capital.* "Work processes, techniques, ... and employee programs that augment and enhance the efficiency of manufacturing or the delivery of services." (Edvinsson and Malone, 1997)

The CIBC modification promotes *Customer capital* (formerly under structural capital and defined as the "valuation of customer relationships") to a third major category equivalent to structural and human capital.

There is something inherently unsatisfying about these schemas. Perhaps they are aesthetically unpleasing in that they seem so lopsided. Also, the categories seem inexact and somehow to overlap with each other. (Are humans not customers?)

However, the primary test of a taxonomy is *whether it works*—whether it helps us to understand, and thereby manage, the knowledge asset base more effectively. And, most importantly, it is here that the Skandia model goes astray. It requires the development of dozens of metrics (total assets, total assets per employee, and so forth—some of which are actual knowledge metrics, others of which measure other intangibles, and still others of which are financial and other operating metrics).

Eventually the Skandia model reduces to a single index that purports to measure all of the intellectual capital of the organization. This, for us, simplifies to the point of being much too simplistic.

Overall Structure of the Knowledge Matrix Taxonomy

The Knowledge Matrix model proposes two distinct and concurrent dimensions along which a "piece" of enterprise knowledge can be classified: its *nature as an asset* and its *content*.

- *Asset.* How does each item of knowledge exist as an asset? For example, is it a book, a magazine, or a database? We will examine four asset classes that together form the *knowledge balance sheet*—in other words, that comprise 100 percent of the knowledge asset base of the enterprise. We will also describe the "gatekeepers" associated with each asset. That is, each of these assets tends to be associated with one (or more) organizational function(s), which typically purchases or develops the asset, and maintains it.

• *Content.* If we turn our asset classes sideways, we see that associated with each item of knowledge is its content—what it is "about." For example, some knowledge elements are related to market opportunities, others to competitive threats that face the enterprise. We will examine five broad classes of knowledge content, which together we call the *knowledge compass,* after its configuration—four directional pointers emanating from a center hub.

The knowledge balance sheet and the knowledge compass form the perpendicular X and Y axes, respectively, of the Knowledge Matrix.

The Knowledge Balance Sheet

The knowledge balance sheet is a structure by which we describe the knowledge asset base of the enterprise. What *form* does knowledge take? Here, we see four major *asset classes* into which we can group various *categories* of knowledge assets. These four asset classes are: protected assets; purchased assets; produced assets; and people (see Figure 16.1).

Figure 16.1   Four major asset classes.

Protected Assets

Protected assets are what we typically think of as "intellectual property." They include the following asset categories:

- *Trademarks.* Trademarks can include the words used to identify a brand (like Kleenex®), as well as the graphic logos used to identify these brands. They also include phrases linked with a brand, like FedEx's "Absolutely, positively overnight."™ Trademarks include registered trademarks (the ones with the little ® following them), and unregistered marks (typically followed by ™ for a product or ^{SM} for a service). In the U.S., trademarks are registered with the Patent and Trademark Office. They are also protected by a variety of international treaties, as well as by the World International Property Organization (WIPO).
- *Patents.* Patents include proprietary formulas, inventions, and (recently) business models and processes. They, too, are registered with the U.S. Patent and Trademark Office.
- *Trade secrets.* Trade secrets are similar in content to patents, but are typically not formally registered, as patents are. In the U.S., various state laws, as well as the Economic Espionage Act of 1996, protect these.
- *Copyrights.* Copyrights are, literally, the rights to copy (and charge for) a piece of intellectual property, e.g., a book, movie, audio recording, and such. These are registered in the U.S. with the Copyright Office, which is part of the Library of Congress.
- *Brands.* Branding is a complex art/science, and the subject of dozens of books and hundreds of articles. In a nutshell, a brand is a trademark consistently associated with a certain type and level of user experience. (For example: If I eat under the "golden arches" of McDonald's, I expect to reliably get a certain type and quality of food and service at a certain price.)

Purchased Assets

Purchased assets typically include assets produced by a third party, and purchased (or licensed) for internal use. They include:

- Periodicals: magazines, newsletters, and so forth (both hard copy and electronic)
- Commercial databases: Factiva, LexisNexis, for-pay Web sites like WallStreetJournal.com and such

- Directories
- Books
- Syndicated reports: produced by research houses such as Information Resources, IMS, Gartner, and such, and available to anyone who pays the subscription fee
- Custom reports: produced on-demand for a particular sponsor or set of sponsors, and not available to anyone else
- Electronic media: CD-ROMs and DVDs that increasingly supplement or replace printed forms of the categories listed above

Produced Assets

Produced assets are knowledge assets (e.g., lists, documents, databases) produced as part of another business process, as either a direct product or a by-product, and that have strategic value for the enterprise as a whole.

Specific categories of produced assets include:

- *Transaction data.* For example, credit card companies maintain huge databases of who charged what items, at what kind of store, at what time and day, and so forth. When aggregated and analyzed, this kind of data can have strategic value. (This is what "data mining," also known as "business intelligence" software, is all about.)
- *Operating data.* Other kinds of data can have value as well, most often when aggregated and analyzed. For example, Dun and Bradstreet, which compiles credit histories of individual companies, is able to aggregate these data points into industry-wide databases that in turn have value as marketing and sales tools.
- *Strategic documents.* Strategic plans, product development memoranda, marketing plans, and sales plans all have great value. These mostly have "defensive" value, meaning their value is realized by maintaining secrecy about what they contain, rather than by selling them in an open marketplace.
- *Customer/client/prospect lists.* During the course of executing the marketing/sales process, lists of customers and prospects are developed and maintained. These may be kept in an integrated customer relationship management (CRM) system, on individual desktops and personal digital assistants, or even on 3 x 5-inch index cards.
- *Local databases.* In a more general sense, there may be other kinds of local databases that have value when aggregated.

- *Proprietary software.* Rather than purchase or license software from a third party (which in our taxonomy would be a "purchased asset"), companies may elect to develop proprietary software themselves. If successful, such software can provide *strategic differentiation* over other firms who compete in the industry. A good example is the proprietary trading algorithms that the largest Wall Street houses develop.
- *Internal best practices.* These may be kept in a formal database, but have value whether or not this occurs.

People

"People are our most important asset." Whether companies actually believe this often-repeated business cliché is best reflected in how they actually care for, develop, and maintain such "assets." But, we quite agree that collectively they are the most important asset of any enterprise, whether engaged in services, manufacturing, government, or not-for-profit work. There is a large body of knowledge and literature regarding the economic value of the "human asset," which goes beyond the scope of this chapter.

Not only are people the most important part of the knowledge balance sheet, their knowledge is also the hardest part to manage. This is because most of their strategic knowledge remains *tacit*, meaning outside the boundaries of documents and databases.[3] Nevertheless, it benefits our taxonomy to be able to take the most important *indicators* of knowledge and begin to codify them, thereby managing them more rigorously.

To simplify (which we must do in the interest of our overall goal of developing a robust taxonomy), the major value categories of people-as-knowledge-asset are as follows:

- *Education and training.* University degrees; training courses, such as those that earn continuing professional education credits; workshops; executive education; and distance learning together constitute an important part of the knowledge base of the enterprise.
- *Experience.* Current and past projects or work-team assignments, completed within the current enterprise or in other organizations, can have strategic value.
- *Contacts.* The "communities of practice" to which an individual belongs or contributes can have great value. These can include:
  - Professional and trade organizations

- Social, civic, charitable, or recreational groups
- Organizational boards
- *Employment contracts.* One of the best ways to assure continued access to an individual's knowledge is to put that person under an employment contract. Even retired employees can be contracted in such a way that the enterprise continues to maintain access to their expertise and contacts.

Management Challenges Presented by the Knowledge Balance Sheet

The primary challenge in managing these various asset classes is that they typically "belong" to widely dispersed and independent groups in the enterprise. Their respective gatekeepers (whose budget power is used to acquire and maintain them) are typically not connected to each other. As a result, the typical enterprise is left with a series of *knowledge tactics*—but little in the way of true *knowledge strategies*.

The typical gatekeepers for the asset classes we reviewed are:

- For protected assets: the legal department (for existing properties); the R&D department (for properties under development); the marketing function and/or outside advertising agencies (for brands)
- For purchased assets: the library
- For produced assets: the respective "producer" business operating units; the IT function
- For people: the human resources department; individual operating units

To manage knowledge strategically, linkages need to be built among these far-flung gatekeeper groups.

The Knowledge Compass

In discussing knowledge as an asset, we have been essentially "content-neutral." For example, all databases may be purchased by the organization's library, regardless of whether their content pertains to business opportunities, competitive threats, patents and technologies, and so forth. However, the functions that *use* these assets are different—sales, competitive intelligence, and R&D, respectively. One of the essential challenges of KM is that *knowledge assets are typically purchased and maintained in different ways than they are used*.

The knowledge compass attempts to manage this paradox by concurrently classifying knowledge assets by a second set of characteristics: by what they are *about* (as a proxy for how they are used). These content categories intersect the asset categories described earlier in matrix fashion. We will keep the categories broad, in order to achieve comprehensiveness while maintaining comprehensibility.

Our categories of what knowledge is about include two major dimensions, each of which has two endpoints (see Figure 16.2). The two major dimensions are knowledge about events, entities, and such that are *internal* to the organization; the other involves *external* events, entities, and so forth.[4] The internal dimension includes *product* knowledge and *process* knowledge. The external dimension includes knowledge of *friends* and *foes* of the organization. At the center of the compass rose is knowledge about *people*, as people exist in both internal and external dimensions.

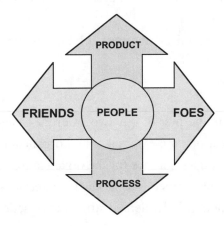

Figure 16.2   The knowledge compass

Product Knowledge

Product knowledge includes knowledge that typically goes into the products (or services) we make and offer for sale. It can include:

- Basic science
- Technologies in the public domain
- Proprietary technologies
- Product features and benefits
- Brands

It is often captured and managed in the form of *intellectual capital*, that is, protected assets as we have defined them here. This includes trademarks, copyrights, patents, and trade secrets.

Process Knowledge

Process knowledge includes the way we do things. It can be comprised of:

- Technology processes, such as how to manufacture a computer chip
- Business processes, such as how to bring that chip to market
- Project results

It can also include comparative elements:

- Internal best practices: the best solution set developed within our organization
- "Best-in-industry" practices: the best solution set developed by *any* company in our industry
- "Best-in-world" practices: the best solution set developed by *any* company in *any* industry

Friends Knowledge

Friends knowledge is the first of our two external categories. It includes all entities, forces, and such that are external to the organization and are primarily *positive*. These represent opportunities for the organization and can include:

- Customers: the end users of our products or services
- Channels: retailers, wholesalers, distributors, resellers
- Suppliers
- Complementors: makers of products that render our products more valuable (for example, PC manufacturers if we produce software)
- Market trends

Foes Knowledge

Conversely, *foes* knowledge includes knowledge of entities, forces, and such that are primarily *negative* to the organization. These represent threats to the enterprise and can include:

- Direct competitors: those who sell what we sell to the same markets to which we sell
- Potential competitors: those who have the basic competencies to become direct competitors, but have not yet done so

- Substitutes: products that, though based on different technologies, offer similar benefits to end-users as our product (for example, trains if we provide local air travel)
- Critical issues: factors that may have interests counter to those of our organization, for example government regulations

People Knowledge

People stand at the crossroads, as they may be "internal to" (that is, employed or otherwise financially engaged by) the enterprise, or they may be "external" (everyone else).

Such people can include:

- Internal experts
- External experts: consultants, academics, channel partners, securities analysts
- Communities of practice: trade associations, professional groups

Several existing management practices already acknowledge the role of such networks:

- *Alumni relations.* Large consulting firms, for example, often retain active networks of former employees. These form a vast knowledge base and are also helpful in gaining new assignments.
- *Analyst relations.* Technology companies, for example, typically have formal programs to cultivate relationships with the analysts who report on their products and services.
- *Academic relations.* Many Silicon Valley companies and investors, for example, maintain active relationships with research universities, such as Stanford University.

Note the distinction between this *knowledge about people* and the asset category of *people*. In the latter, we are talking about people as a vessel for knowledge, as a form that knowledge often takes. In the former, we are talking about the knowledge of *who those people are* who know what they know. (It is admittedly a bit confusing at first.) Here, it is "who knows about X." As an asset, it is the "X knowledge" itself that we are describing.

The Knowledge Matrix and What It Does for Us

We have discussed four major knowledge *asset classes*, and five major knowledge *content classes*. Now we can envision a 4 x 5-inch matrix (see Figure 16.3). Every piece of enterprise knowledge maps into one of the 20 cells in this matrix.

	PRODUCT	PROCESS	PEOPLE	FRIENDS	FOES
PROTECTED					
PURCHASED					
PRODUCED					
PEOPLE					

Figure 16.3 The knowledge matrix.

A database that contains information about possible competitors goes into the "purchased/foes" cell. A trademark for a new product of ours goes into the "protected/products" cell, and so forth.

Each cell is subdivided into the specific asset and content categories listed previously. It is possible that any single asset will fit into more than one cell. A database, for example, can contain information relevant to both customers and competitors.

What is the value of this rationalized taxonomy? We believe there are several major kinds of benefits:

- *Enables a knowledge inventory*. The first step in any serious effort to manage knowledge is the development of an inventory of what that knowledge is. Specific asset values can then be evaluated against their costs, and overlapping assets can be eliminated. Nonproductive assets may be sold or licensed, creating incremental revenue. Thus, the knowledge inventory is the first step in increasing the return on investment for the knowledge process as a whole. The Knowledge Matrix represents a model that can be used as the basis for such an inventory. It represents the "chart of accounts" into which specific knowledge assets can be classified and documented.

- *Increases knowledge accountability*. A knowledge inventory enables a level of *accountability* for each knowledge asset. Specific gatekeepers can be assigned whose responsibility includes maintaining and safeguarding each asset.

- *Promotes knowledge integration*. One of the current roadblocks to managing knowledge effectively is that knowledge is typically *managed by asset class* (for example, lawyers manage the protected assets; librarians manage the purchased assets; and so on). However, knowledge is typically *applied by content class*. The request most often heard by knowledge services providers is "Give me everything we have on topic X." And it usually means just that—everything—regardless of whether it is in a database, a consulting report, or a conversation a salesperson had with a customer that morning. Having this kind of matrix in a relational database, updated in real-time, enables a rapid response to that kind of request.

- *Forms the basis of a knowledge gap analysis.* At least as valuable to knowing what we know, is knowing what we do not know. A matrix such as proposed here enables us to identify and correct gaps in our knowledge base.

- *Heightens knowledge security.* If we are serious about protecting our knowledge assets—and these days, an assault here is a real possibility— we must know where these assets sit in the organization so that these positions can be fortified against unauthorized access and misappropriation.

Conclusion

Notwithstanding the apparent importance of developing strategic taxonomies for enterprise knowledge, various alternative schemas have not been forthcoming. The development of a robust model for enterprise knowledge is a crucial step for KM to take if it is to be an effective management discipline. We offer the Knowledge Matrix model discussed in this chapter as a next stage in the hope that it will be developed and improved in the future.

Endnotes

1. *The New Shorter Oxford English Dictionary*, Oxford University Press, New York, 1993.
2. *Intellectual Capital*, Leif Edvinsson and Michael S. Malone. HarperBusiness, New York, 1997.
3. Indeed, I have argued elsewhere ("Ten Myths About Knowledge Management," address to the 2001 Online Conference, New York, NY) that *all human knowledge is tacit*, and that any explicit or codified "knowledge" is essentially *information*, not true knowledge. The latter distinction I have also explored elsewhere ("The Knowledge Value Chain: How to Fix It When It Breaks," *Proceedings of the 22nd National Online Meeting*, M. E. Williams ed. Information Today, Inc., Medford, NJ, 2001.
4. We acknowledge that, increasingly, knowledge-based management is about making the distinctions between "internal" and "external" seem rather old-fashioned and less useful than it once may have been.

CHAPTER 17

Knowledge Management and Text Mining: Overview and Case Study

Hsinchun Chen, University of Arizona

KM Systems: Background and Overview

Before discussing KM, we need first to understand the unit of analysis, namely, knowledge.

It is generally agreed by IT practitioners that there exists a continuum of data, information, and knowledge (and even wisdom) within any enterprise. The concept of data and the systems to manage them began to be popular in the 1960s. Data are mostly structured, factual, and oftentimes numeric. They often exist as business transactions in database management systems (DBMS), such as Oracle, DB2, and MS SQL. Information, on the other hand, became a hot item for businesses in the 1990s, especially after the Internet Web explosion and the successes of many search engines. Information is factual but unstructured and, in many cases, textual. Web pages and e-mail are good examples of "information" that often exists in search engines, groupware, and document management systems. Knowledge is inferential, abstract, and is needed to support business decisions.

In addition to the IT view of the data-information-knowledge continuum, other researchers have taken a more academic view. According to these researchers, data consist of facts, images, or sounds. When data are combined with interpretation and meaning, information emerges. Information is formatted, filtered, and summarized data that, when combined with action and application, becomes knowledge. Knowledge exists in forms such as instincts, ideas, rules, and procedures that guide actions and decisions.

The concept of knowledge has become prevalent in many disciplines and business practices. For example, information scientists consider taxonomies, subject headings, and classification schemes as representations of knowledge. Artificial intelligence researchers have long been seeking such ways to represent human knowledge as semantic nets, logic, production systems, and frames. Consulting firms have also been actively promoting practices and methodologies to capture corporate knowledge assets and organizational memory. Since the 1990s, KM has become a popular term that appears in many applications, from digital library to search engine, and from data mining to text mining. Despite its apparent popularity, we believe the field is rather disjointed and new KM technologies are relatively foreign to many practitioners.

Definition

We adopt a layperson's definition of KM in this chapter. Knowledge management is the system and managerial approach to collecting, processing, and organizing enterprise-specific knowledge assets for business functions and decisions. Notice that we equally stress both the managerial (consulting) and the system (technology) components.

It is our belief that where a managerial approach lacks a sound technical basis, we will see KM become another casualty of consulting faddism, much as did business process reengineering (BPR) or total quality management (TQM), which, in many cases, did not deliver sustainable values to customers. On the other hand, new KM technologies will fall into misuse or produce unintended consequences if they are not correctly understood and administered in the proper organizational and business context.

In the light of corporate turnover, information overload, and the difficulty of codifying knowledge, KM faces daunting challenges to making high-value corporate information and knowledge assets easily available to support decision making at the lowest, broadest possible levels.

The Landscape

Knowledge management has academic roots in several research communities that have been developing new technologies and researching their organizational impacts.

The National Science Foundation (NSF)-led, multi-agency, multimillion-dollar Digital Library Initiative (DLI) has attracted researchers from computer science, library science, information systems and sciences, and social sciences to research issues related to content creation, information management, knowledge extraction, and organizational adoption of different technologies and practices. Similarly, the NSF Digital Government Initiative, the Knowledge Networking

Initiative, and the Information Technology Research programs aim to make information and knowledge assets more easily available to scientists, policymakers, practitioners, and the general public.

Such federally funded research programs have also fostered involvement of several key-related research disciplines in KM, including data mining, search engines, and information visualization.

While academic communities and federal governments often focus on mid-to-long-term research, IT businesses and consulting firms have eagerly embraced methodologies and frameworks that are suitable for immediate corporate knowledge transformation, although they tend to focus on the managerial dimension, paying less attention to emerging technologies.

Several communities have collectively helped contribute to the development of KM. The consulting community, which is grounded on information system analysis and design methodology, often takes a process perspective. Its members stress best practices, process modeling, learning/education paradigms, human resources, culture and rewards, and systematic methodologies.

Consultants often adopt KM methodologies based on existing and proven technical foundations. Data warehousing, e-mail, enterprise information portals (e-portals), document management systems, and search engines are examples of popular KM implementation platforms. Despite recognition of the importance of methodologies and technical foundations, their systems suffer from an inability to effectively extract and codify corporate information and knowledge assets.

A content management perspective is exemplified by researchers and practitioners trained in information or library science. Stressing content management and system usability, knowledge represented as taxonomies, knowledge maps, or ontologies are created and maintained by information specialists. However, the process of manual knowledge codification is painstaking and error-prone. A system-aided approach is necessary.

A significant (emerging) approach to KM deriving from the content management tradition is represented by researchers and practitioners who attempt to codify and extract knowledge using automated, algorithmic, and data-driven techniques. We define systems that adopt such techniques as knowledge management systems (KMS), a class of new software systems that have begun to contribute to KM practices. A KMS focuses on analysis and is the subject of our discussion in this chapter.

Two of the most relevant subfields within KM are data mining and text mining. Data mining, which is better known within the IT community, performs various statistical and artificial intelligence analyses on structured and numeric data sets. Text mining, a newer field, performs various searching functions, linguistic analysis, and categorizations. A KMS complements existing IT infrastructure and often requires being superimposed on such foundational systems as e-portals or search engines. Methodologies for practicing these new techniques must be developed if they are to be successful.

Consulting Perspective

Many consulting firms and IT vendors have developed methodologies for their practice of KM. Most, however, have limited experiences in adopting automated knowledge codification and analysis techniques.

Dataware Technology has suggested a seven-step KM methodology that includes: (1) identifying the business problem, (2) preparing for change, (3) creating a KM team, (4) performing a knowledge audit and analysis, (5) defining the key features of the solution, (6) implementing the building blocks for KM, and (7) linking knowledge to people. Steps 4, 6, and 7 are problematic unless they are provided with automated, system-aided support.

The Delphi Group's KM practices look at: (1) key concepts and frameworks for KM, (2) how to use KM as a competitive tool, (3) the culture and organization aspects of KM, (4) best practices in KM, (5) the technology of KM, (6) market analysis, (7) justifying KM, and (8) implementing KM. Items 5, 6, and 8 require new KM technologies.

Accenture (formally Andersen Consulting) suggests a simple plan with six-steps: (1) acquire, (2) create, (3) synthesize, (4) share, (5) use to achieve organizational goals, and (6) establish an environment conducive to knowledge sharing. The "create" and "synthesize" phases are often difficult and problematic.

PriceWaterhouseCoopers has adopted a five-step approach: (1) find, (2) filter (for relevance), (3) format (to problem), (4) forward (to the right people), and (5) feedback (from users). Steps 1–4 require system-aided supports.

Ernst & Young, one of the most savvy KM consulting firms, promotes a four-phase KM approach consisting of: (1) knowledge generation, (2) knowledge representation, (3) knowledge codification, and (4) knowledge application. However, like most other major consulting firms, they have only begun to include new data mining and text mining techniques into their KM practices.

KM Survey

A recent survey conducted jointly by the International Data Corporation (IDC) and *Knowledge Management Magazine* in May 2001 reported the status of KM practices in U.S. companies (Dyer and McDonough, 2001). Among the top three reasons for a company's adopting KM are: (1) retaining expertise of personnel, (2) increasing customer satisfaction, and (3) improving profits or increasing revenues. Knowledge management is clearly suited to capturing both internal (employees') and external (customers') knowledge.

The majority of the KM projects (29.6 percent) are cross-functional. In second place, 19.4 percent of KM projects are initiated by a CEO, rather than by other functional executives. More than 50 percent of KM projects are completed within two years.

The most significant KM implementation challenge is not due to lack of skill in KM techniques. The top four implementation challenges are nontechnical in nature: (1) employees have no time for KM, (2) the current culture does not encourage sharing, (3) lack of understanding of KM and its benefits, and (4) inability to measure financial benefits of KM. It seems clear that significant KM education, training, and cultural issues will have to be addressed in most organizations.

Because KM practices are still new to many organizations, it is not surprising that most of the techniques and systems adopted have been basic IT systems, rather than the newer data mining or text mining systems. The most widely used KM software packages, in ranked order of budget allocations, are: e-portal, document management, groupware, workflow, data warehousing, search engine, Web-based training, and messaging e-mail.

KM Functionalities

The Gartner Group arguably appears to have the most complete appreciation and understanding of KMSs. In one of its reports, a multitier KM architecture is presented (Gartner Group, 1999).

At the lowest level, an intranet and extranet that consist of platform services, network services, and distributed object models are often used as a foundation for delivery of KM applications. Databases and workgroup applications (the former deals with data and the latter with assisting people in workgroups) constitute the system components at the next level. In the Gartner Group KM architecture, this next level component is called "knowledge retrieval" (KR), which consists of text and database drivers (to handle various corporate data and information assets), KR functions, and concept and physical knowledge maps. Above the KR level, a Web-user interface is often used in business applications.

Two things are especially notable. First, the Gartner Group's KM architecture consists of applications and services that are layered and have complementary roles. No single infrastructure or system is capable of serving an organization's complete KM needs. Second, KR is considered the newest addition to the existing IT infrastructure and is the core of the entire KM architecture.

The Gartner Group presents KR functions in two dimensions. In the "semantic" dimension, bottom-up system-aided techniques that include data extraction, linguistic analysis (to process text), thesauri, dictionaries, semantic networks, and clustering (categorization/table of contents) are used to create an organization's Concept Yellow Pages. Such Concept Yellow Pages are used as organizational knowledge maps (both conceptual and physical). The proposed techniques consist of both algorithmic processes and ontology generation and usage.

In the second "collaboration" dimension, the goal is to achieve "value recommendations" identified by experts and trust advisors, community building activities, and collaborative filters. Domain experts who hold valuable tacit knowledge in an organization can then be explicitly identified and can be consulted for critical decisions.

The Gartner Group report also presents a KM landscape that consists of several types of industry players. Information retrieval (IR) vendors, such as Verity, Hummingbird, Excalibur, Open Text, and Dataware, are refining their product functioning from text retrieval to KM. They have significant experience in text processing. There are also niche document management companies, such as PCDOC and Documentum, which have developed successful products in managing document content and workflows. Large IT platform companies, such as Oracle, Lotus, and Microsoft, are aiming to improve the KR functionalities of their popular database or workgroup products. Despite their historical successes, these companies lack significant linguistic and analytical (mining) abilities to create ultimate knowledge maps for organizations. They should be referred to as information management vendors instead of KM vendors. There is as of yet little knowledge analysis or support in their systems.

The last type of vendor in the KM landscape consists of smaller, newer start-ups, such as Autonomy, Perspecta, InXight, Semio, Knowledge Computing Corporation

(KCC), and such. This set of companies has new linguistic and analytical technologies but lacks execution experience and integration ability.

Knowledge management start-ups differ widely from many Internet start-ups that often rely on fancy business models or just a fast idea. The KM start-ups often result from multiyear hard-core academic or company research making use of significant algorithmic components. For example, InXight is a technology spin-off from Xerox PARC, Autonomy is a technical company that originated at Cambridge University, and KCC is a spin-off company from The University of Arizona Artificial Intelligence Lab.

TEXT MINING: AN OVERVIEW

IR and Artificial Intelligence

As the core of KMSs, text mining is a cross between IR and artificial intelligence (AI).

Gerald Salton is generally considered one of the pioneers of IR since the 1970s. His vector space model has become the foundation for representing documents in modern IR systems and Web search engines (Salton, 1989).

Information retrieval is a field that has gone through several major generations of development. In the 1960s and 1970s, computational techniques based on inverted indexes and vector spaces were developed and tested in computer systems. In addition, Boolean retrieval methods and simple probabilistic retrieval models based on Bayesian statistics were created. Although more than 30 years old, this set of techniques still forms the basis of modern IR systems.

In the 1980s, coinciding with the developments of new AI techniques, knowledge-based and expert systems that aim to emulate expert searchers and domain specialists were developed. User modeling and natural language processing (NLP) techniques were developed to assist in representing users and documents. Research prototypes were created to represent information specialist (e.g., reference librarian) heuristics for effective online searching.

Realizing the difficulties of creating domain-specific knowledge bases and heuristics, researchers in the 1990s attempted to adopt new machine learning techniques for information analysis. Artificial intelligence techniques, including neural networks, genetic algorithms, and symbolic learning, were tested in IR (Chen, 1995).

Since the mid 1990s, the popularity of search engines and advances in Web spidering, indexing, and link analysis have transformed IR systems into newer and more powerful Internet-content search tools. The diverse multimedia content and the ubiquitous presence of the Web make both commercial users and the general public see the potential for using unstructured information assets in their everyday activities and business decisions.

It is estimated that 80 percent of the world's online content is based on text. We have developed an effective means to deal with structured, numeric content via DBMS, but text processing and analysis is significantly more difficult. The status of KMSs is much like DBMS was 20 years ago. The real challenges, and the potential payoffs for an effective, universal text solution, are equally appealing. It is inevitable that whoever dominates this space will become the next Oracle (in text).

Herbert Simon, a professor at Carnegie Mellon University, is considered one of the founding fathers of AI, which has long been striving to model and represent human intelligence in computational models and systems. Simon and his colleagues pioneered the early research in AI, most notably by creating General Problem Solvers (GPS) that emulated general human problem solving. By the 1970s, computer programs were developed to emulate rudimentary but human-like activities such as cryptarithmetic, chess, games, puzzles, etc. (Newell and Simon, 1972).

In the 1980s, there was an explosion of AI research activities, most notably in expert systems. Many research prototypes were created to emulate expert knowledge and problem solving in domains such as medical and car diagnosis, oil drilling, computer configuration, and so forth. However, the failure of many such systems in commercial arenas led many venture capitalists to back away from any ventures associated with AI. Nevertheless, commercial expert systems have made both researchers and practitioners become realistic about the strengths and weaknesses of such systems. Expert systems may not be silver bullets, but they have been proven to be suited for well-defined domains with willing experts.

In the 1990s, AI-based symbolic learning, neural-network, and genetic-programming technologies generated many significant and useful techniques for both scientific and business applications. The field of data mining is the result of significant research developed in this era. Many companies have since applied such techniques in successful fraud-detection, financial-prediction, Web-mining, and customer-behavioral analysis applications.

Both IR and AI research have contributed to a foundation for knowledge representation. For example, indexing, subject headings, dictionaries, thesauri, taxonomies, and classification schemes are some of the IR knowledge representations still widely used in various KM practices. Artificial intelligence researchers, on the other hand, have developed knowledge representation schemes such as semantic nets, production systems, logic, frames, and scripts.

With the continued expansion and popularity of Web-based scientific, governmental, and e-commerce applications in the 2000s, we foresee active research leading to autonomous Web agents with learning and data mining abilities. The field of Web mining promises to continue to provide a challenging test bed for advancing new IR and AI research.

Text Analysis Techniques

Core KMS text mining analysis techniques can be classified into four main layers: linguistic analysis/natural language processing (NLP); statistical/co-occurrence analysis; statistical and neural networks clustering/categorization; and visualization and human-computer interactions (HCI).

Linguistic Analysis/NLP

At the lowest level, linguistic analysis and natural language processing (NLP) techniques aim to identify key concept descriptors (who/what/when/where) embedded in textual documents. Different types of linguistic analysis techniques have been developed. Word and inverted index can be combined with stemming, morphological analysis, Boolean, proximity, range, and fuzzy search. The unit of analysis is the word. Phrasal analysis, on the other hand, aims to extract meaningful noun phrase units or entities (e.g., people names, organization names, location names). Both linguistic and statistical (such as mutual information) techniques are plausible. Sentence-level analysis including context-free grammar and transformational grammar can be performed to represent grammatically correct sentences. In addition, semantic analysis based on techniques such as semantic grammar and case grammar can be used to represent semantics (meaning) in sentences and stories. Semantic analysis is typically very domain-specific and lacks scalability.

Based on significant research in the IR and computational linguistics research communities, for example, the Text Retrieval Conference (TREC) and Message Understanding Conference (MUC) sponsored by the Defense Advanced Research Projects Agency (DARPA), it is generally agreed that phrasal-level analysis is most suited for coarse but scalable text mining applications. Word-level analysis is noisy and lacks precision. Sentence-level is too structured and lacks practical applications. Semantic analysis often requires a significant knowledge base or a domain lexicon creation effort and, therefore, is not suited for general-purpose text mining across a wide spectrum of domains. It is not coincidental that most of the subject headings and concept descriptors adopted in library classification schemes are noun phrases.

Statistical Co-Occurrence Analysis

Based on statistical and co-occurrence techniques, link analysis is performed to create automatic thesauri or conceptual associations of extracted concepts. Similarity functions such as Jaccard or Cosine are often used to compute co-occurrence probabilities between pairs of concepts (noun phrases). Some systems use bi-gram, tri-gram, N-gram, or Finite State Automata (FSA) to further capture frequent concept association patterns. Existing human-created dictionaries or thesauri can also be integrated with the system-generated concept thesauri.

Statistical and Neural Networks Clustering / Categorization

Statistical-and-neural-networks-based clustering and categorization techniques are often used to group similar documents, queries, or communities in subject hierarchies, which could serve as corporate knowledge maps. Hierarchical clustering (single link or multilink) and statistical clustering (e.g., multidimensional scaling, factor analysis) techniques are precise but often computationally expensive. Neural network clustering, as exemplified by the Kohonen's self-organizing map (SOM) technique, performs well and fast. It is our experience that such a technique is most suited for large-scale text-mining tasks. In addition, the SOM technique lends itself to intuitive, graphical visualization based on such visual parameters as: size (a large region represents a more important topic) and proximity (related topics are grouped in adjacent regions).

Visualization and HCI

Visualization and HCI help reveal conceptual associations and visualize knowledge maps. Different representation structures (e.g., tree, network), display dimensions (1D, 2D, 3D), and interaction techniques (e.g., zooming, spotlight) can be adopted to reveal knowledge more completely. For example, the same 2D SOM representation can be visualized in 3D by using a helicopter-style navigation based on Virtual Reality Modeling Language (VRML). However, such advanced information visualization may not be practical for business applications until more HCI field research has been performed.

It is our belief that the old way of creating subject hierarchies or knowledge maps based on human efforts (such as Yahoo!'s directory structure) is not practical or scalable. The existing amount of business information, the speed of future information acquisition activities, and the amount of human effort involved make the manual approach obsolete. Only by leveraging various system-based computational techniques can we effectively organize and structure the ever-increasing textual (and maybe multimedia) content into a useful Object-Oriented Hierarchical Automatic Yellowpage (OOHAY)—a computational approach in which we believe and which is the reverse of Yahoo!.

Case Study: Medical KM

Based on significant academic research conducted at the Artificial Intelligence Lab of the University of Arizona (http://ai.bpa.arizona.edu), we summarized a case study that used selected text mining technologies in a medical informatics application. We hope to highlight key application characteristics and system functionalities. We also compare our system with several large-scale, existing medical content services.

We would like to acknowledge the support and assistance of the following organizations: National Science Foundation (NSF), National Library of Medicine (NLM), National Institutes of Health (NIH), National Center for Supercomputing Applications (NCSA), Arizona Cancer Center, and The University of Arizona's Eller College of Business and Public Administration.

Introduction

While the problems of information overload and retrieval are prevalent across the many disciplines represented on the Internet, the ability to accurately search for, access, and process information is particularly pressing in the field of medicine. The Internet availability of vast distributed repositories of quality medical information, each with its own unique interface, has placed IR at the center of research.

At the University of Arizona's AI lab, one of our research goals is to develop tools to assist physicians and other health care professionals retrieve quality, relevant medical information and knowledge from the Internet. To this end, we developed a knowledge portal specifically for medical IR called HelpfulMed (http://ai.bpa. arizona.edu/helpfulmed). In the design of this portal, we explored three research questions of relevance to medical text mining: (1) How can linguistic parsing and statistical analysis help extract medical terminology and the relationships between terms? (2) How can medical and general ontologies help improve extraction of medical terminology? (3) How can linguistic parsing, statistical analysis, and ontologies be incorporated in customizable retrieval interfaces? In order to develop this system, we combined existing AI lab techniques for IR, using agent technology, noun phrase indexing (Tolle and Chen, 2000), automatic thesaurus generation (Houston et al., 2000), and data visualization (Chen, Schuffels and Orwig, 1996), along with a metasearch tool designed to search the deep Web of databases. These techniques have been significantly modified and enhanced for medical IR.

Medical Information Needs and Systems

Any attempt to solve the problem of information retrieval for discipline-specific users, such as those in the field of medicine, requires an understanding of the profession's characteristics and the attendant information needs. The occurrence of physicians requiring additional information to answer clinical questions is estimated to be 3.2 questions for every 10 patients seen (Ely et al., 1999). These statistics are more than compelling in light of recent studies that indicate the amount of information available to physicians is increasing while the amount of time outside of daily practice to read has remained constant (Hunt and Newman, 1997).

In addition, *researchers* in the field of medicine generally want information from primary information resources, such as journal articles, while *clinicians* want information from tertiary information resources, such as textbooks or reference sources that will help them answer clinical questions (Hersh et al., 2000). Unfortunately, most physicians and other medical researchers are not able to make full use of these systems because as medical students they are often not adequately trained to use electronic information systems (Hunt and Newman, 1997), making the task of retrieving timely and relevant sources of information even more onerous and time-consuming.

People searching for medical information constitute one of the largest percentages of Internet users (Fox and Rainie, 2001). Numerous sites have been developed to handle the demand for medical information services. We will review three of the online medical search portals currently available: National Library of

Medicine (NLM) Gateway, MD Consult, and HONSelect (Health on the Net). These three services were chosen for their popularity and acceptance in the medical community as well as their similarity to the HelpfulMED system in functionality.

NLM Gateway

The NLM's Gateway is a Web-based system designed to facilitate searching through a single interface among the 11 online retrieval systems published by the NLM, including PubMed, OLDMEDLINE, *LOCATORplus*, MEDLINE*plus,* DIRLINE, and many others. Currently, Gateway maps the terms input by the user to both MeSH terms and to terms in the Unified Medical Language System (UMLS) Metathesaurus, thereby establishing synonymy and providing relationships among 60 source vocabularies.

MD Consult

While the NLM Gateway endeavors to provide quality medical information to consumers without charge, MD Consult relies on individual subscribers or institutions, such as libraries, to pay for access. MD Consult provides access to reference books, journals, practice guidelines, drug information, news, and reports. It relies heavily on humans to assess the quality and relevance of items added to the collection.

HON

Like NLM Gateway and MD Consult, HONSelect provides access to a variety of information through one search interface. Users can choose either to search Web pages through the MedHunt service or to search a variety of databases through the HONSelect service. Web pages in the MedHunt database are collected by MARVIN, HON's Internet search spider. HONSelect is a metasearch engine that includes a collection of medical terms from MeSH, images, bibliographic references, news, and Web sites. This service integrates four databases: MEDLINE; HONMedia, a database of 1,700 medical images; NewsPage, daily medical news; and MedHunt, a full-text search engine.

HelpfulMed System Architecture

The major functionalities of HelpfulMed are: (1) Intelligent Knowledge Portal, the HelpfulMed user interface; (2) Search Medical Web Pages, which consists of search servlet and Web page database; (3) Search Medical Databases, which consists of the metasearch program and the online medical databases; (4) Related

Medical Terms, which consists of the concept space and term co-occurrence files; and (5) Visual Site Browser, which consists of SOM applet and categorization files (see Figure 17.1).

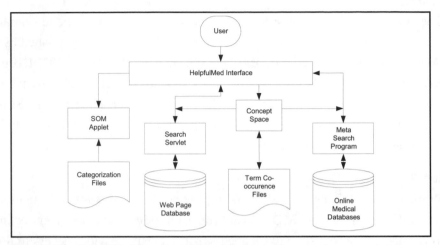

Figure 17.1 HelpfulMed system architecture.

Intelligent Knowledge Portal

A single search interface ties together the Web search, related medical terms, and database search functionalities through the use of an integrated system that allows users to interact with the various technologies offered. This is a vast improvement over conventional multiformat searching, which relies upon the user to seek out and search each database individually in order to gather all of the information available. Our integrated interface increases user satisfaction and productivity by decreasing the amount of time spent searching across multiple formats and databases.

From the initial interface, users can begin searching medical Web sites, related medical terms, and medical databases, or they can browse documents by using the visual site browser shown in Figure 17.2.

Search Medical Web Pages

The HelpfulMed Web-page search engine is designed to filter Web pages to provide not only information on the topic searched but also other high-quality medical information. Figure 17.3 is a diagram of the search engine architecture.

Figure 17.2   The HelpfulMed Intelligent Knowledge Portal.

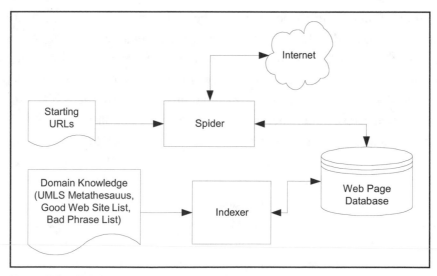

Figure 17.3   HelpfulMed search engine architecture.

A medical spider based on the Hopfield Net spreading activation algorithm is sent to collect Web pages every month and was designed specifically to retrieve medical Web pages (Chau and Chen, 2001). It is equipped with a medical vocabulary knowledge base from the Unified Medical Language System (UMLS). An inlink analysis algorithm, which compares the UMLS knowledge base to the text of the Web page, was developed to allow the spider to assess whether the Web page in question is indeed a medical Web page. In order to provide the highest quality and most finely tuned set of search results, the spider begins its search with a predefined set of high-quality URLs determined by a medical librarian. These pages are stored in the database.

The spider then begins searching the Internet and collecting related Web pages. In order to continue to collect high-quality Web pages, it is assumed that medical pages, such as the American Medical Association or the Mayo Clinic, will point only to those sites that are also of high quality. In addition, the page in question must contain UMLS phrases as consistent with the knowledge base embedded in the spider. In this manner, the spider continually casts a wider and wider net, collecting Web pages. The goal of this process is not to collect and index a large number of Web pages but to collect and index high-quality Web pages in the domain of medical information. Once the Web pages are collected, they are stored in the database and post-processed for retrieval and display.

Post-processing of the documents occurs in four steps. First, the documents are run through a noun phraser developed at the University of Arizona: the Arizona Noun Phraser (AZNP) (Tolle and Chen, 2000). This natural language processing tool is used to extract high-quality noun phrases from text, and can improve retrieval precision because it allows multiword query matching with words present in the document. The AZNP extracts noun phrases from text by, first, processing the raw text, removing any symbols or punctuation without interfering with the textual content and, next, assigning parts of speech to these words.

This implementation of the AZNP incorporates the UMLS Specialist Lexicon in order to correctly identify the parts of speech contained within medical text. Studies conducted previously by the lab have confirmed the ability of this lexicon to improve the extraction of medical phrases from text. The system converts words and parts-of-speech tags into noun phrases. Next, stop words are extracted and the remaining phrases are run against a bad lexicon in order to remove irrelevant or nonsensical phrases, such as "patient with head." Figure 17.4 shows the results from a search for the term "lung cancer."

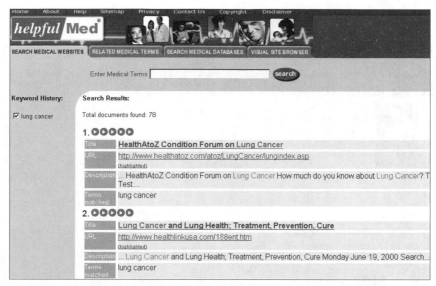

Figure 17.4   Results retrieved from a HelpfulMed search on "lung cancer."

The terms entered by the user are compared against the terms previously extracted during the post-processing phase in order to identify the most relevant Web pages (see Figure 17.5). The system displays the Web pages in ranked order. Ranking of the results is based on the presence of query keywords in the document and the inlink score. An inlink score is computed based on the number of documents that point to a page, following the theory that the more pages that point to a given page, the greater acceptance of the source as reliable. Hopfield Net searching, phrase indexing, UMLS boosting, and inlink ranking combine in our system to collect and present Web pages that are assured to be medical in nature and of high quality (Chau and Chen, 2001).

MD Consult does not provide access to Web pages, while access through NLM Gateway is via one of NLM's other products: Medline*plus*, which is NLM's consumer information gateway. HONSelect provides access to Web pages; however, the keywords are not highlighted in the returned document.

Search Medical Databases

As was mentioned previously, current search engines are able to capture only what is being called the "surface Web," that is, those Web pages that are hyperlinked to other pages over the Web. However, there is also a deep Web of databases

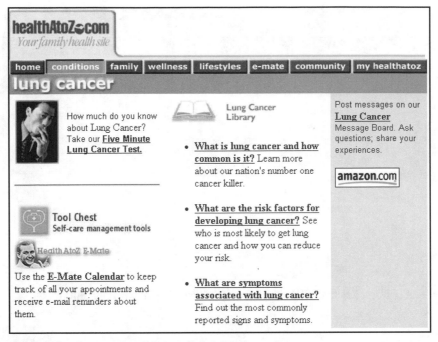

Figure 17.5   Page retrieved from a HelpfulMed search.

and other sites that respond only to specific queries. While an initial page for a database may appear in a collection of Web pages because it has been hyperlinked from another page, the information contained within that database is effectively lost to searchers unless they choose to search it specifically. HelpfulMed provides access to a variety of databases currently publicly available on the Internet. These include citation databases, such as MEDLINE and CANCERLIT, and online reference works, such as the *Merck Manual of Diagnosis and Treatment* and *Physicians Data Query* (PDQ), which provide peer-reviewed summaries on cancer treatment, screening and detection, prevention, genetics, and supportive care. Access is also provided to evidence-based medicine (EBM) databases, such as the American College of Physicians Journal Club (ACP), National Guidelines Clearinghouse (NGC), and the York Database of Abstracts of Reviews of Effectiveness (DARE). Medical librarians at the Arizona Health Sciences library selected these databases as being those with the most comprehensive and accurate information. Access to these systems provides those searching for medical information with a much richer representation

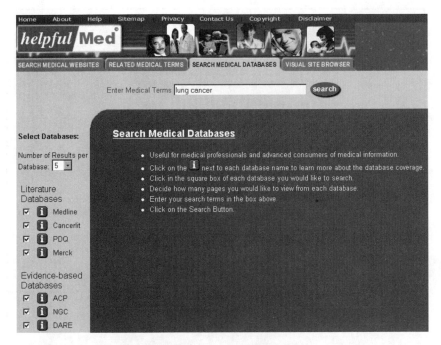

Figure 17.6   Search Medical Databases page in HelpfulMed.

of information for diagnosis and treatment. A growing area for physicians is EBM. Its goal is to combine the expertise of medical personnel with the best evidence available from research.

When searching for information in medical databases via HelpfulMed, the user is able to choose databases of interest. In Figure 17.6, the user has chosen to search all of the available databases by placing a check mark in the boxes next to each of the databases' names. The user can also indicate how many results from each database s/he would like the system to retrieve; the default is five, but the user can choose to see the results in increments of five up through 50. This gives the user some control over the retrieval process and lessens the effects of information overload.

From the retrieved results page (see Figure 17.7), the user is able to follow interesting links and see the terms that are searched as highlighted in the text of the Web page. This helps the user quickly identify whether the document is useful (see Figure 17.8).

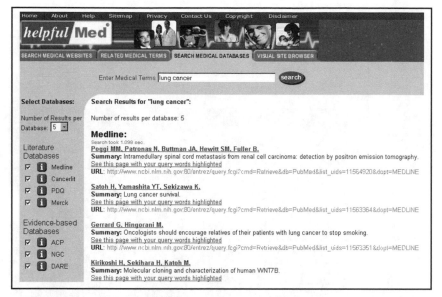

Figure 17.7   Retrieved results list from online medical databases.

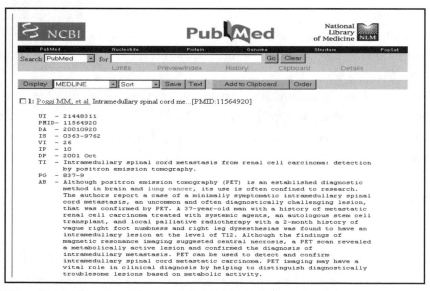

Figure 17.8   Page returned from database search with term highlighted.

The ability to search other databases, particularly MEDLINE, is consistent throughout NLM Gateway, MD Consult, and HONSelect; however, only MD Consult, like HelpfulMed, allows users to search EBM through its interface. National Library of Medicine Gateway provides a link to its EBM, HSTAT, via a link on the left side of the screen; HONSelect does not provide this service.

Related Medical Terms

This section of HelpfulMed is a concept space of medical-related terms. A *concept space* is an automatic thesaurus for domain-specific terms developed by the AI lab. It is called "concept space" because the goal is to create meaningful and understandable domain-specific concept spaces (networks of terms and weighted associations) that could represent the concepts (terms) and their associations for the underlying *information spaces* (i.e., documents in different domain-specific databases). This system also assists in concept-based, cross-domain information retrieval. What differentiates a concept space from traditional subject heading lists or thesauri is that rather than being developed and assigned by human experts, a concept space is created wholly from phrases contained within each of the documents processed. In other words, it is a thesaurus of terms drawn directly from the documents housed in the collection.

Concept space technology uses advanced indexing and analysis techniques to suggest other related and relevant search terms. These techniques are based on the computed relationships between terms. Building a concept space is a four-step process: (1) identifying the document collection, (2) automatic indexing, (3) co-occurrence analysis, and (4) associative retrieval.

In order to create a concept space, a collection of documents must first be identified and analyzed in order to separate unstructured free text from structured data fields. For the medical concept space, we used the MEDLINE collection of about 10 million abstracts. We built two concept spaces, the first of which was based on controlled vocabulary for medical subject headings (MeSH) because this is the vocabulary used to index documents in MEDLINE. The second concept space was built using noun-phrasing techniques. As discussed earlier, noun phrasing parses input files by combining adjacent words into phrases, using punctuation and stop-words as phrase delimiters. Because the application is capable of assigning parts of speech to a word, it generates phrases by making multiple passes through the phrasing rules (Tolle and Chen, 2000).

In order to calculate the importance of each term relative to the content of a document, we used phrase frequency and inverse-document frequency to assign relative importance to documents based on weight. The number of times the phrase occurs in a document (phrase frequency) and the number of documents in which the phrase appears (document frequency) are computed. This weighting of terms ensures that a document containing a brief mention of a topic receives a lower rating than documents that mention the topic quite often, thereby creating a richer representation of a document's content and its relationships to other documents in the collection. The resulting MEDLINE-based concept space consists of 48.5 million terms and 1.7 billion relationships. It was generated by an eight-node SGI/Cray supercomputer at the AI lab and took 18 days to run.

A search in the "Related Cancer Terms" section provides the user with a list of additional terms that might more accurately describe the information needed. If the user inputs "lung cancer" at this point (see Figure 17.9), the system will return a list of related noun phrases (N) and MeSH terms (M), plus a list of authors (A). Thus, the user can decide if s/he wants to search phrases extracted from the text, related medical subjects headings, authors, or any combination of the three. In Figure 17.9, the user has chosen "Occupational Diseases" and "Adenocarcinoma"

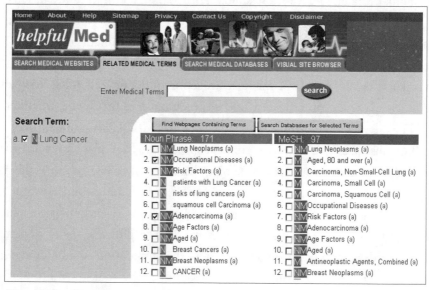

Figure 17.9 Concept space results.

as additional terms to be searched by placing a check mark in the box next to each term. When the user has finished building the search, s/he can choose to either "Find Webpages Containing Terms" or "Search Databases for Selected Terms."

As mentioned previously, NLM Gateway provides users with the ability to expand or refine searches based on vocabulary from both MeSH and the UMLS Metathesaurus, which can boost the precision of results returned. The UMLS Metathesaurus provides high precision and accuracy; the medical concept space provides more fine-grained and high-recall retrieval. The 2001 version of the UMLS Metathesaurus contains 1.9 million terms (National Library of Medicine, 2001), while the medical concept space contains 48.5 million terms.

Visual Site Browser

The Visual Site Browser, also called MEDMap, is a graphical system designed to facilitate the information browsing behavior of users in the domain of medical-related research. The input data to MEDMap consists of 10 million medical abstracts obtained from MEDLINE. By applying indexing, noun phrasing, and SOM techniques, MEDMap generates a subject hierarchy that contains 132,700 categories and 4,586 maps. The MEDMap also combines a text-based alphabetical display and a graphical approach to represent the subject categories generated (see Figure 17.10).

Automatic category generation is a three-step process. Two types of information analysis techniques are used in this process: *automatic indexing* and *clustering*. The third part of the generation process is *expert intervention*, which integrates an expert's domain knowledge with information analysis techniques in order to create meaningful subject categories.

Automatic Indexing is the process of representing a document automatically with a vector of terms (Salton, 1989). The indexing tool used by the CancerMap consists of two parts. The first operation uses the AZNP noun-phrasing tool to identify relevant noun phrases (Tolle and Chen, 2000). The NLP noun-phrasing technique has been used in IR to capture a richer linguistic representation of document content. It has potential over other document indexing techniques to improve precision since it allows multiword (or multiphrase) matching. The second operation is to select a subset of the phrases extracted to represent a document. The indexing tool selects phrases according to the phrase frequency (number of times a phrase occurs in a document) and document frequency (number of documents in which a phrase occurs).

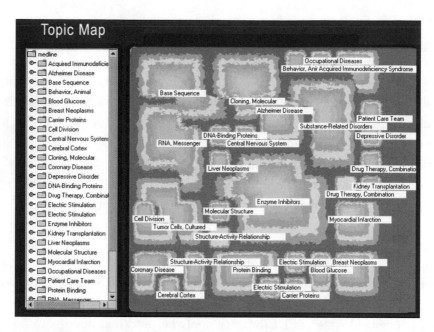

Figure 17.10   Alphabetical list and graphic map of Visual Site Browser.

Clustering is the assignment of items to groups based on semantic association. After examining several neural algorithms in previous research, we concluded that a variant of Kohonen's SOM (Kohonen, 1995) appeared to be the most promising for organizing large volumes of information. For instance, Orwig, Chen, and Nunamaker (1997) applied SOM as a categorization technique to facilitate Internet information browsing, while Ramsey, Chen, Zhu, and Schatz (1999) employed SOM to categorize information in numerical and image media types. During the MEDMap creation, we applied SOM repeatedly to generate hierarchical subject categories in the same way Chen, Houston, Sewell, and Schatz (1998) did in Entertainment (ET)-map generation.

Using the Visual Site Browser, the user is able to "drill down" through the levels of a map, browsing for topics of interest until a collection of documents is eventually reached. In the case shown in Figure 17.11, the user chose to browse the phrase "liver neoplasms," which is circled. Figure 17.12 displays the map for "liver neoplasms." The user chose to explore the phrase "liver cirrhosis," which is circled on the map and in the alphabetic display in Figure 17.12. The user continued refining

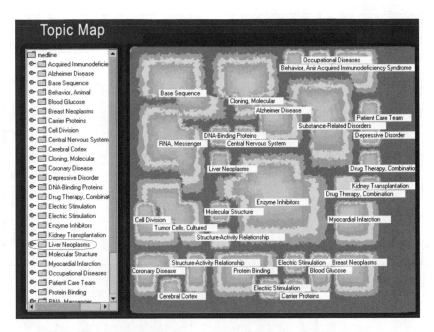

Figure 17.11   First layer of MEDMap with liver neoplasms circled.

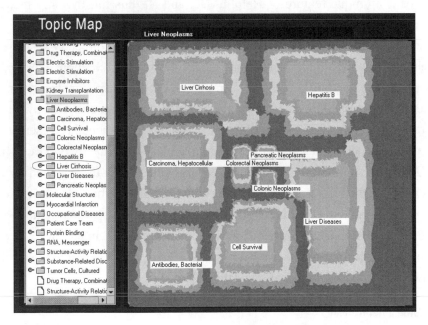

Figure 17.12   Liver neoplasm map with liver cirrhosis circled.

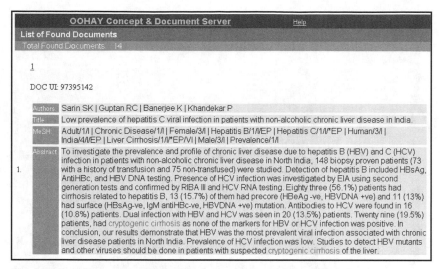

Figure 17.13   Document returned for "cryptogenic cirrhosis."

the search until a relevant document was found (see Figure 17.13). Visual Site Browser is a unique feature of HelpfulMed, and is, thus far, the only medically related online retrieval system known to provide this service.

We believe this approach would be useful when browsing directory systems such as Yahoo!. However, unlike Yahoo! and other directory search engines, Visual Site Browser was created by a computer through a comprehensive analysis of a large collection of quality and time-critical documents rather than designed by humans. The result is a more efficient use of time and a more fine-grained representation of content. The process of creating the MEDMap took approximately two weeks using an SGI/Cray eight-node supercomputer. We also believe that the map and its visual clues facilitate the browsing of large collections. The size of the "islands" represents the size of the content contained below each island, and the spatial proximity of the islands indicates semantic proximity between the categories. In addition, the visual clue of island "layers" represents map "levels." Thus, when clicking on each level, the user is provided with visual orientation clues.

Conclusions: HelpfulMed

In this in-depth case study, we discussed the development of an intelligent medical knowledge portal to serve the information-seeking needs of medical professionals, researchers, and other advanced users. The functionalities of this system have the potential to increase user satisfaction by providing the capability to search multiple information spaces through one interface, and by providing mechanisms that allow users to refine and focus their searches through the use of an automatically generated thesaurus and knowledge maps.

Future development work includes integrating additional technology that will summarize the documents retrieved from the Web and other searchable databases. In addition, a dynamic SOM that categorizes documents retrieved from the Web based on user-chosen attributes, such as noun phrases, is in development, as is a concept-space-based related-terms "suggester," which will present additional terms to the user as the result from a search for Web pages. We are also in the process of conducting a large-scale field study involving user subjects from the Arizona Cancer Center and the Arizona Health Science Library.

The Future

What are the future research areas for KMSs and text mining in general? What are the applications and technologies that may affect future knowledge workers?

Semantic Web

The current Web infrastructure is one of hypertext syntax and structure. The HTML hyperlinks do not suggest any semantic or meaningful relationships between Web pages. We only know that two hyperlinked pages have some sort of relationship. How to represent semantics on the Web and to create a semantic Web of meaningful interconnected Web objects and content is a challenging research topic. Some researchers suggest richer Web content notations and inference rules, such as XML and RDF, others suggest a system-aided machine-learning approach to extracting semantic associations between objects.

Multilingual Web

The Web has increasingly become more international and multicultural. The non-English Web content has experienced the strongest growth over the past few years. In addition, the globalization and e-commerce trend has created much multilingual intranet content for multinational corporations or companies with international partners. How can we create a multilingual knowledge portal so that users can experience seamless cross-lingual information retrieval (e.g., searching for Chinese government regulations using English queries) and real-time machine translation? The most immediate application of a multilingual Web would be in international marketing and intelligence analysis for multinational corporations.

Multimedia Web

We believe multimedia data mining is a trend that cannot be reversed. Although it may not become a dominant part of corporate information assets (unlike structured data and unstructured text), it does fill an important gap in corporate KM.

Wireless Web

Although we believe that the majority of Web content will still be accessed over high-speed wired networks, wireless applications will continue to grow in years to come. They will also emerge and proliferate rapidly in selected high-impact application areas, e.g., e-mail, financial stock quotes, curbside law enforcement alerting (via PDA and cell phone), and so forth. For knowledge workers who are mobile and time-pressed, wireless KM will not be a luxury but a necessity in a not-so-distant future.

KM Killer-apps

We believe KMS researchers and practitioners need to identify areas of high-impact, high-return research and implementations. These applications would allow knowledge workers to better (more effectively and efficiently) perform their tasks in a highly demanding and fast-paced environment. Several application areas come to mind: medical informatics and analysis (as demonstrated in our case study), law enforcement and intelligence analysis (as evident after the 9/11 tragedy), and business and marketing intelligence analysis (as shown in many successful data mining and customer relationships management [CRM] applications in the industry). With more mainstream implementations and success stories, both KMS and text mining will be positioned to make a significant and long-lasting impact on society.

REFERENCES

Chau, M. and Chen H. (2001). A Hopfield Net spreading activation approach to locating domain-specific web pages. AI Lab Technical Report.

Chen, H. (1995). Machine learning for information retrieval: Neural networks, symbolic learning, and genetic algorithms. *Journal of the American Society for Information Science*, 46(3), 194–216.

Chen, H., Houston, A. L., Sewell, R. R., and Schatz, B. R. (1998). Internet browsing and searching: User evaluation of category map and concept space techniques. *Journal of the American Society for Information Science*, 49(7), 582–603.

Chen, H., Schuffels, C., and Orwig, R. (1996). Internet categorization and search: A machine learning approach. *Journal of Visual Communications and Image Representation*, 7(1), 88–102.

Dyer, G. and McDonough, B. (2001). The state of KM. *Knowledge Management*, May, 31–36.

Ely, J.W., Osheroff, J. A., Ebell, M. H., Bergus, G. R., Levy, B. T., Chambliss, M. L. and Evans, E. R. (1999). Analysis of questions asked by family doctors regarding patient care. *British Medical Journal*, 319(7206), 358–361.

Fox, S. and Rainie, L. (2001). The online health care revolution: How the web helps Americans take better care of themselves. http://www.pewinternet.org/ Accessed May 15, 2003.

Gartner Group. (1999). Knowledge Management Report, Summer.

Hersh, W. R., Brown, K. E., Donohoe, L. C., Campbell, E. M., and Horachek, A. E. (1996). CliniWeb: Managing clinical information on the World Wide Web. *Journal of the American Medical Informatics Association*, 3(4), 273–280.

Houston, A. L., Chen, H., Schatz, B. R., Hubbard, S. M., Sewell, R. R. and Ng, T. D. (2000). Exploring the use of concept space to improve medical information retrieval. *International Journal of Decision Support Systems*, 30(2),171–186.

Hunt, R. H. and Newman, R. G. (1997). Medical knowledge overload: A disturbing trend for physicians. *Health Care Management Review*, 22(1), 70–75.

Kohonen, T. (1995). *Self-organizing Map*, Springer-Verlag, Berlin.

MD Consult. (2001). About searching. http://home.mdconsult.com Accessed July 12, 2003.

National Library of Medicine. (2001). UMLS Knowledge Sources. U.S. Dept. of Health and Human Services, National Institutes of Health, National Library of Medicine, Bethesda, MD.

Newell, A. and Simon, H. (1972). *Human Problem Solving*, Prentice-Hall, Englewood Cliffs, NJ.

Orwig, R., Chen, H., and Nunamaker, J. F. (1997). A graphical, self-organizing approach to classifying electronic meeting output. *Journal of the American Society for Information Science*, 48(2), 157–170.

Ramsey, M., Chen, H., Zhu, B., and Schatz, B. R. (1999). A collection of visual thesauri for browsing collections of geographic images. *Journal of the American Society for Information Science*, 50(9), 826–835.

Salton, G. (1989). *Automatic Text Processing*, Addison-Wesley, Reading, MA.

Tolle, K. M. and Chen, H. (2000). Comparing noun phrasing techniques for use with medical digital library tools. *Journal of the American Society for Information Science*, 51(4), 352–370.

CHAPTER 18

A Win–Win Situation: Knowledge Management and the Institutional Archives

Gregory S. Hunter, Long Island University

There are different views about what constitutes KM, but virtually everyone agrees that there is an "explicit" component—knowledge that is already recorded in some way (Platt, 2000; Dalrymple, 2000). One of the major repositories of such recorded knowledge is the institutional archives. However, this resource remains largely untapped in KM initiatives.

I believe there are two reasons for this situation. First, the leaders of KM initiatives do not understand the nature, purpose, and resources of institutional archives. Second, the managers of many institutional archives do not appreciate how they can support KM, thereby increasing the archives' usefulness to the institution. This chapter will explore each aspect.

THE NATURE, PURPOSE, AND RESOURCES OF AN INSTITUTIONAL ARCHIVES

One reason why archives may not be used in KM initiatives involves confusion over terminology. In the past, it was easier to understand the meaning of archives. There was a general sense that archives consisted of items retained for a long period of time. The information age, however, has led to confusion. "Archiving" a word-processing document, for example, now means saving it on a floppy disk, perhaps only for a day or two. Therefore, the distinction between long- and short-term retention has been blurred.

According to archivists, there are three possible meanings of *archives*:

- *Material.* The noncurrent records of an organization or institution preserved because of their enduring value.

- *Place.* The building or part of a building where archival materials are located (also referred to as an archival repository).
- *Agency.* The program office or agency responsible for identifying, preserving, and making available records of enduring value (also referred to as an archival agency, archival institution, or archival program) (Hunter, 1997; O'Toole, 1992).

It is not enough just to have a collection of old records stored in a space unsuitable for any other purpose. For archives to make a contribution to a KM initiative, there must be a program (with trained professionals) as well as historic materials.

The mission of the archivist has three elements: identifying records and papers of enduring value, preserving them, and making them available to patrons.

It is important to note that this mission statement talks about records of enduring rather than permanent value. This subtle change of wording is relatively recent. Archivists know that most records will not last forever, despite our best intentions. Fragile physical media, atmospheric pollutants, and improper handling all take their toll. More importantly, the research value of the records may change over time, making them expendable for historic purposes. If we define archival records as having permanent value, we have bestowed sainthood on them—and have limited our ability to condemn them later. Records of enduring value are beatified—a state below sainthood. In this way, archivists maintain future flexibility while still treating the records with reverential care (Rapport, 1981).

Archivists used to think of the elements of their mission in a linear fashion: from identification through preservation, to reference and access. This reflects the order in which archival tasks usually are accomplished. Today, however, archivists increasingly are taking a cyclical view of their work, focusing more on the objective of their work (use of the collections) than on the progression of activities (Hunter, 1997).

The nature of an archival materials has expanded in recent years. While paper still predominates, many archives have extensive collections of other media: photographs, sound recordings, videotapes, and films. In the corporate world, it also is common to have collections of advertising art, product packaging, and product samples. All of these materials become potential resources for a KM program.

In addition to records and artifacts, institutional archives often conduct oral history interviews. The best oral history programs document more than the facts or events; they seek to document the meaning behind events and actions. In effect, archivists are identifying sources of tacit knowledge (in the memories of people) and making them explicit and transferable through the oral history interview process. Web technologies now are making oral history transcripts and recordings widely accessible within the organization, often for the first time.

In all of these ways, strong institutional archives increasingly are being seen as an essential component of a KM program. Archivists, in turn, must be willing to meet this expanded role.

RELATING THE ARCHIVES TO KM

Thomas H. Davenport and Laurence Prusak (1998) have identified five aspects of "common sense" about KM:

1. Focus first on high-value knowledge.
2. Begin with a focused pilot project, let it build demand, and then pursue other initiatives.
3. Work along the multiple fronts of technology, organization, and culture.
4. Don't put off what gives you the most trouble until it's too late.
5. When necessary, get help from others within the organization as quickly as possible.

These five practical lessons can focus the institutional archivist's entry into KM.

High-value knowledge is something that archives possess in abundance. Not only do archives preserve the various facts of institutional existence, they also capture the meaning and significance of those facts. In particular, archives preserve and transmit the organization's culture—the values, heroes, and rituals that give meaning to organizational life. Similar information is difficult to find elsewhere in the organization.

Focused pilot projects will be a necessity for institutional archives, most of which have small staffs that cannot be diverted from other activities. Several archives have found it useful to begin with audiovisual assets, a perfect resource for sharing and reuse. Beginning small, with photographs or videos heavily used in the past, is an easy way to build demand.

Archivists also need to deal aggressively with difficult problems. One of the most vexing problems facing organizations is how to organize diverse resources. Librarians and archivists would call this "knowledge organization" or "bibliographic control." In several corporations, archivists have either led or been part of task forces to develop taxonomies or classification schemes. The need to control Web resources is pushing this development. An archivist looking to become involved in KM might volunteer to lead taxonomy development, a task that few people in an organization covet.

Archivists are accustomed to getting help from others. For example, successful efforts to manage electronic records feature partnerships with IT and user departments (Hunter, 2000). In fact, because the archivist already deals with individuals throughout the organization, he or she is a valuable ally in many parts of a KM program, such as building directories of tacit/hidden staff expertise.

PRACTICAL ADVICE FROM THE FIELD

For the past five years, a small group of high-level corporate archivists has met to discuss areas of common interest. Calling itself the Corporate Archives Forum (CAF), the group has shared its meeting notes with the wider professional community. On several occasions, group members discussed KM programs. The following comments reflect the front line experiences of working archivists, recounted largely in their own words:

- **From the CAF 2000 Meeting**

  "Knowledge management is what archivists do. We identify and maintain knowledge and make it accessible. Archives are one of the few, real cross-functional areas in a corporation."

  "Archives are a very cost-effective KM component: The information already has been paid for. However, the archives seldom are acknowledged by midlevel people."

  "Very often, KM is equated with technology alone. Archivists have to try to educate people within their corporations that KM also means content." One archivist "found that oral history interviews are key content that can be integrated into KM initiatives." Another archivist has been conducting oral history interviews since 1984. "Oral histories have been used to document new product development, one of the main ways of growing a business."

  "One issue is: Which archival knowledge do we want to make accessible to everyone in the corporation? Full-text oral history interviews may not be at the top of the list. What might be most valuable are case studies produced with training as well as marketing departments."

"One archives has been emphasizing cataloging (sorting and organizing). They are working closely with the corporate Knowledge Architecture committee to create a metadata registry."

"A great deal of effort has gone into developing 'best practices' Web sites within corporations. These sites receive very little use. Employees still call up the archives and ask for information. People don't want to take the time to search the Internet. The self-help tools are not yet in place. There also would need to be a change in corporate culture"

- **From the CAF 1999 Meeting**

"The archivist serves as a 'directional resource' within the company. The archivist has general information about 'who creates what' within the corporation."

"Knowledge management has a 'networking aspect.' The archives need to jump on the bandwagon or be left behind."

"One archives is part of the information sciences (IS) department, which is at the center of KM. The IS department is providing the intellectual framework and the knowledge architecture for the entire company. The archives will provide a layer that people can use for interactions—a controlled vocabulary and schema for dialog."

"The archives 'owns' the product vocabulary database. This is a major contribution to KM. This will form the basis of search systems and knowledge mapping."

"Knowledge management is nothing new, especially for archives. The biggest difference is the networking component. We have not had the technical capabilities before. Capturing and sharing information is new to corporations."

During its 1999 meeting, CAF attendees summarized the elements of a successful archival approach to KM. The five points were as follows:

1. Don't try to run the whole thing.
2. Corporations have technologies that they don't know how to organize. Archival involvement (often with librarians) in thesaurus construction and indexing can make a contribution.
3. Management sees KM as a technology issue, but it goes beyond this. Archives can help with the intellectual components and control. Archives can help with content identification and preservation.

4. Knowledge management vendors are selling tools, not expertise. Archivists have the expertise.

5. Archival involvement on a small KM committee often is a good idea.

Conclusion

As one archivist noted here, capturing and sharing information is new to many organizations. Making full use of the institutional archives also may be a new experience. A KM initiative can make the archives more visible within, and valuable to its parent institution. It also can help the archivist to better understand the organization he/she serves. This is a prerequisite for identifying and preserving an organization's historic records. Clearly, the combination of KM and archives is a win-win situation.

References

Corporate Archives Forum (CAF). Meeting Notes, June 17–18, 1999. Available at http://www.hunterinformation.com/caf1999.htm

Corporate Archives Forum (CAF). Meeting Notes, June 22–23, 2000. Available at http://www.hunterinformation.com/caf2000.htm

Dalrymple, Prudence W. "Knowledge Management in the Health Sciences," in T. Kanti Srikantaiah and Michael E. D. Koenig, eds., *Knowledge Management for the Information Professional*. Medford, NJ: Information Today, Inc. for ASIS, 2000, 389–403.

Daniels, Maygene F., and Timothy Walch, eds. *A Modern Archives Reader: Basic Readings on Archival Theory and Practice*. Chicago: Society of American Archivists, 1984.

Davenport, Thomas H. and Laurence Prusak. *Working Knowledge: How Organizations Manage What They Know*. Boston: Harvard Business School Press, 1998.

Dearstyne, Bruce W. *The Archival Enterprise: Modern Archival Principles, Practices, and Management Techniques*. Chicago: American Library Association, 1993.

Duckett, Kenneth W. *Modern Manuscripts: A Practical Manual for Their Management, Care and Use*. Nashville, TN: American Association for State and Local History, 1975.

Hunter, Gregory S. *Developing and Maintaining Practical Archives*. New York: Neal-Schuman, 1997.

Hunter, Gregory S. *Preserving Digital Information*. New York: Neal-Schuman, 2000.

O'Toole, James M. *Understanding Archives and Manuscripts*. Chicago: Society of American Archivists, 1992.

Platt, Nina. "Knowledge Management: Can It Exist in a Law Office?" in T. Kanti Srikantaiah and Michael E. D. Koenig, eds., *Knowledge Management for the Information Professional*. Medford, NJ: Information Today, Inc. for ASIS, 2000, 405–417.

Rapport, Leonard. "No Grandfather Clause: Reappraising Accessioned Records." *American Archivist*, 44 (spring 1981): 143–150.

Smith, George David. "Dusting Off the Cobwebs: Turning the Business Archives into a Managerial Tool," *American Archivist*, 45 (summer 1982): 287–290.

Part IV

Knowledge Management Applications– Communities of Practice

Knowledge Management Applications— Communities of Practice

Introductory Notes

In terms of what has been implemented, communities of practice are undoubtedly the largest component of KM, and that is likely to be true for some considerable time. For the person or organization looking to get into KM, this is certainly a key area on which to focus. Almost any organization's implementation of KM will centrally involve communities of practice.

It is ironic that much of the enthusiasm for KM, and specifically for communities of practice, derives and descends as Ponzi indicates in Chapter 2 from the writings of Nonaka on tacit knowledge; however, this remains one of the least developed areas of KM. Chapter 24 by Srikantaiah on KM and the World Bank discusses one of the few concrete attempts to harness tacit knowledge.

These and similar themes are described in the Road Map following the Table of Contents.

"Communities of Practice" is a theme elaborated on in that Road Map. A closely related theme is "Roles in KM."

Additional chapters that call attention to those themes but are outside of this section include:

Chapter 4	Critical Success Factors of Knowledge Management Farida Hasanali, American Productivity and Quality Center
Chapter 32	Incentives and Techniques for the Promotion of Knowledge Sharing Ruth A. Palmquist, Dominican University

Alive with the Fire of Shared Understanding: Implementing Knowledge Management in the Department of the Navy

Alex Bennet, Mountain Quest Institute

In 1999, at a U.S. Navy Knowledge Superiority Workshop held at the Naval Academy in Annapolis, Maryland, a senior leadership team recognized the reliance of the Department of the Navy (DON) on the creativity, ingenuity, and intellect of its people. Knowledge superiority was named as a second plank in the maritime concept, alongside the commitment of the Department to forward presence. In vibrant words, the team described the future organization:

> Transcending even our current advantage in physical firepower, our Navy will be alive with the fire of shared understanding. We will do this because we must for our Navy's relevance and readiness in this new era. No foe, present or future, will match our knowledge or our ability to apply it.

In May 2002, the DON was identified as one of North America's Leading Knowledge Enterprises,[1] the only public sector organization to receive this recognition. Other world-class leaders in managing knowledge to deliver superior performance included Accenture, Buckman Laboratories, Clarica Life Insurance, Ernst & Young, General Electric, International Business Machines (IBM), McKinsey & Company, Microsoft, and Xerox. The Navy was specifically noted for the leadership of its knowledge-based programs and initiatives, and for its emphasis on organizational learning.

During the past four years there have been thousands of important initiatives and achievements—and even more learning—as the DON has moved toward knowledge centricity. As a Navy executive and change agent writing about the Department, my usual approach has been from the outside in. I discuss the big enterprise-level initiatives, such as creation of the Navy Marine Corps Intranet (which is being created through the use of a seat management contract!), and the wonderful groundwork laid through early development of an Information Architecture and Standards and, over the past few years, a knowledge taxonomy. These are all significant initiatives. Let's face it, we live in a technology-driven world; where the larger concept of "Defense" is concerned, it is absolutely essential that we as a country stay on the front line of technology insertion. But what we have learned along the way is that all the information in the world—enabled by the best IT—proves insignificant if our decision makers cannot access and use it in support of the organizational mission.

The DON is built around people: a cadre of Naval, Marine Corps, civilian, and contract personnel dedicated to defense of the nation. Most of these people have altruistic reasons for serving and a strong sense of responsibility to larger national ideals. The incredibly high social capital of this organization based on this silent patriotism is enhanced by the fluid movement of people in and out of assignments, across organizational and functional boundaries, and, indeed, in and out of the Department itself. The KM story of the Department, then, begins with them.

THE EVERYDAY LIFE OF DEFENSE

Out on the U.S.S. San Jacinto, deployed in the Indian Ocean, Petty Officer Storm has run into a problem with a winch motor. Last year, when experiencing the same problem, he had to wait until the next port visit to have repairs done. With the advent of the Navy Marine Corps Intranet, he quickly hops to the computer, pulls up a virtual meeting software program, and within minutes via satellite has direct access to a telemaintenance expert at the Naval Surface Warfare Center in Crane, Indiana. During the next 20 minutes, while viewing equipment blueprints on his computer screen, he learns how to effect the repair. Through connectivity and good KM, he has solved the problem within the hour.[2]

While forward deployed, Gunnery Sergeant Jackson notices unusual patterns on his detection device, indicating the possible presence of a biological agent. He reaches back to the Centers for Disease Control and Prevention in Atlanta, Georgia, for advice and via computer transmits the information from his biological agent detection device to their special analysis computers. Using KM systems, historical and other extant data are quickly processed and analyzed to determine the threat level. The gunnery sergeant is immediately linked to the experts at Ft. Dietrick, Maryland, who identify appropriate procedures, which are then downloaded to his laptop. Simultaneously, the Joint Command Center is alerted, and nearby platoons are warned of possible biological attack.[2]

Seaman Nottingham expects his first child in April. While on deployment in the North Atlantic in early March, he receives an urgent message that there are complications and the baby must be delivered immediately by cesarean section. As the expectant father reads information from the Virtual Naval Hospital and researches the procedure on the Internet, beside himself with worry, he is able to open a dialogue with experts at Bethesda Naval Hospital. Shortly after the successful birth, the executive officer of his ship sets up a video teleconference with the hospital and Seaman Nottingham's wife introduces their new daughter.[2]

Through connectivity, access to and exchange of valid information, and the expertise and judgment of people with the right knowledge at the right time to share where and as needed, our forces stay alert and watchful 24/7 in defense of our country. These people are living and working in an organization committed to ubiquitous communication and invisible technology, where through information sharing and organizational learning built on trust and respect, people at all levels can make and implement efficient and agile decisions. And that includes a commitment to providing the best doing and thinking skills possible as the new virtual world continues to emerge.

Building Knowledge from the Inside Out

In the Fall of 2001, the Department published a virtual resource CD entitled Learning in a Virtual World, a reflection of several years of developing and implementing learning programs and breaking old paradigms of traditional approaches to training and education. While focused on operationalizing eLearning throughout the Navy, the toolkit serves as a resource for exploring eLearning through both theory and application. The toolkit provides eLearning tools such as an IT product matrix, an automated career planning tool, and assessment instruments for individuals and organizations to help determine their readiness for eLearning. The toolkit also connects users to communities and collaboration sites, and provides a course on virtual communications.

Systems Thinking

To help facilitate strategic thinking, the Department invested in developing an enterprise learning program based on the Systems Thinking work initiatives by the Massachusetts Institute of Technology and shared broadly through publication of *The Fifth Discipline*.[3] Systems Thinking facilitates both individual and organizational learning. It is an approach to understanding complex systems (such as organizations) that have many elements and relationships, providing a conceptual framework and visual way of describing multiple causality relationships that include both positive and negative feedback loops as well as time delays and nonlinear influences. With the Internet providing availability and access to an ever-increasing amount of data and information, the ability to recognize patterns and relationships among a large amount of data and information becomes essential for good decision making.

The application of Systems Thinking also encourages groups to open a dialogue and develop a common understanding of a complex problem within the organization, thereby learning from each other. Systems Thinking helps restructure views of reality by identifying and challenging prevailing mental models and fundamental assumptions and by promoting double-loop learning. In the process of understanding how organizations work, Systems Thinking encourages exploration of multiple viewpoints to any problem through dialogue and discussion. It is through such knowledge sharing and creation processes that KM and organizational learning benefit each other.

The DON developed a multimedia course on Systems Thinking that addresses the acquisition of cognitive skills at the level of the individual. Available on CD and online through the Navy eLearning Network, the course provides room for the novice and those who have already been introduced to Systems Thinking to expand and test their knowledge and ability to apply it. In the Summer of 2000, the Master Chief of the Navy pulled together all the Master Chiefs in the Navy to learn Systems Thinking skills, before moving toward embedding this individual learning into the training of enlisted personnel.

Information Literacy

Today's workplace demands a new kind of worker. Data is dispatched in picoseconds and gigabits; and this deluge of information must be sorted, evaluated, and applied. It is estimated that the average person spends 150 hours per year looking for information. There is no lack of information in the world; however, the skills needed to search, select, evaluate, and use information can vary from total lack of information skills to some level of literacy. How we solve this discrepancy will depend on our ability to embrace a new basic competency, what is

Here are just a few of the questions addressed in the DON Information Literacy Toolkit, one of a half dozen virtual resources to help the DON—and its partners in government, industry, and academia—stay current in the virtual world:

- Do you recognize when you need information? All the time?
- Can you name at least two search engines?
- Can you find basic facts on the Internet?
- Can you analyze the data you get on the Internet for validity and reliability? Are you always sure where your information comes from?
- Do you know how to identify a computer hoax or urban legend?
- Do you know how to request permission to use information under copyright?
- Do you know the basic steps to ensure your online privacy?
- Do you know what browser you are using?
- Do you know what the deep Web is and that it has 500 times more information than the surface Web we usually surf?

called information literacy (IL), a significant contribution to KM implementation in the DON and the government at large.

Information literacy is a set of information- and knowledge-age skills that enables individuals to recognize when information is and is not needed and how to locate, evaluate, integrate, use, and effectively communicate information. These skills are critical in dealing with the daily barrage of information and in using the broad array of tools to search, organize, and analyze results and to communicate and integrate them for decision making.

Information literacy skills initiate, sustain, and extend lifelong learning, and they complement the aggressive work underway throughout the Department to become a knowledge-centric organization and achieve knowledge superiority.

Knowledge management focuses on ensuring access to data and information through development of connectivity, nodes, and flow. However, gaps exist between peoples' understanding and their ability to access what is needed from the external environment. Knowledge is a moving target, and it is situation- and time-dependent. Information literacy, providing what we could refer to as meta-information (or information about information), helps close these gaps and provides ways of increasing individuals' ability to access what they need from the external information world.

Let me use an analogy to point out the importance of IL. In 1855, pulp paper-making was discovered, providing the opportunity to create paper that was both scaleable and economical. However, only five percent of the U.S. population could read or write. The impact of the invention could not be fully realized until the level of reading proficiency increased. From 1858 through 1899, systematic schooling raised the level of reading proficiency to 85 percent. Continuing the analogy, the late 20th Century ushered in technologies such as the Web and broadband and wireless communications, providing the opportunity to access information from anywhere in the world using mobile devices. But what percentage of people has the capability to use information fully? What percentage of our population is information literate?

As early as 1989, the Presidential Committee on Information Literacy identified IL as a survival skill in the Information Age. The study found that instead of drowning in the abundance of information that floods their lives, information-literate people know how to find, evaluate, and use information effectively to solve a particular problem or make a decision. Since that early identification of the need for IL, academic institutions have been the leaders in understanding IL issues and working to facilitate IL in the United States. The DON developed the first virtual Information Literacy Toolkit for the U.S. government in 2000 as part of their KM program.[4]

Knowing

It is commonly recognized that the world is changing rapidly and in uncertain directions. This is formally described as a nonlinear, dynamic, complex world in which predictability is rare if existent at all. If we accept this observation, then clearly the art of warfare in the current world environment and in the face of new asymmetric threats can no longer rely on the logic of the past to win future engagements. As we move away from predictable conflict patterns susceptible to logic, leaders are increasingly reliant on their "gut" instinct, and internal sense of "knowing." To prepare decision makers to understand current situational assessments and potential threats, it is essential that they learn to make identifications, interpretations, and decisions and then take appropriate actions and counteractions using their sense of knowing.

Knowing enhances the ability to be agile and focused at the point of action without a loss of quick response. In is an integrative competency in that it integrates and enhances other competencies of the individual, thereby leading to improved decision making. Knowing deepens situational awareness and individual understanding of themselves as well as others, in the context of the DON or the enemy. A good top-level description of knowing is "seeing beyond images, hearing beyond words, and sensing beyond appearances."

Knowing has roots in research by both the Department of the Army and the DON. The U.S. Army Research Institute for the Behavioral and Social Sciences held a Situational Awareness Workshop in 1998 that addressed the possibility of making Situational Awareness (SA) a basic, or habitual, way of processing and thinking about sensory inputs. SA applied to the Army is defined as knowledge of a specific situation that enables a commander to place current battlefield events into proper context; to readily share a portrayal of the situation with staff and subordinates; and to predict, expect, and prepare for future states and actions. It focuses on the mental or intellectual processes and results from the ability to derive expected outcomes from conscious and automatic processes, for example, intuition.

In October 1999, the DON hosted an Expert Forum that brought together DON senior leadership with world-class thinkers to focus on the unknown-unknowns driven by IT. The immediate objective was to find ways to better prepare for Y2K by investigating the possibility of recognizing and preparing for unknown-unknowns before they occurred. Out of the plethora of thought that surfaced during this event emerged a series of patterns. The first pattern was an extension of what we see today in the IT world, indicating that as the DON moves from an information-centric enterprise to a knowledge-centric enterprise specific information technologies will rise and wane as the world continues to discover and bring into reality better and better products. The second pattern indicates that both the efficiency and effectiveness of information management (IM) and KM will steadily increase as new processes and products emerge and their full potentials are realized. The third pattern reflects a rapid increase in the need for new skills and capabilities to handle the unknown-unknowns of the knowledge world of tomorrow. These skills and capabilities—using data, information, and imagination to bring about "value transformation"—were described with terms such as the following: intuiting, integrating, innovating, designing, sensing, scanning, patterning, synthesizing, judging, storytelling, persuading, and knowing.

The concept of knowing focuses on the cognitive capabilities of observing and perceiving a situation, that is, the cognitive processing that must occur to understand the external world and make maximal use of our internal thinking capabilities, and the mechanism for creating deep knowledge and acting on that knowledge—what we call "self as an agent of change." The first exposure across the DON to knowing was embedded in the Information Literacy Toolkit. Subsequently this work has been widely distributed across government agencies and was featured at the International Association on Education and Innovation in Business Conference.[5]

Given that the DON successfully executes its holistic IM/IT/KM program, ultimately, the decision maker's ability to navigate and productively integrate and use information comes down to the skills and knowledge of the individual. The individual's ability to do these things successfully depends on the relationships and networks that have been built through collaboration, teams, and communities. This interdependence among systems, groups, and individuals will increase in the future, where the knowledge, skills, abilities, and behaviors of each of us will significantly impact a great many others.

Implementing KM at the Enterprise Level

While ensuring knowledge superiority, KM is also a lynchpin of the DON eGovernment strategy. In the best sense of the word, the Department defines eGovernment as enabled government. Enabled government is government of the people, by the people, and for the people in a virtual world, a collaborative government where technology meets human creativity and where government manages and shares its vast stores of knowledge with, and for the benefit of, the citizen.

Toward this end, the DON has played a strategic role in implementing KM across government, sharing everything it has learned through leadership in governmentwide teams and forums, wide distribution of virtual resources, and the transfer of tacit knowledge in both one-on-one and large group settings. Out of this sharing emerged a comprehensive change strategy that walks organizations through the elements geared toward the following: creating a shared vision;

building the business case; demonstrating leadership commitment; facilitating a common understanding; setting limits; sharing new ideas, words, and behaviors; identifying the strategic approach and thrusts; developing the infrastructure; providing tools, measuring and incentivizing; promoting learning; and envisioning an even greater future.

I will quickly run through some critical steps along this path, beginning with development of the *Department of the Navy Information Management/ Information Technology Strategic Plan*. This plan was mandated by Congress and provided the opportunity for the DON enterprise (the Navy Department, Marine Corps, and Secretariat) to collectively address and reach a consensus on the future in terms of IM/IT. The DON strategic planning process produced a living, breathing document that touched every organizational and functional level and focused on the value of information to the decision maker. One remarkable aspect of this plan is the inclusion of success stories, or what are called pathfinders, in the plan itself. These pathfinders provided visibility to Congress and promoted early implementation as these stories were collected over a six-month time frame prior to publication. All of the goals of the Strategic Plan focused on the information needed by decision makers, with Goal Number 4 specifically calling for the implementation of strategies that facilitate the creation and sharing of knowledge to enable effective and agile decision making.

Looking back one hundred years from now, people will see the beginning of a new age of connecting: people working in innovative and fascinating ways, forming networks and communities across time and distance to organize and create. All of this is taking place in a new space, the global space enabled by the Internet, and transpiring at the new speed, the speed of thought. The KM communities of practice (CoPs) was the first formal community in the Department, evolving from two KM conferences sponsored by the DON in late 1998 and early 1999. From these early beginnings, the KM CoP has grown to include hundreds of members representing over 60 different DON organizations, and a KM community of interest (CoIs) of over 600 has emerged. The KM CoP and KM CoI are focused around knowledge—knowledge of KM—and built on the development of relationships among participants and across the organizational and functional lines of the DON and support organizations of the DON. Communities serve the important knowledge role of intermediation, or knowledge brokering.

Communities are flourishing across the Department. For example, in support of the Fleet, Carrier Team One has created knowledge-sharing networks for the

Carrier Maintenance Community that connect shipyards and ships worldwide. In the words of a participant, people join these communities because they want to learn what other people have already learned, what mistakes have already been made, and because they want to be better at their jobs. The Pacific Fleet (PACFLT) Knowledge Management CoP is an example of a best practices community. PACFLT knowledge managers and leaders use the Community to accelerate KM implementation and to standardize methodology throughout the Fleet to ensure the greatest impact with the least overhead. The Institute for Joint Warfare Analysis is an innovation community that uses KM. Fleet command officers, NATO, the Naval Warfare Development Command, and others use KM technologies to share expertise in various technical and command and control competencies.

To share the successes of the DON and support CoPs as a good practice, the Department became partners with the Federal Aviation Administration and other government and industry organizations to develop and publish the first government virtual tool for building and sustaining CoPs. *Building Communities of Practice: Creating Value Through Knowledge Communities* is a guidebook for championing, developing, and participating in CoPs. The guide provides a set of resources—concepts, principles, models, checklists, and tools—for building CoPs. It also includes ideas that can be shared with executives, champions, and sponsors, and that can assist community members as they establish new professional relationships to support their participation.

Knowledge fairs held in 2000 and 2001 were intermediation events. In complex nonlinear systems, where change occurs in an uneven fashion, consistent "plateau shifts" can be precipitated through formal enterprise-level events. The intent is to quickly raise the awareness and initiate the action of many people to create desired learning and behavior. These knowledge fairs, built on a model used by The World Bank, carried the commitment from senior leaders, provided the opportunity for personal sharing of successful KM and eBusiness initiatives, and included many short demonstrations and learning experiences. They were also fun and memorable. The learning was escalated through the capture on video and CD of the messages, KM initiatives, and points of contact for those initiatives, and by adding context through personal conversations and short, recorded visuals as well as explicit documentation.

The Secretary of the Navy, Chief of Naval Operations, and Commandant of the Marine Corps presented awards at the knowledge fairs. These awards, held in high esteem by the DON work force, recognize project teams whose successful KM efforts are leading the exchange and sharing of information across organizations. For example, a recent award was presented to the Global War Game KM/IT Team. This team contributed extensively to operationalizing the KM concepts in Joint Vision 2020 and in Network Centric Operations, which recognizes that military conflicts will increasingly depend on and revolve around information and communication matters. Information Age modes of conflict will be largely about knowledge, that is, who knows what, when, and where. During the 2001 War Games, The Global War Game KM/IT team focused on how to operationalize Network Centric Operations and its underlying means to exploit and distribute information to dramatically improve the ability of the DON to be well informed and to share and exploit their knowledge.

The DON eBusiness Operations Office won an award for leading implementation of eBusiness in the DON. This office, headquartered at the Naval Supply Systems Command, was established in May 2000 and serves as a clearinghouse for fresh eBusiness ideas for Navy and Marine Corps business processes. In April 2001, this office selected eight (from 360 submissions) pilot projects to be funded during the fiscal year; it also has been paramount in distributing lessons learned and promoting scalability of these pilot projects.

The many winners over the past three and a half years have provided measures and models of success, and come from diverse organizational and functional areas across the DON enterprise. The Naval Facilities Command developed and implemented a CoP/CoI model that has already demonstrated substantial returns on investment. The Naval Sea Systems Command has developed knowledge-sharing networks as an everyday part of carrier maintenance, with significant cost savings and avoidances. There are knowledge portals and digital dashboards, decision support systems and expert systems, community approaches and system approaches, and lots of innovation and sharing.

Metrics are important to the DON. A survey of the responses from a small naval organization implementing a pilot KM initiative demonstrated that the perceived most important factor in successful KM as compared with other factors is culture (29 percent). This is consistent with data from the public sector, as is the recognized level of the much lower importance of technology (4 percent). What is fascinating are the statistics matched to metrics (19 percent) and content (17 percent); that is, there is at least as much if not more concern about measuring than about the content of the system. Recognizing this cultural aspect of the Department, the DON developed a Metrics Guide for Knowledge Management

In early 2000, the DON led an effort to develop learning objectives for the certification of government employees in KM. This effort brought together industry associations, academic institutions, and the federal government to focus on KM and resulted in a clearer understanding of the potential KM offered for the government. The following are the identified learning objectives:

- Have knowledge of the value added by KM to the business proposition, including the return on investment, performance measures, and the ability to develop a business case.
- Have knowledge of the strategies and processes to transfer explicit and tacit knowledge across time, space, and organizational boundaries—including retrieval of critical archived information—enabling ideas to build on ideas.
- Have knowledge of state-of-the-art and evolving technological solutions that promote KM, including portals and collaborative and distributed learning technologies.
- Have knowledge of and the ability to facilitate knowledge creation, sharing, and reuse, including developing partnerships and alliances, designing creative knowledge spaces, and using incentive structures.
- Have knowledge of learning styles and behaviors, strive for continuous improvement, and be actively engaged in exploring new ideas and concepts.
- Have working knowledge of state-of-the-art research and implementation strategies for KM, IM, document and records management, and data management. This includes project management of knowledge initiatives and retrieval of critical archived information.
- Have understanding of the global and economic importance of developing knowledge-based organizations to meet the challenges of the knowledge era.
- Have the ability to use Systems Thinking in implementing solutions.
- Have the ability to design, develop, and sustain CoIs and CoPs.
- Have the ability to create, develop, and sustain the flow of knowledge. This includes understanding the skills needed to leverage virtual teamwork and social networks.
- Have the ability to perform cultural and ethnographic analyses, develop knowledge taxonomies, facilitate knowledge audits, and perform knowledge mapping and needs assessments.
- Have the ability to capture, evaluate, and use best-known practices, including the use of storytelling to transfer these best practices.
- Have the ability to manage change and complex knowledge projects.
- Have the ability to identify customers and stakeholders and tie organizational goals to the needs and requirements of those customers and stakeholders.

Initiatives.[6] Measures serve a number of objectives. They help make a business case for implementation, guide and tune the implementation process by providing feedback, and provide a target or goal. They also measure, retrospectively, the output value of the initial investment decision and lessons learned and serve as benchmarks for future efforts.

The knowledge-centric organizational model uses three types of metrics to assess different levels of KM impact, namely, outcome (enterprise or overall value), output (project or task), and system (technology tool). Based on a review of many high-performing organizations, the DON Metrics Guide for Knowledge Management Initiatives identified several key factors in designing and using performance measures. These factors include using a small number of focused measures aligned to strategic objectives; measuring critical characteristics of the business processes; and recognizing measures as being only valuation tools and not the products of the project.

Working with the Federal Knowledge Management Working Group, the DON led a joint forum of representatives from government, academia, and industry to develop the learning objectives for KM certification programs. The result was a draft set of learning objectives that covers the breadth of what is needed to implement KM successfully in the federal sector. The depth of knowledge and the ability needed in each area are highly dependent on the specific job that needs to be done. These learning objectives help to focus KM for the U.S. government, providing the opportunity to build and share understanding and to stimulate new growth in these focus areas.

AND MORE

The DON KM story is broad and diverse enough to write a great many chapters and even several books. It is a story about technology. It is a story about people. And it is a story about the growth of knowledge and sharing.

In the beginning, the DON began with some closed, structured KM concepts and slowly began to share them across our own organizations and with some trusted partners. As the Department gained confidence in its direction, we increased our connectedness and, recognizing the value offered by KM, began to advance the knowledge of the field and share what we had learned in a broader forum. Today, creating and sharing new thought is part of the strategic approach of the Department. The KM efforts of the DON are aimed at advancing the field and enabling the government to fully leverage the opportunity KM brings. And as the world continues to turn itself inside out with new technologies and new thinking, the Department strives to move forward "alive with the fire of shared understanding."

ENDNOTES

1. Teleos "North American Most Admired Knowledge Enterprises (MAKE) Study," announced May 6, 2002, New York. Using the Delphi research methodology, a panel of 250 leading KM and intellectual capital practitioners nominated organizations delivering superior results against a set of eight knowledge performance criteria: creating a corporate knowledge culture, developing knowledge leaders, delivering knowledge-based products and solutions, maximizing enterprise intellectual capital, creating an environment for collaborative knowledge sharing, creating a learning organization, focusing on customer knowledge, and transforming knowledge into shareholder value.

2. Department of the Navy Knowledge Centric Organization Toolkit. (1999).

3. Senge, Peter M. (1990). *The Fifth Discipline: The Art and Practice of the Learning Organization.* New York: Doubleday.

4. Department of the Navy Information Literacy Toolkit. (2000). The toolkit is available on the DON IM/IT Web site at http://www.don-imit.navy.mil and it can be requested on CD-ROM from the DON CIO.

5. *Knowing: The Art of War 2000* was selected for publication in the best of conference volume, scheduled for 2003 publication by the International Association on Education and Innovation in Business (EDINEB).

6. This guide is available on the Knowledge Centric Organization and cPort (Communities of Practice) Toolkits published by the DON. It is also available at http://www.don-imit.navy.mil

Three Critical Roles for Knowledge Management Workspaces: Moderators, Thought Leaders, and Managers

Mary Durham, Genzyme Corporation

EXECUTIVE SUMMARY

Experience has shown that KM systems do not manage themselves. Left alone, contribution quality and quantity vary unacceptably, interpersonal communications falter, and content stales. How, then, to focus the finite resources available for addressing this need? This chapter presents experiences with moderator, thought leader, and management actions directed toward this pivotal question. For each of these roles, a sequence of recommended practical activities is explored. An action table summarizing a timetable of regular tasks to keep the KM system humming accompanies each discussion.

INTRODUCTION

Knowledge management systems are inherently *people systems*. They provide a platform for social interaction, and they are a reflection of the people who operate and participate in them. In this chapter, I examine three pivotal roles that interact in important ways with KM systems. The perspective is that people will be assuming new roles and can benefit from understanding the ways that others have implemented those roles in similar circumstances. This chapter offers the person who is already enthusiastic about the promise of KM some concrete ways to translate that vigor into effectiveness.

For each of the key roles, a sequence of topics will be considered. Each begins with an overview of the role followed by discussion of the following:

- Locating the pain points
- Setting expectations
- Providing direction
- Keeping people involved
- Following up
- Acknowledging success

End-users are the essence of any successful KM system. Therefore, each topic will be discussed in relation to the end-user population, rather than considering the role unto itself. At the same time, the treatment will benefit someone taking on one of these roles for the first time—to get situated, to understand the basics of the role, and to relate the role to adjacent ones.

The discussion of each role closes with an action table in which is set forth routines relevant to that role. The point here is to get KM "onto the ground" and make it part of daily reality. The action tables are intended to give the sort of practical technique that the author hopes the reader will find both useful and compelling.

I have drawn on experience with the Intellectual Assets Network (IAN) system at Context Integration. This is where my experience is deepest. I also discuss examples from several other KM systems in use at other organizations.

The chapter intends to foreground the pragmatic. The reality is that the resources any organization can devote to KM are finite and, therefore, it is always important to analyze and prioritize the efforts. Fortunately, by its very nature KM engenders open exchange, so the kinds of critiques and lessons learned that enable open exchange are already in your toolkit. The three roles discussed here are key to successful KM efforts.

INTRODUCTION OF THE TOPICS

Drawing on one of the key topics of this chapter, let us begin by doing some expectation setting. Regarding this, I mean to give a brief introduction to each of the topics that will be considered for the individual roles discussed subsequently. Common threads are found amongst them, and an introductory explanation seems in order as we move ahead into the discussion.

Locating the Pain Points

The resources available to any endeavor are finite. Knowledge management teams are well aware of this, particularly in contemporary organizations. The starting point for problem solving is to understand and articulate the problem (or challenge) and its relationship to the environment in which it occurs. Yet many projects fail or fall short because they have tackled the wrong problem. It is therefore essential to solve problems that are genuinely in need of solutions.

The KM team can test this informally. If the vision of the end point generates an enthusiastic, resonating response in end-users, and if the end-users volunteer that this is something that must be addressed, then this is a good initial barometer. Contrast it with a more lukewarm reaction, and hold on to the mental picture of the response that you know you need. Being candid and critical here can add immeasurable value down the road.

Setting Expectations

If KM systems are inherently people systems, as asserted earlier, then it becomes key to get the *people* on board with the thinking as early as possible. Important to setting expectations are having a vision of the end point; involving end-users in the planning, design, and development; and establishing awareness of the end-users' roles. It is important that people know what will be expected of them. If the system introduces new ways of doing things, acquainting users with the concepts and then the activity details—and then the actuality—eases the transition into change. Kotter (1996) makes some excellent points about introducing change successfully.

Developing a marketing strategy applies here, and it involves articulating the vision and its relation to the problem and the ultimate benefits that will touch the individuals. Setting expectations can also be an exercise in repetition, or at least it can feel that way to the KM team—telling, and then retelling, and then telling some more. End-users are far more apt to lose sight of the message than is the KM team, so keep the message coming so that it stays in front of the users. Kotter (1996, pp. 85–100) offers some germane advice on this particular point.

Providing Direction

Good KM systems take advantage of a form of *recursion*. If it is useful to capture lessons learned for the domain being managed; it is also good to capture them for the KM system itself. Providing the necessary details and instructions on how to use the KM system prevents people from having to reinvent the wheel or figure it out individually. Incorporating success stories and other examples and narratives gives end-users a set of fruitful taking-off points on which to begin to build their own initiatives. It also makes the KM system a safe place to work, and this can be quite important when people are being asked to "stretch" and possibly expose the soft spots in their own expertise.

Keeping People Involved

Sustained user involvement makes or breaks a KM system. Many of us have witnessed dramatic launches of worthwhile initiatives that ultimately atrophied into nonexistence. This can happen for a variety of reasons. One of the reasons for having a KM team at all is to sustain the KM system and continually enhance its viability. Many roles are involved in keeping people involved in order to keep energy in the system.

Following Up

Knowledge has a "whole" quality that is absent from information. The KM team contributes to this in various ways. Closure is an important theme discussed in the following paragraphs in relation to the different roles being considered. It means that a topic is brought to completion, the loopholes are closed, and the ambiguities are resolved. The result is that any "knowledge object" is presented as a coherent whole such that a reader coming upon the thread can utilize it without a lot of thrashing around and wasted time.

Other follow-up strategies center around measurement. Because you will have set measurable objectives at the outset, follow-up involves assessing the achievement of those targets. One can learn a lot from failure as well as success, and candor in the assessment is necessary. Again, the "safe" environment plays a part here: If it can be acceptable to fail, then there is more, and richer, material to learn from the next time around.

Acknowledging Success

Sad to say, this author finds acknowledging success routinely short-changed. And it is a bit of a mystery. Building intellectual capital is what this is about, and it is important to take the time, energy, and resources to recognize the victories. Build the success stories, recognize the key contributors, and wave the flag around before moving on to the next challenge. Again, it is recursive.

Three Key KM Roles

With that groundwork laid, let us now turn to examination of three individual roles that I have found to be central to successful KM initiatives: line management, moderator, and thought leaders.

Line Manager

Overview

It is surely unnecessary to introduce the concept of management other than to note that the executive, or senior management level, plays one sort of role, while the supervisor and project manager operate in somewhat different space. Both are important, and both are discussed in the paragraphs that follow.

Locating the Pain Points

There are three key elements to the involvement of senior management in KM initiatives. The first, and far and away most important, is to *recognize the need for and value of the KM initiative*. When senior management sees the KM initiative as crucial to business strategy, KM will achieve a meaningful position within the organization (Zack, 1999). If the KM initiative is viewed as incidental to high-level business purposes, it cannot help but be a more marginal effort. Poised on the brink of joining a KM project, it is a good test to assess the involvement of management. If it is lacking or superficial, this author believes that speaks volumes about the organizational positioning of the initiative. A KM initiative involves too much organizational impact to succeed without active support from senior management. Lacking that, the rest just does not happen. It is senior management who funds any KM initiative, first off, and who provides support in the form of resources (people and otherwise). This is the cornerstone of a successful initiative. Once that foundation has been securely laid, then senior management can actively *champion* and *lead by example*.

On a day-to-day basis, supervisors and project management are the faces of management seen routinely by the troops. The supervisor/project manager emerges as an incredibly key role *vis-à-vis* the KM initiative. End-users may hear their management tell them to use the KM system, but they will perceive quite a different message if the manager then directs them to other work and leaves the KM tasks for "nights and weekends." It is up to the supervisor/project manager to be consistent in walk and talk. Individual contributors will see through any pretense very quickly. This is a key point in determining whether your KM initiative is a "nice-to-have" that people can ignore, or whether it becomes a vital tool in your organization.

Management is most effectively involved in a KM initiative when it occurs at all levels. The executive who keeps the KM initiative in view and keeps its business value in the foreground creates a climate for success. Managers down the line will take this cue from the executive level. At the supervisor/project manager level, the talk turns into daily reality. Project plans include specific tasks and milestones that relate to KM. For example, when a deliverable is produced, it must be published via the KM system in order to be recognized as being complete. The benefit of this by way of byproduct is large—if this technique causes material to reach the KM system that otherwise would not, an important capture-and-preserve step has just joined the toolkit. Supervisors/project managers articulate specific ways of participation in KM and then follow through on them when monitoring staff activity and evaluating performance.

Setting Expectations

The manager should make his or her direct reports aware that participation in the KM system is a specific performance goal. The manager should explain what he or she looks for in evaluating this. Ideally, the manager and the individual contributor will sit down together and do a dry run. If the manager has written criteria, so much the better. Expectations are based on the individual's role, with the more senior staff being expected to demonstrate more leadership.

Managers can also involve KM as a professional development tool. Involvement in the KM system can be brought to the foreground as a way for the individual to demonstrate learning and professional expertise. It can be a growth path to compose and post in the KM workspace, or to take on a thought leadership role there.

The critical message is threefold: the manager expects KM involvement as part of the individual's "day job," the manager will take note of this regularly, and it will have a positive effect on performance evaluation. Bringing in the message of business value is an important complement to the statement that the manager makes.

Providing Direction

Supervisors and project managers monitor and direct people's activities every day. Building the KM activities into routines is a powerful enabler. When the supervisor or project manager directs the individual to both write the report and post it in the KM workspace for comment, then the message is that the report is not complete until it is posted. This sounds simple, doesn't it? If your organization can achieve compliance with this type of activity, you are a long way there with KM. The trick is, very often, to keep the back door closed and not allow the exceptions to gain traction.

At Context Integration, this happened with the staff managers in the Boston practice. They pointed people to IAN (the KM system) repeatedly—relentlessly, one might say. They sent people to IAN rather than answering their questions directly. "Have you looked in IAN?" became a mantra of sorts. New hires learned this, and it spread throughout the office culture such that it was effectively ingrained in second-generation and later employees.

Supervisors/project managers also send a powerful message when they lead by example. Not only do they direct others to work via the KM workspace, they do so themselves. They find creative ways to do essentially everything via the KM workspace. This dissolves the potential disconnect between message and action.

Keeping People Involved

Managers can keep people involved in KM by continuing to utilize and champion it. When a KM system is popular, it may require added resources to sustain system performance levels or to add important enhancements. The support of senior management is demonstrated by funding these improvements and seeing that they happen.

The tone of the KM workspace as a safe environment is important to sustained involvement. If people feel that their contributions are valued, then they will continue. But ego can be a fragile thing, and people may feel slighted or put down in an electronic environment. Electronic words have a way of being colder and harder than spoken ones. Because the organization can achieve a great deal of benefit from an idea machine, such as a well-oiled KM workspace, it is worth some TLC. A big part of this is ensuring an environment where it is understood that every idea is worthy of consideration even if it does not ultimately become the chosen one.

Following Up

Having set expectations with individual contributors at the outset, at review time the supervisor/project manager can ask the individual to show his or her KM contribution highlights over the evaluation period. The supervisor/project manager can meet with the individual and let him or her guide the tour through the key contributions, explaining why each one is valuable. Follow-up and reward as appropriate. If the supervisor/project manager takes it seriously, the direct reports will too—what the manager talks about becomes, by definition, important to his or her direct reports.

Another key technique in follow-up is the lessons learned session. The effective manager will set a tone of examining past actions *in order to learn from them.* Again, the safe environment is important: Create an environment where people are willing to discuss mistakes and come up with better ways to do the job next time. These ideas are excellent KM source material. Further, this activity has social value in team building.

At the organizational level, periodic assessment of performance against strategic objectives is carried out to determine where the KM system is achieving the most, and where the effort might need to be redirected or tuned.

Acknowledging Success

Management is uniquely positioned to recognize and reward. Recognizing individual contributors is certainly important. Managers, too, are worthy of recognition when they have shown leadership in involving their staffs in the KM initiative. Management can also make sure, for instance, that human resources folks are connected with the value of the KM system. Senior management builds the environment for acknowledging success by establishing reward systems, and possibly incentive systems, that incorporate KM work.

Championing has enormous value. The senior executive who "gets it" about the value of knowledge work and brings it up at strategic times does a lot for the visibility and success of the KM initiative. Doing so lets the organization know that it is indeed visible and important. Senior management can also take the opportunity to reward not only long hours but "working smarter" via the KM workspace.

Senior management and the KM team can also collaborate to advantage. Senior executives may well be willing to speak out about the KM initiative and its importance but may not have day-to-day examples readily at hand. The KM team has the awareness of the ways that people are using the KM system but may not commandeer the same sort of audience the executive does. This becomes an opportunity for some good synergy: The KM team can take the initiative to send a steady stream of examples and success stories across the desks of the executives so that they always have material ready when needed. See Table 20.1.

Table 20.1 Action table for line management: A timetable of regular tasks to keep the knowledge management system humming.

Interval	Activity
Daily	• Utilize KM workspace for own work. • Refer questions to the KM workspace rather than answering them directly.
Weekly	• When monitoring progress against the project plan, assume that the KM workspace is the standard environment. • Build KM into status reporting mechanisms, such as using the KM workspace to publish team reports.
Monthly	• Review KM workspace content. What insights can it provide about organizational strengths or need for growth?
At performance review	• Incorporate KM work and assumptions into performance evaluation and rewards. Evaluate individuals both as KM contributors and consumers.
Event-driven	• When working with a new hire, ensure that the person is trained on the KM system and understands its place in the organization.

Moderator

Overview

A moderator is the individual charged with the responsibility to oversee and manage KM workspace content. This may or may not be the individual's only responsibility; however, for purposes of this discussion, it is one that is formally assumed. It needs to be proactive. Depending on the KM workspace design and its attendant rules and practices, the moderator may intercept incoming content for review purposes. The moderator has the authority to remove content and to set and influence the practices of the community. The moderator may act as the go-between among users as well, to resolve problems or questions or to facilitate communications.

Locating the Pain Points

The pain point for many KM workspaces (and I include here listservs, bulletin boards, discussion e-groups, and such) is that they are out of control and no one does anything about it. This can be truly painful! Posts are repetitive or argumentative, answers are nonexistent, and key areas of desired content are missing. Discussions grow unchecked, discussion threads remain unresolved, and the content in place is stale or conflicting. The result of this benign inattention is that users lose willingness to participate, or at least enthusiasm for doing so. The fact that KM systems are people systems translates directly into loss of critical mass and system degradation.

Active management of content and attention to positive social relationships make a significant difference. Thus, the "moderator" role has emerged along with the various forms of KM workspaces. The successful spaces do not manage themselves; they are the ones that have help.

At the design stage of the IAN system at Context Integration, users were polled for requirements. The need for a moderator was so clearly articulated by the user population that a full-time position was created before the system launch. It was an interesting insight that people's prior experience with unmoderated systems was so consistent (and negative) that they loudly asked for someone to take charge of the new system.

Setting Expectations

The most primary expectation to set with users is that the KM workspace has a moderator at all. The existence of the moderator should be stated, and it should be understood what the moderator does and how one communicates with that person. Beyond that, end-users need to understand that the moderator is empowered to manipulate content; that the moderator may ask them to do things; that the moderator is striving for quality and balance; and that if incoming content is filtered, it will be both reviewed and slightly delayed.

The moderating strategy also needs to be visible. Expectations about content and etiquette are best met when they are understood at the outset. If, for instance, the user who poses a question is expected to somehow close out that question—by summarizing results or by describing the solution that worked best—it is only reasonable to keep the users aware of this. On the buslib-l listserv (a popular and active KM workspace among corporate librarians) a very visible theme emerged: The user who asked a question was expected to summarize the answer back to the list as a follow-up posting. With the IAN system at Context Integration, the moderator tracked usage metrics. Not only were all new hires acquainted with this fact but there was a certain amount of traffic within the KM workspace itself on the topic.

Finally—and not to overwork this point, but it is a key one—it is the moderator who regularly ensures that the KM workspace remains a safe environment. The moderator keeps the social system predictable, steering if need be on a one-to-one basis with users.

Providing Direction

The moderator explains how this particular KM workspace runs. What are its practices and rules? How do people typically interact? In the IAN system at Context Integration, this is done in a document called the "social contract" that establishes both the etiquette and the nuts-and-bolts advice, such as the maximum file size to attach to a posting.

The moderator oversees the content from the 10,000-foot level and thus is able to identify areas of needed content. This is one of the key areas where a moderator can make a difference in the overall value of the KM workspace to its user community. When questions are forthcoming but not answers, the moderator can seek out sources of new content and work to get answers added. How this is done depends on the individual KM workspace, but external content (or links to it) is one option. Another is to locate experts and solicit their input. In emerging domains, experts may be few and far between; however, it may be possible to encourage an interested user to take on a task of researching the topic and developing a baseline of content. Another tactic would be to locate experts or discussions elsewhere in the organization and cross-pollinate KM resources. Referring again to the IAN system at Context Integration, at one point it became apparent that there was a need for a type of primary source document in many technical areas, one people could use to get started when working with complex content. Developing a format and template for what came to be called the "roadmap" was an effort spearheaded by the moderator and the associated advisory group.

When key words are used in a KM workspace, the moderator can provide guidance on their application. When the user supplies key words, the moderator can ensure that they align with the vocabulary in use throughout the KM workspace. If users are unsure about key words and their application, the moderator can serve as a resource for explanations and examples.

Keeping People Involved

The moderator can openly encourage people to participate in the KM workspace. Knowing who has specific skills enables the moderator to work with individuals to alert them when content is needed in their domain. Many KM systems include skill data that support this approach.

One-on-one follow-up with a contributor can emphasize the value of a recent contribution. Surveying individual users is an excellent way to connect with people and keep them involved in the KM initiative. One-on-one telephone surveying can be a very productive approach. Not only can it produce valuable survey input but it has considerable public relations and training value. People are often pleasantly surprised at being singled out for a survey, and it presents an opportunity to plumb their use of the system and troubleshoot problems.

The moderator can also work the "back channels" around a KM workspace. For example, the moderator can be alert to conversations around them and suggest that people conduct their discussion via the KM workspace. They can enlist individuals to pose questions and give opinions that are likely to initiate some interesting discussion. Asking for ideas from the user base can have valuable results as well: One user suggested that we hold week-long, asynchronous "conferences" on timely topics as a way to escalate usage.

When ideas originate with end-users, it is especially important that they be acted on promptly. When users see their suggestions taking hold, they are likely to continue to contribute.

Constantly articulating the value proposition of the system is another way that the moderator can sustain user involvement. Likewise, ensuring that management is made aware of valuable contributions and making sure that end-users know that this happens are both important.

Following Up

Timely and disciplined follow through is basic to moderating. When a question is posed in the KM workspace, the moderator can monitor its progress. One tactic is to contact the originator of the question to determine its outcome. The moderator can become involved in unresolved questions to seek their closure. In response to end-user feedback, the moderator ensures that the feedback is addressed and then communicates with the user.

The moderator is involved with system metrics and can use them to judge the effect of functionality changes on the system, the popularity of specific items, and so on.

A special form of following up that the moderator can undertake is weeding. In KM workspaces, less is often more, and a moderator who clears away old postings does a service to the entire KM community. (Clearly a strategy for archiving is a component of doing this well.)

Follow-up differentiates the moderated from the unmoderated KM workspace. The value proposition of a moderator is not only that closure is attained throughout the workspace but that the workspace is not anonymous. Rather, it is a socially based system in which individuals take active part.

Acknowledging Success

Because of the moderator's vantage point, this individual has unique insight into the KM workspace. He or she can assess trends and make others aware of them. Through surveys and focus groups, it is further possible to mine success stories, and to then use them to reinforce usage of the KM workspace. Success stories are valuable tools for management as well. See Table 20.2.

Table 20.2 Action table for the moderator: A timetable of regular tasks to keep the knowledge management system humming.

Interval	Activity
Daily	• Monitor new content. Review for appropriateness and key words. Resolve exceptions. • Follow up on recent posts (including feedback) to ensure closure. • Develop new key words when required. • Maintain measurements of system usage.
Weekly	• Monitor trends in incoming content. Act on them as needed. • Remove old content from active portion of KM workspace. • Survey selected users.
Monthly	• Generate reports to the user base and to management. • Develop new success stories.
Quarterly	• Review training materials, online help, and other documentation. Update as appropriate. • Seek out a new opportunity to integrate the KM workspace with a defined process within the organization.
At performance review	• Provide information to managers as needed. This might take the form of contribution and usage statistics.
Event-driven	• Introduce new users to the KM workspace. Subject matter experts and thought leaders are special types of end-users and may benefit from a customized introduction to the workspace.

Thought Leader

Overview

Next we turn to a group of participants in our KM workspace whose role is less formal and possibly less well understood. These are the thought leaders. Initially, let us distinguish them from subject matter experts. Subject matter experts, as the name implies, hold expertise in their respective subject domains. For purposes of this discussion, that expertise will not be considered synonymous with thought leadership. Thought leadership builds on the notion of subject matter expertise, surely, but goes beyond. "Thought leader" is as much a social role as it is the command of knowledge. It implies leadership, or the willingness to assert direction for others to follow. Thought leaders can articulate vision within their respective domains, and they can home in on the core issues. They possess social capital, affording them influence within their groups of expertise. And finally, they actively mentor others, and their community of practice as a whole. Accordingly, thought leadership becomes a key role in a KM workspace because of the leadership qualities as much as for the domain expertise.

The place of the thought leader within the KM workspace is likewise one of leadership. Thought leaders will challenge other subject matter experts to move to the next level. An example comes from the sigia-l listserv, a discussion community of information architects. In August 2001, Lou Rosenfeld created a posting to kick off the topic of the direction that this quite new profession should be taking. He explicitly stated "… I'm hoping to spur some more discussion. … I'd love to see us discuss our future … as in what it is we will do, both intellectually and practically." He went on to offer six discussion points, and his focused questions generated considerable thought-provoking traffic over the following several weeks.

Thought leaders exercise vision and propose direction. They generate novel ideas and connections. Further, they have earned the respect of their colleagues, and their leadership is not only asserted but acknowledged.

It is an option to explicitly recognize thought leaders for their respective domains and to give them specific responsibilities for the KM workspace.

Locating the Pain Points

Locating the pain points is the challenge of taking the thinking of the organization to the next level that confronts the thought leader. Ours is a fast-paced world in which ideas are important drivers of success. Part of the promise of KM is to free people from solving those repetitive old problems so that they can address new ones. Another part is to do this in a visible, self-documenting fashion. But what is the catalyst that enables this? Thought leadership is at least part of the answer.

Setting Expectations

Thought leadership can go in many directions. The direction we explore herein is that of leading and focusing discussions in the KM workspace. A primary expectation that follows from this is that discussions within a specific domain will have leadership, and not that they will be monopolized, or diversity stifled, but that they will be grounded in experience.

Along with this, the expectation surfaces that the thought leader will be a KM enthusiast. This championing emerges as one of the qualities of an effective thought leader by virtue of being such a strong win–win situation for both the thought leader and the followers of any discussion. It aids the thought leader by allowing him or her to most effectively leverage existing work, and it supports the other participants by providing a channel of accessibility to the thought leader. Thus, the expectation develops that thought leaders can be reached via the KM workspace but it may be difficult to secure their attention elsewhere.

A related example comes from the health care field. Davenport and Glaser (2002) describe the role of high-end experts with the clinical database at Partners HealthCare, which offers treatment information on a demand basis:

> Only clinicians at the top of their game can create and maintain the knowledge repository. Partners [HealthCare] has addressed this issue by forming several committees, and empowering existing ones, to identify, refine, and update the knowledge used in each domain. ... Participation in these groups is viewed as a prestigious activity, so busy physicians are willing to devote extra time to codifying the knowledge within their fields.

Providing Direction

Thought leaders have excellent opportunities to leverage KM systems to the benefit of the overall organization. Directing people to the KM workspace to conduct discussions is one technique that thought leaders might use. Thought leaders are often approached for answers and opinions. In order to achieve maximum benefit from any such interchange, the thought leader can direct it to the KM workspace to ensure that it is captured, shared, and effectively refereed by peers. This has the advantageous side effect that the thought leader need only respond to a question once and can thereafter refer people to the recorded knowledge. At the same time, it exposes new thoughts and ideas to a wider audience, potentially involving participants who would otherwise have missed out on the exchange, and producing a richer variety of input.

Thought leaders can also drive KM workspace participation by trend spotting. Hearing an interesting point, the thought leader can recommend posting it in the KM workspace. This is a ready way to "validate" the notions of someone seeking the opinion of the thought leader. Without too much practice, this can become a habit. Further, it can be fruitful for the thought leader and the moderator to collaborate on developing new domain areas, key words, skill lists, and so on, based on the traffic in the workspace.

The entire approach is reinforced when the thought leader provides timely response or leading edge ideas via the KM workspace.

Keeping People Involved

It may well be the thought leader who drives a discussion to the next level, and this will be of considerable interest to the larger participation group. This happens, for example, if the thought leader poses challenging questions that set forth conceptual challenges and get people thinking about larger issues. The effect can be to develop the business or profession in very new ways. The information architecture case described previously is an example of this.

The thought leader would also be setting the bar high as to technical standards and content. Causing one's colleagues to "stretch" a bit and to push the envelope generates some interesting material. This is, parenthetically, one reason that I recommend making thought leadership an explicit role. This sort of "push" makes sense when it comes from someone occupying such a role; it is less likely to be interpreted as belligerence and more likely to be seen as constructive behavior.

The thought leader also is the logical choice to stay ahead of the curve, bring new topics to the surface, and apply old ones. The person with this inclination makes a natural thought leader; so it also offers a way for the KM team to spot up-and-coming thought leaders.

Following Up

Thought leader follow-up is not too dissimilar from moderator follow-up, and there is actually overlap between the two roles here. If a question is posed, the thought leader ensures that it is addressed. The thought leader encourages people to post results of their work in the KM workspace. The thought leader responds to postings with comments that mentor the colleagues who originated them. Finally, by being a regular participant and predictable presence, the thought leader builds the certainty that the KM workspace is active and productive.

Acknowledging Success

A key way for the thought leader to recognize success is to cite a previous posting. If the KM workspace incorporates a notion of "preferred" or "highest value" content, then the thought leader would be involved in reviewing and recommending the items to be promoted to that state. Beyond this, the thought leader acts as a champion and has a ready catalog of success stories from the KM workspace. These are leveraged when a new topic opens up, or with new participants. See Table 20.3.

Table 20.3 Action table for thought leaders: A timetable of regular tasks to keep the knowledge management system humming.

Interval	Activity
Daily	• Monitor new content. • Participate in discussion threads.
Weekly	• Initiate new topics. • Be a proactive presence.
Monthly	• Review past month's material: summarize and synthesize.
At performance review	• Provide input on participation that has been of special high value.
Event-driven	• Report on a conference that was attended or other event of relevance to the domain.

Conclusion

In this chapter I have attempted to bring out the details and the routines that make real these three KM roles. While the reader surely is familiar with the roles by name, it is on the grounds that the roles take shape and bring vigor to the KM workspace. If the devil is in the details, then it is through the daily, weekly, and monthly actions that a KM system becomes top quality. I hope that the suggestions and insights offered here bring added value to your KM system. If they do, please share your knowledge with the rest of us.

Acknowledgments

This chapter could not have been written without the contributions of Stan Ward (http://www.stanward.com) who brainstormed the entire topic with me, and would have co-authored the chapter if time had permitted.

References

Davenport, T. H., and Glaser, J. (2002). Just-in-time delivery comes to knowledge management. *Harvard Business Review*. July:107–111.

Kotter, J. P. (1996). *Leading Change*. Boston, MA: Harvard Business School Press.

Zack, M. H. (1999). Developing a knowledge strategy. *California Management Review*. 41(3):125–145.

CHAPTER 21

Lessons from Five-Plus Years of Knowledge Management

Jack Borbely, Towers Perrin

The primary purpose of this chapter is to share insights from our real-world experience at Towers Perrin when implementing a global KM operation. To bring these insights into proper focus, the chapter provides background information on Towers Perrin and its KM program.

One of the premier management consulting companies of the world, Towers Perrin helps organizations around the globe manage people, performance, and risk. In fulfilling this mission, the firm supplies knowledge and expertise in the form of advice and assistance to nearly 400 of the world's 500 largest companies and three quarters of the *Fortune* 1000 largest companies. To support its client organizations, Towers Perrin maintains a worldwide presence of 9,000 staff members operating from 78 offices in 23 countries.

As a company that trades in best-practices solutions and strategic advice, Towers Perrin realized early on the importance of KM to its business strategy. To fully leverage the benefits of its intellectual capital for clients, the firm needed a way for its consultants around the world to easily create, share, and find information. Beginning with a mainframe-based application in the late 1980s, the company has progressed through a series of initiatives to make its massive base of best-practices documents, legal advisories, project insights, and client experience available to its consultants.

Today, that early experiment in technology has evolved into full-fledged global KM, with world-class communities of practice (CoPs) environments based on enterprise communication, collaboration, personalized online environments (portals), content management, and search platforms.

KM at Towers Perrin

Towers Perrin defines KM as the capture, maintenance, and sharing of knowledge to help people do their jobs better and add value to work. Properly conceived, KM allows the practitioners of the firm to interact to produce excellent results for clients, learn and keep abreast of developments, and compete effectively. In short, at the micro level, our KM effort concentrates on helping individual staff learn, do, and win. At the macro level, it is about organizational leverage, workplace excellence, and employee engagement.

The impetus for developing a KM system will differ among firms, depending on organizational business needs and structure. In a global consulting firm such as Towers Perrin, there is close linkage between effective KM and meeting the needs of our stakeholders—clients, employees, and shareholders. Being a "knowledge factory" of sorts, we are highly dependent on the continual creation, assimilation, and use of knowledge by expert consultants serving global clients.

More specifically, several of the key goals and strategies of the firm have a strong knowledge–information component and dependency. These include continuously improving the quality and efficiency of work for clients and leveraging our intellectual capital across our consulting population.

Our overarching principle of making significant contributions to the success of our clients dictates that we place a premium on innovation, leverage, efficiency, communication, and growth. These, in turn, have become the basic underlying tenets of our KM efforts:

- **Innovation:** *to deliver innovative and high-impact solutions to our clients.* Before KM, it was much more difficult to access the intellectual capital of the firm, its people, and their individual and collective knowledge.
- **Leverage:** *to leverage fully the intellectual capital of the firm to benefit our clients, our people, and the firm.* Through our CoPs, KM provides worldwide and immediate access to best practices and client learning created anywhere in our global organization.
- **Efficiency:** *to improve the cost-effectiveness of our work environment.* Standardizing the technology infrastructure—within and across enterprises—ensures that the right audience will benefit from the timely and efficient sharing of content. Additionally, it guarantees that the collection and use of knowledge can proceed in a consistent and orderly way.

- **Communication:** *to provide broader access to the critical information and resources needed to serve clients and manage information more effectively.* Our KM environment provides easy links to experts and content, and it supports real-time or synchronous learning or work sessions among geographically dispersed participants.
- **Growth:** *to support profitable revenue growth through both innovation—new methods, client solutions, and services—and continuous improvement.*

The KM effort of the firm supports these tenets through a model based on planned communities, that is, CoPs. Each CoP is enabled by a set of collaborative and interactive capabilities that leverages the best research materials, supporting documents, methodologies, proven practices, and historical data available across the organization and linked to the world beyond as well.

An employee can self-select to become a member of a CoP. However, the premise is that staff members gravitate to community environments that reflect the specific work they do and their line of business. In turn, these environments dictate in large measure their related ongoing requirements for accessing and sharing knowledge. Actuaries and health care specialists need different kinds of knowledge, which will be reflected in their respective online communities.

LESSONS LEARNED FROM KM AT TOWERS PERRIN

The components for building a successful KM environment described in this chapter should work for many different types of organizations. The right approach to implementing and leveraging a successful environment, however, can be highly specific to the structure and business needs of each organization. The details will vary for each firm undertaking such a project. It might be helpful, however, to share some of the observations and experiences of the Towers Perrin team.

Alignment

Alignment is a topic frequently addressed in KM literature. Our experience confirms a central, widely held premise on the importance of maintaining a strong connection to the overall strategy of the organization, that is, a clear line of sight between KM and the business strategy. In the section that follows, we will extend this discussion by highlighting adjustments made as our KM program progressed from the early stages to mature operation. We will share additional insights pertaining to the need for effective alignment of process and technology involved in KM delivery.

Early Lessons

While management sponsorship is important during early stages of KM, putting together the right KM team is perhaps more so. We assembled a diverse group of dedicated people to serve as our core KM team. It included people from different departments and lines of business who brought expertise in communications, technology, Web design, project management, KM, and subject matter. This approach helped us gain broad buy in and engagement at the outset, and combining so much varied expertise and so many perspectives clearly produced a much better result.

Our experience in developing an early prototype community reinforced the premise that content and capabilities must be very relevant to users and usable in the work they do. The online community reacted negatively to what it considered a disproportionate amount of nonessential and general firm-wide information. From this we learned that our people were not engaged or interested when we tended to focus too much on general or corporate information. Nor did building an effective technical system alone result in a positive return on investment. For sustained benefit, the audience must be sufficiently engaged to take ownership and responsibility for the continued use and evolution of the CoP. This means maintaining a line of sight to business priorities.

Since that lesson, our efforts have concentrated on the knowledge and tools needed by people to do their work. Content and capabilities are structured around major knowledge CoPs, and communities and their members are responsible for content development and quality review.

A related lesson learned is that KM is most successful when all constituencies of the KM effort—management, users, and architects of the KM environment—remember several basic elements:

- *Purpose.* Clear line of sight between KM strategy and the goals and business strategies of the organization
- *Culture.* Dedication to learning and knowledge sharing
- *Processes.* Roles, business activities, and management practices that facilitate and sustain the building and sharing of knowledge
- *Connections.* Environment and mechanisms that facilitate interactions among people for knowledge creation, collaboration, and transfer

- *Content.* Actionable information that is relevant, accurate, complete, and appropriate
- *Technology.* Integrated systems that enable easy capture, storage, retrieval, and sharing of knowledge

Call it resistance to change, call it organizational inertia—however you label it—do not underestimate the challenge of changing work habits, even when benefits of the change appear to be clear and compelling.

We rolled out the environment in phases and immediately started leveraging the platform through virtual seminars, hot topic discussions, and other events. Organizations often make a mistake by assuming they are done as soon as the KM system is deployed. In reality, the work has just started. If the KM activity is to take hold and really transform the work environment, the firm must establish a long-term commitment and plan. In addition to sustaining the system, the plan must include efforts to both reinforce the messages and demonstrate the value of the new KM environment. In the end, the challenge is to effect change in behavior up and down the organization; and to succeed, it is necessary to win the hearts and minds of the audience in an ongoing effort. That requires an ongoing effort.

It was equally important during the early stages to listen closely to our audience. We tested the design and overall communication and training plan with groups of people with different skills, needs, and geographical locations; we then made adjustments based on their feedback. Users will give the best and relevant feedback, an approach that increases buy in and connection.

Prove the concept, and then leverage the success. Based on our demonstrated results with the first line of business, each of our other lines of business is now working with our core team developing its own KM environment based on the common technology platform, tools, processing, and staffing models. By achieving this shared vision, we have been able to integrate our knowledge across all practice areas and support complex strategic initiatives of clients, such as managing cost and risk, enhancing human resources service delivery, mergers and acquisitions, and human resource effectiveness.

Transition from the Early Developmental and Launch Phase to Mature Operation

Our experience demonstrates that the factors critical to launching a successful KM effort differ significantly from those critical to sustaining one. Our priority for KM continues to be "market-facing" activities over internal operations. We aim for the KM environment and its use to be directly engaged in enabling and enhancing work done for clients.

As cited, key objectives of the formative stages of KM include engagement, determining a KM approach that fits the organization, identifying and testing opportunities to pursue, and so on. Understandably, trial and error characterized this stage. However, as the KM effort began to mature and investment in it expanded, emphasis heightened on being in close alignment with, and delivering on, strategic organizational priorities.

Moreover, we saw an increase in awareness of the costs and a rise in expectations that KM would demonstrate clear value to the organization, that is, return on investment. While lessons learned regarding KM measurement will be discussed in detail subsequently, one hard learned lesson merits mentioning at this time. Namely, it is both unreasonable and risky to assume that sponsors or management is aware of KM benefits accruing to staff or the firm overall. As is frequently the case with such services, buyers (sponsors) know the cost but often are unfamiliar with the benefits unless they are also direct consumers or participants. The burden of making that connection falls to those in the KM group.

There are several immediate implications of this, but perhaps the most important for this discussion is that clear business sponsorship and commitment takes on heightened importance. We have recently established straightforward but formal roles to clarify and codify what is needed to sustain an effective KM effort, including roles that respective sponsors and members of their organizations perform, from planning through evaluation of communities and KM.

Admittedly, the fact that the consulting practices of Towers Perrin mirror the CoP structure lends itself to creating acceptance for CoP roles. There is a cultural and organization predisposition to some level of direct and ongoing involvement of sponsor staff in support of their KM effort. In large measure, we have simply built on and extended the existing model.

We have made this involvement operational and institutionalized it through codification and implementation of three basic roles performed by or on behalf of *each* community:

- *Overall community sponsor.* Typically a senior business manager of the constituency that the CoP serves who is capable of setting policy, approving the budget, and assessing the value of CoPs to the business unit or endeavor.

- *Champion and liaison to the community.* Typically widely recognized leader of the community who provides closer ongoing guidance, stewardship, and championship and acts as a focal point for constituency; often is a subject matter expert or senior Towers Perrin consultant.
- *Community content manager.* Person responsible for creation, acquisition, selection, processing, and management of content and support to delivery and use of CoP tools.

As will be discussed subsequently, there are complementing KM roles performed by staff of the central KM operations unit.

ALIGNMENT OF KM PROCESSES AND TECHNOLOGY

Some level of "support operation" is required to sustain KM. What should be the organizational strategy and approach to KM operations supporting its CoPs? The answer ranges from a decentralized model, such as making this the responsibility of each CoP to figure out and implement, to various combinations of centrally coordinated, to centrally performed—an enterprise approach centralized at some organizational level, such as regionally, globally, or a combination.

The choices underscore the fundamental decision faced by organizations implementing KM. Namely, should KM be viewed as a collective of individual group efforts with each sponsor–audience responsible for determining its approach and creating and implementing corresponding cultural, process, and technology enablers and supports? Or, conversely, should KM be viewed as an enterprise undertaking that supports the needs of individual constituencies through a common platform? Deciding which approach to take hinges on various factors and considerations specific to each organization.

We have pursued an enterprise strategy and approach to KM operations. Early on, we adopted this as our model and have moved more aggressively to solidify a common, integrated KM process and technology platform. The primary rationales behind this approach are leverage, organizational synergy, seamless flow of knowledge across the enterprise and deployment of robust, scaleable KM technologies.

This approach often creates a natural tension between plans and operations of individual CoPs and the strategy and operations of a common enterprise KM process and technology platform. A key challenge is to recognize where and how flexibility and autonomy at the individual CoP level make sound business sense, such as specialized content and capabilities and maintaining flexibility in cultural aspects of CoPs (incentives, rewards, recognition, and so on), and where they do not. In the end, the most effective case for a CoP to forfeit elements of control is made by delivery of forward-looking, high-quality capabilities and sustained responsive support through enterprise KM operations.

From the inception, Towers Perrin has taken more of an enterprise approach to KM, although early stages were characterized by experimentation and flexibility in core areas. This proved beneficial on several levels. Knowledge management was recognized as an important firmwide endeavor with senior management commitment. An overall strategy and approach to KM and CoP was crafted and approved by management. These developments served as an endorsement that facilitated KM discussions and seed programs with groups in the firm. As important, an enterprise KM group was established with a dual focus to support the divisions of the firm in planning and implementing CoP, and to coordinate the KM processes and technology required.

This top-down approach—overall strategy and a dedicated KM group—was well suited for Towers Perrin and proved critically important to initiating and institutionalizing KM. Within 18 months there were roughly a dozen operational CoPs. Having the expressed commitment of management and active involvement of a global and business-oriented KM group set the KM operations of the firm on sound footing.

In fact, as our KM effort has expanded and matured, we have continued to refine and strengthen our enterprise KM operations and support. One reason has been to create greater transparency and clarity around KM support, that is, who does what.

Over time, we learned that it was necessary to have much tighter alignment and coordination among groups and functions supporting KM systems and processes. While there was clarity pertaining to the go-to group for KM strategy and planning, multiple options existed for acquiring or building KM technology solutions and tools.

We wanted to minimize, if not eliminate, confusion over to whom to turn for support. We also wanted to eliminate the possibility of duplicate or conflicting approaches to both KM applications and underlying KM technology. The primary lesson from this has been the importance of alignment of the KM process and technology delivery comparable to KM alignment with overall business strategy.

Acting on this lesson, the firm has expanded its KM operations unit to encompass the full gamut of KM support, including overall planning, process and technology development, and ongoing support. The rationales underlying this decision are listed in Table 21.1. Knowledge management business sponsors and staff responsible for supporting CoPs, primary "clients" of our KM operations, have responded very positively to the consolidation, citing significant improvement in efficiency and ease of interaction and transparency created from "one-stop" support.

There are similar positive results from improved clarity and focus around roles within KM operations. Table 21.2 represents an effort to clearly communicate the mission and vision of our KM operations unit to senior management, sponsors, and the organization at large. Figures 21.1 and 21.2 provide details of KM operations roles and responsibilities, and are used alternatively with KM staff, sponsors, and management.

Multiple, and often incompatible, KM process and technology approaches develop absent enterprise technology and process platforms. Individual business units often cite speed, specialized needs, and lower direct costs as rationales for addressing KM needs on their own. However, initial benefits realized from acting autonomously are frequently short lived and are typically outweighed by hidden downstream costs from incompatibilities and inconsistencies across content, process, and technology, not to mention duplication of effort and expense. We continue to refine our enterprise approach to ensure it meets the needs of each CoP and division of the firm, as well as delivers on its promises of enterprise leverage and synergy.

Table 21.1   Rationales for formal knowledge management operations unit.

- **Demonstrate to staff and management organizational commitment and values concerning KM**

- **Facilitates global consistency and coordination in face of increasingly complex KM technology environment**

- **Commits resources essential to sustain and evolve KM vision and activities through KM life cycle**

- **Establishes mechanism to better leverage KM investments across an enterprise**

Table 21.2 Mission and vision of Towers Perrin knowledge management operations.

Mission	Vision
Help the firm deliver market-leading service to clients, be recognized by staff as workplace leader, and achieve solid financial performance • By leveraging knowledge and know-how • Through leading-edge collaboration, knowledge creation, and sharing capabilities	Be a world-class global KM operation through leading-edge KM thinking, doing, and measurement

Community Content, Connections, and Capabilities

The essence of a CoP is its content, trusted connections, and capabilities for interacting with content and community members. The following section attempts to provide insights to the processes and approaches needed to create value in each of these areas. It discusses the importance of context and perspective to community content, and also highlights the role of collaborative tools for strong community connections. Finally, it describes methods to sustain a vibrant KM environment community.

It is a statement of the obvious that if leverage and preservation of organizational knowledge and know-how is the *raison d'être* of KM, the success of KM hinges on its ability to generate and sustain valued content and connections. How then to maintain CoP content and connections?

In the case of Towers Perrin, a key part of the answer is the role of community champion and content manager. They are responsible for both content and context. Members of a CoP expect more than just a steady flow of relevant content. They expect their community to provide content and connections readily applicable to their specific business priorities and corresponding activities. The community champion and content manager provide the *context* that enables members to know where, when, and how best to apply content and capabilities.

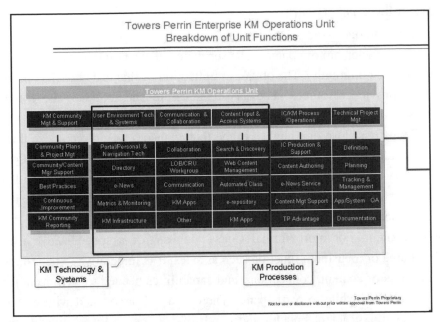

Figure 21.1   Towers Perrin enterprise knowledge management operations unit: breakdown of unit functions.

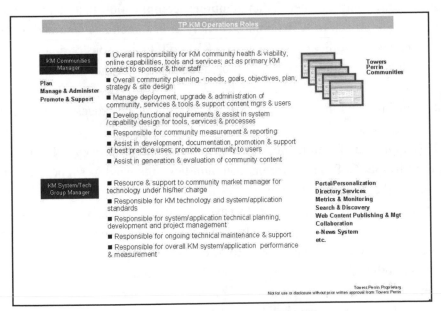

Figure 21.2   Towers Perrin knowledge management operations roles.

Community Ownership of Content

As has been discussed briefly, a foundation of our approach to KM and CoP is community ownership of content. The substance of the community is the responsibility of the community. The obvious implication of this is that each community needs to provide resources necessary to generate and maintain the content it requires.

While at first blush one might assume that sponsors would recognize this as a logical condition of implementing a CoP, this is not necessarily the case. Quite to the contrary, content is typically assumed, sometimes overlooked, and the effort to sustain it is frequently underestimated. Organizations misjudge the role and importance of content and fail to assign sufficient resources to sustain worthwhile community content. For more formal CoPs, such as for a specialized consulting practice area or a business function such as sales, it is imperative to determine the critical mass of content, connections, and capabilities needed to be present for the CoP to be worthwhile to participants. There is a risk associated with going live before having sufficient breadth and depth of content or the ability to sustain. Experience has taught us that when you do not capture the interest and attention of the targeted audience at the first attempt, it is extremely difficult to draw it back.

In our environment, there is an additional complication that stems from our centralized approach to KM support. Namely, it is sometimes assumed that content is the responsibility of the enterprise KM unit. For reasons of quality and relevance, the responsibility for content creation rests with the community and its subject matter experts. In turn, the enterprise KM unit is responsible for the content publishing and management *platform*, as well as the process and systems to leverage content.

This approach of community ownership to content has proven to be successful for both formal CoPs and informal communities organized to support broad initiatives of the firm. Indeed, when a combination of content-related roles are in place and sustained over time, results have been exceptional. By way of example, a triumvirate of overall community champion, content manager, and thought leader as content creator has proven to be an especially effective combination.

Among other things, content managers have demonstrated their value in consistent and sustained performance of content tasks: identify, collect, summarize and provide context, organize, classify content, and highlight "proven practice." In a related vein, thought leaders both seed and augment content within the community, frequently authoring and compiling seminal works for the community at large. As for the community champion, this role has been most effective when performed by a senior manager with formal line responsibilities who assumes leadership commitment and accountability for content. Although the role typically involves a marginal amount of time, the linkage created between leadership group and corresponding community content has enduring benefit and helps to institutionalize content contribution as a valued and recognized behavior. We are exploring the efficacy and making our consulting practice leaders more directly accountable for securing content from practitioners.

Role of KM Operations in KM Content and Capabilities

We have learned that CoPs vary in content and capabilities reflective of differences in consulting service deliverables, corresponding subject matter, methods, and tools. Despite these variations, however, we have found much more similarity than differences in how content is processed and managed, and even in types of content and capabilities across CoPs. This fact is one of the prime motivators for our establishing an enterprise KM operations unit and global KM systems and processes. Simply stated, we look to the KM operations unit to exploit commonality to the benefit of speed to execution, improved content leverage, and overall efficiency in KM activities. Table 21.3 itemizes the current suite of content and capabilities in place and supported by the KM operations unit.

We recently have adopted a "content headwater and stream approach" to the more readily leveraged types of content, such as internally authored position papers, thought pieces, CoP news, and proprietary periodical publications. We consider this to be among the more important insights gleaned from our efforts to leverage relevant content across CoPs.

By content headwater and stream orientation, we mean an approach to Web content publishing and management focused on the content and its logical flow across CoPs, as opposed to treating each CoP or site as a content island unto itself, each with its separate content system and process.

If the content *processes and systems* are predominantly site-centric—the site being the focal point and orientation—the risk increases for creating silo content systems and processes. The consequences frequently are inconsistencies and incompatibilities in content processes and systems, and unwanted duplication in effort. This, in turn, compromises the ability to leverage content and produces inefficiencies. Conversely, orienting toward content streams forces consideration of potential uses, multiple destinations, and delivery devices. For example, we

Table 21.3 Towers Perrin knowledge management suite: content, capabilities, and services.

KM community applications and tools	In the know: keeping users informed
• Client relationship management	• External news feeds: client, practice, and industry news
• Selling information and tools	
• Requests for information	• Community news (internal news feeds)
• Webinars	
• Discussions	• *Towers Perrin HR News Digest*
• Frequently asked questions	• Surveys and reports
• Project management tools	• Business plans
• Practice tools and database links	• Calendar and events
• Ask the expert/issue leader	• Legal and regulatory information
	• Marketing collateral
TP experience: practice-specific intellectual capital	• Vendor information
	• About the practice and community
• Best practices and methodologies	• Site map and index
• Case studies	• Online tutorials
• Legal and regulatory analysis	• People and leadership
• Learning and development	• Leadership announcements

have already established ways for proprietary news common to multiple CoPs to flow from the author who creates the content. While content flows directly to respective internal and external CoPs and sites, it is processed and managed within a single enterprise system.

Meta-tagging is a complementary building block of our content operations platform. We have learned that this KM component is a key enabler for effective, relevant, and consistent content access and personalization, not to mention measurement. Without it, our KM efforts would be compromised, largely as a result of inconsistency, and redundant. The technology centerpiece of our meta-tagging process is the Towers Perrin DataMart, which has been designed as a shared database to be accessible to any CoP system or related applications. Its purpose is twofold: (1) to support consistent tagging of content objects with both descriptive and indicative elements, for example, topical key words, geographic coverage, client name, industry, line of business, author, and so on; and (2) to support personalization among CoP community users.

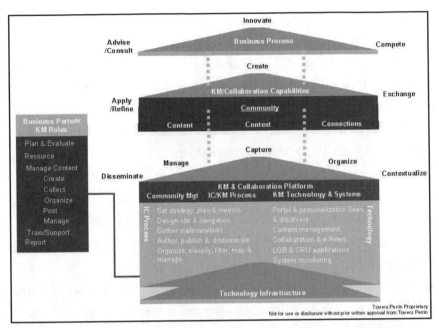

Figure 21.3   Strategy to embed KM and capture and leverage in core business processes.

Embed KM in CoP and CoP in Core Business Process

The conceptual model depicted in Figure 21.3 encapsulates our thinking on how CoP content and capabilities intersect with core business process. Figure 21.3 captures perhaps the most significant lesson learned in the experience with KM within Towers Perrin, which is the paramount importance of embedding KM—leverage, sharing, and capture—within the core business process, and the critical role of CoP in effecting that integration.

While certainly not limited to KM or CoP, notions of just in time, just what's needed, and precisely how it is needed guide our efforts to deliver the KM capabilities of the firm. Hopefully, several examples will demonstrate what we are after and the related lessons learned.

Our "request for information" tool is a quick and easy way to get answers and insights on highly specialized client situations from experts anywhere in our global firm, leveraging expertise and know-how. This simple but powerful tool consists of request posting, targeted canvassing of experts via e-mail distribution, modest workflow, and a feedback mechanism. In addition to addressing the immediate need at hand, we further leverage these insights through capture, distillation, and codification of these exchanges for subsequent access in cases warranting that level of attention. In short, this information is later leveraged as specialists select those answers to distill and add to the knowledge base from the thousands of requests for information.

Tools to work collaboratively online in real time have demonstrated an ability to effectively elicit and communicate the tacit knowledge that is as much a goal of KM systems as explicit information; this includes the facts and other data that systems readily document and codify. Experience-based opinions and perspectives based on insights rather than data alone are the kind of tacit knowledge that emerges in work sessions more often than in textbooks or other documentation.

Our global network of online meeting servers and Web-based electronic project rooms brings online collaboration to individual desktops and conference rooms. We are experiencing steady growth in online meetings directly supporting routine work for clients. Presently, over 2000 such meetings a year, spanning four locations per meeting, involve a combined total of more than 12,000 participants. In addition to being a boon to getting work done, the net of online meetings is resulting in savings in both costs and travel wear and tear. These savings can be sizeable, considering average per person travel costs of roughly $1000. More important, the additional 1000 online meetings with clients extend similar benefits to them.

We believe that rapid adoption of this technology is attributable in no small part to our creation of an "online meeting champion" focused on supporting staff in their use of this capability. This dedicated resource has been in place since the introduction of this capability and is directed at integrating online tools in the fabric of both formal and ad hoc meetings. Responsibilities include assisting senior managers, providing live support for large-scale online events, codifying proven practices for effective online meetings, providing proactive training for influential users and early adopters, maintaining an online collaboration best practices site, and so on. Had it not been for this focused support, especially in the early stages, we likely would not have achieved rapid adoption and the degree of effective use of this capability.

Measurement: The Challenge of Measurement and How It Is Addressed at Towers Perrin

Measurement Challenges

Measurements of the effectiveness of KM are generally of two types: measures of the aggregate impact of KM, largely quantitative and reportable as data, and the more qualitative assessments of individual users' experiences with the system. Both are crucial, especially for a professional service organization and most other organizations where knowledge and its use are critical success factors.

There are several central issues that need to be addressed in a measurement strategy:

- Identify places to invest additional resources and effort to add value to the system for users.
- Determine the effectiveness of the KM system in improving revenue growth and profitability.
- Ascertain which types of users—by function, responsibility level, line of business, or other category—are most and least satisfied by the system, and why.
- Decide which measurements should be tracked over time, especially in the early phases of KM system development, as awareness among users grows and enhancements are introduced.

Technology gives the means for tracking use of a KM system, providing data on quantitative measurements such as hits and online feedback for qualitative response. However, our experience suggests that meaningful KM measurement, particularly its linkage to performance improvement, remains a major challenge. Nonetheless, the importance of measurement increases correspondingly to increases in levels of commitment and investment of an organization to a KM program.

Recognizing the tentative empirical cause-and-effect linkage between KM and business performance, we have been forced to focus measurement on surrogate measures of value, such as use, anecdotal cases, and participant surveys.

Some criticize usage data as a weak, perhaps even misleading, indicator of value, largely because usage is moot on outcomes. Raw usage data does not effectively discern between appropriate and inappropriate use. By extension, a higher level of use does not necessarily translate to desirable outcomes and organizational value, and could indeed produce potentially undesirable effects. Use of knowledge that is wrong for the need at hand is a negative, not a positive.

These are valid concerns. We believe that they can be addressed in large measure by the presence of formal CoP roles, such as CoP champions and content managers performing as subject matter experts, being responsible for maintaining proper context for knowledge shared through the CoP and acting as contact resources. If one accepts that these are effective checks in the process, then usage data can serve as an effective indicator of value. Equally telling as a metric of value is the percentage of the CoP population who are repeat users. Drawing on the Towers Perrin DataMart, we also mine demographic information of our user population to identify use patterns by role, location, service longevity, etc.

Establishing KM Measurement Function

Recognizing the importance of developing and applying meaningful measurements, KM system managers at Towers Perrin developed a strategy that includes both quantitative and qualitative measurements. Interestingly, our experience has been that while the quantitative data are important, and indicate continuing growth in the use and value of the system, the qualitative information gained through user surveys and feedback provides greater insights into ways to improve the system for individuals and user communities.

We have begun to track use over time and correlate it along the lines described in Table 21.4.

Web technology also permits the collection of qualitative information that not only measures the growing use of the Towers Perrin system, but also provides key insights about the features that work well and the improvements that will provide value to users and their clients. We obtain this feedback in two ways:

- Periodic surveys and interviews of Towers Perrin practitioners, with questions focusing on the impact of KM system use in day-to-day work, as well as the value of the system in attracting new business or expanding current assignments
- Feedback buttons throughout the KM system asking users to "rate this page" from a range of perspectives, including ease of locating and need for additional links or information.

Such survey results provide Towers Perrin with key insights into possible missing pieces, improvements in technology, and practical real-world issues in the realm of KM. For example, if the company had previously identified a dozen

Table 21.4   Use analysis and correlations.

USE PROFILE

Quantitative measurements: volume, type, and duration of use

- Visitors by:
  - CoP
  - Level and role
  - Geography
  - Years of service
- CoP overall use over time and by practitioner by:
  - Level and role
  - Geography
  - Years of service
- Content and tools used by:
  - Level and role
  - Geography
  - Years of service

Quantitative business impact measurements

- Add value or quality to client work
- Factor in winning business
- Personal time savings per month
- Degree to which KM makes roles and work easier to perform—personally, teams
- Contribution to new ideas and innovation

subject matter experts who could be called on for a project, and KM has developed and identified 120 with the same level of expertise, then this is a measure of the aggregate value of KM to the organization.

KM MEASUREMENT FOR CONTINUOUS IMPROVEMENT OF KM

Qualitative Assessments

Just as important, however, are measurements based on individual users' experiences with the KM system. Using Web-based tools, users can provide important insights into actual use and perceived value of the system. They can identify content and features that have been helpful, note missing pieces, pose questions, and make suggestions for improving the system to make it more valuable. Online surveys, questions attached to user sessions, or even virtual focus groups can automate the collection of user feedback.

For example, knowledge that originates with the KM system itself can answer such questions as these:

- What types of knowledge delivery formats are most effective in improving performance when time, cost, and performance measurements are taken into consideration?
- Which users or user communities benefit most from KM use? Which benefit least, and why?
- What do usage and user surveys tell us about competency gaps that should be addressed by training, development, staffing, and recruitment functions?
- Which organizational units, functions, or locations seem to have a surplus of intellectual capital, that is, an abundance of high-level users of the KM system and competencies to match?
- Which new competencies—such as the ability to learn and apply strategic planning principles presented in virtual seminars—should the company add to its competency framework and recruit or develop?
- Which individual managers and professionals in the organization contribute most to the KM system by creating and imparting new knowledge? Who are the real thought leaders?

The mechanization of a KM measurement permits real-time tracking of usage, qualitative feedback, and correlation with business performance measurement data and audience demographics generated by human resources and business systems.

CONCLUSION

This chapter has attempted to share insights gained from over five years of experience with a global KM program. In particular, our experience has confirmed the ongoing importance of alignment, content, and measurement to the success of our KM program.

In the area of alignment, our experience has reinforced the need to evolve our thinking and approach, driven as much by environmental change as by a natural growth and maturing of KM—from initial proof of concept to institutionalized global enterprise scale initiative. In short, we recognized a simple but important imperative: Aspects of KM need to change to reflect changes in the broader organizational and business environments and to remain in synch with changing organizational priorities.

As the organization's strategies, goals, and operations change, it is the responsibility of the KM team to ensure and demonstrate continued alignment, such as through periodic reviews and planning sessions with business leaders or reports. Knowledge management should cultivate KM advocates from within the business to assist in this effort and be prepared to demonstrate alignment through KM strategy, plans, and case-study examples.

Our summary observations regarding content center on utility, ownership, and enterprise processes. An obvious requirement of KM is that it be relevant. More than that, however, a CoP must enable individual members to do their jobs more effectively and efficiently. We have come to regard practical utility as an essential requirement. This forces an orientation for KM and CoPs on the individual. Our goal is for the CoP to help staff in broad organizational roles relating to winning business, doing assignments, and learning through content and capabilities that facilitate sharing and application of knowledge and know-how in the context of the work of individual staff. In short, for KM to succeed at the macro, organizational level, it must first succeed at the micro, individual level.

Our experience has also demonstrated the absolute necessity and efficacy of "business" ownership of CoP content. That is, content is the responsibility of subject-matter experts. The challenge to KM remains that of obtaining business commitment to the role and translating that commitment to staff and resources performing ongoing content role.

There is yet another dimension to content that we have found to be equally important, namely, to maintain an enterprise perspective to content. Our KM operations unit must play the role of content-process and technology-platform builder and aggregator to ensure the seamless compatibility and consistency that is essential to leverage knowledge and know-how at the organizational level.

Concerning measurement, we increasingly consider measurement as a practical necessity. Our challenge has been to understand what management values and expects in this area. Our strategy concerning measurement is to consider it a functional requirement of KM processes and systems versus an afterthought. Our goal is to integrate measurement in the fabric of the KM platform.

In summary, we have developed our KM platform and operations to support our strategy for alignment, content, and measurement.

CHAPTER 22

Knowledge Management at the U.S. Department of Labor: A Case Study of Implementing Knowledge Management

Roland G. Droitsch,[1] U.S. Department of Labor

INTRODUCTION

An increasing number of corporations in the private sector have been implementing KM systems in their organizations. Many large companies have chief knowledge officers with an overall responsibility of integrating knowledge-based systems into their operations.[2] While there has been significant movement in this direction in the federal government, KM has not been adopted as broadly as in the corporate sector. Both private and public sectors, however, are facing many of the same pressures from the explosion of information in their organizations, especially the continuing stream of information flowing from their digital systems. This chapter will examine some of the forces at work in the federal sector driving the need for implementing knowledge-based systems and KM through the lens of the U.S. Department of Labor (DOL). It will describe the implementation of a number of key KM systems in the DOL to date. This chapter will also examine the problems of implementing KM in the federal sector broadly, and the preconditions that may be needed for full implementation.

THE EMERGENCE OF KM IN THE CORPORATE SECTOR

Among corporations and private institutions, a number of factors have been identified as the driving forces behind the growing interest in KM. Most would agree that the roots of KM can be found in the computer revolution beginning in the 1950s with the advent of the large mainframe computers. The mainframes were followed by the wave of personal computers in the 1970s and beyond, which contributed further to vast amounts of information produced and captured in digital format.

Building on the increasing power of microprocessors, the marriage of computer technology with telecommunications technology led to the eruption of information collection, processing, and storage that has continued to the present day. Throughout the 1990s, increasingly sophisticated information technologies emerged, enabling institutions to assemble, store, and process ever-larger quantities of information. The advent of the Internet, in particular, unleashed an explosion of information technology that convinced even the most reluctant that we were indeed entering the *information age*.[3]

This dramatic growth in computer-processing speeds, electronic storage, and processing capacity typically were not matched by the ability of organizations to effectively organize their information in ways that would lead to better decision making. In short, much of the raw information that was captured often did not translate into *operationally useful knowledge* for decision makers or those directly involved in managing such operations. The technological ability to collect and maintain increasingly large amounts of information, coupled with the operational need to access critical information, were primary factors contributing to the need for corporations to address the management of this information. Information-intensive sectors, especially health and pharmacological, computer, and telecommunications and manufacturing, came to rely increasingly on more sophisticated information systems for their day-to-day operations. In order to stay competitive, the efficient management of information quickly became a matter of *competitive survival* rather than one of simple efficiency improvement.[4] Recent KM articles (Barth, 2000; Finneran, 1999) have concentrated on KM as a practice implemented to gain a competitive advantage and manage knowledge in ways that directly affect performance and success.[5]

THE EMERGING NEED FOR KM IMPLEMENTATION AT THE DOL

Federal agencies, such as the DOL, have faced many of the same forces that led corporations to adopt better KM techniques. However, federal agencies obviously were not driven by bottom-line considerations or the need to remain competitive like the corporate sector. Rather, a different set of factors has forced the federal sector to address information management—namely the need to sustain program operations in an era of constrained resources and vastly increased information requirements. The DOL presents an excellent example of the impact that these forces have had on energizing the increased use of knowledge-based systems.

The DOL can best be described as a "holding company" that is engaged in a wide variety of activities that relate to the workplace and workforce. Its activities can broadly be categorized into three general areas: (1) administering a large number of employment-related regulatory programs, (2) operating programs that promote employment and training, and (3) collecting and disseminating economic statistics related to the workplace and workforce.[6]

Under the first broad area, the DOL is responsible for administering numerous regulatory statutes that define the relationship between an employer and employee. These statutes, for example, include such areas as the regulation of child labor, the minimum wage, workplace safety, workplace discrimination, and the security of pension and health programs. The administration of these regulatory programs is inherently information intensive. The regulation promulgation process, for example, calls for public comment on proposed regulations, which marks the first step in a lengthy set of procedures leading to the publishing of a final regulation. Thereafter, follows a stream of informational activities involving compliance assistance, interpretive letters, court challenges, and enforcement actions. Each of these activities are intensive information- and knowledge-based processes, such as the analyses of court challenges by legal staff or the desirability of undertaking enforcement action by legal, policy, and enforcement personnel.

Related to the second area of activities, DOL manages a variety of programs to promote employment and training in the private sector. The focus of these programs is to promote employment and employability of American workers either through job placement or through training that increases worker skills. Information about labor markets, the identification of job opportunities, and placement of unemployed workers are core activities. The training of workers, especially those who are not equipped with the skills necessary to easily gain employment in this era of increased technology, has become an increasingly important function. Clearly, these labor market functions, involving either job placement or training, are information intensive and knowledge-based processes.[7]

The responsibility of collecting and publishing workplace statistics by the DOL's Bureau of Labor Statistics (BLS) is yet another facet of DOL's portfolio of activities. The BLS is responsible for publishing such well-known data as the national employment and unemployment statistics, the Consumer Price Index, and the Employment Cost Index. The collection, processing, and subsequent dissemination of statistical information is, by its very nature, an intensive information-based activity. All of the BLS's activities require complex economic and statistical expertise that requires the use of sophisticated knowledge-based processes. Pressed by significant resource constraints and demands to produce new and larger data sets, the adoption of new information processing tools was a necessity rather than a luxury.[8]

Knowledge-based components of each of the DOL's major activities have always been integral to all DOL activities; however, the *vastly increased volume of information* associated with these activities is new. Also new is the fact that an increasing amount of this information is being collected, processed, and distributed in digital format. The DOL, as will be shown later, has begun to use knowledge-based systems to handle these ever-increasing information flows. However, unlike the private sector, the DOL is responding to factors other than the need to be competitive as it increasingly adopts knowledge-based systems and KM in general. Following is a discussion of the more important factors motivating DOL.

First, there has been a substantial increase in the DOL's workload, while resources, particularly in the form of personnel, simultaneously have been constrained. For example, from 1960 to 1974, the number of regulation programs administered by the DOL tripled, growing from 43 to 134.[9] Since then, the number has grown to approximately 180 statutes.[10] Similarly, according to the BLS, the size of the national workforce over that period has increased from 78,678,000 in 1970 to 142,769,000 as of May 2002. Despite these dramatic increases in regulatory programs and the near doubling of the U.S. workforce, the DOL staff, which numbered over 24,000 in 1980, is currently approximately 17,000.

Second, KM is growing in importance because the information content of administering the DOL programs has substantially increased. With regard to regulations, there are a host of new statutory and analytical requirements. Executive Order 12290 on Regulatory Planning and Review requires the preparation of complex Regulatory Impact Analyses that attempt to estimate the costs and benefits a regulation will have to the U.S. economy. The Small Business Regulatory Enforcement and Fairness Act (SBREFA) requires agencies to undertake special measures to ensure that regulations do not disproportionately impact small businesses. To this end, federal agencies must prepare Regulatory Flexibility Analyses that examine the impact a regulation may have on small businesses. The SBREFA also requires the preparation and dissemination of special easy-to-understand compliance assistance information to small businesses.[11] In the area of budgeting and planning, the recently enacted Government Performance and Results Act (GPRA) requires that federal agencies institute a complex strategic planning process along with measurable goals. The Clinger-Cohen Act requires that agencies undertake a similar comprehensive strategic planning activity with respect to their information technology assets. These and many other requirements all demand a substantial amount of information collection, analysis, processing storage, maintenance, retrieval, and so forth.

A third factor promoting the increased use of KM is the growing pressure from the public and Congress demonstrating that government must become more customer-oriented and provide services efficiently. The number of bills introduced in Congress recently that would mandate federal agencies to build electronic government systems has demonstrated this. Responding to these legislative pressures, the Bush Administration testified before the Senate Committee on Government Affairs that it was ...

> This administration's vision to champion a citizen-centric electronic government framework that will result in an order of magnitude improvement in the federal government's value to the citizen. We must simplify business processes to maximize the benefit of technology, resulting in processes that will be faster, cheaper, and more efficient. We must manage information flows and link them across agencies and the federal government so that we can find and use what we collect now and in the future.[12]

Finally, KM is becoming increasingly important to the DOL and other federal agencies due to the demographic makeup of its workforce. Over the next decade, it is expected that roughly half of the federal workforce will retire or turn over.[13] This significant increase in the turnover of the federal workforce will lead to a vast drain of accumulated knowledge resident in those leaving the federal government. In large measure, the impact of this "brain drain" has not been addressed though the importance of its impact is becoming increasingly recognized.

The Emergence of KM at the DOL

In September 1998, the DOL sponsored a workshop on KM opportunities.[14] The purpose of the workshop was to introduce key staff, particularly non-IT staff, to the concepts of KM and to identify approaches for the DOL agencies to implement knowledge-based systems. One of the workshop's findings was that the DOL had already been working on a number of KM tools, without any executive-level management decision to embark on establishing a program of KM at the DOL. The emergence and availability of several KM tools, coupled with the pressures identified previously, led to early adoption of KM practices.

The first important knowledge-based system was the mounting of a DOL-wide Internet Web site in 1995. Like many federal departments, the DOL agencies were beginning to mount information on the Internet, providing the public with knowledge about their programs. As a general rule, departments mounted a home page from which links were established with various agencies within that department. These agencies were generally free to mount information they felt was appropriate without any particular structure. The DOL took a more defined approach. First, agencies were provided with an overall structure to mount specific categories of information in defined fields. Second, agencies were *required* to mount the information. Agency information was then cross-indexed between the DOL's home page and agency home pages. Using this structure, a person seeking information on the DOL Web site could find it either by accessing a specific agency's site, such as the Occupational Safety and Health Administration (OSHA), or by accessing that same information from the main DOL Web site.

With most of DOL's "line" agencies engaged in regulatory activity, this structure was particularly useful to those seeking information about the DOL regulatory programs. Specifically, each regulatory agency had to mount such information as (1) the statutes they administered, (2) the implementing regulations, and (3) the accompanying compliance assistance materials in defined areas of their agency. The user then could collectively view such information across DOL agencies as well as finding agency-specific information on a particular agency's site. By defining the organizational structure for mounting information, the DOL added value to the DOL Internet system, both by improving access to regulatory information and by working towards the goal of assuring that the information mounted on the DOL Web site was timely, accurate, and complete.

The DOL's Employment Laws Assistance for Workers and Small Businesses, or "elaws," were another important KM tool. *Elaws* are a set of expert systems that capture knowledge about particular DOL regulations. These systems emulate the interaction a user might have with a human expert to solve a problem. Expert systems are probably the most established form of artificial intelligence technology and are able to embed complex information into a computer model. The computer model can then be queried on a fact-specific situation and provide the user with an answer to his/her specific question. In short, expert systems perform reasoning using previously established rules in a narrow and well-defined domain. They combine a knowledge base of rules and domain-specific facts with information from clients and users about specific instances of problems in the knowledge domains of these systems.[15]

With the large number of regulations that the DOL administers, providing such compliance assistance has always been a difficult undertaking. The vast number of regulated businesses is relatively small. Of the roughly 6.5 million business establishments in the U.S. that have employees, approximately 99.7 percent have fewer than 250 workers. The challenge to the DOL has been to provide these companies with compliance assistance information tailored to their needs. Often, written materials and pamphlets were too general or were not addressed to the size of firm inquiring about compliance. With voluntary compliance as the backbone of the DOL's regulatory administration, the failure to provide needed information on regulatory compliance was a critical shortcoming. Mounting a system of elaws, expert systems advisors began to fill this critical void.

Each of the existing 24 elaws expert systems or "advisors" provide information about specific laws or regulations, such as the Family and Medical Leave Act (FMLA) and the Fair Labor Standards Act (FLSA). The advisors imitate the interaction that an employer or employee might have with a DOL regulatory expert. They ask questions, provide goal information, and direct the users to the appropriate resolution based on their responses. The goal of elaws is to provide the public with better, timely, and, most importantly, specific information while simultaneously reducing the burden on the DOL personnel of supplying compliance information.

In the area of employment and training, the DOL has undertaken a massive effort to build a nationwide system of posting job opportunities online with America's Job Bank.[16] The Employment and Training Administration worked with state employment security agencies to develop a common taxonomy for job listings and an integrating structure that would allow each state to develop its system within this common framework.

In addition to America's Job Bank, a parallel system, America's Talent Bank, was developed where job seekers could mount their resumes. A site called America's Career Center, which provides information on occupations, their educational requirements, and expected compensation levels, was also added. Currently in progress is the development of a site to be called America's Learning Exchange that lists training opportunities.

This four-element structure—America's Job Bank, America's Talent Bank, Career Center, and America's Learning Exchange—provides the user with all elements of a virtual labor market. At the core, the system seeks primarily to connect job providers with job seekers. In addition to simply connecting job providers and job seekers, the system's occupational outlook section provides career planning information so that a person can improve employment by identifying a new career opportunity *and* by obtaining information regarding any training needed to qualify for the new position.

By the time of the DOL KM workshop, America's Job Bank was receiving an astonishing 300 million hits per month and America's Talent Bank was posting over one million resumes. America's Job Bank and its accompanying knowledge-based systems began to demonstrate the power of organizing large amounts of information and making it easily accessible to the DOL's customers.

In the area of statistics, the BLS has taken the lead in exploring its Web site as a means of organizing and providing information to the public. The BLS spent considerable time on developing a functional site as opposed to one that reflected the agency's organization. Hence, information on the site was displayed in terms of functional areas, such as "employment and unemployment" or "prices and living conditions." The BLS also mounted new information within minutes of its release and implemented intensive security and quality control mechanisms. For each of the functional areas, the BLS developed an e-mail system where a user could request additional information or obtain technical assistance. Therefore, by the time of the KM workshop, the BLS had developed a powerful knowledge-based tool that organized and efficiently disseminated statistical information to the public.

Building Towards a KM Structure at the DOL

Following the KM workshop, no single, coordinated effort was initiated for implementing KM on a departmental or "enterprise-wide" scale, despite the considerable interest expressed among the DOL agencies. The increased awareness of KM and its role, however, stimulated further advances within the DOL agencies to implement new knowledge-based systems or to enhance existing systems.

Perhaps the most notable new KM activity was centered on improving the scope and functionality of the DOL Web site system. With continued advances in Internet use by the public, DOL agencies became increasingly aware of the Web's value as a house for large repositories of information that could be distributed to a variety of users at low cost. Initially, the Web was seen primarily as a tool to inform the public, and, indeed, a limited subset of the public—those with access to the Internet. The rapidly growing access to the Internet by greater segments of the population led to a reduction of the "digital divide" and the recognition that the DOL Web served not just a small elite group but many different users. For the DOL, the two primary user groups were employers and employees. However, other sets were soon identified, which included trade organizations, academics, pension holders, and retirees. It was also recognized that one of these groups was the DOL employees who were increasingly using DOL Web information as an *operational tool*. The diversity of the users and the growing volume of information mounted continue to present the DOL with a significant challenge.

At the initial stages of the DOL Web system, agencies were primarily focused on simply mounting information that was readily available. In a relatively short period of time, several hundred thousand documents were mounted and concerns began to focus on how this information was being *managed*. Was the mounted information accurate? Was outdated material deleted or archived? Was the information that should be mounted on the system? It became increasingly clear that significant measures would need to be taken to better organize the DOL Web information and to implement a means to assure that it was consistently timely, accurate, and complete.

To this end, three actions were taken. First, a Secretary's Order was issued delineating and defining roles and responsibilities regarding the management of the DOL Internet sites.[17] A key distinction was made with respect to the operation and management of the DOL servers (hardware, software, security, etc.) and the organization and management of Web content. The Secretary's Order placed general responsibility for the content of the DOL Web sites under the Office of Policy.

Second, each DOL agency was required to establish procedures whereby its Web content would be placed under the oversight of a senior policy official in that agency, as opposed to an agency's technical staff. Clearly, content or the knowledge responsibilities of Web management were reorganized as a *program* function rather than a *computer technology* function.

The third measure taken to address Web management was to develop metadata for all the information currently on the DOL Web sites and to metatag all new information to be mounted in the future as part of a DOL-wide initiative. Such a fully metatagged site would enable the DOL to dramatically manage, organize, and add significant value to the DOL Web information. The development of a metadata taxonomy covering all aspects of DOL activity has been an enormous undertaking. Several existing metadata formats, initiatives, and standards were examined to provide knowledge about metadata construction and use. These initiatives included the Machine-Assisted Readable Cataloging (MARC) format developed for traditional library cataloging usage, the Government Information Locator System (GILS), and the Dublin Core/Warwick Framework.

The basic structure of the DOL metadata schema was designed to be easily mapped or "cross-walked" to existing categories within these major initiatives, while still using wording specific to the DOL's needs. In this way, if the DOL Metadata Project were later subsumed into a larger cross-government metadata initiative, the schema would be able to convert or coexist with a minimum of "reengineering." In a similar spirit, the DOL system employs the commonly used HTML META tag to format and present the DOL metadata in order to use an existing Web standard and, thereby, provide the metadata to a larger audience than just the DOL as several search engines use the information in META tags as part of their indexing and searching algorithms.

Strong efforts were made to eliminate as much jargon and "buzzword of the week" flavor from the metadata structure and contents as practicable, and to leave room for future additions and changes. Also built into the database supporting the schema was the ability to identify synonyms, related concepts, and several other relationships within the metadata structure and contents, thus, capturing and using semantic relationships and syntactical structures to further broaden and deepen classification and searching using the schema structure. For example, the term "young workers" may be used to classify a Web document aimed at a particular audience. The term is linked to a number of synonyms such as "kids," "youth," "teenagers," plus a closely related subject category of "child labor"—all of which may be terms used by those searching the DOL Web site.

The Metadata Project is clearly a critical and major element in the DOL's efforts to move towards a knowledge-based information system. When completed, the ability to access specific information, to array specific groupings of information, and to tailor responses will add a dramatic knowledge-enhancing capability to the

DOL's Web site. The organization and structure of the information on the Web are rapidly becoming the building blocks of KM in the department.

The Move Towards Integrating DOL's Knowledge-Based Systems

The increase in the quality and functionality of the DOL Web information enabled the department to build other knowledge-based tools and integrate them into an expanded information distribution system. In June of 2001, the Secretary of Labor announced a Four-Point Initiative directed at significantly improving ways by which the DOL could provide compliance assistance to the regulated community.[18] The Four-Point Initiative called for (1) a complete functional redesign of the DOL Web site, (2) the mounting of a DOL-wide toll-free information service, (3) the establishment by each DOL agency of an electronic correspondence system, and (4) the continued development of additional expert system advisors under the elaws program.

Providing compliance assistance to the DOL's regulated community has always been a difficult challenge. The DOL's regulations cover nearly all business establishments in the U.S., with the vast majority of businesses in the U.S. classified as "small" by the Small Business Administration's standards. These organizations' ability to understand and comply with the complex set of regulations promulgated by the DOL is a daunting task.[19] The Secretary's initiative was directed at addressing this problem primarily through the use of technology and knowledge-based systems.

The redesign of the DOL home page was a significant contribution to the use of this knowledge-based tool by radically improving its functionality. The initial DOL Web structure focused on DOL *organizational* units, so that each agency mounted information under that unit. Thus, if you wanted to find information regarding minimum wage, one must first access the Employment Standards Administration's home page and then access the Wage and Hour Division where that information was located. This organizational approach, while serving as a useful initial construct in mounting Web information, detracted from user functionality. The redesign sought to focus on the different audiences that might use the DOL Web information and then organized information around that functional user. The redesign has been a powerful tool enhancing the knowledge content of the DOL Web site, and has received excellent reviews to date.

The improved functionality of the DOL Web provided a cornerstone for building and integrating other information tools that used common Web information. The DOL toll-free information service, for example, employs a desktop interface with information supplied from the DOL Web sites. The electronic correspondence system, in the case of some DOL agencies, is sent first to the Call Center and, only if it cannot be answered there, is sent to the DOL "tier two" staff. A customer service representative at the Call Center might provide a caller with a specific Web address or e-mail him/her the link to the specific elaws advisor that will answer the specific question asked. It is important to note that the elements of the Four-Point Initiative are not free standing; rather, they are an integrated set of tools using common platforms and common information databases. This initiative was clearly an important step towards a more abundant KM environment.

The development by each DOL agency of an electronic correspondence system was also an important step in the process of implementing knowledge-based systems at the DOL. The e-mail response service allows employers and employees to ask questions electronically about DOL issues. The DOL Web site provides users with the ability to choose from a list of topics or internal DOL agencies under the "Contact Us" section. In this way, users are ensured their question will go to the appropriate office and that they will receive a timely and accurate answer.

The last component of the secretary's Four-Point Initiative is the continued development of additional expert system advisors under the elaws program described previously. There are currently 24 elaws advisors and several under development. One of the systems under development seeks to identify which of the DOL major regulations apply to a particular company. Once identified, the system will point the user to the specific elaws advisors that apply to their company's situation.

Planting the Seeds of a Broad-Based KM System

Perhaps the most significant development in knowledge-based systems has occurred in the area of learning technologies. At their best, these technologies can provide interactive user-customized interfaces and modular lessons that allow clients to teach themselves as if they had a flexible one-on-one expert tutor. The DOL has partnered with the Department of Defense (DOD) to develop voluntary standards for Web-based distributed learning: the Advanced Distributed Learning (ADL) Initiative. Learning has always been the central feature in the transference of knowledge. Much of the previous discussion of knowledge-based systems has concerned the collection and organization of information in a way that builds knowledge through better access and distribution of such information. The transfer of knowledge through learning, however, is critical to, and is the lifeblood of, any KM system.

The importance of the ADL Initiative needs to be understood in the context of the roles the two agencies play in U.S. education and training programs for adult workers. The DOD is the largest adult training organization in the world, spending approximately $14 billion annually on such training. Much of this training is directly transferable to post-military, private sector occupations. The DOL is the federal agency primarily responsible for funding and promoting adult learning for workers. Together, these two departments can exercise a powerful influence on the developers and providers of adult computer-based education and training systems. By teaming together, the two most influential departments involved with adult learning in the workplace are uniquely positioned to establish requirements that define how emerging learning technologies will support the 21st century worker as a lifelong learner.

The ADL Initiative emerged out of the 1996 Quadrennial Defense Review conducted by the DOD that had become increasingly aware of the need to dramatically improve its system to deliver complex instructional materials designed to train to higher performance levels. Such instructional material needed to be delivered to far-flung regions, such as Bosnia and Afghanistan, on a real-time basis. Traditional classroom training was found to be increasingly inadequate in the face of complex training requirements that were constantly being updated. Considering this, the DOD undertook an intense review of its computer-based learning systems.

In this review, the DOD learned it had paid for the development of thousands of computer-based instructional systems. These systems, however, were expensive to develop. Once in place, their technology rapidly became obsolete and the systems were not interoperable. Delivery of such instructional materials also presented major problems. The different proprietary systems they used required the maintenance of expensive licensing, making it difficult to share these programs across different services and commands. In addition, different systems were needed to run different proprietary programs. Modifications were expensive and time consuming since the training programs were essentially "hard wired" to specific hardware suites. Delivery via the Internet was impossible for many of the computer-based programs. At first glance, the sum of these problems painted a discouraging picture regarding the worth of investing in computer-based instructional systems, at least in the haphazard and costly manner in which they were currently being handled.

An important positive finding did emerge, however, in that the effectiveness of its teaching capacity, computer-based learning compared very favorably with instructor-based learning. Indeed, those systems that were more advanced and employed higher level interactive and simulation techniques scored substantially higher than instructor-based learning.[20]

In light of these findings, the DOD decided to develop a department-wide strategy to overcome the inefficiencies and technical frustrations in their current arrangement and harness the power of emerging learning technologies to modernize their system of education and training. This strategy was the ADL Initiative.[21]

Shortly after the DOD launched the ADL Initiative, the White House Office of Science and Technology Policy (OSTP) sought to expand the DOD initiative to other federal departments. The OSTP drafted an Executive Memorandum, "Enhancing Learning and Education Through Technology," which referenced the ADL Initiative and charged the DOL to "promote adoption of the best new ways of using technology to enhance training and education programs that provide federal support for education and training."[22] In 1999, the DOD and DOL established the ADL Co-Lab to foster collaborative research, development and assessment of common tools, standards, and content and guidelines for the ADL Initiative. Working with a host of private companies and universities, the ADL Initiative is focused on developing requirements and best practices that will define the structure of "learning objects" so that they can be arrayed in a variety of ways to deliver learning content over the Web. On January 31, 2000, the ADL Initiative's extensive cooperative efforts across public and private sectors culminated in the release of an initial set of specifications and guidelines, called the Shareable Content Object Reference Model (SCORM), version 1.0.[23]

Over the following two years, versions of the SCORM evolved and matured to new levels. The SCORM, version 1.2 release added the ability to package instructional material and metadata for import and export. These XML-based specifications provided the crucial link between learning content repositories and learning management systems. The just released SCORM, version 1.3 defines the internal architecture of course structures within learning modules. Most importantly, version 1.3 deals with the complex issue of sequencing objects so as to be able to array them into a course structure.

To reiterate, the ability to easily capture, store, link, modify, reuse, and distribute learning content is at the heart of KM. Learning objects can take various forms, including verbal, pictorial, video, or written. They can be sequenced or aggregated into refresher learning experiences or full courses. They can be used as instantaneous refreshers for some distinct portion of a course and, hence, are an excellent tool for lifelong learning models. The "granularization" of learning objects makes it possible, for the first time, to deliver learning that is truly learner-centric rather than providing a "one-size-fits-all" course centered around an instructor.

While there is a considerable amount of development yet to be done before the SCORM-based instructional material is made widely available, dramatic progress has been made. One may expect to see a relatively rapid diffusion of this knowledge-based technology for both government and university use in the near future.

THE PROBLEMS AND CHALLENGES OF IMPLEMENTING KM

The DOL has made substantial strides in adopting and implementing a number of important knowledge-based systems. However, it is fair to ask whether or not the DOL has implemented KM. Although the DOL has instituted several department-wide knowledge-based systems, such as the Internet, elaws, and the toll-free information service, the DOL has not instituted an enterprisewide KM structure. While some federal agencies are beginning to explore such a top-down approach, most, including the DOL, have implemented elements of KM on an ad hoc basis based on particular needs and existing opportunities.

There are a number of reasons for adopting this more fragmented approach. First, KM is a relatively new discipline that builds heavily on a number of existing fields, including computer science, artificial intelligence, organizational behavior, and information science. As such, it is not yet well defined in its own right. Karl Wiig, one of the pioneers in KM, provides this definition (found in Droitsch, Medsker, and Demers): "The objective of knowledge management is to make the enterprise act as intelligently as possible to secure its viability and overall success, and otherwise realize the best value of its knowledge assets."[24] Tom Finneran gave the following definition in "The Data Administration Newsletter": "Knowledge Management is the disciple that helps spread knowledge of individuals or groups across organizations in ways that directly affect performance."[25] Steve Barth wrote, "Knowledge management is the practice of harnessing and exploiting intellectual capital to gain competitive advantage and customer commitment through efficient innovation and faster and more effective decision-making."[26] Robert Seiner defined KM similarly and said, "Knowledge Management envisions getting the right information, in the right context, to the right person, at the right time, for the right business purpose."[27]

Such broad definitions do not easily lend themselves to actual implementation. With a lack of clarity as to the objectives and methodology of implementing KM, it is unclear to many precisely what the benefits to be obtained are. The various definitions suggest a variety of different objectives. They also raise the question of what is required and whose responsibility it is to implement KM.

The second reason it is difficult to implement KM top-down revolves around organizational issues. It may be simple to state that KM is the responsibility of a company's CEO (or, in the case of a federal department, the secretary). However, to whom should the latter delegate operational responsibility for implementing KM? In the case of a corporation, as noted previously, an increasing number of companies have designated a chief knowledge officer. While this may work in the private, corporate setting, the question remains as to where the locus of KM activity needs to be placed in the federal sector. Is KM an IT function that is simply an extension of the chief information officer's duties? Or, is KM rooted in the operational needs of program activities that would fall among the duties of program managers? Alternatively, is KM a function that should be housed in a department's human resources (HR) division? These questions raise several of the key problems in implementing KM on an enterprise basis at the federal level.

In fact, KM involves all these component parts and to place the focus on one versus the other skews KM implementation in one particular direction and robs it of its holistic aspects. In the final analysis, it would appear that KM is best rooted in *program operations* with IT and HR, providing critical supporting roles. A core element of KM is to efficiently harness an organization's information and knowledge assets for the purpose of furthering that organization's objectives, be they to generate profits or to administer programs in the most efficient manner possible. Programmatic requirements for identifying, collecting, organizing, and distributing information and knowledge to all those who might benefit from it, again, would appear to be a paramount consideration in implementing KM in the federal sector.

Earlier in this chapter, four factors were identified as forces contributing to the DOL and other federal agencies to adopt knowledge-based systems: increased workloads, dramatic increases in the information content in administering programs, strong political pressure to efficiently deliver program services, and the anticipated brain drain due to the high turnover rate of federal employees in the next decade. These forces will continue to push the DOL and other agencies to adopt efficiency enhancing techniques. However, this ad hoc approach will not ultimately lead to an enterprise-wide effort to fully adopt KM.

Ultimately, it is important for the head of a department or agency to provide the vision and identify responsibilities for KM as an integral part of program operations, not as some added "requirement" imposed from the top but as a strategic philosophy that integrates all the department's information and knowledge-based resources. The strategic focus, as noted earlier, must be driven by program needs and considerations, not by technology. As we continue to move into the 21st century, one of the few certainties is that the information needed and generated by an organization will continue to increase dramatically. The ability to utilize that information and extract operational knowledge from it will determine whether that organization will remain viable. In the case of a private corporation, KM will become a necessity in order to remain competitive. For the federal agency, KM will become a necessity in order to continue to effectively operate and deliver program services to its customers.

ENDNOTES

1. Dr. Droitsch is the deputy assistant secretary for policy at the U.S. DOL. The views expressed in this chapter are his and do not necessarily reflect the policy of the DOL. Throughout the preparation of this chapter, Alyssa Watzman provided substantial research assistance to the author for which he is deeply indebted.

2A. "About 20 percent of the Fortune 500 [companies] have chief knowledge management officers. Four federal agencies have also joined the ranks of the CKO-enabled." From Barquin, R. C. (2000, May). Knowledge management in the public sector. *Performance and Results*, 1(12). © 2000 by Management Concepts, Inc.

2B. The Chief Information Officers Council was established by Executive Order 13011 on July 16, 1996. It's a principal interagency forum for improving practices in the federal government agency information resources. Membership is comprised of chief information officers and deputy CIOs from 28 federal executive agencies, including the DOL.

2C. More than 70 percent of Fortune 500 companies have knowledge programs, according to: Liang, Q., Hernandez, H., Kirch, A, and Prescott, P. (1999, April). "What is knowledge management (KM)?" *Gotcha!* (Web-based magazine) For more information, see: http://www.sims.berkeley.edu/courses/is213/s99/ Projects/P9/web_site/about_km.html

2D. "Major firms, such as BankBoston, Coca-Cola, Ernst & Young, General Electric, Johnson & Johnson, Monsanto, and Pricewaterhouse Coopers already have CKOs and knowledge management programs. . . . Typically, the CKO is a senior-level position, commanding an annual salary ranging from $200,000 to $350,000 per year." From Herschel, R. T. and Hamid, R. N. (2000). Chief knowledge officer: Critical success factors for knowledge management. "Biztech Network Newsletter."

3. For further discussion, see U.S. Department of Labor. (1999). Technology and globalization. *Futurework: Trends and Challenges for Work in the 21st Century*, pp. 60–75. Washington, DC.

4. Droitsch, R., Medsker, L., and Demers, D. (2000, July). Knowledge management at the U.S. Department of Labor. *Artificial Intelligence and Soft Computing Conference Proceedings*, pp. 320. Anaheim, CA; Calgary, AB, Zurich, Switzerland: Proceedings of the International Association of Science and Technology for Development (IASTED).

5A. Barth, S. (2000, July 4). Defining knowledge management. *CRM Magazine*. Available at: http://www.destinationcrm.com/articles/default.asp? ArticleID=1400

5B. Finneran, T. (2000, October). A component-based knowledge management system. "The Data Administration Newsletter." Published by Robert S. Seiner. Available at: http://www.tdan.com/i009hy04.htm

6. See http://www.dol.gov for more detailed information on the DOL's programs and activities.

7. See http://www.doleta.gov for specific program information on the DOL's Employment and Training Administration.

8. See http://www.bls.gov for specific program information on the DOL's BLS.

9. Dunlop, J. T. (1976, February). The limits of legal compulsion. *Labor Law Review*, 27(2): 67–74.

10. U.S. Department of Labor: Office of the Assistant Secretary for Policy. (1993, June 21). "Outline of Statutes and Regulations Affecting the Workplace." A report prepared for the Commission on the Future of Worker-Management Relations. Washington, DC.

11. For a full listing of regulatory promulgation requirements, see: U.S. Department of Labor: Office of the Assistant Secretary for Policy. (2002). *Regulatory Review Handbook*. Washington, DC.

12. O'Keefe, S., Deputy Director, Office of Management and Budget. (2001, July 11). U.S. Senate Committee on Government Affairs.

13. "Many government workers of this generation will soon reach 25 years of service, indicating that they are eligible for pensions. When that wave starts to break, the federal workforce (estimated at 2,922,291 civilians in July 2000 by the Office of Personnel Management) stands to lose half its members." Eisenhart, M. (2001, January). Washington's need to know. *Knowledge Management Magazine*. Available at: http://www.destinationkm.com/articles/default.asp? ArticleID=411

14. Droitsch, R., Medsker, L., and Demers, D. (2000, July). Knowledge management at the U.S. Department of Labor. *Artificial Intelligence and Soft Computing Conference Proceedings*. Anaheim, CA; Calgary, AB, Zurich, Switzerland: Proceedings of the International Association of Science and Technology for Development (IASTED). See also U.S. Department of Labor: Office of the Assistant Secretary for Policy. (1999). *Workshop on Knowledge Management Conference Proceedings*. Washington, DC.

15A. Droitsch, R. (1999, April). Elaws: Using expert systems to deliver complex regulatory information. *Proceedings of the 8th Annual Federal Depository Library* Conference, pp. 96–106. Washington, DC: Federal Depository Library Program, Government Printing Office (GPO).

15B. Distasio, M., Droitsch, R., and Medsker, L. (1999). Web-based expert systems for elaws. *Failure and Lessons Learned in Information Technology Management*, 3: 67–77.

16. See http://www.ajb.org for more information.

17. U.S. Department of Labor. (2000, June). Secretary's Order 2-2000. U.S. Department of Labor Internet Services.

18. U.S. Department of Labor. (2001, June). Proposals announced at the summit. Office of Public Affairs Press Release.

19. For the definition of "small," see the U.S. Small Business Administration, Office of Size Standards at http://www.sba.gov/size. Title 13, Code of Federal Regulations, Part 121, Washington, DC: Office of the Federal Register National Archives and Records Administration, GPO.

20. See bibliography in Fletcher, J. D. and Johnston, R. (2002) Effectiveness and cost benefits of computer-based aids for maintenance troubleshooting, *Computers in Human Behavior*, 18: 717–728.

21. Department of Defense, Office of the Undersecretary of Defense for Personnel and Readiness. (1999, April 30). Department of defense strategic plan for advanced distributed learning, pp. 4–6. Report to the 106th Congress.

22. Executive Office of the President. (1998, January 30). Enhancing learning and education through technology. Memorandum for the Heads of Executive Departments and Agencies.

23. For more information about the ADL Initiative and the Co-Lab, see http://www.adlnet.org

24. Droitsch, R., Medsker, L., and Demers, D. (2000, July). Knowledge management at the U.S. Department of labor. *Artificial Intelligence and Soft Computing Conference Proceedings*, pp. 319. Anaheim, CA; Calgary, AB, Zurich, Switzerland: Proceedings of the International Association of Science and Technology for Development (IASTED).

25. Finneran, T. (2000, October). A component-based knowledge management system. "The Data Administration Newsletter." Published by Robert S. Seiner. Available at: http://www.tdan.com/i009hy04.htm

26. Barth, S. (2000, July 4). Defining knowledge management. *CRM Magazine*. Available at: http://www.destinationcrm.com/articles/default.asp? ArticleID=1400

27. Seiner, R. S. (2000, October). Knowledge management: It's not all about the portal. "The Data Administration Newsletter." Published by Robert S. Seiner. Available at: http://www.tdan.com/i014feo4.htm

CHAPTER 23

Knowledge Management at Caterpillar

Reed Stuedemann, Caterpillar University

Caterpillar, Inc. is a large, globally dispersed company, involved in many different products and services. Like many other companies, Caterpillar will see a significant number of its most experienced employees retire in the next few years. Leveraging our intellectual capital has never been more important. The best way to leverage these assets effectively is to enable our employees as continual learners. On a day-to-day basis, continual learning organizations promote knowledge sharing by learning what we need when we need it. Our knowledge-sharing mission at Caterpillar is to provide efficient, reliable, and easy access to knowledge and collaboration with others across the value chain for the purpose of improving performance.

The Knowledge Network (KN)—built to help address these needs—is a Web-based strategic business asset developed internally at Caterpillar. The KN, delivered via the Internet, effectively leverages the intellectual capital of Caterpillar and its value chain by providing collaborative space and access to expertise through communities of practice (CoPs). Our CoPs are groups of people with a common interest working together to improve performance. They cross the boundaries of business unit, geography, and value chains, and they can range in size from small teams to thousands of people. The KN includes Caterpillar employees, retirees, dealers, customers, and suppliers.

This chapter provides a brief overview of the KN and an explanation of how it is being used today by describing system functionality, benefits realized, and some of the lessons learned.

KN Uses

The KN is used for many things. Some of the more common uses include a place to store information, capture lessons learned, solve problems, identify and locate experts, and more quickly integrate new people into their jobs. It is also used to support and facilitate face-to-face meetings. The KN allows people across our value chain to provide input and gain feedback from all parts of the globe on issues in which they are involved on a daily basis. The KN provides an environment that enables people to take risks, drive innovation, and achieve higher-quality results more quickly than would otherwise be possible.

KN Structure

The KN CoPs are structured in a taxonomy that is based on our business processes. It has been very important to define the scope of our CoPs based on the business needs of the members. Our communities are structured so they align with the day-to-day activities of the members, and their involvement helps them accomplish the tasks needed to do their jobs. The more specific the community purpose, usually the more value it will provide for the members. A CoP may be a group of people working on a project with a limited life, or it may be a group of people involved with a business function that goes on indefinitely. One of the features the system provides is e-mail to community members when new information is posted to the community. With more and more information available to users, it was important that the additional e-mail truly be targeted. As a result, communities are very focused. There are currently over 1,800 CoPs in the KN, with more than 27,000 registered users. At Caterpillar, CoPs with a broad scope have not proven to be successful.

Community Managers

People can play several different roles in a CoP. Every community has a community manager who is responsible for the maintenance and upkeep of his/her community. Maintenance includes the periodic review of content and community participants. The manager plays a critical role in determining appropriate content and should be highly engaged with other users. The manager serves as a role model for the community participants. The manager does not need to be the person with the most knowledge or experience but does need to be someone who is recognized as being involved in the common interest of the community. To be effective, managers must have good communication skills. Selecting and training community managers is an area on which we will spend more resources in the future.

Community Experts

In addition to keeping the information in the community up-to-date, managers are responsible for identifying experts for their community. Experts need to be very knowledgeable in the subject matter on which the community is based. The KN allows a manager to include a description that explains the expert's skill set as it relates to that community. The expert's description is a searchable field, and the KN is considered to be a reliable source where people can go to locate talent. This enables people to "discover" knowledge and expertise, as defined in the CoP, independent of their job title or position. A person may be designated as an expert in multiple CoPs and have a different description in each community based on the role he or she plays in each. Experts cannot leave a CoP unless the community manager removes them as an expert in the community.

Community Delegates

Managers may or may not have delegates, that is, people who assist the manager with the community managerial duties. Delegates have the same authority as the manager and run the community when the manager is traveling or unavailable. It is recommended that a manager have at least one delegate.

Community Members

Members of the CoP are people who are interested in the subject matter but not recognized as experts. Members gain status and recognition by contributing to the community. Members receive e-mail notification whenever something is posted to the community. Members can join or cancel their membership at any time.

Security Issues

A Caterpillar Corporate Web Security ID is required to enter the system. This allows the community managers to control access to their community and to individual entries in their community, based on ID. Access to a community is controlled by the community manager and is defined in one of three ways. Access can be granted based on affiliation (such as Caterpillar employee or supplier), organizational code, name, or any combination of these three. Anyone who meets a community access profile can enter the community. If a person wants to be notified when an entry is added to the community, he or she must join the community and become a member. If an individual chooses not to join the community, he or she still has access to allow for searching or browsing in the future.

Types of Communications

There are two basic types of communications that take place within a CoP in the KN. A community discussion is a quick way to get a message out or ask a question of the community members. It is not validated or approved by the community manager and is sent by e-mail immediately to the community participants. Anyone who has access to the community has access to the community discussions. The other type of communication that takes place is a knowledge entry, which is more formal and has a multipart structure. The community manager must review and approve a knowledge entry before it is sent to community members; however, either the author or community manager can send it to other people to review and comment on before it is approved. Based on this review process, a knowledge entry can be edited at any time by the author or community manager. This process allows for validation and ensures confidence in the information contained in a knowledge entry.

Reference Material on the KN

In addition to the communications that take place within a community, the KN also allows for related reference material to be accessed from the community. In a section called Tools and Guides, the community manager can load or link to documents and files in many different formats that relate to the activities of the community. These documents and links can be organized into folders to provide additional organization, as desired by the community manager. There is also a section called Standards and Specs that allows the community manager to link to frequently used standards documents. These documents may be internal to Caterpillar or externally developed by a standards developing organization. There is no upload feature to the Standards and Specs section, to ensure that community participants are using the controlled sources provided by our suppliers.

History of the KN

The KN was begun in 1998 at the Caterpillar Technical Center as a way to share lessons learned and leverage technical knowledge. Users of the KN quickly recognized that collaborating and learning from each other was a key element for our business units to succeed in a rapidly changing world.

Being an integral part of continual learning, the KN was transferred to Caterpillar University in 2001. However, nontechnical users found the tool unwieldy and difficult to use. Therefore, early in 2001, the National Center for Supercomputing Applications worked with Caterpillar to uncover the usability barriers of the KN that were limiting people's ability to collaborate and participate in CoPs. The primary barriers identified in the study were the fear of embarrassment by not knowing how to use the tool and the lack of computer skills. This information was combined with internal focus group studies to redesign the system completely for improved usability and functionality. The redesigned system was tested in the usability laboratory of Caterpillar University, modified based on the results, and retested until we had a very intuitive and user-friendly system.

Users now report that the new KN is easy to use, and it is now widely accepted by the average, nontechnical person. In addition, on-line help was developed to answer the frequently asked questions.

Value Chain Collaboration

At the same time the redesigned KN was being rolled out as an internal collaboration tool, we were receiving requests from our dealers and customers for a way to collaborate with Caterpillar. In March of 2002, a pilot of the KN was made available on the Internet for our dealers to join select CoPs. These pilot CoPs were organized around committees and work groups already working together. The KN allowed them to improve collaboration by increasing the speed, quality, and acceptance of their work. The pilot program gave the KN team the opportunity to create a KN interface for the entire value chain.

Several system modifications were made in preparation for going across our value chain. In the pilot, all community names and entry titles were displayed in the community structure as well as the search results, even though users were not given access to all communities. For the final rollout, this was modified so that non-Caterpillar people would only be able to see the names and search results of the community to which they have access. Caterpillar personnel see the complete list of all communities with a warning symbol by the community security profile for communities open to external personnel.

An extensive disclaimer agreement was developed by the legal department of Caterpillar and added to the KN for non-Caterpillar people. All external users are required to accept the agreement before being given access to the KN.

In July 2002, the production KN system was made available via the Internet. Dealers, suppliers, and customers are currently involved in our CoPs, as determined by the community manager. The acceptance of the KN by our value chain partners has been extremely positive and quick to show results. It has proven to be an effective tool to convert win–lose situations into win–win opportunities with widespread buy in.

GROWTH RATE

The 12 communities we started with in January of 1999 have grown to over 1,800 today. We anticipate that this growth rate will slow, because many of the business process-related communities have been established. However, we continue to create more project-related communities that will have a finite life.

The number of new users continues to increase dramatically as dealers, customers, and suppliers become involved. Currently, we have approximately 27,000 registered users, with Caterpillar employees making up 21,000 of these users. It is expected that at the current pace, Caterpillar employees will be the minority of the KN users within a year. The KN staff includes two programmers and four knowledge-sharing marketing and support personnel. These six full-time people are assisted by people from each of the major business process areas in establishing communities and training participants in their respective areas. The KN is the prime source of information for many areas of the corporation.

VALUE

A study of the KN has just been completed. It was found that returns on investment (ROI) were in excess of 200 percent for internally focused communities, while externally focused communities have returns on investment in excess of 700 percent. The primary benefits realized by users were improved productivity and quality. Studies show that 67 percent of the people looking for information received the results they needed. Intangible benefits include increased customer satisfaction with Caterpillar equipment, strengthened dealer and supplier relationships, increased retention of knowledge, improved collaboration skills, expanded informal networks, and increased opportunity for continual learning.

LESSONS LEARNED

As we go forward, we will invest more time and effort in the selection and training of community managers because they play a key role in the vitality and success of the community. We are also looking at ways to provide additional support to strategic communities to leverage benefits that the KN provides to the success of our business. We have been amazed at the knowledge and expertise that have surfaced as a result of collaboration on the KN, and from some of the most unlikely places. For example: We had a Caterpillar dealer in Florida developing a hydraulic cylinder repair training module for which they were going to create graphics but thought they would try the KN first. They asked the Service Training Community if anybody had graphics that illustrated our cylinder repair process. The next day, they received a response from our Caterpillar training group based in Moscow with a complete hydraulic repair training module attached. The KN is truly changing the way we work at Caterpillar.

CHAPTER 24

Historical and Contemporary Perspectives on Knowledge Management— and a Look at the Knowledge-Sharing Initiative at the World Bank

T. Kanti Srikantaiah, Dominican University

INTRODUCTION: DEFINITIONS AND ANTECEDENTS OF KM

Knowledge management is a product of the 1990s and a hot topic in organizations, with many practitioners in different disciplines, including business, engineering, information management, communications, education, and epistemology, among others. Knowledge management embraces those disciplines and treats knowledge as an entity dynamically embedded in networks, processes, repositories, and people. Over the last few years, KM has emerged explosively through an interdisciplinary approach dealing with all aspects of knowledge in organizations, including knowledge creation, codification, organization, sharing, and application.

Definitions

Knowledge management is a new way of looking at organizational assets— people, clients, databases, documents, products, processes, and services. Unfortunately, there is no universal agreement on the definition of KM. A survey of the professional literature points out three distinct perspectives: a business perspective emphasizing learning organizations; an engineering perspective concentrating on technology applications; and an information professional perspective focusing on information services. Depending on the perspective, various definitions of KM are offered as witnessed on the Web sites. The following are Web sites containing KM definitions, concepts, and practices:

- http://www.icasit.org
- http://www.sims.berkeley.edu
- http://www.bustexas.edu
- http://www.uts.edu.au
- http://www.apqc.org
- http://www.worldbank.org
- http://www.kmresource.com
- http://www.brint.com
- http://www.cio.com

In general, all definitions agree that KM deals with capturing the collective expertise of an organization. Some examples of definitions follow:

- Knowledge management is a broad process of locating, organizing, transferring, and using information and expertise within an organization (Broadbent, 1998).
- Knowledge management is the utilization of total knowledge assets—both explicit and tacit—in an organization promoting, evaluating, retrieving, and sharing through dissemination, in terms of products, processes, services, customers, and personnel (Srikantaiah and Koenig, 2000).
- Knowledge sharing is the process through which organizations generate value from their intellectual capital and knowledge-based systems (from Bruno Laporte's Power Point presentation at the World Bank, 2001).
- Knowledge management is the systematic process of identifying, capturing, and transferring information and knowledge people can use to create, compete, and improve (American Productivity and Quality Center, 2002).
- Knowledge management is a discipline that promotes an integrated approach to identifying, capturing, evaluating, retrieving, and sharing all of the information assets of an enterprise. These assets may include databases, documents, policies, procedures, and previously uncaptured expertise and experience in individual workers (Gartner Group).
- Knowledge is a fluid mix of framed experience, values, contextual information, and expert insight that provides a framework for evaluating and incorporating new experiences and information. It originates and is applied in the minds of "knowers." In organizations, it often becomes embedded not only in documents or repositories but also in organizational routines, processes, practices, and norms (Davenport and Prusak, 1998).

Definitions stress that managing knowledge involves dealing with the collective expertise of organizations focusing on the tacit knowledge people carry in their possession.

Antecedents

The antecedents of KM had their roots in information management tools and applications. For a long time, knowledge was perceived within the framework of information management and organizations dealt with one major theme—the importance and the skillful use of information to the success of the organization. Various concepts and themes were implemented in organizations for effective information management. Some examples of applications include the following: supply chain management, enterprise resource planning, data warehousing and data mining, business process re-engineering, total quality management (TQM), and information resource management.

- *Supply chain management* is the successor to just-in-time inventory management with the goal of supplying management in general, including one's own production and processing as well as one's relations with suppliers.

- *Enterprise resource planning* is the name for the use of one very large (and very expensive) but modularized commercial data management package to integrate handling of the internal data of an organization.

- *Data warehousing* is the assemblage of selected, filtered, and structured data from a variety of sources into one coherent assembly for the purpose of being able to find meaningful relationships within that data. Data mining is the attempt to extract useful relationships from within large bodies of data.

- *Business process re-engineering* involves redesigning the operations and workflow of the organization to take advantage of the capabilities of electronic communications. Those capabilities, such as real-time operation and the distance independence of modern electronic information systems, permitted radical redesign and, often, dramatic rationalization and simplification of business procedures and systems. Re-engineering helped view organizations as pipelines of horizontal processes rather than vertical departments. It also had a negative impact because it promoted reduction of the workforce and destroyed the social coherence and intellectual integrity of organizations (Stewart, 2001).

- *Total quality management* is the movement to enlarge the responsibility for quality control to include the staff of the organization and the clients served. Quality is not just tolerances and rejection rates, but fitness for use, as the client perceives it. It emphasizes employee involvement in the role of improving the processes and the products. Along with TQM came benchmarking. Benchmarking is the process of examining any process an organization performs, finding out who else needs to undertake the same process, finding out who performs it best, and then using that performance as a benchmark to develop a standard against which to compare other performances.

- *Information resource management* arose in the 1970s and was to an extent the recognition that information is a resource the organization should explicitly pay attention to and manage, just as it manages finance, inventory, and personnel. The concept received additional momentum when, in the Paperwork Reduction Act of 1980, U.S. government agencies were required to assign to a senior administrator the responsibility of information management. Now this application is dated and completely replaced by KM.

Today, all these applications have been modified and have been absorbed by KM.

KM Today

The KM movement had its beginning in intellectual capital. Intellectual capital became popular in the early and mid-1990s. It represented the awareness that, as economists would phrase it, information is a factor of production in the same category as land, labor, capital, and energy (Talero and Gaudette, 1995). In the early and mid-1990s, there was an increasing awareness in organizations that knowledge was an important organizational resource that needed to be nurtured, sustained, and taken into account and measured. Intellectual capital was defined as having two major components: knowledge capital and structural capital. Knowledge capital is the knowledge in the organization—informal and unstructured, as well as formal. Structural capital is the mechanisms in place to take advantage of knowledge capital, the mechanisms to store, retrieve, and communicate that knowledge (Srikantaiah and Koenig, 2000). The intellectual capital movement gained publicity while demonstrating the importance of valuing and nurturing people who carried knowledge in their heads. Thomas Stewart (1994) authored a number of prominently featured articles in *Fortune*, of which the most compelling was "Your company's most valuable assets: Intellectual capital." Stewart also stated that the tangible assets of an organization—cash, land and buildings, plants and equipment, and other balance sheet items—are substantially less valuable than the intangible assets not carried on the books. Most important of these intangible assets are the skills, capabilities, expertise, values, loyalties, and so on, of the staff (Stewart, 2001). In the same period, there were a number of meetings at conferences at which intellectual capital was an important theme.

The notion of a balanced score card was introduced, stating that traditional reporting systems (such as financial systems) were too narrow in their outlook and that they focused only on the present and past, giving no thought to the future. It was argued that there should be a balanced score card that included the traditional measures and that also measured client satisfaction, client inputs, and intellectual capital (Kaplan and Norton, 1992).

In the same period, the Internet burst into the consciousness of organizations, which hitherto was solely used in academia and at not-for-profit institutions. It was soon realized that Internet technology could be used to link together an organization, using the Internet and its conventions for data display and access, leading to intranets. Through intranets, organizations could facilitate communications within as well as with clients (extranets). Of course, the electronic communications with clients had been increasing since the 1970s, electronic data interchange and just-in-time inventory are examples; however, the Internet very much accelerated the process. One consequence of this was an expanded definition of intellectual capital to include client knowledge and input, that is, customer capital.

The large global firms were the first organizations to fully realize the potential of intranets. These firms had long realized that the commodity they deal in is knowledge. The following is an example of a primary concern of such organizations: How can a professional working in a developing country, working for an organization with headquarters in Washington, be made aware of other sources by professionals who worked on similar problems in other developing countries? The organizations saw the intranet as an ideal tool with which to share and disseminate knowledge throughout the scattered offices of the organization worldwide. The organizations recognized that the confluence of the intranet with knowledge as an asset was substantially more than just an expansion of the concept of intellectual capital. The phrase they chose to describe this new confluence and, in particular, the intranet-based systems they were developing, was knowledge management.

The concept of KM continued to expand. Senge's (1990) *The Fifth Discipline: The Art and Practice of the Learning Organization* had a major impact on KM in the 1990s. The learning organization is the belief that what ultimately creates and distinguishes a successful organization is its success in creating and sharing information and knowledge. In short, it is success at learning. The obvious corollary is that to be successful, an organization must create a culture that fosters learning. The concept of the learning organization includes the creation of knowledge. Knowledge management expanded its territory to include the concept of the learning organization.

In terms of KM progress, the first extensive use of information technology to enhance knowledge sharing was the widespread use of e-mail. Next came the broad use of groupware, software designed to help teams work together in an electronic environment. The apex is true KM, including transformation in the culture of the organization to encourage and reward knowledge creation and sharing. Knowledge management has grown into an even broader, more pervasive, and more powerful notion than it originally began as, or than its name would imply. In fact, in some circles it is believed that the term knowledge management is not the appropriate phrase to reflect their undertakings. One suggestion was "knowledge sharing," which the World Bank proposed and implemented and is certainly more descriptive of what KM has evolved to become.

Explicit and Tacit Knowledge

Knowledge management deals with both explicit and tacit knowledge. Explicit knowledge deals with codified knowledge that is documented and is in the domain of structural capital. In contrast, tacit knowledge is the know-how and know-what, the knowledge people hold in their possession, which is the domain of human and customer capital. Knowledge resides with individuals, their conversations, internal records, external publications, data warehouses, internal and external databases, best practices, intranet, and Internet. Nonaka and Takeuchi (1991) identify four basic patterns of explicit and tacit knowledge, addressing it as SECI: socialization, externalization, creation, and internalization.

- *From tacit to tacit.* When an individual shares tacit knowledge with another face-to-face or through other modes (socialization)
- *From explicit to explicit.* When an individual combines discrete pieces of explicit knowledge and creates a new product (creation)

- *From tacit to explicit.* When the organization deals with a knowledge base by codifying experience, insight, and opinion into a form that can be reused by others (externalization)
- *From explicit to tacit.* When staff members internalize new or shared explicit knowledge and then use it to broaden, extend, and rethink their own tacit knowledge (internalization)

The real challenges in KM occur in the last two patterns of knowledge creation: going from tacit to explicit and explicit to tacit. Although it is easier to recognize these patterns in everyday life, how often does this type of knowledge creation occur in organizations? What conditions are conducive to encouraging such forms of managing knowledge? (Broadbent, 1998).

Explicit knowledge exists in organizations in a wide variety of categories. Here is a sample list:

- Commercial print publications (books, periodicals, report literature)
- Internal records (business records, archives)
- Audio and video recordings, graphical materials, and so on
- Data warehouses
- E-mail
- Intranet
- Internet
- Internal and external databases (both text and numerical)
- Best practices
- Groupware
- Self-study materials
- Current awareness
- Newsletters
- Others

Tacit knowledge is vital to KM. Knowledge management practices aim to draw out the tacit knowledge people have, what they carry around with them, and what they observe and learn from experience, rather than what is usually explicitly stated. Davenport and Prusak (1998) state that studies have shown managers get two thirds of their information and knowledge from face-to-face meetings or phone conversations. Many organizations are establishing physical areas that are dedicated and designed to facilitate tacit knowledge transfer.

In the area of tacit knowledge there also is a wide variety of categories. Here are some examples:

- Face-to-face conversations—formal and informal
- Telephone conversations—formal and informal
- Videoconferences and presentations
- Individual knowledge and expertise
- Outside experts
- Mentoring
- Study tours
- E-mail
- Training
- Client knowledge
- Best practices
- Others

By organizing explicit knowledge (both external and internal), capturing tacit knowledge (people skills, ideas, values, motivation, and so on), and transforming this knowledge to the work environment, the organizations of today benefit from KM.

KM in the World Bank and Learning Interaction

Knowledge management is described at the World Bank as knowledge sharing. This creates an environment encouraging and facilitating sharing of useful knowledge. The World Bank has realized that the knowledge it has is its greatest asset, rather than the money it lends to borrowers. The President of the World Bank, Wolfensohn, had this personal reflection to the 1996 Annual Meeting: "We will work with others to build a global knowledge partnership in which the Bank Group can play the role of connector—to capture and disseminate development expertise and experience for our clients and partners." This 1996 commitment resulted in the "Knowledge Bank" taking the role of facilitator, or connector. It includes three broad objectives:

- Improving the efficiency and effectiveness of the Bank by managing knowledge better, and by utilizing modern information technologies.
- Offering clients knowledge, training, and advisory services to help their own development agenda, either bundled with lending or as unbundled products.

- Building client capacity to create, share, and apply knowledge to help clients take charge of their development and to compete more successfully in the global economy.

The challenge exists in the processes in which managing knowledge-related programs and processes, both internal and external, are designed to help clients, partners, and staff learn and access knowledge.

A knowledge-driven reorganization of the Bank took place in 1996. A series of networks were established to cut across the regional "cylinders" (commonly referred to as "silos" in the KM literature). Knowledge management was one of the principal rationales for this matrix structure. A total of seven networks were created, and their organizational structure is listed in the World Bank Directory: the Administrative and Client Support Network; Environmentally and Socially Sustainable Development Network; Finance, Private Sector, and Infrastructure Network; Human Development Network; Information Solutions Network; Operational Core Services Network; and Poverty Reduction and Economic Management Network. These networks had the responsibility to do the following:

- Foster the accumulation of knowledge, determine the skills and training required within each sector, and ensure the quality of projects in the sector.
- Overlay the formal organizational structure in the regions.
- Include families and thematic groups of related specialists who could collectively generate and assess the quality of knowledge.
- Control the budget to facilitate knowledge generation.
- Provide a "human system" of help desks and access to subject experts to provide the information that staff needs in a timely manner.

By drawing on the wider communities of practice (CoPs), thematic groups were later developed. They have the responsibility of capturing the information and knowledge the Bank and other institutions have in their areas of specialty and then processing this information into knowledge. Today, more than 100 thematic groups serve the World Bank community, clients, and partners. Thematic groups have their own Web sites, providing important studies, know-how, sector statistics, and information relevant to the topic and best practices designed to distill the unique experience of the Bank in supporting projects in different countries. Thematic groups also reach out to staff and partners through brown bag lunches, clinics, workshops, study tours, Web sites, and newsletters, as well as supporting task teams enabling staff to apply and adapt the global knowledge to local conditions. Staff members of the thematic groups are mostly front line staff, working in the regions and networks. Leadership and membership in any thematic group are voluntary and open to all staff. Thematic groups are critical to the success of KM.

Twenty advisory services (help-desk facilities) respond to queries from users and serve as the human interface for learning and knowledge sharing. One of their main functions is to provide a "one-stop shop" to respond to information needs on various development topics. The advisory services ensure that responses are given to internal and external questions, usually in 24 to 48 hours. The strength of the advisory services lies in their ability to pull together responses from many information sources and gather experience from a wide range of experts. Although advisory services may use different means to answer queries, they often respond by sharing relevant references, materials, reports, Web site links, and connections to experts. The information collected is used to answer specific queries and then is developed into knowledge products. The knowledge base is used to respond to future queries. Statistics indicate that these advisory services respond to hundreds of queries every week.

The role of information technology as an enabler in managing knowledge in the World Bank has been a success. In managing knowledge, information technology plays a critical role in both the capture and delivery of knowledge. The intranet provides an integrated information infrastructure for internal Bank audiences; the extranet provides the needed knowledge by networking with Bank partners, clients, and the general public, providing the needed knowledge. Knowledge management staff members in the networks and regions provide guidance on content.

The World Bank public site is one of the world's largest Web sites, currently receiving over 10 million page requests per month. The Web site reaches over 600,000 unique visitors a month. E-mail newsletters are an important and growing component of the outreach efforts of the World Bank, amounting to more than 50 newsletters with a total of over 90,000 subscriptions from over 60,000 subscribers. The World Bank intranet is a large and complex decentralized system made up of many servers and systems throughout the Bank that provides knowledge resources and services. Distribution of demand for knowledge is generally rather evenly spread out across sectors, with the exception of high demand for financial sector information.

The current knowledge work of the Bank revolves around three areas: creating, sharing, and applying knowledge. Creating knowledge is done by research (e.g., development economics); economic and social work, pulling together knowledge according to country and assisting in setting strategic priorities for the Bank; and the Operations Evaluation Department and the Quality Assurance Group, producing evaluation reports pointing out what did and did not work.

Efforts of the World Bank to Capture Tacit Knowledge

The Bank uses various direct and indirect programs to capture tacit knowledge. The techniques for direct downloading of tacit knowledge include oral history, mentoring, coaching, strategic staffing, and debriefing. Some indirect programs include CoPs and various other initiatives. The descriptions of these programs provided here derive from different sources in the World Bank, from its Web sites (general, http://www.worldbank.org; knowledge sharing, http://www.worldbank.org/ks), and from the APQC (2002) document.

Direct Downloading of Tacit Knowledge

Oral History Program

The Oral History Program began in 1961 and has been capturing personal recollections of some senior staff members on their tenure in the organization. The program started when Bank management approved a historical project to tape-record a series of interviews with present and former members of the senior staff. Its intended purposes were to build institutional memory, accumulate material for scholarly studies of the history and operations of the Bank, and supplement gaps in its records. From 1993 to 1998, the Oral History Interview Series was one of the main functions of the Office of the Historian; in April 1998, the office was disbanded, and the oral history function became part of the Archives in Information Systems Group. The selection of participants depended on the career significance as well as contribution to, and impact on, historically important Bank activities and operations. Candidates were generally selected from the following categories: executive directors, presidents, managing directors, vice presidents, and directors. In special circumstances, others who influenced the policy of the Bank were also selected.

The interview is conducted in the presence of—other than the interviewer and interviewee—the oral history task manager. The average duration is two hours per session with more than one session needed at times, depending on the material covered. An interview involves the following:

- Formulating questions based on primary and secondary source material to cover educational background and previous Bank experience
- Bank tenure
- Lessons learned and best practices
- Assessment of World Bank presidents
- Conclusions—personal reflections

Candidates are given a set of questions for review before the interview. Once the transcript is prepared, candidates perform an initial review, edit it further, and then finalize it. Candidates are also asked to sign a release agreement stipulating restrictions to access, as deemed appropriate. Traditionally, the oral history function of the Bank has been to capture personal recollections. Recently, interviews have been structured and conducted on the basis of a learned dialogue, in close alignment with Bank objectives and strategy. The primary focus and emphasis lie within the broader institutional objective of building a knowledge bank. The interviews are then disseminated via the Web site in the form of descriptive summaries.

Mentoring Programs

Mentoring programs facilitate the transfer of tacit knowledge from seasoned employee to new recruit, benefiting both parties. For the purposes of knowledge transfer and retention, mentoring programs are excellent but difficult to measure, because the tacit knowledge imparted is impossible to codify.

World Bank Group staff members have always mentored less experienced colleagues. In 1977, a pilot program was launched to examine the effectiveness of a more formal mentoring program. The pilot program matched women from Part II countries (the World Bank euphemism for underdeveloped countries) working in Asia Regions with mentors in management positions. It was very successful, benefiting both "mentees" and mentors. After this success, other units and groups became interested in mentoring and designed and implemented their own programs.

Mentoring at the World Bank is guided by a consideration of the theoretical and research literature on mentoring as well as the special characteristics of the World Bank. Some members of the 1818 Society at the World Bank (World Bank retirees) have served as mentors in the program.

Mentoring programs have sprung up all over the World Bank Group, both at the headquarters and in the field. Currently, several active mentoring programs exist in the World Bank and the International Finance Corporation. Some programs have been successfully concluded. Three new programs are being developed and more are expected in the coming years.

Coaching Program

Coaching is an excellent approach to capture and share tacit knowledge and is applied in many organizations. Coaching is helping people to develop their skills, capabilities, and performance potential in order to achieve individual goals, business goals, and objectives. Coaching helps in capturing the tacit knowledge of experienced staff. The Coaching Skills Program for Task Team Leaders at the World Bank has the following goal: transfer knowledge and experience from senior to junior levels—just in time and on the job.

Strategic Staffing Program

Strategic staffing establishes the systems and actions necessary to ensure that the World Bank has the right numbers, skills mix, and deployment pattern of staff to flexibly support its business strategy. Experienced staff can share their experiences with new staff members.

Debriefing

In the Africa Region, debriefing is part of downloading the tacit knowledge of staff. Debriefing is a systematic process that gives staff members the opportunity to reflect on their experiences and identify lessons learned. In turn, this enables them to share knowledge and helps to create an operational knowledge base for improved quality in project and program design and implementation. Debriefing is done by means of one-on-one or team interviews after assignments to capture and disseminate lessons learned. Elements include a facilitating interview of the selected "debriefee" designed to assist in identifying critical issues to be addressed during missions. The interview includes discussing experiences and identifying what worked, what did not work, and why. The session is videotaped and made available to the debriefee for approval and editing before dissemination to users. The videotape is then edited and made available electronically in its entirety or via shorter clips. Documents and other resources referred to during the debriefing or relevant to the debriefing are also provided and highlighted as red links.

The objectives and activities of the debriefing service of the Bank include the following:

- Capturing experiences
  - Provides time, space, and opportunity for teams to reflect on task issues and achievements
  - Helps identify lessons learned
  - Captures important lessons
- Sharing lessons learned
  - Provides instruments and facilitation for knowledge sharing across teams and networks
  - Disseminates important experiences Bank-wide
  - Contributes to the knowledge base of good practices
  - Provides ground-level feedback on procedures and rules
  - Reinforces the mission and values of sharing and learning
- Interpreting quality at entry and exit
  - Provides pointers to cross-sector and regional knowledge sources, good practices, and relevant local knowledge
  - Identifies critical issues before and after the operational mission
  - Identifies examples of adapting project design to local institutional and cultural format

Debriefing is increasingly applied in public and private corporations to capture and share operational experiences. Debriefing can help learning before, during, and after tasks. It can aid in sharing critical information about task processes and achievements, helping to reduce the risk of future failures. Debriefing is an equal opportunity process that helps create a level playing field for all team members. Debriefing is a key element of the Africa Region's road map for leveraging knowledge into the quality assurance process. Debriefing increases the knowledge base of good practices and helps to avoid repeating mistakes. Debriefing can point to available knowledge resources and identify knowledge gaps. Debriefing helps us to understand what works so that we can improve quality at entry and exit.

The Bank also captures tacit knowledge through audiotaping of individual interviews with subject matter experts. The interviewer asks questions about a given situation, such as "What went well, and why?" "What didn't go well, and why not?" and "What would or could you have done differently, and why?" Subject matter experts conduct the audiotaped interviews with single subjects. The audiotape is then transcribed and edited by the interviewee. A hot link is placed in the text whenever a report or document is mentioned, which creates a fully searchable document that incorporates context with official records. These interviews are also accessible from the Web site. The goal of the Bank in both videotaped and audiotaped interviews is to uncover what it does not know and gather knowledge in these areas.

Indirect Downloading of Tacit Knowledge

Communities of Practice

Communities of practice are an effective approach to capturing and sharing tacit knowledge. The knowledge exchange in CoPs takes place at an informal level. The KM strategy of the World Bank is oriented toward connecting those who need to know with those who do know and collecting what is learned to share both internally and externally with clients, stakeholders, and partners worldwide. It was learned that neither connecting nor collecting could be effectively conducted unless CoPs were in place. Hence, the formation and nurturing of such communities (thematic groups) have become central preoccupations of the KM program. Today, more than 100 thematic groups exist that were developed by drawing on the wider CoPs. Thematic groups work under the overall supervision of sector boards. There are 20 sectors, and each has a sector board comprising representatives from the various business units responsible for directing policy and programs in that sector. Each sector has between three and 12 thematic groups that are communities of practitioners in particular aspects of the sector. Face-to-face contact is an essential aspect of getting the thematic group operating as a CoP. Of staff members, 70 percent are at the headquarters. Each sector holds an annual "sector week" in which staff members worldwide, including those in 60 field offices, and external partners get together to share views in person. "Hub training" in KM also occurs in field offices. Once the community is operating, e-mail is the principal communications tool. At headquarters, brown bag lunches are a ubiquitous feature in the thematic group.

Others

Other services indirectly capture tacit knowledge and make it available in explicit form to staff in the World Bank and its clients. The series of networks established in 1996 enable staff to share their tacit knowledge within networks. Also, Multisector Team Learning captures a considerable amount of tacit knowledge to share. Twenty advisory services also exist that respond to queries from users, and they exchange tacit knowledge. Similarly, the Development Gateway provides access to development knowledge through global and country portals. The Global Development Learning Network conducts distance learning (through videoconferencing) with centers established worldwide. The Global Development Learning Network promotes sharing knowledge and is aimed at policymakers and researchers in developing countries where a considerable amount of tacit knowledge is transferred. The Global Knowledge Partnership Bank acts as a secretariat to a partnership of 40 organizations working on knowledge, ICT, and development issues. Information for Development (infoDEV) channels donor money to innovative projects using ICT and knowledge for development. World Links for Development (WorLD) links schools (students, teachers, policymakers) via the Internet in more than 20 countries to improve education, curricula, teacher training, connectivity, and so on. B-Span, an Internet-based broadcasting station, presents World Bank seminars, workshops, and conferences on a variety of sustainable development and poverty reduction issues. Indigenous knowledge provides users with quick access to syntheses of country sources of knowledge, and Bank-supported projects related to issues of indigenous knowledge. Electronic newsletters offer an opportunity to share knowledge in the form of more than 50 electronic newsletters with thousands of subscribers. Each has its own Web site, and the primary focus is on operational work and technical assistance.

The mission of the knowledge-sharing program is to improve the quality, efficiency, and effectiveness of the operational work of the Bank and to provide direct access to operational knowledge for clients, partners, and stakeholders worldwide. With this mission, the World Bank spends 3 percent of its total budget for KM. Today, the Bank is the only public organization in the top 20 of the Most Admired Knowledge Enterprises Study. The World Bank Group took fourth place in 2001. The organizations in the study are recognized for their world-class efforts in managing knowledge, leading to superior performance.

REFERENCES

American Productivity and Quality Center (APQC). (2002). *Retaining Valuable Knowledge: Proactive Strategies to Deal with Shifting Work Force.* Houston, TX: APQC.

Broadbent, M. (1998). The phenomenon of knowledge management: What does it mean to the library profession?" *Information Outlook.* 2:23–36.

Davenport, T. H., and Prusak, L. (1998). *Working Knowledge: How Organizations Manage What They Know.* Boston, MA: Harvard Business School Press.

Kaplan, R. S., and Norton, D. P. (1992). The balanced scorecard: Measures that drive performance. *Harvard Business Review.* 70:71–79.

Laporte, B. (2001). "Knowledge Sharing at the World Bank," A PowerPoint Presentation. (Available through the Web site http://www.worldbank.org)

Nonaka, I. and Takeuchi, H. (1991). *The Knowledge Creating Company: How Japanese Companies Create the Dynamics of Innovation.* New York: Oxford University Press.

Senge, P. M. (1990). *The Fifth Discipline: The Art and Practice of the Learning Organization.* New York, Currency/Doubleday.

Srikantaiah, T. K., and Koenig, M. E. D. (2000). *Knowledge Management for the Information Professional.* Medford, NJ: Information Today, Inc.

Stewart, T. A. (1994). Your company's most valuable asset: Intellectual capital. *Fortune.* 130:68–74.

Stewart, T. A. (2001). *The Wealth of Knowledge: Intellectual Capital and the Twenty-First Century Organization.* New York, Currency/Doubleday.

Talero, E., and Gaudette, P. (1995). *Harnessing Information for Development: World Bank Group Vision and Strategy.* Draft Document. Washington, DC: World Bank.

World Bank. (1999). *World Development Report.* 1998/99. Washington, DC.

Suggested Readings

Hibbard, J. (1997). Knowing what we know. *Information Week.* 20:46–64.

Stewart, T. A. (1997). *Intellectual Capital: The New Wealth of Organizations.* New York, Currency/Doubleday.

Useful Web Sites

http://www.skyrme.com

http://www.acm.org

http://www.knowledge-nurture.com

http://www.delphic.co.uk

http://www.business innvotion.ey.com

http://www.ibm.com

http://www.kikm.org

http://www.kmworld.com

http://www.scip.org

http://www.sla.org

http://www.sveiby.com

http://www.tfpl.com

http://www.eknowledgecenter.com

http://www.icasit.org

http://www.sims.berkeley.edu

http://www.bustexas.edu

http://www.uts.edu.au

http://www.KMPro.com

http://www.apqc.org

http://www.worldbank.org

http://www.kmresource.com

http://www.brint.com

http://www.cio.com

http://www.kmci.org

Interpersonal Knowledge and Organizational Foresight: The Case of Online Partnership in Micro-Organizations

Elisabeth Davenport, Napier University

INTRODUCTION

This chapter describes a system that addresses a significant KM problem: how to develop human capital in small firm partnerships and networks in a global, distributed economy. The specification presented here is for a novel resource that stores and manipulates profiles of partners' competence, compatibility, and trust. The specification[1] draws on the experience (the lessons learned) of firms that need to find partners online or to configure multidisciplinary teams where work will be distributed, time is short, and little opportunity exists to establish acquaintance. The proposed application extends the concept of human capital beyond competence modeling and includes emotional and moral dimensions.

The Online Partner Lens or OPAL (IST-2000-28295) is a project funded by the European Commission (EC), the goal of which is to establish whether and how a computer application may support team building and partnership. The Online Partner Lens offers an opportunity to explore links between the management of interpersonal knowledge and social capital. The objective is to build and evaluate a computer application that simulates the formation of qualified online partnerships by allowing new candidates to acquire an extensive understanding of a range of potential partners before a contract is signed in situations where time is short and physical interaction is limited. The project focuses on the early stages of interaction during which rapid and robust assessments must be made about partners' competence, compatibility, and confidence in each others' future performance. Each of these is the basis of a system component: the competence layer (layer 1), compatibility layer (layer 2), and confidence layer (layer 3). Evaluation of potential partners in each of these layers has informed the system architecture. The proposed application must support best-matching searches in order to perform at least as well as existing matching technologies. The application may also support reflective practice by broadening both the field of view and decision parameters for informed choice. It does this by providing profiles of a range of partner attributes in each of the three layers that are extracted from a number of sources: questionnaires, interaction patterns, conversation threads, and awareness logs. The sources reflect real-world experience; the resulting profiles combine "insight" derived from current attributes, with "hindsight" derived from track-record data (Table 25.1). One of the research aims of the team is to explore how insight and hindsight intersect by asking system users to reflect on the specific attributes that are in play when partners are selected.

Table 25.1 The Online Partner Lens application layers, insight, and hindsight.

OPAL Layer	OPAL Insight Data	OPAL Hindsight Data
Competence	Current Skills	Certification
		Awards
Compatibility	Shared practices	Reputation
	Shared techniques and tools	Network collaboration
	Shared professional protocols	Mutual collaborators
	Standards compliance	
Confidence	"They do what they say."	Track record and history
	Responsiveness	Endorsements
	Initiative	Recommendations
	Commitment	
	Consistency	

Foresight in organizations is often achieved by means of scenario work. Scenarios allow managers to identify and explore a range of futures that present more or less uncertain conditions (Van der Heijden, 1996; De Geus, 1997). In scenario work, worldviews and planning paths are articulated in narratives based on observations and beliefs about the following:

- The meaning of macrolevel trends
- The significance of cues, signs, and signals in the external environment or milieu
- The likely response to these by the internal environment or milieu
- Organizational prospects in the case of arbitrary events

By examining organizational capability of such emergences and emergencies, planners can assess what action is required, given a range of resources and responses. At this stage, elements are extracted from sets of conventionally hypothesized circumstances that may inform more formal or structured models for allocating resources. In assessing these, hindsight may well play a part—as archives of historical precedents are brought into play through war stories or by means of more structured analysis and pattern matching. Hindsight may be ambivalent: A set of cues and traits may be mistakenly read as indicative of one type of situation when it is indicative of something else, hitherto inexperienced and unique. Thus, it is wise to triangulate interpretations of cues. This may be done by means of insight derived from assessments of the current activity and interaction of the actors involved in the scenario. Foresight emerges from interplay of insight and hindsight that results in a set of reasonable assumptions about future performance.[2]

RESEARCH AND DESIGN RATIONALE

Three commercial companies are involved whose experiences underpin the scenario work of the design team. Within the domain of human computer interaction (HCI), scenario-based design conventionally focuses on the usability of artifacts and their attributes and affordance (or what may be done with them) (Carroll, 1995). In OPAL, as far as partnership and usability are concerned, scenarios carry an added burden: They must yield or deliver insights pertinent to judgments about behavior that involve soft insights about tacit knowledge: trust, rapport, social capital, and social networks. The application provides an opportunity to explore a number of second-generation or reflexive KM issues (Huysman and de Wit, 2002) that are manifest at the local level in social interactions.[3] The approach taken in OPAL is based on two assumptions: that stories and scenarios may be analyzed to produce representations of organizational activity, for example; and that typical scenarios, narratives, and genres are indicative of recognizable social order, and in the case of OPAL, social order at the level of micro, local, mundane work (Dourish, 2001; Davenport, 2002).

Scenario work audits current perceptions and beliefs about the firm; traditionally, it has been applied at a high level in the firm. This chapter is concerned with foresight as a microlevel of organization, specifically with team formation and partnering activity. At this level, scenario work also may be used to provide insight into potential processes and resources and into the climate (tasks, social capital, and emotional capital) conducive to workable arrangements. The subsequent text presents a case study where scenarios drive design and evaluation of the likely performance of future partners in collaborative ventures among small- and medium-sized enterprises (SMEs). Just as scenario work at the level of strategic planning provides a broad field of view for decision making, scenario-based design allows managers and engineers/architects to plan for a range of contingencies and to make parametric judgments about performance. In the case study, judgments about potential partners on the basis of interaction in pertinent scenarios can allow a range of candidate attributes to be identified and tradeoff calculations to be made about the pros and cons of collaboration. Scenarios can be used to derive a field or zone of acceptable behaviors [a pertinent design is offered by Spence and colleagues (2001), the attribute planner] or, as argued subsequently, a field of acceptable candidates who may be ranked according to the priorities of those managing the project. The OPAL team members want to find out if and how hindsight and insight interact in this microlevel local selection process (Table 25.2).

Scenario-based design, then, can be used to probe foresight in organizational relationships. This design takes a number of user stories and re-presents them as a series of an increasingly formal version of the goals, objects, actions, and constraints that characterize the story. In this way, the functionality of a proposed design can be anticipated in specifications whose validity is derived from the observations of users in vivo, and whose reliability is established by means of the identification of abstract or typical stories as the design (or abstraction) process unfolds. The OPAL project has not involved extensive ethnographic work or

Table 25.2 Performance-related judgments about potential partner behavior.

Typical Questions for Online Partnership	Guidance from Direct Experience (Insight)	Guidance from Indirect or Proxy Experience (Hindsight)
Do these people know what they are doing?	Assess their understanding of goals and tools on a trial task.	Rely on reputation or recommendation.
Do they deliver on time?	Set a deadline in a mini-simulation, and see how they perform.	Ask previous collaborators about their track record.
Are they responsive?	Monitor their interaction and conversation patterns in a simulated planning excercise.	Rely on reputation or recommendation.
What is their style of working?	Assess their availability and their initiation and response patterns over a fixed period.	Rely on reports of previous collaborators.

workplace observation. It has used the narratives of experienced practitioners (key informants from the commercial partners of OPAL) to identify relevant narratives of partnership. These have been gathered in written accounts and elaborated on in brainstorming meetings where abstract scenarios have been constructed. Adapting a method described by Benyon and Imaz (1999), the output from the concrete scenarios that have emerged from user scenarios has been presented in the form of interaction patterns that capture regularities of usage and activity. The concept was first applied in architectural design by Alexander in the 1970s, who provided templates for activities in a repertoire of community spaces and proposed that a "pattern language" might improve the design of habitats by taking account of generic human activities (Alexander et al., 1977). Software engineers adopted the concept in the 1980s. It recently has been promoted by Erickson (2000) as a *lingua franca* for interaction design and used as a way of organizing the analysis of ethnographic case studies (Martin et al., 2001). A number of structured formats have been proposed (e.g., Martin et al., 2001; Falconer, 1999) that capture critical dimensions (such as context, problem, constraints, and solutions) of recurring workplace activities.

The initial work on user scenarios with one of the commercial companies that is a partner in the OPAL project has provided data on the roles of insight and hindsight in existing practice. The competence layer of the OPAL platform will focus on hindsight, the substance of traditional job applications, where candidates lodge details of qualifications and credentials, details of endorsements (e.g., evidence of high status in a professional network), referrals to third parties (indirect social capital), and so on. Suggestions for features of the platform include recommender systems and social maps that might reveal overlap across networks and thus be indicative of compatibility. (See, for example, Nardi et al. [2002] and the comments that follow on visualization and foresight.) The compatibility and confidence layers will focus on insight. To design for these, the team has drawn on earlier experience of modeling trust (Davenport et al., 1999; Davenport, 2000) with colleagues whose interests span social computer agents and venture capital interactions. This work suggests that insight into affective or soft factors in interactions can be systematized when observation is focused on structured interaction. Structure may be imposed by means of experimental design or may be implicit in routine or norm-based activity. These are combined in the OPAL project, where users of the application will be asked to engage in semistructured interactions that are based on narratives of the implicit order of the workplace.

Design Challenges

As the preceding discussion indicates, one of the objectives of the project design is to provide a robust partnering mechanism that provides reliable and valid insight into the effectiveness of subsequent collaboration. In traditional face-to-face recruitment and team formation, those who hire and those who recruit interact in a number of conventional or generic social settings (the interview, the aptitude test, eating, a game of golf): these may be seen as high-level structured or rule-based exercises that provide cues about each other's likely behavior in subsequent situations. The design team has defined the "formation of partnerships" in terms of the process or sequence of events and interactions from the first "stimulus to hire" (e.g., a call for tenders) to the signing of a contract, or formal starting point of the process. In initial work on user stories and interaction patterns, the team members (designers and users) were thus able to separate two strands in accounts of user experience of partnerships: stories of the initial phase; and more reflective accounts of the subsequent collaboration, where narrators looked back on the early and later stages of partnerships and commented on points where the process of formation was vulnerable or showed lack of foresight. Team members thus could identify areas where their judgment was impaired and ways in which judgment might be better supported. Practitioners involved in the initial design work welcomed the idea of a system that does not derive an optimal outcome (the perfect partner) but, instead, identifies a range of possible partners whose activities are more or less predictable.

Over a period of three weeks in April 2002, the team worked on a number of initial scenarios that reflected the working contexts of the clients involved: brokering (as project managers and as incubator venture capitalists), recruitment (as software developers), and impresarios (those putting teams together in collaborative projects). A number of generically structured narratives relating to tendering were captured: de novo, forced marriage, client to broker, and broker–recruiter. This chapter focuses on scenarios involving the local commercial partner in the project, a medium-sized database specialist company in Central Scotland.

Interpersonal Knowledge Scenario One

Table 25.3 presents a story that describes a project undertaken five years earlier. With hindsight, the narrator could identify several cues that were missed, which would be more salient in interactions mediated by an application such as OPAL.

Table 25.3   Structured user story of a response to tender invitation.

User Story: Constructing a Team

Part 1.
Company A notices a call for tender in the *Official Journal of the European Communities (OJEC)* to submit a bid for public sector database work. As one of 40 to 50 agencies in this niche market, Denny feels that his company is competent to submit but will need to supplement its skills base. As the niche market works on the basis of a professional network, Denny knows which company he will approach. It is one that has complementary skills and a good reputation, and it has been recommended by a third party with whom Denny has worked.

Part 2.
Contact is made with Company B, which agrees that the tender should be explored and requests a full version of the call.

Part 3.
Both Companies A and B read the full version and agree that they can do this but that they might need to contact a third company to fill a remaining gap in the skills required.

Part 4.
A meeting in Sheffield is arranged to agree on the division of labor and identify the specific skills that are absent. Companies A and B can identify two candidates by their knowledge of the network.

Part 5.
The candidates are approached by phone, and the preferred candidate agrees to a meeting.

Part 6.
Company B goes to the meeting on the premises of Company C. Company C reveals that it wishes to submit its own bid. Company C is not willing to subordinate itself to a small company, because it considers itself a "big player." Company B rejects the offer.

Part 7.
The second candidate is approached by phone and agrees to participate. A meeting is arranged.

Part 8.
All three companies (A, B, and D) meet face-to-face. The meeting is very task oriented. There are a number of identifiable phases:
1. In the exploratory discussion, all parties are very polite and show respect for each other's reputation.
2. They consider the invitation to tender in detail, "forming thoughts on the main elements," and work out a division of labor for writing the bid document.
3. The issue of the "lead" is discussed. All three companies are interested in the lead; however, a pragmatic decision is made that Company B should lead, because it can meet the financial backups and guarantees required by the tender.
4. This raises the issue of cultural clash, because Company B comes from a bureacratic tradition (spin-off from local government) and Companies A and C are entrepreneurial.

Part 9.
A bid is submitted. The bid is successful, and a contract is signed.

This scenario revealed a sequence of activities that combined generic actions (calls for tender, meetings, and preparation of bids and associated documentation and media), using a range of existing technologies (phone, fax, and Web access). Patterns of affect can be identified because confidence and compatibility are tested

in the early stages of collaboration. When time is short (as is the case in most contracts that constitute the business of SMEs), the social network (which offers
some level of reliability by proxy) is used as a source of contact. In the first story
to emerge in the workshop, this took the form of an initial approach to Company
B by Company A on the basis of a third-party recommendation. In a subsequent
face-to-face meeting between Company A and B there was a "sense of strong rapport," as each presented ideas on how to proceed. This perceived agreement led
Company A to entrust B with negotiations that brought to the group a third party,
Company C (identified through the network of Company B).[4] The agreement of
all partners to proceed with a rapid bid was hammered out in an all-day meeting
of the three company directors, where the feel-good factor was strong, This
proved, in hindsight, to be an imperfect indicator, because comparable rapport
was not established among the subordinate colleagues who subsequently had to
work together on the project, a phenomenon that has been observed in many other
partnerships.

In the discussion of this scenario by the design group, a number of issues
emerged related to foresight. First, a better partnership might have emerged if a
wider range of partners had been available as the basis on which to choose. To confirm the competence of Company B, Company A had to rely on the social network
that defines its niche community, given the short time frame. A database with
appropriate hindsight attributes for a number of candidates—experience, endorsement, and so on—would have resulted in a more informed choice. Second, as the
preceding text indicates, small companies such as A depend on multiple submissions of contracts; this pressure may lead to hasty judgments or premature trust. In
the case of Companies A, B, and C, subsequent interaction with B revealed clashes
in organizational culture that were not critical to the survival of the project but did
impact on the "climate" of the team. Some means of sampling each other, by discussing project tasks and plans, and thus experiencing each other's approach over
a wide range of issues (insight data), would have been useful. This might have
flagged the mismatch of styles at lower levels of the organization that undermined
the rapport established by those involved in the initial contract negotiation. After
the event, Company A saw that the rapport experienced in meetings was based on
mutual assumptions and expectations, when a mutually agreed on modus operandi
might have been a more appropriate indicator of compatibility.

The issue for many of the SMEs that are the likely market for OPAL is not to
be forced into premature acceptance or rejection, as is currently the case, but to

have computer support for a more informed selection from a number of candidates who are placed within a tolerance zone. Position (their own and that of others) in the zone will allow partners to understand more fully the implications of subsequent collaboration, to alert themselves to sensitive spots or holes in the road, and to prepare appropriately.

INTERPERSONAL KNOWLEDGE SCENARIO TWO

Scenario Two presents a different set of challenges. In this follow-up to Scenario One, Companies A and B agree to work together on a second bid, because they have successfully completed the project in Scenario One. Despite cultural dissonance, they again seek a third party through the professional network that defines their market niche. At the crucial meeting to write the bid a serious disagreement on the approach occurs, and Companies A and C perceive that Company B is making a bid for sectoral status rather than addressing the specifications of the tender. Despite this, they forge ahead because a month of company time (that most precious commodity) has already been invested: The bid is unsuccessful. Company A observed that a system to support microlevel foresight early in the process might have been useful, before the investment in time made it difficult to pull out; more useful still would have been a system to support multiple concurrent microlevel assessments to allow selection of a broader range of candidates.

INTERPERSONAL KNOWLEDGE SCENARIO THREE

In Scenario Three, Company A is approached by an agency to act as a project manager. Staff members of Company A are happy to work with this agency (a major source of contracts); they are confident that not only can they manage the project but also can undertake many of the tasks. The agency, however, demands that they perform only project management tasks and introduces them to Company D, which will be the subcontractor. The culture of Company D is not compatible with that of A, and the project proves to be unworkable: Company A ended up picking up the pieces and doing the work themselves. Here it would have been useful to have a system to support rapid scanning of alternative partners (and thus provide sufficient insight and hindsight data) to provide counterbids within the extremely tight time frame imposed by the agency.

EMPIRICAL WORK ON TRUST AS A SOURCE
OF ATTRIBUTES FOR FORESIGHT

In each of the previous three scenarios, time was short and prior information about partners was inadequate, either because of lack of prior acquaintance or because previous experience in one situation was not a reliable guide to performance in a different situation. What system features might improve evaluation in the early stages of a project by providing insight and hindsight data to support reasonable assumptions about subsequent performance? In addressing this question, the OPAL design team has drawn on a large corpus of work on interpersonal trust, specifically situated trust in business contexts. Not all of this is pertinent to the OPAL project. Kramer and Tyler (1996) suggest that the treatment of trust by cognitive psychologists has "over-relied on simple mixed-motive games." A social computing approach is required or, as Kramer and Tyler (1996) put it, an exploration of "how trust-related cognitions are influenced by the specific organizational context within which such cognitions are inevitably embedded." This approach draws a distinction between trust cues provided by the individual and those provided by the situation or context, because such cues play a role at least as important as psychological traits. In a detailed exposition of situational trust for the purpose of designing trustworthy computer agents, Marsh (1994), and more recently Zolin et al. (2000), state that the lack of definition has led to confusion. Dibben (2000) provides a comprehensive evaluation of the literature on trust and categorizes the concept into three classifications: dispositional trust, learned trust, and situational trust. For this project, situational trust is most pertinent because it focuses on the situation that the actors are in and on the "amount and quality of communication" (Dibben, 2000). Dibben further notes, "Although one may trust an individual on the whole, one may not do so in certain situations and under certain circumstances."

A number of analytical and empirical studies (many undertaken with student samples) have demonstrated that trust can be effectively decomponentialized, and thus engineered.[5] This process can, as the reference above to Dibben's work indicates, focus interactors' attention on how trust works in a given situation. McKnight et al. (1995) offer a comprehensive and informative analysis of "trust formation in new organizational relationships." Their report covers definitions of trust, the formation process, and the role of emotion in trust. Trust, say the authors, is based on four beliefs about others: their benevolence, their honesty, their competence, and their predictability. The trust formation process early in the relationship is indicative of trust later in the relationship, and five factors will affect the early formation of trust: dispositional trust, situational trust, the categorization mechanisms of interactors, illusory trust, and system trust. Dispositional trust is salient only in situations that are highly ambiguous, novel, or unstructured and that offer few cues about what is going on. It is invoked if no more specific information is available.

Because OPAL targets a business environment, where schemas and genres to some extent drive judgments about whom and what is appropriate, dispositional trust may be disregarded as a key component in design rationale. System trust[6] is not a salient issue either because all those involved in the business partnering process can be assumed to trust the commercial systems within which they operate. From the perspective of the OPAL project, trust is relative to the specific business situations that engage different partners. "Swift trust" is of particular relevance to the OPAL project. Meyerson, Weick, and Kramer (1996) first used this term "to account for the emergence of trust relations in situations where the individuals have a limited history of working together" (Harrison, Dibben, and Mason, 1997). Swift trust has been explored in the context of virtual teams (the case of OPAL) by Jarvenpaa and Leidner (1998) who suggest that, in practice, a clear definition of roles and responsibilities (clarity in order to avoid confusion and disincentive), effective handling of conflict, and "thoughtful exchange of messages at the beginning of the team's existence" (Jarvenpaa and Leidner, 1998) will provide the basis for a successful virtual team. Certain behaviors on the part of the virtual team members distinguish virtual teams with high trust from those with low trust. For example, those teams in the "low initial /low subsequent trust" category lacked social introduction and had a general lack of enthusiasm. Those teams in the "high/high" category experienced the inverse of this, with extensive social introduction and continued enthusiasm.[7]

Synthetic Interaction and Foresight

Recent empirical work on trust-based interactions among both human and computer agents may guide the OPAL team in selecting interactions for layers 2 and 3 of the application that are conducive to insight. The experimental work described by Iacono and Weisband (1997) is highly pertinent to our design rationale. Their work describes a project with distributed electronic teams that must "quickly develop and maintain trust relationships with people that they hardly know and may never meet again, with the goal of producing interdependent work." The time frame for the projects was 24 days. In this situation, say Iacono and Weisband, trust is less about relating than doing, because swift trust is "less an interpersonal form than a cognitive and action form." Temporary systems require quick mutual adjustments so that people can make innovations as required; in online work, technology must support this process. Good communication habits and the ability to multitask and handle remote requests while attending to local demands are key practices: the compatibility layer of OPAL can focus on these areas.

Active participation, say Iacono and Weisband (1997), may be seen as a system of initiations and responses. Initiations involve trust because they "make one's preferences public" (which may incur risk); each initiation strengthens participants' perceptions that trust is reasonable and incurs more initiations. The making of responses "signals and inspires trust" in the group. Action moves forward in a cycle of initiations and responses. We suggest that this activity is appropriate to interactions in the confidence layer of OPAL, because turn-taking is a fundamental or primitive guide to social engagement: Drew (1995) suggests that the "anticipatory interactive planning" (AIP) supported in initiation–response sequences is a defining characteristic of social intelligence. In the fieldwork described by Iacono and Weisband (1997), initiations were categorized as getting together, work-process, work-content, work-technical, needing-contact, and fun-talk initiations. Work-process and work-content initiations correlated with high performance, as did the total number of initiations and the pattern of timing. Within the project period, team members obtained enough social information about each other to reinforce initial trust levels. Age correlated with high performance, and the authors suggest that age may be linked to multitasking. They suggest that working on a temporary distributed team is different from other online social experiences, such as posting to Newsgroups and conversing in chat rooms, a finding that has implications for OPAL.

Weisband (no date) has summarized the findings of a subsequent study (involving 15 teams at two universities): Low performing teams rely on their perceptions of others as a predictor of good performance; high performing teams rely on what people do and say as predictors of good performance. Teams that may not engage in the hard work of doing distant collaboration may feel good about the process and each other; however, such perceptions do not lead to successful outcomes.

Activity awareness information is important, that is, knowing what actions are done at any given moment, as is availability awareness, or knowing whether others can meet or take part in an activity. Process awareness allows people to see where they fit in at any give time and how the project is moving along; perspective awareness gives information (e.g., about beliefs and values) that is helpful in making sense of actions. We suggest that microlevel "shared situational awareness," borrowing a term from macrolevel studies of team-building in the U.S. defense forces (Loughran, 2000) based on Weisband's work, might usefully be built into layer 2 (compatibility), because actual monitoring of progress contributes more to high performance than do feelings about others. In an analogous study of antecedents to trust exploring perceptions of others' ability, integrity, and benevolence, Jarvenpaa, Knoll, and Leidner (1998) indicate that perceptions of others' integrity were important to initial trust and that perceptions of benevolence were least important.

Each of the three layers of the proposed application must deliver attributes that are assembled into profiles. The exercises (or games, as they are called in the OPAL proposal) used for experiential interaction thus must be amenable to formal analysis and representation. As the preceding text indicates, Iacono and Weisband (1997) suggest that initial patterns of initiation and response in an online planning scenario were indicative of successful team performance later in a project, and that these can be captured in a simple visualization. Comparable visualizations are available for moves and presence in a range of online interaction spaces. Preece (2002) presents the goal of these as follows: "to allow participants to more easily gauge such things as, who is present, what they are doing, how long they have been there, who the leaders are and how others judge the value of their contributions." Visual query is a function that OPAL is intended to support, and the design team is currently specifying visualizations as the type of interactions that may generate insightful attribute sets.

Activity and process awareness (two of Weisband's categories) can be supported by proxy systems of the kind described by Erickson et al. (2002). These researchers define a social proxy as "a minimalist visualization of people and their activities," and they describe a number of genres of online interaction (e.g., auction, call-center line) where such proxies can support judgments about how to proceed. Erickson and colleagues (2002) claim that "by making social cues visible, and allowing traces to accumulate over time, we create a resource that allows people—especially those familiar with the interactive context—to draw inferences about what is happening which can, in turn, shape their collective activity." Donath (2002) and Smith (2002) provide examples of comparable work in the specific online contexts of chat rooms and Usenet lists. An indicative typology of awareness types (Weisband, no date) and visualization tools to support awareness are provided in Table 25.4.

Table 25.4   The Online Partner Lens layers, awareness types, and visualization tools for insight, hindsight, and partnerships.

OPAL Layers and Awareness Types	Visualization Tools
Competence layer	ContactMap (Nardi et al., 2002)
Compatibility layer: Activity awareness Perspective awareness	Babble (Erickson et al., 2002) Loom (Donath, 2002) People Garden (Donath, 2002) Threadtracker (Smith, 2002) Coterie (Donath, 2002)
Confidence layer: Process awareness Availability awareness	Time line (Erickson et al., 2002) Babble (Erickson et al., 2002)

DEVELOPING A TRUST MARKUP LANGUAGE

In a recent article, Erickson and colleagues (Thomas et al., 2001) have reviewed a number of social representations and have described the initial work on a markup language for organizational stories ("Story ML"). The OPAL team is considering a comparable modeling exercise, namely, a markup language for interpersonal trust, "Trust ML," that formalizes attributes of trust that are made manifest in interactions that characterize the early stages in the formation of partnerships.

Work with the Scottish commercial partner on the OPAL project (see Scenarios One to Three) suggests that a planning exercise, where potential partners work on the preliminary activities associated with a task, is a useful focal area for judgments to be made about compatibility and confidence early on in the partnering process. Unlike the competence layer, which presents generic attributes of teams and individuals, the confidence and compatibility layers of OPAL address the demands of a particular and immediate project. The judgment made about potential partners will be specific to the circumstances.

Compatibility can be defined in terms of mutually agreed on objectives, procedures, and tools. The term mutually agreed on is not necessarily the same as shared—in some cases, a partnership will be formed to achieve complementarity, not consolidation. In order for OPAL users to assess each other on these dimensions, the design team will provide a conferencing platform that supports a series of structured interactions that relate to the initial planning tasks of a given partnership. In such a structured interaction, topics conducive to judgments about the four dimensions of compatibility can be covered in a systematic way, with intermittent input into standard data collection features, such as dialogue boxes, tick boxes, and checklists.

As OPAL deals with business interactions, the structures that characterize different stages of planning and the shape of the texts that articulate these stages are established and well understood. A long tradition of English language teaching can provide guidance on the structure of business genres (Bargiela-Chiappini and Nickerson, 1999) and the outcomes of each component of such interactions. A parallel analytic tradition in management science has produced tools for mapping and visualizing developing consensus (Eden and Ackerman, 1998). Tools such as these may be useful in extracting attributes from the interactions.

CONCLUSIONS

This chapter has discussed the design and research objectives that underlie the construction of a probe to explore the management of interpersonal knowledge and foresight in organizational relationships. The design process (scenario-based) may be seen as an exploration of theory, because it is based on a premise of a view of organizational learning that is experiential (the hindsight issues addressed in this chapter) and phenomenological (the insight issues). The approach is an example of second-generation KM systems, that is, systems that draw on lessons learned and that support organizational reflexivity. The approach has been synthesized from earlier empirical studies of microlevel routine work and organizational trust. By focusing on the specification of attributes that characterize different levels or layers of partnership, the probe provides a means to assess how insight and hindsight contribute to foresight. A systematic approach to representing foresight by means of a trust markup language ("Trust ML") is proposed.

Acknowledgments

An earlier version of this chapter was presented at a conference at the University of Strathclyde Graduate School of Business: Probing the Future: Foresight Conference, 11–13 July, 2002. The proceedings are available on CD-ROM from the organizers.

I wish to acknowledge the work of my OPAL team colleagues David Benyon, Martin Graham, and Jessie Kennedy, and the work of research assistants Guy van de Walle and Leo McLaughlin.

Endnotes

1. The specification provides design details for the following:
   - Capture of profile data that satisfy minimum requirements for effective partnerships in "temporary organizations" under conditions of "minimal" or "zero" acquaintance
   - Database structure and data models for the different dimensions of competence, social compatibility, and trustworthiness, and the integration of these
   - Mechanisms to evaluate, at a distance, the competence, social compatibility, and trustworthiness of potential partners
   - An archive or "partner library" of profiles that are described in XML
   - A retrieval mechanism that allows efficient access to the archive to retrieve relevant data and that combines advanced and dynamic querying and navigational features based on partner profile and security data
   - A graphical browser or dynamic visual interface
   - A privacy filter

2. A comparable account of the intersection of insight and hindsight is offered in Good (1995).

3. Recent work on "forgotten" categories of knowledge such as "phronesis" and "metis" (Tsoukas and Cummings, 1997; Baumard, 1999) is highly pertinent to the case described here.

4. Prior to the entry of Company C, an abortive approach to Company X led to rejection, because X, a larger firm, wished to be principle in its own bid and did not want to work with a so-called small fry, making an implicit assumption that the culture and competence of Companies A and B would not be appropriate.

5. In a recent edited volume, a number of analyses of trust in contexts relevant to the OPAL project are presented by Castelfranchi and Tan (2001). In this volume, Falcone and Castelfranchi (2001) discuss social trust in terms of a continuum; Rea (2001) considers how trust may be engendered in electronic environments; and Weigand and van den Heuvel (2001) discuss trust in terms of speech acts and work flow modeling (an approach that has some affinities with Weisband's (no date) initiations–responses analysis). A pertinent series of studies from the Electrical Engineering Department at Imperial College of Science, Medicine and Technology, London, can be accessed at http://alfebiite.ee.ic.ac. uk/Templates/papers.htm

6. According to Baier (1986), system trust refers to the roles, responsibilities, promises, and contracts endorsed by interacting parties in a partnership.

7. In the past decade, a number of research studies have explored the validity and reliability of first impressions, specifically in the context of trust at levels of "zero acquaintance" (Albright et al., 1988). It is clear that "first impression" data may contribute to trust assessments, if only on the dimension of "conscientiousness" (Borkenau and Liebler, 1992; 1993).

REFERENCES

Albright, L., Kenny, D., and Malloy, T. (1988). Consensus in personality judgment at zero acquaintance. *Journal of Personality and Social Psychology*. 55:387–395.

Alexander, C., Ishikawa, S., Silverstein, M., Jacobson, M., Fiksdahl-King, I., and Angel, S. (1977). *A Pattern Language: Towns, Buildings, Construction*. Oxford: Oxford University Press.

Baier, A. (1986). Trust and antitrust. *Ethics*. 96:231–260.

Bargiela-Chiappini, F. and Nickerson, C. (1999). Business writing as social action. In: *Writing Business: Genres, Media and Discourses*. Bargiela-Chiappini, F. and Nickerson. C., eds. London: Longman; pp. 1–32.

Baumard, P. (1999). *Tacit Knowledge in Organizations*. London: Sage.

Benyon, D. and Imaz, M. (1999). Metaphors and models: Conceptual foundations of representations in interactive systems development. *Human-Computer Interaction*. 19:159–189.

Borkenau, P. and Liebler, A. (1992). Trait inferences: Sources of validity at zero acquaintance. *Journal of Personality and Social Psychology*. 62(4):645–657.

Borkenau, P. and Liebler, A. (1993). Convergence of stranger ratings of personality and intelligence with self-ratings, partner-ratings, and measured intelligence. *Journal of Personality and Social Psychology*. 65(3):546–553.

Carroll, J. (1995). *Scenario Based Design*. New York: John Wiley.

Castelfranchi, C. and Tan, Y.-H. (2001). *Trust and Deception in Virtual Societies*. Dordrecht: Kluwer Academic Publishers.

Davenport, E. (2002). Mundane knowledge management and micro-level organizational learning: An ethological approach. *Journal of the American Society for Information Science & Technology*. 53 (12):1038–1046.

Davenport, E. (2000). Non-contractual trust, design and human and computer interactions. In: *CHI 2000 Extended Abstracts*. Szwillus, G., and Turner, T., eds. New York: Association for Computing Machinery; pp. 239–240.

Davenport, E., Thimbleby, H., Marsh, S., and Dibben, M. (1999). "Artificial morality": Representations of trust in interactive systems. In: *Human-Computer Interaction INTERACT '99. Swinburne: British Computer Society/International Federation for Information Processing (IFIP)*. Brewster, S., Cawsey, A., and Cockton, G., eds. Amsterdam: IOS Press; pp. 211–212.

De Geus, A. (1997). *The Living Company: Growth, Learning and Longevity in Business*. London: Nicholas Brealey Publishing.

Dibben, M. R. (2000). *Exploring Interpersonal Trust in the Entrepreneurial Venture*. London: Macmillan.

Donath, J. (2002). A semantic approach to visualizing conversation. *Communications of the ACM*. 45(4):45–49.

Dourish, P. (2001). Seeking a foundation for context-aware computing. *Human-Computer Interaction*. 16:229–241.

Drew, P. (1995). Interaction sequences and anticipatory interactive planning. In: *Social Intelligence and Interaction*. Goody, E., ed. Cambridge: Cambridge University Press; pp. 111–138.

Eden, C., and Ackerman, M. (1998). Analyzing and comparing idiographic causal maps. In: *Managerial and Organizational Cognition: Theory, Methods, Research*. Eden, C. and Spender, J.-C., eds. London: Sage; pp. 192–209.

Erickson, T. (2000). Supporting interdisciplinary design: Toward pattern languages for workplaces. In: *Workplace Studies: Recovering Work Practice and Informing System Design*. Luff, P., Hindmarsh, J., and Heath, C., eds. Cambridge: Cambridge University Press; pp. 357–368.

Erickson, T., Halveson, C., Kellogg, W., Laff, M., and Wolf, T. (2002). Social translucence: Designing social infrastructures that make collective activity visible. *Communications of the ACM*. 45(4):40–44.

Falconer, J. (1999). The business pattern: A new tool for organizational knowledge capture and reuse. In: *Proceedings of the 62nd ASIS Annual Meeting: Knowledge Creation, Organization and Use*. Woods, L., ed. Medford, NJ: Information Today, Inc.; pp. 313–330.

Falcone, R., and Castelfranchi, C. (2001). Social trust: A cognitive approach. In: *Trust and Deception in Virtual Societies*. Castelfranchi, C., and Tan, Y.-H., eds. Dordrecht: Kluwer Academic Publishers; pp. 55–90.

Good, D. (1995). Where does foresight end and hindsight begin? In: *Social Intelligence and Interaction*. Goody, E., ed. Cambridge: Cambridge University Press; pp. 139–149.

Harrison, R. T., Dibben, M. R., and Mason, C. M. (1997). The role of trust in the informal investor's investment decision: An exploratory analysis. *Entrepreneurship Theory & Practice*. Special Issue: Informal Venture Capital. 20(2):63–81.

Huysman, M., and de Wit, D. (2002). *Knowledge Sharing in Practice*. Dordrecht: Kluwer Academic Publishers.

Iacono, C. S., and Weisband, S. (1997). Developing trust in virtual teams. In: Proceedings of HICSS-30, Virtual Communities Minitrack, Hawaii, January 2002. Los Alamitos: IEEE. (CD-ROM)

Jarvenpaa, S. L., and Leidner, D. E. (1998). Communication and trust in global virtual teams. *Journal of Computer Mediated Communication*. 3(4). June 1998 at http://www.ascusc.org/jcmc/vol3/issue4/jarvenpaa.html

Jarvenpaa, S. L., Knoll, K., and Leidner, D. (1998). Is anybody out there? Antecedents of trust in global virtual teams. *Journal of Management Information Systems*. 14(4):29–64.

Kramer, M., and Tyler, T., eds. (1996). *Trust in Organizations: Frontiers of Theory and Research*. Thousand Oaks, CA: Sage; pp. 166–195.

Loughran, J. (2000). Working together virtually: The care and feeding of global virtual teams. At http://www.dodccrp.org/2000ICCRTS/cd/papers/Track4/009.pdf

Marsh, S. (1994). Trust in distributed artificial intelligence. In: *Artificial Social Systems, Proceedings 4th European Workshop on Modelling Autonomous Agents in a Multi-Agent World*. Castelfranchi, C., and Werner, E., eds. Italy, 1992, Springer LNAI 830.

Martin, D., Rodden, T., Rouncefield, M., Sommerville, I. and Viller, S. (2001). Finding patterns in the fieldwork. In: *Proceedings of the Seventh European Conference on Computer Supported Cooperative Work*. Prinz, W., Jarke, M., Rogers, Y., Schmidt, K., and Wulf, V. eds. Bonn, Germany, 16–20 September 2001, Dordrecht: Kluwer Academic Publishers; pp. 39–59.

McKnight, D. H., Cummings, L., and Chervany, N. L. (1995). *Trust formation in new organizational relationships*. At http://misrc.umn.edu/wpaper/WorkingPapers

Meyerson, D., Weick, K. E., and Kramer, R. M. (1996). Swift trust and temporary groups. In: *Trust in Organizations: Frontiers of Theory and Research*. Kramer, R. M., and Tyler, T. R., eds. Thousand Oaks, CA: Sage Publications; pp. 166–195.

Nardi, B., Whittaker, S., Isaacs, E., Creech, M., Johnson, J., and Hainsworth, J. (2002). Integrating communication and information through ContactMap. *Communications of the ACM*. 45(4):89–95.

Preece, J. (2002). Supporting community and building social capital. *Communications of the ACM*. 45(4):37–39.

Rea, T. (2001). Engendering trust in electronic environments. In: *Trust and Deception in Virtual Societies*. Castelfranchi, C., and Tan Y.-H., eds. Dordrecht: Kluwer Academic Publishers; pp. 221–236.

Thomas, J. C., Kellogg, W., and Erickson, T. (2001). The knowledge management puzzle: Human and social factors in knowledge management. *IBM Systems Journal*. 40(4):863–883.

Smith, M. (2002). Tools for navigating large social cyberspaces. *Communications of the ACM*. 45(4):51–55.

Spence, R. (2001). *Information Visualization*. New York: ACM Press.

Tsoukas, H., and Cummings, S. (1997). Marginalization and recovery: The emergence of Aristotelian themes in organization studies. *Organization Studies*. 18(4):655–683.

Van der Heijden, K. (1996). *Scenarios: The Art of Strategic Conversation*. Chichester: John Wiley.

Weigand, H., and van den Heuvel, W.-J. (2001). Trust in electronic commerce. In: *Trust and Deception in Virtual Societies*. Castelfranchi, C., and Tan, Y.-H., eds. Dordrecht: Kluwer Academic Publishers; pp. 237–257.

Weisband, S. (no date). *Maintaining awareness in distant team collaboration*. Accessed 4 May, 2002 at http://misdb.bpa.arizona.edu/~lzhao/brownbag/suzie-abstract.html

Zolin. Z., Levitt, R., Fruchter, R., and Hinds, P. (2000). *Modeling and Monitoring Trust in Virtual A/E/C Teams; A Research Proposal*. http://www.stanford.edu/group/CIFE/Publications/index.html

Part V

Knowledge Management Applications— Applications— Competitive Intelligence

Knowledge Management Applications— Competitive Intelligence
Introductory Notes

Competitive intelligence (CI) and KM are logically overlapping areas, but the two communities have remained rather distinct. However, more convergence is likely in the future. This section, to a degree, represents a belief in that theory.

"Competitive Intelligence in KM" is a theme briefly elaborated on in the Road Map; therefore, we discuss it further here. Maag and Flint provide a rather comprehensive introduction to CI in Chapter 26. Shelfer discusses it as a subset of KM, indicating the overlap and reviewing benchmarking as a clear overlap area between CI and KM (see Chapter 27). In Chapter 28, Barth discusses the inherent tension between the knowledge sharing and communication that is inherent in KM, and the necessity to protect knowledge in an environment characterized by increasingly sophisticated CI.

The Role of Corporate Intelligence Gathering in the Modern Business Decision-Making Process

Gary D. Maag and Jeffrey A. Flint, Proactive Worldwide, Inc.

> *What enables the wise sovereign and the good general to strike and conquer, and achieve things beyond the reach of ordinary men, is foreknowledge.*

> *The Art of War*
> Sun Tzu

Today's competitive international business environment can be considered akin to warfare in many ways. It is warfare on friendlier terms to be certain; however, the results can be landscape altering nonetheless. Plant closings, downsizing, bankruptcy, and liquidation often await the uninformed and sluggish.

Consider Sun Tzu's quote above. Substituting the words executive for "sovereign" and product manager for "general," we note that this ancient saying still holds applicable meaning. It does so much so that modern authors have adapted Sun Tzu's teachings into books entitled *Sun Tzu and the Art of Business* and various other reincarnations, including the art of sales, marketing, and management. It is this sense of *fore*knowledge that sets business intelligence (BI) apart as a critical aspect of corporate KM (McNeilly, 2000).

What Is BI?

Business intelligence is the process of legally and ethically obtaining and analyzing raw data in order to make relevant observations about a company's competitive environment and determine actionable, strategic, and tactical options.

These options can then be used by the leaders of the firm in making decisions crucial to its future.

In effect, BI can be considered a portion of the knowledge value chain embodied by KM as a whole. Metaphorically, one corporate executive called BI the keyboard of the KM piano. This keyboard is made up of a variety of information-gathering tools—the keys themselves—most resounding of which are open-source data mining, qualitative and quantitative market research, and competitive intelligence (CI).

Use of the word intelligence in BI can invite connotations of cloak-and-dagger covert operations. Many authors, eager for a headline-grabbing title, have used sensationalistic and erroneous terms such as corporate, economic, or industrial espionage to describe BI. As an often misunderstood field, BI can perhaps be best clarified by explaining what it is not.

- Business intelligence is not espionage. While many former national security operatives have migrated into this field since the early 1990s, the term espionage has strong connotations of the use of illegal means, such as wiretapping or bribery, typically by representatives of a foreign nation. Business intelligence does not incorporate illegal means, and it is sponsored by businesses not governments.

- Business intelligence is not private investigation, although the investigative process can be considered similar in many ways. One main differentiator is that private investigators tend to focus their efforts on personal matters, such as substantiation for divorce, arbitration, or other potentially contentious proceedings. Further, the use of certain means, such as waste archeology or dumpster diving (which are legal under most circumstances but considered too far into the ethical gray zone by most business stakeholders), disassociates this type of investigation from the standard practices of BI.

- Business intelligence is not a software program. Many information technology (IT) and database vendors tout their applications as all-in-one solutions for BI, right down to analysis or filtering of the data gathered. In reality, just as with KM, these systems can dramatically facilitate the BI process but do not encompass it—particularly the analysis portion.

- Business intelligence is not open- or secondary-source data mining; however, the latter is a part of BI, for example, as a key is to our previously mentioned keyboard. Open- and secondary-source data mining *focuses on the past* because it relies on publications, databases, and Web sites. By their nature, these sources are dated, even in this electronic era. Worthy of note is the fact that BI also utilizes data mining to generate possible contacts for the important primary research phase discussed in depth later in this chapter.

- Business intelligence is not traditional market research. Again, market research can be considered an input or another key as part of the BI keyboard; however, it is not one and the same. This is a distinction that even many end-users of BI deliverables fail to recognize—based on more common exposure to market research's rote surveys, focus groups, and statistically significant sampling. Market research is *centered on the present,* not necessarily the future.

In plain terms, BI is about decision support. When corporate leaders confront a critical decision *involving the future* direction of their entity, they turn to the KM infrastructure of the firm for answers. If the sought information does not recognizably reside within the firm, then BI is employed to ascertain the information necessary to assist in making the decision.

Quite often the answers to these critical questions must take into account the competition's likely response: "If we do this, will they react by cutting prices? If we develop this product, will they beat us to market with their product?" The process of ascertaining this sort of information is called CI gathering.

EMERGENCE OF CI

While proprietors have been gauging their competition since the beginning of commerce, CI has been recently "discovered" as a relatively new business research field. Major universities have taught specialized courses on effective market and open-source research for decades; however, as of mid-2002, only 14 U.S. institutions of higher education recognizably offered a CI class—and this number is up by nearly 50 percent over only the three previous years.

From 1986 to 2000, the international membership of the Society of Competitive Intelligence Professionals (SCIP), long considered the premier trade association for CI practitioners, grew from 150 to approximately 7,000 individual members. *This huge increase*—most sharply illustrated in the pharmaceutical, telecommunications, IT, health care, and chemical sectors—can be attributed to several factors, including the following:

- Dynamic speed of change within most markets because of new techno-logical and regulatory environments
- Proliferation of unverified information via the Internet minus the time and ability necessary for effective analysis
- Economic shift from manufacturing to service sectors emphasizing intel-lectual property and capital
- Heightened pace and narrowed nature of merger and acquisitions transactions
- Decreased level of executive and employee loyalty and longevity
- Globalization of business
- Defense breeds offense—attacks on U.S. firms prompt a response

Today, the list of companies employing a BI or CI function reads like the lat-est *Fortune* 500 rankings. For example, 2001 SCIP annual conference attendees included representatives from Ashland, Bayer, Coca-Cola, Eastman Kodak, IBM, Kimberly-Clark, Lucent, General Motors, Motorola, Monsanto, Nestle, Pfizer, Phillip Morris, 3M, and many others.

Large multinational companies are not the only firms to utilize these tools. In fact, one could argue that it was Sam Walton's early application of "do-it-yourself" CI that helped propel his organization to dominance over much larger retailers, such as K-Mart. In the book *Sam Walton: Made in America*, Wal-Mart old-timer Charlie Cate remarks about the seriousness with which his old boss viewed CI:

> I remember him [Sam Walton] saying over and over again: "Go in and check our competition. And, don't look for the bad. Look for the good. If you get one good idea, that's one more than you went into the store with, and we must try to incorporate it into our company."

Walton valued CI so much that he took a hands-on approach that once got him apprehended. In Walton's book he relates the following:

> Once I was in the big Price Club on Marino Avenue in San Diego, and I had my little tape recorder with me—like I always do—and was making notes to myself about prices and merchandising ideas. This guy, a big guy, comes up to me and says, "I am sorry but I'll have to take your tape recorder and erase the material you've got on it. We have a policy against people using them in the stores." Well, we have the same policy, and I knew I was caught.

Chagrined, but impervious, Walton went on to write a note to the head of Price Club stores requesting that earlier portions of the tape be left intact, seeing as they contained observations from other chains. Four days later Walton got his tape back with no portion of it erased.

Goal of CI

In line with Walton's aim of improving displays and increasing sales, the fundamental goal of a CI function must be *to save or make time and money* for the sponsoring firm. Without routinely accomplishing this, any CI function would have to be considered ineffective.

Consider the following two examples.

Example 1. The Decision-Making Dilemma

A consumer goods company is considering the possible acquisition of one of its key suppliers in order to vertically integrate itself. The supplier in question is of particular interest because it has managed to lower prices recently while improving quality; whereas other suppliers have remained static in the marketplace. Because of this unique characteristic of the supplier firm, the consumer goods company is pondering whether to pay a $200 million premium over what similarly sized suppliers are asking in order to effect such a transaction.

Answer by CI

Management at the consumer goods company opts to initiate a CI investigation before making its final offer. In the process, it is learned that the reason for the supplier's ability to lower prices while improving quality is almost entirely due to a manufacturing technology that it has been "beta-testing" under license from another firm. Further research indicates that this nonexclusively licensed technology is soon to be offered to other suppliers of the consumer goods company as well—making the first supplier not unique after all. As a result, negotiators—armed with this intelligence—are able to reduce the premium paid by $150 million.

Example 2. The Decision-Making Dilemma

A major pharmaceutical company produces a popular prescription drug that is due to come off patent in three months, at which time other firms may manufacture a generic equivalent of the drug for sale at a much lower price. The company decides to counter this inevitable development by launching a lower-cost generic drug of its own. However, it is trying to determine when to do so because cannibalization of sales of the branded drug is estimated to reach $8 million per month as soon as this is done. Management is inclined to initiate this launch one month prior to patent expiration. Thus, the implicit risk is that if the company's generic version is launched too early, this move "leaves money on the table" that could have been garnered through normal sales of the branded drug. If the generic version were to be launched too late, it would allow potential competitors to establish a presence in the generic market with their own equivalent products.

Answer by CI

Management at the major pharmaceutical company decides to initiate a CI investigation to learn the intentions of potential competitors regarding the likely timing of a competing generic product. To the surprise of management, it is discovered that no competing product will emerge for another whole year—nine months beyond patent expiration—because of restraints on manufacturing capacity at the facilities of the key competitors. As a result, the generic launch can safely wait for another 11 months—instead of two months—meaning that the company "made" $72 million by not cannibalizing its own branded product one month prior to patent expiration.

Examples Examined

These brief examples illustrate the sort of bottom-line impact that CI can have in saving or making time and money. In the first example, $150 million was saved through intelligence-driven negotiations savvy. In the second example, CI "made" $72 million and an extra nine months for the company employing it.

As the CEO of either the consumer goods or the major pharmaceutical company, how much would you have been willing to spend on the CI investigations in question: $10 million, $5 million, $1 million? In fact, most individual CI engagements involve far smaller amounts than these and represent a tiny fraction of the money they can save or make for those sponsoring them.

In this respect, CI works somewhat like car insurance. Spending money on monthly insurance premiums can seem wasteful for a seasoned automobile driver routinely coursing through known neighborhoods and highways, that is, until the unexpected happens. When business blind spots might otherwise get the best of executives driving the future of their companies down very dynamic roadways, CI can act as a lifesaver for corporate well-being.[1]

CI Performance Metrics

While the goal of CI is clear, sometimes the best way to measure the value of CI within an organization is not. The complexity of putting a number to the impact of CI becomes most pronounced during the budgetary planning process, particularly when corporate cost-cutting initiatives are under way. This is true despite clear indicators that CI activity is linked to increased business performance in multiple areas, such as strategic planning, market performance, and product quality, as substantiated by a 1993 SCIP-sponsored study conducted by Bernard Jaworski and L. C. Wee.

Nevertheless, living on its reputation for speed and accuracy in answering executives' tough questions, one annual challenge every CI unit faces is finding a *quantifiable* way to answer the inevitable query: What have you done for us lately?

In the hunt for a method to illustrate a solid return on investment (ROI) figure for CI deliverables, companies have devised an array of formulas to approximate worth. Some attempt to codify intangible benefits, such as increased decision-making confidence. Some utilize the full value of quantifiable findings, such as those delineated in Examples 1 and 2. Others take a mix of these elements and may use fractions of the value of particular findings due to the involvement of other groups. After all, is the entire $150 million reduction in acquisition price from Example 1 solely a result of the newly provided intelligence or might the negotiators have played a key role as well? Leigh Davison (2001) of Canada's Wilfred Laurier University offers one simplified set of formulas, as shown below:

Value of CI outputs ≥ Value of CI inputs × (acceptable ROI)

Further,

(CI outputs − CI inputs) / CI inputs = Return on CI investment (ROCII)

Davison's formulaic couplet begs the question of how to assign value to CI outputs, with inputs typically being quantifiable elements, such as time, labor, and related fees. In a 1996 study by Jan Herring, former CIA officer and pioneer of the CI function of Motorola, insight was sought as to how corporations value and possibly quantify CI outputs. It was determined, not unexpectedly, that no standard practice exists and that each organization tends to invent its own yardstick. Nevertheless, the study identified five common measures of effectiveness (MOEs) that executives appear to use routinely in assessing the performance of their organizational CI unit:

- Time savings
- Cost savings
- Cost avoidance
- Revenue increase
- Value added

Most intangible of these measures of effectiveness is the value added category. A dominant theme in this area with business leadership is often the increased confidence with which decisions can be made after exposure to CI outputs—even if plans do not necessarily change. This comfort level is hard to track and quantify but is a significant factor, nonetheless.

While Herring's study yielded no broadly applicable formula for measuring the worth of an intelligence function, it did recommend 10 steps crucial to ensuring that the expectations of both CI group leaders and company executives tightly align. These steps to establishing an organization's own CI measuring stick are the following:

1. Involve management from beginning to end.
2. Identify expectations up front.
3. Make expectations and MOEs part of CI planning.
4. Identify and define key performance areas.
5. Align strategic objectives, expectations, and CI operations.
6. Select most appropriate MOEs, including value added.
7. Produce intelligence that links expectations and MOEs.
8. Tailor CI results to the decision-making style of management.
9. Jointly evaluate qualitative results with management.
10. Calculate and communicate quantitative results through users.

In matching the budget of a CI function to expected deliverables, put yourself in the CEO's office suite for a moment and consider what you might have paid for the results found in Examples 1 and 2. Certainly, in these multimillion-dollar examples, where the results are known, CI merits a large budget—but this conclusion benefits from hindsight. What would you have paid *not knowing* what the results would be? What if the intelligence had simply affirmed your preexisting notions of the competitive landscape and was just an all-clear signal to go ahead with what you had planned to do?

Competitive intelligence engagements do not always produce monumental paradigm shifts in the way executives view the competitive environment. However, it can be the exceptions that count. Sadly, some corporate leaders—having devoted their entire career to a specific industry—succumb to complacency about findings that suggest executive perceptions may be amiss and hesitate second-guessing their instincts, even as evidence to the contrary mounts. They do so at the risk of their positions and quite possibly the health of their firms.

GENESIS AND EVOLUTION OF AN INTELLIGENCE FUNCTION

More often than not, corporate intelligence functions are propelled into being by a Big Bang critical event. Companies are either suddenly confronted by a heretofore unrecognized threat or need to make a forward-looking decision that carries with it the fate of the firm and, thus, requires solid research currently unavailable by other means. In some cases, companies become convinced of the value of CI as it is successfully employed against them on a repetitive basis. Suddenly, that competitor seems to beat them to every punch, every product innovation, every new market segment.

This Big Bang event sets in motion a whole sequence of activities that can potentially spiral out of control for any newly designated corporate intelligence manager. Particularly because most employees are exclusively familiar with data mining or traditional market research, the generative process of establishing a trustworthy intelligence network can seem a bit chaotic at first. Born in eruptive crisis, many newly minted intelligence managers launch into work trying to complete a "Mission Impossible" task within a "We need it yesterday" time frame. In nearly all cases, this is a formula for failure. Even amid rapid-fire demand for competitive answers, the new manager needs to take crucial time with the information user(s) in order to separate need-to-know nuggets from nice-to-know items that waste time, money, and effort. Doing so not only helps to align expectations but also serves to identify resources that may be crucial to success in this and future intelligence endeavors—providing bigger bang for every research buck.

An issue that can potentially complicate the creation of any corporate intelligence program and that can have a lasting braking effect on the quality of findings is the method by which a person is selected to head these efforts. If the impetus behind creating an intelligence function is top-down driven, then commonly an executive championing the implementation of CI usage within the firm reaches out to find a right-hand man or woman. Because a critical event for which intelligence is needed on a quick turnaround basis is often driving this decision, it is common for a knowledgeable company market research manager to be tapped for the new responsibility. After all, this is a trusted individual with research experience and little to no industry learning curve. Or is it?

One fallacious assumption made by many executives looking to jump start an intelligence function in order to fulfill immediate decision-making needs is that a company market research manager is going to be able to readily adopt and employ CI techniques. The reality is that while skill sets may be similar in some ways, such a transition takes at least a few months to bear fruit. There is a CI learning curve—not necessarily an industry learning curve—as the designee comes to better understand significant methodological nuances. This learning curve is above and beyond the time necessary to build, tap into, or reactivate an internal/external intelligence-gathering network. Therefore, in meeting abrupt needs, the organization may be best served by engaging a CI agency for quick answers while developing an internal capacity for the long term.

Looking outside for someone to hire as the new head of a fledgling intelligence program may also warrant consideration. First, moving a key employee over to an unfamiliar field may not be in the best interests of the company—a strength is likely to be lost while the learning curve prohibits an imminent CI result. Second, some employees with a market research or library sciences background are bound to view CI as perhaps a less than willful and temporary diversion from their career track, color it in the context of either market research or library sciences, and never fully explore the research options available to a true CI professional. Finally, if identification and clarification of executives' misperceptions or questions with regard to the competitive landscape is in order, why not choose someone with an objective opinion that will come in questioning everything, using CI savvy to substantiate observations with solid findings and analysis.

Ultimately, many companies, such as Motorola, choose to start fresh and often select former national security operatives. These persons may lack industry-specific experience, but they understand intelligence gathering across a broad range of topics and can also competently develop a counterintelligence program. While abilities, of course, differ on an individual level, a generalized list of pros and cons is given in Table 26.1.

Appropriate placement of the intelligence function within an organization is nearly as important as who heads these efforts. Under some circumstances there may be more than one function or more than one location. In determining how best to structure and position the unit, a number of factors must be considered, including the following:

- Proximity to decision makers
- Existing degree of relationship between the function leader and intelligence consumers
- Strategic and tactical focus of anticipated research questions
- Anticipated methods of intelligence collection
- Location of company assets required for research
- Proximity to collection venues and competitive targets

In the book *Millennium Intelligence,* Kenneth Sawka (2000) (a vice president at the consulting firm of Fuld & Co. and former CIA analyst) discusses three frameworks for placement of an intelligence unit. These include centralized, decentralized, and hybrid variants. Paul Kinsinger (2000) (a 20-year CIA veteran and professor at Thunderbird, The American Graduate School of International Management) likewise categorizes BI structural models into several types but expands on the possibilities:

- **Centralized.** Designed to support chief-executive–level strategic decision making; usually found in single business companies where decisions are corporate driven
- **Decentralized.** Designed to support single-business-unit–level strategy and even tactical intelligence needs; found in companies with disparate businesses
- **Hub-and-spoke (hybrid).**[2] Designed to support strategic effort at the corporate level and to coordinate with separate SBU-strategic/tactical effort; found in companies with adjacent businesses
- **CEO-BI "Consigliare."** A senior BI executive who reports directly and sometimes solely to the CEO; rare and always a matter of personal ties
- **BI orchestrator.** Used by SMEs where one person coordinates the needs of internal intelligence with outsource providers
- **Living, breathing intelligence culture.** Where BI becomes second nature in the company; employees recognize the importance of BI and take part in collecting, analyzing, and disseminating critical external intelligence

The evolution of a corporate intelligence function that develops a reputation for providing value to decision makers can be dramatic, even over the space of a few years. A common developmental sequence is for a business to begin with an orchestrator, then move to a centralized or decentralized unit before perhaps adopting a hub-and-spoke model (see Figure 26.1).

Table 26.1   General pros and cons of selecting particular background types to head a new corporate intelligence function.

Background	Market Research	Library and Information Sciences	National Security
Pros:	Typically easy to find in-house with existing company familiarity	May already be in-house with existing company familiarity	Brings a "fresh set of eyes" and objectivity
	Well-versed in the industry at hand and customer perceptions	Likely to be the most competent regarding the implementation and maintenance of a KM system	Thorough understanding of intelligence gathering techniques and methodologies
	Maintains own network of industry contacts	Strong open-source data collection ability	Competent to implement a counterintelligence gathering program as necessary
	Trusted as an insider	Understands accepted company intelligence dissemination process	Views intelligence as a conscious career choice
	Versed in certain types of interviewing and statistically significant sampling	Knowledgeable about the industry at hand and likely to have broad historical recall	Carries "national security" authority regarding intelligence matters
Cons:	Constrained by company and career field paradigms	Must conquer significant learning curve concerning intelligence gathering techniques and methodologies	Likely to require a new hire with a lack of company and possibly industry familiarity
	Transition from existing market research position may be detrimental to other company capabilities	Possibly viewed as having a lack of authority or "librarian" stigma	Must come to know the capabilities of and take time to tap into existing company contact networks
	Must deal with significant learning curve concerning intelligence-gathering techniques and methodologies	May focus on voluminous data dumps versus analyzing for meaning	May be seen by others as a "spook" of questionable intentions
	May view intelligence as a temporary career diversion	Is less believable as a counterintelligence authority	May be less sensitive to limits of business ethics
	Is not believable as a counterintelligence authority	May have difficulties with eliciting aspects of corporate intelligence and may gravitate to secondary source collection	Could become too exclusive of a conduit to understanding the competitive landscape

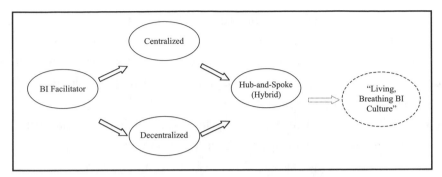

Figure 26.1   Typical business intelligence function developmental sequence.

As the needs of companies evolve, so should their intelligence units. As these intelligence units evolve, so should their budgets, structure, and staffing. Most intelligence functions start as a one-person show loosely associated with a corporate or SBU-specific market research department. Newcomers to SCIP conferences are commonly asked, "How big is your company's intelligence function?" More often than not the response is "You are looking at it!"

Function Size and Outsourcing

Attentive readers may have already noticed that in the section of this chapter entitled Genesis and Evolution of an Intelligence Function, discussion shifted from the specific term and concept of a CI function to the broader "intelligence unit" moniker. This reflects the fact that many companies expect their "unconventional" research unit to handle much more than just gathering information about competitors. An intelligence unit may also be responsible for KM systems, merger and acquisition owing to diligence evaluations, open-source data mining, economic and political risk analysis, counterintelligence investigations, pricing or bid assessments, market opportunities intelligence, and even vendor qualification or potential client pitch support in some cases.

Finding a person who can vibrantly play this research keyboard well enough to smoothly accompany each one of these different informational styles is rare. Most individuals lack depth in one or more areas of this broad range, while educational establishments are only now beginning to recognize the demand for professionals with the focused ability to gather, analyze, provide, and systematize BI in whatever form. Even in finding such a person, the burgeoning demand for quality deliverables and deadline-driven time pressures suggest that outsourcing of activities, additional hiring, or both eventually must take place. Put simply, a single orchestrator cannot do it all and, therefore, must facilitate others in the doing because of time, knowledge, and possibly skill restraints.

It is at this crossroad between merely having a BI facilitator and creating a more extensive centralized or decentralized function that outsourcing commonly becomes an issue. As inexperienced orchestrators initially rely on outside consultants to help establish an internal KM or open-source monitoring system, proselytize counterintelligence basics, or elicit information from competitors, the bills begin to add up. Assuming the value of intelligence deliverables continues to significantly outweigh required company inputs, management extends support but may still seek to integrate and cut costs by either shifting key individuals from other areas into the corporate intelligence function or by bringing new professionals in-house to assist with now proven internal demand for BI products. Determining the right size of a function at this stage becomes crucial to its long-term survival.

Corporate intelligence functions vary widely in staffing and tools. For example, in 2001, pharmaceutical company Merck was reputed to have a largely centralized function staffed with as many as 40 people. The hub-and-spoke function of Eastman Kodak had fewer than half that number. Both are cutting-edge, award-winning operations. Is one just more efficient than the other? Not necessarily.

The difference in size could be due to a variety of causes, a few of which are listed here. First, for instance, it could be largely definitional. Some intelligence functions include traditional market research personnel. Some do not. Some place technical KM system maintenance with IT. Some do not.

Second, it could be due to industry dynamism. The photoproducts market is a fiercely competitive yet relatively stable one, with a handful of entrenched players and infrequent merger activity—although new technologies of potentially great impact routinely emerge. The branded pharmaceuticals industry, in comparison, is a hotbed of potential merger and acquisition activity, even among top-tier companies, and it focuses more on intellectual capital than manufacturing efficiencies to ensure profits.

Third, the size of a BI function is often indicative of its historical term of service and sometimes that of its leader. Merck's function has been in place for at least

15 years. Kodak's CI effort has gained most of its momentum within the last seven years, crowned by a 2001 CI team excellence award from SCIP.

Fourth, different decision makers have different confidence interval requirements, which affect how resources may be allocated. Some executives are ready to move once they are 80 percent certain; others want to be 95 percent sure. The difference in the degree and depth of coverage of key intelligence topics is, over time, largely dependent on the resources allocated to pursue such detail.

On average, mid-sized firms with functions less than 10 years old typically have three to five team members who commonly specialize in certain aspects, such as open-source searchers, KM system updaters, trade show quarterback and collection teams, reverse engineering technicians, public filing experts, counterintelligence penetration testers, and human-source network handlers. Whatever the staffing mix and no matter what the topic of focus, each intelligence unit must be able to adequately perform the fundamental five steps of the process. These steps—planning and direction, collection, processing, analysis and production, and dissemination—as illustrated by a U.S. Central Intelligence Agency Web site diagram in Figure 26.2, inherently comprise a continuous cycle.[3]

One thing common to even the relatively well-staffed intelligence functions at both Merck and Kodak is the need for outsourcing components of intelligence-gathering projects. While involvement of outside entities largely subsides once internal KM, open-source, and human-source networks are up and operating, it is always wise to maintain an outside intelligence collection arsenal available to fill gaps and act as a constant checkpoint for objectivity.

In transitioning from BI facilitator to the centralized or decentralized mode, many companies see their percentage of *internally produced* intelligence dramatically increase from about 20 percent to 30 percent to nearly 80 percent, as new hires, new tools, and training enhance collection capabilities. This increase, in turn, allows the function to more effectively partner with a trusted professional intelligence-gathering firm or two by doing the following: providing prerequisite background materials that significantly streamline the research process, more specifically focus project objective tasking, and decrease engagement costs.

This combination of internally produced intelligence and external deliverables can be powerful when approaching executives who may be averse to what the findings suggest. While some managers might insist on keeping as much of the intelligence activities of the company in-house as is possible due to cost or security issues, this should rarely—if ever—be the case in its entirety. Completely

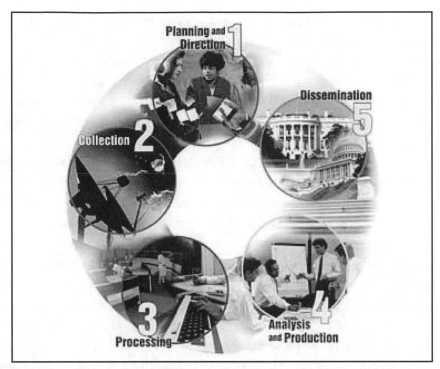

Figure 26.2   The five fundamental steps of intelligence gathering: planning and direction, collection, processing, analysis and production, and dissemination. Accessed from the U.S. Central Intelligence Agency Web site on 20 June, 2002, http://www.cia.gov/publications/facttell/intcycle.htm

inbred intelligence systems have a tendency to lose objectivity and grow complacent until they are exposed by failure to identify an impending critical event.

Consider also that most firms maintain policies that discourage any sort of contact with employees of competing firms. A special mandate exclusively for the intelligence unit would seem suspect and, even if granted, raises the legal and ethical issue of how function members are identifying themselves in speaking with competitors. Further discussion on this topic follows in the section, "Understanding the Legal and Ethical Boundaries of Intelligence Collection." Of course, the better the internal network assets, the less direct contact with competitors and, thus, outsourcing may be needed overall.

INCULCATING COMPANY CULTURE WITH INTELLIGENCE

Few firms ever achieve what Kinsinger terms a "living, breathing business intelligence culture" without a strong KM component also in place. Particularly for non-U.S. organizations, this may not necessarily require a technological platform for the companywide exchange of information. Many foreign entities—and most small firms, no matter where located—rely on low-tech means to ensure dissemination of vital information. The key is having everyone within the firm understand three things: what to keep their eyes and ears open for, to whom they should report insightful nuggets, and that incentives are given for participation.

Building an intelligence savvy culture within an organization can happen without a looming crisis being requisite for unification. Molding such a culture is possible without using money as a reward for participation. Consider the following scenarios:

- A salesperson, during one stop on her monthly route, learns the details of the pitch of a competing firm from a receptionist at a current client company. Included were oblique mentions of new technology being utilized to improve quality and lower cost.
- A delivery driver, in passing the facility of a competitor, notes what appears to be dated machinery being set aside on the lot for disposal.
- A veteran procurer is approached by a manufacturer who, in attempting to presell the upcoming model of his company, hints that a competitor is already involved in beta-testing of this equipment.

Each of these three scenarios possibly infers a competitive development that should interest the employers of these individuals. Reviewed together, the information begins to create a more complete picture of what appears to be an emerging competitive threat. Companies can miss out on insights such as these for a variety of reasons. Perhaps the salesperson resisted informing her district sales manager because the information was, as of yet, sketchy. Perhaps the delivery driver reported his observation, but it was deemed insignificant by a busy supervisor who was more concerned at the time with maintaining a logistical schedule. Perhaps the veteran procurer's claims were dismissed as a scare tactic used to try to upwardly affect the equipment procurement budget of the next cycle.

The fact is that individual nuggets can often be swept under the rug as being alarmist, particularly in industries where the spreading of rumors and misinformation can run rampant. Met with perpetual disdain, employees may shut down as potential sources of useful information. A successful CI manager, to the contrary, activates the entire company as an integrated network of business—and possibly personal—contacts that feeds these nuggets as directly as possible to a core person or group that can then analyze them in the context of the bigger developing picture:

> Hmm. … Based on inputs from one of our salespersons, a delivery driver, and our senior procurement officer, it appears that our major competitor may have already installed and may be testing new production line equipment that could erode our competitive edge. Time to gather additional details and alert senior management!

Assuming that employees will not report such insights without a monetary incentive is more likely an excuse than reality. Unless serious issues of mistrust exist in a firm—which are more poisonous to the organization than any outside competitor—most employees are likely to participate in a KM or CI effort when given the right combination of the following:

- **Attention.** Illustrate attentiveness and concern regarding their observation or finding—do so in the form of brief questions designed to flesh out further detail.
- **Praise.** Congratulate them for taking the initiative to bring this information to the attention of the corporate intelligence group and senior management.
- **Feedback.** Promise to share with them at a later date whether other sources appear to confirm or conflict with the information they have provided, and then follow up with them.
- **Recognition.** If their insight turns out to be accurate and significant for the company, recognize their contribution in front of a supervisor and possibly co-workers as considered appropriate. That is, make them a positive example. (Keep in mind, however, that some individuals may prefer to remain discreet about their input.)
- **Access.** In extraordinary cases, allow them to retell their observation or finding to senior management in a private meeting directly and reward them with a nonmonetary privilege.

Employees who see their interests aligned with those of the firm are ready participants. However, even less loyal associates can find or be shown their own motivation for contributing. For some, being the first to know among peers—and having an independent group validate that they were the first to know—is a status builder. For others, nagging curiosity may drive them to seek confirmation as to whether they were right in their theory or perception. A handful may simply view any association with an intelligence professional as intriguing, a field they may want to learn more about. Providing occasional tidbits gains them the right to do so more closely. For nearly everyone, however, simply taking information without ever letting the provider have some sense of whether, how, and for what it was used is demotivating.

Understanding the psychological drivers behind each source from the internal network of your company is also important in gauging the value of information provided by that person. Time-wasting spreaders of unsubstantiated rumors need to be identified early on and dealt with accordingly. Ulterior motives or experiential backgrounds that can serve to put a spin on information need to be discerned and considered. These factors can also identify the types of rewards this person might find the most pleasing and open up the possibility of enlisting this person's assistance in the future—most likely in seeking answers to follow-up questions or approaching a particular external contact for information. For example, what more could be gained if our salesperson and procurement officer circled back to their sources with additional questions?

Psychological factors need to be addressed not only in dealing with those who volunteer themselves as sources but especially with those that do not. Most large companies will have a broad, silent majority of employees not particularly inclined to pitch in as part of the company intelligence effort. They may consider themselves too busy. They may not yet understand the importance of this function or possibly misperceive its purpose. They may underestimate the value of the knowledge they possess—to them it seems obvious. Not just identifying but overcoming these factors is usually a matter of education.

EXPECTATION MANAGEMENT

Handling information requestors as demand for intelligence deliverables takes off within a company can be as complicated as handling sources. Divergent interests within a company combined with ignorance or misperceptions of the intelligence-gathering process can lead to unrealistic, off-base, and sometimes truly odd requests.

At a 2001 Chicago SCIP chapter meeting, Joseph Goldberg (director of Motorola's corporate BI function and CIA veteran) shared humorous examples of how his group—in place since its inception in 1983 under Herring—is still sometimes misperceived within Motorola itself:

- Library research
- Snitches, narcs, the rat squad, the Inspector General's Office, witch-hunters
- Dumpster divers
- Worldwide Spy Network, which knows everything about every competitor in every country
- Researchers for children's homework [executive education], MBAs, or stock quotes
- [Purely as a] KM system

According to Goldberg, these misperceptions—not unique to individuals within the work force of over 100,000 employees at Motorola—have led to requests such as the following:

- Can you get me 15 or so recent analyst reports on these 10 companies?
- I saw a number somewhere. Can you find out where it was and validate it?
- How big is the Internet?

In some cases for some companies the first question may actually be somewhat appropriate, that is, if your intelligence function also includes a corporate librarian. Goldberg's group does not—a conscious decision made because he constantly strives to have his team members not just dig up material but *add value through analysis*. Goldberg is so focused on this aspect of BI that he considers it an affront to his group when they are asked to dig up data without properly understanding the end goal of the data collection. If the information requestor cannot answer the question "What decision are you trying to make?" then the intelligence function is limited in responding intelligently.

This research hound mentality permeates the mind of the asker of the second inquiry, and yet this question—as well as the third one—is most dangerous in its complete lack of specificity. If this request were to be accepted without further follow-up questions posed by the intelligence provider, then failure to satisfy the requestor's needs is virtually guaranteed. A number about what? Where might you have seen it? What are the measurements to its validity? Why are you looking for it, and what other material might help you make your decision?

As rudimentary as these items would seem, it is not uncommon for modern corporate intelligence functions to receive such requests devoid of detail. More often than not, these requests come in the form of e-mail from a traveling and often unreachable employee, who actually may display disappointment subsequently that his or her mind was not read successfully. Given that these persons also tend to require the information in unrealistic time frames, the point becomes crystal clear. Business intelligence functions must manage the expectations of their end-users, typically executives.

Proactive Worldwide CEO Gary Maag and President David Kalinowski addressed this topic in their 1999 *CI Magazine* article entitled "Expectations management for better CI results." This piece—written for end-users—confronts the pattern of poorly articulated, last-minute, "Get me whatever you can" requests and focuses on having the requestor and intelligence manager work closely together to bring the process out of potential chaos. In order to best ensure that a deliverable delights rather than disappoints, Maag and Kalinowski suggest the following:

- **Be specific with project scope.** Users of CI must ask for *exactly* what they want. Be as granular as possible at the outset.
- **Discuss project do-ability.** Expect CI providers to be upfront and tell it like it is. Nobody wants to hear, "No problem, we can do that in a week," only to be told the day before the report is due that "We really need another month."
- **Agree on realistic time frames.** Take into account and schedule for strategizing with, identifying, and contacting knowledgeable sources; verifying and analyzing research findings; and report writing.
- **Seek perspective, not precision.** Remember, findings may not always need to go to the third number after the decimal point in order to provide sufficient strategic perspective to reach a conclusion.
- **Communicate regularly.** Competitive intelligence engagements can encounter unexpected and exciting turns. Take advantage of them, and know what to expect in the final report by communicating often.
- **Good, fast, or cheap—pick two.** Remember Jerry Maguire, "Help me to help you." Build a win–win partnership.

Relationship building between the intelligence function and end-users is best initiated by first defining who is authorized to request deliverables and how to prioritize research inquiries when resources and time are scarce. In order to avoid last minute requests, even those of a high priority, members of the intelligence function must seek to learn the key intelligence topics of the company, as defined by the end-users and decision makers. In other words, intelligence function members must have them vocalize which issues keep them up at night because of a lack of information or adequate certainty. Issues will range from the strategic to the minutely tactical.

Bringing these topics to the table, even before a commissioned project is required, is extremely helpful for the intelligence-gathering team because it gives them advance notice of where to focus their efforts. This, in turn, can lead to the development of contacts that may later be able to answer crucial questions when time is in short supply. In fact, a well-oiled function will take these key topics and not only develop a contact infrastructure while monitoring events but will proactively attempt to anticipate and answer logical questions for the next step.

UNDERSTANDING WHAT RESONATES WITH END-USERS AND SOURCES

It is not enough to anticipate and answer key questions. Building value into a corporate intelligence process also involves understanding how to best cater intelligence to executives. Does this person prefer at-a-glance charts, well-supported textual argumentation, or just verbal updates? For deliverables to truly be actionable, they must be presented in such a way that important items are easy to find and substantiation is provided to the extent required by the decision maker.

According to a 1995 SCIP conference presentation by Professors Hans Hedin and Katrina Svensson of Lund University in Sweden, two observations are central to discernment of an end-user's decision-making style.[4] The first is the amount of information necessary for the person to decide, and the second is the relative number of alternative solutions that this person tends to consider before arriving at a decision. So, for example, a unifocused person is looking for a single solution whereas a multifocused person wishes to consider many solutions.

Based on these and other variables, Hedin and Svensson developed five personality types that were expanded by Jan P. Herring (see Figure 26.3). These profiles were coupled with fictional and real-world examples, as depicted from top to bottom by the portraits of John Wayne, Bill Clinton, Sherlock Holmes, Steve Jobs, and Inspector Columbo. Next to the portraits are recommendations for dealing with each personality type.

Understanding the personality type of the executive for which an intelligence deliverable is crafted can go a long way toward ensuring that its findings are read and noticed. Steps to success are shown to the right of each portrait in Figure 26.3. Imagine mistakenly approaching a Sherlock Holmes end-user with John Wayne brevities!

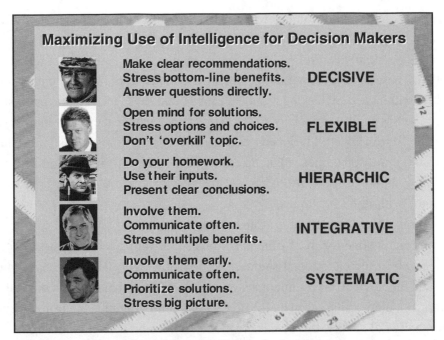

Figure 26.3   Maximizing the use of intelligence for decision makers.

For those personality types who seek explanation as to the hows and whys—namely, the systematic, integrative, hierarchic, and, to a lesser degree, flexible types—it is inevitable that the question of primary sources and whether to reveal none, some, or all of them to decision makers will arise. This is a matter that each BI function needs to broach early on with management, especially because it seems clear that there are at least two sets of circumstances wherein sources should not be revealed.

The first is when a source—whether from an internal or external network—is willing to provide information but only on a "background" or no-name disclosure basis. Journalists and BI professionals alike handle these types of sources with care. Instead of a name, a vague identifier, such as a veteran technical employee or high-level contact, is often used. In essence, this label hopes to provide some gauge of validity while maintaining discretion and the opportunity to reharvest the source's growing crop of information. Suitably, it is not uncommon that the person's job title best approximates his or her likelihood to have access to accurate information on a subject anyway. For example, is it important that Mike Reilly knows of a product coming out next year? Perhaps it is, if Mike Reilly is an advertising executive working with a competitor on the product's campaign.

The second condition under which it is particularly important not to reveal sources is when dissemination of intelligence reports—or information there-from—is not tightly controlled. Newspapers are one thing; intelligence reports are another. These reports are not designed for mass distribution. While contacts must remain within acceptable legal and ethical boundaries, many sources wish to remain anonymous—especially to the party about which they are sharing vital nuggets. To ruin a well-developed external network and expose the strategic hand of a company, sometimes all it takes is one overly informed employee who decides to boast in front of others, is careless with a bound report, or exits the company with illicit intentions.

Since intelligence-gathering professionals are not journalists and cannot rely on a contact's hope for front-page fame, other motivating factors must be found with which to recruit external sources. While ill-fitting to BI, it is interesting to note that the Soviet Union's infamous yet highly effective KGB boiled down these factors to a memorable acronym—MICE—for gaining compliance from potential informants. Put simply, this stands for money, ideology, coercion, and ego.

In BI terms, it is obvious that function members cannot bribe others, nor is it wise to even give cause for suspicion of such. The same goes for coercing others, whether through blackmail, violence, or sexual attention. Ideologically, corporations may have outstanding cultures; however, rarely in this mobile, modern world is loyalty as deep to one's company as it is likely to be to one's country. And, again, devoid of a newspaper reporter's fame-building power, how does a CI professional play on ego?

Building Rapport and "Push-to-Talk" Buttons

Contrary to popular belief, most BI primary research does not take place in smoky bars or by shoulder surfing on airplanes. Most primary research occurs daily right over the phone—a cost-effective, low-risk medium, which usually makes more sense than toneless e-mail or expensive trips to physical locations. This being the case, intelligence professionals often face the routine task of talking to total strangers in order to encourage them to share valuable tidbits about competitors or other important market information. They do so by first establishing appropriate rapport and then utilizing elicitation techniques to slowly unravel details, while upholding the conversant's self-delusion that he or she is in complete control of the conversation.

Compare this with the rote format of most telemarketers or even some survey takers: Name…. Cause…. Sales pitch…. Blah…. Click.

In contrast, professional intelligence elicitors study their potential sources as best as time and resources allow. They quickly become proficient at identifying strategic calling points—those persons who either have answers to the research objectives or are likely to become a gateway to them. Professional elicitors are methodical and practiced, and they recognize individual's push-to-talk buttons even before a call or within a respondent's first few sentences. Pushing buttons then usually is not about making the person angry but, instead, is about engaging the person in such a way that he or she is inclined to continue the conversation and ultimately provide information. Here you see the MICE acronym and scaled down versions fit for CI:

M Money	⇒	"Cha-ching"
I Ideology	⇒	Sympathy
C Coercion	⇒	Quid pro quo
E Ego	⇒	Flattery

We have already mentioned that two of the components are likely to be illegal if employed and that the other two are somewhat sketchy as to whether they truly are fit for use in BI collection efforts. On the right are slightly similar but much more BI-appropriate tactics for enlisting the help of a potential source.

Cha-ching is an onomatopoetic reference to the phenomenon that where a perceived potential sale or cha-ching of the cash register lurks, there also is a loosening of tongues.

Elicitor: I was examining some of your company's product literature and had a few questions….

Conversant: Which model? We mostly sell the R-3050. Customers seem to like its price and dependability. We sold over 400,000 last year….

Sympathy represents the tendency, particularly within certain Western cultures, to assist or teach those in need or in search of something—often with little understanding whatsoever about the requesting party. This tendency seems to generally compound with each expressed degree of similarity between the elicitor and the conversant.

Elicitor: I am fairly new at my job and am just kind of plugging along here. I only graduated from Northwestern last year. I was wondering if you could help me better understand the health care market?

Conversant: New on the job, huh? That can be tough. What specifically did you want to know about health care? 2001 grad? You know I have a daughter who was probably at Northwestern at the same time you were. Small world.

Quid pro quo or tit for tat information is the common currency of business. The more you can illustrate that you have something potentially useful for a source, the more likely the source is to help you with your needs this and the next time around.

Elicitor: Mr. Robbins, I believe I have some information that could be of use to you. I came about it trying to better grasp the dynamics of a technology, which I understand you might know something about.

Conversant: I'd be interested to hear more of your information. Please keep me in the loop if you come across anything new. I'll be certain to tell you when a beta-test observation might be possible.

Flattery exposes each person's need to hear positive things about themselves. Often for nothing more than a few kind and humble words, sources will latch on to the opportunity to speak with you.

Elicitor: I have been hoping to talk with you for some time. I have heard from others in the business community that you are really a guru in your industry.

Conversant: Well, I am not sure I would use the term guru, but I have been around for almost 30 years. There isn't much I have not seen. What is it that you are interested in?

Once through introductions and over the contact's checkpoint of "Will I or will I not speak with you?" professional elicitors employ a variety of techniques to subtly drive the conversation toward the specifics they seek without becoming overbearing or hinting too strongly at what is truly important to them. In fact, using a "macro-micro-macro" approach—as termed "The Conversational Hourglass" by John Nolan—it may never be clear to the contact what exactly the elicitor was looking for and what crucial detail, indeed, was shared. This approach implies wrapping nonthreatening, potentially rapport-building conversational topics around a core of rather specific, albeit often indirect questions. These microissues, the ones a source is likely to be the most hesitant about outwardly answering, are soon forgotten because most persons are inclined to remember the beginning and end of a discussion—unless something unusual dramatically piques their interest or suspicion. This is particularly true when these questions are asked in tandem with other elicitation techniques that appropriately coincide with the push-to-talk approach in use. Table 26.2 provides a list of these techniques, which is not exhaustive. Other combinations also are possible. Table 26.2 merely groups techniques that tend to make sense when used together.

Another key elicitation concept to keep in mind is the outside-in principle. Direct contact with a company is not always necessary in order to first gain information about its activities. Most companies rely on a value chain that often extends far beyond their own operations, and these peripheral entities usually contain knowledgeable sources that have little, if any, reason to guard the information of a company other than their own. For example, suppliers, packagers, engineering or technical consultants, advertisers, and value-added resellers all typically will know

Table 26.2   Collection Technique Consistency

"Push-to-Talk" Button	Related Techniques	Combination Example
"Cha-ching"	Challenging statement Criticism	400,000 units seems high to me. I have an acquaintance who purchased one, and he did not find the motor to be dependable at all.
Sympathy	Instinct to complain Purposely erroneous statement Bracketing	Yes, I felt like I was in over my head the whole first six months. Anyway, I was going to ask you, what is typical market share size for a middle-tier company like yours? 40%? Lower, higher?
Quid pro quo	Quotation of reported facts Oblique reference	You may already be aware of this, but during an earnings call last week one of your suppliers said they had brought on another major account and were shifting portions of production to someplace in Kansas. Have they brought this up with you?
Flattery	Naïveté Word repetition Feigned or real disbelief	Wow, growth over 49%? I never would have thought it could be so high! That is really impressive!

of a new product months to years before it actually reaches the market. As a result, searching for peripheral entities that could be involved in outsourced research and development, design, supply, ramp-up or scale-up, beta-testing, transportation, and myriad other fields is often an effective way to identify other sources with access to important competitive tidbits and less caution regarding sharing them. After all, why attempt to have a company employee describe the inside of his or her facility in detail, when the architectural firm that designed it or the contractor that built it may be inclined to provide photographs that illustrate the quality of their work. Here is a nonexhaustive list of peripheral source possibilities:

Advertising firms
Advertising and promotional design agencies
Allied and partner firms
Architectural firms
Associations
Auditors
Bankers
Benefits companies
Brokerage industry analysts
Building managers
Business park managers
Commercial property agents
Complementary product manufacturers
Construction management firms
Consumer advocates
Contract sales force members
Contractors
Customers
Direct competitors
Distributors
Domain name registration agencies
Educational establishments
End-user organizations and forums
End-users
Equipment dealers, installers, and manufacturers
Ex-employees
Foreign branch offices

Human resource agencies

Internet service providers

Inventors of similar products

Initial public offering underwriters

Journalists

Key opinion and thought leaders

Labor union officials

Lawyers

Local sources: chamber of commerce, dining and entertainment
venues, document preparation shops, lodging establishments,
and vocational programs

Market research companies

Media buying firms

Neighboring entities and persons

Original equipment manufacturers

Outside consultants of any kind

Outsourced call centers

Package designers

Packagers

Public relations agencies

Published and syndicated report authors

Raw materials suppliers

Recent interns

Regulatory agencies: municipal, county, state, and federal

Relatives

Repair and warranty facilitators

Research institutions

Retailers

Returned product handlers

Subcomponent and subassembly companies

Subsidiaries

Suppliers

Telecommunications providers

Temporary staffing agencies

Topic-specific chat rooms

Trade experts

> Trade organizations
> Trademark and patent registration agencies
> Transportation companies
> Value-added resellers
> Warehousing agents
> Waste management firms
> Web site designers
> Wholesalers

Understanding the Legal and Ethical Boundaries of Intelligence Collection

Moving forward with the development of any corporate intelligence function is a truly tremendous and yet exciting undertaking. Amid the hustle and bustle of just in the nick of time deliverables and the innovation of new routes to crucial information, some of the finer points regarding the laws and ethical codes governing business—and particularly competitive—intelligence can become blurred. It is for this reason that forward-thinking function leaders and companies must be proactive enough to well define and document the acceptable limits of these types of activities *before* questionable circumstances arise.

This section is not intended to be an exhaustive discussion of the legal and ethical parameters surrounding BI; however, it is important to point out that the overarching federal law generally deemed to govern this field is the Economic Espionage Act (EEA) of 1996. Put simply, this Act makes it a federal criminal offense for any person to convert a trade secret to his or her own benefit or the benefit of others intending or knowing that the offense will injure any owner of the trade secret.

It is also important to point out that the EEA is often misperceived among those in the general public and media who are aware of it, as well as BI practitioners. When first passed, some parties in SCIP circles speculated that the EEA might seriously hinder CI investigations, if not altogether deem them illegal. This assumption has not been borne out by the relatively limited number of cases in which the EEA has been invoked to prosecute alleged offenders to date. It has also been argued to be erroneous in relation to SCIP members by expert attorneys such as Richard Horowitz. Obviously, over six years after passage of the EEA, BI is still around and actually emerging ever more readily as a routine corporate practice.

One key reason these fears have proved false is that, first, they failed to take into account the historical motivation for the enactment of such a law. In short, the EEA was primarily targeted at foreign spies engaged in economic espionage against U.S. business entities. Ira Winkler's 1997 book entitled *Corporate Espionage* does much to illustrate several cases, which served to precipitate passage of the EEA, such as those of Guillermo Gaede and Karl Heinrich Stohlze. With the Cold War effectively over, international espionage has become decidedly more focused on gaining economic advantage through the illegal collection of trade secrets. The EEA was designed to serve as a vehicle to prosecute such activities.

The second key reason that the EEA has had little to no impact on the BI profession hangs in the balance of what exactly is meant by the term trade secret. Lawyers James Pooley and R. Mark Halligan (2000) maintain that important exceptions to what can be claimed as a trade secret are (1) information that is generally known to professionals in the field; (2) employee skill, that is, the know-how and expertise necessary to do a good job; and (3) readily ascertainable data. This last point is crucial for intelligence practitioners because, as Pooley and Halligan also point out, the burden is on the prosecuting party to illustrate that the trade secret was, in fact, secret; it held value; and reasonable efforts were undertaken by the owner to protect the secrecy of the information. A disincentive exists here for companies to participate in proceedings concerning an alleged violation of EEA in that in order to establish the above, they are likely to wind up exposing much more vital information to the public record than they are defending—with little hope in many cases that the damage, once done, can be effectively reversed.

A third reason for intelligence practitioners to breathe easier is that—short of committing an improper and usually illegal act, such as stealing, bribing, or wiretapping—actual misappropriation of a trade secret is fairly hard to establish. Still, given the choice, most individuals and companies would rather never be implicated versus winning a lawsuit. As a result, most stay a sizable distance from the edge of this legal cliff.

As a result, it is fear of the scourge of negative public opinion that tends to regulate BI practitioners, much more so than the EEA. SCIP maintains a stated code of ethics that if its members simply adhere to, generally removes any significant danger of such allegations. In order to reinforce appropriate behavior and protect themselves legally, most companies with a BI function, particularly those that retain outside BI consultants, demand that intelligence gatherers stay within preestablished legal and ethical limits. Again, being the front-page scandal of tomorrow is avoidable by using a few preventive steps today.

Crafting an Intelligence Deliverable

Assignments differ, but a rule of thumb to consider is that project hour allocation per task tends to approximate the following:
- Planning strategy, 10 percent
- Secondary research, 20 percent
- Primary research, 35 percent
- Write-up, 30 percent
- Client interaction, 5 percent

It may surprise some readers to know that, aside from conducting primary research, intelligence practitioners spend most of their time compiling and writing findings. Just as active police officers spend much of their day doing desk-jockey work in the form of paperwork, so must intelligence practitioners take the time to document important occurrences and findings. This writing process is complicated and elongated by the high degree of accuracy, organization, and analysis required.

In order to customize an intelligence deliverable for an end-user, its author must first be confident in how to sort and organize the material. Inasmuch as possible, this needs to take place *as the informational nuggets come in* to ease deadline pressures and utilize opportunities to issue follow-up instructions to members of the collection team. This can be quite difficult because finding relationships in disparate pieces of the puzzle that may lack obvious connections can be frustrating. Nevertheless, as soon as the collection team begins to encounter repetition or clustered findings, a report shell or template should be put in place. The following are six standard ways of organizing findings as they emerge during what can be very complex investigations:
- By subject category
- By target entity (in alphabetical order)
- By target entity (in order of competitive threat level—greatest to least)
- Direct questions and answers per project objectives
- Logical (inductive and deductive reasoning) progression of indicators concerning the tested hypothesis
- Sequential or historical

The effective conveyance of findings is an art in which one must hold the reader's interest while maintaining a cool sense of objectivity. As with news articles, Western readers tend to expect intelligence deliverables to focus on accurately portraying the facts, effectively leaving them free to draw their own conclusions as to what these facts mean. This does not exclude intelligence report writers from having a forum for expressing their conclusions—and possibly recommendations. It does mean, though, that BI functions need to take extra measures to properly attribute findings and clearly differentiate areas of their reports where their own opinion and analysis are represented.

Similar to how most Western newspapers offset or physically separate op/ed and feature stories—sometimes even with a small photo of the individual providing analysis—BI functions can create perspective sections that provide interpretation and substantive analysis. Over time, as credibility builds, end-users may come to view these sections as the most important portion of the entire deliverable, even if they are disregarded at first.

The importance of the researcher's perspective and finding an appropriate analytical format vary per business culture. For example, Japanese executives have gained a reputation for ignoring the analysis of younger corporate employees. In Russia, reporters and BI practitioners alike commonly convey facts with a heavy dose of commentary—anything less would imply a lack of confidence in the veracity of the information. In general, however, the best route in any culture is to have the findings be so specific and strong that little room is left for doubt as to what is and will take place in the competitive environment studied. If an analysis section is included, consider whether it incorporates the key elements listed here:

- A conclusion/common thread
- Core findings that substantiate the conclusion/common thread
- Caveats and lynchpin assumptions as related to the conclusion/common thread
- Application of the conclusion and caveats to the end-user
- Scenarios, signposts or milestones, and possible next steps for further research

Despite what can be perceived as the crystal-ball nature of BI, effective BI deliverables are not about hedging. In fact, the executive summary sections of most reports—the most often read portions thereof—require terse answers, whether in paragraph, diagrammatic, or bulleted form. The possibility of being flat-out wrong is always present. Fortunately, three issues aid corporate intelligence practitioners.

First, experienced deliverable crafters learn to include key caveats, lynchpin assumptions, scenario matrices, and signpost or milestone events in circumstances where the answers are not so clear. This is not hedging. It is a reflection of reality, particularly where the target entity's management itself may not yet know exactly which strategy it will employ. In effect, the signposts or milestones serve to identify for the reader, even at a much later date, which scenario may actually be occurring and which aspect of the analysis section of a deliverable to focus on at that point. One such case follows:

Background

The client of a BI function sought to understand how a certain company would respond to the introduction of a key product set to occur in a few months within a market sector where the two firms had never competed. Investigation revealed that the target entity's management was completely distracted by another competitor currently making inroads elsewhere and did not even appear to be aware of this impending threat. Further, with the exception of a single up-and-coming product manager, the entity's culture was very passive—likely to yield market share to this larger competitor, instead seeking to bolster newer lines of revenue.

Outcome

Although all indicators showed that the target entity would prove to be a pushover, the BI team was conscientious enough to include one key caveat and signpost in its analysis section: "If the 'up-and-comer' were to be in charge of the product in question at the time of the competitive launch, then he would seek to do everything possible to thwart this assault on the company's—and his—market share." In fact, this is what occurred and although the BI team had leaned toward the pushover scenario in its analysis, it still had correctly portrayed the competitive situation by including this possible nuance.

Second, intelligence practitioners are only as good as their sources. Even when the net is cast wide enough and input from sources is accurately attributed and portrayed, there will still be instances where information either is not available or certain sources thought they knew something that, in fact, they really did not. Misinformation may be afloat, or the target entity may be holding details so close to the vest that they, indeed, may qualify as a trade secret.

Whenever possible, it is certainly the responsibility of the BI function to attempt to triangulate and verify each key nugget of information. However, when this is not possible, due to time constraints, for example, the singularity of sources and the confidence level of the team in this particular piece of information also need to be identified. It must be remembered that a dearth of information also can be telling. Many pharmaceutical companies, for example, tend to go into a form of lock-down mode approximately one to two months before FDA approval of a new drug is anticipated. If the potential drug has questionable chances of being cleared for market, then most often the firm attempts to give fair warning to its stakeholders instead of withholding information.

Third, especially within larger organizations that operate in dynamic markets, there can be a significant time lag between the point when a report is prepared and when certain end-users ultimately get a chance to review it. Just like the news, sometimes as little as a day or a few hours can make a huge impact on the relevancy of a deliverable.

Because intelligence reports are a snapshot in time amidst a constantly changing world and market, they must be viewed promptly for maximum impact. After all, who wants to read last week's news? While it seems absurd, certain executives will rush BI teams into providing a deliverable before they head off on a trip or vacation, promising to read it on the way, and instead declare the findings obsolete when they pull it out of the briefcase for the first time several days or weeks later. If the implications included in an intelligence briefing are not compiled and distributed in a time-sensitive and actionable manner, then they may not be all that valuable.

A Word About Counterintelligence and the Future of Corporate Intelligence

As alluded to by John Nolan and others, intelligence-gathering efforts breed counterintelligence measures—and vice versa. In fact, the two are inextricably connected, albeit many a corporate leader fails to grasp this until having been on the target end of a competitor's probe. As the saying goes, "Fool me once, shame on you. Fool me twice, shame on me." It is also important to remember that not all players play by the same rules, particularly in the international arena.

While security guards, high walls, and metal detectors contain one sort of danger, they rarely seriously inhibit most intelligence practitioners because companies, by their nature, must interact with customers and other parties. This interaction requires the exchange of information, putting into play tidbits that cascade downward from the secret realm to the private and finally public categories of information, according to Thunderbird's Kinsinger (2000). It is up to BI practitioners to catch these tidbits as soon as possible after they move from being prohibitively secret to simply being private—fair game under the EEA.

The best friend of a counterintelligence manager in the corporate environment of today is not a German shepherd or security cameras. As developed economies focus more and more on value-added services, intellectual property is tantamount to success. The best ways to ensure its longevity are a corporate work force that is alert to suspicious activities and knowledgeable about what the nondisclosure agreement (NDA) they signed actually means. Having an NDA with those in the know about the absolutely crucial aspects of one's business is a must, even if they are not direct employees. Certainly this approach is not foolproof, but any close associate or employee unwise enough to divulge protected information would have to be a fool to then not expect to lose their job or relationship with the company, their reputation, and potentially much more.

In gauging the future of business and CI, some have voiced the opinion that events such as those of September 11, 2001, have awakened nations with open cultures such as the United States—and companies that operate in these nations—to their vulnerabilities. As a result, it is argued that corporations will come to share less about themselves and be warier of those asking questions.

Almost two years later, nothing seems further from the truth as companies such as Enron, Arthur Andersen, and Tyco have put the corporate world under even greater scrutiny and fostered more upfront disclosure than seen in recent history. The fact is that so long as these societies remain participatory in the nature of their government and corporate leadership, they will remain fundamentally open in order to continue to profit from the increased overall productivity that this empowers. As a result, those skilled at the scales of the entire KM keyboard will always have room to sound out resonant answers to key questions.

POSTSCRIPT

Shortly after co-authoring this chapter, Jeffrey A. Flint—a dear friend, close colleague, steadfast and beloved husband and father—unexpectedly passed away at the young age of 30 years old. Jeffrey was not near the culmination of his life, yet he managed to leave a deep imprint on the many lives he touched.

Jeffrey embodied many aspects of the BI field about which he felt so passionately. His thirst for knowledge propelled his interest in this chosen field, and inspired him to get involved in interesting and unique life experiences. For example, after two years of study at Brigham Young University in Provo, Utah, he traveled to St. Petersburg, Russia, to serve as a missionary.

Two years later, Jeffrey returned to Brigham Young University; however, he again put his education on hold when he was recruited by United Way International to develop service programs in Naryan-Mar, Russia. He spent 15 months in the remote northern region of Russia and began several exchange programs.

It was there that Jeffrey met Inga, his wife since 1997. He returned to Provo and completed dual bachelor's degrees in communications and Russian in December 1996. After graduation, he worked as a consular assistant in the U.S. consulate in St. Petersburg, assigning visas and assisting international criminal investigations.

Jeffrey returned to the U.S. in 1998 to study international management at Thunderbird, the American Graduate School of International Management, in Glendale, Arizona. He received a master's degree the following year and soon began his career at Proactive Worldwide, Inc., a leading BI research and consulting firm.

At Proactive Worldwide, Inc., he shaped his keen analytical skills and began to lay the bedrock of his BI career. Through his dynamic drive to create heightened industry competition came a desire to teach others the concepts and importance of the intelligence field. To punctuate this desire, Jeffrey began teaching BI courses with Gary D. Maag at Dominican University in 2001.

The enthusiasm and energy he brought to the BI industry will no doubt leave an indelible impression on the community, his close colleagues, and students for many years to come.

Endnotes

1. *Business Blindspots* is the name and concept of a 1993 book by Dr. Ben Gilad.
2. Parentheses are added for the purposes of comparison between categories cited by Kinsinger and Sawka.
3. Accessed on 20 June, 2002 at http://www.cia.gov/cia/publications/facttell/intcycle.htm
4. Hedin, H., and Svensson, K. (1995). Presentation at the 1995 Society of Competitive Intelligence Professionals (SCIP) Conference in Phoenix, Arizona, entitled "Today's intelligence activities don't satisfy organization's dynamic decision makers," as cited by Jan P. Herring in *Measuring the Effectiveness of Competitive Intelligence: Assessing and Communicating CI's Value to Your Organization.*

REFERENCES

Davison L. (2001). Measuring competitive intelligence effectiveness: Insights from the advertising industry. *Competitive Intelligence Review*. 12(4):25–38.

Jaworski, B. and Wee, L. C. (1993). *Competitive Intelligence: Creating Value for the Organization*. Alexandria, VA: SCIP Publications.

Kinsinger, P. (2000). How to begin. *Thunderbird*. 53(3):10.

McNeilly, M. R. (2000). *Sun Tzu and the Art of Business: Six Strategic Principles for Managers*. New York, NY: Oxford University Press.

Pooley, J. and Halligan, R. M. (2000). Intelligence and the law. In: *Millennium Intelligence*. Miller, J., ed. Medford, NJ: CyberAge Books; pp. 171–180.

Sawka, K. A. (2000). Deciding where to locate the intelligence unit. In: *Millennium Intelligence*. Miller, J., ed. Medford, NJ: CyberAge Books; pp. 43–54.

Walton, S. and Huey, J. (1993). *Sam Walton: Made in America: My Story*. New York, NY: Bantam Books.

Winkler, I. (1997). *Corporate Espionage: What It Is, Why It Is Happening in Your Company, What You Must Do about It*. Rocklin, CA: Prima Publishing.

Chapter 27

Using Competitive Intelligence to Improve Knowledge Management

Katherine M. Shelfer, Drexel University

Introduction

Competitive Intelligence

Competitive intelligence (CI) is defined by the Society of Competitive Intelligence Professionals (SCIP) as a

> systematic and ethical program for gathering, analyzing, and managing external information that can affect your company's plans, decisions, and operations. … Specifically, it is the legal collection and analysis of information regarding the capabilities, vulnerabilities, and intentions of business competitors, conducted by using information databases and other "open sources" and through ethical inquiry (http://www.scip.org/ci).

To successfully perform their function, CI practitioners must (1) understand business processes, industry trends, market forces, and strategic impact factors; and (2) differentiate between the unique challenges of various competitors in order to assess their readiness, as expressed by their capability, capacity, and willingness to act. This knowledge will not be useful to their organizations unless CI practitioners are skilled at such tasks as managing projects; extracting value from secondary resources; positioning insights in light of the readiness to act of their own organizations; writing reports; and presenting their findings in appropriate formats in relevant venues and in a timely fashion.

Knowledge Management

The basic value of KM is that it (1) leverages the acquisition, transfer, and management of information; and (2) it encourages the effective reuse of the existing knowledge of the firm. Although KM was first treated as a technology-centric process (http://www.brint.com/km/kmdefs.htm), more recently it has been viewed as a human-centric one:

> Knowledge Management caters to the critical issues of organizational adaption [sic], survival and competence in [the] face of increasingly discontinuous environmental change. ... Essentially, it embodies organizational processes that seek synergistic combination of data and information processing capacity of information technologies, and the creative and innovative capacity of human beings (http://www.brint.com/km/whatis.htm).

A series of structured discussions between this author and information professionals employed by some 70 companies[1] reveals that information professionals are not always able to distinguish between (1) the basic "price of admission" challenges that face every competitor in an industry (e.g., recruitment and retention of skilled employees, commoditization, globalization of markets); and (2) those challenges unique to their own organization (e.g., a family business where the owners have no heirs, reliance on a single expert, unfavorable geographic location, higher production costs). This is because most organizations divide their focus into separate internal and external "stovepipes" and fail to build bridges between them. This approach hinders effective response to changing business conditions for two reasons: First, practitioners of CI are tasked to explore and analyze the external business environment, and to create work products in the form of reports and recommendations. However, if these reports are to be relevant, CI practitioners must have knowledge of the readiness of their own organizations to act in a given manner. This means that they must be aware of capacity, capability, and the assumptions and motivations of the firm. Second, knowledge managers cannot identify and implement the most appropriate and most cost-effective choices of KM processes and systems unless they are aware of new KM advances, are sensitive to industry and competitive pressures, and can appreciate the unique challenges faced by their competitors as well as their own organizations.

Knowledge managers who support the decision makers of government perform essentially the same tasks as their colleagues in the private sector. In both settings, the decision makers generally determine (1) which data to collect, (2) the format that data must take to be most easily understood, and (3) how work products will be provided to the experts who are expected to use them. While knowledge managers have little control over any of this, they are expected to develop effective KM strategies to support such efforts. In order to avoid unpleasant surprises, they must plan KM initiatives that take into consideration the impact of potential changes in the information streams they manage (sources, quantity, formats, contexts of use, timeliness, and so on).

KM may not always appear to be a problem of life or death, but firms do fail, governments do fall, and people are harmed when the credible and useful information does not reach the right expert(s) in a timely fashion. There are published examples of how to use CI to improve KM in the private sector; however, very little has been written about the value that can be derived from integrating a CI perspective into the KM initiatives of the public sector. Events have shown us that failure to integrate the insights gained by bridging the two stovepipes of CI and KM can sometimes have devastating consequences. This chapter focuses on large-scale issues that face knowledge managers in government agencies as they try to protect and serve the public. Two techniques used in both CI and KM are used to demonstrate the value of adding a CI perspective to a KM problem: (1) scenarios and (2) benchmarking, including gap analysis. Discussion of these techniques is accompanied by examples that demonstrate the lesson to be learned.

Scenarios

A scenario is an account or synopsis of a projected course of events. Multiple scenarios are not simply snapshots of the same future taken under different lighting conditions. Rather, the author of the scenario (the scenarist) develops alternative futures based on current conditions and differences in the rate and direction of change at critical junctures that might result in different but equally plausible outcomes. According to Lawrence Wilkinson, scenarios are most helpful when

> "long fuse, big bang" problems ... don't lend themselves to traditional analysis; it's simply impossible to research away the uncertainties on which the success of a key decision will hang. ... The purpose of scenario planning is not to pinpoint future events but to highlight large-scale forces that push the future in different directions. It's about making these forces visible, so

that if they do happen, the planner will at least recognize them. It's about helping make better decisions today (http://www.wired.com/wired/scenarios/build.html

The scenario is crafted by taking a focused issue and exaggerating alternative rates and directions of change for each of the primary motivating factors, which are sometimes called the "four ics":

- Demographics (vital statistics)
- Psychographics (motivating belief systems)
- Geographics (physical environments)
- Politics and legislation (societal constraints on behaviors)

There are two feasibility filters that are often included in the creation of a scenario:

- Economics (production, distribution, and consumption of goods and services)
- Technologies (as primary enablers of change)

Knowledge managers in government agencies support decision makers who are continually bombarded by competing international and intranational agendas. It can be difficult for knowledge managers to predict what information decision makers will need, because all data points and all contexts are not equally relevant in all settings. For this reason, scenarios and springboard stories are useful tools to help knowledge managers focus their thinking (see Figure 27.1).

Figure 27.1   Storytelling.

By isolating each data element demanded by the events of a given scenario, and comparing data elements between scenarios, knowledge managers can (1) identify the critical data elements that would be relevant in multiple scenarios and (2) isolate specific data that would only be critical in one of them. These data can be used to develop time lines and key indicators of change so that KM initiatives can be modified as the information needs of decision makers change. Scenarios encourage knowledge managers to think about the external environment and embed that understanding into KM initiatives that support internal operations. By involving CI practitioners in the scenario exercise, knowledge managers can (1) identify their own biases and improve their sensitivity to issues and events; (2) more accurately assess the potential impact of changes in any of the key variables; (3) improve the comprehensive KM plan to better prepare for alternative futures; and (4) identify the points at which prompt action can have a positive impact.

SCENARIO ONE: SETTING THE STAGE

At the macroeconomic level, according to Finance and Economy Minister Nikos Christodoulakis, the Greek economy

> is experiencing a period of growth, which is more intense than that of the European Union [EU] member-states. ... The main characteristic of the country's growth course is the high rate of [foreign direct] investments in Greece, which is moving at much higher levels than those of member-states of both the EU and the OECD ... [Organization for Economic Cooperation and Development] denationalizations amount to about 1.3 percent of GDP [gross domestic product] on an annual basis. It is a considerable performance, which shows the depth of structural changes in the Greek economy [transferring] property rights to international investors (http://www.greek embassy.org/press/newsflash/2002/June/nflash0627e.html).

On the surface, this economic growth seems commendable; however, at the microeconomic level, the picture is somewhat different. Entire villages are self-sufficient; villagers grow their own food, there are few (if any) retail establishments, and cash is in short supply. Most towns and cities have an active commercial center comprised of small, family-owned businesses. Neighborhood shops provide access to goods and services without adding to the congested automobile traffic of the narrow city streets. Greece is less a semi-industrialized economy than a semi-agrarian one. The chronic lack of employment throughout Greece has resulted in mass migrations to the cities. However, city-dwellers try to escape summer's deadly combination of pollution and heat by returning to their childhood homes in the villages or taking long vacations in privately owned tourist accommodations by the sea. Greece currently faces two nearly insurmountable threats: (1) the invasion of foreign-owned superstores that are starting to pull traffic from the city centers and (2) urban sprawl.

> Sprawl is … "poorly planned, low-density, auto-oriented development … a ring around the dead center" [with] potentially serious environmental and economic issues.
>
> [Today] Wal-Mart is the largest private employer in America, [with more] sales than the Gross Domestic Product of Israel, Greece, Ireland and Egypt. … By the year 2005 just 10 companies, including Wal-Mart, will control 50% of food store sales…[making] it difficult for large numbers of new, small operators to take root and thrive. … The symptoms of retail saturation are everywhere … (http://www.sprawl-busters.com/caseagainstsprawl.html).

There are no easy solutions. Georgios I. Zekos believes that the time of the closed economy is gone and that

> the use of the information technology should be the step which will keep the competitiveness of the whole economy in a certain level. It could be said that [in the United States (AT&T), France (Michelin), Italy (Olivetti), and Germany (Hypo Bank)] downsizing is a common tactic in order to keep competitiveness (http://diavlos.com/zekos/greconomy.htm).

In the first scenario, we look at the growth of superstores and urban sprawl and envision a future that is based on what we know of current conditions. The goal of this exercise is to identify improvements in KM systems that can improve support to decision makers who must identify, monitor, and manage associated risks.

Scenario One: Greece Under Wal-Mart's Benevolent Rule

Wal-Mart is a highly evolved, aggressive, and nimble (primarily) eCommerce company of transnational telecommuters and the major employer of Greece. Most employees have no education beyond high school. In Greece, many are motorcycle couriers; however, delays in the delivery of perishables are so common that bribery is institutionalized. Dependence on the Internet for most transactions makes network invasions and theft of virtual personalities a common problem. Children are self-managed learners who study in Spanish and Chinese (the official languages of the World Union) using content provided by *Wal-Mart.edu*. Few master Greek, although the older generations still use it. One Wal-Mart division employs skilled workers who remotely control robotic minimills to produce customized recyclable goods, such as WallaLegos™ (large, custom-designed interlocking insulated building blocks in soft Mediterranean colors and fantastic shapes. Homeowners have used them to cover the rebar forests on the rooftops of their unfinished country houses, which has turned them into an international tourist attraction). Since employees tend to remain with their families and friends in their villages, Wal-Mart is credited with improving their quality of life. Abandoned city apartments now house refugees from the Balkan wars. These new city-dwellers take weekend excursions into the countryside on Wal-Mart's light rail systems to purchase fresh produce as well as textiles, crafts, and trinkets made with raw materials supplied by Wal-Mart's Unique Boutique® division. Purchases are handled through the Wal-Mart bank over Wal-Mart's wireless networks using Wal-Mart's subdermal chips to authenticate buyers and validate purchases. Wal-Mart pockets the transaction tax, a portion of which is reinvested in improving the communications infrastructure. Some Wal-Mart stores double as administrative offices for nearby theme parks that attract amateur archaeologists. To reduce ethnic conflict, the Wal-Mart peacekeepers receive an international subsidy to convert vacant stores to dormitory-like residences and training centers for refugees. Wal-Mart also receives placement subsidies from the Greek government for finding jobs in other countries for these refugees.

- Which corporate initiatives have taken over existing government functions? What new government functions exist? What impact has this had on sources and uses of funds?
- Describe the information infrastructure that has evolved in response to these changes.
- How will KM systems get there from here?

While somewhat plausible, the value of this particular scenario depends on the scenarist's accurate prediction of the corporate growth strategies of Wal-Mart just as much as it does on awareness of current economic conditions in Greece. In this case, the scenario exercise would revolve around (1) identifying the specific kinds of data needed by decision makers and (2) determining which agencies might benefit from which shared insights. In this case, the government ministers might find it expedient to inquire from others in countries that have already been affected by this issue. However, it is important to recognize that a scenario intended for use in one setting may have little value in other settings if the underlying contextual framework is not recognized or accepted. Because there is a track record of failed family businesses and urban sprawl in the U.S., most Americans can generally follow the logic of the Wal-Mart scenario. In the following scenario, the future of political and social fragmentation is based on social, religious, and cultural conditions that are unique to Greece.

Scenario Two: Setting the Stage

Decisions about database structures often reside with knowledge managers, who need the external awareness provided by CI practitioners to be effective. In the second scenario, there are three lessons to be learned:

- External concerns can have a substantial impact on KM initiatives.
- All variables are not equal, or equally meaningful, in all settings.
- A bleak scenario requires careful handling.

This scenario envisions a bleak future where conditions in Greece deteriorate to the point that the country dissolves in chaos. The value of such a scenario resides in the scenarist's ability to logically derive extremely unpleasant but plausible outcomes based on current conditions that openly acknowledge the down sides of human thoughts and actions in times of stress. When such a future is envisioned, the scenarist must take great care to reduce the push back that results from the participants' resistance to the scenario itself. Opening the scenario exercise with a discussion of the contextual framework on which such a scenario is based allows potential differences in the interpretation and assigned importance of current events to be identified and addressed. For example, the exercise might begin with the following preparatory remarks:

The contextual framework for this scenario exercise is based on the following observations.

First, unemployment is a huge problem. Some college graduates have waited a decade for a job in their major. Greece has responded to external pressures to change its employment practices; however, a recent attempt to squeeze the funnel shut by raising admission standards in order to lower university enrollment has barred many students from higher education for life. This resulted in protests throughout the country and nightly marches in Athens in 2000.

Second, the northern borders of Greece are something of a legal fiction, because some Slavic-speaking people consider themselves Greek, and some Greek-speaking people consider themselves Slavs. Some in the north of Greece fear the expansionist ambitions of the Former Yugoslav Republic of Macedonia (F.I.R.O.M.). The international media call F.I.R.O.M "Macedonia" and researchers point to textbooks from F.I.R.O.M. that treat Macedonia as an occupied province rather than an integral part of Greece. Athens generally ignores and often underfunds public works and social programs in this region.

Third, the government is ill-prepared to absorb the unwelcome influx of Albanian refugees, who are blamed for a significant increase in violent crime, among other things.

Fourth, the Ottoman Empire controlled Greece for over four centuries. Many Greeks express concern over the potential unification of an expansionist and increasingly violent Muslim world with Turkey as the bridge. They are upset about the potential entry of Turkey to a European Union comprised of nominally Christian nations. They think that the United States is being short-sighted in supporting Muslim Turkey over Christian Greece.

Fifth, the recent removal of religion as a personal (and cultural) identifier is seen as an attack on the social fabric of Greece, which is almost completely Greek Orthodox. This situation resulted in street demonstrations in 2002.

Scenario Two: Greece Dissolves in Chaos

Raised to believe that Macedonia is under the hostile occupation of Athens, the people of the Former Yugoslav Republic of Macedonia (F.I.R.O.M.), already called Macedonia by the international press, have staked claim to much of northern Greece. Rebuffed by the European Union (EU), and safe in the knowledge that the Americans need them as allies, Turkey has joined forces with other Muslims in the Balkans to fight F.I.R.O.M. for control of Macedonia. The prize is Thessaloniki, the second largest city in Greece, because it is a major port and the railhead to the Balkans. Through bribery and chicanery that was ignored by Athens, a puppet government is installed in Thessaloniki. Accused as traitors, Greek Orthodox priests, educators, and civic leaders are once again imprisoned. Some are even executed in the White Tower. Frantic to feed themselves and their families in a country with no welfare safety net, waves of Balkan refugees move south, taking what they need to survive. Inflation and unemployment hit all-time highs. The uneducated young, denied entry to state-funded universities and without the ability to pay for a private education, are left with no jobs and no future. The boys join gangs in large numbers. The girls become virtual prisoners in their homes. As parents take their children and flee to Asia and Latin America, the gap between old and young widens, leaving the elderly to become victims of neglect, starvation, and violent crime. Archaeological wonders crumble as those who remain take refuge in smoke-filled Internet cafes. Earthquakes damage natural gas pipelines under narrow streets, engulfing entire cities in flames. The EU expels what is left of Greece when it is not able to achieve its economic goals. Even so, there is no outside help available as the U.S. and European economies disintegrate in the face of the overwhelming combined economic might of China and Brazil.

- Which corporate initiatives have taken over existing government functions? What new government functions exist? What impact has this had on sources and uses of funds?
- Describe the information infrastructure that has evolved in response to these changes.
- How will KM systems get there from here?

In this scenario, the problems lie in (1) determining which data sets are needed to identify the milestones that represent pivotal milestones and (2) providing information to decision makers that is both credible and useful. Context helps knowledge managers develop their awareness of the potential usefulness of specific data fields in ways that are not otherwise apparent, for example. First, this scenario emphasizes the historical significance of religious affiliation that many cultures do not interpret in the same way. While different from the way that religious affiliation is viewed elsewhere (excluded in the U.S. of America and an economic-political distinction in Ireland), the association with Greek Orthodoxy carries additional meaning in Greece that speaks to their survival under centuries of foreign domination. Elimination of this single variable would also make it more difficult to refute those who blame ethnic populations (or anyone else who is *not* Greek Orthodox) for much of the dramatic increase in violent crime. Second, errors of interpretation can happen where (1) the values in a data field do not mean what we think they do and (2) restricted choices force users to enter the wrong values in a data field.[2] The fact that we appear to have relevant data does not always tell us what we really want to know. CI practitioners should be involved in crafting scenarios that inform knowledge managers about the value and meaning of data that might otherwise be eliminated or misinterpreted.

Benchmarking and Gap Analysis

Benchmarking is a common KM tool used by organizations such as the American Productivity and Quality Center (APQC) to help organizations identify, analyze, adapt, and share best practices in ways that promote the emergence and evolution of a learning culture throughout the enterprise (http://www.apqc.org/best). Benchmarking enables a firm to identify superior processes, adapt them to the needs of the firm, and integrate the new processes in ways that reflect the organizational desire and capacity to learn (http://www.apqc.org/best/whatis.cfm). CI practitioners also use benchmarking because its goal is to obtain a strategic, operational, or financial advantage over competitors. Benchmarking has measurable economic benefits. For example, benchmarking projects are reported to save Clearinghouse members $1.4 million per study, and two members each reported more than $1 billion savings from benchmarking (http://www.apqc.org/best/benefits.cfm).

The effectiveness of benchmarking

> ultimately means embracing a robust enthusiasm for finding and adapting ideas and techniques outside the organization. This, in fact, is a key characteristic of the agile learning organization. ... A history of rewarding individual[s] ... make[s] it difficult. ... The really important and useful information for improvement is too complex to put online; too much tacit knowledge is required to make a process work. So, most firms have turned to directory and "pointer" systems that can supplement the search for best practices (http://www.apqc.org/best/keys.cfm).

Practitioners of CI use gap analysis, a component of benchmarking, to quickly identify gaps (e.g., optimal and current business conditions; features and benefits of current product lines) in light of customer needs and expectations. This enables them to identify relative advantages and disadvantages associated with specific courses of action. In the context of information technology, gap analysis is

> the study of the differences between two different information systems or applications, often for the purpose of determining how to get from one state to a new state. A gap is sometimes spoken of as "the space between where we are and where we want to be." Gap analysis is undertaken as a means of bridging that space (http://whatis.techtarget.com/definition/0,,sid9_gci831294,00.html).

Table 27.1 identifies critical failure factors and key indicators of success.

Table 27.1   Benchmarking failure factors and success indicators.

Failure Factors	Success Indicators
Lacks managment or financial support.	Knows its current processes well.
Makes no business case for change.	Involves the right people.
Has a "not invented here" mindset.	Uses the right methodology.
Uses inadequate study methodologies.	Includes all relevant processes.
Ignores relevant processes.	Studies the right firms.
Unable or unwilling to learn and adapt.	Learns and adapts based on results.

Correctly performing a benchmarking study or gap analysis is no guarantee that there will be a successful adaptation of processes if the atmosphere is not conducive to change. A formal benchmarking study is important, however, because even though failure is more likely to result from an informal approach that overlooks important information, there are times, such as the need to respond to a crisis, when even a benchmarking *perspective* can add considerable value.

SETTING THE STAGE: THE CURRENT VISA APPROVAL PROCESS

The mission of the Foreign Terrorism Tracking Task Force (FTTTF), established by Homeland Security Presidential Directive (HPD-2), is to

> ensure that, to the maximum extent permitted by law, Federal agencies coordinate programs to accomplish the following: (1) deny entry into the United States of aliens associated with, suspected of being engaged in, or supporting terrorist activity and (2) locate, detain, prosecute, or deport any such aliens already present in the United States (http://www.whitehouse. gov/news/releases/2001/10/20011030-2.html).

At this point in time, the counterterrorism activities of each of the representative agencies are based on the sources, targets, and locations of the perceived danger. The purpose of the FTTTF is to bring together these agencies to share insights, define roles and responsibilities, and act cooperatively to identify terrorists and deny them the opportunity to harm others. Basically, the FTTTF acts as a bridge between the stovepipes. Merely realigning the reporting structure of these agencies, however, will not make any of them instantly capable of responding effectively to transnational challenges, regardless of whether these have historically been included in their mission.

The current visa approval process is an excellent example of the limitations of the stovepipe approach. The Immigration and Naturalization Service (INS) has the task of denying terrorists access to opportunity through the visa approval process. The overarching goal of the visa approval process is to (1) facilitate entry to the U.S. for those most deserving of it and (2) refuse entry to those who clearly should not be admitted. The current visa approval process is national; however, the terrorists are transnational. Terrorists use shared networks and overlapping criminal modalities to fund and facilitate their activities. The overwhelmed visa analyst has very little time to make a decision about an applicant, and very little decision support. The development of an automated visa risk approval system (AVAS) should support reduction in two types of errors:

Unfair denials. The decision to deny a visa is final, and there is no right of appeal.

Mistaken approvals. This facilitates the entry of criminals, including terrorists.

DESIGNING AN AVAS

An AVAS must incorporate all relevant data into the risk-assessment process if it is to adequately identify and appropriately assess the possibility that an individual might be a terrorist. The conceptual framework of an AVAS is based on the following observations:

- Terrorists may choose to strike at only one of the otherwise separate stovepipes of commerce, national security, or critical infrastructures; however, an attack on just one of these could harm any or all of the others.[3]
- Entry into the U.S. by a foreign terrorist may be legal or illegal. Legal entry takes advantage of weaknesses in the current visa approval system.
- The analyst who must approve or deny a visa application may never see the individual who has made the application. In some cases, for example, travel agents submit groups of applications for visas.
- In times of crisis, there may be a knee-jerk denial of opportunity to those who deserve approval. The analyst might also lack the necessary insight or the time required to identify a dangerous individual.
- The current visa approval process is paper-based. This hinders the effective capture, transfer, and reuse of knowledge between analysts in different countries and across different time zones. This hinders transnational responsiveness to transnational threats.
- The current visa approval system is not able to keep pace with the sheer volume of applications.[4]
- Denial of opportunity to terrorists is based on the effectiveness of both logical and physical access controls.
- Logical and physical access controls are based on (1) the ability to verify that an individual requesting such access is, in fact, who he or she claims to be; and (2) that this individual is actually eligible to access a system or location *at the time and in the manner and for the purpose requested.*

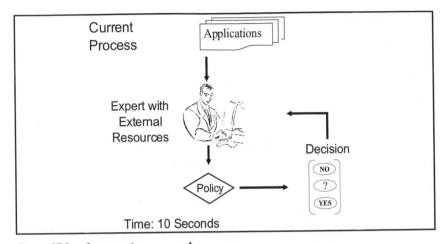

Figure 27.2   Current visa approval process.

Through the current visa approval process, a terrorist can take advantage of an overwhelmed system that is based in large part on the honesty and integrity of the applicant and the effectiveness of the individual analyst (Figure 27.2). More effective methods must be found. The FTTTF supports the INS determination to deny new opportunities to those terrorists who are not (yet) inside the country but who could reasonably expect to enter the country legally by means of the backlogged visa approval process. While it is impossible to improve all systems and all border crossings at once, the INS recognizes that an AVAS could improve both the quantity and quality of the decisions to approve or deny a visa application. There are many reasons for this:

- An AVAS can be updated to reflect improved insights about patterns and processes that are transnational in nature. This would provide more effective decision support to analysts.
- Automation of easy decisions can improve the pace of the approval process. Some approvals currently take six months or more.
- An automated system with remote administration is less likely to be compromised by local conditions.
- A system with embedded legal and ethical constraints is more likely to be trusted. A trusted system is less likely to be bypassed.

SCALING AN AVAS FOR GLOBAL VISA RISK ASSESSMENT

The goal of the AVAS is to automate the easy decisions (both approvals and denials) to provide the analysts with more time to develop and improve insights related to just exactly who does (and does not) constitute a risk. These "no-brainer" decisions can be processed much more quickly, providing the analyst with more time to evaluate complex cases. An AVAS is long overdue if it will prevent knee-jerk post-9/11 reactions, such as the demand of Attorney General Ashcroft for the names of "5,000 Arabs" to interview. The INS reluctantly complied with his request. However, this redirection of already strained resources into such a futile activity resulted in charges of discrimination and a backlash against the INS, further damaging the morale of an already overwhelmed work force.

At the present time, several other countries are willing to participate in the development of a global visa risk assessment system. Still others are considering some form of basic knowledge sharing. Because the INS system may eventually form the basis of a global visa risk assessment system, it must focus on U.S. needs, yet be scalable to support global visa risk assessment and data in a wide variety of formats from a large number of disparate sources. The most obvious approach would be to benchmark systems that are already capable of handling substantial numbers of transactions related to real-time decision support. Such systems must (1) support the assessment of individual risk against known populations for which a simple yes-or-no decision is required, (2) enable retrospective reinterpretation of variables on the basis of improved insight and new information, and (3) embed legal and regulatory constraints.

Whether homegrown or foreign, individual terrorists act like other criminals, in that they falsify personal information, steal identities, and commit economic crimes to fund their activities. The current visa approval system makes it easy for terrorists to hide in plain sight until the damage is done. To determine whether an individual is a terrorist, an AVAS must integrate relevant information about a wide variety of crimes and criminals and include it (where relevant) as part of the risk assessment score of an individual.

Lesson Learned: AVAS Benchmarking

The INS knew about the problems with the existing visa approval processes before 9/11; however, the resources needed to improve the situation were not available. As a result of that event, the INS was able to develop a clearly defensible business case for a KM initiative that was built on evidence of need and accompanied by a strong sense of urgency. The INS received the necessary managerial and financial support for change. In fact, the INS and FTTTF faced enormous public and political pressure to "do something." Of course, agency managers knew that many of the suggestions were inappropriate, even if they were allowable by law (or could become so). Agency managers also were aware of the distrust that resulted from the past reactions of government to horrific events and recognized the need to respond appropriately to the concerns of Arab allies. Agency managers were very willing to learn from others if the relevant KM processes could be identified and adapted to meet their needs. These conditions reduced the likelihood of failure.

The FTTTF and INS knew that learning from existing systems and adapting current processes could help reduce the time required to develop and deploy an AVAS. To undertake a benchmarking study, these agencies needed to locate potentially relevant systems. The FTTTF and INS began with identifying the mission-critical functions of the ideal AVAS:

- Identify and verify an individual's true identity.
- Provide a comparative assessment of that individual's potential risk based on a comparison to known actions of similar populations.
- Focus attention on identifying risks posed by patterns and/or processes (source and use of funds, known criminal associates, previous activities, and so on).
- Embed legal and regulatory constraints that avoid discrimination based on physical characteristics (age, race, gender, place of birth, and so on) and matters of individual choice or circumstances (education, income, religion, and so on).

A review of the literature indicates that there are many systems that might be adapted. When the features and benefits of each were compared, credit scoring systems were found to be the most relevant (see Table 27.2).

Credit scoring systems are designed for many settings. Their function is to authenticate the parties to a given transaction in order to assess the degree of risk that an unknown individual might represent. In eCommerce transactions, for example, the parties to the transaction may never actually meet in person. For this reason, there is a very real need to know that (1) the person or system on each end of a transaction is, in fact, who he or she claims to be; (2) the transaction is a real transaction in which goods or services are actually transferred; and (3) no criminal activity (such as money laundering or economic espionage) is involved.

Table 27.2 Benchmarking an automated visa risk approval system.

Profession/Industry	How Models/Scores Are Used
Nuclear power enigineers	Error—Equipment? Human?
Market segmentation	Europe—north and south different Hispanic and Asian alike—prefer quality over price
Differential diagnosis	Physician treats an unknown patient—fatal disease or a simple burn?
Insurance companies	Cars in different cities
Risk-based premiums	Health and different risk factors
Credit analysts	Limit losses when loosening credit

Lesson Learned: Gap Analysis

It should be noted that (1) the limited sample(s) of known foreign terrorists are not predictive in any statistical sense of the word; and (2) lack of discovery is not equivalent to the absence of a threat, because terrorist activities may still be in the planning stages. As with credit scoring systems, however, insights are expected to improve as the knowledge base grows over time. By benchmarking these and other systems that perform similar decision support functions, the AVAS can be designed to take advantage of specific features that have already proved useful in settings that demonstrate a similar set of requirements

The completed AVAS may eventually resemble the system shown in Figure 27.3. As the existing paper-based system transitions to a transnational automated system, it improves the likelihood that there will be knowledge sharing between analysts. While automating the visa approval process is no guarantee that each individual will be treated fairly, it is hoped that capturing the expertise and past experience of others can be used to improve decision support and reduce the impact of an individual analyst's lack of experience and insight. It might help identify dangerous individuals more quickly and prevent the kinds of errors based on emotional responses to a specific event.

Given the exigencies of the situation, there has simply been no time for a formal benchmarking study and much of the process is classified to prevent strategies from being offset by terrorist masterminds. It should be noted that the current

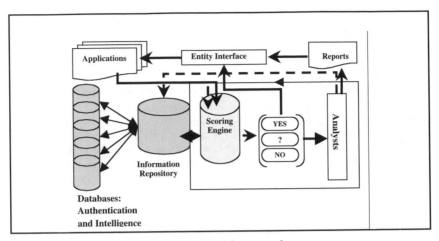

Figure 27.3   Completed automated visa risk approval system.

deputy director of the FTTTF holds a certificate in CI, however, and we can be sure that CI perspectives contributed to that part of the War on Terrorism that involves improvements in the visa approval process.

CONCLUSION

Clearly, knowledge managers can benefit from a range of CI tools and techniques, just as CI practitioners benefit by acquiring a deep understanding of an organization's operational readiness and willingness to evolve and adapt to change. Regardless of the mission, the long-term results of operational decisions are often as important as strategic ones; however, the impact is less readily apparent. For this reason, CI tools and techniques should be part of the toolkits of knowledge managers and should be used to improve the quality of KM initiatives.

ENDNOTES

1. Each employed participant enrolled in Module II (INFO643) of the Drexel CI Certificate Program during 1999–2002 was asked to (1) identify the challenges faced by their industry and (2) compare the specific challenges that distinguished them from their competitors. Most were unable to do so until later in the course.

2. The U.S. government needs to refine its profile of terrorists (as much to avoid wasting resources on those who pose no threat as to allocate resources to those who might). Information provided about the ethnic background of researchers funded by the National Science Foundation is incorrect and potentially dangerous. One reporting function of the FASTLANE system of the

National Science Foundation includes the capture of demographics data about researchers engaged in sponsored research for accountability purposes. This author discovered by chance that the only choice of ethnicity for everyone from the Middle East through the Far East is "Asian." We need only think about the consternation and the impact on resources if the only choice were "Arab."

3. The closing of the Reagan National Airport forced U.S. Airways into bankruptcy, for example.

4. The overwhelmed visa analyst has less than one minute to decide on the average application. Simply verifying the applicant's address can take much longer than that. At the present time, according to the deputy director of the FTTTF, there are over 17,000 applications per day from individuals who appear to have characteristics and backgrounds similar to those of the terrorists involved in the bombing of the World Trade Center.

CHAPTER 28

Integrating Knowledge Management and Competitive Intelligence; Integrating Offense and Defense

Steve Barth, Editor and Publisher, *Knowledge Management* magazine
2002 Visiting Scholar, Harvard University Graduate School of Education

As KM changes the rules of competitive intelligence, offense and defense must merge in a coordinated strategy.

EXECUTIVE SUMMARY

In this postindustrial, post–Cold War world, a general belief exists that we have more to gain from exchanging ideas and information than from locking them away in need-to-know silos. However, many KM and corporate security experts argue that there is a smarter, more controlled way to share knowledge with colleagues, suppliers, customers, and even competitors without giving away a competitive advantage. Whether they are being stolen or simply shared, if your intellectual assets are benefiting your competitors, you are not managing your knowledge effectively.

The increase in both KM and competitive intelligence (CI) cuts both ways. Gathering, organizing, and making accessible the information and intellectual resources of the company benefit managers, workers, customers, suppliers, partners, shareholders, and other stakeholders. However, it makes it harder to keep that knowledge from benefiting competitors as well. Meanwhile, those competitors—known or unknown—are probably getting better at gathering, organizing, and using what they can learn about you.

Acquiring the information that you need to be competitive while safeguarding the information you already have in order to stay competitive is a complicated task. Companies must balance the advantages of openness against its inevitable risks, maximizing the efficiency of electronic communication without making it a magnet for intruders. Experts say that you must integrate offense and defense into a comprehensive strategy, and furthermore, they suggest that it is time to integrate intelligence and security imperatives with other KM strategies and processes.

INTRODUCTION

Discussions about KM frequently begin with the assumption that KM is about sharing knowledge more freely. There is a general belief in the postindustrial, post–Cold War world that we have more to gain from exchanging ideas and information than from locking them away in need-to-know silos. Karl Erik Sveiby (2001), for example, points out that the dynamics of knowledge can be the opposite of capital. "Knowledge grows when shared and grows when used," he says. "Knowledge shared is knowledge doubled." Certainly, businesses can derive many bottom line benefits from such openness: the increased effectiveness of one-to-one marketing, better service and support, improved products as the result of better customer interaction, improved supply-chain efficiency through electronic data exchange, cost savings through cooperative procurement, and greater brand awareness and investor support, just to name a few examples.

If sharing existing knowledge is good, acquiring new knowledge is better. The practice of competitive intelligence (CI) is certainly one of the best examples of the business benefits to be derived from managing knowledge. Compared with the conceptual abstractions of so many KM projects, CI is a business activity with concrete objectives and obvious value. Acceptance of CI as a value-adding practice is increasing and the internal customer base for intelligence products (actionable information) is growing as CI practitioners respond to ad hoc requests for support of far-flung operations as well as deep research for an inner circle of executives. In return, the CI analyst can increasingly draw intelligence from every single employee throughout the organization.

"The essence of CI has changed," says Patrick Bryant, a recent president of the Society of Competitive Intelligence Professionals (SCIP) and a clinical professor at the medical school of the University of Missouri, Kansas City. Bryant also says, "It has become more a part of the company, more widespread and accepted. Information technology (IT) has given it more tools." (Barth, March 2001)

At the same time, however, many KM and corporate security experts voice skepticism about the idea that "information wants to be free." Pretending that knowledge value is always exempt from the laws of supply and demand is dangerous. Expertise is valuable precisely because of its scarcity, which is one reason why senior professionals resist the codification of their experience and expertise. More to the point, trade secrets, if shared with competitors, can definitely diminish share price.

These experts argue that there is a smarter, more controlled way to share knowledge with colleagues, suppliers, customers, and even competitors without giving away existing advantages. Whether they are being stolen or simply shared, if your intellectual assets are benefiting your competitors, you are not managing your knowledge effectively.

"Treating knowledge management as a technique to codify knowledge and share it on databases is just not good enough," warn David Snowden and James Luke (Snowden and Luke, 2000) of IBM Global Services. "Knowledge management is key to the effective management of information, and also to its protection and validation."

Acquiring the information that you need to be competitive while safeguarding the information you already have in order to stay competitive is a complicated task. Companies must balance the advantages of openness against its inevitable risks, maximizing the efficiency of electronic communication without making it a magnet for intruders. Experts say that you must integrate offense and defense into a comprehensive strategy and, furthermore, suggest that it is time to integrate intelligence and security imperatives with other KM strategies and processes.

Background

Intelligence as Knowledge

The aspect of KM relevant to this discussion is the information- and knowledge-gathering process traditionally known as competitive intelligence. However, there seems to be considerable confusion about what CI is really about.

After the breakup of the Soviet empire, focus shifted from geopolitical competition to global economic competition. Intelligence, the most important resource for the former, has become a vital tool for the latter. Mitigating risk is primarily a matter of managing information: collecting, analyzing, and using the right information about competitors and markets, while at the same time preventing your competition from collecting information about you.

As international companies are learning to adapt the strategies and methods of Cold War intelligence and counterintelligence agencies, they are also adopting many of the government agents and analysts now in private practice. Intelligence professionals were managing their knowledge long before KM was in vogue. Whether the goal is military, political, or commercial advantage, intelligence is a discipline that relies on and drives development of KM techniques and technologies. Both CI and information technology have evolved as a result of this symbiosis.

While previous chapters in this volume discuss current thinking in the practice of gathering, analyzing, and capitalizing on intelligence, a few points are worth exploring in terms of developing a comprehensive strategy of offense and defense.

It is one thing to differentiate popular perceptions of CI, which is legal and ethical, from industrial espionage, which is neither. It is another to establish a common understanding about what comprises intelligence and what value it can bring to business. Consider four meanings for three terms:

> **Competitive intelligence** is generally taken in a larger context to include actionable information not only about known competitors but about any factor in the market environment that could impact your competitiveness as a business. Such factors include (but are not limited to) partners, investors, employees, suppliers, customers, government regulators, and critics, as well as competitors.
>
> **Competitor intelligence**, then, would refer specifically to information and analysis about known competitors. In the age of asymmetric threats, however, known competitors are just the tip of the iceberg.
>
> **Business intelligence** (BI) is frequently the preferred term for the previous definition of CI. It is the right way to look at it; however, unfortunately, it has become impossible to distinguish this meaning of BI from another usage for the same phrase that has come into popular use. In many circles, BI has come to mean the collection and manipulation of transaction data in order to mine it for patterns. To make matters worse, this type of BI is sometimes included in definitions of the other.

The goal of CI is not just to react but to anticipate changes in the competitive environment and to support corporate decision making through a rigorous, systematic, legal, and ethical process. This process targets, collects, analyzes, and disseminates critical, forward-looking information about threats and opportunities.

The methodologies of CI professionals are primarily the intelligence cycle, key intelligence topics, analysis of strengths, weaknesses, opportunities, and threats (SWOT), and Porter's five forces. In particular, they rely on the stages of the standard plan-gather-analyze-communicate intelligence cycle:

- Plan
- Gather
- Secondary information (published or posted)
- Primary information (human)
- Analyze
- Communicate

In practice, according to research by CI software vendor Cipher Systems, typical priorities for the CI department are as follows (although Cipher believes companies would be better served if the priorities were inverted) (McKenney, 2001):

1. Ad hoc collection requirements (quick requests for information)
2. Preparing daily or weekly reports
3. Maintaining competitive and competitor profiles
4. Training inside the organization
5. Tactical support for sales and marketing
6. Carrying out market analysis projects for mergers and acquisitions, and so on
7. Strategic planning support
8. Team coordination for task forces
9. Scanning for early-warning indicators
10. Developing and communicating with the network of human sources

Competitive intelligence professionals claim they can supply their clients with 95 percent of the required information without breaking the law. The Society of Competitive Intelligence Professionals (SCIP), with some 8,000 members in 50 chapters worldwide, promotes the acquisition of such information through legal and ethical means.

Without breaking any laws, you can learn a great deal from others and they from you. An executive's travels might indicate a potential new factory or new customer; job postings might reveal labor conflicts or imminent expansion. Political, economic, technological, and consumer trends—all available to the public—have a direct bearing on your business. Information about a competitor company can be had by dissecting newspapers and annual reports—and by dissecting its products. From marketing databases for sale to the public, a little persistent curiosity can reveal targets' household incomes, political leanings, dress sizes, and whether they own a dog or a cat. And although it might be crossing an ethical line, most office dumpsters legally are fair game to any refuse archeologist with the patience and fortitude to sift out the information.

Increasingly, valuable facts are disclosed in digital form. Many of these items are published on the Internet explicitly or can be gleaned implicitly by mining and analyzing the content of aggregated documents and data. Knowledge and information management technologies for storage, retrieval, categorization, and presentation of information can expedite all phases of the CI process, particularly when it comes to distilling intelligence from disparate scraps of information. And just as in the integration of information into knowledge, intelligence is not acquired wholesale. Rather, it is assembled piecemeal from disparate information and reassembled as knowledge by someone else.

The Internet simplifies the task of gathering voluminous, well-organized information on competitors, raising the baseline for companies that do no more CI research than surfing the Web. However, warn CI professionals such as Ernest Brod (former managing director of Kroll International, a risk mitigation company based in New York City, and now CEO of Citigate Global Intelligence & Security), this can quickly lead to an overreliance on Web-based information. Online information can be static, focusing mostly on the past. It can be filtered by whomever posts it. It can also be intentionally misleading. Merely looking online is no substitute for doing the harder work of talking to live sources.

Of course, just because it is legal to scoop up all the information out there, you are not actually required to make it easy for others to do it to you. Every company needs both CI capability and the ability to protect its own information through business counterintelligence.

Synergy

Intelligence as Learning

In the context of CI, KM should be considered in both its strategic and tactical meanings and for both its process and technological implications. Philosophically, KM is the management of information and intellectual assets (experience, expertise, relationships, aggregated data, documents, and so on) for maximum return through better decisions, increased efficiency, customer responsiveness, and so on. In practice, however, KM often comes down to the ability to deliver the right information to the right knowledge worker at the right time. Any of these types of intellectual and information assets can be elements of intelligence if acquired and analyzed through the CI process and applied to make decisions or better understand the competitive position of the company.

On a deeper level, CI must be understood as part of the learning process. According to organizational learning theory, something always causes learning to happen. Stimuli for learning can come from social, legal, economic, political, cultural, and ethical environments. In today's world, however, passive learning about the environment can be too slow.

Edwin M. Epstein, Professor Emeritus from the University of California at Berkeley, argues for active rather than passive awareness of environmental stimuli. "It seems an important responsibility of organizations to absorb various sources of information and strategically use it," Epstein (2001) says. Establishing a CI practice in the organization would be one example. He illustrates with a biblical tale of Moses sending spies into Canaan to report on the situation. The news that was brought back—and the reaction thereto—revealed knowledge about the Canaanites but also about the Israelites.

Epstein explains:

Information which an organization gleans from the environment can inform it not simply about the environment but also about its core values, personnel, resources, and capacity to undertake strategic initiatives. True organizational learning occurs only where the organizational leadership is open to assimilating knowledge acquired about diverse spheres of the environment from diverse sources by diverse persons into the culture and strategic vision of the organization.

Alan Breakspear, president of intelligence consultancy Ibis Research in Ottawa and a former officer in the Canadian Security Intelligence Service, segments what he calls a "value chain" of ascending importance. He says:

Information management helps us understand what has happened. Business intelligence [his term for CI] helps us understand what is likely to happen externally and what our options are. Knowledge management helps us change what is likely to happen, internally and externally, through innovating, reinventing and repositioning (Barth, March 2001).

In short, then, CI is about anticipating and adapting to conditions external to the company. As a larger process, KM looks inward as well as outward, backward as well as forward. It can use CI to create strategies to enhance and protect competitive business advantage.

To the extent that their processes can be facilitated by information and communication technologies, CI and KM share many of the same tools. *CIO* magazine's "CI Toolbox" would sound familiar to any chief knowledge officer (CKO) or chief information officer implementing a knowledge-sharing infrastructure. Gathering secondary source material is facilitated by the Web, electronic news delivery, and automated alert software. Keeping in touch with primary, human sources is easier thanks to expertise profiles, e-mail, instant messaging, cell phones, and so on. Organization and storage are simplified by databases that handle both structured and unstructured information and are protected by information security measures. Analysis can be augmented with data mining, modeling, and visualization tools. And dissemination is more efficient and effective thanks to messaging, intranets, portals, and groupware applications (Breshnahan, 1998).

In both cases, technology can be used to facilitate the process—but must not be allowed to distract attention from the more important issues of process and culture. For evidence of this, consider research by the American Productivity and Quality Center (APQC), which conducts benchmarking and best practices research in both CI and KM. In a study of 12 companies identified as best practices leaders in CI, the APQC identified seven ways technology can be used to facilitate CI activities (Table 28.1).

LESSONS LEARNED

Knowledge management seeks to raise the collective intelligence of a company in terms of organizational IQ. But many of the same values support the argument for spreading another kind of intelligence more widely through the enterprise.

Anecdotal evidence, as well as research by John Prescott (professor of business administration at the University of Pittsburgh's Katz School of Business and past president of SCIP), suggests that there is increasing awareness of the business value of CI (Prescott and Bharwaj, 1995). More companies are doing it, and more people at those companies are involved. Where once CI was presumed to be the esoteric domain of highly skilled experts whispering in the ear of the chief

Table 28.1   Role of technology

How much of a role does information technology play in competitive intelligence (CI) activities (on a scale from 1 to 7)?	
Disseminating intelligence	6.1
Storing information so that it is accessible	6.0
Sharing information between functional groups within the organization	5.3
Collecting information from external sources	5.3
Consolidating different internal and external sources of CI	4.9
Facilitating the usability of CI through filtering, packaging, and so on	4.8
Collecting information from within the organization	4.1
Note: APQC Benchmarking Survey: Best practices in CI (Patton, 2000)	

executive, today every employee can contribute information to the process and every employee can make use of CI.

Knowledge management and CI share the same general drivers in terms of business trends: the globalization and acceleration of competition in almost every industry and economic sector. There is an increased appreciation for the value added by CI to all business processes. There is also an increased awareness of the value added by KM tools and techniques to business processes, including CI. And there is a nascent understanding that CI can be an ideal starting point to foster KM processes and values throughout the enterprise.

According to CI professionals, 80 percent to 95 percent of the information necessary to answer CI research questions already exists somewhere in their own organizations—if only it can be located. Knowledge management offers ways to identify and tap that knowledge. Meanwhile, however, 79 percent of employees polled by a Korn-Ferry study say they still do not have enough information about what competitors are doing. Knowledge management also offers ways to distribute CI to employees who need it in a filtered, useful way.

Lessons learned through often painful experiences with KM to date suggest how CI might be similarly impacted (Barth, October 2002).

Lesson 1: Connection Is as Important as Collection

Early emphasis on repositories and document management distracted KM from focusing on the reality that the most valuable knowledge is the often unarticulated experience and expertise in the heads of workers and managers. The value of technology is therefore in facilitating conversations that, in turn, depend on the trust created in relationships and communities. Competitive intelligence professionals have long understood that the quality of primary, human sources of intelligence outweighs the quantity of documentary material. However, they will need to build out their networks to a wider web of employees, customers, and others.

Lesson 2: Context Is as Important as Content

Only context can turn information into knowledge. This is one reason secondary source material is less valuable. Many CI experts have complained that quality intelligence is being replaced by quantity information, which often does more harm than good.

Lesson 3: Do Not "Do" KM; Apply KM to Specific Problems

Another painful lesson of KM has been to not even try to "manage" knowledge but, rather, to apply KM tools and techniques to specific business problems and to facilitate knowledge work. The trend has been away from enterprisewide infrastructures and universal repositories in favor of small projects—especially "low-hanging fruit" projects, where value can be realized and demonstrated quickly. Competitive intelligence is exactly such a case of low-hanging fruit; however, it faces similar pitfalls as CI processes and practices reach a wider audience.

As practices, both CI and KM have the same fundamental requirements. Each needs a strategic purpose, each depends on having a corporate culture that encourages people to create and share information and knowledge, each requires skills and competencies to carry out the processes involved, and each is facilitated by the same or similar technological tools.

When it comes to integrating CI and KM, however, there is one note of caution, as expressed by Bryant. Carefully consider the procedural and political implications of reorganization. For example, CI professionals feel strongly that they need direct access to top executives, especially when the information they put together on either opportunities or threats can be news that a decision maker does not want to hear.

This raises the issue of whether the chief intelligence officer should report to the head of KM or go directly to the CEO. "Working for a CKO might mean being removed by at least one more layer from the decision-maker," Bryant adds. In whatever way the chain of command is structured, the organization should ensure that critical CI reaches the top. "CI professionals believe that the more people there are between them and the decision-maker, the more chances there are for that intelligence to be repackaged, modified, adulterated, or spun," Bryant says (Barth, March 2001).

Likewise, maximizing the direct connections between seekers of knowledge and those who have the answers they are looking for is good advice for other KM functions.

Like KM, CI requires a cultural shift as well as process and technological changes. When that happens, the results can be dramatic. Because every employee at NutraSweet understands the value of CI, chairman Robert Flynn estimates the company earns—or saves—about $50 million per year (Prescott and Miller, 2001).

Results such as those of NutraSweet have been enough to convince many companies. According to a 1998 survey by The Futures Group, 82 percent of U.S. companies with annual revenues of at least $10 billion had an organized CI system. The figure is 60 percent at companies with revenues of at least $1 billion. The Gartner Group predicted that by the end of 2001, more than 60 percent of *Fortune* 1000 companies would formalize and systematize their CI processes, focusing on markets, competitors, technology, and products and services (Kolb, 2000).

Stop and think about what this means for a moment. It is not just that your company should jump on the bandwagon, although that is an important step in maintaining your competitive position. Perhaps a more urgent implication is that it is extremely likely that someone else has built a CI practice that is watching you!

DOUBLE-EDGED SWORD

The rise of both KM and CI cuts both ways. Gathering, organizing, and making accessible the information and intellectual resources of the company benefit managers, workers, customers, suppliers, partners, shareholders, and other stakeholders. However, doing so also makes it harder to keep that knowledge from benefiting competitors. Meanwhile, those competitors—known or unknown—are probably getting better at gathering, organizing, and using what they can learn about you.

Any aspect of the knowledge, product knowledge, process knowledge, customer knowledge, and so on, of your company becomes intelligence for others if acquired through the CI process and applied to their advantage.

Thanks to increasing digitization of various kinds of information and improved access to that material through powerful applications and networks, your business information is more vulnerable than ever before. In fact, you may be handing over your knowledge without being fully aware that you are doing so, through means such as sales collateral, Web sites, and analyst briefings. Your market positioning information can be as valuable to a competitor as it is to your customers.

More than one CI or security expert has awoken in the middle of the night worrying about this. Here too, however, security is actually hampered by the emphasis on technology and technological solutions. As James Luke (2000) puts it, the pervasive nature of modern communication has resulted in a more relaxed attitude about security in which employees abdicate responsibility to mechanisms such as firewalls and passwords.

In matters of defense, awareness must come first. Many executives fail to understand how easy it is for innocuous public disclosures to be mined, compiled, and analyzed. Business leaders who are savvy about securing their information systems may be clueless about how much competitive information they give away on their Web sites, while briefing analysts, at the coffee urn at conferences, or when chatting on their cellular phones in airport lounges.

Herbert Clough (a former FBI counterintelligence expert and now president of Cointelsys, a security and intelligence consultancy in Los Angeles) warns that it is easy to give away too much when you exchange information with people. CEOs give away too much information when addressing analysts to increase their visibility and stock price. "They love to brag about their products and show off," he says. "It's a thin line you walk when you put at risk your trade secrets and proprietary information. You have to recognize when you are giving away your family jewels" (Barth, March 2001).

You do not have to be a defense contractor to have sensitive information to protect. Your trade secrets are anything that would enable another company to derive economic benefit from your hard work. The long list includes designs and formulas, customer lists, marketing strategies, price structures, new product information, manufacturing processes, and factory locations.

In business, just as in the military, secrets about operational strategies tend to be the most valuable, according to Graham Titterington, senior analyst for technology consultancy Ovum Ltd. in London. "If it's a new soap, the formula is not as valuable as the marketing campaign, the pricing strategy, and where the trial marketing will be," he says (Barth, March 2001).

Not every piece of sensitive information is considered a proprietary secret, however. Unless a company takes definite steps to designate and protect the information, they are not covered by the Economic Espionage Act of 1996. They are more or less fair game.

Requisite Disclosure

All organizations publish data that often reveals more than the company originally intended, both by what is there and what is not. "Organizations need to appreciate that information is transmitted by every action they undertake," says Luke of IBM. "Information on a Web site, recruitment advertisements for specific skills, and even the working hours of staff all represent information transmissions." Such open-source material can offer valuable CI—or it can be manipulated to create distraction and disinformation (Barth, March 2001).

At the same time, the law requires all companies to disclose information that many would rather keep private, such as the ingredients in food and drugs, origins of manufactured goods, names of executives, and details of new products submitted for patent. In the old days, nuggets such as these were safer because they were kept on paper in scattered locations. Today, most of this information is available in electronic format and can be acquired without having to scour warehouses full of documents or microfiche.

Patent data are perhaps the most potent example. During the Cold War, the Soviet Union's intelligence agency, the KGB, created software to monitor patent registration and identify areas of technological development. Today, even small companies can do the same, legally gleaning the secrets of their competitors while spending less on research.

Cloaking Public Information

These realities need not lead to despair. Although you cannot protect all sensitive information, there are ways to give the competition less to work with. John McGonagle (managing partner of the Helicon Group, a CI consultancy in Blandon, Pennsylvania) suggests a process he calls "cloaking" to implement countermeasures to protect your company. "Cloaked competitors don't operate by stealth or clandestine methods," he explains. "Instead, they take some fundamental steps to control the flow of information into the public domain, without trying to stop the flow or taint it with false information" (Barth, March 2001).

McGonagle lists three keys to becoming an effective cloaked competitor: (1) Determine the activities of greatest interest to your competitors and focus on protecting them; (2) understand the channels through which your competitors collect raw data on your firm, and control what goes into them; and (3) discern what techniques your competitor uses to analyze the data, and then deprive it of a few key pieces of data that are necessary to complete the analysis. He also offers some examples of how to do this:

- *Blur numbers.* Instead of giving the exact specs for your warehouse, say that, for example, it is more than 100,000 square feet. If you are expanding, say you will be using three times as many trucks as you do now.

- *Be vague.* Instead of telling people the specific names of software that you use, say that it is state of the art (if it is) or that we use computers that are just right for our needs.

- *Do not overfile.* The Securities and Exchange Commission realizes that some company information is sensitive. Be wary what you include after such forward-looking words as expect, plan, or intend. Volunteer only the minimum required for government paperwork.

- *Code randomly.* Product numbers in catalogs can reveal to your competitor the age of the equipment you use or how long you have used it. Keep those numbers under wraps.

McGonagle also suggests that you can turn the wealth of information disclosed on your Web site to defensive advantage by playing against the overreliance on Web surfing. He says:

The Internet makes collecting historical and near-current data easier than ever. However, it tends to convert CI into reporting about competitors, substituting volume and currency for analysis and thoroughness. Its growth continues to perpetuate the myth that everything is on the Net. If key data is not on the Internet, inherent laziness and time constraints tend to keep many CI researchers from seeking it (Barth, March 2001).

POSTINDUSTRIAL ESPIONAGE

Meanwhile, however, no matter how rigorously a company's CI practice holds itself to strict ethical and legal standards, the same cannot be assumed for your known or unknown competitors. Counterintelligence strategies must be far more comprehensive and assume that others are willing to cross ethical and legal lines. Virtually every company needs to practice CI. And every company must be ready to defend itself against both CI and industrial or economic espionage in real space or cyberspace.

Competitive intelligence professionals emphasize that they can satisfy as much as 95 percent of their client's needs for information about competitors using open, public sources and legal, ethical methods. Most companies stop there—but not all of them. Your secrets are worth big money to your competitors, to foreign governments looking to help their own industries, and to entrepreneurial information brokers who will dig up anything on anybody, then figure out to whom to sell it. This is where CI, which is legal, becomes industrial espionage, which is not legal.

It is essential to understand how far some competitors and foreign governments will go to steal your secrets—even if you are not aware of them as competitors. As economic security replaces military security in a global economy, government agencies supporting national industries and retired spies working for private clients use all the tricks of the Cold War and all the tools of IT. Some have gone as far as to bug first-class seats on certain airlines and staff their own business hotels. Here are two examples of how vulnerable companies can be:

> In September 2000, Irwin Jacobs, founder and chairman of Qualcomm Inc., finished a speech to the Society of American Business Editors and Writers in Irvine, California, and stepped away from the podium in a hotel ballroom. After talking with members of the audience for about 20 minutes, he discovered that his laptop computer was gone. Although local police considered it to have been a commonplace theft of a $4,000 piece of equipment, Jacobs told *The Wall Street Journal* that the information on the hard drive of the laptop could have been far more valuable to foreign governments, with whom he was then negotiating billion-dollar deals. It was later revealed that Jacobs's laptop had been protected by nothing more than a basic Windows password. Security experts say that is no protection at all. Not only do senior executives often carry sensitive financial information and other critical enterprise data on their portables, but if

their laptops enable them to access back-end systems behind the company firewall, it is a backstage pass.

In October 2001, Microsoft discovered someone had gained access, and for three months had been breaking into to the corporate network to look at the source code of products under development. Information was apparently going to a computer address in St. Petersburg, Russia. It is not known how many other documents and e-mails were also accessible to the hacker, but those conceivably could have included contracts, e-mail, marketing documents, and other key components of the business strategy and operations of the company.

Unlike the police view of the theft of Jacob's laptop, Microsoft officials had little doubt that this break-in was an act of industrial espionage. The incident was a reminder that breaking into networks has become a useful tool for illegally cutting corners. Obviously, the protection was not ironclad. However, Microsoft's security team is considered top-notch and few corporations have more resources or greater incentive to maintain the integrity of their information channels. If they cannot keep their knowledge safe, who can?

Traditional approaches to economic espionage, such as eavesdropping on conversations or steaming open envelopes, were labor-intensive and risky and often produced spotty results. Electronic spying adds a new category of threat, whereby unprotected internal and external communications and documents can be accessed by hackers on a continuous basis. However, trade shows are still full of attractive and curious young people taking interest in your products.

CULTURAL ISSUES

Finally, if poor security can compromise the competitive position of a company, so can too much security. Overreliance on technological solutions can disconnect knowledge workers from their constituents as well as from their tasks. Companies sometimes tighten the security of their information systems to the point where employees cannot conduct effective online research or communicate with customers, partners, suppliers, or even colleagues.

The doubt and paranoia that these stifling policies imply can paralyze an organization in a number of ways. When this happens, your competitors are already gaining advantage without gaining intelligence. Here are just a few of the consequences (Snowden and Luke, 2000):

- If people do not trust each other, they will not share.
- If people do not trust information, they will waste their time and effort validating it.
- If valuable information exists, it can be obscured by worthless material.
- If policies and procedures interfere with getting the job done, they will be ignored or subverted.

Titterington says:

> You can't be heavy-handed. It's no good having a system that's 100 percent secure if, at the end of the day, you can't do business efficiently. Protecting assets and enabling employees is a difficult compromise to get right, but it's worth the effort (Barth, March 2001).

Real security can only be guaranteed through behavioral changes in an organization. Anything less is easy to compromise. For example, an onerous password regimen may drive people to write passwords on sticky notes or tape them up in plain sight. Luke urges employees and executives alike to learn how valuable their knowledge is to competitors; how prevalent the dangers are; and how easy they make it by speaking on mobile phones or working on documents in public, such as while traveling (Barth, March 2001).

The best technological solutions are ultimately incomplete and fallible without human behaviors and networks of personal trust. Experienced KM professionals know that loyalty cannot be coerced. Without loyalty and trust, the intellectual capital of any company will always be at risk. "Effective security, like effective KM, should be natural and based on the support and commitment of educated staff," says Luke (Barth, March 2001).

As with other business intangibles, such as quality or ethics, security should be seen as a process rather than as a goal. As with these other factors, security must also come from the top. Unfortunately, one of the most common problems is that senior executives rarely follow the rules they impose on other employees.

Author M. E. Kabay says:

> Because we are primates and social animals, every layer of the hierarchy will strive to emulate them. So when the male baboon who is the chief financial officer refuses to wear a security badge, saying "Everybody knows me," the next layer down will emulate that person in order to acquire his status (Barth, August 1998).

Improving security can be even more problematic at an international company or at an overseas site. Kabay recommends managers bring in representatives from different cultures from throughout the multinational organization to make sure that security policies do not offend traditional sensibilities (Barth, August 1998).

Open Dialogues and Closed Communities

Balancing the benefits of increased openness and increased liability is the same challenge that the national security community has been grappling with in recent years. Its thinking around these issues is now migrating to KM consultants.

Andrew Campbell, senior vice president and CKO, and Carol Willett, executive vice president for innovation and learning, now work for Applied Knowledge Group in Reston, Virginia, which is a consulting company that specializes in virtual teams. Both are former employees of the Central Intelligence Agency (CIA), where they learned to weigh benefits against risks before sharing knowledge.

At the CIA, Campbell recalls:

> It's drummed into our heads from day one that you have to think about information as having differing levels of sensitivity and value. There's a lot of naïveté in American industry. I don't think enough attention is paid to that aspect of knowledge and how it's managed (Barth, March 2001).

Willett says that sensitivity to who needs to know something must be seen in terms of external—not internal—competition. When someone refuses to share with a colleague, for example, the message should be, "It wasn't that I won't tell you because it would give you a leg up on me but because I have responsibility for protecting it," Willett explains (Barth, March 2001).

This kind of thinking has obvious implications for the value KM thinkers place on ad hoc conversations and the innovation that comes from combining bits of knowledge from normally unrelated disciplines. The ex-CIA workers argue that this conflict can be resolved. Campbell says:

> I know it's an oxymoron, but you can have controlled serendipity. Serendipity happens within the community of people who are working on a project. In the experience of the intelligence community, you don't go out and have that serendipity at a public conference, because if you are not careful, there are people who are skilled at cleaning your clock (Barth, March 2001).

Willett, who has taught U.S. government teams that deal with sensitive information, says it is possible to do interdisciplinary problem solving without making all of the details explicit. "There are ways to describe problems using analogies and to ask how someone would do it in their discipline," Willett explains (Barth, March 2001).

Another aspect of this conundrum is that security concerns can make it more difficult for knowledge workers to create reciprocal exchanges of information and experience. Willet says:

> For a good exchange where there is value for all sharing parties, customers, suppliers, and the company need to clarify what they hope to achieve and what they assume the other party is bringing to share. But those conversations rarely happen, so there tends to be mutual disappointment because people don't articulate their expectations (Barth, March 2001).

Campbell adds:

> Some coin has to be used to maintain the balance. This happened all the time with people outside the boundary of the agency, such as academic experts. Anybody I ever ran into who was truly skilled at this kind of transaction was good at paying attention to the relationship capital (Barth, March 2001).

To have productive conversations, Campbell and Willett conclude that people must make decisions about the need to know in real time. A professional skilled in these situations can decide whether the issue can be divorced from its context and the question answered without jeopardizing the strategy or industrial secrets of the organization.

CONCLUSION

If knowledge assets are worth collecting and sharing, it is because they have value. If they have value, those assets must also be considered worth protecting.

Intensifying domestic and international competition has increased the role that intelligence can play. No longer is it a mysterious art practiced only by corporate librarians and retired spy catchers whispering in the ears of executives. Today, every employee can and should contribute to it, just as every employee can and also should benefit from it. This democratization can be facilitated by increasingly robust corporate information structures, such as portals.

The rise of both KM and CI cuts both ways. Gathering, organizing, and making accessible the information and intellectual resources of the company benefit managers, workers, customers, suppliers, partners, shareholders, and other stakeholders. However, it makes it harder to keep that knowledge from benefiting competitors as well. Meanwhile, those competitors—known or unknown—are probably getting better at gathering, organizing, and using what they can learn about you.

ENDNOTE

This chapter includes material adapted from the following references:

Barth, S. (October, 2002). State of the Notion: The collective experience of practitioners in KM and related fields point to key lessons to keep in mind for successful application of KM to business problems. destinationKM. http://www.destinationkm.com

Barth, S. (March 2001). Open yet guarded: As knowledge management changes the rules of CI, offense and defense must merge in a coordinated strategy. *Knowledge Management* magazine.

Barth, S. (July 1998). The professionals: From industrial spies to corrupt officials, the borderless world is full of dangers, but risk management can limit your exposure and safeguard your profits. *World Trade*.

Barth, S. (August 1998). Spy vs. spy: With the Cold War over, spies are targeting companies rather than governments. *World Trade*.

REFERENCES

Breshnahan, J. (July 15, 1998). Legal espionage. CIO Enterprise magazine http://www.cio.com/archive/enterprise/071598_ci.html

Epstein, E. (November 17, 2001). How to learn from the environment about the environment: A prerequisite for organizational well-being. Presented at Organizations in the 21st Century: Knowledge and Learning—the Basis for Growth at the Wissenschaftszentrum Berlin für Sozialforschung (Social Science Research Center), Berlin. http://www.global-insight.com/WZB

Johnson, A. (June, 1998). An introduction to knowledge management as a framework for competitive intelligence. Presented at the International Knowledge Management Executive Summit, San Diego, CA. http://www.aurorawdc.com/essaysindex.htm

Kolb, G. (April, 2000). Entrepreneurial CI. *Competitive Intelligence* 3(2): 56. http://www.scip.org/news/cimagazine_article.asp?id=266

McKenney, P. (January, 2001). A practical approach to competitive intelligence. PowerPoint presentation to the Raleigh, North Carolina, chapter of Society of Competitive Information Professionals.

Patton, S. (1 December, 2000). By the numbers: Competitive intelligence tips. *CIO* magazine.

Prescott, J., and Bharwaj, G. (1995). Competitive intelligence practices: A survey. *Competitive Intelligence Review* 6(2): 4–14.

Prescott, J., and Miller, S. (2001). *Proven Strategies in Competitive Intelligence: Lessons From the Trenches*. Hoboken, NJ: John Wiley.

Snowden, D., and Luke, J. (2000). The knowledge salient: Intelligence and information warfare in a new age of uncertainty. *Knowledge Management* (Ark Group) 3(8).

Sveiby, K. (2001). A knowledge-based theory of the firm to guide strategy formulation. *Journal of Intellectual Capital* 2(4): 344–358.

ADDITIONAL USEFUL MATERIAL FOR THE READER

Ashkinaze, C. (16 June, 2000). Spies like us: You don't need to be James Bond or IBM to use competitive intelligence. *Business Week.*

Brod, S. (1999). Competitive intelligence: Harvesting information to compete and market intelligently. APH Associates white paper.

Butler Group. (July 1999). Knowledge management—management guide: Strategies and technologies. Butler Group white paper.

Butler Group. (February 2001). Competitive intelligence. Butler Group *Enterprise Intelligence Journal.*

Crawford, M. G. (February 1998). Get smart: Your guide to competitive intelligence. *Profit* magazine.

Gross, M. (September 2000). Competitive intelligence: A librarian's empirical approach. *Searcher* magazine.

Imperato, G. (April 1998). Competitive intelligence: Get smart! *Fast Company* magazine. Fast Company's panel of experts provides a six-point program for keeping an eye on your rivals.

Johnson, A. R. On predicting the future: Competitive intelligence as a knowledge management discipline. Arik. http://www.aurorawdc.com/essaysindex.htm

Mellon, D. (30 November, 1999). The art of corporate spying: To go without competitive intelligence would be like going into battle without a weapon. *Ottawa Business Journal.*

Montague Institute. (March 2000). Competitive intelligence: How and where to find it. Montague Institute *Limited Edition* newsletter.

Moon, M. (February 2000). Effective use of information and competitive intelligence. *Information Outlook.*

Part VI

Education and Training—Organizational Learning

Education and Training—
Organizational Learning
INTRODUCTORY NOTES

Although this is the last section of this book, it is by no means the least important. To attest to that, review Chapter 29 for data on the surprisingly large proportion (over half) of KM implementation failures that are attributable to inadequate user training and education.

Both education and training for KM, and organizational learning as a component of KM, are increasingly being recognized as central to its success.

In addition, education and training for KM professionals are required to provide competent and effective services in an enterprise addressing current issues and challenges in the creation, identification, codification, and sharing of knowledge. Knowledge is power, but only if it is really made accessible—organized, analyzed, and delivered to meet the organization's needs. Understanding what knowledge should be made available and how to make it accessible is the key to successful implementation of a KM program. The program may involve capturing strategic knowledge, analyzing markets, and developing databases, policies, and procedures. KM professionals need to understand the language and culture of an organization and to know business and financial practices. For a KM professional, the knowledge required to work competently and effectively requires education and training with an interdisciplinary approach, an approach that we are more frequently observing as new KM training programs emerge.

This section addresses all three of these issues: education and training for users of KM systems, organizational learning as a component of KM, and education and training for KM professionals.

These and similar themes are described in the Road Map following the Table of Contents. "Education for KM and Learning in KM" is a topic elaborated on in that Road Map.

Additional chapters that call attention to those themes but are outside of this section include:

CHAPTER 29

Knowledge Management and User Education: The Unrecognized Achilles' Heel

Michael E. D. Koenig, Long Island University

It is now common to observe that although the phenomenon of management attention upon KM was given birth to a large degree by the appearance of the Internet and its brethren, intranets and extranets, fundamentally KM is more about people and corporate culture than it is about technology.

An important aspect of that human resource side of KM that has not been adequately recognized is the need for user support and user education and training. Fascinating and compelling documentation in regard to that problem is contained in a recent KPMG Consulting (2000) study of more than 400 firms and their status in implementing KM systems. They reported that of the 288 firms with KM systems in place, or that were setting up such a system, there were 137 cases, nearly half, where the benefits failed to meet expectations (and of that base of 288 firms, 127 were still only in the setting up phase). The breakdown of why benefits failed to meet expectations follows in the table:

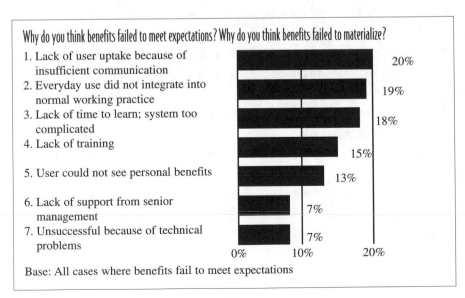

Why do you think benefits failed to meet expectations? Why do you think benefits failed to materialize?

1. Lack of user uptake because of insufficient communication — 20%
2. Everyday use did not integrate into normal working practice — 19%
3. Lack of time to learn; system too complicated — 18%
4. Lack of training — 15%
5. User could not see personal benefits — 13%
6. Lack of support from senior management — 7%
7. Unsuccessful because of technical problems — 7%

Base: All cases where benefits fail to meet expectations

Note: These percentages add to 99 percent due to rounding error; there is no overlap.

It is striking that three reasons provided—lack of user uptake because of insufficient communication, lack of time to learn; system too complicated, and lack of training—are all fundamentally the same reason: inadequate training and user education. With that recognized, the table can be recast in a much more informative fashion:

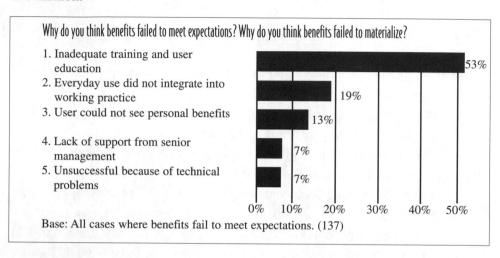

Why do you think benefits failed to meet expectations? Why do you think benefits failed to materialize?

1. Inadequate training and user education — 53%
2. Everyday use did not integrate into working practice — 19%
3. User could not see personal benefits — 13%
4. Lack of support from senior management — 7%
5. Unsuccessful because of technical problems — 7%

Base: All cases where benefits fail to meet expectations. (137)

Note: It is also likely that some component of reason 3, "User could not see personal benefits," is reflective of inadequate training and user education.

First, it is striking that inadequate training and user education is by far the most prominent reason provided for why benefits failed to meet expectations, accounting for the majority of failures and exceeding all other reasons combined.

One small caveat is that, as Davenport and Prusak (1998) observe, sometimes lack of training may take the blame when the real culprit is a combination of naïve expectation and a failure to adequately address the corporate cultural changes needed. Even considering this, however, the predominance of the training-and-user-education factor is striking.

Second, it is striking that the KPMG Consulting report (2000) fails to notice this rather dramatic finding. To their credit, KPMG Consulting does observe: "These responses confirm the fundamental flaw in viewing KM as a technology issue: It is not the technology that is holding organizations back but a lack of strategy and a failure to build KM in the organization's day-to-day operations and its culture in order to encourage end-user buy-in." However, that is as far as they get toward recognizing what their data portrays.

It is interesting to compare that in KPMG Consulting's data, 53 percent reported inadequate training and user education as the principal problem for failure, and seven percent reported lack of support from senior management as the principal problem for failure.

It is not that senior management support is unimportant; however, consider the proportion of KM literature that emphasizes the importance of getting senior management support versus the proportion of KM literature that emphasizes the importance of setting up adequate and extensive support for user education and training. One immediately understands the extent of the Achilles' heel problem. The culture of KM is nowhere near adequately aware of the importance of training and user education, and the KPMG Consulting report illustrates and illuminates the problem in a wonderfully compelling fashion by, ironically enough, not recognizing it.

Lessons Learned

The importance of paying adequate attention to the key role played by training and user education is the obvious lesson learned from the KPMG Consulting analysis. That lesson can be usefully refined and made concrete. One point of departure is to factor in phenomenon that have emerged from the study of information workers and their productivity:

1. The importance of rich communications, browsing, and serendipity.
2. The phenomenon that information workers, from researchers to managers, tend to spend a surprisingly consistent 20 to 25 percent of their work time seeking information.

Rich Communications, Browsing, and Serendipity

There is an extensive body of work documenting the relationships between knowledge worker and organizational productivity, and rich communications, browsing, and serendipity (Koenig, 1990). That work is discussed in Chapter 8, "Knowledge Management and Research on Research: What Has Been Learned." In these studies of the correlates of successful R&D, not only the consistency of the findings is intriguing, but also the phenomenon that when various other factors are considered as well, the information-related factors so consistently jump to the head of the list. Equally intriguing is the tendency of authors to fail to remark upon the phenomenon. Also consistent within the studies is the importance of browsing and serendipity. In Koenig's study of the pharmaceutical industry for example, the researchers at the more productive pharmaceutical companies not only used their corporate library or information center more recently, they used it proportionately much more for browsing and keeping abreast, as opposed to using it to address a specific information need. Indeed at the pharmaceutical company most highly rated for research success, Pfizer, the corporate message encouraging such browsing was abundantly clear. Immediately on entering the library at research headquarters one saw two long tables, one prominently labeled "Today's Journals" and the other prominently labeled "Yesterdays Journals." The researcher was obviously expected to be in the library, to be there frequently, and to be following the most current literature. By contrast, another large company, one very near the bottom of the list, Searle, made it very clear that the researchers should be at the bench doing their job, and when information was needed, they should ask for it to be delivered.

In a similar vein, Mondschein (1990) studied the productivity of researchers in major corporations in several industries, including pharmaceuticals and electronics. He found that scientists who used literature alerting services heavily were more productive (as measured by publication output, patents, and internal evaluations) than their colleagues who either did not use such services or used them only infrequently. Further, the productive researchers were characterized by their use of a wider variety of information sources, particularly by the extent of their efforts to stay current and by their use of patent information sources.

The 20 to 25 Percent Rule, "Satisficing"

An intriguing finding from studies of the work practices of white-collar professional employees is that they spent a rather consistent 20 to 25 percent of their time seeking information. This phenomenon is documented and discussed in more depth in Chapter 10, "Time Saved: Not a Politic Justification for Knowledge Management" (Griffiths, 1982; King, McDonald, & Roderer, 1981; Nelke, 1999a, 1999b; Poppel, 1982; Roderer, King, & Brouard, 1983). This proportion is surprisingly independent of the apparent information intensity of the job domain. Line business managers and administrators spend as much of their time information seeking as do research scientists. There seems to be a sort of homeostasis, or perhaps more accurately a satisficing mechanism at work. Knowledge workers whether managers or administrators or researchers need substantial information input to perform satisfactorily, but when the amount of time devoted to that function approaches roughly 20%, then knowledge workers appear to begin to satisfice, they begin to conclude that they have to get on with the rest of their job, and that if they have not already done so, they will soon run into diminishing returns in their information seeking, and that it is time to proceed based on what they have.

The obvious conclusion is that if knowledge workers are going to spend so much of their time information seeking, then they are likely to perform better if the systems and environment are provided so that their time is spent efficiently. After all, it is unlikely that the 20- to 25-percent figure arises because most knowledge workers coincidentally arrive at the exact information they need at the exact same point. It is rather more likely that they share an intuitive, satisficing mechanism in common, and that they often proceed in their decision making with poorer information than they would have if a more supportive environment and more capable information and knowledge systems were in place.

DOMAINS OF TRAINING AND USER EDUCATION FOR KM

The two points noted previously indicate that there are at least two different domains for training and user education. The 20- to 25-percent satisficing point phenomenon implies the strategy of assisting information workers to apply that 20 to 25 percent of their time as efficiently as possible and creating an environment that makes it easy for them to do so, and even impels them to do so. On the other hand, there is the undoubted utility of serendipity and broad spectrum browsing, and serendipity is, by contrast, inherently somewhat messy and seemingly inefficient. These are clearly two different information environments.

If this distinction is combined with the codification (creating structured information and knowledge sources) versus personalization (facilitating interpersonal contact and access to tacit knowledge) distinction popularized by Hansen, Nohria, and Tierney (1999), then we arrive at Table 29.1.

This table serves as a chart for the different domains that need to be addressed, and allows us to think more clearly about what is needed in training and user education.

Table 29.1   Domains of training and user education for knowledge management.

	Codification	Personalization
Directed Information and Knowledge Search	Databases, external and internal Content architecture Information service support (training required) Data mining Best practices/lessons learned	Community and learning directories, findings and facilitating tools, groupware
Serendipity and Browsing	Cultural support Current awareness profiles and databases Selection of items for alerting purposes/push services Data mining Best practices	Cultural support Spaces, libraries and lounges (literal and virtual), cultural support, groupware Travel and meeting attendance

Table 29.2   Knowledge management strategies.

	COLLECT/stuff	CONNECT/people
Exploit	HARVEST Example: best practices	HARNESS Example: response teams
Explore	HUNTING Example: data mining	HYPOTHESIZE Example: brainstorming scenario analysis

The utility and validity of Table 29.1 is affirmed by its fundamental equivalence to Table 29.2, which has been used for the last several years by IBM to explain and articulate KM, its functions, and its components.

Although not totally identical, the two independently derived tables—one (ours) developed on the basis of knowledge use and knowledge organization, and the other (IBM's) developed on the basis of KM functions and strategy—are remarkably consistent, a fact that is perhaps not too surprising given that KM is about knowledge use and knowledge organization.

Table 29.3   Domains of knowledge management strategy, and of training and user education for knowledge management.

	Collecting (Stuff) and Codification	Connecting (People) and Personalization
Directed Information and Knowledge Search **Exploit**	Databases, external and internal Content architecture Information service support (training required) Data mining Best practices/lessons learned (HARVEST)	Community and learning directories, findings and facilitating tools, groupware Response teams (HARNESS)
Serendipity and Browsing **Explore**	Cultural support Current awareness profiles and databases Selection of items for alerting purposes/push services Data mining Best practices (HUNTING)	Cultural support Spaces, libraries and lounges (literal and virtual), cultural support, groupware Travel and meeting attendance Brainstorming Scenario analysis (HYPOTHESIZE)

They are so congruent that they can quite usefully be combined and superimposed with no major distortions. See Table 29.3.

Scanning Table 29.3 reinforces the observation that KM is a multifaceted undertaking and it also reiterates that user education and training is multifaceted.

DESIGN THE TRAINING AND EDUCATION PROGRAM FIRST

A well worn but very valuable precept in systems analysis is "write the user manual first." Taking time to write the user manual first, or at least very early on in systems development, forces the design team to put themselves in the user's position and to think clearly about what the system will and will not do. It helps avoid the common problem of systems development drifting in the direction of the easily doable, or what the programmer thinks is clever or neat, rather than in the often more prosaic direction of what the user really needs. And, of course, it helps ensure that the system does what is needed in a fashion that is effective and easy to use.

The KM analog of this is "design the training and education program first" or at least as early on as practicable. There are two sets of reasons for this. The first set consists of those reasons provided previously. After all, implementing KM is a systems development project. It is, however, a systems development project in which the cultural aspects are of even more critical importance than in most projects. The second set of reasons derives from the importance of those cultural aspects.

If one thinks about a program for user education and training, one not only has to think about how to use the system, but also has to be prepared to answer the question, "Why?" In asking, and answering this question, the team is forced to address what the system is trying to accomplish, whether it is likely to be accomplished, and what stands in the way, typically cultural issues. Then, the question arises, "What is being done and what can be done to address those issues?"

It is ironic that in a circular fashion those who, as Davenport and Prusak (1998) point out, blame lack of training when the real problem is neglecting the corporate culture change needed may, in an underlying sense, be partially correct in that a lack of planning for training may have led to, or been a major cause of, the lack of awareness of the need for cultural change.

In addition to "design the training and education program first," what specific lessons are there?

Target the Domains

The following sections relate to Table 29.3.

Harvesting

Teach Database Searching

Using and searching databases, external or internal, is not intuitively easy. There is immense literature on database searching attesting to this inconvenient fact. In the welter of publicity during the last several years about the Internet, it is easy to overlook the fact that online database searching goes back three decades and that, while the quantity of material online has mushroomed, the quality of the tools and techniques has changed very little in more than a quarter century. Teaching users how to use database systems effectively is just as mandatory now as it was in 1971 when the world of online databases blossomed (Koenig, 1992).

Teach Database Mining

The use of tools for database mining and manipulation is an area that is particularly nonintuitive. Effective database mining simply will not happen without training.

Hunting

Train Users on the Use of Current Awareness Services

Just like doing an online search, setting up a good profile for a current awareness service, despite what vendors will say, is not easy or intuitive. It requires skill and experience to design a good profile.

Over time, people's interests and responsibilities tend to diverge from these profiles. Profiles need to be updated and maintained. The best way to accomplish this is to set up a procedure whereby an information professional (distinct from an IT professional) periodically makes an appointment with key employees to lead them through an information-requirement determinations interview and update their profile. If users are left to their own devices, profiles seldom are updated since there is no triggering event as the profiles gradually become less relevant. In addition, the revisions will be more effective if an experienced database searcher takes part.

Harness and Hypothesize

Teach the Use of Groupware

Even systems that are designed for easy use are not as simple as they are indicated to be, and people are very reluctant to admit their lack of knowledge. Whether the software in question consists of search engines, word processing, statistical packages, or groupware, there is a consistent set of findings to prove that most users learn only the basic functionalities and their skills plateau after that. With a bit of education, including refresher training, users can make much more effective use of their tools.

THINK IN TERMS OF COACHING

Although the specific teachings of our education and training are beyond the scope of this chapter, and indeed comprise a whole field unto itself, the point needs to be raised here that, in so far as practicable, user education and training for busy professionals should be personal and one-on-one. That is, one should consider and design user education and training as a method of coaching. The most successful KM implementations, a classic example being British Petroleum's virtual teamwork program (Davenport and Prusak, 1998), have been successful because they designed and thought of their user education and training program as coaching.

Conclusion

Inadequate user training and education is by far the most prevalent cause for failure in KM, and it is an easily preventable problem.

The key lessons are:

- *Design the training and user education program first.* The first order effect of this strategy is that it directly addresses the principal reason for KM implementation failure, and the second order effect is that it focuses attention on the "why" of KM and the cultural changes that need to be accomplished.

- *Train users for directed information and knowledge search (and give them good support).* If users fail to do this efficiently, they can squander their information search time up to the 20 to 25 percent satisficing point, and they have inadequate time left for serendipity and browsing for which they need a supportive corporate culture, and more training and user education.

- *Call it and think of it as "coaching," not user training or education.* Not only do users respond better, but it puts the "coaches" in the right frame of mind, emphasizing that the interaction is, or should be, more personal and one-on-one, rather than classroom training and education. It should be an interactive process, not passive.

References

Davenport, Thomas H. and Prusak, Lawrence. 1998. *Working Knowledge*, Boston, MA, Harvard Business School Press.

Hansen, Morten T., Nohria, Nitin, and Thomas Tierney. March-April, 1999. "What's your strategy for managing knowledge?" *Harvard Business Review* 77 (2): 106–116.

Koenig, Michael E. D. 1990. "Information services and downstream productivity," *The Annual Review of Information Science and Technology*, vol. 25, Williams, M. E., ed., New York, Elsevier.

Koenig, Michael E. D. 1992. "The information environment and the productivity of research," *Recent Advances in Chemical Information*, Collier, H., ed., London, Royal Society of Chemistry. Reprinted in *Information Culture and Business Performance*, (Information Strategy, Report 2, prepared for the British Library by Hertis Information and Research), Grimshaw, A., ed., Hatfield, Hertfordshire, U.K., University of Hertfordshire Press, 1995.

KPMG Consulting. 2000. Knowledge Management Research report, London, New York.

CHAPTER 30

Training and Education in Knowledge Management

T. Kanti Srikantaiah, Dominican University

BACKGROUND

Knowledge management is currently a hot topic. Training in KM can mean different things to different people as witnessed on search engines (for example, Google). To see the diversity of what is meant by KM, simply key in the phrase "knowledge management" on a search engine, such as Google. The number and diversity of hits are almost staggering. A close examination of the relevant hits indicates the interdisciplinary and fluid state of KM. This also has resulted in various definitions of KM, depending on one's perspective. Training for KM exists at both individual and organization levels, geared for both experienced KM practitioners and novices who wish to gain a better understanding of the field.

The concept of KM has been interpreted in various ways to meet the needs and purposes of professionals in the field. Since KM has emerged as a new field in business consulting, KM experts have defined the field in many ways. It can be simply defined as the use of total knowledge assets—both explicit and tacit—in an organization, in terms of processes, products, services, information repositories, customers, and personnel. *Explicit knowledge* refers to what has been documented and available to everyone. *Tacit knowledge* refers to what an individual holds in his/her possession. Knowledge resides in individuals, their conversations, internal records, external publications, data warehouses and databases, best practices, and on intranets. Therefore, KM is the result of information products, information management, the experience and skills of staff, and organizational culture. Knowledge management is about connecting people for sharing information and knowledge, experiences, concepts, best practices, and values.

Knowledge management training is offered worldwide by a wide variety of organizations. They include academic institutions, software vendors, consulting firms, and professional organizations. The participants might include: students on the academic campus, practitioners in the field, senior management, IT professionals, information management professionals, and learning organization specialists. One can enhance KM learning through participating in listservs and online forums, and keeping up with the professional literature that has exploded in the form of books, articles, Web sites, and a great number of case studies.

Academic Programs

Unlike many other disciplines that originated in the academic environment and then went outside for practical applications, KM originated in practical applications, mainly in the private sector and particularly among consulting firms. This origin among consulting firms almost immediately provided KM with a relatively theoretical underpinning. Consulting firms like to start at the top of organizations and sell down. To do that, a high-level value proposition, a theoretical underpinning, is needed. That made it easy for academic institutions to initiate programs that train in the area of KM. In academic institutions, training in KM was developed at various levels: academic degree programs, concentration in KM in degree programs, certificate programs, continuing education programs, workshops, and seminars.

Today, academic institutions throughout the world offer training in KM. This training is centered around three central themes: learning organizations, information repositories, and technology.

Graduate Degree Programs

Curricula in KM for graduate programs can vary widely depending on the focus of the training and the school that administers it. A review of the graduate degree programs that offer a more rigorous and longer term commitment indicates that three schools dominate in KM training: library and information science schools, engineering and computer science schools, and business schools.

Library and information science schools regard KM as an extension of information management where the basic premises revolve around identifying information needs, locating information sources, selecting information sources, organizing information, developing taxonomies and classification schemes, and disseminating information. They are primarily concerned with textual (semistructured) data and information; secondarily, with structured information; and only marginally with tacit information.

Engineering and computer science schools train KM specialists with an emphasis on technology (especially software). Engineering schools view KM through IT and computer science. They train individuals in coding techniques, networks, and technology application packages, and cover knowledge production, acquisition, and storage and dissemination.

Business schools emphasize organizational analysis and design, and organization learning aspects, in their KM training. In some cases, there is a management information systems (MIS) emphasis. Some business schools also offer executive management training in KM.

Obviously, the focus of the curricula in these schools is targeted to the constituency. There are also academic campuses that specialize in providing KM training in sector-based training, such as health sciences.

Curricula for the Graduate Degree

Which courses should be included in the curriculum for a graduate degree in KM? An analysis of the three degree programs provided varied results.

The School of Library and Information Science at Kent State University administers a Master's of Science in KM as part of an interdisciplinary Information Architecture and Knowledge Management Program (IAKM). To complete the program, the student must complete an eight-core course module consisting of: Information Architecture and Knowledge Management I, Information Architecture and Knowledge Management II, Information Design in the Digital Age, Structure of Computer Science, Information Technologies, Strategic Information Management, and Economics of Information. The core also includes one of the following courses: Quantitative Methods in Business Administration I, Quantitative Methods in Business Administration II, Research Methods in Communication, Research Methods in Mass Communication, or Research for Decision Making in Libraries and Information Centers. The remaining seven courses are to be selected from the other IAKM areas—Information Architecture and Information Use. A thesis or project is also required for completion of the program. A total of 48 credit hours provides a rigorous and concentrated KM program. The emphasis is on training information professionals.

George Washington University's curriculum has been designed around four major pillars of KM: leadership/management, technology, organizational, and behavioral. The programs are system oriented with the focus on KM technology in organizations and producing KM engineers. The university offers two important degree programs with a concentration in KM, the MEM and MS. Both programs require many of the same courses: The Management of Technical Organizations, Survey of Finance and Engineering Economics, Elements of Problem Solving and Decision Making for Managers, and Systems Engineering I. A concentration in KM includes the following courses: Knowledge Management I; Leadership and Management; The Learning Enterprise; Knowledgeware Technologies; Knowledge Management: Organization and Processes; and Knowledge Management II. After completion of these courses, students can select from a list of approved elective courses. The emphasis is on training KM engineers.

Since fall 2002, Dominican University has offered a master's program in KM. A total of 39 credit hours must be completed to obtain the degree. The program has two tracks: one with an emphasis on management systems and computer information systems and the other with an emphasis on information science. Both tracks share common core courses, which include: Organization of Knowledge, Management Information Systems, Information Policy, Organizational Analysis and Design, Knowledge Technologies, Knowledge Management, and a capstone course/practicum. If the student is following the management systems track, three additional core courses are required: Management Computer Programming I, Accounting, and Financial Management. If the student is following the information science track, two other core courses are required: Database Management and Information Systems Analysis and Design. Then, students can take courses from an approved list of electives. The emphasis is on training information professionals.

Certificate Programs and Workshops

Certificate programs are short-term, catering to professionals to improve their understanding of KM. To obtain a certificate in KM, the universities have different policies. Typically, four three-credit courses are required for obtaining the certificate.

Workshops usually consist of one or two days, occasionally longer, and are very popular on campuses. Sometimes they are customized for specifically targeted audiences. They offer exposure to, and understanding of, the field of KM sufficient enough to pursue the field further. Many campuses use workshops to market their KM degree and certificate programs. In general, these workshops provide CEUs for participants.

Campuses also arrange seminars, manage KM roundtables, and arrange distinguished lectures by well-known KM practitioners to draw attention to their KM programs.

Study of Sample Programs

Three KM-related programs and offerings from academic programs will be discussed here: one from the engineering perspective, George Washington University; one from the library and information science perspective, Dominican University; and one from the management perspective, George Mason University (GMU). A closer look at the curricula of these academic institutions reveals a great deal of diversity.

George Washington University, located in Washington DC, trains KM specialists in three tiers. One is a graduate certificate program in KM upon the completion of six graduate-level courses designed to cover the theory, principles, practices, strategies, processes, tools, and technologies associated with KM. This university also manages a KM roundtable, arranges professional presentations, and has an active Web site. Upon completion of the KM certificate program, a student can continue for a master's degree with a concentration in KM through one of two degree programs: Master's of Engineering Management (MEM) or Master's of Science (MS). Obviously, the training concentrates on the engineering side. The list of courses, concentrations, and other details can be obtained by consulting: http://www.gwu.edu/~mastergw/programs/KM/index.html

Dominican University, located in River Forest, Illinois, offers a certificate program upon the completion of four graduate courses, two in the area of library and information science and two in the area of business and computer science. Dominican University also offers several one- and two-day KM workshops and arranges guest speakers in KM. Since September 2002, this university has been offering a master's degree program in KM. The training emphasis is geared toward information professionals. Further information can be obtained by consulting: http://www.dom.edu

The third example of a KM program is offered at the International Center for Applied Studies in Information Technology (ICASIT) at GMU. This program focuses its efforts on helping organizations understand and implement KM processes. The primary focus is on policy issues that lead to leveraging information technology. The ICASIT offers resources to teach KM courses in degree programs and also is very active in managing a KM roundtable, arranging presentations, and maintaining an active KM Web site with links to many KM activities. An excellent and interesting paper is available through the ICASIT in the KM training area ("A University Based Approach to the Diffusion of Knowledge Management Concepts and Practice," by Stephen Ruth, Jeffrey Theobald, and Virgil Frizzell). This paper addresses the diffusion of KM concepts, principles, and cases into university courses. The faculty is affiliated with the School of Public Policy. For more information, consult: http://www.icasit.org/index.html

There is also sector-specific KM training available on academic campuses. For example, the University of California at San Francisco has a Center for Knowledge Management. It advances healthcare research and instruction through the education, development and organization, and presentation and dissemination of the World's Health Sciences Knowledge Base. For more information, consult: http://www.ckm.ucsf.edu

Peter Gray (pgray@business.queensu.ca) at the Queens University School of Business in Canada has compiled a list of 25 academic institutions that offer courses in organizational learning and/or KM. These include undergraduate, M.S., M.B.A., and Ph.D. courses from business schools, library/information science schools, computer science schools, and certificate programs. Further details on the university, course titles, course outlines, course syllabi, and the course instructors and audience can be obtained by consulting: http://qlink.queensu.ca/~8phg/KMS_Courses.htm

A modified version, listing KM degree programs and other training opportunities that are available on academic campuses, is provided in Table 30.1. Since Peter Gray's compilation is superb in accessing relevant information, the Queens University Web site is referred to in the table for many academic institutions.

NONACADEMIC PROGRAMS

Nonacademic programs include training offered by professional organizations, consulting firms, and software vendors.

There are various enterprises offering KM training in the form of training sessions, workshops at conferences, exclusive workshops, and short courses.

Table 30.1   A modified version of knowledge management degree programs and other training opportunities available on academic campuses.

Institution	Course Number	Course Description	Course Term	Instructor/ Author	URL
American University	MGMT.656. 001B	Business Applications of Knowledge Management	Fall 2000	F. D. Tuggle	http://qlink.qu eensu.ca/~8ph g/SyllabusF00 .doc
Aston University	M739	Knowledge and Process Management		J. S. Edwards	http://qlink.qu eensu.ca/~8ph g/Edwards.doc
California Polytechnic State	CPE/CSC 580	Knowledge Management	Spring 2001	F. J. Kurfess	http://www.cs c.calpoly.edu/ ~fkurfess/Cou rses/CSC-580/S01/Sylla bus.html
Canberra Institute of Technology					http://www.cit .act.edu.au/ welcome/ programs/hb/ hb-61.php3
Dominican University Graduate School of Library Science	LIS 880	Knowledge Management	Fall 2001	K. Srikantaiah	http://qlink.qu eensu.ca/~8ph g/LIS880Sylla bus.doc
George Mason University	MIS 792	Leveraging Information Technology: Knowledge Management	Fall 1998	S. Ruth	http://www.ica sit.org/classes/ mis792fall98/s yllabus.htm
George Washington University	EMSE 270	Knowledge Management I		M. Stankosky	http://km.gwu. edu/km/KM bar.cfm?addr= http://www.em se.gwu.edu/e mse/program/ masters/km. html
George Washington University	HRD 290	Organizational Learning	Spring 2001	A. Casey	http://qlink.qu eensu.ca/~8ph g/HRD290syl. 2001.doc
George Washington University	HRD 381	Adult Learning: Theory, Research, Practice	Fall 2001	C. Kayes	http://qlink.qu eensu.ca/~8ph g/HRD380 syllabus.pdf

Institution	Course Number	Course Description	Course Term	Instructor/ Author	URL
Georgia State University	DSC 8030/ CIS 8260	Knowledge Management	Fall 2001	S. Samaddar	http://www.gsu.edu/~dsc-sss/teachung.dsc_8030/intro.htm
Kent State University	IAKM 60001 & IAKM 60002	Foundations of Information Architecture and Knowledge Management			http://iakm.kent.edu/km.html
Knowledge Management Consortium International		Certified Knowledge and Innovation Manager (CKIM) Program	September 2001	M. McElroy	http://qlink.queensu.ca/~8phg/CKIMAgenda092401v.6.PDF
Lancaster University		Organizational Learning and Knowledge Management	May/June 2001	M. Easterby-Smith	http://qlink.queensu.ca/~8phg/OLKM2001.doc
Lotus Institute		Knowledge Management and Collaborative Technologies		M. Zack/ M. Serino	http://www.lotus.com/services/institute.nsf/550137bfe37d25a18525653a005e8462/000021ca
McMaster University	P727	Knowledge Management	Fall 2001	N. Bontis	http://qlink.queensu.ca/~8phg/BontisOutline.pdf
Monash University	IMS5027	Knowledge Management	Semester 2001	F. Burstein	http://qlink.queensu.ca/~8phg/MonashKM_syllabus2001.pdf
National Defense University		Knowledge Management: Leveraging Intellectual Resources			http://qlink.queensu.ca/~8phg/KNOWLEDGEMANAGEMENTSyllabus.doc
North Carolina State	Bus 590Z	Knowledge Management	Fall 2001	I. Eriksson	http://www4.ncsu.edu/~iverikss.F01GradSyl.doc

Institution	Course Number	Course Description	Course Term	Instructor/ Author	URL
North Carolina State	Distance Education	Knowledge Management	Fall 2001	I. Eriksson	http://www4.ncsu.edu/~iverikss.F01TUCSsyl.doc
Norwegian University of Science	IT-385	Information and Knowledge Management	Fall 2001	M. Dinvitini	http://www.idi.ntnu.no/emner/mnfit385/pensumliste.html
Queens University School of Business	COMM 397	Knowledge Management Systems	Winter 2001	P. Gray	http://qlink.queensu.ca/~8phg/Syllabusfor397.doc
Royal Roads University	KM 510	Knowledge Management Strategies of the Global Business Environment			http://www.royalroads.ca/ste/km/courses.htm#km510
Rutgers University School of Communication, Information, and Library Studies	LIS574	Knowledge Management in Organizations	Fall 2001	C. McInerney	http://qlink.queensu.ca/~8phg/LIS574KnowledgeManagementinOrganizations.htm
Stanford Graduate School of Business	R398	Knowledge Management	Winter 2001	K. Klein	http://www.bsos.umd.edu/psyc/faculty/kklein/knowledgemgtsyllabus.html
Temple University	MIS 594	Knowledge Management Systems in E-Business	Fall 2000	R. Patnayakuni	http://qlink.queensu.ca/~8phg/PatnayakuniSyllabus.rtf
University of Capetown Graduate School of Business		Knowledge Management		K. April/ C. Gorelick	http://qlink.queensu.ca/~8phg/KMCourseOutline.doc
University of Colorado, Denver	ISMG 6440	Knowledge Management	Fall 2000	S. Walczak	http://carbon.cudenver.edu/~swalczak/ISMG6440F00.html

Institution	Course Number	Course Description	Course Term	Instructor/ Author	URL
University of Denver Library Information Science Program	LIS 4201	Knowledge Management	Winter 2001	J. Twining	http://www.du .edu/~jtwin ing/LIS4201/
University of Maryland, College Park	BMGT 305	Knowledge Management	Spring 2002	C. . Weatherford	http://www.ra venrocks.com/ courses.html# knowledge mgmt
University of Melbourne	615-650	Information Management - Competitive Intelligence	February+ 2000	M. Sandow-Quirk	http://qlink.qu eensu.ca/~8ph g/650guide00 1.doc
University of Minnesota	IDSC 6471	Knowledge Management		P. Johnson	http://ids.csom /umn.edu/MB A.htm http://ids.csom /umn.edu/ faculty.asp? person=Paul
University of Missouri	HSM 478	Knowledge Management in Health Care	Fall 2001	J. W. Hales	http://www.h mi.missouri.ed u/Course_Mat erials/Resident ial_Informatic s/semesters/
University of Oklahoma, Norman	In design		Fall 2002		http://www.ou .edu/cas/slis/
University of Technology, Sydney	MC53/MC58	Knowledge Management		E. Tsui	http://qlink.qu eensu.ca/~8ph g/Tsui.htm
University of Texas, Austin	MIS 381N.7	Information and Knowledge Management	Spring 2001	R. McDaniel, Jr.	http://www.bu s.utexas.edu/d ept/msis/cours es/Syllabi_Sp g2001/mis/gra d/
Victoria University, Wellington	MIM 503	Knowledge Management		D. Pauleen	http://qlink.qu eensu.ca/~8ph g/PauleenOutl ine.doc

They are less focused on the theoretical considerations and concentrate on the organizational and business aspects of KM, targeting professionals working in the field. So far, there does not seem to be one universally acceptable accrediting body recognizing these training programs. Some efforts in KM certification are in progress based on ISO and ANSI standards. The Knowledge Management Certification Board (KMCB) is one such body involved in the accreditation of KM programs. It is difficult to evaluate all the training modules available in KM because there is a wide range of KM instructional resources currently available that attract private sector professionals; government workers; sector specialists; academicians; and undergraduate, graduate, and post-graduate students. The coverage of KM in these training modules varies considerably from one to another and, so far, there is no standardization.

Some professional organizations conduct frequent seminars and workshops in KM, often in conjunction with their annual conferences. Several of these organizations follow:

- Special Libraries Association (SLA)
- The Conference Board (usually one East Coast and one West Coast conference each year)
- American Society for Information Science and Technology (ASIST)
- Association for Information and Image Management (AIIM)
- Association for Computing Machinery (ACM) (holds seminars and workshops through one of its important SIGs)
- American Productivity and Quality Center (APQC) (conducts a great deal of research and offers workshops and training on benchmarking)
- Association of Special Libraries and Information Bureau (ASLIB) in the U.K.

A wide variety of workshops and seminars are available to individuals and organizations eager to learn about KM. Typically, KM workshops are sponsored by professional organizations that serve KM communities. The Knowledge Management Professional Society (KMPro), eKnowledge Center, and the Knowledge Management Consortium International (KMCI) are examples of KM bodies promoting KM accreditation and training. Professional organizations offer KM training as separate workshops or attached to their annual and midyear conferences. For instance, the ASIST offers KM workshops during its annual conferences, and one year had a conference theme on KM. Similarly, the SLA, the American Records Management Association, and ACM offer KM training through workshops and other means. High-level conferences are offered by organizations like the Conference Board and APQC. Some conferences are hosted by for-profit organizations, such as Information Today, Inc., publisher of *KM World* and organizer of the conference of the same name.

Workshops and seminars come in many shapes and sizes and are designed for people of all roles and disciplines, including knowledge workers, knowledge managers, knowledge leaders, and enterprise-level leaders. They are designed to bring people up to speed fast so they can participate in KM initiatives in their organization. Some workshops are basic introductions to the field and require no previous exposure to KM; others are more advanced and are designed for experienced KM practitioners who wish to broaden their understanding of the field. Some workshops are designed for individual enrichment; others are designed to market KM to the entire organization. Workshops typically range from half-day to five-day intensive sessions. They are generally face-to-face meetings of individuals at various locations. Consulting firms offer workshops at client sites for the entire organization. The workshop fees are generally on the high side. Similarly, there are many software vendors (such as Microsoft, IBM, Netscape, and other KM software vendors) who offer training once their systems are implemented in organizations. Knowledge management is an important business activity, a major product area, of consulting firms. They work with clients to help them understand their KM needs and provide in-house training.

Knowledge management activity has spread quickly in most organizations dealing with information management and technology. The seminars offered by various organizations and titles reflect the diversity of KM. For example, the title of some recent KM seminars include:

- The Transfer of Knowledge and Best Practices
- Benchmarking: An Executive Overview
- Designing a Knowledge Infrastructure
- Knowledge Discovery, Capture, and Creation
- Boosting Collective IQ
- Competitive Intelligence
- Intellectual Capital
- Measuring Knowledge
- Knowledge Management and eCommerce

In a typical introductory course on KM, the topics should be well balanced to provide an overview of the KM field, which later may be built upon by taking more specifically focused courses. For example, at Dominican University, the introductory course on KM exposes students to all areas of KM in general, which includes:

- KM Overview
- Definitions, Concepts, and Evolution (Antecedents of KM)
- KM Resources
- Trends in Organizations
- KM Domains
- Discussion of Various Sectors, Such as Health, Legal, Business and Finance, Industry, Government, and Such
- KM as Business Strategy
- Knowledge Representation and Database Design
- KM Systems
- Systems Analysis and Design, Development and Implementation
- Case Studies in KM
- KM Projects
- KM in the For-Profit Sector
- Business and Private Enterprises
- KM in the Not-for-Profit Sector
- Government, Academic Institutions, Religious Institutions, and Others
- KM and Ethics
- Business Ethics
- Impact of eCommerce on KM
- B2B
- B2C
- KM Software Tools
- Application Packages
- Knowledge Ecology
- KM Policies
- KM Architecture and Such
- Metrics and Evaluation in KM
- ROI for KM Implementations

This course is designed from the perspective of the information professional. It can be modified to meet the business or technology perspective.

CONCLUSION

We have seen a rapid growth in KM training over the last five to six years, with more and more academic institutions initiating KM certificate and degree programs. There are also concentration studies and sector-based KM training available, particularly in the health sector. Today, there are extensive KM training opportunities available through professional organizations and for-profit and not-for-profit organizations.

As the field of KM is absorbing the concepts of content management and taxonomies, the library and information science schools and programs are taking a greater initiative in KM training. In the academic environment, it is interesting to note that if the academic campus has a library and information science school (only 56 accredited schools in the U.S. do), the KM program will typically start at that school with an interdisciplinary arrangement. Otherwise, the KM program will be absorbed by the business schools and, in special cases, by the engineering schools.

CHAPTER 31

Learning and the Knowledge Worker

David H. Bennet, Mountain Quest Institute

This chapter addresses the relationships among three topics of current interest that are usually addressed separately: KM, learning, and the knowledge worker. When considered together, these three areas form a powerful force for improving organizational performance and accelerating the career growth of individuals who work primarily with knowledge.

There is considerable literature in each of these three areas. The recent attention given to KM has resulted in the recognition of the value of knowledge in improving organizational performance. Learning, both organizational and individual, has seen a resurgence in popularity, driven by the accelerating pace of market changes, the Internet, the opportunities offered by virtual learning, and books such as *The Fifth Discipline: The Art and Practice of the Learning Organization* (Senge, 1990). The knowledge worker is now recognized as a major part of the workforce; that is, those workers that use their experience, education, and mental capacity to deal with the problems and opportunities arising from complexity, uncertainty, and rapid change. Understanding complexity demands knowledge. Making decisions under conditions of uncertainty requires a KM approach to ensure organizational agility and knowledge sharing. Rapid change places high priority on learning and flexibility. Many companies living on the forefront of the emerging landscape have recognized the importance of these three factors. Each of these factors is interdependent with the other, and they are all consistent and synergistic with each other. In a culture that needs workforce competency and empowerment, the growth of KM provides a foundation to leverage and accelerate the improvement of both learning and knowledge worker performance.

Knowledge management is a systematic approach to getting an organization to make the best possible use of knowledge in implementing its mission. Learning, individual and organizational, serves to keep knowledge workers and their organization up to date with changes in the external environment while creating energy, enthusiasm, flexibility, and collaboration among knowledge workers. It is with the knowledge worker that both innovation and action occur. Working in a knowledge-centric and learning culture, knowledge workers, individually and in groups, can create, leverage, and apply knowledge to meet changing needs. Knowledge management provides the emphasis, the enabling information technology, the processes, and the attention to help knowledge workers learn, collaborate, and implement the four major processes—creativity, problem solving, decision making, and taking action. Conversely, knowledge workers can support the objectives of KM and actively increase their own performance by sharing their knowledge and facilitating organizational learning.

It is clear that each of these three aspects of the knowledge organization both supports and needs the other two. The challenge is to bring learning into the knowledge organization and—using the gains that KM and learning techniques can provide—assist those knowledge workers who recognize the need and payoff from managing their own knowledge. Since knowledge management is the foundation of this book, this chapter focuses on learning and the learning processes that help knowledge workers keep up with the fast changing world. It also provides stories of successes.

The Changing World

The past several decades have led to two major changes in the working world. The first is a significant increase in the number of people in the workforce that spend most of their time perceiving, creating, thinking, and acting on data, information, and knowledge. To distinguish them from laborers, Peter Drucker tagged these individuals as knowledge workers (Drucker, 1989). A second major trend is the nature of the environment in which both business and governance is conducted. The landscape may be described as one composed of an increasing rate of change, greater uncertainty in predicting future events, and massive complexity of our systems. Confusion, ambiguity, and anxiety are often direct consequences of this landscape. These trends are expected to continue, and place additional burdens on knowledge workers and organizations in the future.

These two trends, together with their consequences, are putting pressure on leading edge organizations to reflect on their structure and take action to undergo a transformation that will permit them to work more effectively within their environment. Examples of such actions are the recent popularity of total quality management, the transfer of best practices, the rapidly rising interest in KM and organizational learning, and the search for new leadership characteristics and models. The common themes underlying the current and future challenges can be understood as the need for the workforce to possess the *knowledge* to respond effectively and the critical role of *learning* to ensure that knowledge keeps up with the rapidly changing environment.

SOME BASELINE DEFINITIONS

We understand *knowledge* to be the human capacity (potential and actual) to take effective action in varied and uncertain situations. Knowledge is tied to action because it is only through action that changes can occur and results can be obtained. Tying knowledge to action recognizes the importance of tacit and implicit capabilities to take actions. Knowledge also consists of facts, concepts, principles, laws, causal relationships, insights, judgments, intuition, and feelings. It produces understanding and meaning to a situation, often considered as know-how and know-why.

Learning is considered to be the creation and acquisition of knowledge, both potential and actual. Thus, learning and knowledge are closely related but not identical. Learning is a process that creates new meaning from experience and new capabilities for action. Knowledge may be a process (taking action) or an asset (capacity) residing in the minds of knowledge workers. Often, we do not know what we know until we say or do something. Knowledge, like memory, is often created and brought forth from the unconscious mind when we need it.

A *knowledge-centric organization* is one in which knowledge is recognized as a key success factor and is systematically managed through KM best practices. When maximum synergy exists between individuals in the workforce and KM, the organization amplifies its resource effectiveness, thereby providing sustainable competitive advantage and performance excellence. For this to occur, the organization must be able to sustain a dynamic balance wherein the individual and the KM system continuously adapt to each other through cultural expectations, flexibility, and empathy. By *culture*, it is meant the set of beliefs of employees about how the work should be done and what behavior is expected. There are things that the worker can learn, know, and do that will significantly impact organizational learning and performance. At the same time, there are many things the organization can do to support and help their knowledge workers perform more effectively. Both parties will benefit from continuous collaboration and support. As the environment becomes turbulent, nonlinear, and complex, this relationship between knowledge workers and their organization takes on even more importance. Over the past decade, KM has grown up and is now a significant part of many knowledge organizations. The partnership of KM, learning, and the knowledge worker is coming into its own, as we will demonstrate in several examples.

Using these concepts to build a common framework for understanding, there are a number of ways that individuals can learn and some areas that are vital to the success of organizations at the forefront of this new world. We will explore the mutual interdependence between learning and the knowledge worker through a discussion of e-learning, action learning, and accelerated learning. The reader interested in learning and adult performance should consider the following: Druckman and Bjork, 1994; Merriam and Caffarella, 1999; Knowles et al., 1998; and Kolb, 1984.

KNOWLEDGE WORKERS

Knowledge workers do not always work in organizations that recognize the value of knowledge and have processes and technology that support and leverage the creation and application of it. Often, organizations need to be made aware that their performance is determined by the day-to-day actions of all employees. If a clear line of sight from these actions to the mission and purpose of the firm can be made visible, the value and contribution of knowledge workers can be understood. This line of sight is best seen as the interplay between KM, learning, and knowledge workers. Knowledge workers take action because someone makes a decision to do so. That decision, in turn, is the result of some existing situation that needs to be changed. For nontrivial situations, problem solving can become challenging and generate alternative options often as the result of creative thinking and innovative ways of viewing a situation. Knowledge management provides the environment, learning keeps the knowledge up to date, and the knowledge worker both creates and acts on that knowledge.

There are four major processes used in knowledge organizations: creating ideas, solving problems, making decisions, and taking effective actions. Each of these processes can be implemented by an individual knowledge worker or by a team of workers. Each process presents an opportunity for knowledge workers to learn and increase both their knowledge and experience. Teams are particularly effective as learning experiences because many ideas and viewpoints are presented, and dialogue and discussion can help clarify questions and misunderstandings that participants may have, often leading to "a-ha experiences." To get the maximum learning from team meetings, the knowledge worker can take a number of actions. These actions include: keeping an open mind, not taking sides quickly, and always remembering that knowledge is never absolute. The efficacy of knowledge depends on its situational context and the future flow of events. The former is never completely known and the latter is often contingent upon many unpredictable interactions.

The knowledge worker who actively listens and reflects on multiple views will not only achieve understanding and insights that leverage and modulate his/her own knowledge but also develop an objective, systems-oriented perspective that significantly contributes to problem solving and cognitive growth. If the team is interdisciplinary, the awareness and appreciation of other modes of thinking and fields of learning will significantly enhance the knowledge worker's ability to integrate information and balance priorities, thereby preventing the hardening of sides and viewpoints during team discussions. The ability to remain objective and be part of a discussion is a mark of leadership that helps both the knowledge worker and the organization.

Teams have proven their ability to improve decision making and enhance learning (Katzenbach and Smith, 1993). Knowledge workers can improve their learning during team problem solving and decision making by withholding their own beliefs and opinions until late in the dialogue process. A position stated quickly becomes a position defended. When this occurs, the conversation moves from open inquiry to a debate or face-saving challenge. Much learning is lost when debate replaces inquiry. Although debates can certainly be learning experiences, they are much more useful at deeper levels of thought, such as assumptions, context, patterns, relationships, and expectations of the future rather than the higher levels of beliefs, events, and opinions. Beliefs, events, and opinions are surface phenomena that usually represent information, not knowledge. Keeping group discussions at deeper levels requires an open and supportive organizational culture (KM) and continuous team-member attention to learning (Bennet, 1997).

Physical environment, culture, and interpersonal relationships must be taken into account for a team to achieve learning and high performance. The use of groupware, such as whiteboards and computer systems that allow input from every team member and real-time integration and display of ideas, can be very helpful. The physical layout of working spaces also influences the way knowledge workers think and feel during meetings. Good facilitation is essential for productive and open communication among diverse knowledge workers. Individual empowerment of team members gives them confidence and strength of resources. Many of the KM objectives, such as knowledge sharing, knowledge repositories, knowledge systems, storytelling, knowledge flow channels, and communities of practice provide strong support for team performance and individual learning.

Classical research in adult learning has two primary foundations: Malcolm Knowles (1998) research in adult learning and David Kolb's (1984) research in experiential learning. Knowles identifies the conditions in which adults learn best and the human characteristics that drive those conditions. For example, adults are usually driven by real-world problems and learn best from solving problems that are directly related to their current work. They are self-directed and each individual, usually without conscious awareness, has developed a way of learning that is unique and maximizes his/her ability to take in information and create understanding. Although there are many individual learning "styles," a given worker will usually have one particular style that is most effective and most personally satisfying. A knowledge worker who takes time to "learn how to learn" will be able to learn via several styles. Since much learning takes place in situations that are not within the learner's control, being able to learn through images, lectures, reading, dialogue, debate, computers, and so forth will be very helpful over the long term.

Often team or group learning can be very effective if it is planned and run by an experienced leader or facilitator. Learning does not automatically occur among team members simply because they are talking to each other. Simulations can be very effective learning tools for individuals and for teams. Even though their initial development may be expensive, once developed, simulations are very economical for large numbers of learners. Systems Dynamic modeling is one example of coupling groups of managers and computer modeling to clarify issues and help knowledge workers make sense of their organization's behavior and take any necessary corrective actions (Vennix, 1996).

Another challenge for the learning knowledge worker is the increasing number of situations in which learning can take place. As the Internet grows, there will be more learning through browsers, chat rooms, and communities of practice. Normal classroom education will still count, as will conferences, retreats, and other off-site experiences. An often neglected, yet most important source of learning, is the casual conversation that occurs around the coffee pot. An informal question-and-answer exchange concerning issues at work between two colleagues of differing experiences can lead to significant growth in the knowledge of both workers. Organizations that are aware of these gains make special efforts to design their facilities and the knowledge workers' spaces so that they may take advantage of these natural cross-fertilizing opportunities. They also should provide the information technology that supports learning and knowledge sharing. For a good review of IT in support of collaboration see Coleman (1997). While no one can "order" a knowledge worker to learn or share knowledge, the smart organizations nurture and create environments within which learning and sharing occur naturally. We will now look at several of the main trends and methods of learning, particularly those appropriate for the knowledge worker.

E-LEARNING

According to Rosenberg, e-learning refers to the use of Internet technologies to provide many types of solutions to enhance knowledge and performance (Rosenberg, 2001). Note that this definition focuses on the Internet but allows a wide variety of possibilities for learning, creating, and changing knowledge. The advantages of e-learning include reduced cost and time of both instructors and students. Once an e-learning course has been developed, it can be given to a large number of people with minimum expenses. The material can be updated at one time and all students can quickly be notified. Changes and new ideas can be easily inserted into the material. Discussion groups operating in conjunction with e-learning courses allow students and instructors to dialogue and expand upon the material as needed. The main thing missing is the interpersonal interactions that allow in-depth exchange of ideas and insights through facial and other nonverbal communications. While e-learning may not work for learning deep knowledge about complex subjects, it is well structured for many knowledge worker needs.

A good example of e-learning comes from the Department of the Navy. Early in their implementation of KM, the Department of the Navy realized it could not become a knowledge-centric organization without being a learning organization. They also realized that when they coupled the fast pace of change with a geographically dispersed, rotating workforce, e-learning had to become a necessary part of their strategy. The deputy chief of Naval Operations established a high-level taskforce to provide the tools and opportunities that would enable people to learn, grow, and develop into successful leaders who could make a difference in the Navy. In a hierarchal, military structure, direction from senior leadership is the impetus for success. This enterprise-wide effort led to a partnership between the education and information technology leaders to develop a virtual toolkit to operationalize e-learning. The toolkit provides resources and connections that form the network of education and learning in the department. In the spring of 2002, the Department of the Navy was named a "Most Admired Knowledge Enterprise," the only public-sector organization to receive this honor. Alongside such organizations as Microsoft and IBM, the Navy was specifically noted for its emphasis on organizational learning.

ACTION LEARNING

Another form of learning, known as action learning, uses a team or group to solve real, practical problems while deliberately emphasizing learning as they do. The action-learning group takes a systems approach to solutions since their actions are designed to affect all parts of the organization necessary to ensure long-term problem resolution. Thus, action learning enhances individual and group learning, facilitates organizational change, and solves real-world problems.

Action learning is a special form of team learning, problem solving, and implementation. The group has a facilitator, and learns through questioning and reflecting clarified via group dialogue. True to the concept of knowledge, an action-learning group is committed to taking action but only after considerable time is spent in understanding the problem, the situation, and the ramifications of potential actions. In effect, an action-learning group becomes a knowledge creating (learning) team. This process not only improves decision making, it also achieves buy-in by team participants and creates a learning environment within which team individuals and their organization can learn and share their own knowledge. This learning occurs when the group is open to new ideas, questions past and current assumptions, and works collaboratively toward a common interpretation of the problem based on their collective understanding and experience. The organization's role, through KM, is to provide: work spaces that are conducive to open conversation and honest inquiry, effective information technology support and information repositories, and a culture that rewards knowledge sharing.

Although the concept originated many years ago, action learning has now come to the forefront as an effective way to meet the demands of the new world (Marquardt, 1999). There are recognized successes throughout the current literature. Several years ago, a large government program in the Defense Department requested the author to lead a team to identify and evaluate the management risks that could impact program success. The program included seven organizations that had to work together; a complex parts supply chain; two refurbishment and rebuild depots; several ordering and stocking facilities; and private industry participation. Although each organization was competent and dedicated, there was inadequate coordination among the organizations and the knowledge workers had little time for learning. Also, the "not invented here" syndrome made communication difficult.

An action-learning approach was taken and nine carefully selected, highly competent team-members were chosen. The members represented all of the organizations as well as the professional experience needed to assess the problem and identify solutions. During start up, it became clear that, although the team was working well together, they were not aware of what each other's organizational problems, constraints, and true objectives were. Most important, knowledge workers in all of the organizations were not aware of the impact of their own decisions on the other organizations as the consequences of their work flowed through the enterprise. Everyone was too busy to be concerned with each other's work, resulting in each organization doing high-quality work that often created problems for the rest of the enterprise. It was a classic situation of the need to understand risk and become aware of the impact of every part of the complex flow of work on the other parts of the system—a good opportunity for an action-learning group. After reviewing and refining the team's mission, a charter was prepared, submitted to a higher authority, and quickly approved. A series of briefings allowed team members to understand the full scope of the program and the nature of the participating organizations. During this time, the members got to know each other, created their own common language, and addressed a number of basic values.

Many learning sessions on organizational structure were conducted on subjects including the nature of enterprises, systems theory, and risk management and communication. All were closely related to the problems at hand. This enabled team members to broaden their understanding of all organizations within the enterprise and to appreciate their own organization's role. As the various processes and procedures were evaluated, many suggestions and ideas were offered by members who were not participants in these processes but saw them from a new and often insightful perspective. Real learning—that is, being surprised and experiencing a leap of understanding—began after the third day. Formality drifted away and real questioning, response, and counter questioning began when the team developed their own meaning of risk and how it should be defined for their task. There were many discussions on what approach should be used to identify and map out the various risks throughout the enterprise and how to gather the desired information. These interactions were more a learning process than result producing. No one was pressured into accepting someone else's conclusions. Instead, there were many deep dives into what assumptions were behind those beliefs and conclusions. Although heated debates and strong feelings emerged, the team was able to do their own double-loop learning, without being force-fed or lectured.

The outcome of the 35 days that the team spent together was a detailed identification of the specific risk areas and the expected levels of risk, along with ideas on how these risks could be reduced and maintained in the future. A risk-interaction matrix was developed to indicate the likely impact of a negative event in one part of the enterprise on all other dependent work efforts. Such a matrix demonstrated to everyone how important it was to communicate and collaborate with other individuals and organizations that were part of the enterprise. One surprising result was the possibility of turning risk-management practices into opportunity-management practices, with the only difference being that a risk results from a potentially negative event and an opportunity results from a potentially positive event. Another benefit from the action-learning effort was the personal and professional growth that occurred within the team members. The ability to be more receptive to other viewpoints, and to discern differences and discriminate their value is a measure of personal growth. Also, the capability to reintegrate those differences, ideas, or interpretations into a cohesive, meaningful whole is a competency not often found.

Such personal development can occur when a team learns to work together, dissect, and understand major facets of the organization and then bring them back together into a complex system that produces a desired product. Put another way, their domain of action and sources of knowledge expanded as a result of solving a real world problem that was of high interest and importance to them. Not only had they made useful contacts and learned from them, they also saw the enterprise in a new light and understood their own problems in a broader context. While KM was largely unknown to the enterprise at that time, the attitudes of the senior executives and the organization's culture permitted, and even encouraged, such learning. Information technology was used to maintain a team Web site, an intranet was available throughout the enterprise, and a meeting space was found that offered the needed groupware support. However, in the end, it comes down to the human-to-human interactions and the trust and ability to listen and share understanding with each other that spurs learning and creates knowledge.

ACCELERATED LEARNING

Accelerated learning is a systematic process designed to take advantage of our brain's full capabilities through the use of findings in recent research in neuroscience. Recognizing that our brains are highly complex—with five types of memory; right and left hemispheres that specialize in different capabilities; three major parts (a brainstem, limbic, and neocortex) each with different functions; and eight intelligences (language, logic, visual-spatial, musical, kinesthetic, social, interpersonal, and naturalistic) (Gardner, 1993)—accelerated learning is an approach designed to take advantage of the whole brain's capability to learn. Briefly, the process consists of six phases: motivation, getting information, finding meaning or sense making, committing to memory, practicing what you have learned, and reflecting on how you have learned. The techniques used in each of these phases could best be considered as meta-learning since their purpose is to help one learn how to learn. Each of Gardner's eight intelligences is inherent in everyone to varying degrees, and they all can be improved through learning and practice.

While individuals can personally make good use of the ideas and practices of accelerated learning, the best learning often occurs in a low-stress, small-group environment that is positively reinforcing, with some enthusiasm and humor (Rose and Nicholl, 1997). In addition, the knowledge worker must want to learn, that is, the material must be relevant, needed, and applicable. It helps to deliberately involve as many senses as possible. Studying and exploring a problem from each of the eight intelligence areas provides viewpoints, insights, and solutions that may not otherwise surface. Another useful technique is to search for good metaphors and analogies that provide windows to better understand the problem.

The following is an example of how a small professional services firm changed itself through collaborative learning. The company, Dynamic Systems, was in the highly competitive engineering and professional services field, predominately working for the U.S. government. Dynamic Systems grew to about 120 professionals over its ten-year history but was lagging behind its competitors in the application of IT, in the ability to leverage knowledge within the company, and in applying that knowledge to provide fast, high-quality customer support. In other words, it could not use the knowledge it had to create the desired competitive edge. There was also no clear direction for company growth. This was not unusual in this industry since growth was primarily achieved by winning competitive contracts from a wide range of clients.

The company's growth had slowed and senior management recognized that technology was significantly changing the competitive landscape. It also became apparent that there were a number of much larger companies that had been able to achieve what was popularly known as "world-class" status. It was concluded that the organization needed to change within the next few years or the company could easily fall far behind its best competitors. Being a professional services firm, it was recognized that about 90 percent of its value was in the minds and behavior of its employees. Increasing that value had to come from the knowledge workers themselves. Since the employees were motivated and competent professionals, the strategy selected was to make the workforce aware of these concerns and empower them to participate and find solutions. Whatever the solution looked like, it would require employees and senior managers to change their daily actions, in other words, to learn. The tenets of both action and accelerated learning were found to work nicely with the goals of the organization.

They began by analyzing the current and anticipated environment, and identifying those world-class organizations that were demonstrating successful practices in markets similar to Dynamic Systems. Five teams were formed from volunteers throughout the company. The teams dealt with the vision, the use of technology, customer service, the bid-and-proposal process, and the employee management process. Employees from all levels of experience were encouraged to participate, as well as representatives from all departments. This ensured the diversity of thinking and encouraged cross-department communication and systems thinking. All teams were briefed and encouraged to ask questions and add ideas. Using only volunteers and keeping an open dialogue led to highly motivated teams. Charters gave the teams both freedom and empowerment. Funds were allocated and the teams were given six months to research their tasks, develop programs for achieving their objectives, brief senior management, and prepare and present a half-day learning session to every employee in the company. All team members participated in presenting the learning sessions.

As the vision team developed its ideas, they briefed the other teams in order to get feedback and receive direction in terms of the company's long-term objectives. This provided a reference point for the other teams to making sense of their research and focus their efforts. At the briefings and learning sessions, all team members participated in answering questions and generating ideas. During these discussions, care was taken to reflect on the work and its potential effect on both individual and organizational performance. This ensured understanding and buy-in for the implementation of the recommended actions. The results were later used to provide an up-to-date orientation for new employees.

Since about 35 percent of the employees had participated in the learning process, there was enough critical mass to bring the entire company into alignment. Several changes included increased training in technology, much greater use of teams and knowledge sharing, an improved process for customer support, and better customer feedback. A second round of teams were started after 18 months that included a strong effort in KM to formalize the company's internal ability to share knowledge and use technology in order to add value to customer products.

Within three years, the company growth rate went from five to 25 percent per year. There was a significant increase in profitability, a higher rate of employee satisfaction, and a significant increase in the company's market value. As in all organizations, there is never a single cause and effect between planned change and results. Many complex interdependencies are involved. However, by bringing the employees into the challenge and creating an environment in which they learned quickly and practiced what they had learned, the entire organization could work cohesively and move together. Although larger organizations would be more difficult to move, the principles of collaboration, participation, and learning are still fundamental and highly effective.

LEARNING BEYOND THE PROFESSIONAL AREA

As the world moves into the age of complexity and events become more difficult to predict, there are certain areas of knowledge that are becoming essential for career success and for maintaining organizational performance. Because technology and the pace of change will almost surely continue accelerating, successful knowledge workers must be able to learn rapidly, continuously, and flexibly to fulfill their work responsibilities and maintain employability, as well as employment. This means that they must learn how to learn in a variety of situations and in many different ways. Rarely, if ever, do we reflect on how we learn and consciously try to expand the ways we learn. Living in the world of the future, where professionals often deal with five to 10 subject areas in the course of an hour, requires the ability to communicate and share understanding with professionals from other disciplines, and make decisions and solve problems that entail multiple subjects.

Essential areas for most knowledge workers include: learning how to learn, having knowledge about knowledge, systems thinking, complexity thinking, risk management, networks, networking and relationship management, questioning, facilitation, flow, information literacy, judgment and intuition, knowing, sense making, and peripheral discipline awareness. This assumes that the knowledge worker knows his/her professional field and continuously learns to keep up with that field.

The best knowledge workers will be able to learn and apply their knowledge in collaboration with others, while simultaneously recognizing the breadth of information and knowledge needed to comprehend and resolve complex problems and situations. To be successful, they must also be able to manage knowledge in the sense of recognizing, creating, finding, and moving knowledge that is valid, useful, and applicable to the issue at hand. Beyond this, knowledge workers must have the foresight to sense their future knowledge needs and acquire that knowledge to handle challenging problems well before the problems arise. Even though they may not know the specific problems that will be faced, they should be aware of the *types* of issues and challenges that may occur. In the best case, knowledge workers should direct their learning and manage their knowledge so they are well prepared for both present and future challenges. This will be the payoff from learning how and when to learn and from treating their knowledge as a manageable asset that greatly influences career success. Since their competency is the source of the organization's performance, KM and learning become everyone's responsibility and everyone's gain. The trio is thus intertwined, and loss of any one will significantly impact the others.

REFERENCES

Bennet, David. *IPT Learning Campus: Gaining Acquisition Results Through IPTs*. Alexandria, VA: Bellwether Learning Center, 1997.

Coleman, David. *Collaborative Strategies for Corporate LANs and Intranets*. Upper Saddle River, NJ: Prentice Hall, 1997.

Drucker, Peter F. *The New Realities: In Government and Politics/In Economics and Business/In Society and World View*. New York, NY: Harper & Row Publishers, 1989.

Druckman, Daniel and Bjork, Robert A. (eds). *Learning, Remembering, Believing: Enhancing Human Performance*. Washington, DC: National Academy Press, 1994.

Gardner, Howard. *Frames of Mind: The Theory of Multiple Intelligences*, 10th Anniversary Edition. New York, NY: Basic Books, 1993.

Katzenbach, Jon R. and Smith, Douglas K. *The Wisdom of Teams: Creating the High-Performance Organization*. Boston, MA: Harvard Business School Press, 1993.

Knowles, Malcolm S., Holton III, Elwood F., and Swanson, Richard A. *The Adult Learner*. Houston, TX: Gulf Publishing Company, 1998.

Kolb, D. A. *Experiential Learning as the Source of Learning and Development*. Englewood Cliffs, NJ: Prentice-Hall, 1984.

Langer, Ellen J. *The Power of Mindfull Learning*. Reading, MA: Perseus Books, 1997.

Marquardt, Michael J. *Action Learning in Action*. Palo Alto, CA: Davis-Black Publishing, 1999.

Merriam, Sharan B. and Caffarella, Rosemary S. *Learning in Adulthood: A Comprehensive Guide*. San Francisco, CA: Jossey-Bass Publishers, 1999.

Rose, Colin and Nicholl, Malcolm J. *Accelerated Learning for the 21st Century*. New York, NY: Delacorte Press, 1997.

Rosenberg, Marc J. *e-Learning: Strategies for Delivering Knowledge in the Digital Age*. New York, NY: McGraw-Hill, 2001.

Schank, Roger C. *Designing World-Class E-Learning: How IBM, GE, Harvard Business School, & Columbia University Are Succeeding at e Learning*. New York, NY: McGraw-Hill, 2002.

Senge, P. *The Fifth Discipline: The Art & Practice of the Learning Organization*. New York, NY: Doubleday, 1990.

Vennix, Jac A. M. *Group Model Building: Facilitating Team Learning Using System Dynamics*. New York, NY: John Wiley & Sons, 1996.

CHAPTER 32

Incentives and Techniques for the Promotion of Knowledge Sharing

Ruth A. Palmquist, Dominican University

The open society, the unrestricted access to knowledge, the unplanned and uninhibited association of men for its furtherance—these are what may make a vast, complex, ever-growing, ever-changing, evermore specialized and expert technological world, nevertheless a world of human community.

J. Robert Oppenheimer, 1954

INTRODUCTION

The "uninhibited association" that Oppenheimer describes has certainly evolved from the research lab, to the factory floor, to the water cooler. The innovation he envisioned has also been found to grow and be grown by this ease of "unrestricted access to knowledge." As networks of individuals evolve, so do the number of people connected to a network and the information shared and generated. However, the capture, guided encouragement, purposeful transfer, and management of this informal information growth are of growing concern to both KM academics and practitioners (Holsthouse, 1998; Grover and Davenport, 2001). The value of creating a company or organization that "learns to innovate" has become a major priority for KM professionals.

To create this innovative mindset, shared knowledge is a key element. Learning through knowledge that is shared enables a synergy that creates new ideas, and new ideas create the necessary innovation to move an organization forward toward being more competitive and productive. Many companies and organizations, desirous of competing in a new knowledge economy, have recognized that an organizational culture of knowledge sharing is essential. But, how is the knowledge to be transferred so that it reaches other parts of the organization and how can it be used to promote innovation? Surely, such sharing of information happens easily, does it not? In fact, it does not happen easily at all. Employees must be encouraged, in many cases enabled, prodded, and cajoled to share what they know—share their intellectual capital—and they must be encouraged to learn from others within the company, as well.

Early efforts to support such sharing with automated computer-aided tools have been less than successful (McDermott, 1999). The "build it and they will come" software solutions often did not take into account the human elements intrinsic to the act of sharing. An example of this was the idea of a *knowledge warehouse*, a repository of "bright ideas" that could be contributed by anyone who had an innovative idea or practice to communicate to others. There were incentives from cash rewards to frequent flyer miles, and yet there was little activity from employees to build the warehouse. Dixon (2000), in her study of the types of transfer mechanisms that can help companies share their knowledge, found that potential contributors were troubled by this knowledge warehouse concept because the image of a warehouse is primarily that of a storage facility. The members of the organization did not see it as a "reuse environment" for knowledge, and felt little desire to contribute to something that they thought no one would use.

Dixon (2000) and others who are cited in this chapter have found that there are blocks or barriers inherent in both personal and organizational efforts toward knowledge sharing that deter this flow or sharing of knowledge. This chapter is designed to explore a few of the strategies that seem to have been effective in getting individuals to share their tacit knowledge, that is, the knowledge held in one's head but not easily articulated or made explicit.

First, some of the issues that arise within an individual that may block the impulse to share are examined. Second, several approaches that have been shown to be valuable in creating successful "sharing" experiences will be reviewed. This chapter cannot begin to cover every good idea encountered in the readings reviewed; however, it is hoped that the summary will provide some of the "lessons learned" that may be useful to those knowledge managers who have the task of building a sharing culture in their own organization.

Personal Knowledge Acquisition and Sharing

Most efforts for knowledge sharing stem either from the individual knowledge worker or from inducements created by the organization that employs the knowledge worker. Piaget (1960) and others who studied the human ability to learn were the first to formalize some of the elements essential to learning. First, he saw that the ability to bring in new information was dependent upon the ability to accommodate the new information. Second, he observed that the individual needed the right self-image skills to feel capable of learning. The two elements are inexorably intertwined. An incident that provides a challenge to learn—to accommodate something different from a currently understood "truth"—creates an impact, either positive or negative, on the self-image. If one fails to make the accommodation and then understands that failure to be a personal one, damage to the self-image may be sufficient enough to create a similar outcome when the next "new" accommodation is required.

New developments in the science of learning (Bransford et al., 2000) have introduced the notion of "active learning." This emphasizes the importance of helping people take control of their own learning experience. When individuals becomes "active" learners, they become more able to recognize when their understanding or state of knowledge is in need of additional information. The research term for this awareness is *metacognition*, which generally refers to people's ability to predict their current understanding and their ability to perform a particular task. The need to provide information to someone undertaking a new task is more complex than might be seen at first, especially as many of the knowledge sharing mechanisms to be discussed further along make little effort to tailor content to individual learning styles, even though there is recognition that such accommodation should be made. For example, the information given through the company's intranet should be in a form and structure that will be meaningful to the individual who needs it to complete a new task. Teaching methods that have evolved from such active-learning theories have stressed heavily the act of self-assessment and reflection on what has worked and what needs improving.

To follow this approach, knowledge sharing environments must take several "truths" into account. First, the individual will approach the learning activity with a preconceived notion of how the learning should proceed. If this initial understanding is not met, the information to be communicated may be completely lost to the individual. They may fail to grasp the "new" because they cannot accommodate the new with the old model they currently hold. Such models can affect and be affected by the way an individual looks at the company's structure. If that structure is replicated in an intranet, finding key information within that structure can fail if the employee's model does not match the structure provided on the intranet.

INTRANETS AND COMPANY PORTALS

Many of the knowledge sharing strategies mentioned further along in this chapter depend upon the presence of an intranet or at least a company-wide e-mail or voice-mail system. Intranets have proven currently to be strong contenders for the KM mechanism of choice. Considering both the need for contributions to such company intranets to be easy to make, and to be seen as useful to contribute to, Hall (2001) examined a variety of strategies for making the company intranet input-friendly. One suggestion was that the input be addressed to a single e-mail addressee. This would mean that the barrier to participating would be only the acquisition of one additional e-mail address. Also suggested to possibly ease the effort of contribution was to create a method of input that could mimic simple patterns of speech rather than some formal criteria that requires effort on the part of the sharer to reformat the submission into some more complicated form. This more structured approach to soliciting content can also mean that more explicit knowledge is shared rather than garnering the less formal, more socially embedded know-how of colleagues communicating with colleagues, which often takes the form of conversational exchanges rather than some form-filling effort.

Motivations for knowledge sharing to a company intranet were generally found to take the form of some type of reward. These seemed to be either explicit rewards or, less frequently, what Hall (2001) called "soft" rewards. Explicit rewards were one of the following: economic rewards took the form of access provided to additional information/knowledge; or led to some other mechanism that ensured career enhancement and security. Von Krogh and colleagues (2000) indicate that when success in a company is dependent upon expertise demonstrated and not upon the degree to which an individual actually helps others succeed, individuals tend to build up their own hegemonies of knowledge. Sharing more knowledge than is absolutely required is seen as decreasing the sharer's power and working against his/her own self-interest. Hall's (2001) list of "soft" rewards extended to things like an enhanced reputation that may come from a simple acknowledgement that a shared idea had merit or created a value-linked change. Also, the compliment of being invited to join a work group based upon a contributed good idea was found to be rewarding to the invitee even though no direct economic reward was given.

In establishing an effective intranet for knowledge sharing, the notion of critical mass is essential. This mass is usually comprised of three major components: *users* who come to the intranet for information, *content* that is more useful and more relevant than what was available before, and *utilization*. Hall (2001) reports on a study done by Cap Gemini Ernst & Young in the U.K. through Cranfield University in 1999 that found a minimum of 40 percent of the connections to the intranet need to produce some type of utilization in order for the intranet to achieve this critical mass.

Before we leave the role of the individual in knowledge sharing, an interesting book edited by T. Nishida (2000) should be mentioned in the context of creating environments where individuals feel comfortable sharing information. Nishida's contributors created an interdisciplinary study of an environment for the exchange of public opinion and aimed the effort at understanding the facilitation of knowledge networks within a community. Although their interest is clearly in creating the information technology to host such a facilitation, their research into the dynamics of collecting public opinion discussions is quite useful.

Nishida (2000), although primarily concerned about developing theoretical norms for sharing knowledge that can develop community norms and governance standards, is essentially echoing the same issues that are of concern to the KM manager. Through examining a community, Nishida (2000) found that two factors were key in preventing the sort of dynamic knowledge interaction that would be desirable in order to build communities of tolerance and shared experience. First, the pathology of the group was a possible block to such sharing behaviors. If the group was highly cohesive and maintained a fairly stiff structure, this created the limitation of *groupthink* which, simply put, meant that the creativity that might evolve from the collective efforts of such a group cannot exceed the creativity of the individual. Or, put another way, the group's effectiveness may be no better than that of a single individual within the group. An example of this groupthink danger is well illustrated by a military command where a strong leader might assert a solution in the form of some clearly articulated objectives. In such a structure, other group members will hesitate to suggest alternatives for fear of losing the support of others in the group or for fear of removal from the group, thus, the dynamic for knowledge or opinion sharing is stifled.

A second block to creativity in a fairly stiff organizational structure is its tendency to promote hostility toward "out-groups." In stiffly defined groups, the boundaries are clearly marked and those that form out-groups are often perceived as hostile. This, in turn, engenders a tendency on the part of the "in-group" to resort to stereotypes in making inferences about the out-group's behavior or intentions. Sometimes this phenomenon has been called the "not invented here" syndrome. When the knowledge created by other workgroups is not trusted, for example, there is no incentive to learn from the efforts of others. A variety of experimental efforts to demonstrate these effects are given in Nishida's (2000) work, along with the complementary effort of developing from those efforts a conceptual model for understanding groups in terms of their structure, their degree of anonymity or freedom provided to members, and their type of information to be shared.

Organizational Strategies for Improved Knowledge Sharing

An organization's leadership quietly initiates a knowledge-sharing atmosphere through something as simple as agreeing to restructure an organizational routine when someone puts forward a better way to perform some task. The organization's management seeks, or at least welcomes, the sort of improvement that the individual suggests and, if it agrees to the change, it makes the suggested knowledge part of the explicit knowledge of the company by changing a form or a routine. Eventually the change becomes part of the social knowledge of the firm, especially if the routine is shared by many and done frequently enough. The original idea from which the new routine or new form stemmed may become lost, but the social instantiation of the routine and its practice continues to provide benefits in time or effort until the next "bright idea" amends the practice further. Several of the specific approaches mentioned later in this chapter depend on this same socialization process.

Tacit knowledge is less easily brought forward by those who hold it. As Von Krogh and colleagues (2000) explain, tacit knowledge is seldom fully recognized by the knowledge holder and, even less often, able to be made explicit enough for sharing. For the salesperson who has an uncanny sense of the correct moment to close a sale or for the talented medical professional who cannot always account for the various resources brought to bear on a successful medical diagnosis, the reality of tacit knowledge is a highly personalized one. Tacit knowledge is bound to an individual's senses, personal experience, and even the muscular movement of the individual and, as such, it cannot easily be transmitted to others.

Upper-level management has usually been central to the initiation of early approaches to knowledge sharing. These approaches were often IT-driven efforts, such as setting up a database to hold the company's knowledge of outside vendors. Such an approach Kluge and colleagues (2001) would characterize as "knowledge push." As primary leaders of a global survey for McKinsey and Company, these researchers found that there were plenty of companies doing knowledge-push activities but fewer trying to creating an environment within the organization for "information pull." Any heavy reliance on an organization's infrastructure is a symptom of an information-push environment. Also, these organizations often contained management groups that thought they had little need for a KM initiative because the company's database or knowledge warehouse was perceived as performing well.

While not seeking to characterize all "push" as bad and all "pull" as good, the McKinsey and Company survey does describe pull approaches as being better able to capture the full capabilities of everybody in an organization. The pull philosophy sets a standard where all within an organization are encouraged to freely share and constantly seek new knowledge to apply to old problems. These pull approaches are harder to instill since the manager can only indirectly set the right environment; the actual effort to pull knowledge from within his/her skill set has to come from the employee. The strength of the pull approach has to be monitored, but as it becomes stronger it can dramatically affect the organization's culture toward becoming one in which more knowledge sharing occurs. The following techniques and concepts have strong pull aspects in their approach.

Creating a Learning History

Peter Senge, Art Kleiner, George Roth, and others at the Center for Organizational Learning at the Massachusetts Institute of Technology (MIT) attempted to develop a technique for capturing a collective learning history for a project or product development effort (Kleiner and Roth, 1997). This learning history technique helped participants see a project or group accomplishment like a product launch, as a process rather than only as an outcome. The learning history was generally created using two parallel columns of text, right- and left-hand columns that could be of any length. This history was to be a simple narrative of an endeavor currently underway. In the right-hand column, a narrative of critical events in the process of the ensuing project was set down by any of the participants involved in the endeavor. Those involved in creating this on-going narrative were to be a good cross-section of the people involved in the project and, therefore, included all levels of decision makers. Ideally, contributors from all levels of the organization for whom these events had an impact would be involved—those who took part in the event, those on whom the event had a direct impact, and even those who merely observed the event from close range (Farr, 2000; Jacques, 1997). Participants were identified in the narrative by their title only; however, a fairly personal evaluation of events was encouraged rather than just a strict accounting of events. They were to record what they felt went well and what did not.

The left-hand column became a counterpoint narrative that was created by "learning historians." These were individuals who were trained and experienced outsiders. There could also be some who were concerned and knowledgeable insiders as well, usually drawn from the organization's human resources or organizational effectiveness departments. Their job was to distill, find patterns, and pose questions about the various assumptions made by participants throughout the project's life. As Farr (2000) described this process: they were to raise "the unspoken and unspeakable issues that hover just below the surface of the quotations found alongside."

The learning history should be used as the basis for discussions within the work group in the hope that they might learn as the project unfolds. Unlike best practice write-ups that generally are created after the project is complete, these learning history narratives do not omit the mistakes and mishaps. In addition, these narratives could become the stuff of months or even years of additional analysis by learning historians who could further distill the events into meaningful knowledge for the organization (Jacques, 1997). It was intended to show what worked, what did not, and why; thus, becoming a mechanism not only for the project team who generated it, but also as a way to pass the learning to other groups involved in similar efforts in various times and locations. Kleiner and Roth (1997) provide a detailed example and state that in addition to the capture of knowledge that may not be well understood by the participants—a definition often used for tacit knowledge—the process of developing a learning history can build trust. People who may have felt that their opinions were ignored in the past, come to feel their opinions and contributions are validated when they see them become a part of a narrative that will live on after the project has been completed. The group discussions that are generated from the learning history help to provide a time to clear the air about concerns, fears, and assumptions, allowing a more candid environment for sharing ideas.

Although the generation of these learning histories is definitely time and labor intensive, literature indicates that the technique continues to be used and is discussed at about the same level over the past five years since its initial inception at MIT. The effort involved is obviously worth more when these learning histories can be combined to create a body of knowledge for an organization. Kleiner and Roth (1997) would also add that the "hard" results desired by the organization—financial returns, high levels of productivity, and so on—are often found to be a function of the "soft" issues, such as a company's corporate culture or the quality of human interactions that are inspired within the workplace.

Creating a Yellow Pages or Know-How Exchange

Most employees never think about the immense amount of knowledge that an organization needs in order to function. Particularly in global enterprises with multiple interests, the extent of distributed experience at all levels of the organization is virtually unseen. Siemens Industrial Services, headquartered in Erlangen, Germany, is just such a global company. It employs approximately 22,000 people in more than 70 countries. Reported by D'Oosterlinck et al. (2002), the development of Siemens Industrial Services's Know-How Exchange has become one of Siemens Industrial Services's best practices for KM. The idea of a shared know-how "yellow pages" took approximately three years to realize. A database was developed that allowed individual employees to enter their specific know-how and skills, and also provided individuals with some scope in determining how they wished to introduce their skills to others. Employees then had to be prodded, cajoled, and motivated through employee newsletters, personal e-mails, and conferences to get involved in the effort. Every individual, regardless of rank, had to be informed of the Know-How Exchange, and made to understand that the success or failure of the effort depended on him/her personally because it would only be useful if it had a critical mass of participants. The database was enhanced with additional information about partners, products, and technology tools or solutions that have been successfully created by Siemens Industrial Services in the past. This allows a one-stop effort to locate not only company personnel with relevant experience but also customers and outside contacts with useful advice and experience.

The key to the effort was in the development of a culture at Siemens Industrial Services that supported this sort of collaboration. One of Siemens Industrial Services's corporate principles, broadly and frequently expressed, included mottos about the need to share information, for example: "Our cooperation has no limits" and "Learning is the key to continuous improvement." Through combining these sentiments with a more subtly communicated understanding that the expertise held by an individual is his/her value to the company, employees were able to realize that participation could help demonstrate their worth. What better way to show your value to the organization than through the contacts you receive from others who need your expertise.

Two types of employees were identified through the building of the Know-How Exchange. The first group is one that is quite enamored with IT solutions and will quickly get involved, despite early irritations like slow response times. The second group is more hesitant when it comes to something "new," especially if it is something with a learning curve. The second group would not tolerate much browsing before finding exactly what was needed. For the sake of this second group, the system had to be able to deliver results with quick response time and no intense training required. The structure for entries was relatively simple, using the standard qualification descriptions found in job descriptions and allowing a four-level indicator of competence, from support and planning at the low end to administration and in-depth knowledge at the high end. A powerful information structure was also important so that the searcher could navigate without much need for keywords or special terminology. In addition, the interface was optimized for use with a standard Web browser to provide a familiar look and feel. Used just once to provide some element—a contact or a proven solution to a problem—an employee can experience the benefits first hand and will want to participate. Related to this networked exchange, the benefits of human networking are also a plus in enabling knowledge sharing.

Building a Knowledge Networking Infrastructure

Traditionally, apprenticeships and mentoring relationships have long been used to transfer tacit knowledge to new workers in the organization. The benefit of physical proximity between workers has always been key in helping knowledge transference occur. This element of personal contact is still an important characteristic in a successful learning organization but harder to achieve in today's global organization. McKinsey and Company found in their global survey of KM practice that the more successful companies provide space within the organization for personal collaboration (Kluge et al., 2001). Less successful companies do not put as much emphasis on bringing people together and do not provide the space to do so. Collaboration is encouraged to extend beyond the department level and often goes beyond company walls through regional, national, or international conferences and technology fairs.

The approach of developing cross-functional teams has proven to be particularly effective in building an enterprise-wide networking culture. Alongside the deliberate and direct knowledge exchanges that accompany cross-functional team efforts, there is a good deal of informal networking that occurs as well. Cross-functional teams help to quickly highlight the cost to individuals of hoarding knowledge because hoarders quickly become known and gain a reputation for not being team players.

In developing cross-functional teams, one approach is for a project manager to advertise a project and have staff from a variety of departments self-select the effort that they feel they could best contribute. Individuals might be attached to one or two projects at one time, sharing their time across several efforts, perhaps more involved in one than in another. Members of various teams get together with their counterparts on other projects that share the same expertise. This helps everyone maintain an awareness of other participants' activities. These meetings can promote learning that, in turn, helps sharpen one's expertise. This learning can be brought back to the individual's own project team.

Although teams generally stay together only for the duration of a project, the mixing that occurs across various departments means that there is a likelihood that the contacts made during the project will be maintained after the project ends. Also, strong team performance may be rewarded with an "invitation to join" another team effort. Cross-functional teaming emphasizes to the individual the importance and benefits of sharing information and being a good team player, but care must also be taken to set goals for each team participant that extend beyond the team itself in order to avoid internecine rivalries and the "not invented here" dysfunction that can occur between teams.

John Deere was a very hierarchically arranged company that had trouble absorbing new knowledge. It suffered seriously from the "not invented here" syndrome (Kluge et al., 2001). Essentially, this syndrome meant that outside expertise was regarded very skeptically. Globally situated, John Deere had a plant in Mannheim, Germany, that was the largest maker and exporter of tractors worldwide. About 2,200 employees working at the plant produced more than 30,000 units per year. Because of its reputation for a high number of units and a high rate of export, there was resistance, especially among the ranks of the midlevel managers, to implementing change.

To attack this resistance, John Deere made it possible for department managers to get to know each other personally, both within the same plant and across the Atlantic. American managers visited the German plant and vice-versa. It was also possible to receive credit at yearly reviews for being a part of an "absorption" team and spending up to a month visiting another plant that was developing a new process. John Deere fostered a variety of internal exchange opportunities, starting with telecommunicated meetings at line level as well as the managerial level. It soon became an accepted standard that any employee could have an effect upon practice, fostering a stronger desire to know what was happening elsewhere.

Communities of Practice

Closely related to the notion of cross-functional teams is the currently popular "community of practice" approach. Even though it is too broad to be fairly treated here, a few characteristics are provided that seem to make the approach more useful. When the initial wave of using technology to facilitate knowledge sharing became clearly disappointing, an effort to examine the naturally occurring behaviors and cultures that were beneficial for sharing knowledge gave rise to the idea that groups that share a concern, a set of problems, or simply a passion about a topic will deepen their knowledge of the shared concern by interacting in an ongoing manner. These communities do not necessarily work together every day, but they come together because they find value in their interactions. They become informally bound by the value they find in learning together (Wenger et al., 2002).

Seemingly, more intentionally structured than some of the previous techniques, the identification of communities of practice stems from an identification of an organization's critical knowledge "domains." These flow directly from an organization's strategic goals, core competencies, business practices, and key activities. These communities result from intentional management efforts to identify social structures that will allow these communities to function. But once identified, these communities must be allowed to flourish as they will, running the unavoidable risk of dysfunctional behaviors. For each community, there needs to exist a "champion" who believes strongly that the community should exist and who will aggressively support its development through guidance, funds, visibility, and legitimacy. In companies like IBM and Schlumberger, each community has an executive sponsor who provides access to top management and, thus, gives the community a voice in management decisions. In other companies, there are "knowledge boards" that serve this championing function or chief knowledge officers (CKOs) with sufficient resources to provide a point of focus for the work of these communities.

These communities interact with others and tend to form a constellation of communities, testing the management's ability to live with a new level of complexity. The same issues of boundaries and internecine warfare that exist with cross-functional team efforts exist with communities of practice. Communication barriers can also abound when communities take in others that do not share their common language or perceptions. Moving knowledge across these often unseen boundaries can form extremely difficult challenges for the community. Wenger and colleagues (2002) describe this tendency for knowledge to have difficulty transcending the community in order to find application in other parts of the organization as a "stickiness" problem. Boundaries of practice often do not follow organizational boundaries, so the "leakiness" of knowledge becomes a problem as well. Competitors might collaborate to solve a common problem, but the possibility exists that knowledge in one firm will be "leaked" easily to the other because shared practice crosses organizational boundaries. Today's more complex issues create the need to develop partnerships with other organizations and, thus, it becomes important to develop procedures to avoid sharing that which should be private, yet disclose enough to enable communication and mutual learning in the community.

CONCLUSION

Creating environments where knowledge sharing is supported is not easy. Across the several authors reviewed for this chapter, they each seem to indicate that such knowledge enabling will not happen on its own. The key element is people. Developing their understanding of the importance of sharing cannot simply be engineered with some piece of software, a database, or a global voice-mail system. The efforts discussed in this chapter all came from organizational contexts that had an emphasis on innovation and a commitment to the knowledge growth of the individual. This commitment to knowledge sharing has to be endorsed and supported by the highest levels of the organization, but it can seldom be successful if forced. Once there is a clear commitment to such a culture, then the benefits of a sophisticated technology like groupware or a corporate portal can be attempted. The knowledge creating process is quite fragile, and the need to examine each barrier to the process is essential.

In addition to an appropriate knowledge-sharing culture, a variety of enabling ideas must be tried. Conversational opportunity is essential, for example. People must talk with one another in order to share ideas. And face-to-face communication is the best medium, a difficult standard in today's global enterprise. Actively managing conversational opportunities can be essential and often is required to counteract normal competitive tendencies that have long formed the basic culture of organizational life. Von Krogh et al. (2000) advocate for the recruitment of knowledge activists who can identify microcommunities where knowledge sharing, particularly tacit knowledge sharing, is most likely to occur. This is an idea very similar to the knowledge champion for communities of practice found in Wenger et al. (2002). The message from these and other authors is that the process is never finished.

Knowledge creation, through whatever vehicle, is simply a part of a dynamic process that is as changeable as the current global economy. There may be new barriers that arise and new approaches must be created to address those barriers, but the value of connecting people who are able and willing to share the tacit knowledge that they possess has proven to be an essential activity in today's learning organization.

REFERENCES

Bransford, J. D., A. L. Brown, and R. R. Cocking, eds. (2000). *How People Learn: Brain, Mind, Experience*. Washington, D.C.: Commission on Behavioral and Social Sciences Education, National Research Council.

Cameron, P. D. (2002). Managing knowledge assets: The cure for an ailing structure. *CMA Management*. 76(3), 20–23.

Cap Gemini Ernst & Young and Cranfield University. (1999). *Intranet Benchmarking and Business Value*. Report summary available from http://www.capgemini.co.uk.

Davenport, T. H. and L. Prusak. (1998). *Working Knowledge: How Organizations Manage What They Know*. Boston, MA: Harvard Business School Press.

Davenport, T. H. and G. J. B. Probst, eds. (2002). *Knowledge Management Case Book: Siemens Best Practices*. 2nd edition. Erlangen, Germany: Publicis Corporate Publishing (Division of John Wiley & Sons).

Deveau, D. (2002). No brain, no gain. *Computing Canada*. 28(10), 14–15.

Dixon, N. M. (2000). *Common Knowledge: How Companies Thrive by Sharing What They Know*. Boston, MA: Harvard Business School Press.

D'Oosterlinck, M., D. Freitag, and J. Graff. (2002). Siemens Industrial Services: Turning know-how into results. In Davenport, T. H. and G. J. B. Probst, eds., *Knowledge Management Case Book: Siemens Best Practices*. 2nd edition. Erlangen, Germany: Publicis Corporate Publishing (Division of John Wiley & Sons).

Farr, K. (2000). Organizational learning and knowledge managers. *Work Study*. 49(1), 14–17.

Grover, V. and T. H. Davenport. (2001). General perspectives on knowledge management: Fostering a research agenda. *Journal of Management Information Systems*. 18(1), 5–21.

Hall, H. (2001). Input-friendliness: Motivating knowledge sharing across intranets. *Journal of Information Science*. 27(3):139–146.

Holsthouse, D. (1998). Knowledge research issues. *California Management Review*. 40(3): 277–280.

Jacques, M. L. (1997). Learning histories: The S in PDSA of learning. *TQM Magazine*. 9(1), 6.

Kleiner, A. and G. Roth. (1997). How to make experience your company's best teacher. *Harvard Business Review*. September-October, pp. 172–177.

Kluge, J., W. Stein, and T. Licht. (2001). *Knowledge Unplugged: The McKinsey and Company Global Survey on Knowledge Management*. New York, NY: Palgrave (St. Martin's Press).

McDermott, R. (1999). Why information technology inspired but cannot deliver knowledge management. *California Management Review*. 41(4), 103–117.

Min, K. and S. Yoon. (2002). So, what do you know? *Far Eastern Economic Review*. 165(19), 34–36.

Nishida, T., ed. (2000). *Dynamic Knowledge Interaction*. New York, NY: CRC Press.

Oppenheimer, J. Robert. (1954). *Science and the Common Understanding*. New York, NY: Simon and Schuster.

Piaget, Jean. (1960). *The Psychology of Intelligence*. Paterson, N.J.: Littlefield, Adams.

Skyrme, D. J. (1999). *Knowledge Networking: Creating the Collaborative Enterprise*. Boston, MA: Butterworth Heinemann.

Von Krogh, G., K. Ichijo, and I. Nonaka. (2000). *Enabling Knowledge Creation: How to Unlock the Mystery of Tacit Knowledge and Release the Power of Innovation*. New York, NY: Oxford University Press.

Wenger, E., R. McDermott, and W. M. Snyder. (2002). *Cultivating Communities of Practice: A Guide to Managing Knowledge*. Boston, MA: Harvard Business School Press.

Knowledge Management Lessons Learned: A Brief Bibliography

Paul Burden, DeVry University

This is not a comprehensive bibliography to KM. In the predecessor volume to this, *Knowledge Management for the Information Professional* (2000), we included a rather comprehensive bibliography—though by no means a complete one—of more than 600 items. Knowledge management has grown so quickly (see Chapter 2), that such a bibliography is no longer a feasible addendum to a printed source.

This bibliography focuses on citations for sources (both print and online) that discuss KM lessons learned. There are also a few that discuss best practices. We have included them because the step after lessons learned is the creation of a body of knowledge pertaining to best practices. These documents have been placed under subject headings that more precisely describe their contents. The section entitled "General Applications" contains documents that are broad in scope and address more than one subject area. The "General Applications" section also includes case studies. Under "WWW Resources," we have listed Web sites that contain information pertaining to more than just one subject area. We have evaluated these articles, and feel that they have value for the individual(s) trying to gain expertise in the area of lessons learned.

All listed Web sites were revisited and verified during the week of April 5, 2003.

BOOKS

APQC. *Knowledge management: Lessons from the leading edge*. Proceedings from APQC's third Knowledge Management Conference. Houston, TX: APQC, 1998.

Ahmed, Pervaiz K. et al. *Learning through knowledge management*. Boston, MA: Butterworth-Heinemann, 2002.

Bahra, Nicholas. *Competitive knowledge management*. New York, NY: Palgrave, 2001.

Bellaver, Richard F. and John M. Lusa. *Knowledge management strategy and technology.* Boston, MA: Artech House, 2002.

Bernbom, Gerald, ed. *Information alchemy: The art and science of knowledge management.* San Francisco, CA: Jossey-Bass, 2001.

Brooking, Annie. *Corporate memory: Strategies for knowledge management.* New York, NY: International Thomson Business Press, 1999.

East, E. William and Jeffrey G. Kirby. *Corporate lessons learned (CLL system): System decision paper,* Champaign, IL: US Army Corps of Engineers, Engineer Research and Development Center, Construction Engineering Research Laboratory, 2001.

Fuller, Steve. *Knowledge management foundations.* Boston, MA: Butterworth-Heinemann, 2002.

Garvin, D. A. *Learning in action: A guide to putting the learning organization to work.* Boston, MA: Harvard Business School Press, 2000.

Gottschalk, Petter. *Information technology support for knowledge management: Lessons learned from law firms in Norway.* Henley on Thames, U.K.: Henley Research Centre, 1999.

Granatosky, Mark S. *A study of lessons handling in lessons learned systems and application to lessons learned system design.* Monterey, CA; Springfield, VA: Naval Postgraduate School, 2002.

Leondes, Cornelius T. *Expert systems: The technology of knowledge management and decision making for the 21st century.* (6 volumes) San Diego, CA: Academic Press, 2001.

Liebowitz, Jay. *Building organizational intelligence: A knowledge management primer.* Boca Raton, FL: CRC Press, 2000.

Liebowitz, Jay. *Knowledge management: Learning from knowledge engineering.* Boca Raton, FL: CRC Press, 2001.

Malhotra, Yogesh. *Knowledge management and virtual organizations.* Hershey, PA: Idea Group Publishing, 2000.

Mertins, Kai et al. *Knowledge management: Best practices in Europe.* New York, NY: Springer, 2001.

O'Dell, Carla S. *Knowledge management: Consortium benchmarking study: Final report.* Houston, TX: APQC, 1996.

Tiwana, Amrit. *The knowledge management toolkit: Practical techniques for building a knowledge management system.* Upper Saddle River, NJ: Prentice Hall Professional Technical Reference, 2000.

ARTICLES

Best Practices

Despres, Charles and Danielle Chauvel. "Knowledge management(s)." *Journal of Knowledge Management,* 03.02 (1999): 110.

Fyock, Catherine D. "If only we knew what we know: The transfer of internal knowledge and best practice." *HR Magazine,* 44.05 (May 1999): 134.

Jackson, Nicholas. "Knowledge summit '99." *Management Services,* 44.03 (March 2000): 20–23.

"Knowledge management: Best practice sharing extends resources." *PR Newswire,* (April 18, 2002): 01.

"Knowledge management: Best practice sharing optimizes limited resources." *PR Newswire*, (February 20, 2002): 01.

Litman, Joel and Brent Lohrmann. "Innovating with customer intelligence." *Strategic Finance*, 83.07 (January 2002): 11–13.

Martin, Bill. "Knowledge management within the context of management: An evolving relationship." *Management Review*, 22.02 (2000): 17–36.

National Partnership for Reinventing Government. "Balancing measures: Best practices in performance management." (August 1999). Accessible at http://www.npr.gov/npr/library/papers/bkgrd/balmeasure.html

Zairi, Mohamed. "Benchmarking maturity as we approach the millennium?" *Total Quality Management*, 10.04/05 (July 1999): S810–S816.

Competitive Intelligence

Breeding, Bret. "CI and KM convergence: A case study at Shell Services International." *Competitive Intelligence Review*, 11.04 (Fourth Quarter 2000): 12–24.

Shelfer, Katherine. "A roadmap for the successful implementation of competitive intelligence systems." *Information Outlook*, 05.07 (July 2001): 34–44.

Customer Service

Davenport, Tom. "On the right track." *CIO*, 15.03 (November 01, 2001): 92.

e-Commerce

Fahey, L. et al. "Linking e-business and operating processes: The role of knowledge management." *IBM Systems Journal*, 40.04 (2001): 889–907.

General Applications

Bixler, Charlie. "Practical, critical success factors for KM implementation." *KM World*, 11.09 (October 2002): 18.

Burk, Mike. "Knowledge Management: Everyone benefits by sharing information." *Public Roads*, 63.06 (May/June 2000): 26–29.

Carliner, Saul. "Modeling information for three-dimensional space: Lessons learned from museum exhibit design." *Technical Communication*, 48.01 (February 2001): 66–81.

Charles, Susan K. "Knowledge management lessons from the document trenches." *Online*, 26.01 (January/February 2002): 22–24, 26–28.

Clark, Judy and Steven Poruban. "Oil, gas industry makes advances in managing data, knowledge." *Oil and Gas Journal*, 99.50 (December 10, 2001): 74–82.

Combs, Deidre. "Take-home lessons." *Health Management Technology*, 22.04 (April 2001): 48–49.

Denton, D. Keith. "Better decisions: With less information." *Industrial Management*, 43.04 (July/August 2001): 21–25.

Dixon, Nancy M. and Jonathan Ungerleider. "Working paper: Lessons learned." (January 1998). Accessible at http://www.cbi.cgey.com/pub/docs/ Lessons_Learned_Final.doc

Drucker, David. "Knowledge management revised—Theory doesn't equal practice." *InternetWeek*, 846 (January 29, 2001): 01.

Duffy, Jan. "Knowledge management: To be or not to be?" *Information Management Journal*, 34.01 (January 2000): 64–67.

Ellis, Kristine. "Sharing best practices globally." *Training*, 38.07 (July 2001): 32–38.

Empson, Laura. "Fear of exploitation and fear of contamination: Impediments to knowledge transfer in mergers between professional service firms." *Human Relations*, 54.07 (July 2001): 839–862.

"Gotcha! Case Studies." Accessible at http://www.sims.berkeley.edu/courses/is213/s99/Projects/P9/web_site/case_studies.htm

Hanley, Susan and Christine Dawson. "A framework for delivering value with knowledge management: The AMS knowledge centers." *Information Strategy*, 16.04 (Summer 2000): 27–36.

Hirschbuhl, John et al. "Using knowledge management to deliver distance learning." *British Journal of Educational Technology*, 33.01 (January 2002): 89–93.

Holland, Christopher P. and Ben Light. "A stage maturity model for enterprise resource planning systems use." *Database for Advances in Information Systems*, 32.02 (Spring 2001): 34–45.

ICASIT. "KMCentral: KM Resources: Case Studies." (09 April 2003). Accessible at http://www.icasit.org/km/resources/kmcases.htm

Kemp, Linda Larson et al. "Knowledge management: Insights from the trenches." *IEEE Software*, 18.06 (November/December 2001): 66–68. "Knowledge Management: Lessons learned in establishing BSX (a KM system)." Accessible at http://center.dau.mil/job_support_and_cops/knowledge_management/CoP_Archives/Air%20Force%20BSX%20Lessons%20Learned.ppt

Koenig, Michael E. D. "The third stage of KM emerges." *KM World*, 11.03 (March 2002): 20–21.

Kotnour, Tim. "Organizational learning practices in the project management environment." *The International Journal of Quality & Reliability Management*, 17.04/05 (2000): 393.

Lesser, Eric and Laurence Prusak. "Preserving knowledge in an uncertain world." *MIT Sloan Management Review*, 43.01 (Fall 2001): 101–102.

"Lessons Learned." Links to sites concerned with military Lessons Learned. (June 19, 2002). Accessible at http://library.nps.navy.mil/home/lessons.htm

Levett, Gavin P. and Marin D. Guenov. "A methodology for knowledge management implementation." *Journal of Knowledge Management*, 04.03 (2000): 258–270.

McDaniel, Samuel W. "Just-in-time project management." *IIE Solutions*, 33.04 (April 2001): 30–33.

Melymuka, Kathleen. "Profiting from mistakes." *Computerworld*, 35.18 (April 30, 2001): 42–43.

Mullich, Joe. "Growing a knowledge management solution: Lessons learned from pilot projects can nourish your enterprise-wide implementation." (March 2001). Accessible at http://www.kmmag.com/articles/default.asp?ArticleID=515&Keywords=lessons++AND+learned

Murray, Peter. "Knowledge management as a sustained competitive advantage." *Ivey Business Journal*, 66.04 (March 2002): 71–76.

Poister, Theodore H. "Building quality improvement over the long run: Approaches, results, and lessons learned from the PennDot experience." *Public Performance and Management Review*, 24.02 (December 2000): 161–176.

Raths, David. "Practice makes perfect." *InfoWorld*, 23.45 (November 05, 2001): 46–47.

Richert, Andrew. "Lessons from a major cultural change workshop programme." *Industrial and Commercial Training*, 31.07 (1999): 267–271.

Schoech, Dick et al. "From data to intelligence: Introducing the intelligent organization." *Administration in Social Work*, 26.01 (2001): 01–21.

Schultze, Jamie. "Managing knowledge in the comptroller community." *The Armed Forces Comptroller*, 46.01 (Winter 2001): 09–11.

Seeman, Patricia. "A prescription for knowledge management: What Hoffman-Laroche's case can teach others." (07 April 2003). Accessible at http://www.cbi.cgey.com/journal/issue1/features/apresc/index.html

Sooknanan, Ash. "The importance of knowledge management in public sector organizations." (28 May 2001). Accessible at http://www.hc-sc.gc.ca/iacb-dgiac/km-gs/english/sooknanan_en.pdf

"Spread the knowhow." *Business Week*, 3704 (October 23, 2000): 52.

Sumner-Smith, Martin. "Practical knowledge management for drug discovery." *Scientific Computing and Instrumentation*, 17.09 (August 2000): 22–24.

Tan, Jeffrey. "Managing knowledge—How to do it—A practical case study." *The British Journal of Administrative Management*, 19 (March/April 2000): 12–13.

Tapsell, Sherril. "Brain fuel for the future." *New Zealand Management*, 46.06 (July 1999): 42–43.

Taylor, Karla. "Today's lesson: Strategic planning." *Association Management*, 53.01 (January 2001): 65–66, 70–71.

Thomas, J. C. et al. "The knowledge management puzzle: Human and social factors in knowledge management." *IBM Systems Journal*, 40.04 (2001): 863–884.

Truran, William. "The 'cost of quality' in wire and cable industry." *Wire Journal International*, 35.03 (March 2002): 106–112.

Information Audits

Henczel, Susan. "The information audit as a first step towards effective knowledge management." *Information Outlook*, 05.06 (June 2001): 48–57.

Information Professionals

Abell, Angela. "Skills for knowledge environments." *Information Management Journal*, 34.03 (July 2000): 33–41.

Choo, Chun Wei. "Working with knowledge: How information professionals help organisations manage what they know." *Library Management*, 21.08 (2000): 395.

Dearstyne, Bruce W. "Fighting terrorism with information: Issues and opportunities." *Information Outlook*, 06.03 (March 2002): 28–32.

Duffy, Jan. "Knowledge management and its influence on the records and information manager." *Information Management Journal*, 35.03 (July 2001): 62–65.

Duffy, Jan. "Knowledge management: What every information professional should know." *Information Management Journal*, 34.03 (July 2000): 10–14.

Foote, Nathaniel W. "Managing the knowledge manager." *The McKinsey Quarterly*, 10.03 (2001): 120–129.

Miller, Leah. "Wanted: Improved communication." *The Internal Auditor*, 57.05 (October 2000): 13.

O'Donnell, Anthony. "Carrier learns underwriting lessons." *Anthony O'Donnell; Insurance & Technology*, 28.01 (January 2003): 22.

Souder, Laura. "Building organization capacity through knowledge management." *Journal of Interactive Instruction Development*, 13.04 (Spring 2001): 21–25.

Intellectual Capital

Bontis, Nick. "Thought leadership on intellectual capital." *Journal of Intellectual Capital*, 02.03 (2001): 183–191.

Bontis, Nick and John Girardi. "Teaching knowledge management and intellectual capital lessons: An empirical examination of the Tango Simulation." *International Journal of Technology Management*, 20.05 (2000): 545–555.

Cameron, Preston D. "Managing knowledge assets: The cure for an ailing structure." *CMA Management*, 76.03 (May 2002): 20–23.

Dixon, Nancy M. "The neglected receiver of knowledge sharing." *Ivey Business Journal*, 66.04 (March 2002): 35–40.

Downes, Meredith. "Knowledge transfer through expatriation: The U-curve approach to overseas staffing." *Journal of Managerial Issues*, 12.02 (Summer 2000): 131–150.

Downes, Meredith and Anisya S. Thomas. "Managing overseas assignments to build organizational knowledge." *HR. Human Resource Planning*, 22.04 (1999): 33–48.

Koenig, Michael. "The resurgence if intellectual capital." *Information Today*, 17.08 (September 2000): 01–02.

Liebowitz, Jay. "Developing knowledge management metrics for measuring intellectual capital." *Journal of Intellectual Capital*, 01.01 (2000): 54–67.

McElyea, Brian E. "Knowledge management, intellectual capital, and learning organizations: A triad of future management integration." *Futurics*, 26.02 (2002): 59–65.

Knowledge Audit

Santosus, Megan. "Case files: Northrop Grumman: Thanks for the memories." *CIO*, 14.22 (September 01, 2001): 86.

Weber, Rosina O. and David W. Aha. "Intelligent delivery of military lessons learned." *Decision Support Systems*, 34.03 (February 2003): 287.

Knowledge Mapping

Stanford, Xenia. "Map your knowledge strategy." *Information Outlook*, 05.06 (June 2001): 18–24.

Organizational Culture

Armbrecht Jr., F. M. Ross et al. "Knowledge management in research and development." *Research Technology Management*, 44.04 (July/August 2001): 28–48.

Baltazar, Henry. "Overcoming KM's obstacles." *Eweek*, 19.07 (February 18, 2002): 43–44.

Banks, Eric. "Creating a knowledge culture." *Work Study*, 48.01 (1999): 18.

Becerra-Fernandez, Irma. "Organizational knowledge management: A contingency perspective." *Journal of Management Information Systems*, 18.01 (Summer 2001): 23–55.

Brailsford, Thomas W. "Building a knowledge community at Hallmark Cards." *Research Technology Management*, 44.05 (September/October 2001): 18–25.

Brown, E. W. "Toward speech as a knowledge resource." *IBM Systems Journal*, 40.04 (2001): 985–1001.

Burk, Mike. "Communities of practice." *Public Roads*, 63.06 (May/June 2000): 18–21.

Burton-Jones, Alan. "Daunting paradox." *Across the Board*, 39.03 (May/June 2002): 60–63.

Cameron, Preston D. "Managing knowledge assets: The cure for an ailing structure." *CMA Management*, 76.03 (May 2002): 20–23.

Cook, Peter. "I heard it through the grapevine: Making knowledge management work by learning to share knowledge, skills, and experience." *Industrial and Commercial Training*, 31.03 (1999): 101–105.

Connor, Michael. "M & A risk management." *The Journal of Business Strategy*, 22.01 (January/February 2001): 25–27.

Davenport, Tom. "The last big thing." *CIO*, 14.03 (November 01, 2000): 60–62.

De Long, David W. "Diagnosing cultural barriers to knowledge management." *The Academy of Management Executive*, 14.04 (November 2000): 113–127.

Dixon, Nancy M. "The changing face of knowledge." *The Learning Organization*, 06.05 (1999): 212.

Doherty, Paul. "Thinking outside the box." *Facilities Design and Management*, 20.02 (February 2001): 50–51.

Fogarty, Kevin. "Managing the data pack rats." *Computerworld*, 35.42 (October 15, 2001): 58–59.

Greengard, Samuel. "Moving forward with reverse mentoring." *Workforce*, 81.03 (March 2002): 15.

Gross, Arthur E. "Knowledge sharing: The crux of quality." *ASQ's ... Annual Quality Congress Proceedings*. Milwaukee: Quality Congress, 2001.

Grover, Varun. "General perspectives on knowledge management: Fostering a research agenda." *Journal of Management Information Systems*, 18.01 (Summer 2001): 05–22.

Holloway, Pamela. "Tips and techniques for embedding KM in your organization." (07 April 2003). Accessible at http://www.knowledgeharvesting.org/presentations/Tips%20fpr%20Embedding%20KM%20-%20Helsinki.pdf

Horwitch, Mark and Robert Armacost. "Helping knowledge management be all it can be." *Journal of Business Strategy*, 23.03 (May/June 2002): 26–31.

Hyland, Paul and Ron Beckett. "Learning to compete: The value of internal benchmarking." *Benchmarking: An International Journal*, 09.03 (2002): 293–304.

Lee, Sr., James. "Knowledge management: The intellectual revolution." *IIE Solutions*, 32.10 (October 2000): 34–37.

Markus, M. Lynne. "Toward a theory of knowledge reuse: Types of knowledge reuse situations and factors in reuse success." *Journal of Management Information Systems*, 18.01 (Summer 2001): 57–93.

Milne, Patricia. "Rewards, recognition and knowledge sharing: Seeking a causal link." *Australian Academic and Research Libraries*, 32.04 (December 2001): 321–331.

Pangarkar, Ajay M. and Teresa Kirkwood. "Capitalizing on brain power: Tapping into your human capital network." *CMA Management*, 76.01 (March 2002): 24–27.

Parise, Salvatore. "Leveraging knowledge management across strategic alliances." *Ivey Business Journal*, 66.04 (March/April 2002): 41–47.

Pawar, Kulwant S. and Sudi Sharifi. "Managing the product design process: Exchanging knowledge and experiences." *Integrated Manufacturing Systems*, 13.02 (2002): 91–96.

Raub, Steffen and Charles-Clemens Rüling. "The knowledge management tussle—Speech communities and rhetorical strategies in the development of knowledge management." *Journal of Information Technology*, 16.02 (2001): 113–130.

Samuells, Jennifer. "Putting knowledge management to work for real estate organizations." *Real Estate Issues*, 26.01 (Spring 2001): 35–38.

Sbarcea, Kim. "The mystery of knowledge management." *New Zealand Management*, 48.10 (November 2001): 33–36.

Schelin, Elsa. "Recognizing the champions." *E-Learning*, 03.04 (April 2002): 12–19.

Sinclair, Diane. "The latest intelligence." *People Management*, 07.21 (October 25, 2001): 88.

Tan, Jeffrey. "Knowledge management—Just more buzzwords?" *The British Journal of Administrative Management*, 19 (March/April 2000): 10–11.

Turpin, Andrew. "It's about common sense." *Director*, 54.01 (August 2000): 25. "Valuing knowledge behaviors: Microsoft to share knowledge management insights with the Global Benchmarking Council." *PR Newswire*, (March 01, 2002): 01.

Ward, Arian. "Getting strategic value from constellations of communities." *Strategy and Leadership*, 28.04 (March/April 2000): 04.

Zielinski, Dave. "Have you shared a bright idea today?" *Training*, 37.07 (July 2000): 65–68.

Organizational Learning

Becerra-Fernandez, Irma and Joseph Martin Stevenson. "Knowledge management systems and solutions for the school principal as chief learning officer." *Education*, 121.03 (Spring 2001): 508–518.

Bonner, Dede. "Enter the chief knowledge officer." *Training and Development*, 54.02 (February 2000): 36–40.

Bonner, Dede and Stacey Wagner. "Meet the new chief learning officers." *Training and Development*, 56.05 (May 2002): 80–89.

Christie, Anne. "The knowledge harvest: Ensuring you reap what you sow." *Journal of Workplace Learning*, 12.03 (2000): 83–88.

Cross, Rob. "Information seeking in social context: Structural influences and receipt of information." *IEEE Transactions on Systems, Man, and Cybernetics. Part C, Applications and Reviews*, 31.04 (November 2001): 438.

Cross, Rob. "Technology is not enough: Improving performance by building organizational memory." *Sloan Management Review*, 41.03 (Spring 2000): 69–78.

Dixon, Nancy M. "The responsibilities of members in an organization that is learning." *Learning Organization*, 05.04 (1998): 161–167.

Koenig, Michael. "The 2000 Conference Board Conference." *Information Today*, 17.06 (June 2000): 28–29.

Kotnour, Tim. "Building knowledge for and about large-scale organizational transformations." *International Journal of Operations & Production Management*, 21.08 (2001): 1053–1075.

Linde, Charlotte. "Narrative and social tacit knowledge." *Journal of Knowledge Management*, 05.02 (2001): 160–170.

Salopek, Jennifer J. "Common knowledge: How companies thrive by sharing what they know." *Training and Development*, 54.04 (April 2000): 63–64.

Schulz, Martin. "The uncertain relevance of newness: Organizational learning and knowledge flows." *Academy of Management Journal*, 44.04 (August 2001): 661–682.

Stevenson, Joseph Martin. "The modern university provost." *Education*, 121 (Winter 2000): 347–349.

Social Capital

Deuck, G. "Views of knowledge are human views." *IBM Systems Journal*, 40.04 (2001): 885–888.

Gupta, A. K. and V. Govindarajan. "Knowledge management's social dimension: Lessons from Nucor Steel." *Sloan Management Review*, 42.01 (Fall 2000): 71–80.

Talisayon, Serafin D. "Knowledge and people." *BusinessWorld*, 15.200 (May 07, 2002): 01.

Thomas, J. C. "The knowledge management puzzle: Human and social factors in knowledge management." *IBM Systems Journal*, 40.04 (2001): 863–884.

Technology

Abate, Carolyn. "Make the most of company brainpower." *Ziff Davis Smart Business*, 15.06 (June 2002): 52–54.

Armour, Phillip G. "The case for a new business model." *Communications of the ACM*, 43.08 (August 2000): 19–22.

Balla, John, Jennifer Harty, et al. "Knowledge management comes of age." *Inform*, 13.07 (July 1999): 22–29.

Birk, Andreas, Torgeir Dingsovr, et al. "Postmortem: Never leave a project without it." *IEEE Software*, 19.03 (May/June 2002): 43–45.

Borck, James R. "Information building." *InfoWorld*, 23.40 (October 1, 2001): 47–48.

Brizz, Paul "Enterprise information portals: An evolution of knowledge management tools." (June 21, 2001). Accessible at http://www.destinationkm.com/articles/default.asp?ArticleID= 286

Chudnow, Christine. "Knowledge management tools." *Computer Technology Review*, 21.11 (November 2001): 28–29.

Genusa, Angela. "Chaos theory." *CIO*, 14.05 (December 01, 2000): 228.

Gonsalves, Antone. "Employees share pearls of wisdom." *InformationWeek*, 854 (September 10, 2001): 48–49.

Gralla, Preston. "Robo boss." *CIO*, 15.11 (March 15, 2002): 85.

Gregor, Shirley. "Explanations from intelligent systems: Theoretical foundations and implications for practice." *MIS Quarterly*, 23.04 (December 1999): 497–530.

Guenther, Kim. "Knowledge management benefits of intranets." *Online*, 25.03 (May/June 2001): 17–20.

Halpern, Mark. "Broadening vistas of design optimization." *Computer-Aided Engineering*, 19.05 (May 2000): 24–28.

Hildebrand, Carol. "Knowledge fusion." *CIO*, 13.16 (June 01, 2000): 152 .

ICASIT KMCentral: KM Tools and Sharing Knowledge. (07 April 2003). Accessible at http://www.icasit.org/km/tools/share.htm

Kontzer, Tony. "U.S. Army ready to capture and build on information." *InformationWeek*, 884 (April 15, 2002): 50–51.

Lesperance, Yves and Gerd Wagnerg. "AAAI 2000 workshop reports." *AI Magazine*, 22.01 (Spring 2001): 127–135.

Moore, Cathleen. "Tapping knowledge." *InfoWorld*, 23.42 (October 15, 2001): 38.

Parzinger, Monica J. and Mark N. Frolick. "Creating competitive advantage through data warehousing." *Information Strategy*, 17.04 (Summer 2001): 10–15.

Pimm, Fox. "Making support pay." *Computerworld*, 36.11 (March 11 2002): 28.

Pohs, W. "The Lotus Knowledge Discovery System: Tools and experiences." *IBM Systems Journal*, 40.04 (2001): 956–966.

Quesenbery, Whitney. "Lessons from the Novartis InfoWeb: Creating a successful knowledge management system." (1999). Accessible at http://www.cognetics.com/portfolio/whitney/iw-lessons.pdf

Shani, A. B. (Rami), James A. Sena, et al. "Knowledge work teams and groupware technology: Learning from Seagate's experience." *Journal of Knowledge Management*, 04.02 (2000): 111.

Skyrme, David J. "The MIS contribution to knowledge management: Lessons learned?" (09 April 2003). Accessible at http://www.skyrme.com/UPDATES/u23.htm#mis

Trepper, Charles. "Keep your knowledge in-house." *InformationWeek*, 802 (September 04, 2000): 55–59.

Ulrich, Dave and Paige Hinkson. "Net heads. Using technology in leadership development." *People Management*, 07.02 (January 25, 2001): 32–36.

WWW Resources

Air Force Center for Knowledge Sharing Lessons Learned http://knowledge.langley.af.mil/afcks/default.asp

Air Force Knowledge Management Initiatives http://center.dau.mil/job_support_and_cops/knowledge_management/CoP_Archives/AF%20KNOWLEDGE%20MANAGEMENT%20INITIATIVES.doc

Best Practices Database http://www.bestpractices.org

Centre for Advanced Learning Technologies (CALT) Knowledge Management and Workflow http://www.insead.fr/CALT/Encyclopedia/ComputerSciences/ Groupware/Workflow

EPSS InfoSite http://www.pcd-innovations.com/infosite/km.htm

Efforts to Develop Knowledge Management Systems http://center.dau.mil/Topical_Sessions_templates/Knowledge_Management/Efforts_to_develop_KM_Systems.htm

Hokkanen, John and Tricia Bond. "Knowledge management: A bibliographic resource." (15 August 2000). Accessible at http://www.llrx.com/features/ km_bib.htm

ICASIT KMCentral: KM Resources and Articles. (09 April 2003). Accessible at http://www.icasit.org/km/resources/kmarticles.htm

ikon: Warwick Business School http://users.wbs.warwick.ac.uk/ikon

KMWorld Lessons Learned Articles http://www.kmworld.com/search/index.cfm?action=searching&maxrows=25&collection=articles&criteria=lessons%20learned

Knowledge Management Research Group, Business School, Aston University http://knowledge-mgt.abs.aston.ac.uk

Lessons Learned Links (Navy Center for Applied Research in Artificial Intelligence) http://www.aic.nrl.navy.mil/~aha/lessons

Meta Knowledge Management Portal: Lessons Learned http://www.metakm.com/search.php?topic=5

Miesing, Paul. "Organizational Learning." (April 09, 2003). Accessible at http://www.albany.edu/faculty/pm157/teaching/topics/orglearn.html

Office of Environmental Management Lessons Learned Program http://www.em.doe.gov/lessons

UN-Habitat: Best Practices, Knowledge Management http://www.sustainabledevelopment.org/blp/links

WWW Virtual Library on Knowledge Management http://www.brint.com/km

DATABASES CONSULTED IN THE PREPARATION
OF THIS BIBLIOGRAPHY

ABI Inform

Academic Search Elite

Applied Science and Technology

Business Source Elite

Computer Database

Electric Library

Electronic Collections Online

Library Literature

Periodical Abstracts

Wilson Select Plus

WorldCat

About the Contributors

Stephen E. Arnold

Stephen E. Arnold has over 20 years of experience in online information. In addition to helping develop ABI/INFORM, Business Dateline, and the General Business File, he was one of the founders of The Point (Top 5% of the Internet). He provides professional services to organizations worldwide. Arnold is the author of six books and more than 55 journal articles. He provides a range of professional services to organizations worldwide, including the U.S. Senate, the House of Representatives, and the General Services administration. Arnold is on the board of the Sport Information Research Center in Ottawa, and is a member of the Infozen, Inc. board of advisors.

Arnold received the 1998 Thomson/Online award for his article on push technology. In 1989, he received the ASIS/Rutgers University Distinguished Lectureship Award. He holds an A.B.A. and an M.A. from Bradley University. Selected Web-related projects can be reviewed at http://www.arnoldit.com

Richard C. Azzarello

Richard C. Azzarello is the founder and president of Reality Consulting, Inc. Azzarello assists his clients in realizing measurable results from their improvement efforts, primarily in the KM arena, often where prior attempts have failed. He formerly served as a founding member and practice executive for knowledge and content management with the IBM Corporation. Azzarello also served as a member of Ernst & Young's Performance Improvement practice, leading the development of their approach, methods, and tools. He has in-depth experience in knowledge and content management, practice enablement, and organizational change. Azzarello has been making KM approaches real since he began doing so in the manufacturing industry in the early 1980s. He is a frequent speaker on KM topics, as well as a published author of articles and book chapters on KM. He has nearly 30 years of management and project leadership experience in a variety of industries.

Azzarello holds an M.B.A. from Rutgers University and a B.A. degree in Theater from the State University of New York, Buffalo. He is also an accomplished musician and founding member of Patio Daddy-O, a rock band whose philanthropic mission has raised over $100 thousand to date. Azzarello can be contacted at: razzarello@wakeuptoreality.com

Steve Barth

Award-winning journalist Steve Barth specializes in KM, organizational learning, and knowledge-worker productivity. However, over the past 20 years, he has explored a plethora of diverse subjects, including rainforests, trade wars, domestic violence, quantum cosmology, leveraged buyouts, Hawaiian natural history, and canoe paddlers—all of which remain relevant to the subject at hand. He is currently editor and publisher of the online reincarnation of *Knowledge Management* magazine (destinationKM.com), authors the "Personal Toolkit" column in *KMWorld*, and contributes to *Harvard Management Update* and other business publications. He previously held positions at *World Trade*, *Asia Pacific Economic Review*, *Japan Digest*, *U.S.-China Business*, and other publications, while contributing to a variety of magazines, including *Asia Inc.*, *CRM*, *Field Force Automation*, and *Portable Computing*.

In addition, Barth spends much of his time speaking and consulting on KM, organizational learning, and knowledge worker productivity. During 2002, he was also a visiting scholar at the Learning Innovations Laboratory at Harvard University Graduate School of Education, focusing on issues of "organizational intelligence." An extensive archive of his work is available at http://www.global-insight.com. Barth can be contacted at: barth.km@global-insight.com

Denise A. D. Bedford

Denise Bedford is a senior information officer at the World Bank Group in Washington, DC. Since 1997, her duties have included management of the World Bank Group's MetaThesaurus, management of the Bank's core metadata strategy, and being the Bank's lead for usability engineering. She is also a member of their long-term search strategy design team and of the information architecture group.

Bedford is an adjunct associate professor of the faculty of Catholic University of America and Georgetown University.

Bedford received a Ph.D. from University of California, Berkeley, in information sciences; an M.A. from University of Michigan in Russian history; an M.S. in library science from Western Michigan University; and a B.A. in Russian language, German language, and Russian/East European history from University of Michigan. Her experience prior to joining the World Bank Group includes positions at the following: University of California Systemwide, Stanford University, Intel Corporation, NASA, University of Michigan, University of Maryland, University of Southern California. She serves as a member of the Board of Trustees of the Dublin Core Metadata Initiative and the Board of Directors of the Colten Textile Museum, and is a senior fellow for the Montague Institute. Bedford can be contacted at: dbedford@worldbank.org

ALEX BENNET

Alex Bennet, internationally recognized as an expert in KM and an agent for organizational change, is co-founder of Mountain Quest Institute, a research and retreat center. From October 1998 to January 2002, she was the deputy chief information officer for enterprise integration for the U.S. Department of the Navy, serving as the chief knowledge officer for the department. Concurrently, from early 1999 to January 2002, she was the co-chair of the Federal KM Working Group. In 1994, through an exchange agreement between the Department of the Navy and the Department of the Treasury, Bennet spent six months leading strategic planning and development of the IRS Master Plan to educate 120,000 government workers.

Bennet has an M.S. degree in management for organizational effectiveness and an M.A. in human development, is a graduate of the Defense Systems Management College, and a member of the Delta Epsilon Sigma and Golden Key national honor societies. She is currently pursuing her Ph.D. in human and organizational systems.

Bennet has published over 500 articles worldwide, edited several books on KM and e-Government and an upcoming book on the DON CIO implementation strategy. She is currently co-authoring books focused on the knowledge worker and the knowledge organization of the future. Among her many awards and honors, Bennet is the recipient of the Department of the Navy Superior Public Service

Award from the Secretary of the Navy, the National Performance Review Hammer Award from the U.S. Vice President, and the National Knowledge and Intellectual Property Management Task Force Award for distinguished service and exemplary leadership. *Federal Computer Week* named her a member of the Federal 100 for the year 2002.

Bennet can be contacted at: Sabennet@prodigy.net

David H. Bennet

David H. Bennet is co-founder of Mountain Quest Institute. His experience spans 40 years of service in the Navy, Civil Service, and Private Industry. Until October 2001, he was chairperson of the board and chief knowledge officer for Dynamic Systems, Inc., a professional services firm in northern Virginia.

He and his wife, Alex, are now building Mountain Quest Institute: an inn and research and retreat center set in the middle of a 450-acre farm nestled deep in the mountains of the Monongahela National Forest of West Virginia.

Bennet frequently speaks at KM conferences and has authored many papers on topics such as KM, organizational learning, and the Intelligent Complex Adaptive System. He is the author of a comprehensive guide for the application of Integrated Product teams that includes a 250-page virtual book and a System Dynamics Flight Simulator.

A Phi Beta Kappa, Sigma Pi Sigma, and summa cum laude graduate of the University of Texas, Bennet holds degrees in mathematics, physics, nuclear physics and liberal arts, and is currently working on a doctorate in human and organizational systems with a dissertation in KM.

Bennet can be contacted at: Dhbennet@prodigy.net

Jack Borbely

Jack Borbely is a principal at Towers Perrin and the director of KM. He is responsible for the firm's global processes, staff, and technology, supporting KM leverage of intellectual capital and electronic communication and collaboration. This encompasses the firm's communities of practice as well as intranet and .com sites.

In the area of KM process and technology, Borbely oversees the firm's portal, search, content management, and Web publishing. He also oversees electronic communication and collaboration, which includes the Lotus Notes platform. Prior to joining the firm, he spent eight years as manager of information services at AT&T Communications, and was responsible for staff and systems nationwide, providing research support to marketing, sales, competitive analysis, and strategic planning.

Borbely is a member of the Conference Board's Learning and KM Council. He holds a master's degree from Rutgers University. Borbely can be contacted at: borbelj@towers.com

Paul Burden

Paul Burden is a librarian at the Tinley Park, Illinois, campus of DeVry University. He is the principal author of *Knowledge Management: The Bibliography*, published by Information Today, Inc. He gave a presentation at Improving Academic Library Operations Through Knowledge Management Principles, Tools, and Techniques, a workshop sponsored by the Center for KM at Dominican University. Burden has been published in *American Libraries* and is completing a book on basic Internet searching for Scarecrow Press. He has a master's in library and information science from Dominican University. Burden can be contacted at: pburden@ameritech.net

H. Frank Cervone

H. Frank Cervone is the assistant university librarian for IT at Northwestern University where he is responsible for the planning and policy related to information systems that enhance knowledge discovery and access. Prior to this appointment, he was the director of instructional technology development at DePaul University.

Cervone is the author of four books related to IT. He has an M.A. in IT management from DePaul University and an M.S.Ed. in online teaching and learning from the California State University. A frequent speaker at conferences worldwide on issues related to project management, Web site usability and accessibility, and issues related to information architecture and access, Cervone has served as a consultant for library systems and library consortia in the U.S., U.K., and Brazil in areas related to IT implementation, policy, management, and organization, as well as digital library technologies. Cervone can be contacted at: f-cervone@north western.edu

Hsinchun Chen

Hsinchun Chen is a McClelland Endowed Professor of MIS at the University of Arizona and director of the artificial intelligence lab and Hoffman E-Commerce lab. He received his Ph.D. in information systems from New York University in 1989. Chen has been heavily involved in fostering digital library and KM research and education in the U.S. and internationally. He was a principal investigator of the NSF-funded Digital Library Initiative-1 project, and continues to receive major NSF awards from the ongoing Digital Library Initiative-2, Information Technology Research (ITR), National Science Digital Library (NSDL), and Digital Government programs.

Chen is author of more than 100 articles covering KM, text mining, medical informatics, semantic retrieval, intelligence analysis, and Web computing. Chen has served as the conference or program chair for the past five International Conferences of Asian Digital Libraries. He is a recognized advisor for international IT research programs in Asia and Europe. Chen can be contacted at: hchen@eller.arizona.edu

Elisabeth Davenport

Elisabeth Davenport is a research professor in the School of Computing, Napier University, Scotland, where she leads the Social Informatics group, and is a researcher in the International Teledemocracy Centre. For a number of years, she has been a visiting scholar in the School of Library and Information Science at Indiana University. Davenport has published extensively in the areas of information and KM. Her current interests include contextual analysis, strategy and policy for KM, and social aspects of human computer interaction.

Davenport has obtained her Ph.D. and master's in information science by the University of Strathclyde. She also holds master's of letters and M.A. degrees in ancient Greek and English literature from the University of Edinburgh, and is a fellow of the Chartered Institute of Information and Library Professionals. Davenport can be contacted at: e.davenport@napier.ac.uk

ROLAND G. DROITSCH

Roland G. Droitsch is currently the deputy assistant secretary for policy at the U.S. Department of Labor. In this capacity, he serves as policy advisor to the Office of the Secretary of Labor on a variety of issues, including regulatory policy, employment policies, and the impact of technological change on the department's programs.

Droitsch came to the department in 1975 to work for then Secretary of Labor John Dunlop. Recently, he has been focusing on implementing and integrating a number of technology-oriented programs, including the department's Web site, a system of "expert systems" that provides users with guidance on how to comply with the department's regulations, and the establishment of a department-wide Call Center. He also has been working collaboratively with the Department of Defense on the Advanced Distributed Learning initiative, which is developing standards for mounting and distributing object-based instructional material.

Prior to joining the department, Droitsch worked in the Office of the Special Representative for Trade Negotiations in the Executive Office of the President. He also worked in the Policy Planning Office of the Cost of Living Council and the economic forecasting unit of the U.S. Treasury department. Prior to joining the federal government, he worked for the Chase Manhattan Bank. In 1988, Droitsch was the recipient of the Presidential Rank Award of Distinguished Executive; and, in 1993, recipient of the Philip Arnow Award, the highest award presented by the Secretary of Labor to career staff in the Department of Labor.

Droitsch received his B.A. in political science at Columbia University, his M.A. in political science from the Maxwell School of Public Administration at Syracuse University, and his Ph.D. in economics from Georgetown University in Washington, DC. He is the author of numerous articles and monographs, and drafted the sections dealing with technology in the Secretary of Labor's recent report, "Futurework: Trends and Challenges for Work in the 21st Century." His most recent article, "Knowledge Management at the Department of Labor," was presented at the Artificial Intelligence and Soft Computing Conference in July 2000.

Droitsch is married with four children and resides in Washington, DC. He can be contacted at: Droitsch-Roland@dol.gov

MARY DURHAM

Mary Durham is a principal regulatory affairs associate at Genzyme Corporation, where she works with KM initiatives and manages a specialized internal document collection. Prior to joining Genzyme, Durham was the moderator of the Intellectual Assets Network (IAN) at Context Integration, and managed a leading-edge KM system for that consulting organization. Durham also developed the electronic library for Sybase Professional Services, and worked at Bolt, Beranek and Newman during the early times of the Internet.

Durham holds an M.S. in library and information science from Simmons College and an M.A. in linguistic anthropology from Brandeis University. Durham can be contacted at: mjd@bicnet.net

DARLENE FICHTER

Darlene Fichter is the data library coordinator at the University of Saskatchewan library. She has worked in public, academic, and special libraries. As a librarian and an IT consultant, Fichter has been the project leader for several Internet, intranet, digital library, and portal projects.

Usability, user adoption of new technologies, metadata, XML, and KM are areas of particular interest to her. She is also a columnist for *Online* magazine and a frequent conference speaker.

Fichter has a B.A. in philosophy from the University of Saskatchewan and an M.L.S from the University of Toronto. Fichter can be contacted at: Darlene.Fichter@usask.ca

JEFFREY A. FLINT

Jeffrey A. Flint, recently deceased, supervised Proactive Worldwide, Inc.'s extensive and international research operations, spanning several industry-specific practices. Flint was a veteran in the intelligence field and an expert in gathering, analyzing, and reporting difficult-to-obtain information, particularly within the healthcare field where he conducted international business intelligence (BI) research for a wide array of pharmaceutical "majors," biotech companies, medical device manufacturers, and hospital groups.

Prior to joining Proactive Worldwide, Inc. in 1999, Flint served as an investigator for the U.S. Consulate General in St. Petersburg, investigating Russian-organized crime. He was awarded a Meritorious Honor Award by the state department for his efforts in identifying and building cases against international criminals. Flint acted as a consultant on a number of business development projects within Russia, including work for clients such as Conoco International Petroleum Company, Abbott Labs, the U.S. Department of Commerce, and USAID.

Flint had a master's degree specializing in competitive intelligence and global marketing from Thunderbird, the American Graduate School of International Management, and held a B.A. in communications and Russian with university honors from Brigham Young University. Together with Proactive Worldwide, Inc.'s CEO, Gary Maag, Flint taught a graduate-level competitive intelligence course at Dominican University as an adjunct assistant professor.

He was fluent in Russian and conversant in several eastern European languages, plus German and Spanish. He was affiliated with the Dobro Slovo Slavic Honor Society, and served as a Brigham Young University National Development Board member for the College of Humanities.

Flint passed away suddenly and tragically while this book was in development. There is a brief celebratory note about his life and his contribution to the fields of KM and competitive intelligence by his co-author, Gary Maag, at the end of Chapter 26.

Farida Hasanali

Farida Hasanali is the program manager for the American Productivity and Quality Center's (APQC's) Knowledge Sharing Network (KSN). Hasanali led the design and development effort of APQC's KSN, which attracted 2,000 registered users in the first week of launch. In this role, Hasanali is involved in creating the processes and guiding the infrastructure required to promote and share knowledge at APQC. She is responsible for identifying user requirements, selecting vendors, designing the processes, and managing the support structure.

Over the past eight years at APQC, Hasanali has led and been involved in numerous multiclient benchmarking projects, including five focused on KM. Hasanali's involvement in such projects has provided her with the opportunity to learn successful business practices firsthand by visiting numerous Fortune 1000 companies. Hasanali is applying her experience in KM by helping APQC's customers implement KM within their organizations. In this capacity, Hasanali acts as a subject-matter expert to the APQC KM consulting team.

Prior to her involvement in KM, Hasanali spent eight years of her professional career working in IT as a database administrator and, later, as an information analyst. Hasanali's experience in business processes and IT helps her understand both the business and technical issues related to KM.

Hasanali has given presentations at several KM events, for such prestigious organizations as the U.S. Navy, KM World, ContentWorld, InfoWorld, and Society for Petroleum Engineers. She holds a bachelor's degree in psychology from St. Xavier College in Bombay, India. Hasanali can be contacted at: fhasanali@apqc.org

Cindy Hubert

Since helping to launch the American Productivity and Quality Center's (APQC's) KM program in 1995, Cindy Hubert has played an instrumental role in building APQC's reputation as an internationally renowned leader in the KM arena. Over the past seven years, Hubert and her team have worked with more than 250 organizations to provide KM assessments, strategy development, project management, transfer of best practice design and implementation, and internal and external benchmarking studies. As director of KM and learning at APQC, and through her work with Dr. Carla O'Dell, president of APQC, she has guided the center, which has become a national leader in conducting and producing KM studies, workshops, conferences, and publications.

Hubert has worked with a variety of industries, including oil and gas, manufacturing, healthcare, financial, retail, nonprofit, and consumer products. She was recently a keynote presenter at Petroleos de Venezuela, S.A. (PDVSA's) III International KM Forum, and has spoken extensively on KM issues and best practices at conferences worldwide.

With strong interpersonal and facilitation skills, as well as an ability to find solutions, Hubert has played an instrumental role in the development and delivery of APQC's KM education and curriculum. Her role has recently expanded to encompass all of APQC's Connected Learning™ offerings, covering such topics as KM, benchmarking, performance measurement, and process improvement. In addition to developing a practitioner certification program, Hubert also directs APQC's on-site, custom, and computer-based training offerings.

Prior to being named director of KM and learning, Hubert served as a senior consultant in KM and a manager of APQC's custom solutions KM practice area, focusing on business process improvement, including transfer of best practices, quality, benchmarking, measurement, and strategic planning.

Before joining APQC in 1995, Hubert spent 15 years in the oil and gas industry as a controller, and in the retail industry as a general manager. In both positions, Hubert served as a consultant to a number of total-quality, benchmarking, and re-engineering projects. Hubert also has served as an instructor in KM and the transfer of best practices at Rice University's Executive Education Graduate School of Management. A graduate of University of Texas at Austin, Hubert received a bachelor's degree in business administration and marketing with emphasis in accounting and finance. Hubert can be contacted at: chubert@ apqc.org

Gregory S. Hunter

Gregory S. Hunter is a professor in the Palmer School of Library and Information Science at Long Island University. He holds a Ph.D. in American history from New York University and is a certified records manager and a certified archivist. Hunter previously served as manager of corporate records for ITT Corporation's World Headquarters and director of archival programs for the United Negro College Fund, Inc. He is the author of over 25 articles and four books, including *Developing and Maintaining Practical Archives* (Neal-Schuman, 1997) and the award-winning *Preserving Digital Information* (Neal-Schuman, 2000). Hunter can be contacted at: gregory.hunter@liu.edu

Michael E. D. Koenig

Michael E. D. Koenig is currently dean and professor at the College of Information and Computer Science and, simultaneously, dean and professor in the Palmer School of Library and Information Science at Long Island University. His career has included both senior management positions in the information industry and academic postings, including: manager of information services for Pfizer Research; director of development at the Institute for Scientific Information; vice president, North America, at Swets and Zeitlinger; vice president, data management, at Tradenet; associate professor at Columbia University; and dean and professor at Dominican University.

Koenig obtained his Ph.D. in information science from Drexel University. His M.B.A. in mathematical methods and computers and his M.S. in library and information science are from the University of Chicago; and his undergraduate degree, psychology and physics, is from Yale University. A Fulbright scholar in Argentina, he is the author of more than 100 professional and scholarly articles, a member of the editorial board of more than a dozen journals, and past president of the International Society for Scientometrics and Informetrics. Koenig can be contacted at: michael.koenig@liu.edu

Thomas Krichel

Born in Völklingen, Saarland, Thomas Krichel studied economics and social sciences at the universities of Toulouse, Paris, Exeter, and Leicester. He obtained his Ph.D. in economics from University of Surrey. Between February 1993 and April 2001, he lectured in the department of economics at the University of Surrey. In 1993, he founded the NetEc, a consortium of Internet projects for academic economists. In 1997, he founded the RePEc dataset to document economics. RePEc now contains the largest decentralized online academic digital library in the world. Between October and December 2001, he held a visiting professorship at Hitotsubashi University. Since January 2001, he has been an assistant professor in the Palmer School of Library and Information Science at Long Island University. Krichel's prime interests are organizational matters relating to free online scholarship. Krichel can be contacted at: krichel@openlib.org

Gary D. Maag

Gary D. Maag is the chairperson and CEO of Proactive Worldwide, Inc. He has been a part of the business intelligence decision support community for over 12 years. Maag, along with his partner, David Kalinowski, established Proactive Worldwide, Inc. in 1995. He supervises their long-term direction and strategic initiatives. He also orchestrates new business development, marketing, and oversees internal technology-based initiatives. Maag is intimately involved with developing partnerships and alliances for strong long-term growth.

During the last 12 years, he has directed business intelligence (BI) research on dozens of high-profile assignments for both medium-sized and Fortune 500 companies. He has assisted numerous corporations in the development and coordination of BI processes, as well as advised numerous product and task force teams on related issues. Maag has authored numerous articles on BI topics and is a frequent speaker on the relevance and value of BI in today's fast-paced information era.

Prior to co-founding Proactive Worldwide, Inc., Maag worked as a consultant with other BI firms, and held positions in the area of traditional quantitative research with several Chicago-based advertising agencies, including Leo Burnett USA, Well, Rich Greene, and Grant/Jacoby.

Maag is currently an adjunct professor with the Center for Knowledge Management at Dominican University. He also is the Society of Competitive Intelligence Professional's Chicago Chapter coordinator, and an active member of the Strategic Management Association (Chicago Chapter), American Marketing Association, and the Executives' Club of Chicago. Maag can be contacted at: gary@proactiveworldwide.com

Yogesh Malhotra

Before joining Syracuse University, Yogesh Malhotra taught senior executives at the Kellogg School of Management at Northwestern University and the Graduate School of Industrial Administration at Carnegie Mellon University. He is the founder of the BRINT Institute (brint.com), the New-York-based, globally branded e-learning, research, and advisory firm. His advice and vision influence policies and strategies of world governments, United Nations, Fortune 1000 and Global 3000 companies, and international professional associations in all areas of business and technology practice. He has more than 18 years of professional experience as a chief executive, management consultant, and hands-on technology project manager in multiple industry sectors across the U.S. and Asia.

Malhotra is profiled in the Marquis Who's Who in the World, Marquis Who's Who in America, Marquis Who's Who in Finance and Industry, Who's Who in the Internet Commerce Standard, Leaders and Legends of Business Intelligence and Data Warehousing, CRM Leaders and Legends of Intellibusiness, and Knowledge Inc. Top Knowledge Management Experts and Luminaries. He has a Ph.D. in business administration from the University of Pittsburgh, specializing in information systems and KM; a Ph.D. minor in psychology of education from the University of Pittsburgh; an M.B.A. from the University of Nevada, and a bachelor of engineering from University of Delhi, India. Malhotra can be contacted at: Yogesh@syr.edu

Carla O'Dell

Carla O'Dell is president of the APQC and the thought leader of their KM work. She has been with APQC since 1991, and became president in 1994. O'Dell and APQC have been instrumental in bringing the concepts of KM into action, as well as developing the knowledge of best practices, methods for KM, and how to successfully implement KM. Under O'Dell's leadership, the APQC has been active in KM since 1995, and has led 11 major consortium studies on KM.

O'Dell has authored numerous articles, and is co-author with Dr. C. Jackson Grayson of *American Business: A Two Minute Warning* (The Free Press, 1988) and *If Only We Knew What We Know: The Transfer of Internal Knowledge and Best Practices* (Simon and Schuster, 1998), one of the leading KM books. She speaks frequently at executive conferences, writes for major business publications and APQC, and facilitates developing KM strategies for executives. Based on seven years of extensive best-practice research in KM, with the help of over 200 leading companies, government, and nonprofit agencies, O'Dell and the APQC developed its Road Map to Knowledge Management Results: Stages of Implementation framework.

O'Dell obtained her B.A. from Stanford University, M.A. from the University of Oregon, and Ph.D. from the University of Houston. O'Dell can be contacted at: codell@apqc.org

Ruth A. Palmquist

Ruth A. Palmquist has a B.S. in education from the University of Nebraska. She earned an M.A. in library science from the University of Iowa and a Ph.D. from Syracuse University in information transfer. Before coming to Dominican University in River Forest, Illinois, she taught at the University of Texas at Austin. Her teaching and research interests include electronic information retrieval and the cognitive theories that support the study of user search behavior in such environments. She is currently working on a book concerning the cognitive power of metaphors and their ability to convey mental models of complex digital work environments to those new to such environments. Palmquist can be contacted at: rpalmq@dom.edu

Leonard J. Ponzi

Leonard J. Ponzi has 10 years of experience in solving business problems. He was formerly the managing director of Solutions In Research, Inc., and held positions at FIND/SVP and at Microsoft.

He obtained his M.B.A. from Syracuse University, and recently completed his Ph.D. in information studies from Long Island University. His dissertation explores the evolution and intellectual development of KM. Ponzi lives in Manhattan, NY, with his wife, Karen.

Ponzi can be contacted at: lponzi@mindspring.com

Timothy W. Powell

Timothy W. Powell is founder and managing director of TW Powell Co., "The Knowledge Agency" (http://www.knowledgeagency.com), a business research and strategy firm based in New York City. He spent 23 years as a management consultant, including service with the following firms: KPMG, Pricewaterhouse-Coopers, and FIND/SVP. His clients consist of about 100 organizations, including Global 1000 companies, professional services firms, government agencies, and start-ups.

Powell is the author of two books, *The High-Tech Marketing Machine* (Probus/McGraw-Hill) and *Analyzing Your Competition* (FIND/SVP). A Fellow of the Society of Competitive Intelligence Professionals (SCIP), he presents regularly to business groups worldwide. He holds a bachelor's degree in premedical science and psychology from Yale University and an M.B.A. from the Yale School of Management. Further biographic details may be found in Who's Who in Finance and Business and Who's Who in the World. Powell can be contacted at: tim.powell@knowledgeagency.com

Katherine M. Shelfer

Katherine M. Shelfer is an associate professor at the College of Information Science and Technology at Drexel University in Philadelphia, Pennsylvania. She is also the program director for the college's program in Competitive Intelligence. Her teaching interests include business information management; competitive intelligence; and the design, marketing, and analysis of information products and services. Her research interests focus on information needs analysis of entrepreneurs. Shelfer performs strategic needs analyses and manages research projects for a number of enterprises, including business incubator facilities in several states. Shelfer earned her bachelor's, master's, and doctorate degrees while attending Florida State University. Shelfer can be contacted at: kathy.shelfer@cis.drexel.edu

Tom Short

Tom Short is the solution strategy executive for IBM's Global Life Sciences Solution Group. He is a key contributor and thought leader for internal KM efforts related to the coordination of the global IBM life sciences community.

Short's career in consulting has always been focused on making businesses work better internally, using a variety of techniques and methods. Some of these include organizational development, KM, business process redesign, activity-based costing, and organizational restructuring. He is a frequent speaker on the topic of portals for life sciences and KM, and is also a published author with several articles and book chapters on the subject.

Prior to joining IBM, Short worked for various consulting firms, including both boutique and large firms. He also operated a private practice for himself. He attended the University of Michigan, in Ann Arbor, where he earned bachelor's and master's degrees in industrial and operations engineering. Post-graduate education has included scenario planning, video production, and motorcycle road racing. Short can be contacted at: tshort@us.ibm.com

Taverekere (Kanti) Srikantaiah

Taverekere (Kanti) Srikantaiah, director of the Center for KM at Dominican University joined the Dominican faculty in 1997 as an associate professor. He teaches graduate courses in the Graduate School of Library and Information Science (GSLIS) and also cross-disciplined courses with the School of Business (GSB) at Dominican University. Before joining Dominican, Srikantaiah had a distinguished career at the World Bank headquarters in Washington DC (and also at the World Bank's field offices in Africa and Asia) where he headed varied and important assignments in the area of information management.

Srikantaiah received his B.S. in chemistry from the University of Mysore; M.S. in geology from the Karnatak University; M.S.I.S. in library and information science from the University of Southern California; M.P.A. in public administration from the University of Southern California; and Ph.D. in library and information science from the University of Southern California. He worked at the Library of Congress as an area specialist, and taught at California State University as an associate professor. He has also taught for many years as an adjunct faculty member at the Catholic University of America in Washington DC. Srikantaiah's specialization includes: systems analysis, taxonomies, information policy, and KM.

Among others, his research output covers several research studies and project reports at the World Bank and articles and presentations at the International Federation of Library Associations (IFLA) and similar international organizations. He was the chief editor, with Michael E. D. Koenig, of *Knowledge Management for the Information Professional* (Information Today, Inc.) as part of the ASIS monograph series. He has also published two other prominent books: one on systems analysis and the other on quantitative research methods. Srikantaiah can be contacted at: srikant@email.dom.edu

REED STUEDEMANN

Reed Stuedemann has been the knowledge-sharing manager at Caterpillar University since June 2001. He leads a small team that is responsible for transitioning the knowledge network from an internally focused knowledge-sharing collaboration tool to a strategic business asset, spanning the value chain. Stuedemann has been with Caterpillar University for 27 years and has worked in a number of different areas within the company. Previous to his knowledge network position, Stuedemann was responsible for marketing Caterpillar University components to other original equipment manufacturers.

Stuedemann's expansive background also includes positions in manufacturing, purchasing, quality, and product support. He was raised on a farm in Iowa, and has bachelor's and master's degrees from Iowa State University. He is married and has two children. Stuedemann serves on the board of directors of a local credit union, CEFCU, that serves over 200,000 members. Stuedemann can be contacted at: Stuedemann_Reed_A@cat.com

Index

K

Knowledge process mapping (KPM), 36,
3637
Knowledge repository management, 211,
220, 221
Knowledge retrieval (KR), 243–245
Knowledge workers, 511–525, 514–5155
KnowledgeCurve, 108
Knowles, M.S., 514, 516
Koenig, M., 18, 84, 113, 114, 116, 364,
489–490, 494
Kohonen, T., 248, 262
Kolb, D.A., 514, 516
Korn-Ferry study, 468
Kotter, J.T., 295
KPMG Consulting, 127, 487–489
Kraken (e-mail list), 108
Kramer, M., 388, 389

L

Labor
costs, 131, 134
information literacy, 282–284
Labor, Department of (DOL), 333–351
Languages, 181, 265–266, 519. *See also*
vocabularies
Lazard Freres & Co., 142
Leadership. *See also* management
command and control systems, 106
identifying, 46
KM initiatives, 58–59
line business managers, 44–46
strategy development, 68
Learning
accelerated, 521–523
active, 518–521, 529
definition, 513, 520
history of, 533–535
knowledge workers and, 511–525
synergy, 466–468
technological advances, 344–347

Learning in a Virtual World (CD-ROM),
281
Legal issues, 153
Leidner, D., 389, 391
Leonard-Barton, D., 16, 17
Leverage, KM and, 312
Librarian's Index to the Internet, 214
Licensing, barriers, 344–346
Line managers, 44–46, 142, 297–301
Listening skills, 56, 515
Literature surveys
citation counts and, 9–26
disciplinary activity measures, 12–13
journal support measures, 13–14
methodology, 10–11
Price's Index, 18
Loshin, P., 210
Luke, J., 463, 472

M

Maag, G., 423
Machine Readable Cataloging (MARC),
216, 342
Malhotra, Y., 96, 100, 105, 106, 108
Malone, M.S., 137, 226, 227
Management
championing efforts, 297–298
characterization, 114–115
communities of practice, 354–355
of content, 341
control, 105–107
corporate intelligence functions,
412–415
critical roles for, 293–309
failures due to, 487, 488
formal operations unit, 319–320
operations unit functions, 321
support for CM, 167–168
time saved, 142
understanding of processes, 166

P